LEO BAECK INSTITUTE
YEAR BOOK

1999

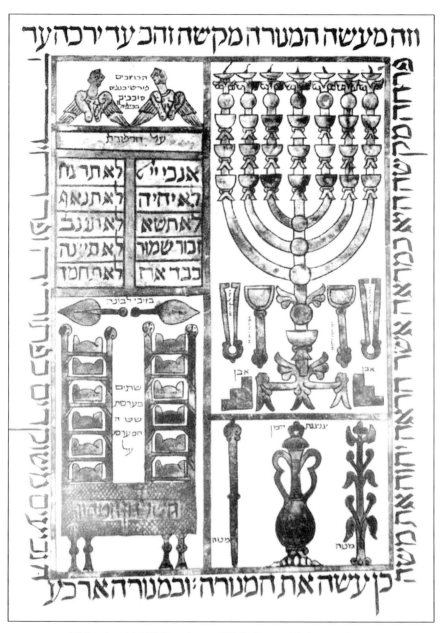

Bible, dated 1299, Perpignan, Bibliothèque Nationale, Paris.

The utensils of the Tabernacle. *Top left*: The Ten Commandments. *Bottom left*: The table with the show breads. *Top right*: The Menorah-Candelabra. *Bottom right*: The staff of Aaron depicted dry to the left and flowering to the right. The Hebrew of the surround is extracted from the text of the instructions for making the utensils, Exodus 25 and 33.

This illustration is taken from Rachel Wischnitzer's study of Jewish art, *Gestalten und Symbole der jüdischen Kunst*, Berlin 1935.

LEO BAECK INSTITUTE

YEAR BOOK
1999

XLIV

SECKER & WARBURG · LONDON
PUBLISHED FOR THE INSTITUTE
LONDON · JERUSALEM · NEW YORK

FOUNDER EDITOR: ROBERT WELTSCH (1956–1978)
EDITOR EMERITUS: ARNOLD PAUCKER (1970–1992)

Editorial office: Leo Baeck Institute
4 Devonshire Street, London W1N 2BH

THE LEO BAECK INSTITUTE

was founded in 1955 for the study of the history and culture of German-speaking Central European Jewry

The Institute is named in honour of the man who was the last representative figure of German Jewry in Germany during the Nazi period

LEO BAECK INSTITUTE

JERUSALEM: 33 Bustanai Street
LONDON: 4 Devonshire Street, W1
NEW YORK: 129 East 73rd Street

© Leo Baeck Institute 1999
Published by Martin Secker & Warburg Limited
Random House, 20 Vauxhall Bridge Road, London SW1V 2SA
ISBN 0 436 20483 5
Photoset by Wilmaset Limited, Birkenhead, Wirral
Printed in Great Britain by Mackays of Chatham PLC

Contents

Illustrations

Errata

The illustration between pages 102 and 103 in Year Book XLIII is of Hermann Cohen which should have accompanied Avi Bernstein-Nahar's article, 'Hermann Cohen's Teaching Concerning Modern Jewish Identity (1904–1918)'.

Preface

There is no time to pause. New generations since the end of national-socialist Germany are confronting the cultural heritage and history of German Jewry and its fate with more urgency and interest than ever before. Nor is this surprising. We search for answers to the destruction of a civilisation of multi-cultural dimensions in an age when multi-culturalism and minorities are continuously and bloodily assaulted. In modern times it was in Germany that the most thorough attempt to "cleanse" Germany from influences not deemed to be part of a self-contained so-called German culture was attempted with unparalleled and ruthless thoroughness. German scholars are distinguishing themselves in seeking answers to the question of how an advanced western society in the forefront of progress could have reversed its own course of history into barbarous perversity. It is also German scholars who keenly research what has been lost; a new generation of scholars is emerging which, fully conversant with Hebrew and Yiddish, will bring new dimensions to the exploration of Jewish life and culture. But these questions cannot be addressed to German history alone, they are of universal significance. Genocidal murders have recurred between peoples who previously had lived peacefully with each other and intermarried, just as German Jews had done. Never has the need to learn from the past been greater. That is why the German-speaking Jewish experience in Europe has not been, and will not simply be, consigned to the history books as if the final chapter had been written.

The universal importance of the issues the German-speaking Jewish experience raises, one threatened minority among others, is recognised by scholars globally as the contributors to the Year Book from every continent demonstrate. Scholars from all over the world thus address questions which had their origins in central Europe. The efforts of Ignatz Bubis, the late leader of the German Jewish community, exemplified the importance of defending human rights wherever they have been and are assailed.

German history is of concern to Germans, but it would be a perversion once more to regard it as the *sole* concern of German scholarship, a belated return to a kind of mono-culturism that would assert that German history should be repatriated to Germany. German governmental institutions have recognised this for many years and continue generously to support the international effort of the Leo Baeck Institute. In this regard, we particularly wish to cite the *Bundesministerium des Innern* and the *Ständige Konferenz der Kultusminister der Länder in der BRD*.

The Year Book with its multi-lingual footnotes and other individual features is by no means an easy or straightforward publication. We have enjoyed invaluable support from the staff of Secker and Warburg since 1972 and especially from the 'hands on' advice of Mary Gibson and her predecessors who have been in charge of the production process. It is with real regret, therefore, that our long and fruitful association with Secker and Warburg will be coming to an end with this year's Year Book. We are pleased to announce, however, that the Year Book will be published from the year 2000 onwards by Berghahn Books of New York and Oxford, who have a special interest in the area of German-Jewish history and culture and our Year Book fits in well with their list. Berghahn Books already handle our North American distribution and now are taking over publication and distribution world wide. They are also the distributors for the first forty volumes of the Year Book on CD-ROM. The creation of a CD-ROM of the combined bibliography, however, is proving an even more challenging undertaking than expected, but we are continuing to tackle the problems still posed to provide as excellent a search mechanism as is already available in the CD-ROM Year Books.

*   *   *   *   *

The death of Dr. Fred Grubel in his ninetieth year on 4th October 1998 should not have been unexpected. And yet, when it occurred, it was still hard to believe that a man of such vitality and creativity who had directed the Leo Baeck Institute in New York for many decades was no longer with us. We miss him personally. He respected and promoted academic scholarship in every way. He lent his support to all the three Institutes, but the Editors of the Year Book in London were able to develop close relations with him on visits to New York. He championed the Year Book as the "flagship" publication of the Leo Baeck Institutes and the joint events organised by the LBI New York and LBI London at the American Historical Association's Annual Conventions became an invaluable forum for involving a wide audience of historians in the work of the Year Book. With his death yet another link with Germany's pre-war Jewish community is severed.

It was with deep regret that we learnt of the death on 6th September 1999 of Janet Langmaid who worked for the Year Book for twenty-two years. Devoted to our work and a superb indexer she compiled the annual index for many years and also the excellent General Index Volume for the years 1976–1994. She undertook these painstaking tasks with delightful cheerfulness and achieved the highest professional standards. We are grateful to our experienced bibliographer, Annette Pringle, who undertook the task of providing this volume with its detailed index at very short notice.

The Year Book editors once again wish to record the excellent support they receive from the staff, the assistant editors and the services of the bibliographers and indexers.

John Grenville   *Julius Carlebach*

*German-Jewish Intellectual Development from the
Late Eighteenth to the Nineteenth Century*

The Similarities and Relationship Between the Jüdisch-Theologisches Seminar *(Breslau)* and the Rabbinical Seminary *(Budapest)* [*]

BY MOSHE CARMILLY-WEINBERGER

The Rabbinical Seminary of Budapest was "created by enlightened Jews", wrote Ludwig Blau, Rector of the Institute. He was correct. Commencing in the second half of the eighteenth century, in the wake of the French Revolution, the *Haskalah* paved the way for a cultural renaissance of the Jewish people. There emerged the need to establish rabbinical seminaries in which rabbis and teachers could be educated for service to Jewish communities. The first such institute, the Istituto Rabbinico Lombardo-Veneto, was established in Padua in 1829 followed by the École Rabbinique-Séminaire Israélite de France in Metz in 1859, which later relocated to Paris. Because of the different Orthodox and Reform trends in Germany, various ideas were considered in the creation of a Jewish Theological Seminary. In 1836 Abraham Geiger (1810–1874), one of the leaders of the Reform movement, had expressed his eagerness to establish a department for Jewish theology in a German university, connected with other departments but independent of any Jewish organisation or community. His attempt was unsuccessful, as had been earlier attempts by Meyer S. Weyl, the *Vize-Oberlandesrabbiner* of Berlin (1824), Ludwig Philippson (1838) and Leopold Zunz (1848).[1]

Geiger was among the first to advocate the creation of a *Jüdisch-Theologisches Seminar* in Breslau, but he was not to be appointed its head as he had "leider eine Richtung eingeschlagen, die ihn unfähig macht, eine vollwichtige Rabbinatswürde zu erteilen". He saw the establishment of the *Hochschule für die Wissenschaft des Judentums* in Berlin in 1872, where he had served the congregation since 1870.[2]

[*]This essay is the revised text of a lecture presented at the hundred and twentieth anniversary of the Rabbinical Seminary of Budapest, 8–10 September 1997.

[1] Ismar Schorsch, 'Emancipation and the Crisis of Religious Authority: the Emergence of the Modern Rabbinate', in *Revolution and Evolution: 1848 in German Jewish History*, ed. by Werner E. Mosse, Arnold Paucker and Reinhard Rürup, Tübingen 1981 (Schriftenreihe wissenschaftlicher Abhandlungen des Leo Baeck Instituts 39), pp. 211–213, 223, 227–228; *Das Breslauer Jüdisch-Theologische Seminar (Fraenkelscher Stiftung) in Breslau, 1854–1938: Gedächtnisschrift*, ed. by Guido Kisch, Tübingen 1963, p. 264; Ludwig Geiger, 'Eine Denkschrift von Zunz', *ibid.* p. 61.

[2] *ibid.*, p. 57; Schorsch, pp. 210–211; Kisch (ed.), *Das BreslauerSeminar*, pp. 45, 47–48, 52; Ludwig Geiger, *Abraham Geigers Leben in Briefen* , Berlin 1878; *idem, Abraham Geiger: Leben und Lebenswerk*, Berlin 1910.

THE *JÜDISCH-THEOLOGISCHES SEMINAR* OF BRESLAU

Zacharias Frankel (1801–1875), Chief Rabbi of Teplitz and later of Dresden, envisaged a Jewish theological seminary which would allow for the preservation of the Jewish heritage of "a thousand generations" to be taught in a scholarly way. Frankel, the son of Yaakov Koppel Frankel and Esther Fischel, was born in 1801 in the ghetto of Prague. In 1848–1849, in the face of resistance from the antisemitic Gentile population the gates of the ghetto were opened by Imperial order. Under Joseph II German became the official language in Austria-Hungary; Hebrew and Yiddish were forbidden in the interest of furthering Jewish assimilation.

In 1831, the year after he received his doctorate from the University of Budapest, Frankel was offered the post of rabbi in Teplitz in northern Bohemia. While in Teplitz, in 1835, he wrote a memorandum addressed to the Minister of Education, Miller, in which he stated: "If the rabbi is to be respected as a learned man, he must be academically trained. To be intimately familiar with the Talmud is not enough, the muses must also not be strange to him... He should be the teacher and guide of the people. Would our age in fact take instruction from a man trained otherwise?"[3] In 1851, Frankel founded the *Monatsschrift für Geschichte und Wissenschaft des Judentums* [*MGWJ*] in order to foster interest in Jewish scholarship. It became one of the most valuable periodicals until the appearance of its last volume, the eighty-third, in 1939. (Its last editor was Isaak Heinemann, who left Nazi Germany in 1938 for Israel.)[4]

It was in the *Monatsschrift* in 1853 that Frankel proposed the establishment of a rabbinical seminary. The leadership of the Jewish communities in Germany approached Leopold Zunz, the director of the Jewish Teachers' Seminary in Berlin (1840–1850) and one of the founding fathers of the *Wissenschaft des Judentums*, with this proposal. Zunz responded that the rabbinical seminary had to be independent, but built in a place where the students would be able to attend courses at a secular university. He proposed a curriculum for the teachers' institute but not for the seminary "aus erwähnten Gründen". It is possible that he wanted to avoid confrontation with Abraham Geiger, who would have had a different point of view on the composition of a curriculum for the seminary, or that Zunz himself was not comfortable with the concept of the "rabbinate". Zunz

---

[3]Isaak Heinemann, 'The Idea of the Jewish Theological Seminary in the Light of Modern Thought', in *Historia Judaica* 16:2 (1954), p. 73; Rivka Horovitz, *Zacharias Frankel and the Origins of Positive-Historical Jewry* [Hebrew], Jerusalem 1984; I. Hermann, J. Teige, Z. Winter, *Das Prager Getto*, Prague 1903; Hans Tramer, 'Prague—City of Three Peoples', in *LBI Year Book IX* (1964), pp. 305–339; Christoph Stölzl, 'Prag', in *Kafka-Handbuch, I. Der Mensch und seine Zeit*, Stuttgart 1979, pp. 52–53, 67, 127; Joseph Karniel, *Die Toleranzpolitik Kaiser Joseph II*, Tel Aviv 1986, (Schriftenreihe des Instituts für Deutsche Geschichte, Universität Tel Aviv, 9); *Encyclopaedia Judaica*, vol. III, col. 1456; Schorsch, p. 211; Saul Pinehas Rabbinovitz, *R. Zeharyja Frankel*, Warsaw 1898, pp. 23–24. In mid-nineteenth century in Germany only about 67 rabbis had a Ph.D. degree. See Schorsch, pp. 212, 214, 216, 245–247.
[4]Markus Brann, 'Zur Geschichte der Monatsschrift', in *Monatsschrift für Geschichte und Wissenschaft des Judentums (MGWJ)* 51 (1907), pp. 1–16; Adolf Kober, 'The Jewish Theological Seminary of Breslau and "Wissenschaft des Judentums" ' in *Historia Judaica* 16:2 (1954), pp. 116–119.

emphasised, as did Frankel, that study of the Talmud is impossible without scholarly method.[5]

On 10 August 1854, the *Jüdisch-Theologisches Seminar-Fraenckel'scher Stiftung* was established in Breslau. In 1931 permission was granted to add the words *Hochschule für Jüdische Theologie* to the seminary's title. The future of the seminary was secured by the *David und Jonas Fraenckel's Stiftung* which donated a portion of the brothers' wealth towards the establishment of a rabbinical seminary and Jewish teachers' institute. Having accepted the invitation to head the seminary, Frankel at the opening declared:

> The Seminary is to be a property of all Jewry. The ideas and ideals of Judaism are to be cultivated and taught here.

In an article published in the first volume of the *MGWJ* Frankel advocated that:

> Jewry has always maintained that Judaism has its essence and fulfillment in research on religion and in intellectual activities connected with the religious sphere. *Wissenschaft des Judentums* is its powerful lever, without it there is no Judaism. Judaism degenerates if it ceases to love its *Wissenschaft*.[6]

It was a clear definition.

Frankel, the scholar, with his immense knowledge of Talmud and *Halakhah*, laid down the foundation of the seminary and defined its direction. He invited Heinrich Graetz, the great Jewish historian, Jacob Bernays, the son of Isaac Bernays, Chief Rabbi of Hamburg, who banned the "reformed" German prayer book, Israel Lewy, author of Talmudic studies, and Manuel Joel, one of the great scholars of medieval Jewish philosophy to teach there.[7]

The establishment of the *Jüdisch-Theologisches Seminar* was not accepted with great joy, either by the Reformer Abraham Geiger, the leader of the Reform movement, or by the neo-Orthodox leader Samson Raphael Hirsch (1808–1888), *Landesrabbiner* of Oldenburg and later of Frankfurt am Main. Geiger was not happy with Frankel's traditional attitude and Hirsch considered its ideology unclear. Hirsch wrote to Frankel asking him to define his view concerning Oral Law. Did he believe it to be of divine origin? Frankel in his *Darkhei ha-Mishnah*[8] had not mentioned the divine origin of the Oral Law. A pamphlet, *Meor Einayyim. Beleuchtung des Frankel'schen Streites,* published anonymously in Vienna in 1861, contained harsh attacks against Frankel and Graetz, who was called a "ketzerriechender Klausner". The seminar was described as an institute "der Ketzerei und des Abfalls". Frankel answered Hirsch's inquiry in a short article entitled *Erklärung, die Schrift "Hodegetik in die Mischna" betreffend,* in which he rejected the

[5]Kisch (ed.), *Das Breslauer Seminar*, pp. 55–64; Schorsch, pp. 206, 239–247

[6]A. Kober, p. 90; *MGWJ* 3 (1853), pp. 293–308; Rabbinovitz, p. 347.

[7]On Samson Raphael Hirsch and Zacharias Frankel see Isaak Heinemann, *Ta'ame Hamitzwoth BeSafruth Yisrael II*, Jerusalem 1956, pp. 91–182; David Philipson, *The Reform Movement in Judaism*, New York 1931, p. 75; Moshe Carmilly-Weinberger, *Censorship and Freedom of Expression in Jewish History*, New York 1977, pp. 141–142; for Manuel Joel, see *MGWJ* 70 (1926), pp. 305, 315, 324, 330, 347, 351.

[8]Zacharias Frankel, *Darkhei ha-Mishnah*, Leipzig 1859, reprint. 1867.

accusations by stating that every page of his work *Darkhe ha-Mishnah* "athmet die tiefste Verehrung für die mündliche Lehre".[9]

Neither these attacks nor a financial crisis in 1858, when L. Volkmar and M. Kalisch contested the Fraenckel brothers' will,[10] halted the great educational and scholarly work of the seminary. During its eighty-four years of existence under the leadership of *Seminar-Rabbiner* (Frankel, Leyser Lazarus, David Joel, Israel Lewy, Saul Horovitz, Michael Guttmann, Israel Rabin and Samuel Moses Ochs and Professors David Rosin, Jacob Freudenthal, Markus Brann, Albert Lewkovitz, Isaak Heinemann, Heinrich Speyer, Hirsch Zimmels, Nahum Wahrmann, Ephraim Elimelech Urbach and Ernst Hoffmann) it became the most prestigious institute of Jewish learning. It followed Frankel's objective: to teach and research "positive historical Judaism" – neither Reform nor ultra-Orthodoxy but conservative Judaism, in which the traditional, fundamental heritage was combined with *Wissenschaft des Judentums*, (which today is called *Torah u-Mada* [Torah-learning and scholarship]). Hundreds of rabbis were educated and ordained in that spirit at the *Jüdisch-Theologisches Seminar* of Breslau by world-renowned scholars and professors of Bible and biblical exegesis, Talmud, Jewish history and literature, philosophy of religion, ethics, homiletics, as well as Hebrew and Aramaic. Modern Hebrew was introduced at the beginning of 1921.[11] Modern Hebrew reading (*neu-hebräische Lektüre*), proposed by Frankel, was modified.

Wilhelm Bacher and David Kaufmann, graduates of the Breslau Seminar, were among the first professors of the Rabbinical Seminary of Budapest when it opened its doors in 1877.[12]

[9]*MGWJ* 10 (1861), pp. 159-160; Heinrich Graetz, *The Structure of Jewish History and Other Essays*, transl., ed., and introduced by Ismar Schorsch, New York 1975; *Meor Einayyim (Beleuchtung des Frankel'schen Streites)*,Vienna 1861, pp. 10–13, 16–17, 20, 26, 37; Yedidyah Gottlieb-Fischer, Rabbi of Stuhlweissenburg (Székesfehérvár, Hungary), was one of Frankel's attackers. He opposed the Reform movement in a booklet entitled *Delathayyim u-Variach le-Mei ha-Shiloah*, Vienna 1853, and in essays, Rabbinovitz, pp. 203–218; *Zsidó Lexicon*, Budapest 1929, p. 280; Yitzhak Yosef Cohen, *Hakhme Hungaryah* (Sages of Hungary and Her Torah Literature), Jerusalem 1995, p. 392; Moshe Idel, ' "That Wondrous Occult Power": Some Reflections on Modern Perceptions of Jewish History', in *Studia Judaica* 7 (1998), pp. 59–61.

[10]*Die Erbeseinsetzung der Fraenckelschen Stiftung; Nichtigkeits-Beschwerde in Sachen des Dr. M. Kalisch zu Berlin, Imploranten, Wider die Commerzienrath Fraenckelschen Stiftungs – Curatoren, Imploranten von L. Volkmar,* Berlin 1858.

[11]Markus Brann, 'Verzeichnis der Schriften und Abhandlungen Zacharias Frankels', in MGWJ 45 (1901) pp. 336–352; idem, *Geschichte des Jüdisch-Theologischen Seminars (Fraenckel'sche Stiftung) in Breslau: Festschrift zum Fünfzig Jaehrigen Jubilaeum der Anstalt,* Breslau 1905, (Publication of the Jüdisch-Theologisches Seminar*)* pp. 140–207; Alfred Jospe, *Faculty and Students, 1904–1938,* Tübingen 1963, (originally published in *Das BreslauerSeminar*); Adolf Kober, 'The Seminary's Curriculum and Faculties', in *Historia Judaica* 16:2 (1954), pp. 10, 91–116; Kurt Wilhelm, 'Etwas vom Jüdisch-Theologischen Seminar in Breslau', in *Paul Lazarus gedenkend: Beiträge zur Würdigung der letzten Rabbinergeneration in Deutschland* (Jerusalem 1961), pp. 52–59. On Frankel's positive-historical Judaism see Michael A. Meyer, *Response to Modernity: A history of the Reform movement in Judaism*, New York–Oxford 1990, pp. 84–87, 414–415, footnotes 91–99.

[12]*The Rabbincal Seminary of Budapest, 1877–1977: A Centennial Volume*, ed. by Moshe Carmilly-Weinberger, New York 1986.

Rabbinical Seminary, Budapest

Group picture of ordained rabbis taken on the occasion of the fiftieth anniversary
of the Rabbinical Seminary, Budapest, 1927.

THE RABBINICAL SEMINARY OF BUDAPEST

A strong relationship was forged between the seminars of Breslau and Budapest. The establishment of the rabbinical seminary was mooted in 1806 by an enlightened, erudite Hebrew scholar, David ha-Cohen Friesenhausen who came from Friesenhausen (Bavaria) to Hunsdorf (Hunfalva, now in Slovakia). After studying at the Yeshiva in Fürth with Rabbi Joseph Steinhardt, Friesenhausen went to Berlin, the centre of *Haskalah*. In 1806, he travelled to Vienna and presented a memorandum to Palatin Joseph which reads:

> In a time when under his [Joseph's] reign care was taken of deaf and mute people, why should the suffering of hundreds of thousands of Jews be forgotten? The Jewish people needs to have an institute where rabbis and leaders would be educated so they would be able to teach the people to understand their obligations as human beings and as citizens.[13]

However, the Jews did not have the financial foundation to enable them to sustain such an institute especially at a time when a heavier *Toleranz*-tax was being demanded. Moreover, the government's intention to integrate the Jewish people and Friesenhausen's project of a rabbinical seminary would enhance their separateness. Attendance at secular schools was therefore perceived to eradicate the need for Jewish schools. Friesenhausen described his project and the curriculum of the rabbinical seminary in his book *Mos'doth Tevel* (The Foundations of the World).[14]

The idea of establishing a rabbinical seminary in Budapest was reintroduced in articles written by Leopold Löw in 1844 and 1859.[15] It received an important impetus when, on 20 September 1850 the Emperor Franz Joseph eliminated the massive fine imposed on the Jews in Hungary by General Haynau for their participation in the Hungarian Revolution of 1848–1849. With the mobilisation of an additional one million florint a Jewish education fund, supported by the Emperor, was to be established in order to create a rabbinical seminary and a teachers' institute.

The Hungarian authorities requested that a committee of rabbis draft the statutes and regulations for the rabbinical seminary. The *Elaboratum* was published in 1864 prescribing the curriculum of Jewish and secular studies for the three year programme of the theological department (subsequently extended to five years), and for the the secondary school five year programme. A special paragraph defined the spiritual and intellectual goals of the seminary, keeping in mind the principles of "positive historical Judaism" advocated by Zacharias Frankel. The *Elaboratum* emphasised: "in no part of the curriculum should the basis of positive-historical Judaism be neglected".[16] The objective was to imbue

---

[13]The cultural and other activities, the personality, the religious world outlook, and the scholarly works of David ha-Cohen Friesenhausen are discussed in Meir Gilon's excellent essay 'R. David Friesenhausen between Haskalah and Hassidism', *ibid.*, pp. 3–5; 19–54 (Hebrew section).

[14]*ibid.*

[15]*Pesti Hirlap*, Budapest 2 June 1844; and *Ben Hananyah*, II, Szeged 1859, pp. 341–343.

[16]'Adalékok a Ferencz József Országos Rabbiképö Intézet történetéhez', in *Az Intézet fennállása negyvenedik évfordulója ünnepére (1877 október 4–1917 október 4)* (Documents on the history of the Franz Joseph

students with the desire to study and to preserve Judaism, the inherited teachings of the past, combined with scholarly research. It is not surprising that the curriculum committee required that the candidates for the Rabbinate study for a Ph.D. at a secular university before they could be ordained and receive their diplomas (*Hatarath Hora'ah*). The original curriculum of the seminary in Budapest followed that of Breslau until 1912, when it was revised. Ludwig Blau, the third rector of the seminary, recommended that a comparison be made of the curricula of the two institutes.[17]

In Germany, the struggle was not against the establishment of a seminary but about the clarification of its direction. In Budapest, a bitter attack was directed against the founding of such an institution based on the composition of the Jewish population. More Jews had emigrated from Eastern Europe to Hungary than to Germany. The Hassidic, ultra-Orthodox elements of the Hungarian-Jewish population represented a powerful voice against any innovation in Jewish religious life. Orthodox rabbis held a meeting, which took place on 15 March 1864 in Nyiregyháza under the leadership of Rabbi Jehuda Aszód, Rabbi of Dunaszerdahely. Ninety two rabbis signed a petition against the seminary and a delegation of six rabbis was sent to Emperor Franz Joseph I to request that he reject the proposal. For the ultra-Orthodox, the seminary presented a great danger to Judaism. The staunchly conservative Emperor sympathised with the request and promised his good will. The delegation returned satisfied from Vienna and the peril of the establishment of a seminary in Budapest was averted. There was, however, a strong Western influence developing in Hungary, especially in the large cities. On 28 November 1865, a conference was held in Nagymihály (Mihalovce), convened by Hillel Lichtenstein, Rabbi of Szikszó and student of Rabbi Moses Sopher, HeHatham Sopher of Pressburg (1762–1839). He followed the teachings of his master, one of the greatest rabbinical authorities, who fought against the Reform movement in Hungary and Germany. HeHatham Sopher forbade any innovations, stating "any changes [in the *Halakhah*] are forbidden" (*hadash assur min ha-Torah*). At the Mihalovce meeting, a *pesaq-din* (rabbinic decision) was formulated which forbade any innovations in Jewish religious life. These included prohibitions against sermons delivered in German or Hungarian; against entering the so-called *Chorsynagogen*, in which the cantor wore robes similar to those used by the Christian clergy, choirs sang and men and women were seated together and against changes in traditional synagogue architecture. The reading table for the Torah (*bimah*) was to be placed in the centre of the synagogue.[18] The establishment of the seminary was not discussed at the Mihalovce

---

Rabbinical Seminary on the occasion of the fortieth anniversary of its existence), ed. by Dr. Blau Lajos, Rector, Budapest 1917, p. 29 (hereafter: *Documents*).

[17]*ibid.*, p. 15.

[18]Jacob Katz, *The Unhealed Breach: The Secession of Orthodox Jews from the General Community in Hungary and Germany* [in Hebrew], Jerusalem 1995, pp. 73–99; Moshe Samet, *Halakhah and Reform*, Ph.D. diss. Hebrew University of Jerusalem, 1976; Jacob Katz, 'Contributions Towards a Biography of R. Moses Sofer', in *Studies in Mysticism and Religion Presented to G. Scholem on His Seventieth Birthday By Pupils, Colleagues and Friends* [in Hebrew], Jerusalem 1967, pp. 140–144; Moshe Carmilly-Weinberger,

meeting but it became one of the focal points of the General Congress convened by Joseph Eötvös on 14 December 1867. The purpose of the Congress was to create an autonomous organisation of the Jewish communities in Hungary, and the establishment of a rabbinical seminary was on the agenda. The representatives of Orthodox Jewish communities and rabbis rejected, after a passionate debate, the idea of a seminary. Azriel Hildesheimer (born in 1820 in Halberstadt), a German-educated rabbi (of Eisenstadt, Kismarton and cities in Burgenland), favoured establishing a seminary according to the philosophy of Samson Raphael Hirsch, based upon "Torah im Derekh Eretz". (Yeshiva University in New York, where traditional Torah-learning is not in opposition to scientific knowledge, followed this path). Hildesheimer introduced secular subjects in his *yeshiva* in Eisenstadt. He saw the need to teach his students general secular subjects without this affecting the traditional *yeshiva* education. He was unhappy with the seminaries of Padua and Breslau. At the 1868–1869 Congress in Budapest,[19] Hildesheimer alone remained in favour of a seminary based on his philosophy and with perhaps himself as rector. He left the Congress and accepted the call of the *Adath Yisrael* congregation in Berlin, where in 1873 he founded a rabbinical seminary which became the most important institute for the education of modern-Orthodox rabbis.[20]

On 21 February 1869, the Congress decided to establish the Rabbinical Seminary where Talmud and Codes would be taught, but which would consider at the same time the cultural and scientific gains of the nineteenth century. A committee of six rabbis was appointed to work out a curriculum.[21] The adversaries of the rabbinical seminary renewed their struggle, opposing the use of the

---

'The Jewish Reform Movement in Transylvania and Banat: Rabbi Aaron Chorin', in *Studia Judaica* 5 (1996), pp. 13–60; Joseph Schweitzer, 'The Seminary in Responsa Literature', in Carmilly-Weinberger, *Rabbinical Seminary of Budapest*, pp. 95–105; *Ben Hananya* 45 (11 May 1864), pp. 7, 906–910.

[19]On 23 February 1869 this congress was adjourned with the tragic result of dividing the Jewish communities into three separate and autonomous factions, namely Orthodox, Neolog and Status Quo Ante. This fatal chapter in the history of Hungarian Jewry is discussed in Jacob Katz's excellent work, *The Unhealed Breach*.

[20]Nathaniel Katzburg, 'The Jewish Congress, Hungary, 1868–1869', in *Areshet* 4 (1966), pp. 322–367; Jacob Katz, *The Unhealed Breach*, pp. 92–99; Joseph Eötvös, *A zsidók emancipációja* (The Emancipation of the Jews), Budapest 1840, pp. 142, 293–294 (note 14); Yitzhak Yosef Cohen, *Hakhme Hungaryah*, p. 381; Rabbi Hillel Lichtenstein attacked Rabbi Azriel Hildesheimer in a twelve-page pamphlet entitled *Tokhahah Megulah ve-Sefer Torath ha-Ken'aot*, Kolomea 1873; M. Eliav, 'Meqomo shel ha-Rav A. Hildesheimer ba-Ma'avak al Demutah ha-Ruhanit shel Yahadut Hungaryah' (The place of Rabbi A. Hildesheimer in the Struggle for the Spiritual Image of Hungarian Jewry), in *Zion* 27, pp. 59–86.

[21]*Documents*, pp. 10–11; Carmilly-Weinberger, *Rabbinical Seminary of Budapest*, pp. 910; 'Denkschrift in Angelegenheit des Rabbiner-Bildungs-Institutes, im Auftrage des königl. ungar. Ministers für Cultus und Unterricht, verfasst von J. Rannicher, Sections-Rath', in *Adalékok a Ferencz József országos Rabbi-Képző Intézet történetéhez* (Separatbeilage des *Pester Lloyd* zu Nr. 55, Freitag, 6 März, 1874), in *Documents*, pp. 60–78. Prior to that, on 3 February 1864, at the suggestion of the Hungarian authorities, rabbis drafted statutes and regulations for the Seminary which were published under the title *Das Elaborat der Rabbiner Commission*, Arad 1864; *Ben Hananya* 19 (11 May 1864); *Documents*, pp. 15–43; 'A Kongresszusi szakbizottság tervezete' (Elaboration of the Congressional Committee upon the Decisions of the Congress), (21 February 1869) in *Documents*, pp. 45–59.

Jewish Education Fund for the establishment of the seminary, with the argument that the Orthodox population had also contributed to the fine imposed by General Haynau. In 1871, a delegation of rabbis travelled a second time to Vienna and begged Emperor Franz Joseph I to cancel the seminary project, but this time in vain.[22] On 6 May 1873, the Emperor granted permission for the establishment of a seminary to be financed by the Jewish Education Fund. Rabbi Moses Bloch, the elected Rector, lit the *Ner Tamid* (eternal flame) on 5 October 1877 in the seminary's synagogue. Heinrich Graetz, among other dignitaries, conveyed the congratulations of the *Jüdisch-Theologisches Seminar* of Breslau:

> The Breslau Theological Seminary may consider itself the mother of this newly created institute. Not only does it feel joy that its deserving disciples [Wilhelm Bacher and David Kaufmann] have been appointed professors of the Jewish Theological Seminary in Budapest, but it also has the satisfaction that several of its no less deserving disciples [Ludwig Venetianer, Alexander Kohut] also serve in Hungary as rabbis in highly regarded positions and have participated diligently in establishing this new theological institute of learning.

Graetz expressed the hope that the "young institution would pursue the same goals which have also been those of the Breslau Seminary from its inception."[23]

Breslau became the model for the seminary in Budapest, as it was for those in Vienna, London and New York.

The election of Rabbi Moses Bloch was an excellent decision. Bloch, the grandson of Rabbi Eleazar Trietsch, author of the Responsa *Shemen Roke'ah*, was born in Ronsperg (Bohemia) on 1 February 1815. He spent seven years in Nagy-Tapolcsány (now Topolcany in Slovakia), at the *yeshiva* of his uncle, Rabbi Binyamin Wolf, whose *Sha'arei Torah* had made him famous, before studying philosophy, logic and physics at Pilsen and Prague. He served as rabbi in the communities of Wottitz (Votice) and Hermanuv-Mestetz (Hermanau-Mestec), both in Slovakia, and in Leipnik, Moravia. Bloch founded a *yeshiva* in Leipnik, which attracted students from all over Europe. His Talmudic and secular knowledge and his experience as head of great *yeshivot* prepared him to guide the newly-established Rabbinical Seminary of Budapest from 1877 until his retirement in 1907 at the age of ninety-two. He taught Talmud for thirty years and found time to publish his magnum opus, *Sha'arei Torath ha-Takanoth*,[24] in which he dealt with the development of the laws, customs and regulations (*takanot*) promulgated from biblical times until the sixteenth century. On his eightieth birthday, Emperor Franz Joseph I honoured him by conferring on him the *Franz-Joseph-Orden*. To mark his eightieth and ninetieth birthdays, jubilee volumes were published by his students and members of the faculty. Bloch died on 6 August 1910, recognised by the Jewish and Gentile world as a great

---

[22] Carmilly-Weinberger, *Rabbinical Seminary of Budapest*, p. 10; *Documents*, p. 60; *Areshet* 4 (1966), p. 364, No. 298.

[23] Carmilly-Weinberger, *Rabbinical Seminary of Budapest*, pp. 12–13, 50–51.

[24] Moses Bloch, *Sha'arei Torath ha Takanoth*, Vienna 1879; Budapest 1906.

Talmudic scholar, who had laid down a solid foundation for the Rabbinical Seminary in Budapest.[25]

THE "BRESLAU SPIRIT"

Following Bloch's death, Wilhelm Bacher became Rector of the seminary. Bacher had been ordained in 1876 at the *Jüdisch-Theologisches Seminar* of Breslau and received his Ph.D. at Friedrich Wilhelm University, Breslau, before returning to Budapest. He and David Kaufmann, another graduate of the Breslau seminary, introduced the "Breslau spirit" of learning to the Rabbinical Seminary of Budapest. They had assisted Bloch in guiding the institute through its "turbulent times". Both were influenced by Frankel, Graetz, the philosopher Manuel Joel, David Rosin, the exegete, and the Hellenist Jacob Freudenthal. Bacher became a renowned scholar in Talmudic and Biblical studies and his research in *Halakhah* and *Aggadah* have "lasting influence". Kaufmann wrote more than thirty books and hundreds of articles about Jewish philosophy, genealogy, cultural history and art.[26]

On 22 January 1905, Bacher and many former students left Budapest for Breslau to participate there in the celebrations of the seminary's twenty-fifth anniversary. Blau, in an article written for that occasion, praised the Breslau Seminary and its relations with the Rabbinical Seminary of Budapest.[27] Bacher and Kaufmann maintained a relationship with their *alma mater*. Kaufmann, from 1892 until his death in 1899, co-edited with Markus Brann the *Monatsschrift für Geschichte und Wissenschaft des Judentums* in which scholars at the Budapest seminary published essays.[28] Students of the Budapest seminary were attracted

[25]Carmilly-Weinberger, *Rabbinical Seminary of Budapest*, pp. 14–15; *Die Achtzigjaehrige Geburtstagsfeier des Professors und der Landes-Rabbinerschule Rabb[iner] Moses Bloch*, Budapest 1895; *Jubilee Volume in Honor of M. Bloch at His Ninetieth Birthday* (in Hungarian, with an additional part in Hebrew entitled *Sefer ha-Yovel li-Khevod R. Moshe Arye Bloch*), Budapest 1905; Michael Guttmann, 'Bloch Mózes', in József Bànóczy and Ignácz Gábor (eds.), *Zsidó Plutarchos* II, Budapest 1927, pp. 45–54; a Hebrew poem written by Ignácz Gábor in honour of Moses Bloch can be found in *ibid.*, pp. 39–44.
[26]Carmilly-Weinberger, *Rabbinical Seminary of Budapest*, pp. 16–20; Raphael Patai, 'W. Bacher', *ibid.*, pp. 157–161; Aron Dotan, 'Wilhelm Bacher, Linguist', in *ibid.*, pp. 255–264; Jacob I. Dienstag, 'The Seminary and Maimonidean Scholarship', in *ibid.*, pp. 270–273; Bernát Heller, 'Vilmos Bacher', in Bànóczy and Gábor (eds.), *Zsidó Plutarchos* II pp. 9–38; Ludwig Blau, *Bibliographie der Schriften Wilhelm Bachers*, Frankfurt am Main 1910; Dionysius Friedmann, *Nachtrag zu L. Blau's Bibliographie der Schriften Wilhelm Bachers*, Frankfurt am Main 1928; *Historia Judaica* 16:2 (1954), pp. 103, 116–119; Jacob I. Dienstag, 'The Seminary and Maimonidean Scholarship' in Carmilly-Weinberger, *Rabbinical Seminary of Budapest*, pp. 282–284.
[27]'A boroszlói rabbiszeminárium' (The Rabbinical Seminary of Breslau), in *Magyar Zsidó Szemle*, XII, pp. 97–99.
[28]Markus Brann, 'Zur Geschichte der Monatsschrift', in *MGWJ* 51 (1907), pp. 1–16; *Generalregister zu den Jahrgängen 1-75 der MGWJ*, I–II, Breslau 1938; Kurt Wilhelm, 'Die Monatsschrift für Geschichte und Wissenschaft des Judentums: Ein geistesgeschichtlicher Versuch', in Kisch (ed.), *Das Breslauer Seminar*, pp. 327–380; Leo Baerwald, 'Register für die Jahrgaenge 76 bis 83 der Monatsschrift', in *ibid.*, pp. 351–353; Samuel Krauss, *David Kaufmann: Eine Biographie von Dr. Samuel Krauss*, Breslau 1901; Markus Brann (ed.) *Gesammelte Schriften von David Kaufmann*, Frankfurt am Main 1908; Carmilly-Weinberger, *Rabbinical Seminary of Budapest*, pp. 41–42. Wilhelm Bacher, Ludwig Blau, Adolf Büchler, Ignáz Goldziher, Michael Guttmann, Bernát Heller, George Alexander Kohut,

to Breslau. Among the first were Adolf Büchler, later Principal of Jews' College, London; Joseph Gerson, later a rabbi in Szabadka (Subotica); Ludwig Venetianer, later a rabbi in Ujpest and lecturer at the rabbinical seminary; and Ignaz Ziegler, later a rabbi in Karlsbad. Büchler's main objective was to promote the *Wissenschaft des Judentums*. His dissertation, *Untersuchungen zur Entstehung und Entwicklung der hebräischen Accente*, was published in the *Sitzungsberichte der kaiserlichen Akademie der Wissenschaften* in Vienna in 1891, although his main interest lay in the period of the Second Temple.[29]

In the 1920s and 1930s more than fifteen students of the Budapest Seminary spent some semesters in Breslau and returned influenced by the intellectual world of the Breslau school. Among them was David Samuel Löwinger, who was to be Rector of the Seminary between 1942 and 1950. Together with another student of Breslau, Bernard Dov Weinryb, Löwinger prepared two catalogues of manuscripts held in the library of the *Jüdisch-Theologisches Seminar* of Breslau.[30]

In 1921, Michael Guttmann was invited to be *Seminarrabbiner* of the *Jüdisch-Theologisches Seminar* of Breslau, where he served until 1933, returning as Rector to his *alma mater* in Budapest following the death of Ludwig Blau in 1932. He strengthened the relationship between the two seminaries, restructuring the curriculum in Breslau in 1926 along the lines of the Budapest curriculum. For example, the division of the curriculum into three *Abteilungen* in Breslau is similar to the *Unter- und Oberabteilung* (alsó és felsö-osztály) in Budapest. In 1887, the undergraduate (*Gymnasium*) classes in Jewish and classical studies were eliminated in Breslau. In Budapest, the *Gymnasium* (lower division), consisting of five classes, continued until 1944. Freshmen and senior students in Breslau, as in Budapest, sat in the same classrooms and participated together in Bible, Talmud, Jewish history and philosophy courses.[31]

Many who had studied at both institutes became university professors:

Samuel Krauss and Immanuel Löw contributed to *MGWJ* during its existence. Samuel David Löwinger and Bernard Dov Weinryb, *Jiddische Handschriften in Breslau*, Budapest 1936; 2nd edn. 1965.

[29] Adolf Büchler, *Das grosse Synhedrion in Jerusalem*, Vienna 1902.

[30] Carmilly-Weinberger, *Rabbinical Seminary of Budapest*, pp. 145–146; Alfred Jospe, 'Biographies and Bibliographies' and 'Verzeichnis der Lehrer und Schüler des Seminars, sowie ihrer Schriften, 1904–1938', in Kisch (ed.), *Das Breslauer Seminar*, pp. 405–442; Hugo Neczerka, 'Die Herkunft der Studierenden des Jüdisch-Theologischen Seminars zur Breslau, 1854–1938', in *Zeitschrift für Ostforschung* 35, 1/2 (1986), pp. 88–139. Some students of the Budapest Seminary (Naphtali Blumgrund, Gyula Diamant, Lipót Kecskeméti, Lajós Kún, Ferencz Löwy, Béla Vajda and Ignàc Ziegler) studied at the *Lehranstalt für die Wissenschaft des Judentums* in Berlin; Miksa Even-Eckstein, Ottó Komlós, Gábor Schwartz and Ernö Szrulyovitz studied at the *Jüdisch-Theologische Lehranstalt* in Vienna. Alexander Scheiber studied for one year (1939) in London and Oxford. The catalogues prepared by Weinryb and Löwinger are *The Catalogue of the Hebrew Manuscripts*, Wiesbaden 1965 and the *Jiddische Handschriften*, Budapest 1936, 2nd ed. 1965.

[31] Kisch (ed.), *Das Breslauer Seminar*, p. 88; *Studien und Prüfungsordnung des Jüdisch-Theologischen Seminars (Fraenckelscher Stiftung) in Breslau*, Breslau 1926; Miksa Klein, 'Courses Given at the Ober- and Unter Abteilung (Gymnasium) of the Rabbinical Seminary of Budapest in the Years 1877–1927', in Dr. L. Blau, Rector and Dr. Miksa Klein, Secretary, *Jubilee Volume of the Fiftieth Anniversary of Francz Joseph Rabbinical Seminary, 1877–1927*, vol. I, Budapest 1927, pp. 43–61.

Raphael Patai (Fairleigh Dickinson University in Rutherford, N.J.), Moses Weinberger (Carmilly) (Yeshiva University, New York), Ödön Kálmán (lecturer at the Rabbinical Seminary of Budapest), Alexander Guttmann (Hebrew Union College, Cincinnati) and Heinrich Guttmann (Rabbinical Seminary of Budapest), the sons of Michael Guttmann, Professor of Talmud at the Rabbinical Seminary of Budapest.

BIBLE AND TALMUD

Bible and Talmud were important parts of the curriculum of both seminaries. Modern methods of scholarship were introduced, although biblical criticism was not accepted. Julius Wellhausen's radical Bible criticism had an antisemitic undertone. Heinrich Graetz, who opposed Protestant biblical scholarship, approved traditional explanations of the five books of Moses although he was liberal in his interpretation of the Hagiographa (Kohelet, Proverbs and the Psalms).[32] Israel Rabin, Bible lecturer (and later *Seminarrabbiner*) also opposed Bible criticism as did Jacob Benno, a graduate of the Breslau Seminary and rabbi of Göttingen and later of Dortmund.[33]

In Budapest, Wilhelm Bacher's approach to the Bible was similarly conservative. He believed "in the divine origin of the religious content of the Holy Scripture".[34] Ludwig Blau rejected the radical Protestant Bible criticism of Julius Wellhausen with its antisemitic undertones and any proposed corrections to the biblical text remarking: "In 1925, someone living on the third floor at 37 Königstrasse in Göttingen, wants to know Hebrew better than the Prophet Ezekiel." When the Hebrew University established two chairs in Bible Studies in 1920, Blau was among the scholars considered for these posts.[35]

Academic freedom prevailed at the seminaries of Breslau and Budapest but restraint was appreciated in Bible teaching. At the establishment of the Rabbinical Seminary in Budapest, Ignáz Goldziher, a world-renowned scholar of Islam, who took part in the preliminary work leading up to its foundation, was not invited to join its faculty. His work, *Der Mythos bei den Hebräern und seine geschichtliche Entwicklung*[36], caused consternation because of its mythological explana-

---

[32]Kisch (ed.), *Das Breslauer Seminar*, pp. 270–271; Julius Wellhausen, *Prolegomena zur Geschichte Israels*, Edinburgh 1885; *idem, Prolegomena to the History of Israel*, Atlanta 1994.

[33]Israel Rabin, 'Studien zur vormosaischen Gottesvorstellung', in *Festschrift zum 75 jährigen Bestehen des Jüdisch-Theologischen Seminars*, Breslau 1929; Jacob Benno, *Der Pentateuch: Exegetisch-kritische Forschungen*, n.p. 1905; Kisch (ed.), *Das Breslauer Seminar*, pp. 271, 420; *Historia Judaica* 16:2 (1954), pp. 96–97.

[34]Wilhelm Bacher, *Die Bibelexegese Moses Maimunis*, Budapest–Straßburg 1897; reprint. 1972, pp. VI, 152–153.

[35]Carmilly-Weinberger, *Rabbinical Seminary of Budapest*, pp. 78–79; Sara Japheth, 'Research and Academic Teaching of the Bible in Israel', in *Jewish Studies: Forum of the World Union of Jewish Studies* 32 (1992), pp. 15, 23–24; Jacob Haberman, 'Some Changing Aspects of Jewish Scholarship', in *Jewish Quarterly Review*, 35:2 (1986), pp. 191–192; Nathan Rotenstreich, 'The "Science of Judaism" and Its Transformation', in *Jewish Studies* 32 (1986), p. 11.

[36]Ignàz Goldziher, *Der Mythos bei den Hebräern und seine geschichtliche Entwicklung*, Leipzig 1876; reprint. 1987

tions. However, following the sudden death of David Kaufmann in 1899, Gold-ziher was asked to join. He taught philosophy and subjects related to Islam and the works of Saadiah, Bahya ibn Pakuda, Abraham ibn Daud, Yehudah ha-Levi and Maimonides, bringing prestige and honour to the Budapest seminary.[37]

The second important subject taught at both seminaries was the Talmud. From the beginning, these institutes were blessed with great Talmudic lumin-aries: Rabbi Zacharias Frankel in Breslau and Rabbi Moshe Bloch in Budapest. Each made an impact. Ephraim Elimelech Urbach, one of the most outstanding contemporary Talmudic scholars and a student at the Breslau Seminary, wrote:

> Jewish scholarship in which the impact of the Seminary of Breslau is uniquely and ostensibly visible, which somehow deviated from its envisaged goal, is the research of Talmudic literature and it penetrated into the orthodox and liberal movements.[38]

Urbach excelled not only in Talmudic but also in Jewish scholarship as a whole.[39] He clearly exemplified Frankel's dictum: "Judaism and scholarship must be brought closer to each other", and his belief in the holy desire for research and scholarship was echoed in the title of the lectures he delivered in Jerusalem in 1926: 'The new should become holy and the holy should become new (*He-Hadash yitkadesh veha-kadosh yithadesh*).'[40] Urbach was not satisfied with philological-critical explanations and emendations of Talmudic texts but was also concerned with their historical and cultural meanings as his monumental work *Ba'alei ha-Tosafot: toldotehem, hiburehem ve-shitatam* (The Tosafists: their history, works and methods) shows.[41] "One of the most fundamental works in Jewish scholarship", wrote Jacob Katz of this work, "which will be needed by all who deal with the Middle Ages from historical and halakhic points of view."[42]

Zacharias Frankel defined the objectives and methods of Talmudic scholar-ship: history and philology are the auxiliary tools by means of which Talmudic literature is researched.[43] Frankel was followed by Israel Lewy, who in *Über einige Fragmente aus der Mishnah Abba Saul* (1876) and in other works made use of the philological method. The third professor who belonged to the philological school was Saul Horovitz (born in Szántó, Hungary), a student of, and successor to, Israel Lewy.[44]

---

[37] Carmilly-Weinberger, *Rabbinical Seminary of Budapest*, pp. 20–23; Raphael Patai, 'The Seminary and Oriental Studies', *ibid.*, pp. 187–193, 278–279.

[38] Ephraim E. Urbach, *Shloshet Morei ha-Talmud shel ha-Seminar be-Breslau* (The Three Talmud Teachers of the Seminary in Breslau); Kisch (ed.), *Das Breslauer Seminar*, p. 175.

[39] His life and scholarship were discussed in a special issue of *Jewish Studies*, which carried the title: 'E.E. Urbach: A Bio-Bibliography' in *Supplement to Jewish Studies: Forum of the World Union of Jewish Studies*, ed. by David Assaf, No. 1, Jerusalem 1993.

[40] *ibid.*, p. 123, No. 121; p. 124, No. 141.

[41] Bitya Ben-Shammai, 'Prof. Ephraim Elimelech Urbach: A Biobibliography', *ibid.,*, p. 120, Nos. 51, 62, 133, 237, 300.

[42] Jacob Sussman, 'The Scholarly Oeuvre of Prof. Ephraim Elimelech Urbach', *ibid.*, pp. 26, 107–114.

[43] Kisch (ed.), *Das Breslauer Seminar*, p. 185; Zacharias Frankel, *Darkhei ha-Mishnah*, 1859; *idem, Mevo ha-Yerushalmi*, Breslau 1870.

[44] Shaul Horowitz, *Die Psychologie bei den jüdischen Religionsphilosophen des Mittelalters von Saadia bis Maimuni*, Breslau 1898; Kisch (ed.), *Das Breslauer Seminar*, pp. 183–185, 273–277.

Bloch and Bacher, Blau and Michael Guttmann, who was *Seminar-Rabbiner* and Professor of Talmud in Breslau between 1921 and 1933, all became well-known Talmudic scholars. Bacher's works *Die Agada der Tannaiten, Die Agada der palästinensischen Amoräer* and *Die Agada der babylonischen Amoräer*[45] dealt with the history and the statements of the *Tannaim* and the *Amoraim*. Bacher's works have not only been reprinted but have also been translated into Hebrew.[46] They are invaluable contributions to the study of the development of Jewish religious beliefs. These monumental Talmudic works were prepared through a "penetrating critique of the midrashic works", according to their author and have remained of "lasting importance" to Talmudic research. Bacher's *Tradition und Tradenten in den Schulen Palästinas und Babyloniens: Studien und Materialien zur Entstehungsgeschichte des Talmuds*[47] deals with the construction design of the Talmud and the transmissions of traditions through the generations and their incorporation into the Babylonian and Palestinian Talmuds.[48] Bacher critically researched and organised the immense material of Jewish traditions and so helps us to understand the *Entstehungsgeschichte* of the Talmud. Ludwig Blau completed and published the *Tradition und Tradenten* because of Bacher's failing health.[49]

Blau was an important and recognised Talmud scholar who understood that modern Jewish scholarship is a bridge between Jewish disciplines (Bible and Talmud) and secular studies. "The Talmud must be placed in the lectures within the cycle of all other literatures so that the student may find in the Talmud ample points of contact with other branches of study, and thus his interest in learning will be increased", he wrote in 'Methods of Teaching the Talmud in the Past and in the Present'.[50] In his German-language Talmud classes Blau demonstrated the usefulness of this method: "The object of teaching the Talmud is not to master single portions dialectically but to acquire knowledge of its contents, its spirit, its doctrines and principles" in doing so, Blau was convinced, "that the students will learn the life and habits of the ancients".[51] For example, on the debate between the schools of Hillel and Shammai in the first *mishnah* of tractate Betzah on whether it is permissible to eat an egg laid during a Holy Day, Blau concluded that it illustrated "the miserable condition of the Palestinian Jew" under the Roman oppression demonstrating the prevailing difficult economic conditions under which a poor Jewish woman was confronted

[45]Wilhelm Bacher, *Die Agada der Tannaiten*, I-II, Straßburg 1890, reprint. 1965–1966; *idem, Die Agada der palestinensischen Amoräer*, I–III, Straßburg 1892–1899, reprint. 1965; *idem, Die Agada der babylonischen Amoräer*, Straßburg 1878, 2nd ed. Frankfurt 1913, reprint. 1965.

[46]Alexander Siskind Rabinowitz translated many of Bacher's works. Aron Dotan, 'Wilhelm Bacher the Linguist', in Carmilly-Weinberger, *Rabbinical Seminary of Budapest*, pp. 260–261.

[47]Wilhelm Bacher, *Tradition und Tradenten in den Schulen Palästinas und Babyloniens: Studien und Materialien zur Entstehungsgeschichte des Talmuds*, Leipzig 1914, reprint. Berlin 1966.

[48]See Blau's foreword to Michael Guttmann's *Register des hebräischen Materials*, Leipzig 1914; reprint. Berlin 1966; Carmilly-Weinberger, *Rabbinical Seminary of Budapest*, pp. 155–161 (note 28 on p. 161).

[49]Wilhelm Bacher and Ludwig Blau, *Tradition und Tradenten in den Schulen Palästinas und Babyloniens*, Leipzig 1914; reprint. Berlin 1966; Ludwig Blau, *Bibliographie der Schriften Wilhelm Bachers*, Frankfurt am Main 1910; Friedmann, *Nachtrag*, Frankfurt am Main 1928; Dotan, pp. 255–264.

[50]Ludwig Blau, 'Methods of Teaching the Talmud in the Past and in the Present', in *Jewish Quarterly Review*, 15 (1903), pp. 131–132.

[51]*ibid.*

with this religious problem. Blau recommended that the "history of exegesis of the Talmud" be included in the curriculum in addition to the "introduction to the *Mishnah* and the Talmud".[52] Blau applied the same methodological approach to his scientific scholarly works. In addition to biblical themes for instance his *Massoretische Untersuchungen* (1891) or *Zur Einleitung in die Heilige Schrift* (1894), he dealt with Talmudic issues in the light of modern scholarship.

At Breslau, eight hours per week in each semester were dedicated to learning Talmud with the commentary of the Tosafot. Students were accepted by the Seminary on condition that they could demonstrate knowledge of ten pages of the Talmud together with the commentary of Rashi. In Budapest, there was a lower (gymnasial) division, which consisted of a five-year course of study into which students who had a minimal knowledge of Talmud and who were tutored by those students who came from *yeshivot* were accepted. They continued their studies in the upper division, which also consisted of five years. In the whole ten years they learned approximately 250 to 300 pages of Talmud with commentaries (Rashi and Tosafot).[53] "The most significant field of instruction and research at the Budapest Seminary was the Talmud", stated Alexander Guttmann, a student at both seminaries and subsequently a professor at the Hebrew Union College in Cincinnati.[54]

According to Kurt Wilhelm, however, some students were not happy with the Talmud instruction at the Breslau seminary. Students who were admitted with knowledge of only ten pages of Talmud were unable to follow the lectures of great Talmudic scholars, the "Begründer der wissenschaftlichen Talmudkritik", such as Zacharias Frankel, Israel Lewy and Saul Horovitz. Those students who came from the *yeshivot* of Eastern Europe enjoyed the instruction and guidance of these great teachers and were able to pursue their *wissenschaftlich* studies.[55] In the final examinations for ordination in Budapest, the candidate, after having successfully passed the preliminary examinations in the first and third years, had to prove his knowledge, both orally and in written form, in Bible, Talmud, Codes, Jewish philosophy and history. In Breslau, examinations were administered in Bible, Talmud, Jewish history and literature, history of philosophy, pedagogy and homiletics.[56]

GOTTESDIENST

With the establishment of the seminaries, special places were set aside for synagogue services. A synagogue was opened on the second floor of the building at

[52]Ludwig Blau, *Festschrift zum 50 jährigen Bestehen der Franz-Josef Landes Rabbiner Schule in Budapest,* Budapest 1927, pp. 47–57.

[53]Wilhelm, *Etwas vom Seminar in Breslau*, pp. 52–59. A detailed programme of Talmudic tractates taught at the Budapest seminary can be found in *Festschrift zum 50 jährigen Bestehens der Franz-Josef Landes Rabbiner Schule*, pp. 47–57.

[54]Carmilly-Weinberger, *Rabbinical Seminary of Budapest*, p. 180.

[55]Wilhelm, *Etwas vom Seminar in Breslau*, pp. 53–54.

[56]*Studien-Ordnung für das jüdisch-theologische Seminar in Breslau festgestellt im Jahre 1873, revidiert im Jahre 1895. Nebst einem Anhange: Vorschriften für die Prüfungs-Candidaten,* Breslau 1885, pp. 9–12.

Waldstrasse 14 in Breslau.[57] In Budapest, a synagogue was built as an addition to the seminary building. It had a carved-wood ark and the *bimah,* when opened up, served as a pulpit. Students, especially those who resided in the dormitory, participated in the daily services. On Sabbaths and Holy Days, the rector and some of the professors attended the services and listened to sermons delivered in Hungarian by students of the upper division. Some students who had studied in Breslau, delivered sermons in German upon their return. The first teacher of homiletics was David Kaufmann, "einer der besten Kanzelredner der Neuzeit", who, requested by the Hungarian authorities to do so, learned Hungarian in four years.[58] Blau excelled in homiletics, as a teacher and as a speaker, basing his well-prepared sermons on biblical texts and speaking freely when preaching. The addresses he delivered at rabbinical ordination ceremonies were intended to serve as a guide for the newly ordained rabbis in the important and responsible tasks facing them in Jewish communities. He published a special homiletic supplement to the *Magyar Zsidó Szemle* (Hungarian Jewish Review).[59]

Between 1930 and 1943, Simon Hevesi, Chief Rabbi of Budapest and a renowned orator, was Professor of Homiletics. Students read their sermons, which were delivered in the synagogue of the seminary, to Hevesi in class. He analysed and criticised and, sometimes, "reshaped" the sermons in order to instruct his students.[60]

Isaak Heinemann, the great professor of Jewish-Hellenistic literature, also taught homiletics. He lived outside the seminary and therefore held his classes on weekdays in the classroom and in the synagogue. He was an outstanding orator and possessed the ability, despite his hearing difficulties, to guide the rabbinical candidates, who revered their teacher.[61] Students conducted the services at both seminaries. Some of them were blessed with excellent musical voices and talents. Following the Second World War, the synagogue adjoining the Budapest Seminary was rebuilt and reopened its doors.

MODERN HEBREW LANGUAGE AND LITERATURE

The study of modern Hebrew language was introduced in Breslau as this was felt to be an urgent matter. Those who proved their knowledge of Hebrew were immediately accepted into *Abteilung B* and, after a short stay there and on passing an examination, were moved to *Abteilung A.* It appears that *Seminar-Rabbiner* Michael Guttmann, who mastered the modern Hebrew language and

---

[57]Wilhelm, *Etwas vom Seminar in Breslau,* pp. 57–58.
[58]David Kaufmann, *Achtzehn Predigten,* ed. by Ludwig Blau and Max Weisz, Budapest 1931; Bertalan Kohlbach, *The First Decade,* in Carmilly-Weinberger, *Rabbinical Seminary of Budapest,* pp. 55, 65.
[59]Carmilly-Weinberger, *Rabbinical Seminary of Budapest,* p. 171.
[60]*ibid.,* pp. 85–87.
[61]Adolf Kober, 'The Jewish Theological Seminary of Breslau and "Wissenschaft des Judentums" ', in Kisch (ed.), *Das Breslauer Seminar,* pp. 273, 395–397; Raphael Patai, *Apprentice in Budapest,* 1988, p. 337; Isaak Heinemann, *Die Stimme Gottes in der Kraft des Einzelnen. Predigt gehalten in der Synagoge des Seminars am Wochenfeste 5687,* Breslau 1927; idem, *Der Tag der Versoehnungen. Predigt gehalten am Versoeh-nungstage 5683 in der Synagoge des jüdisch-theologischen Seminars in Breslau,* [in Hebrew], Breslau 1923.

had an interest in Hebrew literature and poetry, was eager to reinforce *Neuhe-bräisch* into the curriculum. In 1925, he was invited to head the Institute of Jewish Studies and to teach Talmud at the Hebrew University in Jerusalem. After one year in Jerusalem, he returned to Breslau and his desire to have modern Hebrew taught at the seminary was strengthened.

At the Budapest Seminary, Wilhelm Bacher and David Kaufmann were also concerned with modern Hebrew literature. Bacher, Blau, Samuel Krauss and Goldziher aided and guided Eliezer ben Yehuda in writing and publishing his modern Hebrew vocabulary.[62] In 1894, Bacher published his father's *Sha'ar Shimon*,[63] the first representative volume of Hebrew poetry in Hungary. He also translated Schiller's poem *Der Jüngling am Bache* into Hebrew.[64] Between 1862 and 1868 Bacher wrote twenty-eight Hebrew poems, now in the library of the Budapest seminary.

In 1940, a special *Hug Ivri* (Hebrew Society) was established, where lectures in modern Hebrew were given weekly. Josef Kastein, the renowned German-Jewish author, was invited to discuss "the cultural problems of Eretz Israel". In 1943, a memorial service was held for Joseph Trumpeldor.

Students of the rabbinical seminary, especially those who arrived from the Hebrew high schools of Ungvar (Uzhorod) and Munkács (Mucacevo), promoted Zionism inside and outside the Institute. Some of the professors were pro-Zionist. After the Balfour Declaration on 2 November 1917, Rector Ludwig Blau declared: "Prompted by our religious ideas and feelings of religious brotherhood, we have cleaved and do cleave to the Holy Land. We warmly welcome and support any effort exerted in its interest."[65]

Blau had a durable connection with the Breslau seminary. He was a member of the board of the *Gesellschaft zur Förderung der Wissenschaft des Judentums* in Germany and of the *Mekize Nirdamim* society, which was founded in 1862 by E. L. Silbermann (Lyck) with the assistance of Chief Rabbi Nathan Adler of London. The objective was to publish Hebrew manuscripts in order to enhance interest in Jewish scholarship. Following a hiatus of almost ten years, it renewed its activities

[62]Eliezer Ben-Yehuda's letters to Ignáz Goldziher were published by Alexander Scheiber in *Orlogin*, 1957, pp. 318–319; Moshe Carmilly-Weinberger, 'Eliezer ben Yehuda's Modern Hebrew Dictionary and Jewish Scholarship', in *Studia Judaica* 8 (1999); Samuel David Löwinger, 'Mikhteve Eliezer ben Yehuda (Jerusalem) el Prof. Bacher (Budapest)', in *Antal Mark Emlékkönyv* [Memorial volume to Antal Mark], ed. by Moses Weinberger, Kolozsvár 1943, pp. 145–147 [in Hungarian] and pp. I–XIII [in Hebrew].

[63]Wilhelm Bacher (ed.), *Sha'ar Shimon. Hebräische Dichtungen von Simon Bacher. Aus den gedruckten Schriften und dem handschriftlichen Nachlasse des verewigten Verfassers ausgewählt und herausgegeben von seinem Sohne Wilhelm Bacher*, I-III, Vienna 1894.

[64]'Ha-Na'ar al ha-Ayyin', transl. by Wilhelm Bacher in *Kokhave Yitzhak*, 32 (1865), pp. 60–61. He also translated from Arabic (*La'amiyah al Arab*) and two poems by Sándor Petöfi from Hungarian.

[65]Adolf Kober, 'The Jewish Theological Seminary of Breslau and "Wissenschaft des Judentums"', in *Historia Judaica* 16:2 (1954), p. 92, reprint. in Kisch (ed.), *Das Breslauer Seminar*, pp. 261–293; *Studien und Prüfungsordnung*, p. 5, para. 9; Moshe Carmilly-Weinberger, 'Hebrew Language and Literature', in *idem*, *Rabbinical Seminary of Budapest*, pp. 205–214; *idem*, *Yalkut ha-Meshorerim ha-Ivriyyim me-Hungaryah* [Hebrew poets of Hungary], Tel-Aviv 1977; Eliyahu Yeshurun, 'The Seminary, Zionism and Israel', in Carmilly-Weinberger, *Rabbinical Seminary of Budapest*, pp. 123–142.

in 1885 under the impetus of David Kaufmann who remained an active member of its board until his death in 1899.[66]

Blau's love of Hebrew scholarship and literature is visible in his role of founder and editor of *Hatzofeh leHohmath Yisrael meEretz Hagar* [The Review from the Land of Hungary]. From 1911 to 1931 fifteen issues appeared and the annual became a forum for Jewish scholars from all over the world. *Hatzofeh* received essays in Hebrew from Johannesburg, London, Amsterdam, New York, Warsaw, Cracow, Tangier and Cairo. Blau also edited the fifth volume of *Otzar Yisrael* and contributed many articles.[67]

Interest in modern Hebrew language and literature was not confined to the faculty members of the rabbinical seminary in Budapest. Students were influenced by their teachers and wrote Hebrew poetry. Joseph Patai dedicated his first volume of Hebrew poetry *Sha'ashu'ei Alumim*,[68] and Avigdor Hameiri-Feuerstein dedicated one of his poems, to Bacher. Hameiri became one of the most eloquent Hebrew writers and secured for himself a place in the history of modern Hebrew literature. In 1912 his first volume of Hebrew poems, *Me-Shire Avigdor Feuerstein*, was published in Budapest.

STUDENT LIFE

The student body in Breslau was formed into an independent, recognised student organisation. The organisation had its representatives, unlike that in Budapest, where the various student societies had no official standing. In Budapest their task was to conduct cultural events, with lectures delivered by students, to organise public meetings on national remembrance days and to publish jubilee volumes (Moses Bloch, Abraham Hoffer) and memorial volumes (Leopold Zunz, David Kaufmann, Ignáz Goldziher). The student body of the seminary in Budapest was more homogeneous than the one in Breslau, which had students from Poland, Hungary, Romania, Czechoslovakia and Switzerland.

In 1885–1866, the students of the Theological faculty in Budapest planned to establish a Hungarian *Burschenschaft* in imitation of the *Amicitia* of Breslau. Wilhelm Bacher, then a student at the Breslau Seminary (1868–1876), established the *Boroszlói Magyar Olvasó Társulat* (the Hungarian Cultural Society in Breslau) together with Ignáz Goldziher, then a student at the *Friedrich Wilhelm*

[66]Samuel Krauss, *David Kaufmann: Eine Biographie*, Breslau 1901, p. 24; *Hevrath Mekitzei Nirdamim, 1864–1964, Ephraim E. Urbach's discourse at the one hundredth anniversary of "Hevrath Mekitzei Nirdamim,* Jerusalem 1964; Bityah Ben-Shammai , 'Professor Ephraim Elimelech Urbach: A Bibliography' in *Supplement to Jewish Studies*, p.122, No. 102; *Encyclopaedia Judaica*, vol. XI, cols. 1270–1271.

[67]Samuel D. Löwinger, 'Ludwig Blau', in Carmilly-Weinberger, *Rabbinical Seminary of Budapest*, pp. 162–177; *Jubilee Volume of Ludwig Blau at His Sixty-Fifth Birthday and Forty Years of Scholarship*, (in Hungarian), edited by Simon Hevesi, Miksa Klein and Dionysius Friedmann, Budapest 1926; Simon Hevesi, Bernát Heller and Miksa Klein (eds.) *Ve-Zoth li-Yehuda*, Vienna, 1926; Simon Hevesi, Michael Guttmann and Samuel David Löwinger (eds.) *Zikhron Yehuda: Studies in Memory of L. Blau*, Budapest 1938, (hereafter *Zikhron Yehuda*); Dionysius Friedmann, *Bibliographie der Schriften Ludwig Blau's, 1886–1926*, Budapest 1926; Joseph Bakonyi and Dionysius Friedman, 'The Literary Work of L. Blau in the Last Years of His Life, 1926–1936', in *Zikhron Yehuda*, p. 18

[68]Joseph Patai, *Sha'ashu'ei Alumim*, Budapest 1903.

Universität. Bacher returned to Hungary after completing his studies, bringing with him the documents and seal of this society. The *Burschenschaft* never materialised, however. Ironically, in the 1930s, students from the Breslau Seminary carried the paraphernalia of a German *Burschenschaft* at a time when Nazism was conquering Germany. The antisemitic *Die Peitsche*, the German university students' paper, was posted on the bulletin board of the seminary as an indication of the danger to the future of the Jewish community in Germany and to the *Jüdisch-Theologisches Seminar* in Breslau.[69]

In the 1920s, the economic situation in Germany became more difficult daily. The students of the Breslau seminar who came from different parts of Europe, eager to learn, were confronted with difficulties in securing lodging and food. Students who required financial assistance were aided by the *Liwyath Hen* society, which was established in 1885 and which provided daily meals in the *Mittelstands-küche*. In Budapest, the *Etz Hayyim* and other foundations provided financial help for lodging and other expenses for students from neighbouring cities. The housing crisis, during which ten to twelve students were lodged in the former laboratory in the main building, was solved in 1931–1932, when an adjoining building, purchased in 1918 with a donation of 600,000 crowns, was turned into a dormitory. The American Jewish Joint Distribution Committee (AJDC) opened the *Mensa*, where students enjoyed three meals every day. Students in the Theological Faculty were given the opportunity by the *Hevrah Kadishah* of Budapest to serve for one month as auxiliary rabbis at funerals. With the fees they received, they were able to cover the costs of printing their doctoral theses. In 1941–1944, the financial situation worsened and students were forced into slave labour camps.[70]

THE SECOND WORLD WAR AND ITS CONSEQUENCES

820,000 Jews lived in Hungary in the years 1936–1944. They were subjected to the anti-Jewish legislation created by five premiers—Kálmán Darányi, Béla Imrédy, Count Pál Teleky, László Bárdossy and Miklós Kállay—who served under Regent Miklós Horthy. In a letter to Teleky Horthy declared: "I have been an antisemite all of my life. I haven't socialised with Jews . . . perhaps I was the first who loudly voiced antisemitism, but I cannot silently allow inhumanity, sadism and humiliation when we still need them."[71] This sentiment notwithstanding, he urged the enactment of "racial legislation". The *numerus clausus* restrictions, which limited the number of Jewish students in higher education to six per cent of the total number of students, were introduced in 1920.[72] Anti-

[69]Carmilly-Weinberger, 'Students at the Rabbinical Seminary of Budapest' in, *Rabbinical Seminary of Budapest*, p. 31; Vidor Pál, *History of the Literary Society of the Rabbinical Seminary of Budapest*, Budapest 1928); Jospe, pp. 384–388; Géza Komoróczy (ed.), *A zsidó Budapest*, Budapest 1995, p. 313.
[70]'Assistance to the Students', in *Jubilee Volume of the Fiftieth Anniversary*, I (1927), pp. 78–95; 'Students', in Carmilly-Weinberger, *Rabbinical Seminary of Budapest*, pp. 146–147.
[71]Miklós Szinai and László Szücs (eds.), *Horthy Miklós titkos iratai* [The Secret Papers of Miklós Horthy], 4th edition, Budapest 1972, pp. 136–138, 221–222, 261–262.
[72]Nathaniel Katzburg, *Hungary and the Jews: Policy and Legislation, 1920–1944*, Ramat Gan 1981, [in Hebrew], pp. 60–79; Judith Horváth, 'The Seminary and the Budapest University', in Carmilly-

Jewish laws were promulgated in 1938–1942; in the eyes of the antisemitic politicians such legislation was needed to more effectively safeguard the equilibrium in social and economic life, to curb Jewish social-economic activities and to protect the race from Jews. In 1940, the Hungarian authorities introduced these laws into the North-Transylvanian territory, annexed from Romania under the Vienna Dictate of 30 August 1940.

All of these anti-Jewish laws worked to ruin the entire infrastructure of Jewish life. Thousands of families lost their means of livelihood.[73] In 1941, an Executive Decree approved by Regent Horthy, forced tens of thousands of Jews between the ages of eighteen and forty-eight into labour detachments which were then sent to the German-Russian battlefields, where they were exposed to inhuman and brutal treatment by the Hungarian officers and soldiers. A majority lost their lives.[74]

The *Wehrmacht* entered Hungary on 19 March 1944 and this event sealed the fate of Hungarian Jewry.[75] The Hungarian government and administration, under the former ambassador to Berlin Döme Sztójay, under the guidance of the German military command and with the co-operation of an SS detachment, deported within six weeks 600,000 Jewish Hungarian citizens to Auschwitz-Birkenau, Mauthausen and other death-camps, where they perished after indescribable suffering, together with millions of their Jewish brethren.[76]

AFTER 1945

On 10 November 1938 the doors of the great Institute on Wallstrasse 14 were closed: "In the eighty-fourth year of its existence the *Jüdisch-Theologisches Seminar* fell victim to extreme violence. In those horror-filled days of November

Weinberger, *Rabbinical Seminary of Budapest*, pp. 106–112; Yehuda Don, *Anti-Semitic Legislations in Hungary and Their Implementation in Budapest*, New York 1986.

[73] Katzburg, *Hungary and the Jews*, p. 94; *idem*, *Antisemitism in Hungary, 1867–1914*, Tel Aviv 1969; Victor Karády, 'Les Juifs d'Hongroie sous les lois antisemites', in *Actes de la Recherche en Sciences Sociales* 56 (1985), pp. 3–30; Yehuda Don, 'Antisemitic legislations in Hungary, 1938–1944', in *East European Quarterly* 20 (1986), pp. 477–485; Moshe Carmilly-Weinberger, *Memorial Volume for the Jews of Cluj-Kolozsvár*, New York 1970, reprint. 1988; *idem*, 'The Tragedy of the North-Transylvanian Jewry', in *Yad Vashem Bulletin* 5 (1964); Béla Vágó, 'The Destruction of the Jews of Transylvania', in *Hungarian-Jewish Studies* I, New York 1966, pp. 171–221; Maria Schmidt, *Collaboration or Cooperation* (in Hungarian), Budapest 1990.

[74] Elek Karsai, *They Stood Without Arms on the Minefield* [in Hungarian], Budapest 1962; Vitéz Nagybaczoni Nagy Vilmos, *Végzetes esztendők* [Fateful Years], Budapest 1986, pp. 15, 17, 99–101, 107–108, 118–119, 125–127, 138, 149–150, 157, 161–165, 167–169, 172–179; Ádám Revitzky, *Vesztes háboruk megnyert csaták* [Lost Wars and Gained Battles], Budapest 1985; Gabriel Bar-Shaked and Mizzi Herbst (eds.), *Names of Jews Lost in Labor Battalions in the East*, Jerusalem 1991.

[75] György Ránki, *1944. március 19.* [The German Occupation of Hungary], Budapest 1978.

[76] Jean-Claude Pressac, *Auschwitz: Technique and Operation of the Gas Chambers*, transl. by Peter Moss, New York 1989; *Indictment of Nazism: Documents for the History of Jewish Persecution in Hungary, from the German Occupation until the Beginning of the Deportation (March 19, 1944–May 15, 1944)* [in Hungarian], Budapest 1958; Piper Franciszek, *Die Zahl der Opfer von Auschwitz: auf Grund der Quellen und der Erträge der Forschung, 1945 bis 1990*, Oswiecim 1993; Béla Ötvös and Ernö Horvát, *Porrá és Hamuvá* [Into Dust and Ashes], with a preface by Bishop József Tempfli, Nagyvárad 1997.

1938, during which barbaric violence was exerted on the places of worship throughout the land ... the Breslau seminary was destroyed together with all the other places of Jewish faith, Jewish learning and Jewish culture.'' The surviving professors and students found shelter in the United States, Israel and elsewhere, and provided a professional reservoir for nearly every theological institute in the Western world.[77]

The rabbinical seminary in Budapest had been seized by the SS and became a transit prison for thousands of Jews on their journey to Auschwitz-Birkenau. In the last month of the war, the bombardment of Budapest damaged the seminary building, and the library containing 300,000 volumes collapsed. (Valuable manuscripts and *incunabulae* from the library had been placed in an underground vault before the war and were thus saved). Hundreds of students, ordained rabbis, professors and teachers, were among the 600,000 Jews deported from Hungary. Of 160 practising rabbis only sixty survived. When the war ended, the need for the rabbinical seminary to continue was questioned and resolved: 120,000 Jews remained alive in Budapest, among them Samuel Löwinger, the rector of the institute and some rabbis and teachers, including Alexander Scheiber, rabbi of Dunaföldvár. With the financial assistance of the AJDC, the Central British Fund for Jewish Relief, and other Jewish organisations, the partially destroyed building was restored. On 22 March 1945, the Rabbinical Seminary of Budapest, with thirty students in the Theological Department (upper division) and four in the secondary school (lower division), resumed its important educational task. On 10 March 1946, seven rabbis were ordained. In 1950, Löwinger left for Israel and Alexander Scheiber was entrusted with guiding the newly re-opened institute, which became, the centre of Jewish and Hebrew cultural life under his leadership.[78] The *Jüdisch-Theologisches Seminar* in Breslau and the Rabbinical Seminary of Budapest were like the two bronze columns Jachin and Boaz, which stood at the entrance to the *Beth ha-Mikdash* in Jerusalem. They laid down the foundation of modern Jewish scholarship and strengthened the future of the Jewish people.

---

[77]Jospe, pp. 388–390; Konrad Fuchs, 'Zur Entstehung und Schliessung des Jüdisch-Theologischen Seminars zu Breslau (Fraenckelsche Stiftung)', in *Jahrbuch des Schlesischen Friedrich-Wilhelms-Universitaet zu Breslau* 31 (1990), p. 305; Guido Kisch, 'In Memoriam', in *idem, Das Breslauer Seminar*, pp. 11–13. "Im vierundachtzigsten Jahr seines Bestehens fiel das Jüdisch-Theologisches Seminar roher Gewalt zum Opfer. In den von Grauen erfüllten Novembertagen des Jahres 1938, in denen mit barbarischer Gewalt gegen die Gottesstätten im Lande vorgegangen wurde... ging mit den übrigen Stätten jüdischen Glaubens, jüdischen Wissens und jüdischer Kultur auch das Breslauer Seminar unter."

[78]After Scheiber's sudden death on 3 March 1985, Joseph Schweitzer was appointed to head the seminary. Imre Benoschofsky (ed.) *Shearith Yisrael (maradék – zsidóság): the Hungarian Jews in 1945/46*, n.p. 1947; Carmilly-Weinberger, *Rabbinical Seminary of Budapest*, p. 147; György Ránki, *1944. március 19. Magyarország német megszállása* [The German Occupation of Hungary], Budapest 1978; Moshe Carmilly-Weinberger, *The Road to Life: Tthe Rescue Operation of Jewish Refugees on the Hungarian-Romanian Border, 1936–1944*, New York 1994, pp. 33–44, 94–99; *idem, The History of the Jews in Transylvania (1623–1944)* [in Hungarian], Budapest 1995, pp. 282–317.

The Deutsche Encyclopädie *and the* Jews*

BY EDWARD BREUER

The appearance of the *Deutsche Encyclopädie* between 1778 and 1807 came at a propitious juncture in German-Jewish history.[1] As a work that promoted the enlightened values of reason, toleration and pluralism, the encyclopaedia reflected the many changes that were taking root in German-speaking lands. With regard to the Jews, these changes engendered a lively debate concerning their civic status and the question of whether it was possible – or advisable – to repeal the numerous laws which sought to restrict them socially and economically. As this debate moved into the public realm, the issue of Jewish civil equality also turned increasingly to a question that, in the minds of many Germans, defined the crux of the matter: could Jews, so alien and distinctive, really fit into German society? Did Jewish rites render them indelibly foreign? Jews, for their part, were fully cognisant of the issues and their implications. Could they expect civil equality as a newly articulated right, or would they need to demonstrate their ability to integrate, at least socially and culturally, before gaining a measure of economic and even political parity?

It is not surprising that a work such as the *Deutsche Encyclopädie* mirrored and contributed to this debate in important ways. In the culture of eighteenth-century Europe, encyclopaedias were more than mere reference works that sought to convey information. In their scope and attitude they embodied the intellectual spirit and optimism of the age, especially the sense that significant social and intellectual advances were at hand. With all the self-conscious ambitiousness of the Enlightenment, works of this *genre* sought to address contemporary issues and shape their outcome. Questions concerning the legal and social status of the Jews were no exception. The debate over Jews was integral to many of the broader themes of late eighteenth-century discourse, and as a result the *Deutsche Encyclopädie* took up various issues regarding Jews and Judaism.

After much neglect on the part of historians and students of German literature, the *Deutsche Encyclopädie* has only recently been given serious attention.[2] In two

*The author wishes to thank Willi Goetschel for drawing his attention to the *Deutsche Encyclopädie* over a decade ago, and for reading an early draft of this paper. The author's thanks also go to Christina Kraenzle for obtaining copies of some of the material discussed here, and for her assistance in a number of the translations.

[1] *Deutsche Encyclopädie oder Allgemeines Real-Wörterbuch aller Künste und Wissenschaften von einer Gesellschaft Gelehrten*, 24 vols., Frankfurt am Main 1778–1807.
[2] The standard survey of encyclopaedias, Robert Collison, *Encyclopedias: Their History throughout the Ages*, New York 1966, focused on encyclopaedias written from the eighteenth century onwards, but only briefly mentions the *Deutsche Encyclopädie* on p. 110.

collections of studies on European encyclopaedias of this period, Willi Goetschel, Catriona MacLeod and Emery Snyder co-produced the most thorough and comprehensive examination of this work to date, outlining its cultural and intellectual significance and describing it as a distinctly German manifestation of contemporary encyclopaedism.[3] These studies draw attention to the fact that one of the most innovative aspects of this encyclopaedia was its sustained interest in Jews and Judaism.[4] They suggest that, on the whole, the *Deutsche Encyclopädie* approached non-Christian religions in general, and Judaism in particular, with a measure of open-mindedness, presenting information and issues without engaging in polemics. Although a certain anti-Jewish hostility does occasionally emerge, the spirit of this encyclopaedia was one which sought to make encounters with Jews as free from prejudice as possible.

The present study seeks to build on this scholarly interest in the *Deutsche Encyclopädie* and its treatment of Jews and Judaism. This encyclopaedia, as we shall see, serves as an excellent means through which to capture the complexities of this historical moment. Beyond the important shift to a more tolerant and accepting view of Jews, there are many facets of the relationship between Jews and Germans that can be explored here. One must, for example, be aware of the fact that as much as the *Deutsche Encyclopädie* presented a view of the Jews to the German reading public, it was also presenting a notion of what enlightened religion was and what an enlightened Judaism might look like. In the context of the debate concerning Jews and the possibility of their integration into German society, such notions about Judaism were far-reaching. An encyclopaedia that addressed itself to a wide variety of Jewish texts, rituals and beliefs would implicitly, if not explicitly, address itself to the question of what Jews could or should do to ease their integration into German society. It is also notable that this encyclopaedia was published at a time when Jews had begun to interact with, and contribute to, German culture, and as such, we may therefore also examine the way in which these encyclopaedists read and reacted to contemporary Jewish writings.

Even by eighteenth-century standards, the *Deutsche Encyclopädie* was an ambitious undertaking. Germans, to be sure, had a habit of producing encyclopaedias of immense and unwieldy proportions: Johann Heinrich Zedler's *Grosses vollständiges Universal Lexicon* (1732–1750) extended to sixty-eight volumes, while Johann Georg Krünitz's *Oeconomische Encyclopädie*, published between 1773 and 1858, extended to no less than two hundred and forty-two volumes. The *Deutsche*

---

[3]See Willi Goetschel, Catriona MacLeod and Emery Snyder, 'The *Deutsche Encyclopädie*', in Frank Kafker (ed.), *Notable Encyclopedias of the Late Eighteenth Century: Eleven Successors of the Encyclopédie* (*Studies on Voltaire 315*), Oxford 1994, pp. 257–333; idem, 'The *Deutsche Encyclopädie* and Encyclopedism in Eighteenth-Century Germany', in Clorinda Donato and Robert M. Maniquis (eds.) *The Encyclopédie and the Age of Revolution*, Boston 1992, pp. 55–61.

[4]Before the articles by Goetschel *et al.*, the question of the Jews in the *Deutsche Encyclopädie* had been addressed by Barbara Suchy, *Lexikographie und Juden im 18. Jahrhundert*, Cologne 1979, pp. 248–256. However, Suchy fails to place the *Deutsche Encyclopädie* in its proper historical context, and its treatment of Jews and Judaism is examined without regard to the themes and concerns of the encyclopaedia as a whole.

Encyclopädie ceased publication with the volume for the letter K, but with twenty-four volumes (and, unlike Zedler, with no biographical or geographical entries) its density surpassed even these.[5]

In its quintessentially enlightened German way, the *Deutsche Encyclopädie* simultaneously drew upon and rejected the two publications that influenced it most, the English *Cyclopaedia* (1728) of Ephraim Chambers, and the French *Encyclopédie* (1751–1772) of Diderot and d'Alembert.[6] The idea for this endeavour began in the mid-1770s, when a Frankfurt publisher had the idea of translating Chambers' popular work into German. Heinrich M.G. Köster (1734–1802), the Giessen University professor appointed to the task, recruited a number of other Hessian academics, but they quickly decided to change course and produce an original German work that would be more contemporary and suitable for a German audience. Köster remained the general editor until 1794, when the editorship was assumed by another Giessen professor, Johann Friedrich Roos (1757–1804). With Roos's death, the project foundered and was never completed.[7]

This German encyclopaedia drew on its French predecessor in at least two important and related ways. First, unlike many other encyclopaedias of the eighteenth century, the *Deutsche Encyclopädie* was a truly collaborative affair involving more than sixty contributors. The benefit of this collaborative effort was mixed; like the French *Encyclopédie*, it allowed a broader range of scholars to focus on their own areas of expertise, although it led to a certain unevenness in quality. It also had the not unintended effect of allowing for differing, even contradictory views. The second feature was that, from the third volume onwards, the authorship of each article was identified through a system of personal numbers, and a list of contributors matching most numbers was included in the preface to the fifteenth volume. As a result, the *Deutsche Encyclopädie* was not a faceless work, and since many of the contributors were known through their other writings, one can appreciate the multiplicity of voices in light of the spirited intellectual debates of the time.[8]

In other ways, the *Deutsche Encyclopädie* displayed a Germanic world view that eschewed the French work of the *philosophes*. In this German encyclopaedia, the enlightened penchant for reasonable and practical ideas manifested itself in an approach which was thoroughly sensible and moderate in tone. Written by academics, pastors, and others in established positions, this work was more conservative than the French *Encyclopédie*; it sought to challenge and enlighten without attempting to radically transform the world around it. The *Deutsche Encyclopädie*, furthermore, steered clear of sweeping social criticism, and as such was not per-

---

[5]Collison, pp. 104–105, 108–109; on Zedler, see also Peter E. Carels and Dan Flory, 'Johann Heinrich Zedler's *Universal Lexicon*', in Frank Kafker (ed.), *Notable Encyclopedias of the Seventeenth and Eighteenth Centuries: Nine Predecessors of the Encyclopédie (Studies on Voltaire 194)*, Oxford 1981, pp. 165–196.
[6]With regard to the *Deutsche Encyclopädie* and its relationship to other eighteenth-century encyclopaedias, see the preface to the first volume, p. 2b; and see the entry for "Encyclopädie" in volume VIII, pp. 379–380.
[7]The full story of this encyclopaedia is told in Goetschel *et al.*, pp. 258–268.
[8]*ibid.*, pp. 262–263.

ceived as antagonistic to territorial and ecclesiastical authorities.[9] The respectful
and moderate tone of the work, finally, was also evident in the encyclopaedia's
handling of Christianity. Although the contributors to this encyclopaedia
roundly condemned superstition, they distanced this from thoughtful religious
belief and saved some of their most acerbic condemnations for atheism. When
the *Deutsche Encyclopädie* voiced its occasional criticism of Christian beliefs and
rituals, it did so not from a position of scepticism or anti-religious hostility, but
as a result of distinctly enlightened Protestant leanings.[10] The *Deutsche Encyclopädie*'s treatment of Jews and Judaism was very much in this spirit. How did this
approach compare to those of other eighteenth-century encyclopaedias? Generally speaking, the encyclopaedias of this age attempted to present the reader with
some factual observations and basic information about Jews and their religious
practices, both ancient and contemporary, but, not unexpectedly, such articles
also regularly included comments regarding the absurdity of a particular Jewish
belief or the superstitious quality of a particular ritual. In many, however, the
animus towards Jews and Judaism tended to be rather mild in comparison to
the treatment meted out to Catholics or Christian sectarians; Jews, it seems,
could safely be regarded as a non-threatening curiosity, something which could
not be said about the way in which Christians of different denominations viewed
each other.[11] There were, of course, some notable exceptions. Diderot's *Encyclopédie*, for example, was thoroughly hostile towards Jews, although in this instance
it was accompanied by a critical approach to religion in general.[12] Beyond the
issue of attitude, however, it is fair to say that perhaps the most consistent
feature of these articles on Jews was their uneven quality: although they demonstrated the occasional insight into Judaism and Jewish history, their treatment of
the subject was rather shallow, a problem exacerbated by the fact that many
encyclopaedias simply reproduced the entries of earlier ones.[13]

The situation in Germany was in many respects different. From the early part
of the century, much information about Jews and Judaism was available for the
educated reader. Between 1714 and 1718, Johann Jacob Schudt published
Jüdische Merckwürdigkeiten, a dense multi-volume work describing contemporary
Jewish life in great detail. More important was Johann Christoph Wolf's *Bibliotheca Hebraea* (1715–1733), a masterly four-volume work that provided an
unprecedented wealth of biographical and literary information. Zedler's *Grosses
vollständiges Universal Lexicon*, which contained a large number of biographical
entries, drew heavily on Wolf and others. Although this work stood out for its

[9]See Frank Kafker, 'The Influence of the *Encyclopédie* on the Eighteenth-Century Encyclopedic Tradition', in *idem*. (ed.), *Notable Encyclopedias of the Late Eighteenth Century*, p. 395.
[10]See Goetschel *et al.*, pp. 304–307.
[11]See, for example, the discussion of Judaism in eighteenth-century British encyclopaedias in Suchy,
pp. 67–93; Lael Ely Bradshaw, 'Ephraim Chambers' *Cyclopedia*', in Kafker(ed.), *Notable Encyclopedias of the Seventeenth and Eighteenth Centuries*, pp. 134–135; *idem*, 'Thomas Dyche's *New General English
Dictionary*', *ibid.*, pp. 156–158; Frank Kafker, 'William Smellie's Edition of the *Encyclopedia Britanni-
ca*', *idem* (ed.), *Notable Encyclopedias of the Late Eighteenth Century*, pp. 171–172.
[12]See Arthur Hertzberg, *The French Enlightenment and the Jews*, New York 1968, pp. 281–282.
[13]See note 11 above.

unmitigated hostility towards Jews – an enmity that was clearly informed by a traditional Christian animus – Zedler managed to produce a reference work that devoted more attention to Judaica than any of its contemporaries.[14]

As the century progressed, German universities and scholarship began to flourish, and Judaism became the subject of increasingly sophisticated scholarly inquiry. Drawing on this intellectual climate, the *Deutsche Encyclopädie* went well beyond other non-German encyclopaedias of the late eighteenth century and their basic treatment of Jewish literature, history and religion. The scholarly tone of the articles relating to Jews and Judaism was set in the entry for 'Ebräische Alterthümer':

> [Hebrew antiquities] refer to those traditions, laws, and customs, that were common among the Jews in earlier times. Among a people that experienced many eras, there is no doubt that these things changed from one period to another. Nevertheless, since the Jews retain their basic perspective as much as circumstances allow, it is certainly worth the effort to learn about their antiquities.[15]

The author for this entry was Johann Georg Purmann (1733–1813), a rector of the Frankfurt Gymnasium and a prolific author who contributed extensively to this encyclopaedia. True to his exhortation, Purmann demonstrated astonishing scholarly breadth by authoring the vast majority of articles relating to Jews, including those on religious practices, language, literature, and history.[16] In this entry for 'Ebräische Alterthümer', Purmann underlined the value of such knowledge in both antiquarian and contemporary terms. Learning about Jewish traditions and law, he suggested, was important because they

> affect not only their religious outlook and the resulting customs, but also their civic and domestic outlook as well. Without an exact knowledge of these, one will not understand many Biblical passages in both the Old and New Testaments, and similarly, a large portion of their history will be incomprehensible to us. Hebrew antiquities are also noteworthy in another sense: the Jews are in every respect a people whose fate and history distinguish them from that of many other peoples. Their customs and laws are relics of a very distant era and of the most ancient law-making wisdom. Even the philosopher who contemplates the history of mankind cannot dispense with it.[17]

Perusing the *Deutsche Encyclopädie*, there is little doubt about the thoroughness and seriousness with which the editors went about presenting information about Jews and Judaism. In the fifth volume of this work, for example, we find not only entries for 'Canon der heiligen Schrift (kritisch-historisch)', 'Chaldaische Sprache', 'Chanukafest', "Copulation der Juden" and 'Coscher', but also for 'Capporah' (the customary form of expiation on the eve of the Day of Atonement), 'Chalil' (flute), 'Challel Bittho' (prostitution of one's daughter), 'Challah' (bread traditionally used for the Sabbath meal), 'Chateph' (a form of grammatical notation), and 'Chattan hattorah' (associated with the completion of the annual cycle of Torah readings on Simhat Torah), and 'Col Nidre', (a

---

[14]See Suchy, pp. 234–246; and Carels and Flory, p. 191.
[15]*Deutsche Encyclopädie*, vol. VII, p. 805.
[16]See Goetschel *et. al.*, pp. 301, 330.
[17]*Deutsche Encyclopädie*, vol. VII, p. 805.

renunciation of vows recited at the onset of the Day of Atonement). Throughout this encyclopaedia, we also find that Jewish themes are regularly inserted as subsections of larger articles. Under the general entry for 'Abkürzungen der Wörter, Abbreviaturen', for example, we find a subsection for 'Abkürzungen in der hebräischen Schrift' listing fifty common literary abbreviations and acronyms;[18] and similarly, the entry for 'Auslegungskunst (Hermeneutik)' was followed by numerous articles relating to Catholic and Protestant interpretations of Scripture, which was in turn matched by an article entitled 'Auslegungskunst der heiligen Schrift, nach der Meynung der Rabbinen'.[19] The subject of Judaism, broadly conceived, was thus everywhere incorporated into the expansive intellectual breadth of this work.

This increased intellectual sophistication combined with the *Deutsche Encyclopädie*'s enlightened religious sensibilities produced a work that approached Jews and Judaism not only as an object of antiquarian interest, but as a living entity that deserved to be understood and appreciated in its own terms. Unlike Zedler's more traditional view, the Jews were not measured in Christian terms and subjected to vilification and ridicule. On the contrary, this German encyclopaedia even went out of its way to scorn traditional anti-Jewish polemic.[20] The *Deutsche Encyclopädie* thus set out self-consciously to create a work that would be "equally useful to all religious parties and all philosophical sects";[21] and although the authors of these words were in all probability thinking mainly of Christian parties and sects, they sought to extend this level of understanding to Jews as well.

Perhaps the best way to illustrate this attitude, and especially its limitations and complexities, is to turn to the general articles on Jews. Reflecting its organisational refinement and collaborative nature, the eighteenth volume of the *Deutsche Encyclopädie*, published in 1794, included four different general entries under *Juden*, each written by a different author. The first article, 'Juden überhaupt', was written by Purmann, the author of the entry for 'Ebräische Alterthümer' cited above. In this general article, Purmann took a curious, if telling, approach: he chose to focus not on Jewish history or the basics of Jewish faith and practice, but on how ancient Greek writers had reported on Jews. Rather than offering a substantive overview of the subject at hand, Purmann chose to educate the reader regarding the tendentiousness and unreliability of ancient

---

[18]*ibid.*, vol. I, pp. 68–71.

[19]*ibid.*, vol. II, pp. 488–491.

[20]In the article 'Ebräische, oder hebräische Sprache', vol. VII, p. 810, for example, Johann Georg Purmann referred to Psalms 2:7, "…The Lord said to me, 'You are my son, I have fathered you [*yelidetikha*] this day'", and the classical polemical claim that this verse referred to Jesus as the Son of God. After stating that some Christian exegetes based this Christological reading on the appearance of the word *yelidetikha* (rather than *yeladetikha*), Purmann added: "Who can understand what [the vowel] 'i' substituted for [the vowel] 'a' has to do with supernatural procreation? Does one not make the truth itself ridiculous through such an arbitrary explanation? What must the Jew think when one approaches with such miserable evidence?" On the history of the polemical use of this verse, see David Berger, *The Jewish-Christian Debate in the High Middle Ages*, Philadelphia 1979, pp. 137, 294–295.

[21]*Deutsche Encyclopädie*, vol. I, Vorrede, p. 3.

accounts, upon which so much historical writing was based. His tone extended beyond merely counselling scepticism and caution with regard to such historical sources. He expressed his dismay at the fact that instead of being enlightened and informed, the reader was instead confronted with polemic and open enmity. In adopting a critical approach to historiography, however, this article also tacitly gave shape to the way in which contemporary Jews were to be regarded. When Purmann commented that deeply-rooted religious hatred all too often hampered intelligent insight, there is little doubt that he did not have only ancient writers in mind. Indeed, he lamented the fact that Christians denied the Jews their basic humanity for the sole reason that they were Jews.[22]

This general entry on Jews was followed by two other, somewhat overlapping, articles on Jewish legal status in historical and judicial terms. The first of these, 'Juden (juristisch)', was written by Christian Gottlieb Gmelin (1749–1818), a professor of law who had already published a scholarly treatise on criminal law as it applied to the Jews.[23] Gmelin expressed clear empathy for the position of the Jews, especially the legal arbitrariness to which they were regularly, and unfairly, subject. Openly decrying the "unchristian" way in which Jews had been dealt with historically, he ended by asserting that "in accordance with common sense, humanity, and justice" one could not maintain different criminal laws for Christians and Jews.[24] Even though this article touched regularly on issues of legal status and jurisdiction in German lands, the *Deutsche Encyclopädie* followed with an entry entitled 'Juden (nach ihren Rechtsverhältnissen in Deutschland überhaupt betrachtet)', written by another law professor, Johann Gottfried Büchner (1754–1821). Büchner was not known as a writer on Jewish matters, and it is unclear why he was asked to be a contributor. Much of this article focused on the nature of the privileges and protection that Jews obtained from territorial authorities. Although his tone was less indignant than Gmelin's, Büchner decried the treatment of Jews, noting that the *Leibzoll* – the body tax paid by Jews – effectively reduced them to the status of animals when they crossed national borders.[25] He went on to explain that when, historically, the Jews went from being imperial subjects to finding protection at the hands of territorial authorities, certain rights and privileges were not retained, and Jews were discriminated against in a variety of new ways. The reason for this, Büchner stated flatly, was "arbitrariness and religious hatred".[26]

There was, in these articles, an evident expression of enlightened pique, informed not so much by a genuine warmth or concern for the Jews as by indig-

---

[22]*ibid.*, vol. XVIII, p. 202: "Eingewurzelter Religionshass verblendet nur gar zu oft die bessern Einsichten des Verstandes. Giebt es doch wohl auch Leute unter den Christen, die den Juden blos deswegen die Pflichten der Menschlichkeit versagen, weil sie Juden sind."

[23]Christian Gottlieb Gmelin, *Abhandlung von den besondern Rechten der Juden in peinlichen Sachen*, Tübingen 1785.

[24]*Deutsche Encyclopädie*, vol. XVIII, p. 207: "... so ist es sowohl der gesunden Vernunft, der Menschlichkeit und Billigkeit, als auch den Gesetzen gemäss, dass wir niemals unterschiedene Rechte der Christen und Juden in peinlichen Sachen behaupten." See also Goetschel *et al.*, p. 302.

[25]*ibid.*, p. 208: "Doch fordert man von jedem reisenden Juden einen Leibzoll, wodurch derselbe leider bis zum Vieh herabgewürdiget wird."

[26]*ibid.*, p. 209: "Willkühr und Religionshass sind hiervon die Ursache."

nation about the inconsistency and injustice of extant policies. The *Deutsche Ency-clopädie*, in fact, included among its editors and contributors a number of individuals who had publicly called for changes in the civil status of the Jews. Johann August Schlettwein (1731–1802), for example, published an essay in 1776 which drew attention to the general social and economic harm caused by existing discriminatory regulations, and proposed that Jews be allowed to work as artisans. He also suggested that special Jewish taxes and duties be eliminated.[27] More significantly, Christian Wilhelm von Dohm (1751–1783) published *Über die bürgerliche Verbesserung der Juden* in 1781, in which he argued forcefully against the continued separate legal status of Jews and for a large measure of Jewish social, economic, and political equality.[28] Dohm's work was widely noted and discussed, and in the early 1780s at least, it became the touchstone of the public debate on Jewish equality.

Despite the fact that these individuals were involved with the *Deutsche Encyclopädie* from an early stage,[29] the articles written by Purmann, Gmelin and Büchner did not advocate any kind of broad legal amelioration of the Jews' status in the form of civil equality. The volume in which their articles appeared was published in 1794, when the idea of Jewish civil equality had been debated for well over a decade: the campaign for Jewish rights was still a contentious matter, but it was hardly an issue that would have identified its supporters as radical. The *Deutsche Encyclopädie*, however, was politically cautious and generally eschewed a reformist stance; at some level, a decision was apparently taken not to advocate forcefully the elimination of the Jews' separate legal and economic status.[30]

Like German society as a whole, however, the *Deutsche Encyclopädie* yielded a far more conflicting view regarding Jewish civil equality than the articles cited indicate. Indeed, the fourth and final general article on Jews, 'Juden (politisch)', gave strong expression to those who would caution against the social and economic integration of Jews. The opening line of this article, whose author was never identified,[31] established its forthright tone and placed the issue squarely before the reader: "Questions have often been raised as to whether Jews are useful or harmful for a state, and whether they are to be tolerated or not."[32] The author began by suggesting that while some humanitarians believed that it was

---

[27] Johann August Schlettwein, 'Bitte an die Grossen wegen der Juden zu Verhütung Trauriger Folgen in den Staaten' in *Ephemeriden der Menschheit*, No. 10, (1776), pp. 41–47; and see Robert Liberles, 'From Toleration to *Verbesserung*: German and English Debates on the Jews in the Eighteenth Century', in *Central European History* 22 (1989), pp. 6–7.

[28] On Dohm see Ilsegret Dambacher, *Christian Wilhelm von Dohm*, Frankfurt am Main 1974; on his writing on behalf of the Jews, see Horst Möller, 'Aufklärung, Judenemanzipation und Staat. Ursprung und Wirkung von Dohms Schrift "Über die bürgerliche Verbesserung der Juden"' in W. Grab (ed.) *Deutsche Aufklärung und Judenemanzipation*, Tel Aviv 1980, pp. 119–149; and Robert Liberles, 'Dohm's Treatise on the Jews: A Defence of the Enlightenment', in *LBI Year Book XXXIII* (1988), pp. 29–42.

[29] See Goetschel *et al.*, pp. 326, 331, and also p. 287 note 67.

[30] On this encyclopaedia's cautious approach to politically liberal ideas, see *ibid.*, pp. 307–309; and see above, note 9.

[31] With regard to the anonymity of some contributors, see *ibid.*, pp. 263, 323.

[32] *Deutsche Encyclopädie*, vol. XVIII, p. 209. All the quotations below are found on the same page. For the German original see Appendix A.

precisely the responsibility of the state to make the Jews useful, the problem was not all that simple:

> It is also, in fact, a noble idea to transform [*umzubilden*] such a degraded nation that dwells among us, so that it can supply society with useful members. The zeal with which one pursues this transformation always remains commendable, but while attending to this important matter, one must not overlook the difficulties that must first be eliminated before one can endeavour towards the realisation of this charitable plan. People insist that the Jews should learn professions and become soldiers, but they forgot to raise the question: can the Jew become a professional or a soldier *qua* Jew? Will he, as a Jew, be useful to the state?

After raising the idea of apprenticing Jews to Christian masters, this author points to the problems that might ensue:

> How different are the religious customs of Master and [Jewish] youth? The latter may not begin any work before performing his morning prayer, and this may not take place before daybreak ... With the sundown on Friday, he must stop working, and he must sanctify the Sabbath. If he were to work on Sunday, it would be unfair to have him work alone, and the master could say: "my Sabbath is as holy as yours". One could further consider the kind of obstacles added by the numerous holidays, during which the Jew often cannot work for an eight day period. These difficulties, to which many more could still be added, occur in an even greater degree in the case of soldiers.

Even if a Jew were to become a master himself, the effect on the public good would not be negligible. The Jew's many religious obligations and holidays, not to mention the special taxes owed the state, would force him to raise prices: "[The Jew] becomes a profiteer in his profession, as he was before; one has therefore gained nothing, but simply made a change in form which is actually not advantageous to society."

The arguments contained here were not, in fact, novel, and many of them were rehearsed over a decade before the appearance of this volume of *Deutsche Encyclopädie*. In his *Über die bürgerliche Verbesserung der Juden*, Dohm had already anticipated such criticisms by arguing that Judaism had no inherent "antisocial principles (*ungesellige Grundsätze*)" that would justify the continued separate legal status of Jews.[33] What he had in mind were objections that would point, for example, to the observance of the Jewish Sabbath as an impediment to military service.[34] Dohm set forth a variety of arguments explaining why the Sabbath laws would not inhibit the fulfilment of military duties or any other civic responsibilities, but few were convinced. The noted orientalist Johann David Michaelis was quick to criticise this treatise in a review, and his objections centred on the fact that Jewish practices and beliefs served as obstacles – both practical and attitudinal – to any kind of meaningful integration.[35] Moses Mendelssohn, for his part, certainly believed that Jews could live as responsible and

---

[33]Christian Wilhelm Dohm, *Über die bürgerliche Verbesserung der Juden*, Berlin und Stettin 1781, pp. 16–17.

[34]*ibid.*, pp. 133ff.

[35]Johann David Michaelis, *Orientalische und Exegetische Bibliothek*, 19 (1782), pp. 1–40; reprinted in full in the second volume of Dohm's treatise (1783), pp. 31–71.

productive citizens, and he appreciated Dohm's position that Jews had a right to
expect civil equality without preconditions.[36] Throughout the 1780s, however,
there was no lack of voices objecting to the unrealistic and even undesirable
nature of Dohm's proposals to integrate the Jews into German society.[37]

This article in the *Deutsche Encyclopädie* gave expression to the earlier debate
concerning Jewish equality in another important way as well. One of the issues
that all German writers addressed was the inflexible, if not obdurate, nature of
Jewish law. Dohm, for example, had praised the Jews for their unyielding
devotion to their religious practices, but he had also written about "the dete-
rioration of [Jewish] religious law" and the stiflingly "anxious observance of
certain customs and holidays".[38] Although he argued that religious reform
should not be demanded of Jews as a precondition for legal and economic
parity, Dohm made no secret of the fact that he expected that such changes
would occur as a natural effect of social and economic integration.[39] Michaelis's
disagreement with Dohm stemmed, in part, from the former's belief that Jewish
separatism was constitutionally ingrained in this tradition, and that Jews therefore would not, and could not, integrate with surrounding communities.[40]

Along these lines, after pointing out a variety of problems that would mitigate
against successful Jewish integration, the anonymous author of the article 'Juden
(politisch)' turned to the crux of the matter:

> The Jew will and must appear useless for all civil operations as long as he remains
> forced into his oppressive situation by the yoke of his religious laws. These are what
> prevent him from becoming what he should and could be, and what he can never
> become as long as these restraints are not lifted, at least to some degree. Here one
> must ask: can these obstacles be removed, and if so, how should one remove them?
> The remedy for this can be nothing other than complete reform in accordance with
> the circumstances.[41]

In clear and unambiguous terms, this author, like so many others, was arguing
that Jewish civil equality would be unworkable in the absence of a straightforward *quid pro quo* in which Jews were expected to adjust their religious practices
to contemporary social and economic realities. The writer, for his part, realised
that this was a complex endeavour which would take much time, patience and
foresight. Education, too, was an important factor:

---

[36] Mendelssohn articulated his position in *Manasseh Ben Israel Rettung der Juden Aus dem Englischen übersetzt. Nebst einer Vorrede von Moses Mendelssohn...* Berlin 1782 reprinted in F. Bamberger, A. Altmann
et al. (eds.), *Moses Mendelssohn Gesammelte Schriften Jubiläumsausgabe*, vol. VI, Stuttgart 1971–, pp. 1–
25; and *idem*, *Jerusalem, oder über religiöse Macht und Judentum* Berlin, 1783; reprinted in *Gesammelte
Schriften Jubiläumsausgabe*, vol VIII, pp. 99–204. Mendelssohn's response to Michaelis was also published in the second volume of Dohm's treatise, pp. 72–77.

[37] See Jacob Katz, *From Prejudice to Destruction: Anti-Semitism, 1700–1933* Cambridge, Mass. 1980,
pp. 52–62; and Liberles pp. 15–20.

[38] Dohm, *Bürgerliche Verbesserung*, pp. 93–94, 137, 142–143; and see my 'Politics, Tradition, History:
Rabbinic Judaism and the Eighteenth Century Struggle for Civil Equality', in *Harvard Theological
Review* 85 (3), 1992, pp. 363–367.

[39] *ibid.*, pp. 143–44.

[40] See note 35.

[41] *Deutsche Encyclopädie*, vol. XVIII, p. 209.

Every moral improvement of a nation must be carried out step by step if it is to reach a certain stage of maturity. Enlightenment of the intellect and education of the heart are the foundations upon which the future building can and must be erected. For this, men of insight and great importance from the nation itself are required.[42]

This contributor to the *Deutsche Encyclopädie* did not follow Michaelis in eschewing the very possibility of Jewish integration into German society, but he did shun the more liberal position advanced by Dohm. With appropriate reforms, this writer suggested, the Jews could indeed successfully adapt themselves to their surrounding environment; but in order to make their integration possible, they would have to undertake these reforms in advance, or at least in conjunction with the loosening of economic and legal restrictions.

The articles examined here expressed a degree of empathy for the Jews and an enlightened desire to effect positive, if moderate, socio-economic and cultural changes. Even the author of the entry 'Juden (politisch)', after all, appreciated the oppressiveness of the situation and was, in principle, open to Jewish integration. There is some evidence that Purmann, the main contributor of entries pertaining to Judaism, recognised that the situation within the Jewish communities was already changing. In his article on 'Bann bey den Juden', he described at some length the effect of excommunication on the tragic life of Uriel Da Costa.[43] Towards the end of the article, however, he paused to comment that:

in more recent times, the practice of this aspect of the Jewish religion has changed very much. [The Jews] no longer make as much of excommunication as they once did. In general, it is clear that excommunication no longer results in exclusion from the community, and that many individuals have been excommunicated but nevertheless do as they wish.[44]

Even in light of this recognition, most of Purmann's numerous articles on Jewish religious practices refrained from commenting upon what an enlightened or modern Judaism was to look like. It may be that this contributor simply disagreed with the position of the anonymous contributor who penned the articles 'Juden (politisch)' or that he was uncomfortable using the encyclopaedia for this kind of activism. Even beyond Purmann's own work, the *Deutsche Encyclopädie* appears to have taken the position that the reforms and adaptations necessary to expedite Jewish integration into German society were an internal Jewish matter: the encyclopaedia was to limit itself to the presentation of Jewish rituals in a non-judgmental and informative manner.

It is significant and unsurprising that the one aspect of Judaica subject to explicit criticism in the *Deutsche Encyclopädie* was that of rabbinic Judaism. Christian scholars had long harboured an anti-rabbinic animus; often polemically motivated, they ridiculed rabbinic literature for its pettiness and absurdities, and for its interpretative corruption of the Bible. In the eighteenth century, hos-

---

[42]*ibid.*, pp. 209–210.
[43]On Da Costa, see most recently Yirmiyahu Yovel, *Spinoza and Other Heretics*, vol. I, Princeton 1989, pp. 42–54.
[44]*Deutsche Encyclopädie*, vol. II, p. 777.

tility towards rabbinic Judaism lost a good deal of its religious thrust, but not its immediacy and relevance.[45] In the German debate concerning Jewish civil equality, the subject of rabbinic Judaism emerged as a significant problem, for it was in the writings and teachings of the rabbinic sages that the most obdurate and non-integratable aspects of Judaism were located. If Jews could only shed the worst rabbinic accretions of their tradition, the thinking went, they would be in a far better position to effect their integration into German society.[46]

The *Deutsche Encyclopädie*'s writings on Judaism reflected this critical view of post-biblical Judaism. This German encyclopaedia, to be sure, did yield the occasional reference to rabbinic literature that was factual in content and neutral in tone. The entry for 'Babylonischer Talmud', for example, described the content and provenance of this text in brief and helpful terms.[47] Similarly in 'Ebräische Alterthümer', Purmann listed six ancient primary sources that a scholar must consult on any subject relating to Jewish antiquity, including the Talmud and rabbinic explanations of the Bible. Although he quickly added that not all of these sources were equally useful, his comment was a broad expression of scholarly scepticism that did not single out the rabbinic texts.[48] Indeed, rabbinic sources were judiciously used in several articles on Judaism.[49]

More typical, however, was the attitude voiced in the article 'Ebräische, oder hebräische Sprache', in which Purmann traced the study of Hebrew in its historical context. Having argued that the spirit and distinctiveness of the Hebrew language could only be learned from the Hebrew Bible, Purmann disparaged post-biblical Jewish scholars for failing to plumb the depths of biblical language.[50] The point was that rabbinic sages were not textually equipped to read the Hebrew Bible with sufficient discipline and sophistication. Thus, in the article on 'Draschah', which was defined as "an allegorical explanation of a

---

[45]See Arnold Ages, *French Enlightenment and the Rabbinic Tradition*, Frankfurt am Main, 1970, pp. 28–47.

[46]The issue of rabbinic Judaism in the eighteenth-century debate over civil equality is discussed in my 'Politics, Tradition, History,' pp. 357–383.

[47]*Deutsche Encyclopädie*, vol. II, p. 643. The reader is referred to a more extensive handling of the subject in the entry for Talmud, which, of course, was never published.

[48]*ibid.*, vol. VII, pp. 805–06.

[49]See, for example, the entry 'Bann bey den Juden', in vol. II, p. 775; 'Bibel (critisch protestantisch)', in vol. III, p. 623; 'Cabbala', in vol. IV, p. 702; and 'Jom Chibbur', in vol. XVIII, p. 55.

[50]*ibid.*, vol VII, p. 809: "[Die Bibel] ist das einzige Buch, das uns aus dem lebenden Alter dieser Sprache übrig ist. Was in den folgenden Zeiten hebräisch geschrieben ist, stösst so sehr gegen die Regeln der Grammatik an, dass man schlechte Regeln daraus wird schöpfen können. Und dieses ist die Ursache, warum wir unter den Juden so wenig gute Hebräer antreffen, weil sie sich zum Voraus durch das Lesen der Rabbinen verderben." It is interesting to note that some of Purmann's most hostile comments regarding Jewish culture were written in connection with Jewish linguistic traditions. Perhaps his harshest comments along these lines came in the entry "Judendeutsch", vol. XVIII, pp. 213–214: "Judendeutsch, nennt man denjenigen verdorbenen Dialect der deutschen Sprache, dessen sich die Juden sowohl in täglichen Reden als auch im Schreiben bedienen. Aus der abergläubischen Anhänglichkeit an die Sprache ihrer Vorfahren, haben die Juden überall, wo sie sich aufhalten, die Landessprache verdorben ... und wenn sie sich auch bey zunehmenden Jahren Mühe geben, reines Deutsch zu sprechen, so können sie doch ihre von Kindheit auf angewöhnte Aussprache nicht ganz ablegen, so dass man sie auch noch an getauften Juden, lange Zeit nach ihrem Uebertritt, gewahr wird." Purmann went on to complain that Jews had given German a foreign tone and sound, and had garbled its words, on top of which they added Hebrew words which were mangled by applying German conjugations to them.

biblical verse", Purmann wrote dismissively that such interpretations sometimes yielded readings which only individuals with a 'rabbinic head' could produce. After referring to the many collections of such interpretations, he ended by stating flatly that one would not get much edification from such writings.[51]

Perhaps the most intriguing and culturally complex instance of such anti-rabbinic sentiment was the entry 'Auslegungskunst der heiligen Schrift, nach der Meynung der Rabbinen'.[52] This erudite and learned article, also written by Purmann, drew together an impressive number of texts and ideas which high-lighted the hermeneutical sophistication of the sages. The article included an explication of the fourfold medieval approach to the interpretation of Scripture (represented in Jewish literature by the acronym *PaRDeS*), as well as a discussion of the interpretative tools used in Talmudic texts, especially the thirteen herme-neutical principles articulated by R. Ishmael. One of the most interesting features of this article, however, was the fact that the first section, the explication of the fourfold *PaRDeS*, was actually drawn without acknowledging Moses Men-delssohn's Hebrew commentary on Ecclesiastes published a decade earlier.[53] In the introduction to this commentary, Mendelssohn had focused mainly on two of the four classical interpretative modes – the plain sense *(peshat)* and rabbinic *(derush)* – in order to explain how it was that Scripture could yield different inter-pretations that were equally and simultaneously true, despite the fact that they contained distinct, even contradictory, meanings. The thrust of his exposition was oriented towards the presentation of rabbinic exegesis as hermeneutically sophisticated and textually well-grounded, and as such, Mendelssohn's introduc-tion was intended to serve as a defence of rabbinic interpretations of Scripture.[54]

Mendelssohn's introduction and commentary on Ecclesiastes was translated into German soon after its publication by the Hebraic scholar Johann Jacob Rabe, and for an encyclopaedist like Purmann, it was a natural source to utilise.[55] His article in the *Deutsche Encyclopädie*, however, altogether obscured Mendelssohn's intentions. Purmann, like Rabe, did not fully grasp the nuance of some of Mendelssohn's original Hebrew terminology and as a result, was unable to grasp the fact that the Jewish author was attempting to give organic root to rabbinic exegesis.[56] Purmann's article did not simply fall victim to the difficulties of cross-cultural translation, however. In his discussion of the rabbinic mode of interpretation, Purmann used a passage from the writings of the twelfth-century biblical scholar Abraham ibn Ezra that expressed a different sensibility towards rabbinic exegesis, especially in its comment that rabbinic

---

[51]*ibid.*, vol. VII, pp. 621–622: "Manchmal bedienen sie sich der besondern Auslegungsregeln, davon wir oben gehandelt haben, und bringen einen Verstand heraus, den sonst kein Mensch, als nur ein rabbinischer Kopf, herausbringen konnte ... Viel Erklärung ist nicht darinnen zu holen."

[52]*ibid.*, vol. II, pp. 488–491.

[53]Moses Mendelssohn, *Sefer Megillat Kohelet*, Berlin 1770, reprinted in *Gesammelte Schriften Jubiläum-sausgabe*, vol. XIV, pp. 145–207.

[54]I have discussed this introduction at length in *The Limits of Enlightenment: Jews, Germans, and the Eight-eenth-Century Study of Scripture*, Cambridge 1996, pp. 184–191.

[55]The German translation appeared as *Der Prediger Salomo, mit einer Kurzen and Zureichenden Erklärung nach dem Wort-Verstand zum Nutzen der Studierenden von dem Verfasser des Phaedon*, Ansbach 1771.

[56]See Breuer, *Limits of Enlightenment*, pp. 192–193.

midrash was sometimes comparable to fine silk, other times to crude sackcloth.[57] The ultimate indication of Purmann's attitude towards rabbinic literature, and his failure, ironically, to appreciate the very Mendelssohnian texts he appropriated, came at the end of the article, in which he concluded with the following reflection on the rabbinic interpretation of Scripture:

> While among these rules there are many that are good and correct, there are also many that are doubtful. In general, the rabbis are wanting in most of the [exegetical] devices that make a good exegete. If one examines their explanations [of Scripture] as found in their writings, [one often finds that] common sense suffers; but still, it cannot be denied that occasionally one can find something good . . . Examine everything, and retain what is good.[58]

For all the general erudition of this article, Purmann, like so many of his contemporaries, could not refrain from expressing his anti-rabbinic sentiments.

The *Deutsche Encyclopädie*, then, yields a number of important inconsistencies and ambiguities which reflect the transitional nature of attitudes towards Jews at the end of the eighteenth century. On the one hand, the encyclopaedia gave voice to those progressive and empathetic *Aufklärer* who decried the way in which Jews had been historically treated and called for change. In doing so, on the other hand, at least one key contributor made it clear that he was uncomfortable with the notion of accepting the Jews as they were. Rather, he envisaged the shaping of an enlightened, modern Judaism, a view no doubt informed by the sensibilities of the German *Aufklärung*. One important feature of this new enlightened Judaism was a reconsideration of rabbinic teachings, for the undisciplined and unsound quality of rabbinic Judaism and its literature was deemed unworthy of the modern age. In the context of the debate about the Jews and the possibility of their integration, this kind of exposition had serious political and cultural ramifications. By shaping the way in which Jews and Judaism were regarded, the *Deutsche Encyclopädie* not only shaped German attitudes towards the Jews, but also articulated a set of expectations with which, directly or indirectly, the Jews were confronted.

APPENDIX A

Entry for 'Juden (politisch)' in the *Deutsche Encyclopädie*

Man hat oft die Fragen aufgeworfen, ob die Juden einem Staate nützlich oder schädlich sind, ob sie zu dulden sind oder nicht, und wenn einige sie für schädli-

---

[57] *Deutsche Encyclopädie*, vol. II, p. 488; the citation from Ibn Ezra is taken from the introductory passage to his commentary to Lamentations. My thanks to Marty Lockshin for pinpointing the citation in Ibn Ezra's *oeuvre*.

[58] *Deutsche Encyclopädie*, vol. II, p. 491: "Auch von diesen Regeln sind viele ganz gut und richtig; viele aber auch unbestimmt. Im ganzen genommen, fehlt es den Rabbinen an den meisten Hülfsmitteln, die einen guten Exegeten bilden. Sieht man ihre Erklärungen an, wie sie in ihren Schriften vorkommen, so leidet meistens der gesunde Menschenverstand; doch ist auch nicht zu leugnen, dass hier und dar noch etwas gutes darinnen ist . . . Prüfet alles, und das Gute behaltet."

che Leute erklärten, so fanden sich nicht minder Menschenfreunde und weise Männer, welche glaubten, das es blos auf die Regierungen ankomme, diese Leute für den Staat nützlich zu machen, welches um so leichter bewerkstelliget werden könnte, da sie über dieselben weit freyere Hände haben, als in vielen Ländern über andere Classen von Unterthanen. Es ist auch in der That ein edler Gedanke, eine unter uns wohnende, so sehr herabgesunkene Nation, so umzubilden, dass sie der Gesellschaft brauchbare Mitglieder liefern kann. Der Eifer, mit dem man diese Umbildung betreibt, bleibt immer lobenswürdig, aber man muss bey diesem wichtigen Geschäfte die Schwierigkeiten nicht übersehen welche erst gehoben werden müssen, bevor man zur Ausführung jenes wohlthätigen Planes schreiten kann. Man drang darauf, der Jude soll Professionen erlernen, soll Soldat werden, aber man vergass die Frage zu erörtern: kann der Jude als Jude Professonist werden, Soldat seyn? Wird er als Jude dem Staate dadurch nützlicher? Wird er sich dadurch glücklicher sehen? Die jüdische Jugend soll bey christlichen Meistern in die Lehre gehen. Gewiss giebt es gutdenkende, vorurtheilfreye Männer, die zu redlich denken, als dass sie es den jüdischen Lehrling sollten fühlen lassen, das er ein Jude ist. Wer will aber diese redlichen Männer aus dem grossen Haufen heraussuchen, und ohne sie zu suchen, möchten sie bis jetzt noch in manchen Städten schwer zu finden seyn. Soll man die christlichen Meister zwingen, Juden in die Lehre zu nehmen, so lässt sich der Erfolg voraus sehen. Wie verschieden sind überdiess die religiösen Gebräuche des Meisters und des Jungen? Dieser darf zu keiner Arbeit schreiten, bevor er sein Morgengebet verrichtet hat, und diess darf nicht vor Tages Anbruch geschehen. Ja von Rechtswegen soll er dieses Gebet in der Synagoge verrichten. Freytages mit Untergang der Sonne muss er aufhören zu arbeiten. Den Sabbath muss er heiligen. Sollte er dafür am Sonntage arbeiten; so wäre es unbillig ihn allein arbeiten zu lassen, und dann könnte der Meister sagen, mein Sabbath ist so heilig wie der deinige. Man erwäge ferner, was für Hindernisse die vielen Feyertage noch hervorbringen, an welchen der Jude oft ganzer 8 Tage lang nicht arbeiten darf? Diese Schwierigkeiten, wovon noch weit mehrere angeführt werden könnten, finden bey dem jüdischen Soldaten noch in einem höhern Grade Statt. Gesetzt aber in jenem Falle, brächte es der Jude bis zum Meisterwerden. Hier kann er mit christlichen Professionisten weder gleich arbeiten, noch gleiche Preise halten. Er hat unendlich mehr Abhaltungen, als: die vielen Feyer-, Bet- und Fastäge, Todesfälle in der Verwandtschaft, und bey weitem mehr Ausgaben, die seine Religion, die Verfassung, in welcher er in dem Staate lebt, verursachen. Der jüdische Meister sieht sich also immer gezwungen, sich auf irgend eine andere Art schadlos zu halten. Er sucht Schleichwege, wird ein Wucherer in seiner Profession, wie er es zuvor war, und man hat also nichts gewonnen, sondern nur eine kleine Veränderung in der Form, und in der That keine der Gesellschaft vortheilhafte, bewirkt. Kurz, der Jude wird und muss zu allen bürgerlichen Handthierungen so lange unbrauchbar erscheinen, so lange er noch durch das Joch seiner Religionsgesetze in seine drückende Lage eingezwängt bleibt. Diese sind es, die ihn hindern, das zu seyn, was er seyn sollte und könnte, und was er nie werden kann, so lange diese Hindernisse nicht wenigstens zum Theil gehoben sind. Hier fragt sichs nun: sind diese Hindernisse zu heben, wie soll man sie denn heben? Das Mittel hierzu kann kein anderes seyn, als eine den Umständen angemessene vollkommene Reform. Dazu aber wird eine hinlängliche Zeit, Vorsicht, ausdauernde Stetigkeit erfordert; denn gewaltsame Mittel würden diese Nation noch unbrauchbarer und unglücklicher machen, als sie es jetzt schon ist. Das Schwierige dabey liegt darinnen, dass Umreissen und Aufbauen, und zwar nicht nur etwas Neues, sondern etwas Bessers aufbauen, bey einander seyn müssen. Pädagogik ist die erste Grundlinie, woraus figurirt werden muss, aber an eine vollständige Pädagogik hat man noch nicht gedacht. Jede moralische Besserung einer Nation muss stufenweise bey ihr fortgeführt werden, wenn sie einen gewissen Grad der Reife erlangen soll. Aufklärung des Verstandes und Bildung des Herzens, diese sind das Fundament, auf welchem das künftige Gebäude aufgeführt werden kann und muss. Dazu gehören Männer von Einsicht und grossem Gewicht unter der Nation selbst.

[The article ends with a bibliography of contemporary writings on the Jews' political status].

The Beginnings of Jewish Children's Literature in High German: Three Schoolbooks from Berlin (1779), Prague (1781) and Dessau (1782)

BY MICHAEL NAGEL

THE MODERNISATION OF THE JEWISH SCHOOL AND CHILDREN'S LITERATURE IN GERMANY: JEWISH OR NON-JEWISH INFLUENCES, OR AN INTERACTION OF BOTH?

Research into the history of the German Jews since the *Haskalah* raises the question as to whether the general change in Jewish life, starting in the last decades of the eighteenth century, was primarily brought about by Jewish or non-Jewish initiatives. Examples include the use of High German, the modernisation of religious rituals, the increasing access to new professions, and thereby the slow separation from traditional values and lifestyles. Was all this caused by the endeavours of Jewish individuals or through Christian initiatives, as for instance by the state?

This perspective of an either Jewish or non-Jewish dominated development can best be shown in the history of Jew hatred and antisemitism. In this context there is a clear answer as to the question of origins and influences. The difference between active persecution and passive suffering is obvious, even in the case of defence against antisemitic statements and actions.

However, the history of German Jewry cannot be solely interpreted through the aspects of Jew hatred and antisemitism. It is much richer, more complex and also shaped by many internal influences. This is especially true in the case of the *Haskalah* which combined both traditional and modern concepts and which quickly spread from its beginnings in late eighteenth-century Berlin to other towns and countries, bringing about considerable changes in a relatively short space of time. Nevertheless, even in this era of relative religious tolerance one can detect strong non-Jewish influences.[1] The ideology of the Enlightenment did not approve of the persecution of the Jews in the past and distanced itself particularly from the popular religious and folkloristic elements of earlier Jew hatred. However, was this not replaced by more subtle forms of violence and domination used against the minority? To what extent were German Jews

---

[1]Still worth reading on the interplay of Jewish and non-Jewish influences in the era of Enlightenment, Jacob Katz, *Die Entstehung der Judenassimilation in Deutschland und deren Ideologie*, Inaugural Dissertation, Frankfurt am Main 1935.

allowed their own path to modernisation, or how much of this was prescribed or even forced upon them by the majority?

In studying the development of the Jewish education system in German-speaking countries since the last third of the 18th century, the model of just one dominating influence (whether Jewish or non-Jewish) proves to be too narrow a base. Especially in this area we see an interplay of intellectual stimulation. The establishment of the modern Jewish school, beginning in 1778, is just one example. In the case of the first Jewish schoolbooks (manuals and text books on religious education) these contacts can be characterised as a pedagogical and literary cooperation.

These first Jewish schoolbooks mark the beginning of a specifically Jewish children's literature in High German, which was something new to Ashkenasi Jewry. To understand this break with tradition, a short glance back to the traditional education system and children's literature before the *Haskalah* will be useful. Furthermore, we will examine some details of the comparative Jewish and non-Jewish contribution to the contents and publishing history of these (apparently) first three schoolbooks in High German.[2] Since this essay is part of a series of research projects on the history of Jewish children's literature in German-speaking countries undertaken within the last ten years, a survey of some recent contributions by Israeli and German scholars will be given first.

When Zohar Shavit published her fine article on the beginnings of Hebrew children's literature in Germany in the *LBI Year Book*,[3] systematic research on the subject of Jewish children's literature was a *desideratum*.[4] Despite the fact that studies in children's literature of the past can give useful and new insight into literary and pedagogical questions, and can also make a contribution to the understanding of social and moral history, the books written for Jewish children in Germany had been neglected by academic research up to this time.

Now, ten years later this situation has changed considerably. Due to cooperative bi-national bibliographical/biographical research carried out by the Porter Institute at Tel Aviv University (under the direction of Zohar Shavit), the *Institut für Jugendbuchforschung*, Frankfurt University (led by Hans-Heino Ewers) and the *Institut für Popularkultur und Kinderkultur*, Bremen University (under Dieter Richter), a bibliography of more than 2,400 German, Hebrew and bilingual books from the Berlin *Haskalah* up to 1945 has been compiled. Many of these titles have also been annotated. The *vitae* of the authors – mainly teachers and rabbis – and the history of publishing houses of Jewish children's literature are

---

[2] Moses Mendelssohn's High German *Pentateuch* (starting with the 1780 edition and at first printed in Hebrew letters) will not be the subject of this article, although it was translated especially for young readers.

[3] Zohar Shavit, 'From Friedländer's Lesebuch to the Jewish Campe. The Beginning of Hebrew Children's Literature in Germany' in *LBI Year Book XXXIII* (1988) pp. 385–415.

[4] There are a few publications by Jewish scholars and teachers in Germany on that subject dating from the early 20th century, for example Hermann Levi, *Lehrbuch und Jugendbuch im jüdischen Erziehungswesen des 19. Jahrhunderts. Versuch einer entwicklungsgeschichtlichen Darstellung nach Inhalt und Methode*, Diss. University of Cologne, Cologne 1933; Elias Gut, 'Zur Geschichte der jüdischen Jugendliteratur', in Otto Driesen (ed.), *Bausteine praktischer Pädagogik*, Frankfurt am Main 1929, pp. 91–102.

described as well. The bibliographical handbook *Deutsch-Jüdische Kinder- und Jugendliteratur*[5] provides a solid basis for further studies.[6]

TEACHING AND READING MATERIALS FOR CHILDREN BEFORE THE *HASKALAH*

Up to the time of Moses Mendelssohn few Jews were able to read and speak High German. The economic, social and cultural conditions of Jewish life did not require a thorough acquaintance with the language of their Christian fellow-citizens.[7] In the centuries preceeding the *Haskalah*, adults as well as children and juveniles rarely had access to literature in Latin or German. For their education and entertainment they had to rely on a relatively fixed canon of literature, written in Hebrew and Yiddish and printed in Hebrew letters. Hebrew texts were mostly on spiritual-religious matters, and normally intended to be read by male children, juveniles and adults, whereas the Yiddish books, some of a more profane and entertaining nature, were meant mainly for girls and women, as well as for less educated men. With young readers in mind, some characteristic features common to both Hebrew and Yiddish literature can be found:

1. Normally the books were meant to be read by all age-groups, with little differentiation between young or adult readers. This is in contrast to non-Jewish books of the same period.
2. As to contents, there are only a few points of contact with non-Jewish education and reading customs.
3. For male children and juveniles reading matter related exclusively to religious subjects.

These contents and aims of reading for children and juveniles are subject of numerous guidelines on the proper use of books in moral instructions, spiritual testaments and so on.[8]

[5]Zohar Shavit and Hans-Heino Ewers (eds.), *Deutsch-jüdische Kinder-und Jugendliteratur von der Haskalah bis 1945. Die deutsch- und hebräischsprachigen Schriften des deutschsprachigen Raums. Ein bibliographisches Handbuch*, vols. I and II, Stuttgart and Weimar 1996.

[6]For a brief survey of the history of Jewish children's literature in High German from the Enlightenment to 1938 see Michael Nagel, 'Motive der deutschsprachigen jüdischen Kinder- und Jugendliteratur von der Aufklärung bis zum Dritten Reich', in *Zeitschrift für Religions- und Geistesgeschichte*, vol. IIL, No. 3, pp. 193–214 and *idem*, 'Jüdische Kinderbücher im deutschsprachigen Raum vom 18. bis zum 20. Jahrhundert', in Michael Nagel (ed.), *Begegnung und Erinnerung. Universitätssymposion Haifa-Bremen 1994*, Bremen 1995, pp. 189–215. On the intentions of authors, on contemporary reviews and on the inner-Jewish discussion about the use and the contents of Jewish children's literature see Gabriele von Glasenapp and Michael Nagel, *Das jüdische Jugendbuch. Von der Aufklärung bis zum Dritten Reich*, Stuttgart 1996; Michael Nagel, *"Emancipation des Juden im Roman" oder "Tendenz zur Isolierung"? Das deutsch-jüdische Jugendbuch in der Diskussion zwischen Aufklärung, Reform und Orthodoxie (1780–1860)*, Hildesheim–Zürich–New York 1999.

[7]On the transition to the use of High German see, for example, Jacob Toury, 'Die Sprache als Problem der jüdischen Einordnung im deutschen Kulturraum', in *Jahrbuch des Instituts für deutsche Geschichte*, Beiheft 4, Tel Aviv 1982, pp. 75–96.

[8]For a brief survey of reading instructions before the *Haskalah* see Michael Nagel, 'Jüdische Lektürepädagogik im deutschsprachigen Raum von der Berliner Haskala bis zur Neo-Orthodoxie', in Glasenapp and Nagel, pp. 6–19.

Moses Mendelssohn's translation of the Hebrew bible into High German, begun in 1774 primarily with the aim of introducing a new style of teaching children and juveniles, was the starting point for changing both the reading methods for the young and the Jewish school itself. The *maskilim*, the followers of Jewish Enlightenment in Berlin, wanted to introduce a system closer to the non-Jewish education system. Through this they hoped to gain full emancipation, i.e. full civil rights, within a relatively short space of time. This expectation seemed to be justified: Christian advocates of Jewish emancipation, for example Christian Wilhelm von Dohm in 1781, had tied the question of civil rights for the Jews to a thorough modernisation of their education system.[9] Without really being familiar with traditional Jewish teaching, non-Jews distrusted it. In their prejudiced opinion this system was partially responsible for the peculiar and difficult position of Jewry in society.

LESEBUCH FÜR JÜDISCHE KINDER, ZUM BESTEN DER JÜDISCHEN FREYSCHULE, BERLIN 1779 (READER FOR JEWISH CHILDREN, FOR THE BENEFIT OF THE JEWISH FREE SCHOOL)

"Matrimonial love has room on the blade of a knife, for matrimonial hatred a sixty-foot bed is too small."[10] This "talmudic" quotation seems strangely out of place in a book, which appears to be addressed mainly to younger school children. This first German-language Jewish school-textbook of 1779 is also different in many other respects from contemporary non-Jewish school literature. Its forty-six pages make it a rather "slight" reading manual, without a very defined character. It seems neither to address a particular age group nor to convey a straightforward pedagogical message. On the one hand it appears to be a normal primer, on the other hand it looks like a non-denominational religious instruction manual. Other sections consist of a collection of Jewish moral fables from the Middle Ages, better suited to an adult audience, as well as talmudic quotations and contemporary German poetry and passages from non-Jewish readers. The (anonymous) editor, David Friedländer, a Berlin merchant and friend of Moses Mendelssohn, apparently wanted to focus on two aspects. He emphasised the universality of Jewish monotheism and he tried to bring into harmony the popular philosophy of the Enlightenment with Jewish literary tradition. His sources are mainly non-Jewish readers and traditional Jewish texts, most of the latter translated and edited by Moses Mendelssohn.[11]

---

[9]Christian Wilhelm [von] Dohm, *Über die bürgerliche Verbesserung der Juden*, Berlin 1781, parts 1 and 2 repr. in one vol., Hildesheim 1973. It is well known that Dohm, member of the Prussian civil service, had written his widely-discussed essay influenced by ideas of and conversations with Moses Mendelssohn.

[10]From the above mentioned reader, p. 34 (repr. in Moritz Stern, 'Aus Moses Mendelssohns und David Friedländers wiederaufgefundenem 'Lesebuch für jüdische Kinder', in *Gemeindeblatt der jüdischen Gemeinde zu Berlin*, vol. XVII, No.1, 7 January 1927). ("Eheliche Liebe findet auf einer Messerschneide Raum, ehelichem Haße ist ein sechzigfuß breites Bett zu eng.") For an analysis of the book and its sources see Zohar Shavit, *David Friedländer. Lesebuch für jüdische Kinder*, Frankfurt am Main 1989.

[11]Shavit, *David Friedländer*.

The first pages of the book contain reading exercises and rules for correct German pronunciation, followed by the alphabet in Latin letters. A copper engraving shows the Hebrew alphabet in script and the sacred prayer *Schema Israel* in High German, also written in Hebrew letters. This page, written in Hebrew, shows the only typographical evidence that this a Jewish text book, apart from the title page, which displays the Hebrew symbol of the Jewish Free School in Berlin. This is followed by Moses Maimonides's thirteen articles of faith in the more modern translation by Moses Mendelssohn. Instead of the traditional recurrent opening "I believe...", it says "I hold as true and certain" (*Ich erkenne für wahr und gewiß*). Maimonides's articles are followed by the ten commandments, which in turn are followed by six animal fables by Berachia ben Natronai ha-Nakdan, also in a Mendelssohn translation. 'Moral tales' (*Moralische Erzählungen*) from the Talmud are the next topic, then *Andachtsübung eines Weltweisen*, a philosophical prayer by Mendelssohn which could be used by any monotheistic religion or Christian denomination. The same universal and inter-denominational character appears in another prayer, *Vorbereitungsgebet*, which Mendelssohn had based on a poem by the medieval Spanish writer Jehuda Halevi. Addressed to a universal God, it emphasises the longing for paradise and the transitoriness of life. The next chapter *Sittensprüche und Sprichwörter aus dem Talmud* 'Moral quotations and proverbs from the Talmud' offers, besides the sentence on matrimonial love and hatred cited above, several other quotations hardly suitable for the young reader, for example, "When the thief cannot steal, he plays the honest man." (*Wenn der Dieb nicht stehlen kann, so spielt er den ehrlichen Mann*). The book closes with passages from non-Jewish readers and fables.

According to the contemporary philanthrophic view concerning children's literature, the language, contents and style of such texts had to be adapted to the level of understanding of their young readers.[12] From this point of view, the Berlin Jewish reader from 1779 could not be considered suitable literature for children. Nevertheless, the subtitle of this textbook refers to the *Jüdische Freyschule* in Berlin.[13] But it does not say "for use by the Jewish Free School". It simply states "for the benefit of the Jewish Free School" (*Zum Besten der jüdischen Freyschule*). Indeed, there is some evidence that the book had not been edited primarily for the use by the Jewish Free School:

1. The Jewish Free School was in its infancy in 1779. Even three years later there was only a total of seventy-three pupils.[14] One can question the value of printing a book for such a small group of readers.

---

[12] See, for example, Christian Gotthilf Salzmann, *Conrad Kiefer oder Anweisung zu einer vernünftigen Erziehung der Kinder: ein Buch für's Volk*, Ulm 1796 (2nd edition).

[13] The Jewish Free School – free meant a nonfeepaying school for the poor – had been founded in 1778 by the Berlin merchants David Friedländer and Daniel Itzig. It was the first school in the history of Ashkenasi Jewry to use the vernacular and to teach non-religious subjects.

[14] For the number of pupils see [August Friedrich Cranz], *Berlinische Correspondenz historischen und litterarischen Inhalts. Eine periodische Schrift von dem Verfasser der Lieblingsstunden. Viertes Stück, Dritter Brief*, Berlin, 7 December 1782, p. 61. Up to 1784 the number of pupils remained unchanged, see Moritz Stern, 'Die Konzession zur Errichtung der orientalischen Buchdruckerei und Buchhandlung in Berlin 1784', in *Zeitschrift für die Geschichte der Juden in Deutschland* 1929–1938, vol. VI (1935), pp. 168–171, especially p. 169.

2. Contemporary accounts of the Free School – as far as they are available today – do not mention the book at all.[15]

Can one surmise, then, that the book had been published for home reading? This is not very likely either. Only a few wealthy Jewish homes possessed books in High German. What purpose did this manual serve then?

Presumably, its initial purpose was to introduce to the public a fundamentally changed and substantially modernised Jewish educational system. It was supposed to serve as a sign to fellow Christians that an enlightened *avantgarde* within German Jewry was ready to assimilate with the non-Jewish majority and share their cultural and educational values. At the same time, the selected texts from the Hebrew literature – most of them translated and arranged by Moses Mendelssohn – could demonstrate that the principal ideas of the Enlightenment were nothing new to the *maskilim*. Furthermore, this was seen as an opportunity to show the educated non-Jewish public that traditional Jewish literature could add interesting and original aspects to the contemporary literary scene:

1. The chapter 'Samples of Rabbinic wisdom' (Proben rabbinischer Weisheit), in which Mendelssohn presented a selection of talmudic and other traditional tales, had already been published two years earlier in the enlightened literary journal *Der Philosoph für die Welt* edited by Johann Jacob Engel and had been favourably reviewed in the *Allgemeine Deutsche Bibliothek* (a leading German journal for literary criticism in the second half of the eighteenth century). It was hailed as innovative in introducing traditional Jewish literature to non-Jewish German readers: "The samples of rabbinical wisdom are truly drawn from rabbinic literature and are indeed a valuable example of the attitudes and ideas of earlier Jewish writers. The translation shows the inimitable hand of a Moses Mendelssohn in combining the characteristically oriental with a true German style."[16]
2. The fables by Berachia ben Natronai had first been published in the literary journal *Bibliothek der schönen Wissenschaften und der freyen Künste*, edited by Moses Mendelssohn and Friedrich Nicolai.[17]

The contemporary reviews by Christian teachers and literati show that it was clearly understood and agreed upon that the main purpose of the "*Lesebuch für jüdische Kinder*" was to serve as a signal to the non-Jewish population. Georg

---

[15]See, for example, Daniel Itzig, David Friedländer, *Nachricht von dem gegenwärtigen Zustand, bisherigen Fortgang, und eigentlichem (sic) Endzweck der Freischule . . . zu Berlin, wie auch Erklärung des Institutes, unter welchen Bedingungen es gesinnt sei, von ihrem (sic) ersten Plane abzugehen und den Unterricht ausgebreiteter und nützlicher zu machen* (Berlin 1783). This four-page programme, one of the first of the *Jüdische Freyschule*, is in High German using Hebrew letters.

[16]*Allgemeine Deutsche Bibliothek*, vol. XXXV, part 2, Berlin 1778, pp. 330–336. ("Sie ['Proben rabbinischer Weisheit'] sind wirklich aus rabbinischen Büchern gezogen, und in der That ein schätzbarer Beytrag zur Kenntniß der Gesinnungen der ältern jüdischen Schriftsteller. Man erkennet übrigens auch in dieser Uebersetzung bald die Feder eines Moses Mendelssohn, an der unnachahmlichen Wendung, mit der er das eigenthümliche orientalische durchscheinen läßt, und doch ganz deutsch schreibt.")

[17]*Bibliothek der schönen Wissenschaften und der freyen Künste* (first edition 1757), vol. III, part 1 (1759), here cited from the second edition Leipzig 1762 (reprint. Hildesheim 1979), pp. 73 ff.

Friedrich Goetz, *Informator* (private tutor) to the Hessian court, remarked in his rather critical annotated bibliography *Children's books for parents and educators*: "This booklet also deserves to be mentioned because of its well-selected contributions."[18] Johann Erich Biester, secretary to the Prussian Minister Karl Abraham von Zedlitz, writes in more detail, but in the same positive vein: "We take pleasure in the existence of a Jewish Free School and in the publication of the Jewish reader too, even though from the pedagogical point of view not all pieces are chosen well."[19] The theologian Samuel Baur expressed a similar opinion: "Indeed some parts are not suitable for children, but the booklet contains so many excellent things which even deserve to be included in our own school books, so that every reader will want to thank Herr Friedländer for having compiled such a fine collection."[20]

The friendly interest of the non-Jewish reviewers is directed at the establishment of a modern Jewish school system in Germany, teaching in High German, as represented by the Jewish Free School in Berlin. The educational shortcomings of the reader of 1779 are benignly overlooked. Another author, Friedrich Nicolai, who had a special and critical interest in contemporary education, does not mention the weaknesses of the textbook at all. In his biographical work on Berlin scholars, Nicolai writes about the editor, David Friedländer: "Merchant and owner of a silk factory. He is well known and respected for the publication of a very useful children's reader for the Jewish people..."[21]

David Friedländer, however, was not very eager to acknowledge publicly his role as the editor of this reader. He possibly felt uneasy about the educational dilettantism. Over the next few decades he worked ceaselessly on improving the Jewish school system in Prussia and certainly wanted to avoid the impression of being an amateur in this field. Even his own comments on the reader forty years later do not refer to him being the editor, but they do confirm the impression that the book had been published with non-Jewish public opinion in mind and not just as a reader for the Jewish Free School: "The *Lesebuch für jüdische Kinder*, today forgotten for good reasons, caused a sensation when it was first published. To

[18]Georg Friedrich Goetz, *Kinderbibliothek für Aeltern und Erzieher*, part 2, Frankfurt am Main 1781, p. 14. ("Auch dieß Büchelchen verdient wohl hier eine Anzeige, da eine gute Auswahl in Demselben herrscht.")

[19]*Allgemeine Deutsche Bibliothek*, vol. LII, part 1, pp. 206 ff. ("Es erfreut der Gedanke an eine jüdische Freischule und so auch der Anblick eines solchen jüdischen Lesebuchs, obgleich nicht alle Stücke pädagogisch richtig berechnet sind.")

[20][Samuel Baur], *Charakteristik der Erziehungsschriftsteller Deutschlands. Ein Handbuch für Erzieher*, Leipzig 1790. ("Für Kinder ist freilich manches nicht; aber das Büchlein enthält doch so viel trefliches, welches höchlich verdient in unsere Bücher selbst zur Bildung junger Leute aufgenommen zu werden, daß es jeder Leser dem Herrn Friedländer Dank wissen wird, eine so schöne Sammlung veranstaltet zu haben.")

[21]Friedrich Nicolai, 'Anzeige der vornehmsten jetzt in Berlin, Potsdam, und der umliegenden Gegend lebenden Gelehrten, Künstler und Musiker', in *Beschreibung der Königlichen Residenzstädte Berlin und Potsdam, aller daselbst befindlicher Merkwürdigkeiten, und der umliegenden Gegend*, vol. III, appendix 3, Berlin 1786, p. 7. ("Hr. David Friedländer, Kaufmann und Inhaber einer Seidenmanufaktur. Er ist durch ein vorzüglich brauchbares Lesebuch für Kinder Jüdischer Nation ... rühmlich bekannt.")

Christian scholars it came as a real surprise in a way that we today find hard to understand."[22]

The *Lesebuch* was reprinted in Prague in 1781.[23] There, this new edition with only one slight alteration in the title, was supposed to fulfil the same purpose as in Berlin. It was intended as a symbol for enlightened Jews to bring Jewish traditional thinking into line with a modern Christian educational system. As in Berlin it was never used in the Jewish schools of Prague. The traditional *chedarim* concentrated on religious education and did not teach in High German, and the modern Jewish school (*Jüdische Normalschule*), founded by the Austrian administration in 1782, used another reader altogether, namely the *Lesebuch für die jüdische Jugend*.

LESEBUCH FÜR DIE JÜDISCHE JUGEND DER DEUTSCHEN SCHULEN IM KÖNIGREICHE BÖHMEN. BESTEHEND IN DER ANLEITUNG ZUR RECHTSCHAFFENHEIT, PRAG: KAISERL. KÖNIGL. NORMALSCHULE 1781 (READER FOR JEWISH JUVENILES IN GERMAN SCHOOLS IN THE KINGDOM OF BOHEMIA: A GUIDE TO RIGHTEOUS LIVING)

This book, another early reader in High German for Jewish children, suggests a rather different approach to modern Jewish education. Although the first edition seems to have been lost without trace, it is possible to reconstruct its contents from contemporary school reports and correspondence, as well as from a review and a travelogue of a journey to Prague. These sources offer useful information on the origin and intentions of the book.[24]

The Jewish Free School in Berlin had been founded on the initiative of local Jewish merchants together with Jewish followers of the Enlightenment with active encouragement from the Christian *avantgarde*. The German-speaking Jewish *Normalschule*, on the other hand, had been established by the government (though paid for by the Prague Jewish community).[25] Six years before, under the

---

[22]David Friedländer, 'Moses Mendelssohn. Von ihm und über ihn, vom Stadtrath D. Friedländer. 5. Unterhaltung mit Mendelssohn, aus der Erinnerung niedergeschrieben. Zweites Fragment', in *Jedidja*, vol. II, No. 1 (Berlin 1818–1819), pp. 143–153, here p. 147. ("Das 'Lesebuch für jüdische Kinder', jetzt und mit Recht vergessen, machte damals als eine unerwartete Erscheinung bei christlichen Gelehrten eine gegenwärtig unbegreiflich scheinende Sensation.").

[23]Otto Muneles, 'Bibliographical survey of Jewish Prague', in Hana Volavková (ed.), *Jewish Monuments in Bohemia and Moravia*, vol. I, Prague 1952, p. 91.

[24]The book is mentioned by Bernhard Mandl, *Das jüdische Schulwesen in Ungarn unter Kaiser Josef II (1780–1790)*, Frankfurt am Main 1902. See also G[erson] Wolf, *Geschichte der Juden in Wien (1156–1876)*, suppl. No. 32, Vienna 1876 (facsimile reprint with comments by Erika Weinzierl, Vienna 1974), p. 267.

[25]On the founding of this modern Jewish school in Prague see Moses Wiener (one of the first teachers), *Nachricht von dem Ursprunge und dem Fortgange der deutschen jüdischen Hauptschule zu Prag*, Prague 1785. See also Ignatz Böhm, *Historische Nachricht von der Entstehungsart und der Verbreitung des Normalschulinstituts in Böhmen*, Prague 1784; and Emanuel Böhm (probably identical to the previous), *Fortsetzung der historischen Nachricht, I. Heft für die Jahre 1784 und 1785*, Prague 1785. *II. Heft für die Jahre 1785 und 1786*, Prague 1787. These reports, although written from the administration's point of view, give interesting and detailed information.

reign of Maria Theresia, a previous attempt by the administration to modernise the Jewish school system had been rejected by the Jewish community, and since then the feeling of distrust towards the state had remained in the Jewish population of Prague.[26] Due to the skilled policy of Ferdinand Kindermann Ritter von Schulstein in his role as chief inspector for the school system in Bohemia during the reign of Joseph II, a compromise was reached between the administration and the Jewish community.[27]

The traditional religious education of the *chedarim* and the *Talmud-Thora*-schools remained unchanged. In addition to this, from the age of ten, children – meaning boys – would be taught every afternoon in the secular *Normalschule* too, but only for two hours in the winter and four hours in the summer. The Jewish teachers of the *Normalschule* (primarily Jews were to be employed) had to first be trained and qualify in Christian schools. The Chief Rabbi of Prague was particularly anxious to keep the modern secular teaching in High German strictly separate from traditional religious instruction.

The compromise meant a success for Ferdinand von Schulstein and the policies of "tolerance" and Germanisation under Joseph II. The opening of the school on 2 May in 1782 was celebrated with great extravagance: The day was declared a holiday for the Jews of Prague. Beginning in the early morning, prayers for the government were said in all synagogues. The Chief Rabbi had written special prayers,[28] which were sung in the great synagogue "by the famous Jewish vocalists from Mannheim", attended by all the dignitaries and elders of the Jewish community.[29] This was followed by a festive procession of nobles and commoners alike to the newly built school. Then several speeches were made accompanied by music, and this was followed in the evening by a fireworks display ". . . in which the words *Vivat Josephus secundus* did shine brightly . . ."[30] The *Wiener Zeitung*, a prominent Austrian newspaper, published a euphoric report on the event and gave the following as the primary goal of the newly inaugurated school, ". . . to transform the young people of the Jewish nation into upright and active members of the state."[31]

The ceremony and the public attention given to the school's inauguration, indicate the importance given to Jewish emancipation by Joseph II's enlightened reform movement. The drawback of this reform lay in the fact that this modern Jewish school had not been established through a Jewish initiative. Could this

---

[26]See, for example, the report by Johann Wanniczek (later headmaster of this school), *Geschichte der Prager Haupt- Trivial- und Mädchenschule der Israeliten, deren Verfassung und merkwürdigen Vorfälle von ihrer Gründung bis auf gegenwärtige Zeiten. Verfaßt von Johann Wanniczek, Direktor dieser Hauptschule, zur Erinnerung des 50 jährigen Jubelfestes derselben im Jahre 1832*, Prague 1832, p. 8.

[27]On the modernisation of the Jewish school in Prague see, for example, Ruth Kestenberg-Gladstein, *Neuere Geschichte der Juden in den böhmischen Ländern. Erster Teil: Das Zeitalter der Aufklärung 1780–1830*, Tübingen 1969 (Schriftenreihe wissenschaftlicher Abhandlungen des Leo Baeck Instituts 18/1).

[28][Ezechiel Landau], *Dankgebet, welches den 2. May 1782 bey der feyerlichen Einsegnung der deutschen Schule in der Judenstadt in Prag, von den besten jüdischen Schulsängern unter Musik abgesungen wird . . . in Versen verfasst und von einem Prager Juden aus dem Hebräischen übersetzt*, Prague 1782, see Muneles, p. 92.

[29]Wiener, p. 32.

[30]Wiener, p. 34.

[31]*Wiener Zeitung*, No. 39, Wednesday, 15 May 1782. (". . .den jungen Nachwuchs ihrer Nation zu rechtschaffenen und thätigen Gliedern des Staates umschaffen zu können.")

modernisation therefore be seen as a form of "pressure to conform in school and language (*Schul- und Sprachzwang*)", as the historian Simon Dubnow contended?[32] However, the upper class of the Prague community seemed quite willing to adopt secular elements and the use of High German into their children's education.[33]

Just like the establishment of the *Normalschule*, the creation of this school manual was not initiated by Jews either. Who then was responsible for it? Ferdinand Kindermann von Schulstein was the anonymous editor. He had taken most of the text from a modern Austrian non-Jewish reader, carefully removing all traces of Christian elements.[34] In contrast to the Berlin reader of 1779, Jewish tradition and literature are not represented in this model. In their place, the book tries to engender a sense of social and moral values in its young readers. Being a typical product of the Enlightenment, it tries to promote a sensible, hardworking and economically-aware lifestyle. The subtitle "guide to righteous living" (*Anleitung zur Rechtschaffenheit*) is to be understood as an agenda: the attainment of polite, modest, and amiable behaviour, first in school and later in society are extolled as principal goals of the reader. Correspondence between Ferdinand Kindermann von Schulstein and Moses Mendelssohn from 1783 throws further light on the intentions of the editor. The Austrian school inspector had sent Mendelssohn a copy of the reader and had asked the Berlin philosopher for a thorough evaluation of it, at the same time expanding on his own views on modernising the Jewish educational system, and specifically on the goals of the manual. Jewish youth should become "socially aware", they should be encouraged to abandon their typically "rough and unpolished behaviour (*Rohigkeit*)" and to adopt good manners and integrity.[35] The chapter headings reflect this aim: "1. On the righteous behaviour of students at school (including subheadings: The students' appearance in school and on their way to school. The conduct of pupils during the lessons; their conduct when leaving school.) 2. On the decency or righteousness of human beings as reflected in their convictions and beliefs, in their deeds and in their conduct (including the subheadings: On order. On industriousness. On domesticity. On thrift. On what constitutes good behaviour. On walking. On sitting. On the form of greeting. . . . On gracefulness in gestures and dress and other things. 3. On the society in which man is destined by God to live and on social obligations. 4. On the art of housekeeping. 5. On patriotism."[36]

[32]Simon Dubnow, *Weltgeschichte des jüdischen Volkes. Von seinen Uranfängen bis zur Gegenwart. Die Neuzeit*, vol. VII, Berlin 1928, p. 373.

[33]See, for example, Hillel J. Kieval, 'Caution's Progress: The Modernization of Jewish Life in Prague, 1780–1830' in Jacob Katz (ed.), *Toward Modernity. The European Jewish Model*, New York 1987, pp. 71–105.

[34]See Wiener, p. 27. On the non-Jewish reader, which served as a model, see Joseph A. Freiherr von Helfert, *Die österreichische Volksschule. Geschichte, System, Statistik. Erster Band. Die Gründung der österreichischen Volksschule durch Maria Theresia*, Prague 1860, p. 536.

[35]Ferdinand Kindermann Ritter von Schulstein, 'Brief an Moses Mendelssohn vom 5. 1. 1783', in Moses Mendelssohn, *Briefwechsel II. Bearbeitet von Alexander Altmann, Gesammelte Schriften, Jubiläumsausgabe*, vol. XIII, No. 586, Stuttgart 1977, p. 88.

[36]Cited from a positive review of the reader in *Hameasef: Erste Zugabe des zweyten Jahrgangs zu der hebräischen Monatsschrift* [in Hebrew letters: *Hameasef*] *dem Sammler. Herausgegeben von einer Gesellschaft*

The above correspondence reveals that Moses Mendelssohn was sceptical about the so-called "roughness" and other social vices of Jewish youth, as characterised by Ferdinand von Schulstein in keeping with popular prejudice. He had mixed feelings about the new *Normalschule* in Prague as well, because he mistrusted Joseph II's politics of tolerance. In 1784 he wrote to his friend – and his son's former teacher – Herz Homberg: "As long as the system of (religious) unification is still lurking in the background, these glossy attempts at tolerance seem to be more dangerous than open persecution."[37]

In his polite answer to Ferdinand Kindermann von Schulstein Mendelssohn avoids giving a detailed evaluation of the reader, although that had been the explicit request by the Bohemian school inspector.[38] Instead, he asks for von Schulstein's assistance in promoting the sale of his own High German translation of the Bible in Prague and remarks with friendly irony ". . . as you are willing to make allowances for some of my co-religionist's impoliteness, you will surely forgive me, too, if I appear rude and intrusive."[39]

In the following editions (1784, 1788, 1811), all of them based on the first one,[40] the Prague reader continued to demonstrate the rather mundane attempt of the Jewish *Normalschule* to impart values of social morality and usefulnes to its students. The second edition from 1784 is described in detail by the Dutch statesman, writer, and traveller J. Meermann Freiherr von Dalem. He had visited the Jewish *Normalschule* in Prague, at that time a tourist attraction, in November of 1791. One of the teachers showed him the manual.[41]

---

hebräischer Literaturfreunde zu Königsberg, Königsberg, December 1784, pp. 7-14. ("1. Von der Rechtschaffenheit der Schüler in der Schule [Unterabschnitte: Wie die Schüler in der Schule erscheinen und in dieselbe gehen sollen. Wie sich Schüler während des Unterrichts verhalten sollen. Wie sich Schüler bey dem Herausgehen aus der Schule verhalten sollen]. 2. Von der Sittsamkeit oder Rechtschaffenheit eines Menschen in seinen Gesinnungen, Handlungen und in seiner Aufführung [Unterabschnitte: Von der Ordnung. Von der Arbeitsamkeit. Von der Häuslichkeit. Von der Sparsamkeit. Von dem, was zur Artigkeit gehöret. Vom Gehen. Vom Sitzen. Vom Grüßen ... Von der Artigkeit in Gebärden. Von der Artigkeit in Kleidungen und Sachen.] 3. Von der Gesellschaft, darinn die Menschen zu leben von Gott bestimmet sind und von den gesellschaftlichen Pflichten. 4. Von der Haushaltungskunst. 5. Von der Vaterlandsliebe.")

[37]Moses Mendelssohn, 'Brief an Herz Homberg vom 1.3.1784' in Mendelssohn, *Briefwechsel III* No. 634, pp. 177–181, p. 179. ("So lange noch das Vereinigungssystem im Hinterhalte lauert, scheint mir diese Toleranzgleißnerey noch gefährlicher als offene Verfolgung.") Herz Homberg, who became official Inspector for the Jewish schools in Galicia in 1787, lived in Vienna at this time.

[38]Kindermann Ritter von Schulstein, 'Brief an Moses Mendelssohn vom 5. 1. 1783' in Mendelssohn, *Briefwechsel II*, No. 586, p. 88.

[39]Moses Mendelssohn, 'Brief an Ferdinand Kindermann Ritter von Schulstein', April 1783, *ibid.*, *III* No. 591, p. 98. (". . . da Sie so manchem meiner Glaubensgenossen Unhöflichkeit zu gute halten, so werden sie auch mir vergeben, wenn ich zudringlich seyn sollte.")

[40]Some scholars believed Moses Wiener to be the author/editor of the later Prague readers and not Ferdinand von Schulstein, see Alexander Altmann, *Moses Mendelssohn. A Biographical Study*, London 1973, pp. 488 and 836, note 113; Haim Borodianski, 'Anmerkung zu Brief 281', in Moses Mendelssohn, *Hebräische Schriften* III, Jubiläumsausgabe (JubA) vol. XIX, Stuttgart 1974, p. XCVIII; Kestenberg-Gladstein, pp. 53–55; Kieval, p. 92. These later readers are simply new editions of Schulstein's reader from 1781, see in detail Nagel, *Jüdische Lektürepädagogik*, p. 195.

[41]J. Meermann Freiherr v. Dalem, *J. Meermanns Freyherrn von Dalem Reise durch Preussen, Oesterreich, Sicilien und einige an jene Monarchien angrenzende Länder. Aus dem Holländischen übersetzt vom Professor Lueder in Braunschweig, Zweyter Theil*, Braunschweig 1794, p. 33.

WOLF ABRAHAM BEN NATHAN, *JÜDISCHE RELIGIONSSTÜTZE,
ODER GRUNDSÄTZE DER JÜDISCHEN RELIGION AUS DEN HEILIGEN
BÜCHERN, TALMUD UND DEN VORZÜGLICHSTEN RABBINEN
ZUSAMMENGETRAGEN*, DESSAU 1782
(SUPPORT FOR THE JEWISH RELIGION, OR THE PRINCIPLES OF
THE JEWISH RELIGION COMPILED FROM THE HOLY
SCRIPTURES, THE TALMUD AND BY MOST EMINENT RABBIS.)

Whereas the Prague reader for Jewish children had been published without much
consideration for the educational goals of the Berlin *Haskalah*, the emergence of
our third early Jewish schoolbook shows a closer connection to the Mendelssohn
circle and deals with religious instruction.[42] The author Wolf Abraham ben
Nathan – sometimes known as Wolf Dessau – was a traditional Jewish teacher
and scholar in Dessau. His book appears to be the first religious textbook written
in High German not using Hebrew letters.[43] The chapters are entitled: "The
Creation (*Von der Schöpfung*)"; "The prophetic spirit (*Von dem prophetischen Geist*)";
"On the Meschiah, or, according to Christian pronunciation, Messias (*Vom
Meschiah, oder, nach Aussprache der Christen, Messias*)"; "On the sufferings of the
Meschiah (*Von den Leiden des Meschiah*)"; "Eternity and salvation (*Von der Ewigkeit
und Seligkeit*)"; "On punishment (*Von der Bestrafung*)"; "On Paradise and Hell (*Von
dem Paradiese und der Hölle*)"; "The resurrection of the dead (*Von der Auferstehung der
Todten*)." The goal of the rather slim volume – 126 pages – is to draw attention to
some concepts of the Jewish faith, based mainly on the thirteen articles by Moses
Maimonides. There is a deliberate tendency to present the universal perspective
in the Jewish faith, that is to look at Christianity with an open mind and without
prejudice. The selection of passages from traditional authors is designed to
emphasise Jewish tolerance towards other monotheistic religions.

In addition to being an elementary teacher in Dessau, the author Wolf
Abraham ben Nathan was also a knowledgeable scholar of traditional classic
Jewish learning. He was well acquainted not only with men of his own faith, but
also with several Christian teachers of the Dessau *Philanthropin*, the famous educational institution of the enlightened elite in Germany which was supported by the
sovereign. Christian Gotthilf Salzmann, a teacher of religion at the *Philanthropin*,
had encouraged his close friend Wolf Abraham ben Nathan to write a textbook
on the basic principles of the Jewish religion. The language of this book should be
High German, so that it was not restricted to a Jewish readership, but could be

---

[42] For the origins and publication history of this text as well as contemporary reactions, see Max Freudenthal, 'R.[abbi] Wolf Dessau', in *Beiträge zur Geschichte der deutschen Juden. Festschrift zum siebzigsten
Geburtstage Martin Philippsons*, Leipzig 1916, pp. 184 ff.

[43] In the same year, 1782, another modernised religious textbook had been published in the vernacular. It had the appearance of a catechism and was intended for Jewish children in the Austrian part
of Italy, see Simone Calimani (Simcha ben Abraham Calimani), *Esame ossia Catechismo ad un giovine
israelite istruito nella sua religione*, Venice 1782, other editions Gorizia (or Triest?) 1783, Triest 1784,
Triest 1786, Verona 1821. This catechism (the 1786 edition can be found at the British Library)
differs significantly from the Dessau book, due to the unique development of the Upper-Italian
Haskalah. For more see, Moritz Steinschneider, 'Die italienische Litteratur der Juden. Das XVIII.
Jahrhundert', in *Monatsschrift für Geschichte und Wissenschaft des Judenthums*, vol. XLIII (1899), p. 567.

read by Christians, too. Christian Gotthilf Salzmann, an outstanding teacher and theoretician of the late Enlightenment in Germany, was an advocate of religious tolerance (he had asked several members from different Christian denominations to assist in the baptism of his daughter born in 1782).[44] His aim for this religious reader by his friend Wolf Abraham ben Nathan was to serve as a counterbalance to German literature on Jewry written by Christian authors. Quite a few of these articles and books were filled with prejudices and antisemitic sentiments even in the age of Enlightenment.

One can be sure that the proposal by his philanthropic friend caused some uneasiness at first in Wolf Abraham ben Nathan. It would be an almost impossible task to compress all Jewish religious principles and concepts, as traditionally understood, into a 126-page reader. How could one reduce the infinite "sea of the Talmud", the numerous other scriptures, commentaries and supra-commentaries into one comprehensive systematic survey? The author, nevertheless, tried his best, recognising the importance of his task, because he harboured great doubts about the recent attempts under Joseph II to integrate and "educate" Austrian Jewry. For his part, Christian Gotthilf Salzmann collected money from Dessau citizens for the costs of publication at the local *avantgarde* publishing house, the *Buchhandlung der Gelehrten*. We have reason to believe that he also assisted in the writing of the manuscript by making suggestions concerning contents, style, and language.[45]

This *Jüdische Religionsstütze*, the first attempt at religious instruction in High German, differs in a singular way from the catechisms and religious textbooks of the Jewish reform movement which had appeared since the beginning of the nineteenth century. Wolf Abraham ben Nathan, not only teacher but also learned talmudist, presents his arguments and considerations in rather a 'discursive' manner, rooted in tradition and still far removed from the rather homogenous and unequivocal style of the later reform catechisms.[46] On specific topics of the Jewish faith, a variety of belief systems and commentaries inherited from the learned elders were presented, sometimes complementing, sometimes even contradicting each other. This feature of the book particularly appealed to Moses Mendelssohn.[47] Nathan's religious reader represented to some extent the traditional way of continuous learning, searching and discourse. But, according to contemporary Christian theories regarding children's literature, this booklet was no suitable reading for the young either.

The author was not certain who his readership should be. On the one hand children should not be reading the book alone, but, rather, under adult supervision. On the other hand, Wolf Abraham ben Nathan did not expect the already

---

[44]Ernst Gundert, 'Christian Gotthilf Salzmann in Schnepfenthal', in Karl Adolf Schmid, *Geschichte der Erziehung vom Anfang an bis auf unsere Zeit*, vol. IV, part 2, Stuttgart 1898, reprint Aalen 1970, p. 357.

[45]Freudenthal, pp. 202–204.

[46]See the survey and analysis by Jakob J. Petuchowski, 'Manuals and Catechisms of the Jewish Religion in the Early Period of Emancipation', in Alexander Altmann (ed.), *Studies in Nineteenth-Century Jewish Intellectual History*, Cambridge, Mass. 1964, pp. 47–64.

[47]Moses Mendelssohn, 'Brief an Wolf Dessau vom 11. Juni 1782', in Mendelssohn, *Briefwechsel III*. No. 573, pp. 68–71.

overworked and poorly paid teachers to have to learn a new method of teaching either. In his introduction he stated: "One aim of my reader is to satisfy the curiosity of Christians, who asked me to give them a short summary of Genesis, of Moses' miracles, of the spirit of the prophets, of the redemption of our Messiah, of reward and punishment, of paradise and hell, of the resurrection of the dead, all this taken from tradition and transformed to suit today's beliefs."[48] Then he comes to a central point: "Yes, I have occasionally found in some Christian literature opinions expressed on our education system, as if it instils in our children hatred, disgust and unkindness against other nations who do not share our beliefs. But this cannot be stated with any fairness about the more reasonable elements of our nation."[49] The Dessau teacher and talmudist and his Christian friend made it their task to counteract prejudices like this. The author wants to introduce interested Christians to some central concepts of the Jewish religion which hitherto were either unknown to them or only known in distorted and selective versions. The contents of his book confirm this intention: the author tries to forge a connection between the Jewish faith and the ideas of the Enlightenment. In this attempt, we can compare his book to the Berlin *Lesebuch* from 1779.

Like the Berlin reader, the Dessau textbook on Jewish religion was not used in Jewish schools either, be they modern or traditional. However, there is evidence that Wolf Abraham ben Nathan was attacked by some conservative members of the Dessau Jewish Community because of the book. To settle this dispute, Moses Mendelssohn advised the author to change one paragraph of the already printed introduction in which he had harshly criticised prejudices that some of his co-religionists harboured against the Christian religion.[50] Even the Christian teachers Christian Gotthilf Salzmann and Johann Bernhard Basedow, both of them part of the *Philanthropin* and also acquainted with Mendelssohn, became involved in mediating this inner-Jewish dispute in order to avoid bringing it before the sovereign.

CONCLUSION

All three Jewish schoolbooks written in High German have the common characteristic of reflecting the transition from the traditional to a modern system of education. Up to the time of Moses Mendelssohn, Jewish schools in German-speaking countries were almost exclusively devoted to religious matters and

---

[48] Abraham ben Nathan, *Jüdische Religionsstütze*, pp. 10, 11. ("Auch will ich hiermit die Neubegierde der Christen stillen, die mich darum ersucht, einen kurzen Auszug von der Schöpfung, von den Wundern Mosis, von dem prophetischen Geist, von der Erlösung unseres Messiah, von der Belohnung und Bestrafung, von dem Paradies und der Hölle, von der Auferstehung der Todten, alles so, wie es heut zu Tage nach der Tradition angenommen und geglaubet wird, zu machen.")

[49] Abraham ben Nathan, pp. 4, 5. ("Ja, ich habe zuweilen in christlichen Büchern die Meynung von unserer Erziehungsart gefunden, als wenn unsern Kindern von Jugend auf Haß, Ekel oder Lieblosigkeit gegen andere Nationen, die nicht in Glaubensverwandtschaft mit uns stehen, beygebracht würde. Dieses aber kann wahrlich auf keine Weise von dem einigermaßen verständigen Theile unsrer Nation mit Recht gesagt werden.")

[50] Moses Mendelssohn, 'Brief an Wolf Dessau', in Mendelssohn, *Briefwechsel III*, p. 50. A copy of the first version of the *Religionsstütze* with the original introduction could not be located.

their principal aim was to promote the ability of lifelong study of the scriptures. Almost from the beginning of his schooling, the young male child was required to participate in the study and discussion of these religious texts as an intellectual equal. Therefore, he did not require other age-related reading materials, once he was able to read and write Hebrew.[51]

With the beginning of Jewish Enlightenment these attitudes began to change. Together with the gradual opening of the Jewish school to non-Jewish educational influences, the *maskilim* adopted new ideas on the nature of childhood and of children's literature which Christian philanthropists, influenced by Rousseau, had developed: Childhood was seen as a period of preparation for adult life. In the light of this, the young needed special books for study and entertainment. To be sure, this concept can only be seen in a rudimentary form in the two books of truly Jewish origin, the Berlin *Lesebuch für jüdische Kinder* and the Dessau *Jüdische Religionsstütze*. These two textbooks were not really meant for children, but to promote Christian understanding of the newly introduced modernisations of the Jewish education system.

Returning finally to the initial question of Jewish or non-Jewish influences in the origins and uses of the three early Jewish schoolbooks in High German, we find that there is no simple answer. The Berlin reader originates from the Mendelssohn circle of *maskilim*[52] – with numerous contributions by Moses Mendelssohn himself – and tries to combine traditional Jewish with modern non-Jewish ideas. Some of the Christian reviewers of the book not only understand this purpose, but explicitly support it. The Dessau *Religionsstütze*, on the other hand, was developed jointly by a Jewish and a Christian pedagogue. Wolf Abraham ben Nathan compiled the text combining traditional religious concepts with modern methods. The manuscript was then "... prepared for publication in Dessau by Prof. Salzmann *(von dem Herrn Prof. Salzmann in Dessau zum Drucke befördert)*".[53]

This leaves the Prague reader. Can this book, edited by a professional Christian pedagogue in accordance with Joseph II's enlightenment policy towards the Jews, be seen only as an act of coercion by the state? Were Jewish interests totally ignored in this case? After all, Ferdinand Kindermann von Schulstein had anonymously edited the reader in agreement with the elders of the Prague Jewish community and, prior to publication, as Moses Wiener reports, "... a proof-reader had been employed, who read each page to the Chief Rabbi for final signed approval".[54]

---

[51]Primers and spelling books were sometimes used for school beginners.

[52]The 'Mendelssohn circle of *maskilim*' should not be considered a uniform group and Mendelssohn should not be held responsible for the *Haskalah* as a whole. For this see Shmuel Feiner, 'Mendelssohn and "Mendelssohn's Disciples". A Re-examination', in *LBI Year Book XL* (1995), pp. 133–167. However, the origins of Jewish children's literature in High German show the important part Mendelssohn played in the modernisation of the Jewish school.

[53]'Fortgesetztes Verzeichniß der Werke, die in der Buchhandlung der Gelehrten zu haben sind', in *Berichte der allgemeinen Buchhandlung der Gelehrten vom Jahre 1782*, Siebentes Stück, Dessau (1782), pp. 35 ff., especially p. 40.

[54]Wiener, p. 27. The proof-reader mentioned in this report may have been Moses Wiener himself. ("Beym Abdrucke wurde ein Korektor bestellt, der jeden Bogen dem hiesigen Oberrabiner vorlas, und vor der Auflage zur Unterfertigung überreichte.")

In her article in *LBI Year Book XXXIII* of 1988, Zohar Shavit dealt with Jewish children's literature in Hebrew. She came to the conclusion that the main motive for the authors and/or translators into Hebrew had been ideological in nature. They had tried to demonstrate a relationship between certain elements of the Jewish religious tradition with central Enlightenment principles. However, they had obviously translated (and changed) the non-Jewish German texts they had selected to serve their own purpose, without assistance from or reference to non-Jewish writers. We can therefore safely say that these translations had been written and published by Jews alone.

If we look at early initiatives for Jewish children's books in High German, the context proves to be quite different. Zohar Shavit has referred to intellectual and social contacts between Jewish and non-Jewish representatives of the Enlightenment era, for example, between Moses Mendelssohn and Joachim Heinrich Campe. The first three books in High German bear witness to more than just an intellectual or verbal connection. They show evidence of a practical literary cooperation between *maskilim* and Christian scholars. Although there are obvious differences for each book in the circumstances of this cooperation, the origins of these three manuals consistently point to the combined efforts of the *Haskalah* and the Christian Enlightenment in the years around 1780.

When Did Haskalah Begin? Establishing the Beginning of Haskalah Literature and the Definition of "Modernism"*

BY MOSHE PELLI

When did modern Hebrew literature begin? Does its beginning coincide with the beginning of *Haskalah* literature? Is there a literary personality who signals the beginning of the new trends in modern Hebrew literature? These were some of the questions discussed by several literary historians in the early days of *Haskalah* historiography. For some time, such questions were frequently debated, but after a while, literary historians and critics apparently lost interest in them. The topic has recently been revisited by a few contemporary *Haskalah* scholars. The questions now being asked echo earlier themes, though more profound queries have emerged: What is "modern" in "modern Hebrew literature", and how is "Hebrew modernism" defined?

The most significant trend in *Haskalah* historiography has highlighted the elements, which distinguish *Haskalah* literature from the corpus of traditional Hebrew literature through the ages. *Haskalah* was considered to be new, modern and different. Proponents of this notion designated *Haskalah* as the beginning of modern Hebrew literature, while endeavouring to identify a major writer or group of writers who, to them, signal the beginning of *Haskalah*. There was, however, another trend, the major spokesman of which was Dov Sadan (and perhaps also, to some extent, Shmuel Werses, as discussed below). Sadan did not emphasise the distinctions between bodies of literature. Instead, he established different outlooks, which group together various types of literature and form a different concept of periodisation. He considered *Haskalah* literature to be part of the corpus of Hebrew literature in its historical perspective, without paying attention to the criteria which characterised its modern or secular inclinations.

* This article is a revised and expanded version of a paper presented at the conference on "New Perspectives on the *Haskalah*" at the Oxford Centre for Hebrew and Jewish Studies, Yarnton Manor, Oxford, 27 July – 3 August 1994. Some of the ideas in this article were expressed briefly in an earlier article published in *Jewish Education and Learning*, ed. by Glenda Abramson and Tudor Parfitt, published in honour of Dr. David Patterson, Switzerland 1994. A Hebrew version was published in *Beirs Historiah Lesifrut*, ed. by Stanley Nash, Israel 1997, pp. 335–369.

The main assumption of most historians of Hebrew literature who have dealt with this topic was that the beginning of modern Hebrew literature also signals the beginning of modern Jewish history.[1] From the start, the discussion of *Haskalah* encompassed both historical and literary domains. Terms were flowing from one discipline to another, from the literary to the historical and vice versa. Consequently, the ensuing discussion will address issues in the domain of both disciplines, namely, establishing the beginning of *Haskalah* literature and attempting to probe modernism and its manifestations in the context of *Haskalah*. The combination of the two scholarly areas, however, may be problematic because of the different methodologies applied in each discipline. In spite of this risk, an interdisciplinary approach to *Haskalah* may be welcomed, with the understanding that it will not substitute for a historical or socio-historical treatment of the subject matter. Our discussion will concentrate on the literary and the intellectual history aspects of *Haskalah*.

The question of the periodisation of Jewish history and of establishing the beginning of modern times in the annals of the Jewish people has already been widely discussed. Historians such as Jost, Graetz, Dubnow, Dinur, Ettinger and Baron, as well as a philosopher, Krochmal, and a *Kabbalah* scholar, Scholem, have contributed to the historical conceptualisation of Jewish history. Historians have attempted to establish a transition from the Middle Ages to modern times (as seen in Shohet's statement below). They have often endeavoured to identify a major historical personality, such as Moses Mendelssohn (proposed by Graetz), as the initiator of that change. Others, such as Dubnow, suggested that the signalling change should be related to an important historical event; for example, the French Revolution may be considered the initiation point of modern times in Jewish history. Such historical analyses were examined a few years ago by Michael Meyer. He concluded his discussion by questioning the significance of establishing a definite date for the beginning of modern times in Jewish history.[2]

The topic of modernism in its broader context has become very popular recently, especially as it is extended to the discussion of "post-modernism". Both "modernism" and "post-modernism" have been used in a variety of disciplines, from history to literature, encompassing a wide range of historical periods, from the European Enlightenment to our own day and age. Understandably, such a broad use of identical terms may result in generalisation and ambiguity, leading to errors and misconceptions. As fashionable as "modernism" sounds, it is a

---

[1] See F. Lachover, *Toldot Hasifrut Haivrit Hahadashah*, I, Tel Aviv 1928, p. 1: "... It [modern Hebrew literaure] echoes the modern times [*ha'et hahadashah*]"; Joseph Klausner, *Historiah Shel Hasifrut Haivrit Hahadashah*, I, 3rd edn., Jerusalem 1960, p. 9: "The name 'Modern Hebrew Literature' should be referred to as the Hebrew literature of the modern times [*ha'et hahadashah*]."; H. N. Shapira, *Toldot Hasifrut Haivrit Hahadashah*, 2nd edn, Ramat Gan 1967, p. 59: "Modern Hebrew literature was born ... in the great change that occurred in the Jewish people on the threshold of our new history."; Shimon Halkin, *Derachim Vetzidei Derachim Basifrut*, I, Jerusalem 1970, p. 155: "Modern times in the history of the world and the nation gave birth to modern Hebrew literature." (The above quotations originally in Hebrew, as are all quotations from Hebrew sources; translation is mine.) The term "modern" in Hebrew is often expressed by the word *hadash* [new] as well as *moderni* [modern].

[2] Michael A. Meyer, 'Where Does the Modern Period of Jewish History Begin?', *Judaism*, vol. XXIV, No. 95 (Summer 1975), pp. 327–338.

relative term, the meaning of which changes with context. Our context is Jewish and Hebrew modernism in relation to eighteenth-century Hebrew *Haskalah*. My working hypothesis is that this "modernism" began at the end of that century. Questions related to modernism, modernity, or post-modernism in other contexts will not be discussed in this study.

One of the most frustrating aspects of reviewing past discussions concerning the beginning of *Haskalah* stems from the fact that the terms "modernism" and "secularism" have not been defined. It has been generally assumed that "modernism" is exemplified in an alleged clear-cut transition from traditional, normative Judaism to "secularism". As will be shown, my approach towards a definition of modernism is different, and it will be developed step by step.

By the term "*Haskalah*" (which Shavit has recently examined[3]) this article refers to Hebrew *Haskalah* literature in Germany in the last quarter of the eighteenth century and the early part of the nineteenth century. The controversy of whether a distinction should be made between *Haskalah* literature and the *Haskalah* movement is not addressed here. For the purpose of our discussion, it is assumed that the two were closely bound together, especially at this early stage.

LITERARY AND HISTORICAL THEORIES: SECULARISM AND MODERNISM

Joseph Klausner, who in many respects has laid the groundwork for *Haskalah* research (although he was not the first literary historian to explore the topic), will be the starting point of our discussion. It was Klausner who enunciated his views on the "essence and the beginning of new [modern] Hebrew literature". In the introduction to his monumental work *The History of Modern Hebrew Literature*, a seminal work consulted to this day, he characterised the "new" Hebrew culture as "essentially secular". Klausner asserted that "it started a new direction – to enlighten the people and resemble in its form and contents more or less the literatures of all European peoples".[4]

The terms "new direction" and "to enlighten" may signal the criteria for modernism which Klausner had in mind. This is due to the use of the term "new" in Hebrew to designate "modern" as well (*Sifrut Ivrit Hadashah*). However, this meaning is not obvious from the text itself. Unfortunately, Klausner did not clarify what he meant by the term "secular". Nor was Klausner the first to highlight the notion of secularism as a criterion of modernism in *Haskalah*. Early in the century, Nahum Slouschz employed the term "secular literature" and "secularism" to characterise *Haskalah* literature. He discovered in *Hame'asef* (The Gatherer) "a great innovation whose value will last for generations to come, in its secular contents and format, and in disrobing the religious attire from language and literature". Slouschz considered the publication of *Hame'asef* to be a modern phenomenon: "It opened by its very publication the gate to modern

---

[3]Uzi Shavit, 'Ha"*Haskalah*" Mahi: Leverur Musag Ha"*Haskalah*" Basifrut Haivrit', *Mehkerei Yerushalayim Besifrut Ivrit*, XII (1990), pp. 51–83.
[4]Klausner, *Historiah Shel Hasifrut Haivrit Hahadashah*, p. 9.

literature, and became the forerunner of the modern period, the period of *Haskalah*."[5] Yet, it is obvious that the term "secular" (*Hol*), as used by Slouschz, is not identical to a similar term used by Klausner (*Hiloni*). Slouschz does refer to "secular" in terms of form and contents, but it is not entirely certain that he also meant "secular" as an intrinsic essence.

In the second decade of our century, Yaakov Rabinowitz discussed the periodisation of Hebrew literature throughout Jewish history and observed that modern Hebrew literature, in distinction from its predecessors, is "essentially secular". What did he mean by "secular"? Rabinowitz defined it as literature "that came to free the individual and the people and to resuscitate them". To him, the corpus of Hebrew literature is distinguished by its religiosity. Even secular concepts which were cited in it are merely "proverbial [references] for God and the people of Israel". The guiding principle of modern Hebrew literature, on the other hand, is "the desire for normal life based on a humane and national foundation".[6]

Other critics and literary historians, such as Jerucham F. Lachover[7] and later Abraham Shaanan[8], continued to use the term "secular" without defining clearly the essence of this concept and what they meant by it.

Both terms, "modern" or "modernity" and "secular" or "secularism", were first offered on an intuitive level. Only after the 1930s and 1950s do we find serious efforts to explain the nature of secularism. General historians and social historians of the old generation, such as Bernard Weinryb, Jacob Katz, Azriel Shohet and Shmuel Ettinger, probed the social phenomena that had prevailed among West European Jews prior to *Haskalah*. They alleged the existence of the phenomena of "secularism" even before the "modern" age of the Jewish Enlightenment. Thus, some of them endeavoured to advance the *Haskalah* to the first part of the eighteenth century. In another vein, Gershom Scholem argued his case for "a clear dialectical development leading from the belief in Shabbetai Zvi to the religious nihilism of Shabbetianism and Frankism . . . to the new world of *Haskalah*".[9] Historians of the middle generation, such as Michael Meyer, Emmanuel Etkes and younger historians, David Sorkin and Shmuel Feiner and others, have reviewed and scrutinised accepted notions in Jewish historiography.[10] Etkes, for example, questioned Shohet's observations and

[5]Nahum Slouschz, *Korot Hasifrut Haivrit Hahadashah*, I, Warsaw 1905/6, pp. 27 and 9; see also his English book, *The Renascence of Hebrew Literature (1743–1885)*, Philadelphia 1909, pp. 29–34.

[6]Yaakov Rabinowitz, 'Letoldot Hasifrut Haivrit Hahadashah', *Maslulei Sifrut*, I, Jerusalem 1971, p. 5; the article was first published in 1919/20.

[7]Lachover, *Toldot Hasifrut Haivrit Hahadashah*, I, p. 4: "the inclination this time was towards secularism". See discussion below.

[8]Avraham Shaanan, *Hasifrut Haivrit Hahadashah Lizrame'ah*, I, Tel Aviv 1962, p. 18: "the process of penetration of secularism into the Jewish world of beliefs and ideas".

[9]Gershom Scholem, 'Mitzvah Haba'ah Ba'averah', *Knesset*, II, Tel Aviv 1937, p. 351. See also Shmuel Werses, *Haskalah Veshabta'ut*, Jerusalem 1988, pp. 11–14.

[10]Dov Weinryb, 'Gormim Kalkaliyim Vesotzialiyim Bahaskalah Hayehudit Begermanyah', *Knesset*, III Tel Aviv 1938, pp. 416–436; *idem*, 'Hame'ah Hasheva Esreh Kehakdamah Litkufat Hahaskalah', *Perakim*, IV (1966), pp. 113–142; Jacob Katz, *Masoret Umashber*, Jerusalem 1958, chaps. 20, 21, 23, 24; *idem*, *Tradition and Crisis*, New York 1977 3rd edn.; Azriel Shohet, *Im Hilufei Tekufot*, Jerusalem 1960; *idem*, 'Resheet Hahaskalah Beyahadut Germanyah', *Molad*, XXIII, Nos. 203–204 (Sep-

complained about the lack of clarity in his definition of terms. He noted that Shohet did not distinguish between the phenomena of assimilation, exiting the ghetto, and "*Haskalah*". Thus, "the distinction between *Haskalah* and phenomena which were concurrent to it but not identical with it is completely blurred". Etkes proposed to define the essence of the Jewish Enlightenment movement (in Eastern Europe, only) by delineating its ideological stand in the subjects of theology, *halakhah,* the study of Torah, the Hebrew language, and attitudes towards European society and Western culture. He has also probed the subject of the early forerunners of *Haskalah.*[11]

KLAUSNER'S SELECTION OF WESSELY

It is possible to deduce the meaning of Klausner's terminology elsewhere from his continued discussion of the beginnings of modern Hebrew literature. He developed his literary theory by applying it to a literary personality, whom he designated to mark the beginning of the *Haskalah* period. As is known, Klausner rejected Lachover's choice of Moshe Hayim Luzzatto as the originator of modern Hebrew literature. Instead, Klausner ostensibly preferred Naphtali Herz Wessely. However, Klausner's discussion of the beginning of modern Hebrew literature and its originator is not without ambiguity. As early as 1926, Klausner established the beginning of modern Hebrew literature "from the *me'asfim* generation, more accurately from the publication of the first pamphlet of *Divrei Shalom Ve'emet* (Words of Peace and Truth) by Naphtali Herz Wessely (1781)".[12] Klausner did *not* select the *me'asfim* (the editors and writers of the journal *Hame'asef*), but the generation of the *me'asfim,* and specifically, one person in that generation, namely Wessely. Klausner explained his choice by saying that Wessely was "a new man" who "fought for a new life, a new education, and a new Hebrew style".[13] Elsewhere in his book, Klausner writes that Wessely "was the initiator and the creator of that period".[14]

Klausner's selection of Wessely to represent the beginning of modern Hebrew literature, for the stated reasons, is problematic. It raises the question whether

---

tember 1965), pp. 328–334; Shmuel Ettinger, *Toldot Am Yisra'el Ba'et Hahadashah,* Tel Aviv 1969, pp. 66–67; see references to Michael Meyer and Shmuel Feiner, above, note 2, and below. Also see Moshe H. Graupe, *Hayahadut Hamodernit Behithavutah,* Jerusalem and Tel Aviv 1990, and David Sorkin, *The Transformation of German Jewry 1780–1840,* New York 1987. I just received Shmuel Feiner's 'Early Haskalah in Eighteenth-Century Jewry' *Tarbitz,* LXVII, No. 2 (1998), pp. 189–240, dealing with the phenomena of early Haskalah.

[11]Emmanuel Etkes, 'Lishe'elat Mevasrei Hahaskalah Bemizrah Eiropah', *Tarbitz,* LVII, No. 1 (Tishrei-Kislev 1988), pp. 95–114; reprinted in the anthology *Hadat Vehahayim: Tenu'at Hahaskalah Hayehudit Bemizrah Eiropah,* Jerusalem 1993, pp. 25–44. A number of studies on modernity were published in *Toward Modernity: the European Jewish Model,* ed. by Jacob Katz, New Brunswick 1987. (Publication of the Leo Baeck Institute.)

[12]Klausner, *Historiah Shel Hasifrut Haivrit Hahadashah,* I, p. 9. Klausner used similar expressions in his earlier article, 'Shalosh Tekufot Beafrut Hahaskalah Haivrit', *Mada'ei Hayahadut,* Jerusalem 1926, p. 7. The publication date is 1782 and not 1781, as stated erroneously by Klausner.

[13]Klausner, *Historiah Shel Hasifrut Haivrit Hahadashah,* I, p. 10.

[14]*ibid.,* p. 42.

Wessely was indeed "a new man". Klausner did not make it clear what he meant by the term. However, if we assume that this expression encompasses the new *Weltanschauung* envisioned by the *maskilim*, as depicted in scores of articles, stories, fables and other works, it would be improper to consider Wessely as the representation of the new man of Hebrew *Haskalah*. It should be noted, nonetheless, that the *maskilim* did consider Wessely an exemplary figure in Hebrew poetry.

Reading Wessely's writings in totality, and not only *Divrei Shalom Ve'emet*, one is impressed that Wessely was essentially a traditionalist, representing the normative viewpoint of Judaism. More than any other writer in early Hebrew *Haskalah*, Wessely epitomised in most of his writings – with the exception of *Divrei Shalom Ve'emet* – the traditional values of Judaism. He represented the norms of traditional Judaism, rather than the as yet undefined "modern secularism". Thus, naming him "a new man" without the necessary elucidation, is indeed questionable. Paradoxically, his writings did contain a major innovation, which Klausner failed to discern, and which will be discussed below.[15]

The attitudes of Klausner and the school of his followers towards *Haskalah* literature may in fact be understood as an antithesis, when viewed against the backdrop of the criticism of *Haskalah* waged in the previous generation. Klausner was able to achieve a perspective that enabled him to assess critically and unemotionally the contribution of early *Haskalah* and its writers to Hebrew literature. Attitudes towards early *Haskalah* went through variegated developments, representing a myriad of viewpoints in the nineteenth century. What started as a very positive attitude, in the first part of the *Haskalah* period, evolved into the negative attitude that Perez Smolenskin, in his harsh criticism of Mendelssohn, expressed. This negative attitude continued during the next literary period, known as *Hamahalach Hehadash* (the New Move). Concurrently, an attitude of some disrespect was exhibited towards the authors of *Haskalah*. Mordechai Ehrenpreis offered a complete rejection of *Haskalah* in his article entitled 'Le'an?' (Whither?). Published in the first volume of *Hashilo'ah* in 1897, it represented the transition that had taken place between the literary periods.[16] Certainly, Ehrenpreis attempted to create a polarity between the earlier period of *Haskalah* literature and contemporary Hebrew literature, which was represented by *Hamahalach Hehadash*. He expressed his views without any ambiguity, writing: "The literary work in which we are engaged now is not a *continuation* of the work of earlier generations from the *me'asfim* on, but indeed the *beginning* of an entirely different undertaking which is new in its form and contents".[17] According to his assessment, the *me'asfim* did not have any "programme" (plan), and their intention was, in effect, to annul the concept of "literature". It stands to

[15]Cf. Moshe Pelli, *The Age of Haskalah*, Leiden 1979, chap. 6; *idem, Bema'avkei Temurah*, Tel Aviv 1988, pp. 47–55; see also H. N. Shapira, *Toldot Hasifrut Haivrit Hahadashah*, p. 57, for his rejection of Wessely's choice as the author marking the new age; and Mordechai Ehrenpreis's article (see note 16), pp. 491–492.
[16]Mordechai Ehrenpreis, 'Le'an?', *Hashilo'ah*, I (1897), pp. 489–503. Republished in *Le'an?*, Jerusalem 1998, pp. 105–133, ed. by Avner Holtzman.
[17]*ibid.*, p. 489.

reason that this kind of rejection did not represent a balanced historical analysis, but is certainly a rejection based on ideological considerations. Ehrenpreis was obviously ignoring the subject which Y. E. Trivush raised three years later in *Ahi'asaf*, asserting modern Hebrew literature's indebtedness to *Haskalah*: "They have to be very grateful to the early *maskilim*, for only because of them have we arrived at this point. It is not our generation that created modern Hebrew literature, but those poor *maskilim*. They were the ones who resuscitated it, they toiled over it, they fought for it, and were the ones who went begging for it".[18]

LACHOVER: LUZZATTO ORIGINATOR OF MODERN HEBREW LITERATURE

In 1928, Lachover began publishing his *History of Modern Hebrew Literature*, in which he traced the signs of "the new spirit", ostensibly exemplifying the beginning of modern Hebrew literature, to the figure of Moshe Hayim Luzzatto and his literary work. This literary historian seemed to be following in the footsteps of H. N. Bialik's classic article on Luzzatto.[19] Concurrent with his selection of Luzzatto (a mystic, Kabbalist, and moralist, who considered himself a Messiah) as the originator of modernity, Lachover adopted the notion of secularism as characterising modernity. He expressed this notion of modernity as "Hebrew secular literature", which represents "the new spirit" in Hebrew literature in Italy and in Holland. He also asserted that the inclination of modern Hebrew literature towards secularism is manifested through "free humanism". "The eyes were searching for 'Torat Ha'adam'", he wrote, using the term Wessely employed to designate humanism.[20] Although these additional definitions shed light on the concept of "secularism" they are still rather vague and overly general. In addition, Lachover's attempt to combine two seemingly contradictory notions, namely the selection of Luzzatto with the criterion of "secularism", made it easy for his critics (Klausner, Kleinman,[21] Shapira, and others) to dismiss his choice of Luzzatto as a modernist. They did this mainly on the grounds that Luzzatto's world was completely ruled by the old order and the traditional way of life, as were his Kabbalistic tendencies and his spiritual outlook. Importantly, Lachover acknowledged that Germany was the locus of the new literary movement in Hebrew letters, rather than Italy, where Luzzatto functioned. Nevertheless, other scholars, such as Meyer Waxman and recently

---

[18]Y. E. Trivush, 'Bichvod Hahaskalah', *Ahi'asaf*, VIII (1900), n.p.

[19]H. N. Bialik, 'Habahur Mipadova', *Kitvei H. N. Bialik*, II, Tel Aviv 1935, pp. 307–310.

[20]Lachover, *Toldot Hasifrut Haivrit Hahadashah*, p. 4. Others, too, selected Luzzatto. In 1907, Bar-Tuviah wrote an article, 'Bresheet Sifrutenu Hahadashah', *Hashilo'ah*, XVI (1907), pp. 18–23, in which he considered Moshe Hayim Luzzatto and Abraham Mapu as the creators of modern Hebrew literature. However, his observation is more poetic than critical, as it lacks the detailed discussion and critical analysis. The fact that he combined different periods and localities cast doubt about his proposal. Bar-Tuviah is identified as Dr. P.[?] Frankel in *Otzar Beduyei Hashaem*, Vienna 1933, p. 81.

[21]Moshe Kleinman, *Demuyot Vekomot*, Paris 1928, p. 13.

Uzi Shavit, continued to support Lachover's position concerning Luzzatto's alleged "modernism".[22]

Among literary historians, it was H. N. Shapira who selected the *me'asfim* as the initiators of modern Hebrew literature, referring to them as "the new people of Israel".[23] He stipulated that *Haskalah*'s major distinction from previous Hebrew literature is its demand to return to the real, mundane, and terrestrial world. Shapira identified the direction of *Haskalah* – both the movement and the literature – as "introcentric national orientation", encompassing the revival of "terrialism". It is known that Shapira's usage of his own coined terms and formed expressions in Hebrew are somewhat esoteric and unclear. They become clearer as he delineates the perimeters and characteristics of *Haskalah* literature, which "turned its back to personal Judaism and to its anchored spirituality". He asserted that *Haskalah* "exhibits a strong and mighty desire for a fundamental, earthly existence, and . . . longing for nature and natural life". "All the *maskilim* in Germany were introcentric, 'terrialistic' people. They all desired to be free men, liberated from the yoke of any subjugating spiritualism. They were inclined to subject themselves to the soaring, free spirit and to the dictates of earthly life, rooted in mother Earth, and glued and consolidated to its resources and real assets."[24] I believe that Shapira's selection of the *me'asfim* is correct. Some of his observations may be somewhat exaggerated, but in general they do summarise several trends of *Haskalah*.

The question of the beginning of modern Hebrew literature was raised again in 1947 by Hayim Bar-Dayan at the World Congress for Jewish Studies. A student of Klausner, Bar-Dayan rejected Lachover's selection of Luzzatto, whom he considered "the forerunner of the period in our literature", but not "its father and its initiator". Bar-Dayan, like Klausner, selected Wessely "who was fit in many respects to fulfil this role". Bar-Dayan saw in Moses Mendelssohn "the person who paved the road and prepared the grounds for the establishment of the new literature, but not as its founder". In his view, the revival of modern Hebrew literature stems "from the appearance of a major, central personality, who possessed great creative power, and was aware of its mission, carrying new ideas and establishing a well-developed, enlightened generation of students". He added several other factors: "the historical and social circumstances, and the readiness and preparation of a certain public, having a certain economical class and living in a populous, homogenous community, to absorb and cultivate the new".[25]

---

[22]See for example Meyer Waxman's article 'Yoseph Klausner Kehistoryon Shel Hasifrut Haivrit Hahadashah," *Bitzaron*, 39, No. 2 [205] (Kislev 1959), p. 109; in his book *A History of Jewish Literature*, III, New York 1936, p. 107, Waxman asserted that Luzzatto was a forerunner of *Haskalah*, and that Wessely was the initiator of the period. On Shavit, see below.

[23]H. N. Shapira, *Toldot Hasifrut Haivrit Hahadashah*, pp. 57–58. Yaakov Rabinowitz selected the *me'asfim* before Shapira, see *Maslulei Sifrut*, I, pp. 16, 44.

[24]*ibid.*, Shapira, p. 67.

[25]H. Bar-Dayan, 'Lishe'elat Resheetah Shel Sifrutenu Hahadashah', *Hakinus Ha'olami Lemada'ei Hayahadut*, Summer 1947 (1952), pp. 302–306.

KURZWEIL: METAMORPHOSIS OF HEBREW LITERATURE

The subject of "secularism", raised earlier by several historians, gained recognition in the 1950s in the writings of Baruch Kurzweil. He made a concerted effort to examine and define secularism, while emphasising his theory of the unique "secular" nature of modern Hebrew literature. He asserted that there was a major gap between traditional Hebrew literature, as it developed throughout the ages, and modern Hebrew literature. Kurzweil further argued that the corpus of Hebrew letters functioned on the foundations of a sacral world. However, modern Hebrew literature has emerged out of a "spiritual world that was void of its primordial religious certainty" which encompasses the totality of life and provides the sole criterion for its values.[26] Kurzweil considered "secularism" as the most dominant feature of the new Hebrew literature. This secularism is not merely dealing with secular subjects as compared with sacral literature, such as liturgy, *piyut*, found in traditional Hebrew literature; it is the totality of its spiritual world that has been completely changed. There is one major problem in the thesis of Kurzweil and other theoreticians. Kurzweil undertook to define "modern Hebrew literature" *in toto*, and not necessarily the beginning of *Haskalah* literature. As a result, his approach to the topic is overgeneralised and erroneous. It contains an anachronistic application of late phenomena to early *Haskalah*. This point will be elaborated on below.

In his lectures of the 1950s, Shimon Halkin addressed the issue of modernism, suggesting that the "appearance of humanism in Jewish history and in Jewish literature" exemplified the modern tendencies in Judaism. Accordingly, modern Hebrew literature is characterised by the shift from theocentricity in traditional Judaism (regarding man's relations to God) to the homocentricity in modern Judaism. The latter outlook is based on contemporary European Enlightenment thought, in which man is the centre of interest. Halkin borrowed this concept from European Enlightenment and applied it to *Haskalah*, while stressing that the European humanists were indeed men of religious conviction. Accordingly, modern Hebrew literature's shift towards humanism should not be viewed as a "revolution" (a notion Kurzweil advocated), "which detaches the past from its roots, but as a continuity, affecting some serious changes".[27]

In the 1950s, Isaac Barzilay published a series of articles concerning the German and Italian *Haskalah*, in which he ostensibly makes a distinction between the two. He proposes a definition of the Berlin *Haskalah*, and analyses its principal values and ideology. Among these values he lists the following: the ideal of reason, the brotherhood of man, and the return to reality (which he divides into the return to nature, hedonism, love, heroism, the pursuit of beauty,

---

[26]Baruch Kurzweil, *Sifrutenu Hahadashah Masoret O Mahapechah*, Tel Aviv and Jerusalem 1960, p. 16. Also, p. 44: "modrn Hebrew literature is secular because it comes out of a world void of divine holiness that had been hovering over the unity of Jewish culture".

[27]Simon Halkin, *Zeramim Vetzurot Basifrut Haivrit Hahadashah*, I, Jerusalem 1984, p. 29. Halkin had formulated his views earlier in *Modern Hebrew Literature*, New York 1970 [first published in 1950], p. 36. Halkin's lectures from the 1950s were published in *Mavo Lasiporet Haivrit*, Jerusalem 1978, pp. 9–12.

the economic rehabilitation of Jewry, and education). His articles provide the appropriate textual citations to support his thesis, which shed light on the tenets of *Haskalah*.[28]

In 1967, Avraham Holtz presented an overview of existing trends in the historiography of *Haskalah*, and proposed a revision in the approach to its study. He argues against the existing theories of Klausner, Lachover, and those literary historians who have followed in their footsteps. In his view, these theories are rather weak because they rely on non-literary theses. Some of their arguments, he claims, were cited out of context. Others were based on summaries of poetical and prose texts for the purpose of presenting an ideology of the reviewed material, rather than treating it as a work of art. Holtz adds that these theories are deficient, since they do not pay attention to important bodies of Hebrew letters, such as oriental Jewish literature as well as *Hasidic* and *Mitnagdic* writings. He also considers the use of the prevailing terms, "secular" and "modern", as another weakness of these theories. Holtz insisted that Hebrew literature should be approached as literature. Consequently, the student of Hebrew literature should examine the Hebrew literary tradition for its linguistic, stylistic, and generic characteristics. In sum, Holtz called for a revision of the critical literature of *Haskalah*.[29]

In the early 1980s there had been very little discussion on the beginnings or perimeters of *Haskalah*. When Yehuda Friedlander surveyed the existing views regarding *Haskalah* in 1980, he did not even mention it as a topic worthy of discussion. Neither has the subject of its beginning been touched in my two articles on trends, attitudes, goals and achievements of *Haskalah*.[30] It would appear that the subject matter had been exhausted in the existing theories. A few years later, Werses likewise suggested that current research showed a lack of interest in the question of periodisation in Hebrew literature.[31]

SHAVIT: BELIEF IN INTELLECT, GOD AND BEAUTY

We find another trend emerging during the 1980s in Hebrew *Haskalah* scholarship, as a few contemporary scholars offered new ways to approach the study of

[28] Isaac Eisenstein-Barzilay, 'The Ideology of the Berlin Haskalah', *Proceedings of the American Academy for Jewish Research*, XXV (1956), pp. 1–37; *idem*, 'The Jew in the Literature of the Enlightenment', *Jewish Social Studies*, XVII, 4 (October 1956), pp. 243–261; *idem*, 'The Background of the Berlin Haskalah', *Essays on Jewish Life and Thought*, New York 1959, pp.183–197; *idem*, 'The Italian and Berlin Haskalah', *Proceedings of the American Academy for Jewish Research*, XXIX (1960–1961), pp. 17–52; *idem*, 'Livdikat Mahut Hahaskalah Uvikortah', *Hado'ar*, XLIII, Nos. 19 & 20 (1964), pp. 320–321, 347–348.

[29] Avraham Holtz, 'Prolegomenon to a Literary History of Modern Hebrew Literature', *Literature East and West*, XI, No. 3, (1967), pp. 253–270.

[30] Yehuda Friedlander, 'Be'ayot Yesod Babikoret Uvamehkar Al Sifrut Hahaskalah', *Peles*, Tel Aviv 1980, pp. 33–45. See Moshe Pelli, 'Haskalah Literature Trends and Attitudes', *Jewish Book Annual*, 39 (1981/1982), pp. 92–101; and *idem*, 'Ye'adim Vehesegim: Megamot Unetiyot Besifrut HaHaskalah Ha'ivrit Beresheetah', *Hadoar*, LXI, Nos. 34, 35, 36, (10, 24 September, 15 October 1982), pp. 558–560, 586–587, 604–605.

[31] Shmuel Werses, 'Al Mehkar Sifrut Hahaskalah Beyameinu', *Megamot Vetzurot Besifrut Hahaskalah*, Jerusalem 1990, p. 358, published first in the *Yedi'on*, the Newsletter of the World Union of Jewish Studies, 25 (Summer 1985) and 26 (Winter 1986).

Haskalah. Uzi Shavit, for example, argued against Kurzweil's notion of "secularism", as related to modern Hebrew literature. Shavit claims that such "secularism", which reflects, according to Kurzweil, "a spiritual world that was void of its primordial religious certainty", is inappropriate for early *Haskalah.* According to Shavit, these statements do not fit "the world of the *Haskalah* fathers, led by Mendelssohn, Wessely, and the editors of *Hame'asef*'. Nor do they fit the spiritual world of next generation *maskilim* in the nineteenth century, such as Shmuel David Luzzatto, Shlomo Yehuda Rappaport, and Nachman Krochmal.[32] Indeed, Kurzweil's error, duplicated by some literary historians, is that he failed to distinguish between early and late *Haskalah.* As mentioned earlier, he conceptualised the complex phenomena of *Haskalah,* covering more than a century and several geographical locations, in a generalised way.

In my opinion, the spiritual world of the early Hebrew *maskilim* was not portrayed accurately by Kurzweil. Even those who were dichotomous in their viewpoint, exhibiting some dualism and ambiguity about *Haskalah,* tradition and modernity, could not be characterised as *telushim.* They were not detached, uprooted and lost (as this Hebrew term implies), as were some of the late nineteenth-century authors and their literary protagonists. Mendelssohn and Wessely, to cite the major figures, were completely immersed in traditional Judaism while also adhering to their *Haskalah* point of view. Even a *maskil* such as Rabbi Saul Berlin, by far among the more extreme and radical of the *maskilim* in his religious outlook, was totally immersed in the world of tradition. His pseudo-epigraphic writing (to use Werses's terminology) is ingrained in the world of *halakhah,* as his work, *Besamim Rosh* (Incense of Spices), exemplifies. Isaac Euchel, and Isaac Satanow as well, hovered next to the world of traditional Judaism.

Shavit presented his own case, arguing that it is not "secularism" that characterises these early and late proponents of *Haskalah.* It is, rather, "the belief in man's intellect, the power of free thinking and enlightenment, and the assurance that, as a result of the rule of reason, understanding and science, humanity – and Jews as part of it – was destined in the foreseeable future to achieve a better, improved society, where each individual would be able to live in it safely, freely and peacefully".[33] Subsequently, Shavit cites some of the characteristics of *Haskalah* literature, which are definitely correct. In his opinion, the most important characteristic of modern Hebrew literature is not its alleged secularism, but rather its *hofshiyut,* its libertarianism, freedom, and freethinking.[34] Shavit borrowed these terms from Yosef H. Brenner, who used the expressions "free Jews" or "free Hebrews".

This characterisation of "free Jews" does not apply easily, in my view, to figures such as Mendelssohn and Wessely, or even to Euchel, Satanow and Saul Berlin. Clearly, the term is vague, and may result in some misconceptions. If "free" refers to Jews who were "free" from the observance of the *mitzvot,* and were totally "liberated" from traditional Judaism, it is evident that most of the

---

[32]Uzi Shavit, *Shirah Ve'ideologyah,* Tel Aviv 1987, pp. 14–15.
[33]*ibid.,* p. 15.
[34]*ibid.,* p. 16.

early Hebrew *maskilim* were not such persons. If this term means that these Jews believed in free thinking or libertarianism, (and there is no question that the more extreme did so), this by itself would not make all the *maskilim* "free Jews". They still operated within the framework of organised Jewish communal life, or in its margins even though they endeavoured to reform it. Euchel was trying to set up a substitute for the organised Jewish community, while Saul Berlin still functioned within the very rabbinic institution which he attempted to destroy.[35]

One may further deduce the meaning of *hofshiyut* from Shavit's reliance on Brenner. The combination of "Jew" and "Hebrew" on one hand, and the notion of a "free Hebrew" on the other, related to an identity phenomenon that had not existed during the period of early *Haskalah*. It would be inappropriate to attribute it to the *maskilim* themselves, as it was completely anachronistic to their thinking. It is interesting to note that Shapira used a similar expression ("the modern Hebrew man") which *Haskalah*, in his view, began to personify (*legalem*). However, Shapira intended this concept as an imaginative, literary portrayal, and not as depicting actual personalities.[36] In addition, it is rather difficult to reconcile this theory of *hofshiyut* and Shavit's choice of Luzzatto as the initiator of *Haskalah*, because of the great influence he exerted on it.[37] Was Luzzatto also a "free Jew", or a "free Hebrew", according to Shavit? It is inconceivable to think of this Kabbalist and traditionalist as a "free Jew".

Shavit dealt at length with the question of Luzzatto's role in *Haskalah*, and reached the conclusion that the roots of *Haskalah* literature originated in the previous generation with Luzzatto, who exerted a great influence on it. Shavit's most convincing argument concerns Luzzatto's reception among the *maskilim*. In a hundred years of *Haskalah*, there were 23 published editions of Luzzatto's *Layesharim Tehilah* (Praise for the Upright). In Shavit's words: "It can be confirmed with certainty that indeed Luzzatto (together with Mendelssohn, Wessely and the editors of *Hame'asef*) is the 'initiator [opener] of the period'."[38] He argues that *Layesharim Tehilah* must be viewed as "an allegorical drama based on reality [actuality], which clearly expresses the spiritual climate of its time, that of the stages of the scientific revolution, rationalism and *Haskalah*".[39]

It is ironic that Shavit's criticism of Kurzweil and the latter's definition of secularism may be applied to his own concept of "libertarianism", and in effect may cancel it altogether. Apparently, Shavit himself sensed that his attempt to characterise *Haskalah* through one criterion had an inherent weakness. He proceeded to propose three criteria, "three fundamental and basic principles", which, he

---

[35]See the chapters in Pelli, *The Age of Haskalah* and *idem, Bema'avkei Temurah*, on Euchel, Berlin and Satanow, respectively. See also Shmuel Feiner, 'Yitzhak Eichel – Ha"yazam" Shel Tenu'at Hahaskalah Begermanyah', *Zion*, 52, No. 4 (1987), pp. 427–469. On Brenner's attitude towards tradition and his use of "Hofshiut", see Shmuel Schneider, *Olam Hamasoret Hayehudit Bechitvei Yoseph Hayim Brenner*, Tel Aviv 1994, pp. 81, 84.
[36]Shapira, *Toldot Hasifrut Haivrit Hahadashah*, p. 572.
[37]Shavit, *Shirah Ve'ideologyah*, p. 98.
[38]Uzi Shavit, 'Layesharim Tehilah Leramhal: Hitbonenut Mehudeshet (He'arot Hadashot Leviku'ah Yashan: Mesayem Tekufah O Pote'ah Tekufah?)', *Mehkarim Al Toldot Yahadut Holland*, IV, Jerusalem 1984, pp. 179–217; see especially quotations on pages 214–215.
[39]*ibid.*, p. 213.

believes, served as the basis of the *Haskalah* movement from the 1780s to the middle of the nineteenth century. In his opinion, these principles complemented each other, and constituted the basis for "one, wholesome and harmonious spiritual world". The three principles consisted of "the belief in the human intellect, in understanding and in science", "the belief in God and in the religion of revelation", and "the belief in the power of beauty and the sublime".[40] Shavit's criteria suit the early *Haskalah*, to be sure. However, it should be asked whether these criteria shared the same weight in the late *Haskalah*. Even if they are correct and indeed characterise the Hebrew *Haskalah*, they do not reflect the *essence* of modernism in *Haskalah* literature, as will be discussed below.

BAND: MODERNISM TRACED TO BERDICZEWSKI

In 1988, Arnold Band explored the question of modernism and the beginning of modern Hebrew literature. He reviewed existing theories, and applied Hans Robert Jauss's theory about the reception of literary texts by a certain audience to Wessely's *Shirei Tiferet* (Songs of Glory) and Luzzatto's *Layesharim Tehilah*. Indeed, both works of these writers were influential during early *Haskalah* and exerted seminal influence on subsequent *Haskalah* writers. However, no one has considered any of them as "modern" in the sense of being "secular" or as works that contain rationalistic ideology. Band proceeded to offer his own theory of modernism, suggesting that the beginning of modernism in Hebrew literature be traced to the works of Micha Josef Berdyczewski.[41] Certainly, Berdyczewski was considered as *Aher* (the "other") in his time. Nevertheless, when compared to such contemporary writers as David Frischmann, Ahad Ha'am, Hayim Nachmann Bialik, and Shaul Tschernichowsky, there is no justification to assign the notion of "modernism" uniquely to Berdyczewski. Even if Berdyczewski had advocated a non-normative Judaic orientation, he could not be exclusively termed a "modernist" just because of that. He and the other authors cited above were products of *Haskalah*. Upon its demise, they remained active in literature, each of them experiencing differently the changing of the literary guard and the rise of Jewish nationalism. For example, Berdyczewski's unique stature as *Aher* is diminished somewhat when compared to Frischmann. Nevertheless, there is nothing in that to belittle Berdyczewski's literary importance and contribution to Hebrew literature. Certainly, the 1890s represent a new direction in Hebrew letters and epitomise modernism at its height. However, the beginnings of that very modernism had appeared earlier in *Haskalah*.

Also in 1988, Hayim Shoham was attempting to address the question "What is Hebrew-Jewish *Haskalah*?". He, too, believed that "the essential beginnings of Hebrew *Haskalah* literature, as part of *Haskalah* movement, should be found in the latter third of the eighteenth century". He selected this period because it was marked by the publication of "*Hame'asef*, the first secular Hebrew period-

---

[40]Shavit, *Shirah Ve'ideologyah*, p. 25.
[41]Arnold Band, 'The Beginnings of Modern Hebrew Literature: Perspectives on "Modernity"', *AJS Review*, XIII (Spring-Fall 1988), pp. 1–26.

ical" and "Wessely's *Shirei Tiferet,* the secular biblical epic". According to Shoham, it is then that Hebrew literature became a continuous and successive secular literature.[42]

In the 1990s Shmuel Werses took stock of his own research activities, and characterised his approach to the study of *Haskalah* in terms of adhering to its broader and more comprehensive concept. His approach differed from the trends of *Haskalah* historiosophy, which tended "to highlight *Haskalah*'s defined and confined perimeters, in accordance to its stages of development and periodisation". These trends in the study of *Haskalah,* he writes, attempted to emphasise the essential differences between *Haskalah* literature and the types of Hebrew literature preceding and following it. In his research he also pursued the phenomena of continuity and succession in Hebrew literature, apparently following in the footsteps of Dov Sadan.[43] Indeed, Werses's studies testify to the existence of affinities between traditional literature and modern Hebrew literature, manifesting aspects of continuity. Yet, he also dwells on various new aspects of this literature and its indebtedness to European literatures.

SUMMARY OF THEORIES:
SYMPTOMS AND RESULTS BUT NOT THE ESSENCE

The variety of the generally perceptive viewpoints regarding *Haskalah* is impressive, but there is a lack of textual reference and substantive proof based on literary sources. This has enabled successive Hebrew critics to question their validity and their applicability to the totality of *Haskalah* literature, and even to refute them altogether. Many literary theoreticians did exactly that, while they formulated their own new theories of the beginning of modern Hebrew literature and the notion of modernism in Hebrew letters.

Some of these definitions are so general that they purport to encompass several periods in Hebrew literature, during *Haskalah* and even post-*Haskalah,* while retaining some common denominator within *Haskalah* literature *per se.* It is for this reason that we must ascertain whether they exclusively define the beginning of modern Hebrew literature (which is to be found in *Haskalah* literature). Even though they may have some relevance, they cannot qualify as a unique definition of *Haskalah.* Some definitions contain deficiencies that may preclude their use for Hebrew *Haskalah.*

Other definitions appear to be based on generalities, which address complex and complicated issues in a simplified, and perhaps even an oversimplified manner. They attempt to attribute a complex social process and major ideological and cultural changes to a single individual or to a single idea that they consider represents the new trends.

Additionally, while some of these observations relate to aspects of the new

---

[42]Hayim Shoham, 'Mahi Haskalah Ivrit-Yehudit?', *Hado'ar,* 67, Nos. 33 & 34 (1988), pp. 16–18; 46–48; reprinted in *Betzel Haskalat Berlin,* Tel Aviv 1996, pp. 9–21.
[43]Shmuel Werses, 'Orhot Ushevilim Beheker Sifrut Hahaskalah', *Mehkerei Yerushalayim Besifrut Ivrit,* XIII (1992), p. 19.

trends, they are not necessarily the only criteria, as is asserted. Consequently, some of these criteria for evaluating modernism or the new trends are only partially correct.

In order to define these criteria critics have explored the question, "what characteristics are common to *Haskalah* writers?" They identified various religious, spiritual, cultural, social, and/or literary phenomena, and asserted that they, and only they, reflect the shift towards modernism.

Some of the criteria cited in the critical literature as representing the tenets of Enlightenment and its counterparts in *Haskalah* are listed below:

> Emphasis on mundane, this-worldly matters, in contrast to other-worldly matters, and an emphasis on man and humanism;

> Critical attitude towards religious institutions, the deterioration of the stature of the church and the rabbinate, and the decline of the authority of religion and the Scriptures;

> Belief in man's reason as the ultimate criterion for the evaluation of all phenomena of life; freedom, freedom of thought, freedom from prejudice and superstitions; scepticism and rationalism;

> Belief in a universal truth and the ability to discover it through the use of man's reason; belief in progress and in a better future; belief in the brotherhood of man and a desire to improve man's lot and humanity's future; optimism;

> Universalism, utilitarianism, pragmatism, and empiricism; emphasis on science and secular studies, etc.

These criteria, representing tendencies in European Enlightenment which were adopted by Hebrew *Haskalah*, are undoubtedly correct. They summarise, on different levels of importance, various aspects of the general Enlightenment. Some of them represent a philosophy of life and modes of expression, while others form social or ideological trends. All in all, they characterise in one way or another the tenets and tenor of European Enlightenment, which were applied to *Haskalah*.

These concepts appear to reflect the transformation into modernism, and indeed may serve as authentic characteristics of *Haskalah*. Moreover, these notions occurred concurrent with these changes. Nevertheless, they were the *results* of the occurring changes and *not* their common denominators. They were symptoms of the transition process that has brought about modernism. They certainly characterise this transition, but they do not constitute the main components nor the unique aspects of this transition. Many of the criteria cited above may be helpful in identifying aspects of the Enlightenment. However, they do not represent the essence and uniqueness of modernism in *Haskalah*.

The modernism that we are trying to identify is a combination of *mega-trends* which epitomise the all-encompassing phenomena of modernism in *Haskalah*.

HYPOTHESES IN EVALUATING MODERNISM

A discussion of Hebrew modernism must be predicated on a few fundamental premises. First, it is assumed that changes have taken place in Jewish society, its ways of life and its culture (as have always occurred to some degree), but that there were also phenomena of continuity. We assume that modernism is a process, which could be traced and reconstructed on the basis of such components as discussed below and not only through overt changes in the social and cultural order. Since our discussion is based on literary research, we shall look for manifestations of these changes in works of literature and in their periphery (as well as in other related areas of human endeavour).

Another basic assumption is that modern-day students of *Haskalah* are able to discern the tenets of these changes as well as trends of continuity. Furthermore, it is assumed that they are able to establish the proper criteria to distinguish between the two periods or two types of literature being discussed. We must, however, take into consideration that the notion of changes during the first generation *Haskalah* in Germany is not universally accepted. Ahad Ha'am (Asher Ginzberg), for example, was of the opinion that the early *maskilim*, such as Wessely and Salomon Maimon, did not desire to create a new Hebrew literature with a new base, but wanted to develop the traditional Hebrew literature that had ceased to grow.[44]

A more modern scholar, Dov Sadan, who was cited before, expanded the perimeters of modern Hebrew literature to encompass *Hasidic* and *Mitnagdic* literatures, in addition to *Haskalah* literature. Sadan also broadened the linguistic framework beyond Hebrew, to include Yiddish and other European languages employed in Jewish literature.[45] In Sadan's theory, the question of modernism does not concern itself with the criterion of secularism as epitomising the modern age. Thus, the concept of modernism becomes even more nebulous.

Second, we should consider the fact that the process of change was gradual, and that its scope was relatively limited within the framework of Jewish society, as applied to the individual, or in literature. We should note that the process of *Haskalah* and its acceptance among the ranks of the Jewish people was limited in its magnitude and intensity, especially at its inception. Certainly, *Haskalah* did not embrace the totality of the people (even in the centres of Enlightenment in Western and later in Eastern Europe), nor did it cover the totality of Jewish experience in the Diaspora. We should not assume that the shift to *Haskalah* was universal or uniform, even within a group of writers who identified themselves as *maskilim*. The *maskilim* represented the wide spectrum of *Haskalah*. Some of them were more extreme than the others, some were more moderate, and some were even conservative. Therefore, any attempt to achieve a single definition should be considered only as an attempt to establish a boundary, whose total applicability is not guaranteed even by the definition itself.

Moreover, we are dealing with phenomena in the realm of culture and the humanities, bordering in the imaginative and creative arts. These phenomena

---

[44]'Halashon Vesifrutah', 'Lishe'elat Halashon', *Kol Kitvei Ahad Ha'am*, Tel Aviv 1956 5th edn., p. 95. See also Z. Kalmanovitch, 'Ahad Ha'am Utehumei Hasifrut Haivrit', *Molad*, XII (1954–1955), pp. 510–520.

[45]Dov Sadan, *Al Sifrutenu Masat Mavo*, Jerusalem 1950, pp. 1–9; first chapter published earlier in 'Al Tehumei Sifrutenu Hahadashah', *Molad*, II (1948–1949), pp. 38–41. Sadan reiterated his views in other articles and in 'Al Sifrutenu – Masat Hitum', *Yerushalayim*, XI-XII (1977), pp. 162–171.

attest to intellectual self-scrutiny, and to a probe and a quest for secularism, as manifested in literature. They are spiritually tantalising, soul searching, creative and cultural inner struggles. They are indicative of covert imaginative and intellectual processes of changes within the individual that may not have materialised externally at this point. This concept of change is an inner perception that came to fruition only later. This is the most important aspect of our search for the early manifestations of secularism and modernism in their inception in *Haskalah*. As suggested by the Enlightenment historian Norman Hampson, "the Enlightenment was an attitude of mind rather than a course in science and philosophy".[46] These precautious perceptions, still hidden in the innermost thoughts of *Haskalah*, expressed the spirit of modern times in Judaism and in Hebrew letters.

Third, in light of past attempts to define modernism, it is incumbent upon us to abandon a single-sentence definition attempting to encompass the meaning of modernism in Hebrew literature. It is a complicated subject, involving a complex process in many areas of human endeavour within Jewish society. This process was manifested in the realm of society, religion, culture, and literature. No magic formula could contain the total scope of the new phenomenon of modernism.

Thus, we must acknowledge the complexity and the multiplicity of the *Haskalah* phenomena as a basis for our discussion. The term *"Haskalah"*, which, as mentioned earlier, has recently been reviewed and re-examined by Uzi Shavit,[47] and the term *"maskilim"*, were applied to various individuals and groups, in several localities and in different times, as if they were all identical in their *"Haskalah"*. Even within a single group of *maskilim*, in the same place and the same time, we can discern diverse positions. Ostensibly, some of them embraced a *Haskalah* viewpoint with an individual interpretation of *Haskalah* ideology, different from the one advocated by the others. Some also differed in the way they applied their ideology in a practical and empirical fashion. *Haskalah*, as has been shown elsewhere, cannot be delineated as a straight, direct line, but rather as a spiral, advancing and then, to some extent, regressing.[48] It is my conclusion that we should not expect to find the answer to modernism in one person or one definition.

Another premise, adopted for the purpose of identifying modernism in Hebrew literature, acknowledges that its beginnings can probably be found in the early period of German *Haskalah*, while some of its forerunners may be traced to certain phenomena in Italy. It is my working hypothesis that the dominant and decisive beginning of modernism will not be found in later literary periods, such as the *Tehiyah* (Rejuvenation). The phenomena of this late period belong to different currents in Hebrew literature. This hypothesis does not preclude the examination of other periods and other arenas with the same tools. The purpose of such

---

[46]Norman Hampson, *The Enlightenment*, London 1968, p. 146.

[47]Uzi Shavit, 'Ha"haskalah" Mahi', pp. 51–83.

[48]*Bema'avkei Temurah*, chap. on 'Haskalah Vehitmaskelut', pp. 35–40. See Feiner's new article cited in note 10.

an examination is to locate and identify aspects of the modern period and its literature which are significantly different from those of the previous period. My working premise is based on my studies and research in this field. This research has established that Hebrew *Haskalah* in Germany, more than any other single literary phenomenon that preceded it, contains definite signs that mark the beginning of the trends leading into "modernism" (a term that is still to be defined). This premise does not purport to negate any theory of continuity, from medieval or renaissance Hebrew letters to the modern phenomena. Nor does it reject the notion that there were definite signs of the development of earlier literary genres and styles in *Haskalah* literature. *Haskalah*, as we conceive of it, does not only represent innovation; it combines continuity as well as change. This dual tendency complicates our question and poses additional challenges to the scholar who explores it. For now it is his duty to identify literary phenomena that belong to the new currents, as well as those phenomena indicative of indebtedness to a traditional literature.

Lastly, and most importantly, the definition of modernism should come from the literature itself. Our definition will not be content with only the modern scholar's interpretations, based on his research in *Haskalah*. Neither will we only cite *Haskalah* sources that, according to our interpretation, characterise modernism. We will demand that *Haskalah* literature itself will present its own concept of modernism. It would be preferable if we found the appropriate text where *Haskalah* itself offered a definition of modernity, or an attempt at a definition. If our premise is correct, we should search contemporary literary works for a proper definition, or else we should search for the proper literary phenomena that represent the new orientation in Hebrew literature.

However, we must make a clear distinction between *symptoms* of modernism that are indeed important, relevant and correct, and a *major* transformation in *Weltanschauung*, which is the essence of modernism. It is this major shift (unlike the symptoms of the changes) that signifies the beginning of the all-encompassing spiritual, intellectual, and cultural mega-trends, constituting a revised outlook on Judaism. It represents a revised attitude towards Jewish existence and Jewish values. It also incorporates a revised Jewish self-concept as related to Jewish heritage and Jewish view of the surrounding cultures and societies. Yet, these changes did not mark the "spiritual world void of its primordial religious certainty" suggested by Kurzweil.

The need to find a definition from within the corpus of these writings is appropriate for literature, which is by nature able to register overt and covert expressions of the changing spiritual and cultural trends. Thus, it can be argued that literature may offer special insights into the essence of modernism, which may surpass in their value any other social or historical record.

AWARENESS OF TRANSFORMATION

In order to define the awareness of modernism, which began to permeate Hebrew writings, the literary historian and critic will have to identify and track this ostensible feeling of modernism. He will have to scrutinise the literary and linguistic expressions of that perception of transformation, as manifested in the writings of the early Hebrew *maskilim*. Subsequently, he will have to interpret those expressions critically, as he would any other literary text or literary phenomena for accuracy and insight. He should be especially sensitive to the linguistic manifestations which exemplify the transformation occurring in the Hebrew language. To do that, he must be attuned to the rhythm of the period, listen to the nuances of transition, and be familiar with the formation of new linguistic patterns, as the "holy tongue" was being transformed into mundane, secular Hebrew. For language itself was one of the tools leading to change and simultaneously undergoing this very change itself.

The modern critic should not automatically assume that every *Haskalah* author possessed this awareness of modernism, nor that he was necessarily aware of the changes that were taking shape. Neither can it be easily assumed that the historical, cultural, and spiritual processes of change were expressed in his writings. Obviously, not every author was sensitive to this metamorphosis, and not every one reacted to it. However, upon identifying such reactions, we should examine them and weigh the possibility that they represent timely observations and perhaps contain significant insight into these processes. On the other hand, it can be argued that certain timely phrases which we selected to represent modernism may reflect the author's contemporary enthusiasm, reacting uncritically to events that appear to him at that moment as momentous and earthshaking. In historical perspective, however, they may turn out to be of lesser significance. In addition, the "artificiality" of *Haskalah* Hebrew, and its inclination to resort to euphuism, the high-flown turgid style of *melitzah*, may exaggerate an event beyond its objective importance. Therefore, it is incumbent upon the student of *Haskalah* to watch out for linguistic and conceptual traps. We must question whether we can rely on the historical ability of contemporary individuals to evaluate the essence of an occurring change, and to discern properly the historical, cultural, or spiritual developments of that change. Likewise, we must weigh our ability to rely on our own reading of these historical texts, and actually to discern change by means of the Hebrew language. We must be certain that there indeed is a change, and that it is not merely a linguistic ornament, or a lexical *Fata Morgana*, reflecting something that had not actually occurred.

Another methodological problem related to the interpretation of *Haskalah* texts stems from the intention of *Haskalah* writers to spread the notion of change as part of their ideology. It is not inconceivable that they purposely exaggerated their depiction of change in order to disseminate their cultural and social agenda. Therefore, we must not rely blindly on their writings, but should assess them critically and historically. Additionally, we should not rely on one source, but look for a number of textual proofs, which will be interpreted in context.

DIRECT STATEMENTS ON THE CHANGE:
OVERT AWARENESS OF THE NEW TIMES

As we look for overt manifestations of an awareness of the new times, we should pay attention to several expressions, by the early Hebrew *maskilim* in Germany, found in *Hame'asef*. Its prospectus, *Nahal Habesor* (the Brook Besor, or Good Tidings) contains explicit expressions concerning the new times. The editors proclaimed the emergence of a new age by saying: "And behold wisdom now cries aloud outside." While employing a paraphrase from Proverbs I:20, the statement highlights three important concepts relevant to the new components of change during the Enlightenment: the concept of time ("now"), the principle of wisdom, and the dichotomy between "inside" and "outside". A call for immediate action follows: "Hurry up to call her in, hasten to bring her indoors."[49] The use of the biblical idiom and the parallelism between the two components of the statement intensify the message and suggest the image of a bridge, leading from the outside world into Jewish society.

These statements are indicative of a profound awareness of metamorphosis (possibly leading into modernism). The editors accompanied these phrases by demands that their fellow Jews follow in the footsteps of European Enlightenment and adopt its new ideology. The *maskilim* believed that the times demanded a change from the traditional Jewish way of life, to a more updated (and perhaps "modern") course. Many of these statements heralded the dawn of the new age of reason in Europe, constituting the litmus test for discerning the emerging modernism. They are euphoric, hopeful, high-flown, and naive. However, they certainly form the literary and linguistic expression of the awareness of the changing times which we are trying to identify.

The Book of Proverbs, from which the paraphrased quotation came, served like some other similar pronouncements, as a source of slogans for promoting and inaugurating the new age. The use of the sacral biblical idiom to present a new, contemporary concept, related to the new times, is of special interest. It signals the accepted method, during early (and late) *Haskalah*, of employing "the sacred tongue" to express secular concepts. The Hebrew language itself – the revived vehicle for communication – subtly reflected, in its sensitivity, the complex transition to modernity. Modernism was exemplified by the use of the traditional "holy tongue" to express new, modern, and perhaps secular notions. Thus, it should be reiterated that our study of *Haskalah* must focus on the problems of the resuscitated Hebrew language.[50]

Haskalah writers sensed that a new age had emerged in Europe. They referred to it as "the days of the first fruits of knowledge and love in all the countries of Europe".[51] It is significant to note that the two concepts signifying the new epoch are "knowledge" and "love", that is "tolerance", and that the two are

---

[49] *Nahal Habesor* bound with *Hame'asef*, I (1783–1784), p. 3.
[50] The topic of the revival of the Hebrew language during the *Haskalah* is discussed in an article submitted by the author to *Leshonenu La'am* 1999.
[51] *Nahal Habesor*, p. 3.

connected. In other words, this phrase suggests that receptivity to happenings in the areas of culture and the humanities in Europe may impact on the social level in human relations and in the attitude towards the Jews.

This feeling intensified in the early years of the publication of *Hame'asef*, as seen in the writings of the *maskilim*. In the news section 'Toldot Hazman' (Chronicles), published in the first volume in 1784, Hayim Keslin portrayed the new age with the familiar metaphors: "Ever since the light of knowledge has shone among the nations, and ever since the veil of ignorance has been lifted from the face of the peoples among whom we dwell, God has remembered us as well and has made their leaders act in our favour . . . and they [now] consider us as brothers."[52]

Discerning the change in 1786, the Italian *maskil* Eliyahu Morpurgo used a similar metaphor: "Now that the sun of wisdom has come out on the earth in this wise generation."[53] He highlighted this changing time by comparing it to the earlier period: "Now it is unlike the early days for the remnants of this people, as the seed of peace has given its fruits, fig and vine have brought forth their crop – the crop of wisdom – and the tree of knowledge has given its fruits . . . and a clear spirit [wind] has passed throughout the world, a cloud will spread its lightening [light], and will saturate it under the entire heavens, and its light [will reign] over the corners of the earth."[54]

The *maskilim* argued that recognising the emerging changes on the (non-Jewish) European scene necessitated that Jews, too, pursue a course of action to implement that change among themselves. They proclaimed that: "The age of knowledge has arrived among all the nations; day and night they do not cease teaching their children [both] language and book. And we, why should we sit idly by? Brethren, let us get up and revive [those] stones from the heaps of dust."[55]

The commitment to the mission which *Haskalah* undertook upon itself and the strong sense of urgency to act permeate Shimon Baraz's poem '*Ma'archei Lev*' ('Preparations of the Heart'). The poem was published in 1785, at the first anniversary of the founding of the Society for the Seekers of the Hebrew Language, the umbrella organisation of the *maskilim*. This Hebrew writer used the seasonal revival of nature as the metaphor for the revival of the Jewish people and Jewish society. He emphasises the notion of the group working together for a unifying goal so as "to teach understanding to those who erred in spirit; enlightenment and knowledge to the impatient; and the earth should be full of knowledge as the water [cover the sea]".[56] The latter part is a partial biblical citation, based on Isaiah, purposefully omitting the name of God. Another *maskil*, David Friedrichsfeld, summarised the goals of *Haskalah* in this new age, expressing his wish in the form of a prayer: "May God make this community [of *maskilim*] the

---

[52]H. K. (Hayim Keslin), in *Hame'asef*, I (1784), p. 111.
[53]Eliyahu Morpurgo, in *Hame'asef*, III (1786), p. 131.
[54]*ibid.*, p. 68, based on Job XXXVII:11.
[55]*Nahal Habesor*, p. 13.
[56]Shimon Baraz, *Ma'archei Lev*, Koenigsberg 1785, based on verses from Isaiah XXIX:24; XXXV:4; XI:9.

teachers of knowledge and the clarifiers of good tidings, so that the children of Israel will walk in their light.''[57]

It may be argued that these statements carry a tone of exaggeration and essentially propagandise the *Haskalah* agenda. Thus, they ought not to be taken as naive, innocent observations, authentically reflecting the current condition. However, even if these are attempts to disseminate propaganda, they represent a clear indication of the *maskilim*'s awareness of the changing times. To reiterate, this awareness of the ensuing change undoubtedly was coupled with the *maskilim*'s strong desire for such a change. It was part of their recognition that this change was possible and that they were committed to pursue it. These tendencies represent a new and innovative thrust, signalling a transition from a rather passive attitude towards Jewish existence to a more active one. The occurring change transforms a lofty slogan into an ideal that must be realised and into an enterprise that must be brought to fruition. Since its inception, and for some time to come, Hebrew *Haskalah* literature has been a tendentious literature, whose goal was to revive the Jewish people and its culture. Hebrew literature undertook a "national" mission: to bring about a cultural revival for the ultimate rehabilitation of the Jewish people, and had adopted a revolutionary goal and had mobilised its resources to initiate action to effect the change. The clear signals of modernism that began to emerge from within the pages of *Hame'asef* were thus manifested by the awareness of the need for change, striving to define it, and struggling to execute it. These expressions of modernism, in its myriad, complex forms, continued to gain momentum. Even this awareness gained momentum, while leaving its cumulative impact on the beginning of modern times among the European Jews. It did not occur in one day, nor in one place. Yet, the theme repeated itself like a leitmotif, indicative of this historical trend and attesting to the validity of our observations.

The feeling of newness, innovation, and regeneration was the thrust of the first proclamation the new editors presented in *Nahal Habesor*. The publication of the periodical was noted as a new phenomenon: "A new publication which has never materialized in our times" (of course, they were in error, for they apparently were not aware, at that time, of the earlier publication of *Kohelet Musar* [Preacher of Morals]).

Undoubtedly, the editors of *Hame'asef* discerned that a momentous change had taken place in Europe. They advocated that their fellow European Jews partake in this process and reap its fruits. As *Haskalah* progressed, their concerted efforts to introduce the ideas of European Enlightenment started to bear fruit. In a long, continuous process lasting over a century, they effected acute change in the attitude of modern Jews towards traditional Judaism. These Hebrew *maskilim* were cognisant of the innovative nature of their activities and of the fact that they had formed a new social and cultural framework. They knew that they had created a new ideology which spoke on behalf of the new movement. They established a new literary centre, aiming to produce a new type of Hebrew literature, even if they did not name it "*Haskalah*". The *maskilim* did not refer to this new

[57]David Friedrichsfeld, 'Hadlah Mimlitzat Yehudit Hatif'eret', *Hame'asef*, II (1784–1785), p. 34.

orientation as *Haskalah* literature, the *Haskalah* movement, or the *Haskalah* period, as Shavit has recently pointed out.[58] However, as Shmuel Feiner proved in his dissertation, the eighteenth-century *maskilim* developed a full historical awareness, and it served them in shaping the self-consciousness of the period.[59]

MESSIANIC CONCEPTS APPLIED TO THE NEW AGE

Awareness such as this usually surfaced in public manifestos, which targeted a certain audience and carried a social message. A writer of such a proclamation usually felt the need to cite the occurring change as the reason for implementing a reform, as he was arguing his position and advocating his cause. One such manifesto was published in *Hame'asef* in 1790 by Mendel Bresslau, an editor of the periodical. Bresslau called on contemporary rabbis to form a rabbinic assembly in order to alleviate the burden of religious ordinances.[60] He cited the new age as reason for his demand, saying: "And who is too blind to see that the day of the Lord is coming, and in a short while wisdom and knowledge will become the faith of the times".[61] Bresslau's phraseology is based on messianic hopes that were transformed and applied to the new age. In spite of the traditional metaphors, the reference to the proverbial Prophet Elijah, and the designation of the forthcoming great day as "the day of the Lord", Bresslau was far from considering it a divine or heavenly phenomenon; rather, he deemed it an earthly one. "You should pay attention to the splendid and awesome things that God has amazingly done in our times. And whosoever would not close his eyes in malice will indeed notice that it is God's hand ... And why are you indolent to arouse the heart of the people, who are seeking to benefit our people in their toil, to re-establish the name of Jacob ... My heart cries because of the evil that is happening in Israel ... Not so are the ways of the other peoples around us, for they are improving the ways, and remove falsehood from the truth ... Be ashamed, the house of Israel, for you have been doing the opposite, and truth is wanting."

These words are charged with great emotional vigour and attest to the great excitement among the Hebrew *maskilim*. It has been demonstrated elsewhere that Bresslau's article was written against the background of the call by the English deist Joseph Priestley for the "return of the Jews", in his book *Letters to the Jews*.[62] Bresslau's article is indicative of the awareness of the pending changes. Evidently, the Hebrew language is deceiving us, playing a game of allusion and illusion,

---

[58]Shavit, 'Ha"haskalah" Mahi', p. 51. Shavit argues that the *maskilim* were not aware that they were "*maskilim*". I tend to disagree with his notion if by this he meant that they did not consider themselves as *maskilim*.

[59]Shmuel Feiner, *Hahaskalah Beyahasah Lahistoryah – Hakarat He'avar Vetifkudo Bitnu'at Hahaskalah Hayehudit (1781–1881)*, A Doctoral Dissertation, Jerusalem 1990, in the introduction and chapter one. Published as *Haskalah Vehistoryah*, Jerusalem 1995.

[60]Mendel Bresslau, 'El Rodfei Zedek Vedorshei Shelom Aheinu Bnei Yisrael', *Hame'asef*, VI (1790), pp. 301–314. See *Bema'avkei Temurah*, chap. 5 on Bresslau.

[61]*ibid.*, p. 301.

[62]See Joseph Priestley, *Letters to the Jews*, New York 1794 [first edition: 1787]. See Pelli, *Bema'avkei Temurah*, pp. 167–174.

replete with sacred expressions and hope for a heavenly redemption. Nevertheless, the thrust of the article is completely secular, and its intent and tenor are mundane and earthly. The problem is that the author makes use of the "holy tongue", with its religious and biblical allusions, in order to communicate with his contemporary readers. However, to read it naively and literally is incorrect.

Bresslau's article and his use of the Hebrew language raise questions about our reading of the text. Is our reading tendentious? Do we read in the text what we wish to see in it? Is it possible that we interpret the above statements out of context? Could these statements be naive expressions which are based on textual allusions in the style of *Haskalah* and rabbinic writings of the time? Or perhaps these expressions represent emotional outpouring, uttered in a lofty, turgid language, while the author did not have in mind any new phenomena at all. Even if he did, was he correct in his observations about the so-called "new phenomena"? These questions – which were alluded to before – will continue to confront us in our discussion below. Yet, we should not be misled by Bresslau's quasi-religious statements to think that all the *maskilim* – even the early ones – were devout supporters of the rabbinic establishment. Nor were all of them very strict about the religious observance of the *mitzvot* in a full-fledged, rabbinic manner. Many of the *maskilim*'s pronouncements were said in a certain way in order to appease the rabbis. Many of these statements were intended as lip service to placate the apprehensions of the Orthodox circles so as to win the support of the moderates among them, who were proverbially "sitting on the fence." Bresslau "recruited" the Almighty to serve the *Haskalah* as it were, employing the messianic concept of "the day of the Lord" in order to assure his audience that his intentions were honourable.

KOHELET MUSAR AND DIVREI SHALOM VE'EMET EXAMINED FOR NEW AWARENESS

In order to examine the validity of our observations, we will apply the same method to search for overt expressions of the changing times in the early periodical *Kohelet Musar*, published by Mendelssohn in the 1750s. No such expressions are to be found in that ephemeral publication. There are references to the author's contemplations on the world, citing "various changes", but they allude to seasonal changes in nature. The thrust of those statements reflects certain aspects of contemporary *Weltanschauung*. There is an emphasis on man as the crown of creation, but this concept is found also in traditional Judaic sources. Gilon's contention that *Kohelet Musar* "opens, in the humanities, the period of modern Judaism",[63] will not be discussed here as it exceeds the scope of this article.

[63] *Kohelet Musar*, Issue I, p. 1, a copy of the edition at the British Library, London. Meir Gilon, *Kohelet Musar Lemoshe Mendelssohn Al Reka Tekufato*, Jerusalem 1979, p. 1. Gilon found in this periodical "the first attempt to form a *Weltanschauung* that is a synthesis of both the teaching of Judaism and the culture of European Enlightenment, and by this it opens up, in the realm of the humanities, the period of modern Judaism". I discuss Gilon's stand in the introduction to my book (temporary title) *Hame'asef Index*, submitted recently. This is also discussed in Pelli, 'Hame'asef: Michtav Hadash Asher Aden Beyamenu Lo Hayah', to *Hebrew Studies*, 1999.

A very interesting reference to the passing times is found in the original, hand-written comment that Shlomo Dubno marked on his personal copy of *Kohelet Musar*. On the cover page, which is now at the British Museum, he wrote: "This pamphlet has been composed by two individuals who are well-versed in Torah ... and it was their intention by that to awaken the sleepy ones and to revive the slumbering persons out of the slumber of time, so as to get them accustomed to morality, by improving their manners, and to stir hearts by the beauty of the rhetoric of the holy tongue, which had been lost from us because of our own ini-quities." However, Dubno's reference about the changing times does not address the kind of changes we are looking for, namely: quintessential and far-reaching "mega-changes". No doubt, Dubno cited important changes that the editors of *Kohelet Musar* were attempting to effect. These were secondary signs of contem-porary innovation with an emphasis on the aesthetic of language, which indeed was one of the tenets of the modern age.

A comparable search in Naphtali Herz Wessely's timely writing, *Divrei Shalom Ve'emet*, will bring similar results. Even though this work contains many overt expressions relevant to the notion of modern times, it is generally immersed in a totally traditional ethos that was not indicative of the new age. Unlike Bresslau's external use of the "holy tongue" – the only one available to him – Wessely's tenor is traditional, as is typical of his other writings. For example, Wessely wrote: "In our generation the kings of Europe are wise, man-loving and virtuous, and they display benevolence and compassion towards us, may God remember it in their favour."[64] While Wessely's style may resemble that of Bresslau, the thrust of Wessely's text is totally ingrained in normative Judaism. He portrays contemporary events in the European arena as initiated by the Almighty – "he who announced the generations from the start" (based on Isaiah, XLI:4). Note that as Wessely proposed to enact the desired change, there appeared to be some hesitation in the thrust of his message: "And perhaps it is the assigned time to remove the hatred from the people's heart".[65]

Interestingly enough, in another comparable search of a *maskil's* writings sixty years later we find an echo similar to the one in *Hame'asef* concerning the changing times. Mordechai Aharon Ginsburg proclaimed in 1843: "Behold the new age comes upon you, and we, the authors, are the scouts that she has sent before her, to herald her coming, and to command you to search out a resting place for her and to prepare for her needs."[66]

If our observations in these examples are correct, the editors of *Hame'asef* and several of the writers who contributed to the journal were indeed the representa-tives of modernism, and were among those who promoted it in the last quarter of the eighteenth century.[67] We have certainly noted the beginnings of the aware-

---

[64]*Divrei Shalom Ve'emet*, I, Berlin 1782, p. 14 [my pagination].

[65]*ibid.*, p. 15.

[66]Mordechai Aharon Ginsburg, 'Kikayon Deyonah', *Hamoriyah*, Warsaw 1878, pp. 47–48, which was written in 1843, and published posthumously.

[67]H. N. Shapira selected the writers of *Hame'asef* as those that opened the new era, as cited above, in his book, *Toldot Hasifrut Haivrit Hahadashah*: "Modern Hebrew literature does not have one initiator, but initiators, and they are the authors who published and participated in *Hame'asef* the literary

ness of change in their writings. Of course, not everything in their writings indicated change, as I have shown in some of the other examples. Change may be noticed not only in this early period, but also in later periods of *Haskalah*. Moreover, in this early generation of transition, one can find manifestations of both the old and the new in the same writing.

COVERT EXPRESSIONS OF CHANGE: JUDAISM SUBSERVIENT TO WESTERN CULTURE AND DEPENDENT ON IT

The forthcoming change towards modernism was expressed not only overtly, as discussed above, but also covertly in the works of several *Haskalah* writers. Unlike the overt expressions, covert enunciations were subconscious and clandestine. They are indicative of existing undercurrents and growing sensitivities with regard to phenomena which had barely begun to emerge. Nevertheless, these suggestions of awareness have foreshadowed the forthcoming new trends. They may be even more important than the overt expressions because of the latent message which they harboured concerning Judaism and the Jewish religion in modern times. Those subtle signs found in Hebrew literature manifested the emerging notion that normative Judaism, as it had been transmitted and practised throughout the ages, was no longer self-sufficient and self-contained. The *maskilim*, who expressed their innermost thoughts, inferred that Judaism could no longer continue to exist as an entity on its own, independent of the surrounding cultures, and could no longer provide total support to its adherents. Indeed, there was a strong feeling of the inadequacy of rabbinic Judaism to address the needs of modern man. In order for Judaism to survive, they argued, it could not continue to be isolated as in the past, but it must adjust to the new circumstances.

Moreover, the transformation of these Hebrew writers' outlook assumed another tone, manifested by the notion that traditional Judaism was subordinated and subservient to Western civilisation, inferior to it and dependent on it. This notion should not be interpreted to mean that these *maskilim* had any inferiority complex because of their adherence to Judaism. On the contrary, many of them expressed their pride in the pristine form of Judaism. They did consider contemporary rabbinic Judaism, which had allegedly deteriorated as a result of *galut* (exile), to be inferior, in contrast to the original form of Judaism. In fact, one of the *maskilim*, Satanow, expressed his opinion about the superiority of ancient Judaism, and implied that the Jewish Enlightenment should advocate a return to it.

This awareness represented a new phenomenon in eighteenth-century Judaism. The new awareness shattered the notion taken for granted in traditional Judaism, that the latter was an all-encompassing way of life. Judaism was considered to have addressed the needs of the individual Jew and Jewish society.

---

organ of the new people of Israel. From this *Hame'asef*, that is from 1784, we have to start reckoning modern Hebrew literature.'', p. 58.

The change in outlook did not occur instantly. Jewish intellectuals were transforming their behaviour and viewpoints in a process that took place over a long period of time. The process involved spiritual and intellectual debate, tantalising questioning, and soul-searching, representing the desire to bridge two worlds and to narrow the gap between two civilisations.

Halkin was correct in his observation that "the Jew's total contentment with his inner life is what typifies him in his living within the walls up until the eighteenth century". With the ushering in of that century, Halkin stated, "his contentment with his inner life begins to dissipate", and he feels free to address "the hunger of a regular human being for the good life on this earth". It was Halkin who related the appearance of modern Hebrew literature to the Jewish tendency towards the external civilisation, combined with the strong desire of these Jews to remain Jewish.[68] The tension between these two tendencies brought about the advent of modern Hebrew literature, according to Halkin.

WESSELY: JUDAISM SUBSERVIENT TO EUROPEAN CIVILISATION

Significantly, this new awareness regarding Judaism's alleged inferiority, subordination to, and dependence on Western civilisation was first detected in the writings of the moderate *maskil*, Naphtali Herz Wessely. It is remarkable that even *maskilim* with a traditional orientation such as Wessely shared this feeling of the alleged inferiority of contemporary rabbinic Judaism to Western culture in the modern age, and that they expressed it covertly in their writings. I base these conclusions on my previous works on Wessely, and on my interpretation of his book *Divrei Shalom Ve'emet*, which deals with reforming Jewish education.

Wessely articulated his educational theory in relation to his perception of Judaism. He argued that Judaism incorporates two major entities: *Torat Hashem,* the laws of God, which consists of the laws or teaching of God, and *Torat Ha'adam*, the laws of man. He further expanded the first entity, *Torat Hashem,* to include not only the laws of God, but also Judaism and the Judaic corpus in general. Similarly, Wessely extended the concept of *Torat Ha'adam* to include not only the laws of man, but also Natural Law, or the "seven Noahide laws", all secular disciplines – scientific knowledge, social customs, and Western civilisation *in toto*. Wessely developed his theory on both the educational level and the historical level. He argued that historically and chronologically the law of God, namely, Judaism, was subservient to the law of man. Now, in the modern age, it was completely dependent on Western civilisation. Accordingly, this traditionalist *maskil* took a position that Judaism in modern times could not remain an independent entity. It was subjugated to Western culture, which he considered to be superior. His position manifested a major revision in Judaic *Weltanschauung*. It looked as though Judaism was no longer a self-sufficient entity, whose spiritual strength supported all its needs. It was felt that Judaism at this

[68]Halkin, *Derachim Vetzidei Derachim Basifrut*, I, pp. 156–157; Halkin, *Zeramim Vetzurot Basifrut Haivrit Hahadashah*, I, p. 11.

modern age should extract itself from its particularistic isolation and assume its previously held character of universalism.[69]

Wessely's reflections should be interpreted, neither as an attempt to assimilate, nor as self-denial *vis-à-vis* Western culture. Wessely was a devout Jew who was proud of his Jewish heritage. Wessely's *Torat Ha'adam* was not foreign to pristine Judaism. It was indeed integrated in it, although it had been neglected as a result of the Diaspora experience. This was a modern re-interpretation of Judaism, an attempt to rehabilitate it on the basis of its own inherent principles. Undoubtedly, this view represented a revolutionary revision of values of *Haskalah* Judaism. This was a complete about-face from the viewpoint of traditional Judaism. Thus, one of the important indicators of modernism in Judaism was in its deviation from the traditional outlook that viewed Judaism as a self-reliant, self-sufficient, all-encompassing entity. Instead, modernism considered Judaism in its present state to be inferior and subservient to European civilisation.

Wessely presumably expressed these ideas without realising fully and consciously their revolutionary nature. For this reason, his utterances have been classified within the *covert* statements. They are the most significant aspect of the modern period, because they expressed the social, cultural and spiritual undercurrents leading to the changes that were about to take place. Wessely was not and could not have been "a new man" "fighting for new life," as suggested by Klausner. He displayed a profound expression of the changes he sensed, although, I believe, he was not consciously aware of them, and did not intend them to be so extreme. Therefore, while Wessely's literary work was already within the perimeters of *Haskalah*, he should not be considered as one of the "heralds" of *Haskalah*, such as Emden, due to his traditional orientation. The early *maskilim*'s inner world was not devoid of their Jewishness, as Kurzweil attempted to portray it. It was the beginning of a change that evolved into a complex process of transformation, a process that should not be entirely delineated only as linear, progressive and continuous.

JUDAISM RE-DEFINED

An important aspect of modernism in Hebrew *Haskalah* was manifested through conscious attempts to re-define Judaism. In the writings of the Hebrew *maskil* Isaac Satanow an allusion to rejecting the claim by contemporary rabbinic Judaism for the exclusive right to represent and interpret authentic Judaism may be found. Satanow identified a historical model which he thought represented the original, authentic form of Judaism. In his view, this historical Judaism should be emulated by *Haskalah* in order to revitalise the Jewish religion in modern times. Significantly, Satanow found the epitome of authentic Judaism in *early* rabbinic Judaism. He considered the periods of Mishnaic and Talmudic Judaism as representing Judaism at its highest point of flourishing,

---

[69]See detailed discussion, Pelli, *Bema'avkei Temurah*, pp. 58–59, 76–77 (notes 80–81); *idem, The Age of Haskalah*, pp. 122, 127–128.

creativity, scholarship, and knowledge. It was in this period that Jewish civilisation made its lasting contribution to knowledge and humanism. The selection of earlier periods in the history of rabbinic Judaism was intended to crystallise the contrast between them and contemporary rabbinic Judaism. It aimed to return to the original, authentic Judaism, which should be adopted by *Haskalah* Judaism.[70]

Thus began the modern trend in Jewish circles to be liberated from the rabbinic "birthright" and its exclusive, almost divine, religious authority over the definition of Judaism. In order to prove that historical Judaism embodied a multiplicity of viewpoints, the *maskilim* quoted repeatedly the passage, *"Elu ve'elu divrei elohim hayim"* (these and these are the words of a living God). To them, it showed that authentic Judaism encompassed ideologies that at times contradicted each other, and that the Talmudic sages showed no consternation in accepting them. Obviously, the *maskilim* wished to emphasise the openness of Judaism and the inherent freedom to interpret its tenets without resorting to a restrictive Orthodox position. Accordingly, the *maskilim*'s views of Judaism were as legitimate as those of contemporary rabbis. They believed that their views embodied an attempt to present an alternative to rabbinic Judaism.[71]

Modernism, therefore, may reflect not only secular trends, as is customarily accepted by most literary historians and critics, but also the religious tendency to re-define Judaism on the basis of a past model. Replacing normative rabbinic tradition with a re-defined, neo-traditional, modern version of Judaism was indeed the aspiration of many of the moderate *maskilim*. The phenomena referred to as the "forerunners of *Haskalah*" is not addressed here. However, Rabbi Jacob Emden, for example, is not considered part of *Haskalah* proper because of his *Weltanschauung*, his rabbinic post and orientation, and the tenets expressed in his writings.[72] Thus, the axiom that modernism in modern Hebrew literature is essentially secular-orientated should not be accepted at face value. It should be re-examined for its validity *vis-à-vis* the reality of early *Haskalah*. For indeed we have found an all-encompassing and a more meaningful criteria that characterized the evolving modernism within the Hebraic and Judaic spheres of influence. The developing change did not distinguish itself necessarily by its "secularism", although it is definitely characterised by revision in values.

Thus, it is incumbent upon us to review and re-assess some of the accepted notions in *Haskalah* criticism and its historiography concerning the attitude of the Hebrew *maskilim* towards Jewish tradition. One of the accepted myths, which I have established as erroneous, was the claim that the Hebrew *maskilim* possessed a negative attitude towards the Talmud, and that they had rejected its scholarship and learning. As I have demonstrated, this assertion should be revised because it is not applicable to many of the early *maskilim*.[73] Surely, the

---

[70]Cf. *ibid., The Age of Haskalah,* chap. 8; Pelli, *Bema'avkei Temurah,* pp. 120–122.

[71]*ibid.,* pp. 170–171, and the related footnotes where I cited the sources in *Haskalah* literature.

[72]See Shohet, *Im Hilufei Tekufot,* chap. 10, 'The Buds of *Haskalah*', and pp. 220 ff. on Emden. See Feiner's article cited in note 10.

[73]See Pelli, *The Age of Haskalah,* chap. 3, on the attitude of the *maskilim* towards the Talmud.

more extreme *maskilim* embraced a radical "secularism", which in effect removed them from the mainstream of Hebrew *Haskalah*. Thus, they are outside our domain and are naturally excluded from our discussion. The extreme religious reform orientation which occurred in German Jewry some seventy years later did not originate directly from early Hebrew *Haskalah*, some influence notwithstanding. We should not adopt the argument used by *Haskalah*'s Orthodox opponents in its time and afterwards about the alleged heresy of *Haskalah* as valid for a balanced, historical evaluation. This applies not only to the first period of *Haskalah*, but also to the later period. We do not refer to the more moderate of the *maskilim*, such as S. D. Luzzatto and Eliezer Zweifel, who were known for their traditionalist, moderate stand,[74] but to the more mainstream *maskilim*. For example, recently Israel Bartal studied Mordechai Aharon Ginzburg's stand on modernity and concluded that Ginzburg was a very moderate *maskil* in spite of the image portrayed by the Orthodoxy to the contrary. Bartal concluded that Ginsburg "looks much closer to Orthodoxy than to the radical *maskilim* with whom he disagreed in his writings".[75]

It is evident that throughout the course of *Haskalah*, the *maskilim* themselves were very careful to make a clear distinction between the "true *maskil*" and the "false *maskil*", and warned against confusing the two.[76] In time, however, the notion that *Haskalah* was leading to assimilation and conversion prevailed not only in Orthodoxy's criticism (for example, Asher Pritzker's writings), but also in general criticism.[77] A different notion prevailed during *Haskalah* itself, in its early period and even in the 1860s, as expressed by Abramowitz (Mendele Mocher Sfarim), to the effect that the *maskilim* wished to reconcile faith and *Haskalah*.[78]

Haskalah criticism must, therefore, re-examine the cultural, neo-traditional elements in *Haskalah* Judaism. The term "neo-traditional" should not be interpreted as implying a complete Orthodox observance of the *mitzvot*, or "modern Orthodoxy" in the fashion of our contemporary Judaism. It is for this reason that Kurzweil's concept of a total "revolution" in *Haskalah* is incorrect. Kurzweil anachronistically advanced the latter phenomenon, and makes a

---

[74]See Shmuel Feiner's article, 'Eliezer Zwifel Vehahaskalah Hametunah Berusyah', *Hadat Vehahayim: Tenu'at Hahaskalah Hayehudit Bemizrah Eiropah*, Jerusalem 1993, pp. 336–379.

[75]Israel Bartal, 'Mordechai Aharon Ginzburg – Maskil Lita'i Mul Hamodernah', *Hadat Vehahayim: Tenu'at Hahaskalah Hayehudit Bemizah Eiropah*, pp. 109–125.

[76]In early *Haskalah*, the "false *maskil*" is described in Euchel's letters, *Hame'asef*, II (1785), p. 140. In the later part of *Haskalah* the theme is addressed in Brandstaedter's stories.

[77]See, for example, Ruth Kastenberg-Gladstein, 'Ofyah Hale'umi Shel Haskalat Prag', *Molad*, XXIII, Nos. 201–202, (Tamuz-Av, 1965), p. 221: "we see the beginning of *Haskalah* movement, the 'Berlin *Haskalah*', as leading to assimilation, and also to conversion to Christianity". See also Asher Pritzker's books, *Sefer Hame'ilah*, Tel Aviv 1957; and *Sefer Hagut*, Tel Aviv 1958.

[78]Abramowitz, in his article 'Kilkul Haminim', *Mishpat Shalom*, published in Shimon Halkin's *Mekorot Letoldot Habikoret Haivrit Bitkufat Hahaskalah*, Jerusalem 1961, p. 287 [facsimile]. *Hamelitz* had the permanent motto on its masthead: "Hamelitz bein am yeshurun vehamemshalah, bein ha'emunah vehahaskalah." ("Hamelitz [interpreter, mediator] between the people of Yeshurun and the government, between faith and *Haskalah*.") In early *Haskalah*, such a notion may be found in Satanow's writings (see below); see Pelli, *Bema'avkei Temurah*, pp. 93–99. This topic should be further discussed.

generalisation about that which was unique to a different period. It was not a "revolution", as suggested by Kurzweil; rather, one can safely characterise *Haskalah* Judaism as advocating the continuation of the *status quo* with an eye on revolution. Kurzweil's error is that he presented his view as a dichotomy in order to emphasise his point. However, the two polarities which he selected did not fit the reality of *Haskalah*. The latter encompassed a series of internal overt and covert processes, which represented progress (if this is the right word) as well as "retreat". The "revolution" Kurzweil talks about came on the heels of *Haskalah* or at its end. However, this revolution has never been a complete one, typifying all *maskilim*.

REVISION OF THE JUDAIC VALUE SYSTEM

There was another covert expression of the pending shift about to take place in *Haskalah* Judaism. It was detected in the pronouncements of *Haskalah* ideology, as fundamental values in normative Judaism were questioned. These values formed the foundations of Judaism for many generations, and have been accepted as an integral part of Jewish tradition. Now, however, they became the target of probe and doubt. This phenomenon epitomised the beginning of great changes, which were about to occur in Judaism. As emphasised earlier, this was an internal, rather than external change.

Satanow's creative writings and thought best reflect the Jewish experience in the emerging modern age. In his multi-faceted writings, Satanow alludes (according to my interpretation) to major changes in the perception of Judaism. Well-established fundamental values in the make-up of Judaism were scrutinized by this *maskil*. In his early work, Satanow, attempts to reconcile faith and *Haskalah*, and proposes an ideal unity between *hochmah* (wisdom) and Torah, an affinity between tradition and free investigation, which he presents as "twin sisters". From this position, Satanow moves on later in his writing career to destroy the harmony that he had previously attempted to build.

Because of the epigrammatic and proverbial nature of some of his works, emulating the style of biblical wisdom literature, and his pseudo-traditional commentary offered on its side after the style of full-fledged biblical commentary, it is possible to trace Satanow's changing views almost step by step. Thus, we can reconstruct his changing outlook (although it is impossible to prove its exact consecutive development). Viewing his reconstructed standpoint, it seems that Satanow was weighing the relations between freethinking, as a modern representation, and the traditional concept of fear of God, using the terms *hochmah* and *yir'ah* (fear of God). At first, Satanow placed *hochmah* and *yir'ah* as equals, saying that both "*Yir'ah* and *hochmah* are riding together."[79] In the same vein he writes: "There is no contradiction between *hochmah* and Torah," for the "true *hochmah* . . . will not object to Torah". He reiterates: "It is best to have both *hochmah* and Torah, and when these two combine with one another . . . they will inseminate

---

[79] Isaac Satanow, *Kuntres Misefer Hazohar*, Berlin 1783, on the title page.

and bring forth truth."[80] Subsequently, Satanow modifies this notion, saying that the two entities complement each other: "*Yir'ah* and *hochmah* both may bring a person to the realm of perfection."[81] Ultimately, he revised his position, once again, saying that the two were interdependent: "[For] one who denies *hochmah*, it is as if he denied the very seal [of the Almighty], which is truth."[82]

Satanow's personal path to enlightenment went through a transformation in viewpoint as he established the dependence of Judaism on secular *hochmah*. He writes: "The perfect person will not be able to know Him [God] except through *hochmah*."[83] Similarly, he writes: "Faith without *hochmah* is like an open city without a wall."[84] He then establishes that Judaism was subordinated to man's reason, saying that *hochmah* "will probe faith, whether it is based on truth or on falsehood, for any faith which denies reason should not be trusted".[85] Subsequently, he makes an about face similar to the one we found in Wessely's writings: "Whereas *yir'ah* has a temporal priority over *hochmah*, behold *hochmah* possesses a virtuous priority over *yir'ah*, because it is the very essence of *yir'ah* and its objective".[86] In this struggle between *yir'ah* and *hochmah*, between Judaism and Western culture, the latter seems to triumph.

The next stage in the development of Satanow's viewpoint further crystallises the difference between *yir'ah* and *hochmah* and establishes the contradiction between the two. Here Satanow dares to touch upon the essence of Judaism, the *mitzvot*, saying that "the observance of the *mitzvah* and the existence of *hochmah* are two opposites".[87] It appears that Faith, as an entity by itself, cannot compete with Truth, which to him is identical with *Haskalah*, and would not be able even to co-exist as an equal because of the polarity that exists between the two.

Thus, Satanow began his quest, groping for some form of semi-secular Judaism of the future, designated for modern Jews. He alludes to the solution that emerged, annulling the conflict between observing the *mitzvot* and the dictates of modern times. Accordingly, the new form of modern Judaism may have a different attitude towards the *mitzvot* — a position similar to Euchel's (see below). In spite of this extreme position, Satanow should not be regarded as a free or secular Jew because he was anchored in the old world, drawing his creative energies and inner experience from it. Perhaps he was indeed "half a heretic and half a believer", as was said about him. However, in his sensitivity he foreshadowed the very problem which modern Judaism was destined to face in the future.[88]

In his writings we find the tantalising spiritual and intellectual struggle with the viability of basic tenets of traditional Judaism and the probability of their

---

[80]*idem, Sefer Hahizayon*, Berlin [1785], p. 4a.
[81]*idem, Mishlei Asaf*, I, Berlin 1789, p. 12a.
[82]*ibid.*, I, pp. 7b-8a.
[83]*ibid.*, I, p. 9b.
[84]Isaac Satanów, *Imrei Binah*, [Berlin] 1784, p. 12a.
[85]*idem, Mishlei Asaf*, II, Berlin 1792, p. 61a.
[86]*ibid.*, I, p. 1b.
[87]*ibid.*, II, p. 18a.
[88]See detailed discussion in Pelli, *Bema'avkei Temurah*, chapter on Satanow.

annulment in modern times. These articulations constitute the "measuring rod" of modernism, namely, the very changes in values that began to form inwardly and clandestinely in the thinking of this *maskil*. For example, Satanow began to question the tenet of *Bitahon Bashem*, which meant a total unequivocal trust in the God of Israel and in His personal providence, and is considered one of the basic principles of traditional Judaism. These assessments are based on my interpretation of selections from Satanow's *Mishlei Asaf*. In the text, he writes: "Trust and action met, choice and decree touched."[89] In his commentary to the text, the author explains that trust (in God) and man's freedom of action contradict each other because "whoever trusts his master that He will provide his food, yet is actively looking for food, proves that his trust in his master is not complete". Similarly, he stipulates that free choice and providence are contradictory.[90]

Satanow goes on to examine and scrutinise other basic concepts of traditional Judaism. He reinterprets *Yir'at Hashem*, fear of God, and *Ahavat Hashem*, love of God, both basic tenets of Judaism, on the basis of his revised perception of Judaism. Satanow implies in the sub-text that *Yir'at Hashem*, in its classical meaning of an all-encompassing faith in God, is no longer obligatory in the modern age. God "will not blame you for not learning to fear him", he asserts in a complex commentary to a verse in his text, while fostering additional doubts concerning the knowledge of God on the basis of tradition, as compared to the knowledge of God stemming from rational inner conviction.[91]

Satanow continues to examine the concept of *Ahavat Hashem* and concludes that a pure love of God, love for love's sake, which lacks any ulterior motive, can no longer be achieved. "There is no love in the world which is caused by the love of the object alone, for self-love is the cause of all, so that the lover should benefit in some way from his love ... and also all those who worship God with love, love Him because they love themselves, for their own benefit in this world and in the world to come, be it materially or spiritually."[92]

Instead of these fundamental values, Satanow proposes *Haskalah*'s substitute. No longer is it "trust in God" and "love of God", but their antithesis; scepticism and doubt are the alternative values of modern Judaism, according to Satanow.

---

[89]Satanow, *Mishlei Asaf I*, p. 4b.

[90]"Mivtah va'alilah nifgashu, behirah ugzerah nashaku." ("Trust and action met, choice and decree kissed.") Satanow's commentary is complex, at times ambiguous, and requires logical deduction which follows the pattern of biblical parallelism. For example: since the second part of the verse deals with divine providence and free choice, one is led to conclude – based on biblical parallelism – that the first part of the verse deals with divine matters, and thus the commentary follows the same orientation, and the term "master" refers to the Almighty. Thus, the trust is "trust in God", which contradicts man's action. Satanow proposes a compromise, saying that this basic contradiction was intended by God "who makes peace between them" (verse 2, in the text), for man must "trust God as a righteous man trusts [him], and adhere to diligence [in his actions] as if he did not trust God" (commentary to verse 3). At the end, the basic contradiction has not been satisfactorily resolved, and at least there remains some scepticism concerning the possibility of a complete trust in God. See the discussion in Pelli, *Bema'avkei Temurah*, p. 127. Compare, for example, the traditional notion of "trust in God" exemplified a hundred years earlier by Glückel in her autobiography, *The Life of Glückel of Hameln*, New York 1963, p. 6.

[91]See detailed discussion in Pelli, *Bema'avkei Temurah*, p. 127, note 57.

[92]See details *ibid.*, p. 127, note 58.

He expresses it in the following passage: "Those who pass through the depths of confusion, for the reason that one does not fully comprehend the dictum of the Torah unless he had stumbled upon it; this confusion will become as a flowing fountain, which is the source of wisdom, and they will go from strength to strength in their understanding."[93]

Thus, Satanow was re-forming the ideological, spiritual and ethical values of modern Judaism, modelled on the European Enlightenment. This trend should be considered as the budding of modern, secular Judaism, which began its long course of development in German *Haskalah*, and has continued to our days.

NEW PERCEPTION OF JEWISH HISTORY, CALENDAR AND TIME

Another way to identify modernism during this period is to probe the *maskilim*'s perception of Jewish history and the historical processes occurring in it. We can discern the formation of significant changes in their view of Jewish history and their attitude towards it. The perception of Jewish history in *Haskalah* has been previously discussed by Reuven Michael. However, he dwelled on the legitimate historical corpus, namely those works written specifically within history proper – not literature – and the attitude of the *maskilim* towards the study of history.[94] Shmuel Feiner, too, dealt with the attitude of *Haskalah* towards history. He concentrated on the awareness of the historical past and its utilisation to promote the goals and ideology of *Haskalah*.[95]

I found a unique perception of Jewish history in a literary piece during this period of *Haskalah*. It appears to be the first time that a Hebrew writer questioned the inevitability of Jewish history and expressed his doubts about its predestined course. It was an attempt to fathom the meaning of Jewish history and the historical significance of Jewish existence. The very efforts of Hebrew *Haskalah*, as a literature and as a social and cultural movement, to change somehow the course of Jewish history from within manifested the modern aspect of eighteenth-century Judaism.

The exponent of this new attitude was Saul Berlin, a rabbi and one of the most outspoken Hebrew writers of early *Haskalah* in Germany. His views of Jewish historiosophy are expressed in the satire *Ktav Yosher* (An Epistle of Righteousness), published in 1794, but in fact written ten years earlier in defence of Wessely. In this satire Saul Berlin, like Satanow, undertook to annul certain accepted concepts and basic tenets deemed as revered values of Judaism. He also attempted to debunk sacred myths in Jewish historiography. This extreme stand, with its acrimonious forceful tone and criticism concerning the very essence of Jewish existence, had not been heard prior to this time. These views represent a major aspect of modernism to be reckoned with.

Saul Berlin's medium is biting satire, which, as a literary vehicle, is part of the

---

[93] *Mishlei Asaf*, I, p. 25b, and see discussion in Pelli, *The Age of Haskalah*, pp. 169–170.
[94] Reuven Michael, *Haktivah Hahistorit Hayehudit*, Jerusalem 1992, pp. 96–113.
[95] Feiner, *Hahaskalah Beyahasah Lahistoryah – Hakarat He'avar Vetifkudo Bitnu'at Hahaskalah Hayehudit (1781–1881)*.

struggle for change. Berlin ridicules the revered attitude towards *Kidush Hashem*, martyrdom, a concept that has been sanctified in Jewish history. He criticises the Jews' willingness to accept their persecutions and catastrophes without any question or protest, as if they were divinely pre-destined and as if Jewish history must immanently lead to death and destruction. "Since the day the temple was destroyed and the sacrifices were abolished God does not enjoy anything better than to have us slaughtered and killed, like a sacrifice and a burnt offering for the sanctification of His great name ... may I, the poor and humble, too, be worthy to be killed or hanged for the sanctification of His name", he writes scathingly. "And if because of their hatred, our foes are many ... may we be worthy to sanctify heaven's name in the eyes of all the nations."[96] In so doing, this Hebrew writer criticises not only the mentality of the Jews, but also protests bitterly against the divine providence that singled out the Jews, and deplores this Jewish fate and destiny.

Berlin intensifies his criticism beyond examining the historical aspect of Jewish time and the individual Jew's attitude towards it. He begins by probing the concept of the Jewish calendar, that is, the essence of Jewish time, in its contemporary manifestation, and the individual's interaction with it. "And those who were killed in the [1648/9] Chmielnicki massacres in Poland were meritorious because the twentieth day of Sivan was designated for fasting and great lamentation to commemorate their killing. And therefore, why shouldn't we envy them for the great privilege that they had received and bestowed upon others as well".[97] The Jewish calendar – that system of daily sacred symbols – is saturated with memorial days for those historical calamities. The Jew is described as someone who experiences this twisted Jewish history also in his daily life. Saul Berlin now asserts that this practice be changed. He seems to have criticised the synoptic concept of Jewish history that considered every individual Jew in every generation as though that person had been a "participant" in every historical event in Judaism. Perhaps it is the beginning of the orientation that would transform the Jew from his atemporality back to time's normality, placing the Jewish people back into the course of human history.[98]

This aspect of modernism is exemplified in Saul Berlin's attempt to crush some basic paradigms of Jewish existence, embraced wholeheartedly by traditional Judaism. For example, the concept of *galut* (state of exile) is scrutinised by Berlin together with its counterpart, *ge'ulah* (divine redemption). He employs the distorted mirror of satire, claiming that Jews have become so used to the state of exile and to their low ebb that they do not want to be extricated from it. It may be concluded from his writings that this condition is not irreversible and that it could and should be rectified in the modern age, which has witnessed a different

---

[96]Saul Berlin, *Ktav Yosher*, Berlin 1794, p. 4b.

[97]*ibid.*, p. 5a.

[98]Detailed discussion on Saul Berlin may be found in the respective chapters in Pelli, *The Age of Haskalah* and *idem, Bema'avkei Temura*, and in my two articles on *Ktav Yosher:* 'Saul Berlin's Ktav Yosher – The Beginning of Satire in Modern Hebrew Literature of the Haskalah in Germany', in *LBI Year Book XX* (1975), pp. 109–127; and 'Aspects of Hebrew Enlightenment Satire – Saul Berlin: Involvement and Detachment', *LBI Year Book XXII* (1977), pp. 93–107.

relationship with the peoples of Europe. The hope for redemption is depicted by this *maskil*, not as the Jews' desire to be redeemed, but as a limited manifestation of their worship.[99] In addition, Berlin implies that messianic redemption is no longer conceived as a divine act, and that it may be materialised in a mundane way through the person of a leader in their time. This contemporary redeemer "was destined to clear the way and to pave the road",[100] and Saul Berlin implied that it was none other than . . . Moses Mendelssohn.[101]

Another criterion designated to identify the transition to modern times in Jewish history was the desire to normalise the relations between the Jewish people and the other peoples of Europe, a goal undertaken by *Haskalah*. This aspect of Jewish modernism raised the question of the Jewish isolationism and the attitude of the Jews towards Western civilisation, both marked as targets for Berlin's satire. In his caustic satire, the author asserts that the gentiles' hatred for the Jews was benevolent because it facilitated Jewish martyrdom, *Kidush Hashem*. Accordingly, these Jews were better off, he suggests (aiming his satiric arrow), for they attained the same exalted eminence as the righteous people who had become martyrs. In order to achieve this desired goal, he contends, it is better not to seek the well being of the non-Jews. Ostensibly, Saul Berlin also attempts to reject the idea of the "chosenness" of Israel, showing in effect that this "chosenness" in effect brings a total annihilation to the Jews. He thus creates a satirical paradox, whose purpose is to place the existence of the people above the concept of Israel's "chosenness".[102]

Those are intrepid expressions which marked the watershed point in Jewish history and Hebrew letters. They reflect the sense of change in the perception of Jewish history that certainly marked the advent of modernism in *Haskalah* Judaism. They epitomise a revised attitude towards Jewish history. No longer is there a passive, submissive acceptance of persecutions and catastrophes as God's punishments. Now, a pungent, accusatory, and defying protest emerged that would eventually lead to active implementation of the desired changes in Jewish

---

[99]Berlin, *Ktav Yosher*, p. 5a: "And when we pray about the *galut* and for the coming of the Messiah, it is not in order that God will ameliorate our condition and give us pleasure and goodness, but in order that we may worship Him and perform the multitude of *mitzvot* which the contemporary rabbis place upon us, and it is not because of the poverty, destitution and grief that we have endured, for all of this does not bother us. On the contrary, this is what we desire. For the bitter *galut* and the hatred of the nations cleanse our iniquities."

[100]*ibid.*, p. 15b.

[101]See Pelli, 'Aspects of Hebrew Enlightenment Satire – Saul Berlin: Involvement and Detachment', in *LBI Year Book, XXII* (1977), where this was written about in detail, citing the sources and analysing the text.

[102]Berlin, *Ktav Yosher*, p. 4b: "Since the destruction of the temple and the abolishing of the sacrifices, God does not enjoy anything better than to have us slaughtered and killed like a sacrifice and burnt offering for the sanctification of His great name. And happy were our forefathers and our forefathers' fathers in ancient times when the hatred of the nations prevailed, and every day our enemies were rising against them, slaughtering men, women, and children, young men and women, bridegrooms and brides, old men and women by the hundreds and thousands as the sanctified sheep were slaughtered on the holidays in Jerusalem on the altar, and their blood atoned as a sacrifice and burnt offering. And then their souls ascended to heaven, and Michael the archangel stood and slaughtered them again and spilled their blood on the heavenly altar, and happy are they that they achieved such great merit."

society. All of these notions were expressed in the writings of this enigmatic obser-
vant rabbi, a scion of a respectable rabbinic family, who turned out to be one of
the most eloquent spokesmen of *Haskalah*. In the very dual role of his life and his
personality, Rabbi Saul Berlin exemplifies the generation of *maskilim* in transition, advancing towards the forthcoming modernism.

SEARCH FOR HAPPINESS AND DISREGARD FOR *MITZVOT*

Another decisive mega-trend in the changing perception of modern Judaism sig-
nified the great transition between *Haskalah* and the preceding period. For the
first time in the modern age (excluding the Sabbatian and Frankist phenomena),
the question arose as to whether traditional Judaism can bring happiness to the
modern Jew. Two *Haskalah* writers, Isaac Euchel, the editor of *Hame'asef*, and
Saul Berlin expressed their agonising doubts whether traditional Judaism could
bring happiness to the Jew as an individual and to Jewish society as a whole. It
was European Enlightenment ideology that demanded the individual's right to
achieve happiness. Several of the early *maskilim* adopted this ideal of Enlightenment in its concept of mundane happiness and arrived at a radical interpretation
of Judaism. As a result, they demanded change in traditional Judaism.

Isaac Euchel planted the early seeds of scepticism in his satire 'Igrot Meshulam
ben Uriyah Ha'eshtemo'i' ('The Letters of Meshulam ...'). Serialised in
Hame'asef in 1790, this epistolary satire is set in modern-day Spain. Euchel
describes the Marranos' clandestine practice of Judaism, barely observing the
mitzvot. The protagonist, Meshulam, poses a naive, though consequential,
question:

> According to my thinking the success [happiness] of the Israelite lies in the obser-
> vance of the *mitzvot* alone, and if it were possible to be wholesome [achieve perfection]
> and happy without observance of the *mitzvot*, would not Socrates the Greek and
> Zoroaster the Hindu be as wholesome [achieving perfection] and happy as any Israe-
> lite?[103]

On the threshold of modern times, Euchel's intention was to express his doubts
about the happiness that a Jew may derive from the observance of the *mitzvot*,
and to infer that the modern Jew can achieve his happiness without fulfilling the
mitzvot. As Judaism ceased to be the sole provider of happiness for the Jews, the
door was opened to the "brave new world" of Western civilisation. This is the
signal of the emergence of modernism, as it took shape in the minds and hearts
of the early *maskilim*.

Three years later, Saul Berlin expressed a more extreme stand *vis-à-vis* the
Jew's happiness, in his *responsa* book, *Besamim Rosh*, where he examines, among
other things, the probability of abrogating the *mitzvot*. He presents it in a
hypothetical question as follows: "And if, God forbid, it could be envisioned
that there would come a time when the laws of the Torah and its precepts will
cause harm to our people ... or even if it could be envisioned that they would

[103]Isaac Euchel, 'Igrot Meshulam ben Uriyah Ha'eshtemo'i', *Hame'asef*, VI (1790), p. 44.

not bring happiness at all, then we should remove its yoke from our neck."[104] As a *halakhic* authority, Saul Berlin was not satisfied with hints about the possibility of abolishing the *mitzvot* "le'atid lavo" – in the future, or in Messianic times (based on Niddah, 61b), as was done by some of the *maskilim*, but addressed the issue directly.

These two *maskilim* identified one of the most important tenets of the change into modernism: the desire of modern Jews to achieve mundane and immediate happiness, rather than the time-honoured promises for the transcendental world to come. Their stand attested to a mega-trend leading towards secularism, which manifests itself in modern Judaism to this day.

This outlook of the *mizvot* seems to represent an advanced development pursuant to Wessely's re-assessment of the relations between Judaism and Western culture. Upon the removal of the exclusiveness from Judaism, as the only source providing the complete happiness for the Jew, the gate to modernism was thrown wide open, even for those who continued to observe the *mitzvot* and the tenets of Judaism.

WHAT IS SECULARISM?

At this point we must ask: What then is secularism? The dictionary definition of secularism (*Hiloniyut* in Hebrew) does not cover the whole gamut of meanings discussed above, as exemplified in *Haskalah* literature. *Hamilon Hehadash* (The New Dictionary) by Even-Shoshan defines the Hebrew word *Hol* as "anything that does not contain sacredness". *Hiloniyut* is defined as "non-religiousness, lack of connection to the sacred" and *Hiloni* is "non-sacred, that which is not con-nected to religion". *Hilun* is explained as "secularisation, abolishing sacredness, making secular".[105] The Hebrew definition tends to approach secularism nega-tively, as something that is not sacred. Actually, the English definition is much broader in its approach to the subject, using positive terminology. Thus, Webster defines "secular" as: "Worldly, pagan. Of or related to the worldly or temporal as distinguished from the spiritual or eternal; not sacred; mundane. b. not overtly or specifically religious."[106]

Several scholars who studied the phenomena and meaning of secularism attempted to define the term "secular". Wagar, in the introduction to *The Secular Mind*, examines several definitions and cites their weakness. It results from the ambiguity of the term which originates from the Latin *saeculum*, meaning the world. By convention, "secularism" means "to repugn or ignore religious considerations and substitute for them the values of this world".[107] However, secularism is much more complex a phenomenon. Wagar dismisses Chadwick's definition, stating that secularisation "is supposed to mean, a growing tendency in mankind to do without religion, or to try to do without

[104] Saul Berlin, *Besamim Rosh*, Berlin 1793, p. 77a, item 251.
[105] Avraham Even-Shoshan, *Hamilon Hehadash*, II, Jerusalem 1966, pp. 764, 769.
[106] *Webster's Third New International Dictionary*, New York 1971, p. 2053.
[107] W. Warren Wagar, ed., 'Introduction', *The Secular Mind*, New York 1982, p. 2.

religion",[108] as inadequate. Certainly, in context of the modern trends in *Haskalah* Judaism, Wagar's position is accepted.

The issue becomes even more complex when viewed against Harvey Cox's "secular theology" theory. Accordingly, secularisation "is the passage to a society characterized by the anonymity and mobility of urban living, by pluralism, tolerance, pragmatism, and profanity – the last defined as the disappearance from consciousness of any supermundane reality".[109] At this point, one feels the necessity for a definition of the adjective "religious". Martin defines it as "an acceptance of a level of reality beyond the observable world known to science, to which are ascribed meanings and purposes completing and transcending those of the purely human realm".[110] "Secularization is nothing less than the decline of religious beliefs and institutions."[111]

We will not readily follow Wagar's contention that, facing the problematics of the question, "one is tempted to take refuge in Hermann Lübbe's elastic definition of secularization as the historical relationship in which modern civilization stands to its indelibly Christian past".[112] We may possibly consider this notion when "converted" to ... "the Jewish past".

As we have noted in our discussion, the dictionary definition of "secularism" in its meaning of "this-worldliness", "temporality", and "mundane", does not fit the unique case of Hebrew *Haskalah*. Furthermore, the definition of secularism as "non-sacred", or "not connected to religion", is also unsatisfactory. As we have seen, the *maskilim*'s unique predicament was characterised by a spiritual struggle between the old and the new, between the desire to adopt European cultural criteria and the simultaneous desire to remain loyal to Jewish heritage. This precludes any clear-cut classification based on a dictionary definition. The *maskilim*'s Hebrew and Jewish culture cannot be defined solely on either the religious or the secular level. It floats in the spheres of the undefined culture which cannot be classified uniquely as secular or religious. This very problem – the ambivalence between the sacred and the secular – is the epitome of Jewish modernism. Therefore, our definition concentrates more on the inner spiritual and intellectual struggle, the feeling of the new, and the awareness of the pending change.

LITERARY CRITERIA FOR MODERNISM

Our discussion so far has focussed on attempts to define modernism on the basis of non-literary criteria that were borrowed from non-literary disciplines and applied to literature. Since our main subject is literature and literary periodisation, it is incumbent upon us to approach the definition of modernism also in

---

[108]Owen Chadwick, *The Secularization of the European Mind in the Nineteenth Century*, London 1975, p. 17; Wagar, *The Secular Mind*, p. 2.
[109]As cited *ibid.*, p. 3.
[110]David Martin, *A General Theory of Secularization*, Oxford 1978, p. 12. See Wagar, *The Secular Mind*, p. 4.
[111]Martin, *A General Theory of Secularization*, p. 12; Wagar, *The Secular Mind*, p. 5.
[112]*ibid.*

literary terms. One of the most promising prospects for a literary definition is the renewed research on emerging new literary genres and new literary phenomena in Hebrew *Haskalah*, which should result in a new or revised concept of modernism in Hebrew letters. It is assumed that this new definition should concentrate on the transition from traditional Hebrew literature, found in the classical corpus, to the "new" literature. It should discern this transition by identifying new literary genres that were introduced to *Haskalah* or the new literary aesthetics adopted by it.

Until recently Hebrew scholarship has not produced a comprehensive study of the genres of Hebrew *Haskalah* literature, and Holtz has already pointed out this lacuna.[113] An exception is my own recent book, delineating ten major literary genres, mostly in early *Haskalah*.[114] However, the task is far from being completed as many more genres need to be studied, such as poetry and drama, as well as periods of *Haskalah*. Upon completion of such an endeavour, it will be possible to establish satisfactory literary definitions based on the phenomena of genres in *Haskalah* literature. For the time being conclusions based on my book will be used to guide us in this task.

Based on this research in the literary genres of *Haskalah* that encompass ten literary genres, it is possible to discern a dual tendency. On the one hand, there is definitely a trend of continuity in *Haskalah*'s use of literary genres. Many of the *maskilim* continued to use genres prevalent in the corpus of Jewish *belles lettres*. The fables, parables, and epigrams are examples of continued genres. Likewise, the use of the medium of *responsa* by Saul Berlin, in *Besamim Rosh*, for the purpose of parody and criticism, represents this trend of continuity with some slant. Obviously, the contents of these traditional genres reflect the backdrop of the new period.

As part of this tendency to adopt known genres in classical Hebrew letters, there was also a secondary trend to adopt an established genre and present it as authentic classical writing. This was the case of Satanow's *Mishlei Asaf* (The Proverbs of Asaf), allegedly based on an ancient manuscript found by the author to which he only added his commentary, thus enriching it with a fascinating literary dimension. At times, the genre was re-introduced in the classical mould without the guise of a discovered ancient manuscript. Such was Satanow's *Divrei Rivot* (Words, or Matters, of Dispute), patterned after *Hakuzari*. Thus, these revived genres should be considered as indicative of the new literary trends towards modernism.

Another dimension of modernism in Hebrew literature is manifested by the introduction of European genres into *Haskalah*. In my research I have identified and analysed several of these genres. They are: satire, epistolary writings, travelogues, biographies, autobiographies, dialogues of the dead, and utopia, to

---

[113]Holtz, 'Prolegomenon to a Literary History of Modern Hebrew Literature', p. 268. See also Werses's summary of *Haskalah* research, 'Al Mehkar Sifrut Hahaskalah Beyameinu', *Megamot Vetzurot Besifrut Hahaskalah*, pp. 356–408, and 'Mehkarim Hadashim Vegam Yeshanim Besifrut Hahaskalah Utekufatah', *Mada'ei Hayahadut*, 36 (1996), pp. 43–69.

[114]Moshe Pelli, *Sugot Vesugyot Besifrut Hahaskalah Haivrit*, Israel 1999.

mention a few.[115] These genres represent a strong European influence combined with a Hebraic colouring, stemming from the classical tradition of Hebrew letters. If we were to select a single writer as contributing most to the introduction of these genres to Hebrew literature, it would be none other than Isaac Euchel. It is Euchel who wrote the first modern biography in Hebrew, an epistolary satire, a brief travelogue, a utopia, and others. However, as cited earlier, no single person and no single work can represent the beginning of modern Hebrew literature.

These new and renewed genres served the goals of *Haskalah* and promoted its ideology. Through the new genre of biography, *Haskalah* authors presented exemplary personalities whose character and achievements exemplified the ideals of *Haskalah*. The genre of utopia, for instance, envisioned and illustrated new modes of life, new social orders, and an ideal Jewish society. Satire, by its nature, attacked the old order and attempted to promote its own truth, a new agenda for modern times. The genre of the dialogues of the dead brought to life, in a manner of speaking, authoritative personalities from Jewish history in an ideological confrontation with contemporary rabbinic opponents of *Haskalah* to approve the stand of Hebrew Enlightenment.

Thus, it may be said that modern Hebrew literature began with the introduction of European literary genres into it. This change represents a major literary shift that we consider as modernism.

The search for literary definitions of modernism must take into consideration the subtle processes of change occurring within the Hebrew language. The secularisation process of the Hebrew language must be included in any study of modernism in *Haskalah*, as it reflects not only the changing viewpoint of literature, but also the new *Weltanschauung* of the Jewish people. Many sacred concepts and expressions, sanctified and venerated throughout the ages, underwent significant, though subtle, changes, and assumed secular, modern meaning. This is certainly part of the process of secularisation related to modernity. The secularisation of language bordered at times with its profanation. Indeed, the subject of language as part of modernism in Hebrew letters merits a separate study.

Haskalah aspired to resuscitate Judaism by reconstructing it from within. The *maskilim* were apprehensive that if they did not address the lurking, pressing problems confronting Judaism, it would not survive; thus the very existence of the Jewish people would be in jeopardy. The Italian *maskil* Eliyahu Morpurgo expressed this feeling best in an article about the need to introduce changes into Jewish education. He called on rabbis and community leaders to adopt *Haskalah* and modern education, "before your children's light is extinguished and before your feet stumble upon the mountains of twilight".[116]

Hebrew modernity is the awareness of change permeating *Haskalah* literature in the 1780s. It is manifested in the consciousness of the urgent need to implement such change. It is further expressed by the strong faith in the *Haskalah*'s ability to

---

[115]These genres are discussed in my book, cited in the previous note.
[116]*Hame'asef*, III (1786), p. 131, based on Jeremiah XIII: 16.

realise this change in order to save Judaism from extinction. All of this was expressed in *Haskalah*'s endeavour to revive Judaism and to re-define it, as seen above in the cited texts of *Haskalah*.

Joel Brill's epigrammatic observation regarding the old and the new – tradition and modernity – reverberates now as it did some two hundred years ago:

> Do not cast your eye upon the glass whether it is new or old
> Set your eye at the wine itself
> For there is new [glass] full with old
> Yet also old, where there none to drink.[117]

---

[117]J. Brill, 'Al Na Bakos', *Hame'asef*, V (1789), p. 1.

Thus Spoke Herzl:
Nietzsche's Presence in Herzl's Life and Work

While working on my forthcoming book for Cornell University Press, *Nietzsche in Zion*, I uncovered material that sheds new light on Nietzsche's impact on the father of political Zionism. The material convinced me that research on Nietzsche's intellectual influence on Zionists has failed to deal with his spiritual impact on Herzl.[1] Indeed the vast and, until now, completely unexplored material testifies to Herzl's strong attraction to Nietzsche. This essay will present this material and will explicate several Nietzschean ideas that are essential in fully appreciating Herzl's *Weltanschauung* and his motives for embarking on the Zionist enterprise. It will also try to fill in a gap in modern Jewish and Zionist history. The prevalent accounts of Zionism – especially those written in Israel – emphasise the national and social objective of Zionism: the establishment of a Jewish egalitarian society in Palestine. They tend to disregard some of its more implicit ideological aspirations, such as the attempt to foster a new image of an "authentic" Jew. This essay will throw these ideas into sharper relief.

The main pretext for ignoring any trace of Nietzsche's influence on Herzl is a diary entry of 28 June 1895,[2] in which Herzl reported a conversation with Leo Franckel:

> I explained to him why I am against the democracies. "So you are a disciple of Nietzsche?" he said. I: "Not at all. Nietzsche is a madman. But one can only govern aristocratically." Franckel: "How are you going to establish this aristocratic government? I: "There are all kinds of ways. Here is just one example ... The French

---

[1]Some historians reject the possibility of Nietzschean impact on Herzl, though without exploring carefully the latter's library and his personal letters and diaries. See, for example, Steven E. Aschheim, who in his otherwise instructive book, *The Nietzsche Legacy in Germany, 1890–1990*, Berkeley 1992, p. 104, claims that "Herzl himself [unlike Nordau] paid little attention to Nietzsche, referring to him only once, as a 'madman' ". He repeats this claim on p. 204 of his 'Nietzsche and the Nietzschean Moment', in *LBI Year Book XXVII* (1992), pp. 189–212. In his defence it might be argued that he was not the only one to make this controversial claim. Steven Beller, *Herzl*, London 1991, p. 70, also claimed that "despite the fact that Herzl fervently believed in the power of the human will, he thought Nietzsche's ideas to be the thought of a madman". This statement, however, does not prevent Beller from claiming that "Herzl, as Arthur Hertzberg has accurately pointed out, manages to combine the two poles of nineteenth-century thought, Marx and Nietzsche", *ibid.*, p. 48. Beller refers to Hertzberg's quite penetrating, though too general, observation that "[the] Nietzschean strain in Herzl is more personal ... As a 'Nietzschean', Herzl came to Zionism in order to change history", Arthur Hertzberg, *The Zionist Idea*, New York 1959, pp. 47–48."
[2]Both Aschheim and Beller quote this entry. See above.

Academy constitutes an elective aristocracy ...".
Franckel: "That way everything can be arranged *collectivistically*." I: "By no means.
The *individual* must not be done away with."[3]

This passage illuminates the paradox that, whereas Nietzsche's philosophy
focuses on the individual and is mainly concerned with enticing the reader to
embrace subjective patterns of personal authenticity,[4] Zionism and its main ideo-
logues were concerned with establishing a Jewish state and securing a safe shelter
for the Jewish people; many of its original leaders were also preoccupied with the
founding of socialist-collectivist institutions in *Eretz Israel*. The scholar dealing
with Nietzsche's impact on Zionist leaders, writers and thinkers must therefore
provide a reasonable explanation of how such a profound fascination with
Nietzsche was possible at all.[5] In Herzl's case the paradox is only an apparent
one: he rejected the collectivist ideology and elsewhere vehemently objected to
socialism.[6] Unlike his Eastern European Jewish followers, who were profoundly
influenced by Socialist and Marxist trends, Herzl's socio-political thought was
primarily based on the liberal British paradigm and was open to the needs of individuals to express their personal identity. As Jacob Talmon perceptively
observed, "Herzl's Jewish nationalism derives from liberal and individualistic
categories of thought".[7]

Herzl's Jewish state purported to foster an authentic identity for those Jews
who were unwilling to assimilate or to embrace Christianity. Indeed, Herzl was
interested in the effect of Zionism on the individual, and with the ways in which
Zionism might shape, change and even create a new image of the Jew who, by
embracing a new ideology and a secular way of life, could substitute traditional
religious terms of reference. This existential relevance of Nietzsche to
"marginal" Zionist intellectuals[8] was one of the crucial factors that attracted
Herzl to his thought.

---

[3] *The Complete Diaries of Theodor Herzl*, ed. by Raphael Patai, transl. by Harry Zohn, 5 vols., London
1960, vol. I, p. 191. This edition does not include Herzl's diaries from 1882–1887, which are found in
Theodor Herzl: Briefe und Tagebücher, ed. by Alex Bein, Hermann Greive, Moshe Schärf, Julius H.
Shoeps, vol. I, Berlin 1983, pp. 585–648 (hereafter *HBT*). When necessary, I have translated from
this edition.
[4] Jacob Golomb, *Nietzsche's Enticing Psychology of Power*, Ames–Jerusalem 1989, esp. pp. 267–331; *idem*,
In Search of Authenticity from Kierkegaard to Camus, London 1995, pp. 68–87. Cf. *idem*, 'Nietzsche on
Authenticity', in *Philosophy Today*, vol. 34 (1990), pp. 243–258.
[5] See the forthcoming Hebrew collection of essays ed. by Jacob Golomb, *Nietzsche in Hebrew Culture*,
Jerusalem.
[6] See, for example, Herzl's letter to Georg Brandes of 13 January 1897, in which he exclaims: "*Ich bin
kein Sozialist*", quoted in Klaus Bohnen, 'Ein Dialog als Provokation. Unveröffentlichter Briefwechsel
zwischen Theodor Herzl und Georg Brandes', in *Emuna: Israel Forum*, No. 4, (1977), pp. 1–8, and in
HBT, vol. IV, 1990, p. 178.
[7] Jacob L. Talmon, 'Types of Jewish Self-Awareness: Herzl's *Jewish State* after Seventy Years (1896–
1966)', in *idem*, *Israel among the Nations*, London 1970, pp. 88–127. Cf. Ernst Ludwig Ehrlich, 'Liberal-
ismus und Zionismus', in *Theodor Herzl Symposion*, Vienna 1996, pp. 35–43. Robert Weltsch also understood this so far rather neglected ramification of the Zionist revolution: "Zionism is a personal
task imposed upon every individual ... the whole life of the young Jew undergoes a transformation."
Robert Weltsch, 'Theodor Herzl and We', in *The Young Jew Series*, 2, (1929), pp. 24, 23.
[8] See Jacob Golomb, 'Nietzsche and the Marginal Jews', in *idem* (ed.), *Nietzsche and Jewish Culture*,
London–New York 1997, pp. 158–192.

The English translation of the phrase Herzl used to describe Nietzsche – "madman" – is undoubtedly derogatory. If this is what Herzl meant, it is reasonable to believe that he took this phrase from the unbridled attack on Nietzsche penned by his close friend and collaborator, Max Nordau. In his *Degeneration*, Nordau wrote: "Nietzsche was obviously insane from birth, and his books bear on every page the imprint of insanity."[9] Herzl's German original reads, "Nietzsche ist ein Irrsinniger".[10] An Anglo-German dictionary of 1900 defines *Irrsinn* as "mentally deranged", indicating an actual mental illness and not therefore what Germans, referring to a state of mind or behaviour, would call *verrückt or wahnsinnig* (crazy).[11] Nordau uses this latter term when he writes that Nietzsche is "von Geburt an *wahnsinnig* und seine Bücher tragen auf jeder Seite den Stempel des *Wahnsinns* [my emphasis]".[12] In contrast to Nordau, Herzl's term quite correctly describes Nietzsche's mental state in 1895. Nietzsche spent the last ten years of his life (1890–1900) suffering from a general paralysis, some of its symptoms being prolonged unconsciousness and mental derangement. It is therefore quite reasonable to assume that Herzl meant to imply that he could not follow a man who was then (at the time of Herzl's conversation with Franckel) functioning neither mentally nor physically. If correct, this shows that Herzl was quite aware of Nietzsche's state and was far from deriding him as Nordau had.[13] The number of volumes by Nietzsche found in Herzl's private library begs the question that if it is true that Herzl believed Nietzsche was a "madman" why would he have read so much of his work? There is enough historical evidence to contradict the view that Herzl was ignorant of Nietzsche's philosophy and legacy, that the issue is not whether Herzl knew Nietzsche's work but how could he not have known it.

I. THE HISTORICAL TESTIMONY

Most of the books from Herzl's home in Vienna are located in Jerusalem, in the Central Zionist Archives and in the Herzl Museum, where they are exhibited to the public in a reconstruction of his study. Here, even a cursory glance discloses Herzl's preference for philosophy in general and Nietzsche in particular.[14] Amost all of Nietzsche's works are to be found in Herzl's library and their expensive leather covers suggest the owner's willingness to invest significantly in Nietzsche's writings.[15]

---

[9]Max Nordau, *Degeneration*, Lincoln and London, 1968, p. 453.

[10]*HBT*, vol. II, p. 206.

[11]See also the editors' note on this passage in *Theodor Herzl: Briefe and Tagebücher*, which stresses that Nietzsche was at that time "in geistiger Umnachtung", meaning, as I do here, that he was temporarily mentally deranged, *HBT*, vol. II, p. 803, note 22.

[12]Max Nordau, *Entartung*, Berlin 1893, 2nd ed., vol. II, p. 363. This volume can be found in Herzl's library in the Herzl Museum, Jerusalem.

[13]See chapter 2 of my forthcoming *Nietzsche in Zion*, Ithaca – London.

[14]Among the items found in Herzl's private library (in the Central Zionist Archives and in Herzl's Museum) are a heavily scored French edition of Francis Bacon; a four-volume edition of Herder; Kant's *Kritik der reinen Vernunft*; five volumes by Lessing; volumes by Rousseau; and a twelve-volume edition of Schopenhauer, the second volume of which is missing.

[15]Herzl's private library contains the following of Nietzsche's works: *Jenseits von Gut und Böse*; *Zur Genealogie der Moral*; *Morgenröte* ; *Also sprach Zarathustra*; *Die fröhliche Wissenschaft*; *Die Geburt der Tragödie*:

Several primary and secondary sources unmistakably indicate Herzl's familiarity with Nietzsche. Herzl paid him considerably more attention than is usually assumed by most scholars.[16] One of the major primary sources consists of references to and quotations from Nietzsche in Herzl's own diaries, letters and other writings. In a letter to an unidentified theatre critic, Herzl invokes Nietzsche's "explanation" of the desire to be "modern": that "man does not yet know what a comedy he has to play for the new acquaintance".[17] Another reference appears in a letter Herzl wrote to Nordau in which he apologises for not including Nordau's essay on Nietzsche in the recent *Neue Freie Presse*.[18] Nordau's article eventually appeared after the philosopher's death, on 3 October 1900.[19] It is significant that, under Herzl's editorship, seven consecutive issues of the *Neue Freie Presse* were dedicated to obituaries of Nietzsche. Another remark on Nietzsche appeared in the final sentence of Herzl's essay 'Frankreich im Jahre 1891': "However, the 'European man', the new type that Nietzsche sees coming closer and closer to us, is still a very remote figure."[20] The Nietzschean ideal of a "new European man" is close to Herzl's ideal of a "new Jew", and the close resemblance between these types should not surprise us. Neither should Herzl's belief that the "new man" was more likely to materialise as the "new Jew" in Zion, that is, as the creative and authentic Jew who, like the Nietzschean *Übermensch*, would become the father of his own destiny and would freely shape the course of his life.

During Herzl's early days at the University of Vienna, it was not necessary to have studied Nietzsche directly to be permeated with his thought, given that he was quoted, reviewed, and discussed in every circle (especially within the circles to which Herzl belonged) and in every journal and newspaper.[21] Nietzschean

---

oder *Griechentum und Pessimismus*; *Der Fall Wagner*; *Menschliches, Allzumenschliches*; *Unzeitgemässe Betrachtungen*; and *Götzen-Dämmerung*.

[16]For example, one of the most authoritative biographers, Alex Bein, makes no mention of Nietzsche in his *Theodor Herzl: A Biography of the Founder of Modern Zionism*, transl. by Maurice Samuel, New York 1970 (1934 in German). Those few scholars who mention Nietzsche *vis-à-vis* Herzl do so in descriptions of the *Zeitgeist* in which Herzl operated and which was greatly shaped by Nietzsche's ideas. Even Jacques Kornberg's *Theodor Herzl: From Assimilation to Zionism*, Bloomington 1993, pp. 52, 56, 109, refers to Nietzsche only in context of racism and the nationalist atmosphere prevailing in Vienna in general and among the students of the University of Vienna in particular. (See also *idem* "Theodor Herzl: a re-evaluation", *Journal of Modern History*, 52 (1980), pp. 226–252). Kornberg is too eager to blame Nietzsche for fostering German nationalism and antisemitism, mentioning him with "Wagner and Heinrich von Treitschke" (p. 56) and overlooking the simple fact that Nietzsche opposed German nationalism. Cf. the forthcoming *Nietzsche: the Godfather of Fascism?*, ed. by Jacob Golomb and Robert S. Wistrich, Princeton.

[17]"*Nietzsche würde das vielleicht damit erklären, dass man noch nicht weiss, welche Komödie man dem neuen Bekannten vorspielen soll.*" (letter written in Vienna, 22 April 1891), *HBT*, vol. I, p. 438.

[18]Nordau's manuscript arrived only after the issue of *Neue Freie Presse* had gone to print. Letter written in Vienna, 14 September 1900, *ibid.*, vol. VI, p. 38.

[19]Max Nordau, 'Individualismuß, Solidarismuß', in *Neue Freie Presse* (hereafter *NFP*), No. 12971, pp. 1–3.

[20]Herzl, *NFP*, No. 9823, 31 December 1891 (my translation).

[21]Significantly also in Zionist newspapers and those directed at wider Jewish intellectual circles. It is worth mentioning the German-Jewish newspaper *Ost und West: Illustrierte Monatsschrift für Modernes Judentum*, Berlin. Its editors, Hermann Cohen, Ludwig Geiger, Otto Warburg, Martin Buber, Max

concepts and ideas were widespread among Jewish intellectuals and philoso-phers. If some of them were rather critical of his teaching, they were at least familiar with it and were even emotionally stirred by it, as Nordau's case clearly indicates.

In his freshman year at university, Herzl joined the *Akademische Lesehalle*, the original membership of which comprised an eclectic mix of German, Slav, Hun-garian, and Jewish students. It was politically neutral and dedicated mainly to social and cultural affairs.[22] From the start Herzl was active on committees, organised literary meetings, and participated in debates. Moreover, although he was not a formal member, Herzl was quite close to some of the leading members of the Pernerstorfer circle, which comprised some of Nietzsche's first influential admirers and which was nicknamed "Nietzsche's Society in Vienna".[23] To the Pernerstorfer circle belonged the socialist leader Viktor Adler, Hermann Bahr, the Austrian socialist Heinrich Braun, Joseph Ruben Ehrlich (the journalist and Austrian writer who wrote an idolising letter to Nietzsche in April 1876 and signed it as "his most devoted admirers in Vienna"),[24] Max Gruber, Siegfried Lipiner – writer and friend of Nietzsche, Joseph Paneth (who corresponded intensively with Nietzsche) and Arthur Schnitzler.[25] It is absurd to assume that while these men were preoccupied with Nietzsche, Herzl was not.

Two main paths, delineated by Nietzsche, led out of European culture. One was the Zionist project to form an authentic Jewish identity. The other was the Nietzschean attempt to become what Nietzsche had called "a free spirit" like the one embodied in the person of Stefan Zweig, the most marginal Jew who main-tained Nietzsche's cultural ideal of a Europe without national borders until his suicide in Petropolis, Brazil, in 1942.

Nordau and Jakob Wassermann, belonged to the intellectual Jewish elite. It was not a coincidence that the first issue included a manifesto that shaped Western-European Zionism and that was heavily coloured by Nietzschean motifs: Martin Buber, 'Jüdische Renaissance', *Ost und West*, vol. I (1901), pp. 7–10. For analysis of this essay, see Golomb 'Nietzsche and the Marginal Jews', pp. 169ff.

[22]This contrasted to the pan-German *Leseverein der deutschen Studenten*, founded in 1872, which became the famous *Albia* that was disbanded by the authorities following antisemitic riots. Details of this affair are provided by Ernst Pawel, *The Labyrinth of Exile: A Life of Theodor Herzl*, New York 1980, pp. 46–48, 66, 70. In spring 1881, Herzl joined this duelling fraternity but the following year he distanced himself from the *Albia*'s social life and stopped contributing to its official publication. The fraternity at the time still included a fair number of Jews and ex-Jews among both student members and alumni.

[23]Cf. William J. McGrath, 'Student Radicalism in Vienna', *Journal of Contemporary History*, 2 (1967), pp. 183–201; *idem*, 'Mahler and the Vienna Nietzsche Society', in *Nietzsche and Jewish Culture*, pp. 218–232.

[24]*Kritische Gesamtausgabe, Nietzsche Briefwechsel (KGB)*, ed. by Giorgio Colli and Mazzino Montinari, Berlin–New York, 1975–1993, vol. II 6/2, p. 314.

[25]In *HBT*, vol. I, Herzl refers extensively in several letters to Arthur Schnitzler. Herzl's copy of Schnitzler's *Frau Bertha* contains a personal dedication by the author, dated April 1901. Nietzsche's impact on Schnitzler is documented in my essay 'Nietzsche and the Marginal Jews', esp. note 21 on pp. 181–182. Cf. Olga Schnitzler, *Spiegelbild der Freundschaft*, Salzburg 1962, for a description of the close relationships Schnitzler had with Herzl, Hermann Bahr, Brandes, Karl Kraus, Jakob Wasser-mann and Gerhart Hauptmann – all of them enthusiastic admirers of Nietzsche.

Stefan Zweig, whose admiration of Nietzsche is well known,[26] met Herzl in
1900, when the latter was the feature editor of the *Neue Freie Presse*. Zweig
claimed that it was because of Herzl, who made an enduring impression on him
and who accepted his first essay for publication,[27] that he became a writer.[28] The
friendship lasted until Herzl's death. During their numerous meetings, however,
Herzl never succeeded in enlisting Zweig, the *"Europäer"*,[29] to the Zionist cause,
though in 1901 Zweig contributed several poems and one story to the main
Zionist organ, *Die Welt*.[30] In an autobiographical note, Zweig wrote of Herzl:
"I had read all his essays ever since I had been able to read at all; they served to
educate me, and filled me with admiration for his culture."[31]

Herzl aspired to be more than just a serious connoisseur of philosophy. In his
Jugendtagebuch 1882–1887,[32] he refers to Plato, Aristotle, Kant, Feuerbach, Schopenhauer, Fichte, Hegel, Schelling and Brentano. In a diary entry of 21 March
1897,[33] he notes that he had sent his book, *Der Judenstaat*, to Herbert Spencer with
a short letter in which he calls Spencer a "great spirit". It appears that Herzl, not
satisfied to approach only businessmen and politicians, was eager to ensure the
support of the leading philosophers of his time for his Zionist project. Elsewhere
in his diary, he is critical of Rousseau,[34] and he quotes works by Kant, More and
Voltaire that can be still found in his private library.[35] Leon Kellner claims that
after Herzl had moved with his family from Budapest to Vienna in 1878 and had
begun studying at the law faculty of Vienna University, he attended Brentano's
lectures on practical philosophy.[36] Sigmund Freud, whose interest in philosophy

[26]See, for example, Stefan Zweig, 'Friedrich Nietzsche', in *Der Kampf mit dem Dämon*, Leipzig 1925,
pp. 231–322 (the second volume of his *Die Baumeister der Welt*,. transl. by Eden and Cedar Paul as
Master Builders, New York 1939, pp. 441–530); 'Nietzsche und der Freund' [Franz Overbeck], *Neue
Freie Presse* (Vienna), 21 December 1916, pp. 1–5, reprinted in *Insel Almanach auf das Jahr 1919*,
Leipzig, pp. 111–123 and in *Menschen und Schicksale*, ed. by Knut Beck, Frankfurt am Main 1981,
pp. 114–123. See also *idem* 'Mater Dolorosa: Die Briefe von Nietzsches Mutter an Overbeck', *Neues
Wiener Tageblatt*, 21 December 1937, pp. 2–3, reprinted in *Zeiten und Schicksale. Aufsätze und Vorträge
aus den Jahren 1902–1942*, ed. by Knut Beck, Frankfurt am Main 1990, pp. 317–324. On Zweig's re-
lationship with Nietzsche, see Golomb, 'Nietzsche and the Marginal Jews'.
[27]Zweig's first story, *'Die Liebe der Erika Ewald'*, was published in the *Neue Freie Presse* in 1901. Another,
'Die Wanderung' was published on 11 April 1902. (I am indebted to Sylvia Patsch from ORF, to Prof.
Salaquarda from the University of Vienna and to the Jewish Museum, Vienna, for this information.)
[28]Stefan Zweig, 'König Der Juden: The Man of Letters and the Man of Action', in *Theodor Herzl: A
Memorial* (hereafter *Herzl Memorial*), ed. by Meyer W. Weisgal, New York 1929, pp. 55–62. See also
Friderike M. Zweig, in *Stefan Zweig: Eine Bildbiographie*, Munich 1961, p. 16, who reports on Zweig's
attitude towards Herzl; Otto Zarek, 'Stefan Zweig – A Jewish Tragedy', in Hanns Arens (ed.),
Stefan Zweig: A Tribute to his Life and Work, London n.d., pp. 178–191.
[29]Hence the title of Zweig's last autobiographical work: *Die Welt von Gestern: Erinnerungen eines Euro-
päers*. Cf. Harry Zohn, 'Stefan Zweig, the European and the Jew', *LBI Year Book XXVII* (1982),
pp. 322–336.
[30]Cf. Tovia Preschel, 'Stefan Zweig and *Die Welt*', in *Herzl Year Book*, vol. IV, 1961–1962, pp. 305–
308. On Zweig's ambivalent attitude towards Judaism, see Stephen H. Garrin, 'Stefan Zweig's
Judaism', *Modern Austrian Literature*, vol. XIV (1981), pp. 271–290.
[31]Stefan Zweig, 'König der Juden', in *Herzl Memorial*, p. 56.
[32]*HBT*, vol. I, *Theodor Herzl Briefe und Autobiographische Notizen 1866–1895*, pp. 647–648.
[33]*Theodor Herzl Zionistisches Tagebuch 1895–1899*, vol. II, Berlin 1983, p. 492.
[34]*ibid*, p. 76.
[35]*ibid*., p. 131; Paris, 16 June 1895, p. 143; Paris, 19 June 1895 , in which Herzl refers to Thomas
More's *Utopia*; p. 220; 22 July 1895, in which he quotes (in French) from Voltaire's *Candide*.
[36]Leon Kellner, *Theodor Herzls Lehrjahre (1860–1895)*, Vienna–Berlin 1920, p. 25.

is well known, also attended Brentano's lectures while studying medicine at the university as a contemporary of Herzl. It may well be that these two great Jewish thinkers met – they even for some time lived in the same street – without, however, becoming friends.[37]

The publication of the first edition of Nietzsche's collected works in 1892 was a major intellectual event in the German-speaking world.[38] Two years later, a study of Nietzsche by his close friend Lou Andreas-Salomé was published in Vienna,[39] and in 1895 Nietzsche's sister, Elisabeth Förster-Nietzsche, published the first volume of her biography of her brother.[40] The same year saw the publication of Nietzsche's most provocative works, *The Antichrist* and *Nietzsche contra Wagner*.

In his capacity as the chief features editor of the *Neue Freie Presse*, Herzl was exposed to many articles on Nietzsche[41] and collaborated with many Nietzschean writers and intellectuals. He became editor of the newspaper in September 1895, having worked on it for four years. Nietzsche's fame began to soar in the early 1890s, when Herzl was the newspaper's Paris correspondent, and the period between 1895 and 1902 is the most crucial for determining Nietzsche's impact on Herzl.

Herzl was operating within an intellectual *Zeitgeist* permeated by Nietzsche's presence. However, the most conclusive first hand evidence that Herzl was familiar with Nietzsche's work and thought is provided by Herzl's cousin, the playwright and novelist, Raoul Auernheimer (1876–1948). Auernheimer, who also specialised in literary journalism, was associated together with Herzl with the "Young Vienna" circle, to which Arthur Schnitzler, Hermann Bahr and Stefan Zweig also belonged.[42] In the memorial book to Herzl he claimed that his cousin was not a "causeur" at all as far as his literary writings are concerned

[37]See, for example, some of the essays in *Nietzsche and Depth Psychology*, ed. by Jacob Golomb, Weaver Santaniello and Ron Lehrer, Albany 1999.

[38]Under the title *Gesamtausgabe*, ed. by Peter Gast, Leipzig 1892 ff, and discontinued after volume V.

[39]Lou Andreas Salomé, *Friedrich Nietzsche in seinen Werken*, Vienna 1894 .

[40]Elisabeth Förster-Nietzsche, *Das Leben Friedrich Nietzsche*, 2 vols., Leipzig 1895–1904.

[41]Ola Hansson, 'Nietzscheanismus in Skandinavien', No. 9031, 15 October 1889 (3 pp.); Malvida von Meysenbug, 'Erinnerungen an Friedrich Nietzsche', No. 10349, 16 and 17 June 1893; *ibid*, 'Aus meinem Tagebuch über Nietzsche', No. 10469, 14 October 1893 (3 pp.); Dr Karl Federn, 'R.W. Emerson und Friedrich Nietzsche', No. 10732, 10 July 1894, (4 pp.); Moritz Necker, 'Nietzsche's Jugend', No. 11182, 11 October 1895 (3 pp.); Dr Ludwig Stein, 'Friedrich Nietzsche als 'philosphischer Klassiker', No.11803, 3 July 1897 (3 pp.), No. 12934 from 26 August 1900 contains two articles on Nietzsche's death (by Hugo Ganz and Ludwig Stein); Karl Bulcke, 'Die Trauerfeierlichkeit am Sarge Friedrich Nietzsche's', No. 12938, 30 August 1900; Georg Brandes, 'Friedrich Nietzsche 1844–1900', No. 12952, 14 September 1900 (2 pp.); Malvida von Meysenbug, 'Der erste Nietzsche', five articles between 18 and 28 September 1900, *Neue Freie Presse*, Nos. 12956–60 and 12966; Gabriele Reuter, 'Eine Nietzsche-Büste', 31 October 1901 in *NFP*. To these we must add also Nordau's article on Nietzsche (see above). Richard Frank Krummel, in his *Nietzsche und der deutsche Geist: Ein Schrifttumsverzeichnis der Jahre 1867–1900*, Berlin 1974, p.24, refers also to one of the first articles ever published on Nietzsche in the *Neue Freie Presse*: Karl Hillebrand, 'Über historisches Wissen und historischen Sinn', *NFP*, Nos. 3542 and 3544, 7 and 9 July 1874. Krummel, however, omits Nordau's article on Nietzsche of 3 October 1900, *NFP*, No. 12971.

[42]Cf. Harry Zohn, 'The Herzl Diaries: A Self-Portrait of the Man and the Leader', *Herzl Year Book*, vol. II, New York 1960, pp. 207–215.

but was actually "a philosopher. In his reading of Nietzsche, that destroyer of old conventions and of all the false romanticism of his age, he may have encountered the passage that contemptuously addresses the feuilletonists as the "court fool" of His Majesty the Public".[43] Previously he had compared Herzl's literary style to Nietzsche's:

> Following upon the classical age of the Viennese arts piece, he opened its modern period, and the rosy light of this dawn shimmered through his youthful prose. He who wrote it has not only, like the other feuilletonists, read Schiller, Heine and all the French memoirists, but was also familiar with Nietzsche, whose influence inaugurated a new era in German publicistic writing; and he had, perhaps, only half consciously, absorbed his style . . .[44]

These remarks from an expert who was so intimate with Herzl's work and background corroborate the opinion of many of Herzl's readers that he was, like Nietzsche, a master of the aphorism. It is no coincidence that some of Herzl's editors could not resist naming several collections of his aphorisms with titles that bear a direct association with Nietzsche's *Thus Spoke Zarathustra*[45].

This historical part of the article would be quite meaningless were we unable to discern certain Nietzschean imprints on Herzl's writings and life. The second part of this essay is therefore dedicated to a theoretical analysis of Nietzsche's impact on Herzl's thought and life, on his plays and "philosophical" and psychological stories.

II. FROM THEATRE TO AUTHENTICITY: HERZL'S TRANSFIGURATION FROM THE *GRENZ-JUDE* OF *DAS NEUE GHETTO* TO ZIONISM

Herzl's references to Nietzsche show an interesting, though hardly surprising, pattern. While engaged in his search for personal authenticity and identity, that is, while still living in the quasi-limbo of the suspended identity of a *Grenz-jude*, Herzl evoked Nietzsche's name and played with philosophical ideas using ironic posture, dissimulation and distance. These years – from the beginning of his studies at Vienna University to his growing preoccupation with Zionist activity and movement – were marked by "marginality". Herzl, at that time, was still the *Grenzjude* who had sought success and fame within European culture by trying to distinguish himself in *belles-lettres*. At the same time Herzl disguised his personal search for authentic identity with irony and with what Nietzsche called in his *Die fröhliche Wissenschaft* the attitude of the *gaya scienza*. And indeed, with *Der Judenstaat* in 1895, and the crystallisation of his identity as a secular Zionist Jew, Herzl epitomised the class of the German-speaking

[43]Raul Auernheimer, 'Uncle Dori: Memories of a Cousin and a Literary Colleague', in *Herzl Memorial*, p. 35.
[44]*ibid*. Cf. also a chapter of Herzl's autobiography translated by Harry Zohn as 'Beard of the Prophet', in *Herzl Year Book*, vol. VI, New York 1964–1965, pp. 69–76.
[45]See, for example, the Hebrew collection of Herzl's aphorisms entitled: *Ko Amar Herzl (Thus Spoke Herzl)*, ed. by Herzl's secretary, A. Pollack, and printed in Tel Aviv [Palestine] in 1940.

Jews labeled *Grenzjuden*.[46] These highly creative and prominent Jewish women and men of letters (including Else Lasker-Schüler, Arthur Schnitzler, Jacob Wassermann, Lion Feuchtwanger, Stefan Zweig, Alfred Döblin, Franz Kafka, Theodor Lessing, Kurt Tucholsky, Walter Benjamin, Carl Sternheim, Karl Kraus, Ernst Toller and Sigmund Freud) were "marginal Jews" in that they had lost their religion but had not assimilated into secular German or Austrian society.[47] For some, hatred of their ancestral roots led to self-destruction and breakdown. These individuals lacked an identity: they rejected any affinity with the Jewish community but at the same time were not welcome among their non-Jewish contemporaries. Jakob Wassermann describes them from within as "religiously and socially speaking floating in the air ... the physical ghetto has become a mental and moral one".[48]

Herzl sought to liberate himself from such a "new ghetto". According to Gershom Scholem, these marginal Jews, "because they no longer had any other inner ties to the Jewish tradition, let alone to the Jewish people ... constituted one of the most shocking phenomena of this whole process of alienation".[49] Yet despite their desperate attempts to be accepted by the Germans as German, most recognised the traumatic truth that "for a Jew, especially in public life, it was impossible to disregard the fact that he was a Jew".[50] Herzl understood this and wrote bitterly that all the political experience he had gained while working as a correspondent for the *Neue Freie Presse* in France had been for nothing. "It will only benefit those who have the opportunity to enter political life. But for myself? A Jew in Austria!"[51]

The first secular Zionists, among them Herzl himself, found many aspects of Nietzsche conducive to their aspirations. Intellectual Zionists realised that they had been suffering from a divided personality, that as marginal Jews they were torn between their secular aspirations and their own Jewish religious tradition. As such they could not obtain an harmonious self; and living on the margins of all identities, neither could they behave authentically nor feel authentic. Sensitive and proud, Herzl could not bear such a schizoid existence. Assimilation brought him only to a dead end. His inability to reject his Jewish origins altogether, his unwillingness to return to the old ghetto with its Orthodox Jewish lore, and above all his proud rejection of the fact that he did not belong on equal terms within Gentile Viennese society had a destructive potential (as suicides testified, notably the one committed by Otto Weininger) and drove him to find a solution.

[46]See Solomon Liptzin, *Germany's Stepchildren*, Philadelphia 1944; Frederic V. Grunfeld, *Prophets without Honour*, London 1979.
[47]Of course, with regard to Eastern European Jewry, the case is essentially different. They were not "marginal" from the perspective of their Jewish culture. Western Jews, especially German-speaking ones, wanted to assimilate into the main currents of secular German culture.
[48]Jacob Wassermann, *The Maurizius Case*, London 1930, p. 297.
[49]Gershom Sholem, 'Jews and Germans', *Commentary*, November 1966, p. 35.
[50]My translation from Arthur Schnitzler's *Jugend in Wien*, ed. by Therese Nickl and Heinrich Schnitzler, Vienna 1968, p. 328.
[51]Herzl's letter to Hugo Wittmann, dated 30 March 1893.

Initially, Herzl considered solving the problem of his own marginality by mass conversion to Christianity, in which he would help the Pope to conduct the conversion ceremony on the steps of St Stephen's Cathedral in Vienna.[52] Then he tried to assimilate completely into Austrian society, to follow in the footsteps of the best Viennese artists and playwrights without demanding a separate personal identity. During this period Herzl became part of the frivolous atmosphere of Vienna's *fin de siècle*, not merely as a passive spectator but as an active contributor. However, Herzl flinched from Vienna's stages even before the Dreyfus affair. In November 1894 he wrote *Das Neue Ghetto*.

Das Neue Ghetto is a semi-autobiographical play about lost honour, and more concretely, about the wounded honour of Jewish *Grenzjude* Dr Jacob Samuel, a lawyer in Vienna (like Herzl himself), who regained control over his life through a duel with an antisemite. The play describes the existential vulnerability of a *Grenzjude* who strives to overcome his marginality after realising that he had "betrayed his own self" since he made the Gentile world and his Gentile friends the sole focus of imitation and reference for shaping his own personal identity. This attempt to assimilate had not succeeded because his friend "leaves me and simply abandons me after I made him my example, absorbed his habits, have spoken his language, have thought his thoughts".[53]

Das Neue Ghetto expressed Herzl's realisation that assimilation was an illusion, and that Jews' estrangement from themselves was fruitless. The play's conclusion is that these Jews should authentically shape (without the Book of Books from the Old Ghetto) a new image of the Jew who is proud of his or her historical past and origins but will not necessarily express this identity by observing the traditional religious rites. *Das Neue Ghetto* was written before *Der Judenstaat*, hence its importance for Herzl's mission of attaining personal authenticity which required him to overcome his existential patterns of marginality. This was a stage of his transfiguration which exposed Herzl to an intensive and significant dialogue with Nietzsche through his literary writings. Fiction, according to Nietzsche and other more recent theorists of authenticity, is the most appropriate medium to express the subjective pathos of authenticity, which can neither be defined or communicated by direct language nor prescribed by rational persuasion.[54]

The play portrays three negative reactions to marginality: conversion to Christianity, as represented by Dr Bichler, who confesses that "nothing was

[52] In 1895 Herzl wrote in his diary: "About two years ago I wanted to solve the Jewish Question, at least in Austria, with the help of the Catholic Church. I wished to gain access to the Pope . . . and say to him: Help us against the anti-Semites and I will start a great movement for the free and honourable conversion of Jews to Christianity . . . The conversion was to take place in broad daylight, Sundays at noon, in Saint Stephen's Cathedral, with festive processions and amidst the pealing of bells. Not in shame, as individuals have converted up to now, but with proud gestures. . ." *The Complete Diaries of Theodor Herzl*, vol. I, p. 7; cf. Jacques Kornberg, *Theodor Herzl: From Assimilation to Zionism*, Bloomington 1993, pp. 115, 118–121.

[53] My translation from Act II, Scene VI. An abridged English translation (by Heinz Norden) of *The New Ghetto* appears in *Theodor Herzl: A Portrait for this Age*, ed. by Ludwig Lewisohn, Cleveland and New York 1955, pp. 152–193.

[54] On the intimate relations between fiction and philosophy in the existential philosophies of authenticity see Golomb, *In Search of Authenticity*, London–New York 1995, chap. 2.

solved this way"; the reaction of traditional Judaism, namely, to return to the old Ghetto with its traditional values and faith; and the popular reaction of the uneducated Jewish masses, symbolised by the crude figure of the stock-exchange Jew, Wasserstein, who expresses a shrewd adjustment to the prevalent antisemitic image of Jews as materialistic and greedy and therefore acts accordingly to amass a fortune since he "has to buy everything with money". This hard-working and despised Jew, however, recognises a fourth reaction to marginality: even if he claims that "everything revolves around money", he admits that honour is equally important. To Wasserstein, Jacob is far superior, an individual who "soars above us like a bird". Jacob, who transcends the existential limits of marginality over the walls of *Das Neue Ghetto*, becomes, then, a kind of a Nietzschean *Über-Jude*, or a new type of a Jew – the fourth, and only acceptable, solution to the problem of marginality, according to Herzl's narrative. Jacob resembles Zarathustra's eagle, the authentic and unique individual who does not belong to the herd but soars alone high above the new (and the old) ghettos. Jacob manifests many of the character traits and spiritual power with which Nietzsche endowed his authentic hero. Jacob is a master-figure who behaves nobly and proudly with no *ressentiment*. He despises the stock exchange but that does not lead him to shun Wasserstein, whom he prefers to Franz, the Gentile who "did not feel comfortable in the society of such people". "It is not his fault", Jacob claims, referring to Wasserstein's occupation. "It was not even nature that made us what we are, but history. It was your people who rubbed our noses in money – but now we are told to despise it."[55]

Jacob, like Nietzsche's Zarathustra, strives to create new norms and values. He seeks to form the "moral element" and embarks upon the journey of self-over-coming (*Selbstüberwindung*), or, more exactly, "overcoming" his old marginal self. He no longer wishes to live passively and reactively within Gentile history but prefers to initiate a new history – of his own making and for himself. Although at the beginning of his existential journey, at the stage of his assimila-tion, he internalises and imitates the behavioural patterns and ethos of his Gentile neighbours, this was, as he admits now to Franz, "only a transitory period on my way to becoming a free citizen". "Now I can continue my journey by myself", he says to Franz, thereby obeying Zarathustra's prescription that if his followers wish to stay loyal to his teachings, they must abandon him and go alone on their own ways, even if this meant attempting to overcome their master, as Jacob is trying to do *vis-à-vis* Franz and the Western European culture that had brought upon the Jews the unbearable predicament of marginality and estrangement.

However, is not Jacob's emphasis on the honourable duel an indication of his strong dependence on Gentile values? The dignity of human beings and their

[55]*ibid.*, p. 169. Nietzsche, after claiming that "perhaps the young stock-exchange Jew is altogether the most disgusting invention of mankind" asks his readers: "In spite of that, I should like to know how much one must forgive a people in a total accounting when they have had the most painful history of all peoples, not without the fault of all of us, and when one owes them the noblest man (Christ), the purest sage (Spinoza), the most powerful book, and the most effective moral law in the world." *Human-all-too-Human*, section 475 of *The Portable Nietzsche*, transl. by Walter Kaufmann, New York 1968, p. 62.

authentic spiritual power are not Christian inventions; as Nietzsche stressed, "freedom, pride and nobility"[56] are ancient Hebrew values. Hence Jacob returns here to the origins of personal power, pride and dignity. Nietzsche elevated these above the Christian values of pity, meekness, and humility. Likewise, Herzl does not seek to foster here a Christian European set of values but the free, powerful and creative individual capable of defining his own values and norms. It was this kind of honour that was prevalent within the old ghetto, the origins of which are to be found in biblical Zion.[57] In Nietzsche's *Zarathustra* the journey to personal authenticity, to the state of a "child's innocence", passes a second stage: that of the "lion" overcoming the hump of the "camel" which bears all the values and norms of the old tradition and teachings.[58] Although Herzl overcame most of the Jewish tradition, he (and his contemporary Western European Jews) were afflicted by the curse of marginality in the new ghetto, which prevented them from attaining genuine self-liberation. To overcome the agonies of such a marginality is for Herzl already a positive way out that will lead him to the third and more constructive stage of liberation of his self: Zionism.

Up to this point the play has not proposed a way out of the ghetto for the marginal Jew. There is an ellipsis in Jacob's final sentence before his death, and the outcome is destructive for someone who has dared to soar like an eagle over and above *Das Neue Ghetto*. For Herzl, this negation of the negation pointed to a concrete solution: a land in which the values according to which Jacob aspired to live by were originally manifested and genuinely invented for the first time. The journey towards personal authenticity will also include negative ramifications, according to Nietzsche's well-known statement: "If a temple is to be erected, *a temple must be destroyed*."[59] Interestingly, Herzl used almost the same version in *Der Judenstaat*: "If I wish to substitute a new building for an old one, I must demolish before I construct",[60] almost five years before Micha Joseph Berdyczewsky adopted this Nietzschean aphorism as an epigram for his polemical Hebrew-language essay.[61] Nietzsche propagated the dialectic of suffering under the dictum "What does not destroy me makes me stronger". Herzl's struggle was not waged with a sword but with words and with the exhausting political activity which eventually killed him, but not before liberating him from his most hated role – that of the despised *Grenzjude*.

---

[56]See, for example, his *Gay Science*, section 137; cf. Golomb, 'Nietzsche on Jews and Judaism', *Archiv für Geschichte der Philosophie*, 67 (1985), pp. 139–161; *idem*, 'Nietzsche's Judaism of Power', *Revue des études juives*, 147 (1988), pp. 353–385.

[57]Although Herzl incorporates into his play a short story about Moshe from Magenza, who functioned for Jacob as an exemplary figure and who behaved as authentically and humanly as a genuine *Mensch*, his humanity originated with the ancient Hebrews, though it was preserved within the Jewish tradition.

[58]The first part of *Thus Spoke Zarathustra*, in the chapter entitled 'On the three Metamorphoses', in *The Portable Nietzsche*, pp. 137–140.

[59]Nietzsche, *Genealogy of Morals*, second essay, section 24, in *Basic Writings of Nietzsche*, transl. and ed. by Walter Kaufmann, New York 1968, p. 531.

[60]Herzl, *The Jewish State*, transl. by Sylvie D'Avigdor, London 1936, p. 21.

[61]Micha-Joseph Berdiczewsky, 'Zikna ubaharut', [in Hebrew], in *Mimizrah Umimaarav*, vol. I, n.p. 1898.

The dialectic of suffering is expressed in another of Herzl's plays, *Solon in Lydien*.[62] This play, written in 1900, belongs to the Zionist period of Herzl's life, during which the Nietzschean motifs were not altogether discarded. The hero of this play is Solon of ancient Athens, who represents Herzl. When Eucosmos discovers a way to produce wheat without toil, Solon becomes worried. Solon, according to his declaration, "glanced beyond the veil that disguises things", and he seeks to expel or to kill Eucosmos because the latter's invention, the elimination of poverty and of existential anxiety, will bring about only chaos and the end of human culture. Solon claims that Eucosmos is striving to take from people "the most precious things they are blessed with – hunger" and as a result "the fundamentals of culture will disappear as well". Solon believed in the Nietzschean principle of the sublimation of Dionysian instincts through creative work.[63] As an echo of Nietzsche's statement about ancient Greeks and their culture ("How much did this people have to suffer to be able to become so beautiful!"), Herzl writes: "They need poverty! It urges them to create and invent . . . work flourishes sublimely to the level of art, as much as the thought about the private advantages of human beings is raised to the level of sublime philosophy."[64] Herzl mentions the ancient Greek god Apollo several times, thereby enhancing the impression that we have here the dramatisation of Nietzschean anthropological insights expressed in his *Birth of Tragedy* within the framework of an imaginary state, Atlantis (Zion?). In any case, it follows that Herzl's desperate search for personal authenticity and a unique identity did not take place in a vacuum but was pursued in an ambience saturated by Nietzsche's ideas.[65]

The Zionist movement, as envisioned by Herzl, was mobilised to encourage the creation of a new and unique (that is, authentic) image of the Jew in a society without God, dogmas, or "isms". This anti-dogmatic and Nietzschean libertarianism was wrongly regarded as shrewd pragmatism. Hence this examination of the father of political Zionism through the Nietzschean prism reveals the exciting historical experiment of fostering personal authenticity by creating it for the whole nation. This perspective stresses the fact that *Der Judenstaat* was not written solely as a reaction to the failures of emancipation and assimilation, but also as an attempt to provide a personal and constructive solution to the

---

[62]Herzl, *Philosophische Erzählungen* (hereafter *P.E.*), Berlin–Vienna 1919, pp.1–23. All translations from this volume are mine.

[63]On Nietzsche's psychological theory of sublimation and its impact on Freudian psychoanalysis see Golomb, *Nietzsche's Enticing Psychology of Power*, 1989, chap. 1.

[64]My translation. Nathan Rotenstreich realised that in this play "Herzl regarded the emotional state of radical despair, whether individual or collective, and the objective state of affliction, as powers capable of motivating individual and collective action", Rotenstreich, 'On the Groundwork of Herzl's Ideas', in *Herzl Year Book*, vol. III, 1960, p. 167. The exact content of this "radical despair", however, which strongly motivated Herzl and his Jewish friends, was the predicament of marginality.

[65]The biographical circumstances of Nietzsche's emergence as the theorist of personal authenticity were strikingly similar to those of Herzl and the other *Grenzjuden*. He grew up in a rigidly devout home to a Lutheran pastor father and undertook a speedy and painful process of secularisation which left him without roots, identity or nationality. Nietzsche always felt estranged in his homeland and bitterly attacks the Germans, even spreading the myth of his Polish origins. Cf. Walter Kaufmann, *Nietzsche: Philosopher, Psychologist, Antichrist*, Princeton 1968, p. 288.

syndrome of marginality that at the individual level was the most hideous symptom of this failure.

In 1891 Herzl had already referred to the " 'European man', the new type that Nietzsche sees coming closer and closer to us".[66] This "type" showed Herzl the way to the "new Jew". According to Herzl's view, such a type was still "a very remote figure".[67] The European Jew (and Herzl is thinking here primarily of himself) cannot shape his character in Europe, despite Nietzsche's plea for the Jews to become the spearhead of a new cultural Renaissance, because Europe did not want Jews within it. From this perspective, Jewish emancipation had failed completely. Herzl's acute personal experience of marginality and estrangement prevented him from adopting Nietzsche's European ideal, and he sought to transfer it to more fruitful soil. Herzl believed that the proud, free, creative and authentic Jew would be more likely to evolve in Zion, on virgin ground unstained by what his friend Max Nordau called European "degenerated culture". Thus, under Nietzsche's influence, Herzl arrived at the ideal of the authentic human being and sought to apply it first of all to himself and then to other European *Grenzjuden*. The Zionist solution was more authentic than the continuation of assimilation, dissimulation and disguise, and prolongation of the dangerous game of being a "free spirit" in Europe when European national and antisemitic repression had inflicted upon the Jews the crisis of identity that had brought many of them, including Herzl himself, to the desperate search for personal authenticity.

It is therefore possible to delineate the profile of Nietzsche's impact upon Herzl according to his existential stages of assimilation, marginality and Zionist identity. If we adopt Nietzsche's formula for authenticity, then Herzl "becomes what he is"[68] by overcoming what he was not: Herzl was not an Orthodox Jew; he was not a Christian; and finally, he was not a marginal Jew. He had overcome these potential sources of identity until he became what he wanted to be: a free secular Zionist and an authentically creative Jew, who proudly belonged to his people according to his famous definition of the Jewish nation in *Der Judenstaat*: "a historic group with unmistakable characteristics common to us all".[69] Only the Zionist journey would assist the *Grenzjuden* in overcoming the syndromes of marginality and split personality; and only Zionism, Herzl believed, would shape them into *individua* and help them to overcome their socio-psychological *dividua*. Nietzsche claims that in the prevalent European morality "one is splitting one's essence and for part of it one sacrifices all the rest", namely, European man "treats himself not as *individuum* but as *dividuum*".[70] These words are especially applicable to the complex existential reality of the German-speaking marginal Jews who were obliged to suppress some of their most vital elements. By doing so they were prevented from attaining personal harmony and from

---

[66]See note 20.

[67]*ibid.*

[68]This is the subtitle of Nietzsche's autobiography, *Ecce Homo*, transl. by W. Kaufmann, New York 1969.

[69] Herzl, *The Jewish State*, p. 21.

[70]Nietzsche, *Human, All Too Human*, transl. by R.J. Hollingdale, Cambridge 1986, p. 42.

spontaneously expressing their essence, as Herzl, the herald of Jewish authenticity, claims: "The very act of going this way will change us into different people. We regain once more our inner unity that we have lost and together with it we also gain some character, namely our own, not the false and adopted character of the marranos."[71] By the time he left Paris in 1895, Herzl had abandoned his dream of becoming a famous playwrite or writer and had ceased to live in quasi-limbo, or in his own words, in the "new ghetto". With his *Der Judenstaat*, Herzl committed himself to a Jewish-Zionist identity. Thereafter, as in the case of Martin Buber after his arrival in Palestine, Nietzsche ceased to be the catalyst in Herzl's life: his function as a temporary scaffold for climbing to the highest ladder of genuine authenticity had been fulfilled. The posture of ironic disguise and narrative distance is quite conspicuous in the *Philosophische Erzählungen*,[72] the name Herzl insisted on calling his collection of fictive short stories – a fact that points out his aspiration to be considered as a thinker, not only as a capable minor journalist.

As the *Philosophische Erzählungen* show, Herzl was attracted by Nietzsche's genealogical method of "unmasking" the human psyche. Nietzsche used this method to attain selfhood by freezing the motivation to uphold any religious, metaphysical or social ideologies that had previously provided ready-made and inauthentic identities. Following the death of the Father – the Jewish God – and the decline of the authority of the father, who was responsible for bringing his sons into the schizophrenic state they now found themselves in in the typical Jewish family, the *Grenzjuden* (and Herzl) sought to establish an identity which would draw its content not from faith and tradition but solely from their own mental resources. Nietzsche encouraged this process by showing how one could liberate oneself from dependence on habits of thought and conventions. Yet Herzl had to come to terms with his own paralysing human-all-too-human elements. Nietzsche becomes a model of such self-knowledge since he delineates the basic conflict between the negative, weak, reactive, sick and decadent and the positively powerful, vital, active and dynamically creative expression of personal spiritual power.[73] Such neurotic fluctuations between two mental kinds of pathos are frequently described by Herzl: "I do not contemplate death, but think of life full of heroic deeds that overcome anything low, wild and complicated that perhaps once was within myself ... in these days I am frequently afraid that I will completely lose my mind."[74] Nietzsche assists Herzl in expressing the gap between the optimal authentic power of the *Übermensch* and the depth of weakness that looms below the human-all-too-human, which must be overcome if the authority and dignity of the free Jew is to be attained. Indeed, careful reading of Herzl's writings shows that most of the traits he attaches to the marginal Jews in the Diaspora belong to the patterns of negative power ascribed by Nietzsche to the "morality of the slaves" and the "crowd", whereas the main objective of Herzl's

[71] My translation of a speech before the Israeli Union in, *Thus Spoke Herzl* [in Hebrew], p. 30.
[72] See note 62.
[73] For details see Golomb, *Nietzsche's Enticing Psychology of Power*, part III.
[74] *Thus Spoke Herzl*, pp. 15–16.

Zionist revolution is to strengthen and solidify the powerful patterns of "nobility" and "morality of the masters" (to use enticing and provocative Nietzschean terms). Herzl's disdain for the masses (especially the Jewish uneducated masses) and his will to transform these into something more sublime and noble is well known. His revolution aimed to foster anew in the life of the marginal Jew moral patterns and qualities once prevalent among the ancient Hebrews: "In order to remain in its place and also to wander the race should be first improved. It is necessary to strengthen its power for war, to instill in it the joy of working and all good virtues."[75]

The Zionist revolution would enable the "new Jew" to decide whether to go to Zion or stay in Europe. However, for such a mental transfiguration Herzl needs some form of psychology, which Nietzsche called the "bitter psychology" that unmasks those weaknesses which must be overcome. Herzl frequently conducts these psychological examinations: "I found out that the great are petty, as petty as myself." However, Herzl's "petty self" aspired to attain the greatness of a Bismarck, who was, like Nietzsche, an "active psychologist who read individual souls as well as of the soul of the crowd".[76] Such a reading of the human soul is impressively manifested in the *Philosophische Erzählungen*. These stories were written a little while before and after Herzl's transfiguration to a new figure of a Zionist Jew and, actually the very act of writing them, assisted him in this painful process of self-transfiguration. Indeed, these stories express some Nietzschean characteristic notions:

1. The search for an authentic existence beyond the dissimulation and deceit of some of the heroes and heroines of these stories, as well as that of their author.
2. The transfiguration of one's character from its low level of passive and feeble existence to active, proud and vital patterns.
3. Insights into the nature of human beings and their human-all-too-human elements – insights which purport to assist in the transfiguration of the self.

It is worth pointing out that not only does the content of these stories bear a distinctive Nietzschean imprint but also that they possess an impressionistic and unsystematic form, with a flow of spontaneous associations that are more concerned with aphoristic brilliance than with the systematic consistence of the expressed content. All these literary characteristics of Herzl's writings corroborate Raul Auernheimer's observation that Herzl owed a large debt to Nietzsche's style and literary genius[77].

More importantly however, the content of these stories also bears a considerable Nietzschean imprint. One of the stories, 'The Mind Reader', depicts the search for authenticity and the rejection of falsehood. The story, written in 1887 at the beginning of Herzl's Zionist period, is a kind of Nietzschean thought-experiment. It plays with a man who "sees the falseness everywhere", that is, who observes the shifts from *echt* (genuine) patterns of behaviour to *unecht* ones.

---

[75] *ibid.*, p. 21
[76] *ibid.*, pp.108, 89
[77] See Auernheimer, 'Uncle Dori', in *Herzl Memorial*; *ibid.*, 'Beard of the Prophet', in *Herzl Year Book*, vol. VI, note 44.

This example was influenced by Nietzsche's hypothetical construct of *homo Heraclitus*, who

> did not possess the power of forgetting at all and who was thus condemned to see everywhere a state of becoming: such a man would no longer believe in his own being, would no longer believe in himself ... and would lose himself in this stream of becoming: like a true pupil of Heraclitus, he would in the end hardly dare to raise his finger.[78]

Similarly, Herzl's hero claims that "it is a disaster to know how to read our thoughts". The term *echt*, as used by Herzl, is synonymous with Nietzsche's term for authenticity, *Wahrhaftigkeit*. However, fully authentic life is not possible in European society, as Nietzsche had also claimed, locating his hero of optimal authenticity, Zarathustra, in a cave, far removed from human society.[79] In contrast to Nietzsche's hero, the hero of Herzl's story has "social inclinations" and is married (though, like Herzl, not happily). Herzl, who at that time was also preoccupied in finding a political solution to the problem of Jewish authenticity, could not entertain Nietzsche's idea of the splendid isolation of the authentic *Übermensch*, and he had not severed authenticity so radically from the social sphere. The problem of identification between authentic and inauthentic personalities, and the problem of recognising authentic human beings – both problems that had not found an adequate solution in Nietzsche's thought – were solved by Herzl through a kind of *deus ex machina* since he believed that "in principle, every human being is born a good person, and becomes untruthful only in due course".[80]

But Herzl, unlike Nietzsche, does not attempt to uncover the various mechanisms which change us into inauthentic beings and he does not aspire to answer the crucial question asked by the Scottish poet Edward Young: "Born originals, how comes it to pass that we die copies?"[81] It is significant that during his intensive search for a political solution to the Jewish Question Herzl was also deeply preoccupied with the issue of authenticity that had bothered him as a *Grenzjude*. He deals with this existentially crucial problem by a conscious use of Nietzschean formulae. For example, the key formula of Nietzschean authenticity: "How does one become what one is?", is phrased by Herzl in 'The Mind Reader' in a similar version: "This is the question of experiences that makes me what I am."[82] Herzl adopts also the psychologising attitude when he embarks, with the hero of his story, onto "all the ugliness and filth that stirs and lives in the soul".[83] These Nietzschean motifs reappear in two other stories in this "philosophical" collection: 'Die Garderobe' and 'Pygmalion', but this time another Nietzschean *leitmotif* is added: the belief in our ability to transfigure ourselves so that we become

---

[78]Friedrich Nietzsche, 'On the Uses and Disadvantages of History for Life', in *Untimely Meditations*, transl. by R.J. Hollingdale, Cambridge 1983, p. 62.
[79]Cf. Golomb, 'Nietzsche on Authenticity', in *Philosophy Today* vol. XXXIV (1990) pp. 243–258.
[80]Author's translation from the Hebrew edition.
[81]Edward Young, The Complaint, or Night Thoughts on Life, Death and Immortality (1742–1744), vol. IV, p. 629.
[82]Author's translation.
[83]Author's translation.

what we are. A fateful change takes place in the heroine behind the mask of make-up in the theatre, in 'Die Garderobe', and she becomes "completely different from what she was". In 'Pygmalion' it appears that Herzl, like Nietzsche and other existential thinkers such as Sartre, does not believe in a rigid and permanent human essence. Instead, he adopts the dynamic-evolutionary view of the organisation and creation of personality. The impresario of the story, who represents Herzl himself, undergoes a significant transformation from playwright to political director on the stage of the reborn nation. In other stories, estrangement is prevalent, and their wandering heroes manifest syndromes of marginality and fluctuate from one definition of identity to another. Herzl himself, from the dubious status of an assimilatory *Grenzjude,* underwent "a fateful shift" (like some of the heroes of his stories) and "a full transfiguration of the spirit" (as Nietzsche would put it), to become a proud statesman with a definite vision. However, for such a transfiguration Herzl had to choose a firm anchor to create his identity in his writings and political activity.

Such an aesthetic staging of identity is conducted by Herzl under the ironic disguise of the figure of the impresario, the narrator and hero of the 1888 story, 'Der Aufruhr von Amalfi'. Herzl's theatrical experience is applied in this story to arouse the dormant Jewish masses for a significant move from the new and old ghettos. "The real impresario is capable of staging street-shows"[84] and political theatre, in which Herzl famously excelled. Thus the impresario of this story, who adopts a condescending, paternalistic and aristocratic tone towards the "mob", arranges an ecstatic mass orgy in which the "mob" wants to tear the impresario apart as a result of "the crazy and wild drives that erupted".[85] Nietzsche's descriptions of the "Dionysian barbarian ... mixture of sensuality and cruelty"[86] are echoed here, as are his insights about our human-all-too-human souls. Herzl deals in this story with the lowest driving forces: unrestrained greed. He uncovers these regions of the psyche and immediately translates them into political activity. His writings become a kind of a psychological laboratory whose findings he applies in life itself: "The market place in Amalfi is the world and this ugly riot-life."[87]

Herzl also expresses the inner pathos of his protagonists, their reflections and introspection in their attempts to comprehend their "roots" and their existential experiences. In 'Die schöne Rosalinde', Herzl presents the extreme experience of a character who sees his own skeleton and draws existential conclusion from this encounter with finality and death.[88] Another Nietzschean motif appears here: overcoming sickness to attain psychologically penetrating insights. "The sickbed made more than one into a philosopher", Herzl claims[89] in a truly

---

[84]Herzl, *P.E.*, p. 91.
[85]*ibid.*
[86]Nietzsche, *The Birth of Tragedy*, p. 39.
[87]Herzl, *P.E.*, p. 93.
[88]Herzl, 'Die schöne Rosalinde', p. 177. Karl Jaspers referred to *Grenzsituationen* (boundary situations), the vital importance of which in matters of authenticity are discussed in Golomb, *In Search of Authenticity*, chap. 2.
[89]Herzl, *P.E.*, p. 179.

Nietzschean spirit, which is also expressed in his reference to the "birth-pangs of a self-knowledge" by a character who wishes to return from his inauthentic "escape" from himself.[90] In this context Herzl mentions the search by the "modern man" for "a remedy" and meaning, and reflects about "philosophy" and "true poetry" and about the disabling effects of reflection with which Nietzsche has dealt in most of his writings, especially in 'On the Uses and Disadvantages of History for Life'.

The "small letters" of the human-all-too-human soul, our most secret driving forces, appear as a motto in 'Eine gute Tat'. The motto reads: "You have done a good deed, be careful to conceal its reasons."[91] This aphorism and the theme of the story shows a deep suspicion of our conscious motives for actions. The motif finds its expression in the aphorism that so excited Freud who, like Herzl, was deeply influenced by Nietzschean psychology:[92] " 'I have done that', says my memory. 'I cannot have done that', says my pride, and remains inexorable. Eventually – memory yields."[93] This last motif recurs in several stories, conspicuously in 'Die Raupe', in which the hero, Fritz, reads a chapter from Hyppolite Taine's *De l'intelligence* on the "metamorphosis of the caterpillar into a butterfly".[94] 'Das Wirtshaus zum Anilin', written the same year *Der Judenstaat* was published, expresses the belief that a new image of man can be created and shaped by sublimating despair.[95] This typically Nietzschean story focuses on the sublimation of "the most offensive material"[96] where Herzl intentionally uses chemical terms which lie at the root of the concept of *Sublimierung*, and the existential significance of death for self-overcoming on the way to greatness since "one cannot reach philosophical height if one had not squarely faced death".[97]

Herzl deals in most of these stories with the "attractive power of the abyss" and returns to the fundamental idea of his play *Solon in Lydien*, namely that "we human beings, cannot live without distress".[98] These Nietzschean motifs of sublimating our more basic drives to create artistic artefacts of aesthetic and cultural value and of the "metaphysical comfort" of art (the leitmotif of Nietzsche's *Birth of Tragedy*) reappear in the story 'Sarah Holzmann' about "a little Jewess" who sings and plays music out of sublimation of her sufferings since "our best achievements were reached out of our torments".[99] This idea is

---

[90] *ibid.*

[91] *ibid.*, p. 221.

[92] See Golomb, *Nietzsche's Enticing Psychology of Power*, pp. 62–67.

[93] Nietzsche, *Beyond Good and Evil*, section 68, in *Basic Writings of Nietzsche*, p. 270. Herzl could also have employed this aphorism for 'Sarah Holzmann', *P. E.*, p. 50, in which he states that "the motives for our actions are sometimes quite odd and most of the time very gloomy". These actions are rooted mainly in the unconscious, as he indicates by quoting the term *unbewußt* from a poem by Friedrich Rückert, *ibid.*, p. 52.

[94] *ibid.*, p. 214. Stefan Zweig wrote a dissertation on Taine's philosophy at the University of Vienna in which he enthusiastically referred to Nietzsche's ideal of an authentic life (cf. Golomb, 'Nietzsche and the Marginal Jews', p. 162). Herzl's reference to Taine indicates his familiarity with the philosophical publications of his time.

[95] Herzl, *P. E.*, p. 264.

[96] *ibid.*, p. 263

[97] *ibid.*, p. 264.

[98] 'Die Heilung vom Spleen', in *ibid.*, p. 205.

[99] 'Sarah Holzmann', in *ibid.*, p. 45.

nicely put by Nietzsche: "The beast that bears you faster to perfection is suffering."[100] The conclusion of this story is presented directly by the narrator, who confesses: "Art has always been a great comforter in my life, because it is capable of turning pain into flowers that give joy to other people, especially to those who are troubled and oppressed."[101] This remark is clearly autobiographical. Herzl, with his own troubled personal life, sublimates his marginality through creative writing and overcomes it through political activity. The main aim of this activity is to provide the right conditions for the creation of a new image of a Jew who sublimates his sufferings as the marginal "slave" to become a "master".

Although Herzl cites Schopenhauer, "the great pessimist",[102] in 'Die Güter des Lebens', written in 1898, he emphatically rejects Schopenhauer's metaphysical pessimism. Instead he opts for Nietzsche's optimistic *Weltanschauung*. Indeed, the first sentences echo formulations found in Nietzsche's 'Schopenhauer as Educator'. In this one of his *Untimely Meditations,* Nietzsche demands from us that we should be "responsible to ourselves for our own existence; consequently we want to be the true helmsmen of this existence and refuse to allow our existence to resemble a mindless act of chance".[103] Herzl follows this prescription: "No longer does chance toss us this way or that. We ourselves are at the helm of the ship."[104] Nietzsche raises in his essay penetrating existential questions – "Why do I live? What lesson have I to learn from life? How have I become what I am?"[105] – which Herzl tries to answer: "I know what I am after, though I don't know whether I'll reach it. Even so, I've already been raised above the vulgar throng, because I have this consciousness of self."[106] Nietzsche deals with the obstacle to authenticity, namely how to arrive at the nucleus of one's personality beyond the layers of cultural and social conditioning. To overcome these, Nietzsche does not employ self-analysis and direct introspection because, as a sober psychologist, he does not consider them reliable, but adopts the indirect way to self-knowledge:

> Let the youthful soul look back on life with the question: what have you truly loved up to now, what has drawn your soul aloft, what has mastered it and at the same time blessed it? Set up these revered objects before you and perhaps their nature and their sequence will give you a law, the fundamental law of your own true self.[107]

This is exactly what Herzl does in his literary-philosophical experiment about the pre-arranged meeting of four friends twenty years after they graduated, each having followed his own path to find some meaning and value in life. Three of them depict their disappointments in the materialistic value of wealth, in the shallow and illusory value of honour, and in the emptiness of the values of family

---

[100]Nietzsche, 'Schopenhauer as Educator', in *Untimely Meditations,* p. 158.
[101]Herzl, 'Sarah Holzmann', in *P.E.*, p. 55.
[102]Herzl, 'The Good Things of Life', in *HPA*, pp. 121, 129.
[103]Nietzsche, 'Schopenhauer as Educator', op. cit., see note 78, p. 128.
[104]Herzl, 'The Good Things', op. cit. p. 120.
[105]Nietzsche, 'Schopenhauer as Educator', p. 154.
[106]Herzl, 'The Good Things', op. cit., p. 120.
[107]Nietzsche, 'Schopenhauer as Educator', op. cit., p. 129.

and subsistence. Only the fourth friend, who asked at the start of his existential journey for "that which fulfills a man"[108] succeeds in gaining the "internal results of the success" in "this philosophical wager" in which appearances and external layers are illusions and there are no guarantees for attaining a truthful life or a meaningful answer to the existential question of "why" and "what for". He, Wilhelm, like Herzl himself "when he finished his studies at the university tried for a while to be a writer". He went "on trips to England and France" to learn "about modern movements of social welfare".[109] This was undoubtedly Herzl's hint about the nature and the objectives of his Zionist project. Important, however, is the fact that in sharp contrast to Schopenhauer's view of "blind Will" and its manifestations as the pure expressions of evil, Herzl emphasises the sober optimism that values the very act of willing and of hope as ends in themselves since belief in the future "is the only thing in which one is never disappointed".[110] Thus Herzl adopts the attitude expressed in most of Nietzsche's writing, that the path is the goal. A similar idea is presented here by Herzl: only Wilhelm, who sought an existential goal that cannot be fully reached, namely personal authenticity, attained his goal. This existential insight is expressed politically by Herzl's famous claim: "Zionism is the Jewish people *on the road*."[111] Herzl, who according to the popular simplistic perception was considered to be a "romantic dreamer" or "a naïve prophet", appears here as a cautious, realistic optimist.

Although Herzl ends most of these stories with moralistic lessons, we cannot avoid the impression that the writer is floating, as it were, above Nietzschean insights and is not seriously involved with them. He is flirting with Nietzsche, but, in contrast to Stefan Zweig for example, he has not been able to maintain a firm alliance. It is likely that Zionism, which engrossed Herzl during the writing of these stories, and which successfully sealed his troubled journey to shape his own authentic identity, is what prevented him from becoming seriously engaged with the psychological *fröhliche Wissenschaft*. Thus his distance from Nietzsche was actually an indication of the philosopher's positive impact on Herzl who, as a genuine "impresario" or composer of his own life, managed to transfigure it, and in doing so attain his own authentic identity. It may be that Herzl was even more optimistic than Nietzsche. Perhaps Nietzsche's optimism was too weak and restrained for Herzl. We should not forget that Herzl sought to advance the Jewish people and their culture to the sublime achievements represented in 'Die Güter des Lebens', in which he expresses his enthusiasm for "our great cultural achievements. For we live in a time that reminds one of the glorious age of the Renaissance and the Reformation".[112]

Was not Nietzsche's scepticism towards such technological and cultural

---

[108]Herzl, 'The Good Things', op. cit., p. 121.

[109]*ibid.*, p. 129.

[110]Herzl, 'The Good Things', op. cit., p. 129. Cf. a statement in which he explicitly admits that he is fed up with Schopenhauer's philosophy: "The beauty no longer attracts my heart. The world for me is no more appearance but a will.", *Thus Spoke Herzl*, p. 48.

[111]Herzl, 'The Good Things', op. cit. p. 36.

[112]*ibid.*, p. 128.

"progress" the main factor behind the cooling of Herzl's attraction to a thinker who had been so formative in shaping his world-view? In fact, the common opinion that Herzl believed unreservedly in progress and in the "heaven" that science and technology would bring to humankind and to Zion is far from exact.[113] In a fable on Zionism which is like 'Das lenkbare Luftschiff [The Dirigible Airship]', one of his "technological" stories, Herzl tempers his enthusiasm for this revolutionary invention. Employing a Nietzschean tone, he asserts that "people are not worthy of flying. As they now are – crawling is still good for them".[114] There is therefore a good chance that they will misuse this invention for evil deeds and thereby "bring new forms of misery".[115] He repeats his warning against technological progress elsewhere: "The scientific revolutionaries prepare the salvation from the known distresses thereby immediately instigating new miseries."[116] It appears that Herzl's faith in technological progress stemmed solely from pragmatic Zionist needs and that, like Nietzsche, he harboured no illusions about it. Such an attitude is incompatible with the optimistic outlook of someone who unreservedly believed in Enlightenment, progress, education, human reason and the moral improvement of humankind resulting from the advancement of science. However, it seems that despite these sober reservations about our human-all-too-human nature and about the increasing gap between ever-improving technological knowledge and deteriorating morality, an element of optimism does appear, since these technological inventions will bring "an improvement in the welfare and moralities" of humankind.[117] This Nietzschean optimism clashes with his metaphysical doctrine concerning the conservative and static elements of the "eternal recurrence of the same" expounded in his later work. Herzl's optimism is tempered by the human-all-too-human nature that could turn technological and scientific progress into a moral nightmare.

It seems that Herzl accepts this technological advancement as a hard necessity out of the sober and affirmative Nietzschean attitude of *amor fati*, for "there is no way to salvation but by giving up what is already lost". This development therefore "cannot be restrained and halted",[118] and Herzl pragmatically sought to harness the technological progress and the positive potential of 'Das Automobil'[119]. As a genuine liberal pragmatist, Herzl sought to use technological inventions for the well-being and freedom of the individual. (This is the motif of his story about 'Radfahren'.[120]) But Herzl is well aware of Enlightenment flaws and of the price to be paid for it, hence his cautious and sometimes ironic attitude. This irony reaches a pinnacle in his story 'Das Automobil', written in 1899: "The machine has, as it were, the capacity to be improved, which cannot be said with the same

[113]For example, David Ben-Gurion's statement that Herzl "had faith in science and technology" requires serious reservation. See his preface to *Theodor Herzl: A Portrait for this Age*, op. cit., p. 14.
[114]Herzl, *P.E.*, p. 38.
[115]*ibid.*
[116] Herzl, *Thus Spoke Herzl*, p. 88.
[117]*ibid.*
[118] Herzl, 'Der sterbende Fiaker', *NFP*, 17 April 1898.
[119]Herzl, 'Das Automobil', in *NFP*, 6 August 1899.
[120]Herzl, 'Radfahren', *NFP*, 1 November 1896.

certainty about the living creatures."[121] Here, Herzl ironically terms the crisis of modernity, pace Hobbes, *"Bellum omnium contra omnibus"*.[122] Given all this, one can certainly detect that Herzl's psychology softened his pragmatic "technological" inclinations. "How quick becomes our driving ... how slow is our wisdom", he declares in a Nietzschean aphorism characteristic of that period of his life during which he began his transfiguration from "caterpillar" to authentic "butterfly", from marginality to Zionism.[123] Under Nietzsche's influence, Herzl downgrades ideas of Enlightenment and progress. This influence increased even further because Nietzsche's psychology enables him to understand one of the most despicable phenomena from which marginal Jews, Herzl among them, suffered: namely antisemitism and its analogue, Jewish self-hatred.

In the second part of *Genealogie der Moral*, in which Nietzsche deals with the phenomena of *ressentiment* and *Verinnerlichung*, he argues that the powerful masters are responsible for the phenomenon of "internalisation", in which most of man's instincts are turned "inward" against "man himself"; they evoke in the weak the feeling of *ressentiment* which characterises the first stage of the "slave morality", becoming "bad conscience" in the second stage, when the "instinct for freedom [is] pushed back and repressed ... [and is] finally able to discharge and vent itself only on itself".[124] As a result, the intimidated individual becomes a schizoid personality engaged in constant internal strife. This exposition was also applied by Herzl to the antisemite, who is a weak and psychologically unstable individual with the character of a "slave". Antisemitism as a phenomenon can be elucidated with reference to the psychological patterns of the weak and impoverished personality described in Nietzsche's major writings, beginning with *Die fröhliche Wissenschaft*. Lacking personal power, and as a result of *ressentiment* and mental impoverishment, the antisemite is dependent upon certain external surroundings for self-determination. He needs acts of violence and cruel exploitation of others to enhance his feeble sense of power.[125] He is a vengeful and reactive person who uses his hatred out of fear, to attain some security and self-identity.[126] It follows that the antisemite is actually the "slave" and not the "master". This insight provided Herzl with the conceptual framework to understand the mental mechanism that gives rise to antisemitism. Equally importantly, he used it to grasp the roots of his own self-hatred: "There is no other nation but the Jewish People about which so many wide-spread prejudices are being told. Indeed, due to our historical distresses we have become so depressed and broken-hearted that we ourselves repeat these prejudices and begin to believe them as they do."[127]

---

[121]Herzl, 'Das Automobil', op. cit.

[122]*ibid.*

[123] *ibid.*

[124]Nietzsche, *On the Genealogy of Morals*, transl. by Walter Kaufmann, in *Basic Writings of Nietzsche*, note 59, Second Essay, Section 17.

[125]Nietzsche, *Die fröhliche Wissenschaft*, section 359.

[126]*ibid.*, section 379.

[127]Herzl, *Thus Spoke Herzl*, p. 18. The documentation illustrating Jacques Kornberg's claim that Herzl internalised prevalent antisemitic views shows the depth of Herzl's self-hatred (Cf. note 52 above.);

Already in his *Jugendtagebuch 1882–1887,* Herzl analyses the antisemitism of
Dühring's *Die Judenfrage.*[128] He employs a Nietzschean psychological dissection
of the motives for Dühring's antisemitism, describing him as a weak person with a
"slave's mentality", vengeful and frustrated because of his personal failures: in
short, as a man driven to antisemitism by the instinct of *ressentiment*: "This professor, who was expelled from his teaching position, is overwhelmed by a revengeful
and impotent rage."[129] On the next page, Dühring is compared to a "dismissed
servant".[130] He and other antisemites are afraid of Jewish competitors; hence
they want them "out!",[131] acting hypocritically like the "Jesuiten".[132] Already
in 1882 (the year he wrote this note) Herzl describes Dühring's personality and
his outlook in distinctly Nietzschean terms.[133] Herzl also employs Nietzschean
psychological tactics that can be summed up as "Show me who your enemies
are and I will tell you who you are", and which derive from the hatred of antisemites some positive conclusions about the Jewish people: "We are hated by no
lesser degree also because of our virtues than because of our vices", for "our
national personality is famous for its glory in history and despite all the humilia-
tions it is too significantly high to ask for its disappearance".[134] Instead, despair-
ing at pervasive antisemitic sentiments, Herzl suggests a proud inversion of
values and calls upon his brothers: "The nickname *Judenjungen* was so far an
insult. Reverse the order and it will become a term of honour: *Junge Juden.*"[135]
And I would add "new Jews" who, following Nietzsche's inspiration, dared to
embark on a brave journey for the sake of their transfiguration. Interestingly,
Herzl does not discuss this issue in religious terms – this cannot be explained
solely by the historical fact that Viennese antisemitism in Herzl's time was
driven more by racial-biological motives than by religious ones. Herzl does not
refer to Judaism in his attacks against the antisemites because he has lost his religious faith. However, it was Nietzsche, the most famous God-slayer of the time,
who, with Spinoza, legitimises Jewish atheism and sheer immanence devoid of
transcendental and divine intervention.

One of the basic intuitions of Nietzsche's thought is the concept of complete
immanence, formulated in sections 108–125 of *Die fröhliche Wissenschaft.* For
Nietzsche, transcendental entities do not exist; there is no "pure reason", no
other world, no domain different from, or superior to, our own. After the death
of God, one has to adopt for oneself the formerly divine responsibility for originat-
ing truth. The absence of a "pre-established harmony" between our cognition

---

see Ritchie Roberston, 'The Problem of Jewish Self-Hatred in Herzl, Kraus and Kafka', *Oxford German Studies,* 16 (1985), pp. 81–108.

[128]Eugen Dühring, *Die Judenfrage als Racen-, Sitten- und Culturfrage,* Karlsruhe 1881.

[129]Herzl, *Jugendtagebuch 1882–1887,* in *HBT,* vol. I, p. 611.

[130]*ibid.,* p. 612.

[131]*ibid.,* p. 615.

[132]*ibid.*

[133]See Nietzsche's critique of Eugen Dühring, in his *Jenseits von Gut und Böse,* p. 204; *idem, Zur Genealogie der Moral,* second essay p. 11; third essay p. 14, p. 26.

[134]Herzl, *Thus Spoke Herzl,* pp. 26, 24.

[135]*ibid.,* pp. 33–34.

and reality allows us to shift our emphasis to the creation of ourselves. This outlook was the most relevant philosophical message for the marginal Jews in general and for Herzl in particular.

For religiously uprooted Jews in the midst of secularisation, the problem of faith and direction was acute.[136] The simplicity and difficulty of Nietzsche's atheistic solution fascinated them. His call to embrace the idea of complete immanence and to do away with all gods appealed to marginal Jews who desperately needed support through the "twilight of the idols", the journey away from their ancient tradition. The impotence of metaphysics and religion felt so keenly by Jewish intellectuals at the turn of the century attracted them to Nietzsche, who posited the antithesis of salvation from the hardship of life: salvation from the transcendental doctrine of salvation. From this perspective, Nietzsche's existential tendency was similar to that of Spinoza.[137] Perhaps it was easier to identify with Spinoza, the most prominent early Jewish heretic, who had emerged from the tradition from which the *Grenzjuden* now felt completely estranged. But in the twentieth century it seemed far too late to turn to metaphysics, one of the "dead God's shadows", as Nietzsche put it. Nietzsche, who went radically beyond the "metaphysical crutch" and tried to inspire modern humanity to live creatively in a completely immanent world, had far greater appeal for modern secular Jews, and decisively won the ideological battle with Spinoza, at least in the minds of the marginal Jews. His model allowed liberation from the constraints of the various doctrine of metaphysical salvation and was therefore more relevant to their existential concerns than Spinoza's traditional model of salvation, which was powerless to sustain them.

However, the marginal Jews still fluctuated between these two models of Spinoza and Nietzsche. When Herzl became deeply involved in Zionist activity, Spinoza became the main philosophical focus of his outlook. This perhaps explains a short passage of praise that Herzl wrote about Spinoza while writing on Hess' book *Rome and Jersualem* in 1901.[138] In a piece written in 1902 Herzl returns to Spinoza, but this time ironically: "This Spinoza was a polisher of lenses. For a philosopher it is a quite appropriate and decent living."[139] Herzl's radical secularism suggests that he was closer to Nietzsche than to Spinoza. Herzl, like Nietzsche and unlike Spinoza – the "God-drunken sage", as Heine called him – believes in free will; and Spinoza did not stress the significant and

---

[136]"The problem of religion occupied me more than ever before ... it had to flow together with the basic questions of philosophy ... It is nonsense to say 'As God wills'. We will, God has to." Arthur Schnitzler, *My Youth in Vienna*, transl. by Catherine Hutter, New York, pp. 77–78. See also Wassermann's *My Life as German and Jew*, transl. by S. N. Brainin, New York 1933, p. 19, in which he confesses that "[t]he Jewish God was a mere shadow" for him.

[137]The Spinozistic model of salvation, which preferred a metaphysical and rationalistic *amor dei intellectualis*, was a worthy if anachronistic rival of the Nietzschean *amor fati*. See the chapter on Spinoza and Nietzsche in volume II of Yirmiyahu Yovel, *Spinoza and Other Heretics*, Princeton 1989; Joan Stambaugh, '*Amor dei* and *Amor fati*: Spinoza and Nietzsche', in James C. O'Flaherty (ed.), *Studies in Nietzsche and the Judaeo-Christian Tradition*, Chapel Hill 1985, pp. 130–141.

[138]Herzl, *Thus Spoke Herzl*, p. 54.

[139]Herzl, 'Die Brille', *NFP*, 28 November 1902. In this story the hero admits that with his age he became "honest with himself".

task-oriented activity sought by Herzl to attain the existential transfiguration of his nature and the nature of his people. Hence the critical tone of a diary entry of 1895, in which Herzl confesses: " My perception of God is a Spinozistic one and tends to the monistic philosophy of nature. However, Spinoza's substance is somewhat too inert [and] incomprehensible."[140] It is not only the fact that Herzl's private library contains not a single volume by Spinoza that leads me to claim here that his real influence on Herzl's *Weltanschauung* was much more negligible than that of Nietzsche's, but also Herzl's tendency to adopt the monumental historical consciousness that stresses decisive and heroic action – which has no definitive place in Spinoza's more static philosophy.

The traditional Talmudic patterns of learning of the "Old Ghetto" could not be incorporated within the assimilatory "New Ghetto". Marginal Jews therefore considered Orthodoxy, in the words of one of their eloquent spokesmen, Franz Werfel, to be "holiest fossilisation". Herzl's image of the "New Jew" demanded that the Jews overcome their rabbinical consciousness, around which they had structured their Jewish "antiquarian" (to use Nietzschean expression) identity in the Diaspora. Herzl stipulated that instead they adopt a "monumental" approach centred around the grandeur of their glorious days in ancient Israel. This incitement to "monumental history", which focuses on dramatic historical events, disregarding everyday life, is expressed in Nietzsche's essay 'On the Uses and Disadvantages of History for Life', in which he asserts that "monumental" historical consciousness lends support to creative and powerful individuals. It makes possible an emphatic identification with exemplary figures, and reassures those who aspire to greatness by showing them that "the greatness that once existed was in any event once *possible* and may thus be possible again".[141] The ambitious individual is encouraged to reject uncertainty and to pursue the path of glory and creation. Thus Herzl's project for the vital regeneration of the Jewish people, and his insistence that they recreate their ancient glory, is actually a faithful adoption of Nietzsche's attitude towards monumental history. Herzl, who returns "home", insisted upon returning to the historical sources of Jewish people: "Zionism is a return to Israel before the return to *Eretz Israel*", and "though we had to become a new people, we will not deny our ancient race".[142]

Nietzsche believes in the slow but more reliable process of education, cultivation and development of habits of thought and living, that is, in the creation of a "second nature". Here also lies the relevance of his teaching for Jews fluctuating between the traditional *cheder* and secular university education. To them, Nietzsche would recommend adopting monumental historical consciousness, which would assist them in withstanding the torments of transfiguration and help them to attain their glorious future.[143] The necessary condition for assistance from "monumental consciousness" is the aspiration and the will to make

[140]Herzl, *Theodor Herzl Zionistisches Tagebuch*, p. 241.
[141]Nietzsche, *Untimely Meditations*, p. 69 (emphasis in original).
[142]Herzl, *Thus Spoke Herzl*, pp. 13, 76.
[143]See Golomb, 'Nietzsche on Jews and Judaism', in *Archiv für Geschichte der Philosophie*, No. 67 (1985), pp. 139–161, and 'Niezsche's Judaism of Power', *Revue des études juives*, 147 (1988), pp. 353–385.

an imprint upon human history – or at least Jewish history. Herzl nurtured such a monumental mission and distinguished between mundane history and glorious history: "All these petty, unknown, noisy and insignificant men, who plot plots, overturn governments, and do not feel where they are directed . . . act in history . . . without any objective and choice."[144] Herzl stresses his own monumental vocation: "I feel within myself a great power which is ever-increasing toward the splendid mission."[145] He looks to the past of Jewish people through the selective prism of monumental consciousness and asserts that "owing to all our troubles we became decadent and the opposite of what we have once been: a nation gifted with tremendous talent, if during the last two thousands years we are being killed but cannot be completely annihilated".[146] He refers to heroic ages and seeks to revive their greatness: "I believe that on this earth will grow a generation of wonderful Jews. The Maccabees once more will come into being."[147] As the leader of a national revival of the glorious past, Herzl sees himself and his companions from the monumental historical perspective: "I will fight courageously. But all these who are accompanying me will all become historically great persons."[148] He reflects on the fate of an eminent leader *vis-à-vis* the pettiness of the masses: "The great men of spirit . . . are estranged from their people as well as the people are strangers to them . . . I know that the highest objective of democracy is to get rid of the singular individuals for the sake of the common good."[149]

He does not shun greatness because "he who seeks greatness is in my eyes a great man – not the one who has attained it".[150] He draws the strength for his determination and his aspirations for personal and national greatness from the splendid past of his people. Zionism is a political-practical materialisation and revival of this monumental past: "I am not presenting before you a new ideal; on the contrary it is a very old one. This is the idea that dwells in each of us, it is as ancient as our people, who never have forgotten it."[151] Therefore "we need Maccabees who know how to work: spiritual and manual work".[152] Indeed, the provision of role models is, for Nietzsche, the main function of monumental consciousness for the active and ambitious man, "the man of deeds and power, for him who fights a great fight, who needs models, teachers, comforters and cannot find them among his contemporaries".[153]

Martin Buber argued that two thousand years in the Diaspora had forced the Jews to transform their physical energy into purely spiritual energy.[154] This

---

[144]Herzl, *Thus Spoke Herzl*, pp. 83–84.
[145]*ibid.*, p. 16.
[146]*ibid.*, p. 18.
[147]*ibid.*, p. 72.
[148]*ibid.*, p. 106.
[149]*ibid.*, pp. 92, 87.
[150]*ibid.*, p. 92.
[151]*ibid.*, p. 31.
[152]*ibid.*, p. 7. Herzl identified with another leader of ancient Israel, Moses, about whom he planned to write "a biblical drama". *ibid.*, p. 109.
[153]Nietzsche, 'On the Uses and Disadvantages of History for Life' in *Untimely Meditations*, p. 67.
[154]Martin Buber, 'Jüdische Renaissance', *Ost und West*, vol. I, Berlin 1901, pp. 7–10.

affected their alienation from nature and a loss of balance between their physical and spiritual being. Buber called upon modern Jews to liberate themselves from "fettered spirituality[*unfreie Geistigkeit*]" and regain a "completely harmonious sense of living". This call for de-spiritualisation of Jewish life (shared by Herzl) also echoes Nietzsche's teachings.

In *Die Geburt der Tragödie* (which, as we have seen, Herzl read quite closely) Nietzsche claimed that the dominance of the Apollonian-rational element over Dionysian drives diminished the vitality of human creative powers. This spiritual asceticism, he claimed, is caused by excessive repression of instincts and "spiritualisation (*Vergeistigung*)".[155] To reverse these destructive tendencies, Nietzsche advocates a return to the vitality of the senses and a full sensual life. Marginal Jews, acutely aware of their anomalous existence and longing for healthy and natural life, responded enthusiastically to this injunction. In his speeches and writings, Herzl emphasised the "normal" work that New Jews would undertake in their *neu-alt* state. To arrive at this, of course, he had to align himself with the Jewish masses in the Diaspora.

Despite his aristocratic aversion to the Jewish masses in the Diaspora, Herzl was well aware that his Zionist revolution needed masses. Like Nietzsche, Herzl sought to entice his people, using symbolic rituals to enable them to uncover in themselves personal and national powers that had lain dormant in the Diaspora.[156] Herzl posits the flag as a means of enticement: "With a flag we are leading the people to a place we want to, even to *Eretz Israel*. For the flag they live and die, it is also the only thing for which they die in masses if they are trained to do so." And since "we do not have a flag, we need it. If we want to lead many people, we need a symbol to be raised above their heads".[157] The masses also needed slogans: "The public knows only slogans. It is silly but that is what they are."[158] Hence this charismatic man supplies the Jewish masses with slogans and phrases in his attempt to entice them to renew themselves. However, Herzl does not employ the most decisive enticement to self-transfiguration and to the attainment of personal authenticity, but is engaged in the fruitful, mostly hidden, dialogue with Nietzsche, the teacher of personal transfiguration. He confines his personal journey to authenticity, a journey of overcoming mental "ghettos" to his subjective life. This takes place in the deepest mental recesses of Herzl's soul since "we ourselves want to advance to a new morality" and "one who wants to attain to greatness has first of all to conquer his own self".[159]

[155]GM II-16.
[156]See the concluding chapter of Golomb, *Nietzsche's Enticing Psychology of Power*.
[157]Herzl, *Thus Spoke Herzl*, pp. 68, 67. On Herzl's use of icons and symbols and cultivation of myth, see the illuminating essay by Robert S. Wistrich, 'Theodor Herzl: Zionist Icon, Myth-Maker and Social Utopian', in *The Shaping of Israeli Identity*, ed. by Robert Wistrich and David Ohana, London 1995, pp. 1–37.
[158]*ibid.*, p. 85.
[159]Herzl, *Thus Spoke Herzl*, pp. 90, 97.

Jewish Communities in the Nineteenth Century

The Province versus Berlin?
Relations between Berlin and the other Communities as a Factor in German Jewish Organisational History at the End of the Nineteenth Century

BY JACOB BORUT

The relationship between the Jews of Berlin and the other German-Jewish communities had an important influence on the public activities and collective action of German Jews, especially the activities of nation-wide organisations. Modern historiographical research has largely ignored this important subject. Many researchers assume that in the nineteenth century German Jews considered Berlin Jews to be their leaders, even their "masters".[1] In reality, the relationship was much more complicated. This essay will attempt to describe the relationship between Berlin and "provincial"[2] Jews, first by a short characterisation, and then by demonstrating their effect on the activities of three important Jewish organisations active during the early 1890s.[3]

RELATIONS BETWEEN BERLIN JEWS AND PROVINCIAL JEWS

Very little love was lost in Germany between the metropolitan centre, the "*Reichshauptstadt*",[4] and the more traditional and conservative populations of small towns and rural milieu. This reflected the well known trend of repudiation

[1]Peter Gay, 'The Berlin-Jewish Spirit. A Dogma in Search of some Doubts', in *idem., Freud, Jews and other Germans: Masters and Victims in Modernist Culture*, Oxford 1978, p. 172

[2]The term "province" as opposed to Berlin was widely used at the time, and has been followed here. The position of the other big Jewish communities, which were not "provincial", such as Hamburg, Frankfurt am Main, Breslau etc. was not discussed at the time. They were in a midway position between Berlin and the provinces. For a neutral article on the subject listing the advantages and deficiencies of bigger and smaller communities, see *Allgemeine Zeitung des Judentums*, 53, No. 44 (31 October 1889), pp. 687–689. The *Allgemeine Zeitung* was published in Leipzig in 1889 and expressed opinions representing both sides.

[3]In this article it has not been possible to deal with the differences between the various regions that constituted the "province". I hope to deal with this subject elsewhere. For more details see, Jacob Borut, '*A New Spirit among our Brethren in Ashkenaz' – German Jewry's change in Direction at the End of the 19th Century*, Jerusalem 1999, pp. 233–237, 272–274, 280 [Hebrew].

[4]On Berlin's position in the *Reich*, see Wolfgang Schroeder, 'Berlin als Hauptstadt des Deutschen Kaiserreichs', *Zeitschrift für Geschichtswissenschaft* 35 (1987), pp. 698–707 (esp. pp. 698–701, and the references there, and see also *ibid.*, pp. 546–548).

of urbanisation by conservative forces and rejection of the modern, permissive lifestyle that developed in the big cities.[5] In Germany there were other important towns besides Berlin.[6] For the German Jewish community, however, Berlin was *the* metropolis. The number of its members and the financial resources it commanded were several times higher than that of any other Jewish community. In 1910, for example, there were 90,013 Jews in Berlin, excluding the tens of thousands in the suburbs such as Charlottenburg or Wilmersdorf. Bavaria housed the second largest Jewish population at 55,100. If we include the suburbs, the Berlin Jewish population reached 142,289, which represented 29.6% of the entire Jewish population in the *Reich* in 1910. This concentration of Jews in Berlin increased steadily as Berlin was the target for continuing immigration from the province.[7]

Apart from their numerical strength, Berlin Jews held a considerable economic and cultural importance. Tax revenues indicate that they were, on average, wealthier than Jews of other towns.[8] Many Berlin Jews held influential positions in German society – in various cultural fields, in commerce and the economy, and even within the social élite.[9] Although Jews had won similar positions in other parts of the country, such positions were especially significant in the capital. The combination of commanding the largest financial resources among German Jewry, and its leaders' accessibility to the power centres of the *Reich*, gave the Berlin Jewish community leadership a position unequal to, and incontestable by, any other Jewish community or institution.

However, although the community of Berlin was the leading Jewish community in Germany, its aspirations for leadership were not always looked upon favourably by other Jews. Tensions founded on mutual sets of stereotypes between provincial and Berlin Jewry were visible. Those stereotypes appear in memoirs, in private letters, and in articles in the Jewish press. Many Berlin Jews looked down on provincial Jews as too conservative, too naïve and unsophisticated. Provincial Jews saw Berlin Jews as arrogant and insolent, incurably materialistic, and as extreme assimilationists far removed from Judaism. Following a lecture tour in central and south Germany in 1882, Karl Emil Franzos described in a private letter the reaction of local Jews to antisemitism: "Die Berliner Juden sind so arrogant, da war's nur natürlich!" (At the time of the tour, antisemitism –

---

[5]See Klaus Bergmann, *Agrarromantik und Grosstadtfeindschaft*, Meisenheim am Glan 1970.

[6]See, for example, Henning Koehler, 'Die "goldenen zwanziger Jahre" – Kultur und Unterhaltung in Berlin', in Wolfgang Ribbe (ed.), *Geschichte Berlins*, vol. II, München 1988, pp. 876–877.

[7]Monika Richarz (ed.), *Jüdisches Leben in Deutschland. Bd. 2, Selbstzeugnisse zur Sozialgeschichte im Kaiserreich*, Stuttgart 1979 (*Veröffentlichungen des Leo Baeck Instituts*), pp. 21–22; Esra Bennathan, 'Die demographische und wirtschaftliche Struktur der Juden', in Werner E. Mosse and Arnold Paucker (eds.), *Entscheidungsjahr 1932. Zur Judenfrage in der Endphase der Weimarer Republik. Ein Sammelband*, Tübingen 1965 (Schriftenreihe Wissenschaftlicher Abhandlungen des Leo Baeck Instituts 13), p. 90

[8]Avraham Barkai, *Jüdische Minderheit und Industrialisierung*, Tübingen 1988, p. 8

[9]About the strong presence of Jews in the social life of the bourgeois élite in Berlin, and their influence on those circles, as opposed to the lack of Jews among the social and economic élite in the Rhineland, see Dolores L. Augustine, 'Arriving in the upper Class: The Wealthy Business Elite of Wilhelmine Germany', in D. Blackbourn and Richard J. Evans (eds.), *The German Bourgeoisie*, London and New York 1991, pp. 56–63, 65, 70–71.

led by Adolf Stoecker and Heinrich von Treitschke – was conceived as a Berlin phenomenon.)[10] In another letter, Heinrich Kempenich from Geldern described Jewish life in Berlin as "Frivolitaet, Herzlosigkeit, Interesselosigkeit für alles, was nicht das goldene Kalb und das weibliche Geschlecht betrifft".[11]

Berlin Jewry's indifference towards Judaism was strongly attacked by Jewish papers in the province, especially by the *Israelitische Wochenschrift* of Magdeburg, and not only by the editor and staff writers, but also by reporters from throughout the *Reich*. The Berliners were admonished in that newspaper not so much for their religious laxity but for distancing themselves from Judaism and Jewry, taking no interest in the problems of their fellow Jews or in the issues that stood on Jewry's public agenda. Berlin Jews donated more money to Christian than to Jewish institutions, according to these reporters, and preferred to promote their personal and economic interests by assimilating into Gentile society. Thus, the writer of a report about the agricultural school in Ahlem sharply criticised Berlin Jews for ignoring requests to support that institution. In an adjoining letter to the editors, which was also printed, the reporter specifically asked that "denjenigen Theil des Artikels, welcher die Lauheit unserer Berliner Glaubensgenossen gegenüber der Anstalt und deren Bestrebungen zum Ausdruck bringt" would not be shortened:

> Es ist der Ansicht vieler unserer besten und hervorragendsten Kämpfer für das Judenthum, dass die indolenten oder Protzenhaften Elemente unserer Glaubensgenossen, vom denen ein grosser Procentsatz in Berlin wohnt... durch energische Ermahnungen an ihre 'Pflicht' erinnert werden müssen.[12]

Berlin Jewry's leadership within German Jewry provoked resentment and opposition, as described by a writer "from the Elba region":

> ... sich in der Reichshauptstadt ... eine gewisse Selbstüberschätzung herausbildet, welche gegen die Bewohner der Provinzen eine gewisse Missachtung bewirkt und sich eine Suprematie über dieselbe zueignet... Man hält sich deshalb daselbst den Provinzen weit überlegen, beachtet die Erzeugnisse derselben als secundär ... und hält sich für berufen, den Provinzialbewohnern Vorbild zu geben und Vorschriften zu machen.[13]

The ambitions attributed to Berlin aroused resentful comments about the lack of "Jewish feelings" in Berlin, as demonstrated by the lack of Jewish schools there, or the phenomenon of the "three days a year Jews", not unique to Berlin but conceived as characteristic of it at that time.[14]

It is hard to find in the Jewish newspapers direct expressions of disregard by Berliners towards provincial Jews. After all, this was not the sort of material that a respected writer from Berlin would print in a newspaper. Still, ample testimony of their attitude is found in articles that deal indirectly with provincial

---

[10]Karl Emil Franzos to Moritz Lazarus, 1 April 1882, in Moritz Lazarus Archive, Jewish National Library, Jerusalem, Department of Collections and Manuscripts, Ms.Var 298/94.

[11]Heinrich Kempenich (Berlin) to Max Bodenheimer, 16 November 1894, in Bodenheimer Archiv, Central Zionist Archive (Jerusalem), A15\II\15.

[12]*Israelitische Wochenschrift*, 24, No. 27 (30 June 1893), p. 209.

[13]*Allgemeine Zeitung des Judentums*, 53, No. 40 (6 October 1889), p. 626.

[14]*ibid*. For a similar article that emphasised the spiritual potential in the provinces, see *ibid.*, No. 14, (4 April 1889), p. 211.

Jewry and their role in Jewish life. A good example is an article in which a writer
from Berlin suggested the convening of an international Jewish conference to deal
with means of fighting antisemitism. Regarding the method by which delegates
should be chosen, he stated that those would have to be elected by the Jews of the
central community within each country, to ensure that the elected delegates
would be highly intelligent (*hochintelligent*).[15]

Examples of the ambition of Berlin Jews to lead provincial Jewry, in spiritual
as well as in other matters, are abundant. They are found, for example, in articles
and lectures by Berlin Jews that emphasised Berlin's position as a centre of
German Jewry, and shared a common perception of Berlin having an intellectual
and spiritual supremacy over the provinces. A typical lecture was delivered by
Justizrat Hermann Makower, the former chairman of Berlin community's *Repräsentantenversammlung*. Makower had emphasized Berlin's position as the centre of
Prussian and German Jewry, and noted that this position entailed *noblesse oblige*.
"Die grössere Pflicht besteht nämlich darin, die Institutionen der hiesigen
Gemeinde so einzurichten, dass sie nicht blos unseren Zwecken dienen, sondern
dass sie auch den schwächeren Gemeinden... von Nutzen werden". The precondition for this was "dass die anderen Gemeinden freiwillig ihrer Führung folgen".
Makower described at length ways by which Berlin should guide the other communities in the realms of education, rite and culture. One of his propositions was
to appoint a chief rabbi for German Jewry, whose seat would be in Berlin.[16]

Such opinions, and especially Makower's suggestions, aroused furious reactions
on the pages of the provincial press. One article, for example, declared that Berlin
was neither the spiritual nor the cultural centre of the *Reich*, (but was the centre of
the antisemitic movement), and neither should it be.[17] Another described the idea
of laymen, such as Berlin community's leaders, taking decisions on religious
matters for a religious community as absurd, and was typical of the *Machthunger*
of Berlin's leaders. The same article, however, ended by treating the relations
between Berlin and the provinces more realistically than most others. It had
admitted that provincial communities did in fact expect Berlin to lead, and that
Berlin had a task to fulfill, though this should be achieved not through dictates, but
by consultation and consideration for the will of others.[18]

Indeed, provincial Jews, in spite of their grumbling, did accept Berlin's leadership. Whenever a need arose for a nation-wide operation, provincial Jews never
initiated a response of their own, but awaited Berlin's initiative and followed it.
Berlin Jews themselves were well aware of their role as leaders and initiators of
German Jewry in any matter that required collective action. It was the Berlin
community, for example, which initiated, on occasion of the Berlin Congress of
1878, a Jewish national appeal to the Congress for improvement of the situation
of Romanian Jewry. The other communities followed Berlin's lead.[19]

[15] *Allgemeine Zeitung des Judentums*, 53, No. 8 (21 February 1889), p. 118.
[16] *Allgemeine Zeitung des Judentums*, 57, No. 43 (27 October 1893), pp. 506–510. (Quotations from
    p. 507)
[17] *Israelitische Wochenschrift*, 24, No. 44 (3 November 1893), pp. 344–345.
[18] *Israelitische Wochenschrift*, 24, No. 45 (10 November 1893), pp. 349–350.
[19] N. M. Gelber, 'The Jewish Question before the Congress of Berlin in 1878', *Zion* VIII (1943), pp. 38–
    39 (Hebrew).

In the second half of the nineteenth century there were some attempts to form national Jewish organisations outside Berlin, but this only demonstrated Berlin's supremacy. These attempts included the *Deutsch-Israelitischer Gemeindebund* (DIGB), founded in Leipzig in 1869, and the *Zionistische Vereinigung für Deutschland* (ZVfD), whose authoritative leader, Max Bodenheimer, lived in Cologne, and – with Theodor Herzl's support – established the city as the national centre of German Zionism. In both cases, the leadership of both organisations later moved to Berlin. The DIGB moved its headquarters there in 1882 (it had wanted to do so earlier, but the community leadership in Berlin had objected),[20] and, in spite of Bodenheimer's efforts to retain Cologne as the centre of German Zionism, a gradual erosion ocurred in its leadership,[21] until finally in 1910 all leadership of the ZVfD was transferred to Berlin, and Bodenheimer quit his position as chairman.[22] A provincial centre such as Cologne could not compete with Berlin as the centre of a national organisation. The attempts of the *Austritts-orthodoxie* of Frankfurt to organise Orthodox Jews on a national level should also be mentioned. The attempt subsequently succeeded, but its future success was not at all apparent at the end of the nineteenth century.

The complicated set of relations between the leadership in Berlin and the rest of German Jewry was an important factor in the process of establishing and organising Jewish national organisations. There was a regular pattern for those organisations: when a pressing problem arose which could not be handled by the existing organisational network, various Jewish communities responded first by establishing committees and organisations that dealt with that particular problem on their local level. The Berlin leadership responded by forming an organisation in Berlin, which aimed to lead the whole of German Jewry dealing with that problem. Most of the other Jewish organisations then joined this Berlin organisation and accepted its authority. Still, this acceptance was not full and unconditional, and some of the non-Berlin leaders demanded that the Berliners show consideration towards their needs and views, and let them take part in the decision making processes. An excellent example for this set of relations can be seen in the activities aimed at helping Jewish refugees from Russia.

THE *DEUTSCHES CENTRAL-COMITE FÜR DIE RUSSISCHEN JUDEN*

Jewish immigration from Russia was clearly a subject the handling of which required Jewish organisations to form on a national level.[23] Pogroms and legisla-

---

[20]Ismar Schorsch, *Jewish Reactions to German Anti-Semitism 1870–1914*, Philadelphia 1972, pp. 48–52.

[21]This process is described in Yehuda Eloni, *Zionism in Germany*, Tel Aviv 1991, pp. 122–124, 130–134, 137–141, 174–176.

[22]*ibid.*, pp. 196–203; Jehuda Reinharz (ed.), *Dokumente zur Geschichte des deutschen Zionismus 1882–1933*, Tübingen 1981 (Schriftenreihe wissenschaftlicher Abhandlungen des Leo Baeck Instituts 37), p. 94 and note 2.

[23]On the immigrants and views of German Jews, see Steven E. Aschheim, *Brothers and Strangers*, Madison 1982; J. Wertheimer, ' "The Unwanted Element": East European Jews in Imperial Germany', in *LBI Year Book XXVI* (1981), p. 23–46; *idem, Unwelcome Strangers. East European Jews in Imperial Germany*, New York 1987, Part III. On the Weimar period, with references to the *Kaiserreich*, see Trude Maurer, *Ostjuden in Deutschland 1918–1933*, Hamburg 1986.

tion by the Russian authorities led to large waves of immigration as hundreds of thousands of Jews fled the country, many of them passing through Germany in their search to find a better place to live.

The masses of immigrants created two kinds of problems for German Jewry. The first was financial, as the refugees required aid such as food, accommodation, medical treatment, train tickets and other kinds of aid. The second problem was the outer appearance of immigrants, many of whom had earlocks and long beards and wore the old Jewish kaftans which aroused among the Jews fear of unfavourable reactions among the German population.[24] Because of these problems, coordination and concentration of relief activities became vital. Financially, it was necessary to collect money all over the country – as well as abroad – and distribute it to where it was most required. As for the problems caused by the refugees' appearance, they were rapidly transfered from border to harbour towns and then oversees. Both of these problems necessitated the formation of a national organisation to deal with them. Such was the case in 1891, following a series of anti-Jewish decrees and deportations from numerous places including Moscow. Then, in the face of a mass immigration of homeless Jews, organisations to help the immigrants were founded all over Germany.[25] They were followed by the foundation of the *Deutsches Central-Comité für die russischen Juden* in Berlin. This committee – as indicated by its name – aimed to be the central organisation to concentrate and co-ordinate relief activities all over Germany (and, in fact, it expanded its field of activities beyond Germany).[26] Of all the organisations, only the one in Berlin aimed at leading the activities all over the country. The same pattern also took place in 1882: following the mass immigration of refugees fleeing the Pogroms, local relief groups were formed all over the *Reich*, while in Berlin a Central Committee was formed, the *Deutsche Central-Comité für die russisch-jüdischen Flüchtlinge*, aimed at directing the activities of the local organisations all over Germany.[27] Both committees, in 1882 and 1891, were founded and led by the Jewish notables of Berlin – community leaders and members of the economic and social élite.[28]

The network of Jewish relief groups for the refugees spread all over Germany, and the Central Committee acted quickly to put the expanding network under its aegis.[29] But not all local organisations had willingly accepted the supremacy of that committee. (It is noteworthy that, though its official name was *Deutsches*

---

[24]For a background on this subject, see Aschheim, chaps. 1–3; Wertheimer, 'Unwanted Element'.

[25]See Borut, *New Spirit*, pp. 50–52.

[26]For a general description of its activities, see Moshe Zimermann, 'German Jews and the emigration from Russia', in Selwyn Ilan Troen, Benjamim Pinkus (eds.), *Organising Rescue: National Jewish solidarity in the modern period*, London 1992, pp. 127–140.

[27]See Itta Shedlezky, 'The Jewish Press in Germany, 1879–1882: It's Reactions to the Pogroms in Russia and to the Beginning of the National Awakening on the Background of the Rise of Anti-Semitism in Germany', M.A. Thesis, Jerusalem 1976, pp. 37–39 [Hebrew], and the sources cited there.

[28]On the members of the committee in 1891 see *Allgemeine Zeitung des Judentums* 55, No. 23 (5 June 1891), Gemeindebote, p. 1; *Der Israelit*, 32, No. 43 (1 June 1891), p. 800; *Israelitische Wochenschrift* 22, No. 23 (4 June 1891), p. 178.

[29]Refer to notes 26 and 28, and also *Israelitische Wochenschrift*, 22, No. 24 (11 June 1891), p. 184.

Central-Comité, the press usually referred to it as the *Berliner Central-Comité*). Frictions had occurred already during the first meeting of representatives convened by the Central Committee. A source from that committee criticized the behaviour of the delegates from the other committees in Germany. While the non-German delegates willingly accepted the suggestions of Berlin, he complained, there were delegates from German towns that preferred to break the unity.[30] It should be noted, on that occasion, that the presidency and the secretariat of the meeting were composed of representatives from Berlin and from major towns outside Germany, with no representation from other German towns.

Due to the huge expenses of the relief activities, the local committees would have collapsed very quickly without help from Berlin, the richest community, which was able to collect large sums of money in donations from its members.[31] It was not only their financial clout that was important to the local committees. The members of the Berlin committee were highly appreciated for their competence, leadership experience, organisational skills and their contacts in the governing bodies. It would have been impossible to form a national organisation for such widespread activities without the leaders from Berlin. On the other hand, the Central Committee relied on the co-operation of the local groups. The committee wanted to direct the relief activities and to act as their representative. It therefore, needed to have its leadership accepted throughout the *Reich*. The co-operation of the communities along the eastern border, in which the first contacts with the incoming immigrants were made, and the committees in the harbour towns, from which the refugees were shipped overseas, was most important for it. Besides, the Berlin Jews could not cope alone with the large financial expenses. The committee relied on the donations from the other communities and organisations.

This was a recipe for co-operation between Berlin and the other relief committees. The Central Committee supplied the leadership, the organisational guidelines and the finances, while the other committees (including local committees in Berlin itself) carried out the actual tasks, helping the refugees and collecting money. The organisational network that developed with its proven efficiency created a situation where there was no alternative to the leadership of the Central Committee, even though some local leaders were not happy to accept it. The more successful the activities led by the Central Committee, the more its prestige in Germany and beyond grew, and more and more committees joined the organisational network.

The Berliners in the Central Committee made no secret of their intention to concentrate all activities under their leadership, that they, and only they, were capable of managing such a task. Articles written by Central Committee activists

---

[30] *Allgemeine Zeitung des Judentums*, 55, No. 24 (12 June 1891), Gemeindebote, p. 1.

[31] The *Israelit*, which led a fund raising campaign for the refugees, praised the response to its appeal and reported that "several thousands of Mk." were already collected. Two small communities in Baden were praised for collecting 72 and 68 Mk., which were good contributions for such communities. *Der Israelit*, 32, No. 43 (1 June 1891), pp. 792, 797. On one Saturday in Berlin, by comparison, stock exchange members donated 120,000 Mk. for the refugees. *Israelitische Wochenschrift*, 22, No. 23 (4 June 1891), p. 178.

emphasised that a large relief movement could only be run from Berlin.[32] Most of the opposition to Berlin's leadership pretensions came from the bigger communities in the south and west, and especially from Frankfurt. Those communities were less troubled by the presence of refugees and did not need financial assistance. A direct confrontation between the supporters of centralism in Berlin and the demands for maximum independence of the local committees took place at the end of October 1891, when the Central Committee held a big meeting of representatives of the big committees inside and outside Germany in Berlin.[33] A motion was presented at this meeting that all the money collected in Germany and Austria would be concentrated in one central fund run by the Berlin Central Committee which would channel the money to where it was required. As could be expected, the motion aroused strong opposition. The most outspoken critic of the motion, as well as of Berlin centralism in general, was the jurist Julius Plotke of Frankfurt.[34] Plotke demanded that financial control be left in the hands of the local committees and announced that even if the motion were to be accepted, the Frankfurt people would not see it as binding, and would continue to keep their autonomy as before.

Plotke's position exemplifies the positions held by many, on different occasions, on their attitude towards Berlin. The Jews of Frankfurt, declared Plotke in his speech, had done a lot for the refugees. "We have collected half of the money collected in Germany. Under those circumstances we have a right", he said, "we want to have a voice" (*mitreden*). "As well as the Berlin committee had operated, and I shall be the last to deny it," he added, "it will always be the committee of Berlin. We in the West and in the whole of Germany, who would deliver our money to it, will remain without a possibility to have a voice. All Jewry should have a voice, and thus turn the committee into a real Central Committee". This position, although it represented a minority among the delegates, won support among a few delegations. Moreover – several delegations from outside Germany had decided to stay out of the conflict, and abstained in the vote on the motion. The delegations that openly expressed their opposition also abstained, so the motion was accepted without opposition. But the Berliners were furious. Their spokesman declared: "*Wir sind nicht willens, nur ein Local Comité zu bilden, das von dem guten Willen und dem Gutdünken der einzelnen abhängt*", and announced that if within four weeks they did not get the support of those committees both inside and outside Germany, they would quit their positions. The committee of Berlin demanded to have full control of the activities, or not operate at all. This characterised the position taken by Berlin all along the way.

The threats from Berlin aroused the anxiety of the other delegates, who pre-

[32] *Allgemeine Zeitung des Judentums*, 55, No. 34 (21 August 1891), p. 398; *ibid.*, No. 35 (28 August 1891), p. 409; see also *Israelitische Wochenschrift*, 22, No. 46 (12 November 1891), p. 355

[33] For the following, see the protocols of the meeting: *Jüdische Presse*, 22, No. 46 (12 November 1891), pp. 553–554; *Allgemeine Zeitung des Judentums*, 55, No. 46 (13 November 1891), pp. 541–543; *Der Israelit*, 32, No. 88 (12 November 1891), pp. 1647–1648; *Israelitische Wochenschrift*, 22, No. 47 (19 November 1891), pp. 363–364.

[34] On Plotke, see Paul Arnsberg, *Die Geschichte der Frankfurter Juden seit der Französischen Revolution*, Darmstadt 1983, vol. III, pp. 348–350.

sented some motions to pacify the Berliners and prevent their resignation. They were thus satisfied and the discussions continued as before. The threat by Berlin removed most of the opposition and the Central Committee regained control. Its members promised to involve representatives from other towns to its discussions. There is no information, however, as to whether, and to what extent, this promise was fulfilled.[35] In any case, representatives who did not reside in Berlin could achieve only a very limited influence. The expenses involved in travelling to Berlin and staying there were a factor that allowed only a few people to visit Berlin for some very few meetings. The ongoing management of the activity could only be done by Berliners. And even when delegates from other towns were present, it is doubtful whether those few representatives could have had any influence on resolute Berliners who formed the great majority.

To sum up, the activities of the Central Committee displayed a pattern within which the leadership of Berlin came under no dispute. No local committee tried to found a national organisation before it was initiated by the elites of Berlin, and no local committee tried to contest Berlin's claim for a national leadership and control, let alone compete with it. The arguments, when they arose, concerned the question of whether Jews from the rest of Germany could achieve some influence on the decision making process, whether they could have a voice. When the leaders in Berlin were not sensitive enough and were not willing to make suggestions that could, at least formally, satisfy the other groups, they found themselves facing a resistance they did not expect.

A NEW REGARD FOR THE PERIPHERY

The relief committees, and the Central Committee among them, were run by the community and social élites of German Jewry and operated according to the patterns characteristic of German Jewish group-action throughout most of the nineteenth century. At the beginning of the 1890s a major change in the social and political relations of the *Reich* took place, which also encompassed German Jewry. The developments can be summed up by saying that German society took on some forms of mass society, and its politics took on some characteristics of mass politics. These changes, one might even call them transformations, caused a change in the Jewish group mentality, as expressed in its group actions. New groups and organisations were founded which were not apprehensive of appearing in public as specifically Jewish organisations, operating for the Jews and on behalf of their interests. They had thus abandoned the fears, so common in the past, that such activities would provide ammunition for the antisemites, who might claim that the Jews still wanted to remain a separate "state within a

---

[35]Information about the *Central-Comité* was not supplied in the Jewish press after 1891, although it was officially disbanded only several years later. It simply stopped operating in public. The German Jewish press of the period was not an invesitgating press like the papers of today, but relied solely on information supplied to it by outside sources (see Jacob Borut, 'Die deutsch-jüdische Presse am Ende des 19. Jahrhunderts als historische Quelle' *Menorah* 7 (1996), pp. 43–60) and, therefore, once an organisation stopped reporting its activities to the press it would not be mentioned anymore.

state", not willing to really become German.[36] It is necessary to examine the two most important organisations that initiated those changes within the Jewish realm – the *Centralverein deutscher Staatsbürger jüdischen Glaubens* (C.V.) and the *Verband der Vereine für jüdische Geschichte und Literatur* – in order to see how their relations with the provinces were connected with the change in Jewish group action.

We shall start by noting that those two organisations, which were advocating a break with the accepted patterns and norms of Jewish group action in Germany, encountered a resolute resistance by the old guard of community leaders, especially the leaders of the Berlin community. That resistance was never expressed openly – this was also one of the rules of the game of Jewish group action – but we have enough evidence for it behind the scenes. It is important to point out that during the 1880s such opposition to the break with traditional norms was enough to stifle any attempts – such as that by the *Comité vom 1. Dezember* led by Moritz Lazarus in Berlin in 1881 – to break with the norms.[37]

One of the major characteristics of the changed German – and Jewish – groups was a new regard towards the periphery, both social and geographical. The lower social strata (workers, small peasants) and the provinces became objects of a new attention, even subjects to court by various political groupings that wanted their support. The new Jewish organisations that were founded at that time treated the "Jewish periphery" in a similar manner, quite different to that of the Jewish élites. This change was especially conspicuous in the attitude of the leaders of the new organisations towards the Jews of the provinces, which was quite different from the patronising attitude shown by the old Berlin leadership.

THE *CENTRALVEREIN DEUTSCHER STAATSBÜRGER JÜDISCHEN GLAUBENS*

The C.V. was founded in 1893, after widespread Jewish defence activities against antisemitism had been organised and calls for the creation of a national organisation that would concentrate those activities.[38] The C.V. aimed from the beginning to become a national organisation, representative of the whole of German Jewry. Its leaders wanted to turn it into a Jewish interest group, similar to other interest groups that had been founded in that period, which achieved a mass

[36]This major subject is discussed in Borut, *New Spirit*. For a shorter description see Jacob Borut, 'Jewish Politics and generational change in Wilhelmine Germany', in Mark Roseman (ed.), *Generations in Conflict: Youth revolt and generation formation in Germany 1770–1968*, Cambridge 1995, pp. 105–120. Concerning the 1890s as a "watershed" period in German politics, see Geoff Eley, 'Notable Politics: The crisis of German Liberalism, and the Electoral Transition of the 1890's', in Konrad H. Jarausch and Larry Eugine Jones (eds.), *In Search of Liberal Germany: Studies in the History of German Liberalism from 1789 to the Present*, New York 1990, pp. 187–216. The challenge to it by Margaret Lavinia Anderson, 'Voter, Junker, *Landrat*, Priest: The Old Authorities and the New Franchise in Imperial Germany', *American Historical Review*, 98 (1993), pp. 1470–1471 and note 73, is not immune to criticism.

[37]On the *Comité vom 1. Dezember* see Schorsch, *Jewish Reactions*, pp. 59–65; Sanford Ragins, *Jewish Responses to Antisemitism in Germany 1870–1914*, Cincinnati 1980, pp. 33–35; Borut, *New Spirit*, pp. 77–86; and *ibid.*, pp. 78–79, on the opposition behind the scenes against that group.

[38]See Jacob Borut, 'The Rise of Jewish Defence Agitation in Germany, 1890–1895: A Pre-History of the C.V.?', *LBI Year Book XXXVI* (1991), pp. 59–96.

membership and gained dominant political influence, such as the *Bund der Land-wirte*.[39] Its leaders, therefore, devoted a lot of effort to win support in the provinces, although they were faced at first with the typical suspicion which provincial Jews felt towards Berlin organisations.[40]

The C.V. leaders did not show any feelings of superiority towards the provinces. Suggestions for action from the provinces were seriously considered and willingly accepted. This willingness is manifested in the protocols of the meetings of the C.V. executive. For example, an important campaign against the *Umsturz-vorlage* in 1894 was initiated by a letter from Mainz.[41] In many cases, the C.V. publicised its actions as having been initiated by suggestions from the provinces. This attitude proved to be a major cause for the success of the C.V. in expanding into the provinces and mobilising wide support there.[42] This was in contrast to another defence organisation founded in Berlin in the same year, the *Comite zur Abwehr Antisemitischen Angriffe*.[43] This organisation, founded by Berlin notables, aimed, like the C.V., to combat antisemitism. Its leaders also wanted to mobilise the support of provincial Jewry and planned to build a network of local branches,[44] but those ambitions failed. The reason for the varying degrees of success of these two organisations lies in their different treatment of provincial Jewry. Unlike the C.V., the leaders of the *Comite* displayed the paternalistic attitude characteristic of the old Berlin leadership. In a circular sent to community leaders throughout Germany, for example, they asked for financial donations, but emphasised that management must come from Berlin.[45]

On the other hand, however, an analysis of the C.V.'s activities indicates that although suggestions from the provinces did influence its operations, the decisions were always made by the leaders in Berlin. The C.V. did not create any local branches in the period under discussion, and refused to cooperate with regional defence organisations. When the leadership of the *Vereinigung Badischer Israeliten*, an anti-antisemitic defence organisation from Baden, offered to join

---

[39]Marjory Lamberti, *Jewish Activism in Imperial Germany*, New Haven 1978, p. 15; Borut, *New Spirit*, pp. 206–222. For statements of C.V. leaders to that affect see Martin Mendelssohn, *Die Pflicht der Selbstverteidigung*, Berlin 1894, p. 14; Eugen Fuchs' speech of April 1894, published in Eugen Fuchs, *Um Deutschtum und Judentum, Gesammelte Reden und Aufsätze 1894–1919*, Frankfurt am Main 1919, p. 21; *idem*, 'Die Bestrebungen und Ziele des Central-Vereins', (Speech in October 1895), published in *Um Deutschtum und Judentum*, pp. 56, 61; and his speech of February 1896, published in *Im Deutschen Reich* II, 3, (March 1896), p. 170.

[40]For examples for such suspicions see: *Israelitische Wochenschrift* 24, No. 10 (3 March 1893), pp. 74–75, *ibid.*, No. 44 (3 November 1893), pp. 342–343.

[41]The protocols are located at the Central Archives for the History of the Jewish People, Jerusalem, (CAHJP) Inv/124a. For the case we mentioned, See the protocol of 4 February 1895, p. 8.

[42]See Jacob Borut, ' "Not a Small Number of Notables." The Geographical and Occupational Structure of the Central Verein Membership During Its First Years', *Jewish History* IX (1995), No. 1, pp. 51–77.

[43]On the *Comité* see Paul Rieger, *Ein Vierteljahrhundert im Kampf um das Recht und die Zukunft der deutschen Juden*, Berlin 1918, pp. 12, 18–19; Schorsch, *Jewish Reactions*, pp. 113–115; Ragins, *Jewish Responses*, pp. 38–39; Jehuda Reinharz, *Fatherland or Promised Land*, Michigan 1975, pp. 44–45; Borut, *New Spirit*, pp. 195–202.

[44]See letter from November 1893 to the *Vertrauensmänner* of the organisation, entitled 'Lokale Organisationen', CAHJP, Inv 1412/2.

[45]CAHJP, Kn II A II 3, No. 168.

the C.V., its leaders refused the affiliation of an independent group and wrote
back that they would gladly accept the *Vereinigung* leaders if they joined as individuals (which they did).[46] There was only one member of the C.V.'s *Vorstand* that
was not a resident of Berlin and he did not attend any of its meetings. (A second
was accepted at the end of 1895). Arnold Paucker has also written that in its first
years the C.V. was a very centralised organisation, not allowing local members
any measure of independence.[47] Does this information not contradict the view of
the C.V. as responsive to the provinces?

The answer lies in the fact that in its first years the C.V. was a centralised organisation, compared to fifteen years later when the C.V. was far less centralised. In
1893, or 1895, the provincial Jews were unable to make such comparisons. They
could only compare the attitude of the C.V. leaders towards them with the
attitude shown by leaders of other organisations such as the *Central-comité für die
Russischen Juden* or the *Comité zur Abwehr*. And from the provinces' point of view,
the C.V. was clearly favourable. What the Jews outside Berlin wanted to was, in
their own words "*mitreden*", and the C.V. allowed them this. Their queries were
answered. They made suggestions which were considered, and in many cases
accepted. The organisation openly expressed its will to consult with provincial
leaders and its gratitude for their assistance. Although the provincial leaders
were not in a position to make independent decisions on the activities in their
own regions, at this stage they did not demand it. Such demands appeared successfully at later stages.[48]

THE *VERBAND DER VEREINE FÜR JÜDISCHE GESCHICHTE UND LITERATUR*

The Association of the societies for Jewish History and Literature (JGL)[49] was at
the centre of an important process which had begun in the same period: a huge
rise in interest in that subject, and the formation of a large network of societies
throughout Germany.[50] The familiar pattern of relations encountered between
Berlin and the provinces and their influence on the moves towards the formation
of a nation-wide organisation was repeated in the *Verband*'s case. First, a wave of

[46]Protocols of the C.V. *Vorstand* meetings, CAHJP, Inv./124a, 4 February 1895, 7 May 1895.

[47]Arnold Paucker, 'Zur Problematik einer jüdischen Abwehrstrategie in der deutschen Gesellschaft',
in Werner E. Mosse and Arnold Paucker (eds.), *Juden im Wilhelminischen Deutschland 1890–1914, Ein
Sammelband*, Tübingen 1976 (Schriftenreihe wissenschaftlicher Abhandlungen des Leo Baeck Instituts 33), pp. 483, n. 500.

[48]For the beginnings of the decentralisation in the C.V. see especially Lamberti, *Jewish Activism*, chap.
5.

[49]On the *Verband* see Werner Habel, *Deutsch-Jüdische Geschichte am Ausgang des 19. Jahrhunderts*, Kastel-
laun 1977, pp. 126–129; Schorsch, *Jewish Reactions*, pp. 111–113; Chaim Schatzker, *Jüdische Jugend
im zweiten Kaiserreich*, Frankfurt am Main 1988, pp. 169–178; Shulamit Volkov, *Die Juden in Deutschland 1780–1918*, München 1994, p. 61; Borut, *New Spirit*, pp. 265–274.

[50]See Jacob Borut, 'The Rise of Societies for Jewish History and Literature in Germany, 1890–1895',
in *Proceedings of the Tenth World Congress of Jewish Studies*, Part B, vol. I, Jerusalem 1989, pp. 251–258
(Hebrew); *idem*, '*Vereine fuer jüdische Geschichte und Literatur* at the End of the 19th Century', *LBI Year
Book XLI* (1996), pp. 89–114.

local activities in the field – in this case, the field of JGL – arose throughout the *Reich*. No initiative was taken by one of the local activists or societies to form a national organisation, and all expectations for such were directed towards Berlin.[51] The Berliners regarded themselves as fit to lead the Jews of the *Reich*, and initiated the formation of a national organisation in December 1893.[52] This initiative, and the actual activity of the organisation, encountered resistance by local activists and organisations who wanted to maintain their independence. Resentment was expressed towards the Berliners and their ambitions to dominate German Jewry.[53] But most of the local societies and activists accepted the leadership of the new organisation, and gradually the great majority of local societies joined it.

Unlike the C.V., the *Verband der Vereine für jüdische Geschichte und Literatur* gave much more weight to the provinces. In its *Vorstand* the Berliners were in a minority. The *Verband* was meant to act as an umbrella organisation (*Dachverband*), not involving itself in what was going on in the local groups. Its activities were concerned with the co-ordination of the various groups and the personalities involved in the field; it did not become involved in the internal affairs of its member societies. In fact, it allowed quite early the formation of *Provinzialverbände* within the overall organisation. The first one was established in Westphalia in 1894. The C.V. accepted provincial *Verbände* only in 1907, and then only after a bitter struggle.[54] Nevertheless, Berlin retained the overwhelming influence. All executive posts in the *Vorstand* were held by Berliners; they also ran all its activities. The other *Vorstand* members had to travel to Berlin if they wanted to participate in the actual running of the organisation, which they rarely did.[55] The local societies were independent, but the *Verband* in Berlin had an overwhelming influence on their character and activities due to its prestige as well as to the influence of its leaders; many of the local societies, moreover, were founded following their personal efforts. The society in Berlin acted as a model which was followed by most other societies whose activities had similar characteristics. A contemporary journalist wrote about the Berlin society: "Out of her stems the learning (Torah) to the other societies, which are like branches to her, and they follow her deeds and her spirit".[56]

REGIONAL VARIATIONS

The reactions from the various provinces towards the new organisations were not similar. The differences between the various regions that constituted the

[51]See, For example, an expression of hope for it in a letter from Cologne, *Allgemeine Zeitung des Judentums* 56, No. 13 (25 March 1892), *Gemeindebote*, p. 2.

[52]*Israelitische Wochenschrift* 24, No. 52 (29 December 1893), p. 411; *Allgemeine Zeitung des Judentums* 58, No. 1 (5 January 1894), *Gemeindebote*, p 3; *Juedische Presse* 25 (4 January 1894), No. 1, p. 5.

[53]For a typical example see *Israelitische Wochenschrift* 25, No. 34 (25 August 1894), p. 270.

[54]Lamberti, op. cit.

[55]See the comments of Moritz Rahmer in the *Israelitische Wochenschrift* 25, No. 38 (21 September 1894), p. 302.

[56]*Hatzfira* (Warsaw) 21, No. 46 (23 February/7 March 1894), p. 184. (Hebrew. The double date stands for the Gregorian and Julian calendars.).

"province" cannot here be discussed in detail.[57] It should be noted briefly, however, that membership of both the C.V. and the *Verband der Vereine für jüdische Geschichte und Literatur* had similarities in geographical location, and these organisations had similar forms of expansion during their first years.

The major centres of mobilisation outside Berlin were the eastern provinces of Prussia, especially Posen and Silesia. When compared with other provinces and states, the eastern provinces were more open, or less resistant, to organisational initiatives from Berlin.[58] They did not have what could be referred to as a "regional mentality" that emphasised regional independence in facing up to lea- dership pretensions from Berlin (as was the case in Westphalia), or opposing Prussia as a whole (as was the case in Bavaria).

The new organisations found it much harder to infiltrate southern and western Germany and (in the C.V.'s case) the province and duchy of Hesse. These were areas with local tradition and pride, both among the non-Jewish and Jewish populations, and with anti-Prussian traditions. Bavaria is a good example of a state that was most inhospitable to nation-wide organisational initiatives stemming from outside. This was true for both the Christian and the Jewish populations.[59] In these regions new organisations were greeted with deep suspi- cion; they could only succeed in overcoming such suspicion after a considerable amount of time. Westphalia had its own style of reaction. Without overtly opposing Berlin, its communities, (which had joined together in a self created provincial organisation – the *Verband der Synagogen-Gemeinden Westfalens*), tried to assert their independence and operate independently within or alongside national organisations. No wonder that they were the first to organize their own *Provinzialverband* for JGL.[60] The neighbouring Rhine province communities sometimes acted in the same manner.

But these are generalisations; in fact, the attitudes towards Berlin, the C.V. and the *Verband der Vereine füer Jüdische Geschichte und Literatur*, as well as towards the *Central-Comité für die russischen Juden* were diverse, and different individuals and communities had differing views on the subject. Even in Silesia, where the mobi- lisation efforts to arouse support were largely successful, opinions varied from one community to another.[61] Still, when decisions had to be made, communities in a

---

[57] See note 3.

[58] For a discussion, see Borut, 'Not a Small Number', pp. 58–59.

[59] For a Christian example concerning an attempt to form a nation-wide Catholic organisation, see Jonathan Sperber, *Popular Catholicism in Nineteenth Century Germany*, Princeton 1984, pp. 211–212.

[60] Another testimony of its aspirations towards independent action was the desire of the *Verband der Synagogen-Gemeinden Westfalens* to organize autonomous activities for the benefit of Russian refugees. See Katzenstein to Steinberg, 11 February 1892, CAHJPS/384/5. At the end of 1894 the Westphalian groups for JGL formed their own *Provinzialverband*, whose first meeting discussed whether to continue to belong to the national *Verband*. See *Allgemeine Zeitung des Judentums* 59, No. 1 (4 January 1895), *Gemeindebote*, pp. 2–3.

[61] For example, see the discussion among Upper-Silesian communities on their attitude towards the Berlin-controlled *Deutsches Central-Comité für die russischen Juden. Der Israelit* 32, No. 51 (29 June 1891), p. 945; *Jüdische Presse* 22, No. 25 (18 June 1891), pp. 296–297. And see Borut, 'Not a small number', p. 59, for a list of Silesian communities where *Centralverein* membership was very low or non-existent.

certain province or *Land* mostly did act in a unified way, typical for their province.

CONCLUSION

To sum up, the evidence shows that the general attitude towards Berlin and its Jews was an important factor in the *Rezeptionsgeschichte* of the new organisations, which were considered Berliner organisations. The new organisations that wanted to mobilise provincial Jewry, and were willing to satisfy their desire to have a voice, managed to overcome their initial resistance. By 1895 the CV and the *Verband der Vereine für jüdische Geschichte und Literatur* managed to gain strongholds even in Bavaria, and became powerful nation-wide organisations. In fact, in 1895 the Berlin leadership also abandoned its resistance to the new organisations, and this also happened in other big communities which had previously resisted. This was related to the heated election campaign in Berlin, and the appearance of a strong opposition within that community.[62] The fact remains that the new organisations, with a relatively unknown leadership, defeated a resistance by what was the most powerful leadership organ of German Jewry. Their success was achieved by the wide mobilisation of support throughout the country. Thus, the Jews of the provinces had now taken part in shaping the new form of Jewish group-action. They actually "had a voice".

The question as to the reasons why provincial Jews and community leaders were willing to support these changes when the leaders of the big communities resisted them is beyond the scope of this paper. A working assumption might be that because those leaders did not lead Jewish group action they felt less committed to its former norms and were ready to break with them when they felt that the time was right – and the political atmosphere in Germany of the 1890s indicated that the time was right. The Jews of the eastern provinces, who were the first to join the new organisations in large numbers, were also more open to accept a pattern of group action based on openly expressing one's Jewishness. Besides, the attitudes of the new organisations towards the provinces undoubtedly played a major part in attracting those Jews to their organisations. Thus, the support of wide parts of the periphery enabled those groups to reach a position of national leadership. The rules of Jewish group action changed, and the provinces could now play a bigger part.

The relationship between the Jews of Berlin and the other communities constituted a major element of the organisational history of German Jewry. Berlin Jews wanted, and saw themselves fit, to lead the rest of German Jewry. The other Jews did not wholeheartedly accept that will, and had strong reservations about it. In reality, they could not contest Berlin's leadership ambitions, and did not present any viable alternative to it. But they wanted the Berliners to respect them and make it possible for them to participate in the leadership and in the decision

[62]Borut, *New Spirit*, pp. 138–142, 230–231, 271, 280.

making processes. Those desires led to conflicts among the traditional leadership strata – community leaders and notables.

Early in the 1890s a major change occurred within German Jewry (and the *Reich* as a whole) and a new leadership arose – a leadership that led organisations of a new type. One major characteristic of those changes was a new attitude towards the peripheries, including the geographical periphery. The new organisations wanted to mobilise provincial Jewry, and gave them the opportunities to communicate their opinions to the organisational top and influence its activities. But, although the provinces were allowed some influence, the leaders in Berlin kept, at this stage, the actual authority in their hands, and – especially in the CV – had the final word on every subject. The change in that respect occurred later, during the first decade of the twentieth century. By then, a new provincial leadership arose, that demanded more influence, and a real participation in the organisation's management and decision making. But that is a subject for a different paper.

The Israelitische Gebetbücher
of Abraham Geiger and Manuel Joël:
A Study in Nineteenth-Century German-Jewish
Communal Liturgy and Religion

BY DAVID ELLENSON

The nineteenth century was a time of great liturgical ferment in the life of the Liberal German-Jewish community.[1] Reform Judaism bounded onto the stage of history in the 1810s as a movement of liturgical change, and Hebrew prayerbook creativity, as evidenced in the production of a constant stream of new *siddurim*, remained unabated among all the religious streams in Germany throughout the 1800s. These prayerbooks played a central role in the religious developments and conflicts of the nineteenth century German-Jewish community, and the theological nuances and sensibilities of the leaders in these denominational struggles were constantly reflected in the many prayerbooks they produced. The *siddurim* of this time and place are therefore ideal barometers for measuring the moods and attitudes of the variegated religious streams of Judaism in Germany in modern times. In this essay, the Hebrew liturgical creativity of two authors – Abraham Geiger and Manuel Joël – will be analysed so that the nature and course of those streams – their moods and attitudes – can be measured.[2]

Abraham Geiger has of course long been famed as the outstanding Reform figure of his day, and he first wrote his *Israelitisches Gebetbuch* in 1854 while serving as *Rabbiner der israelitischen Gemeinde zu Breslau*. Joël, in contrast, has long been asso-

[1]This paper was originally delivered at the Jewish Theological Seminary on 11 November 1997, at a conference entitled, "Voices of Ashkenaz: An International Conference on the Music and Culture of German and Central European Jewry", presented by The Jewish Theological Seminary and Hebrew Union College-Jewish Institute of Religion, in cooperation with The Leo Baeck Institute and The Elaine Kaufman Cultural Center. The author would like to express special gratitude to three colleagues, Professor Neil Levin of JTS, Professor Michael Meyer of HUC-JIR, Cincinnati, and Professor Eliyahu Schleifer of HUC-JIR, Jerusalem, for their assistance in formulating and researching this topic. He would also acknowledge the support of The Institute for Advanced Studies at the Hebrew University of Jerusalem, under whose sponsorship he engaged in this research during autumn 1997, when he served as a Fellow at the Institute.
[2]Jakob Petuchowski, in his seminal *Prayerbook Reform in Europe*, New York 1968, has been the foremost scholar to point all this out. Robert Liberles has followed Petuchowski and in 'The So-Called Quiet Years of German-Jewry 1849–1869: A Reconsideration', *LBI Year Book XLI* (1996), p. 72, emphasised the importance of these works as sources for the construction of modern Jewish religious history.

ciated with the Positive-Historical wing of *Liberales Judentum* in Germany and he served in the Religious Philosophy Faculty at the Breslau Rabbinical Seminary. Joël succeeded Geiger as *Rabbiner der israelitischen Gemeinde zu Breslau* in 1863, and his *Israelitisches Gebetbuch* was composed in 1872. By analysing the contents of the *siddurim* of these two men within the nineteenth-century context that fostered and informed them, this paper will illuminate the nature of German Liberal Judaism. The sensibilities that united the Reform and Positive-Historical wings of nineteenth-century *Liberales Judentum* will be made manifest, as will the differences between these religious trends. In this way, this paper – through the lens provided by the prayerbook – will contribute towards a fuller understanding of nineteenth-century German-Jewish religious denominationalism.[3]

THE LEGACY OF HAMBURG

In analysing the character and content of Geiger's and Joël's *Gebetbücher*, it is essential to note that their liturgical work did not arise in a vacuum. They did not have to confront the task of composing a communal *Gebetbuch de novo*. Indeed, Joël's *Israelitisches Gebetbuch* was based upon the 1854 *Israelitisches Gebetbuch* written by Geiger. Geiger, in turn, was highly cognizant of attempts made by German predecessors earlier in the century to reformulate Jewish liturgy in keeping with the attitudes and conditions of a novel era. By the time he wrote his 1854 *Israelitisches Gebetbuch*, which bore the Hebrew title *Seder Tefilah D'var Yom B'yomo*, Geiger had already published a number of articles and opinions expressing his views on the subject of Jewish prayer. Indeed, he had been an active participant in the acrimonious debates that had surrounded the Hamburg *Gebetbuch* of 1841, and an analysis of his words on that occasion, as

[3] In this paper, I travel further down the path of prayerbook research initiated by Petuchowski. I also consciously take up the suggestions offered by both Michael Meyer and Robert Liberles concerning the need for more historical research into the Positive-Historical trend in nineteenth-century Germany. In his article, 'Recent Historiography on the Jewish Religion', *LBI Year Book XXXV* (1990), pp. 10–11, Meyer stated: "While the field of recent German-Jewish Orthodoxy has been well ploughed in recent scholarship, that of Positive-Historical Judaism has lain almost fallow." He therefore called for new research on those he termed "middle of the road figures", persons such as "Michael Sachs in Berlin, Isaac Noah Mannheimer in Vienna, and Manuel Joël in Breslau". Robert Liberles, in 'The So-Called Quite Years of German Jewry', pp. 71ff., has repeated this call and has asserted: "Until recently, German Jewry was strongly associated with the Reformers in its midst. ... But over the past two decades, several writers ... have contributed to a richer and more varied perspective on German-Jewish life by focusing on its more traditional sectors. It is to be hoped that this perspective will be broadened to include studies of Positive-Historical Judaism." Therefore, this study purposefully centres upon the Joël *siddur*, in conjunction with that of Geiger, so that a fuller understanding of Positive-Historical Judaism in particular, as well as the contours of German-Jewish religious denominationalism in general, can emerge. Since the article by Meyer was written, Franz D. Lucas and Heike Frank have published their book, *Michael Sachs: Der konservative Mittelweg*, Tübingen 1992. On p. 6, they explicitly note the suggestions made by Meyer. In addition, my essay, 'The Mannheimer Prayerbooks and Central European Communal Liturgies', in David Ellenson, *Between Tradition and Culture: The Dialectics of Modern Jewish Religion and Identity*, Atlanta 1994, pp. 59–78, devotes itself to an element of Mannheimer and his work. This essay will treat the third figure specifically mentioned by Meyer and identified by Liberles as central to an understanding of Positive-Historical Judaism, Manuel Joël.

well as an understanding of the prayerbook upon which he was commenting, are crucial if we are to grasp Geiger's own attitudes towards Jewish liturgy.

The Hamburg Temple prayerbook of 1841, entitled *Gebetbuch für die öffentliche häusliche Andacht der Israeliten, nach dem Gebrauch des Neuen Israelitischen Tempels in Hamburg*, was a revision and expansion of the famous 1819 *Gebetbuch* published by the Hamburg Temple. Limited to services for the Sabbath and Festivals, the 1819 prayerbook was influenced by the Berlin 1817 *siddur* of *Die Deutsche Synagoge oder Ordnung des Gottesdienstes fuer die Sabbath- und Festtage des ganzen Jahres, zum Gebrauche der Gemeinden, die sich deutscher Gebete bedienen*, edited by Eduard Kley and C.S. Guensburg. The 1819 Hamburg rite was dedicated to Israel Jacobson and has been identified by Michael Meyer as "the first comprehensive Reform liturgy".[4] This 1819 liturgy expressed the concerns and aspirations of a nascent Reform Movement, the postures and rituals of which were not fully formed. Much of the 1819 prayerbook was composed in Hebrew and the order and structure of the traditional service were retained in their entirety. Indeed, its editors, Meyer Israel Bresselau and Seckel Isaak Frankel, were anxious to affirm their ties to Jewish tradition and they asserted that they did not want to foster division within the community. As a result, they did not intend a radical reform.

At the same time, Bresselau and Frankel were informed by the rational ideology of the Enlightenment, and they were excited by the opportunity emancipation afforded Jews for full participation in Gentile society. They were anxious to author a prayerbook the manifest content of which would be consistent with the spirit and aesthetic of this new age. The 1819 *Gebetbuch* therefore opened from left to right and contained prayers composed in the vernacular. There was also a pronounced tendency to favour Sephardic formulae over the Ashkenazic liturgy that had guided German Jews in prayer for years. As Ismar Schorsch explains, "As construed by Ashkenazic intellectuals, the Sephardic image facilitated a religious posture marked by cultural openness, philosophic thinking, and an appreciation for the aesthetic."[5] Thus, only Sephardic *piyutim* were included in the Hamburg rite. The Sephardic *L'Moshe Tzivita* was substituted for the Ashkenazic *Tikanta Shabbat* in the Sabbath *Musaf* service while *M'nuhah N'chonah* replaced *El Malei Rahamim* as contained in the *Hazkarat N'shamot* memorial prayer of the Polish rite that had been favoured in northern Germany during the previous century.

Other dimensions of the manifest content of the received Ashkenazic liturgical rite of the previous century were also deemed problematic by the Hamburg Reformers and elements of that rite were rejected or reformulated in keeping with what the editors of the Hamburg *Gebetbuch* perceived as the modern ethos. Prayers concerned with the restoration of the sacrificial cult and those expressing a desire for a physical return to Jerusalem and Zion were among those regarded as particularly troublesome, as were prayers that affirmed a belief in a personal messiah and angelology, and those that articulated what the editors regarded as

[4] Michael Meyer, *Response to Modernity: A History of the Reform Movement in Judaism*, New York – Oxford 1988, p. 56.
[5] Ismar Schorsch, 'The Myth of Sephardic Supremacy', in Schorsch, *From Text to Context: The Turn to History in Modern Judaism*, Hanover 1994, p. 71.

offensive attitudes towards Gentiles. Bresselau and Frankel saw these prayers as inappropriate for Jews living in the modern era and they addressed the issues these prayers raised in their *siddur*. A representative survey of some of these prayers will indicate how they handled these issues, as well as illuminating the character of the prayerbook they composed. [6]

The Hamburg liturgists expressed their distance from those prayers that expressed a hope for the reinstitution of the sacrificial cult by amending the text for the *Shabbat Musaf* service, with its call for a restoration of sacrificial worship, to read, "May it therefore be Your will, O Lord our God and God of our fathers, to accept in mercy and with favor the expression of our lips in place of our obligatory sacrifices." Similarly, in the *Musaf* service for the Pilgrimage Festivals, the same phrase, "to accept in mercy and with favour the expression of our lips in place of our obligatory sacrifices" was placed in the *Mipnei Hataeinu* prayer and the phrases, "And bring near our dispersed from among the nations" and the line which asserts, "And gather us to Zion Your city in joy" were completely removed from this prayer.

These last changes express an antipathy towards more than the Temple with its mode of sacrificial worship. They reflect an opposition to a call for Jewish national restoration as well, and this hostility is contained in other places in the Hamburg *Gebetbuch*. Indeed, the entire traditional content of the *Kedushah* for the Sabbath *Shaharit* service was deleted and the *Kedushah* for *Musaf* was substituted in its stead so that the paragraph which begins with the words, "From Your place, our King, You will appear", and asks, "When will You reign in Zion", and asserts in response, "May You be exalted and sanctified within Jerusalem, Your city", could be removed. Hence, the sentence beginning with the words, "O, may You cause a new light to shine upon Zion" is also deleted from the 1819 Hamburg *Gebetbuch* as is the line from the prayer prior to the recitation of the *Sh'ma* which reads, "And bring us forth in peace from the four corners of the earth, and cause us to walk upright into our land". Instead, this line is replaced by the words, "Bring blessing and peace upon us" in accordance with the Spanish-Portuguese rite, though the Hamburg prayer does not contain the words, "And break the yoke of the gentiles from upon us", as does the Sephardic ritual. [7] The conditions of oppression that had prompted this prayer no longer existed, in the opinion

---

[6] For these points as well a complete account of the posture these men adopted in their approach to their prayerbook, see Seckel I. Frankel, *Schutzschrift des zu Hamburg erschienenen Israelitischen Gebetbuchs*, Hamburg 1819.

[7] Indeed, in making this change, as well as the previous two which have been mentioned, the authors of the 1819 Hamburg *Gebetbuch* employed elements of other accepted Jewish liturgies as precedents for the legitimisation of their ritual. In the case of the *Kedushah*, they had the precedent of Yom Kippur, where the *Kedushah* service on that day in both *Shaharit* and *Musaf* was based on the *Musaf Kedushah*, while many prayerbooks, as far back as the *siddur* of Saadia Gaon in the tenth century, had omitted the line "*Or Hadash*". The fact that the Hamburg Reformers drew upon traditional Jewish practices as warrants for their changes is historically noteworthy, and indicates how deeply embedded they remained in the rabbinic tradition. At the same time, this should not obscure the fact that they drew upon these warrants rather selectively, and that they selected them so as to forge a new Jewish communal identity over and against the traditional rabbinic establishment and because these precedents allowed them to compose a liturgy whose manifest content was more in keeping with their own beliefs than was that of the traditional Ashkenazic rite that was their immediate patrimony.

of Bresselau and Frankel, in Germany. As a result, its sentiments seemed inappropriate and, in keeping with this view, they omitted the line from the High Holy Day liturgy that read, "Our Father, our King, avenge the blood of Your servants that has been shed" as well as the sentence from the Sabbath morning *Tefilah* which states of the Sabbath, "You did not give it, O Lord our God, to the nations of the earth, nor did You make it the inheritance, our King, of the worshipers of graven idols. And in its rest the uncircumcised shall not abide".

At the same time, the Hamburg Temple *Gebetbuch*, in view of the sensibilities of its authors, displayed – in certain respects – a surprising fidelity to tradition.[8] While the authors possessed a definite antipathy towards angelology and the notion of a personal messiah, the weight of centuries of tradition and their own determination to compose a liturgy that could appeal to a broad spectrum of the community, caused them to retain the Hebrew of traditional prayers that incorporated these themes. Hence, the *Kedushat d' Yotzer*, a staple part of the morning service replete with references to angelology, was retained in its entirety and *go'el* (redeemer) was maintained in the first benediction of the *Amidah*. In so doing, Bresselau and Frankel signalled that their intention was twofold – to reformulate the old order of prayer to avoid the creation of a sectarian prayerbook, while bearing in mind contemporary sensibilities. However, in instances such as these, where they retained the Hebrew prayer intact despite the problems they felt with its manifest content, they employed translation as a vehicle to mute or transform the meaning of the Hebrew. Thus, the word "Creatures" in the *Kedushat d' Yotzer* was translated as "Lichtgestalten" (figures of light). The manifest content of the entire prayer was thereby changed. The words of the liturgy no longer referred to heavenly creatures in a mystical sense; instead, they were transformed – at least in German translation – into metaphors for the powers of nature. In the same vein, while "go'el" was maintained in the Hebrew, the 1819 Hamburg *Gebetbuch* translated it not as "Erlöser" (redeemer) but as "Erlösung" (redemption). This tactic – retaining the Hebrew while employing translation as a tool to obviate meanings that were perceived as objectionable – was to become a hallmark of countless numbers of subsequent Liberal liturgies.

The appreciation for as well as ambivalence towards tradition that such an approach displays was evidenced by the 1819 Hamburg Temple prayerbook in other ways as well. Despite the hostility the authors of the *Gebetbuch* had for those prayers that called for the restoration of the sacrificial cult and the return of the Jewish people to Zion, the 1819 liturgy maintained the prerogatives classically assigned the *kehunah*, the priesthood, in Jewish liturgy. A *cohen*, a man of priestly descent, was assigned the first *aliyah* to the Torah in the Hamburg rite and the ritual of *duchenen*, where the priests ascend the *bimah* (prayer platform) to bless the people on Holy Days, was retained. In addition, the passage in the *Shemoneh Esreh* which reads, "Restore the sacrificial worship to Your sanctuary, and accept Israel's fire offerings and their prayer with love and favour" was retained in its

---

[8]Baruch Mevorach, 'The Belief in the Messiah in Early Reform Polemics', in *Zion* (1969) [Hebrew], pp. 189–218, has noted this with regard to the doctrine of the messiah, and has explained why this was so with regard to this particular notion, in this thorough and insightful piece.

entirety and translated into German. Similarly, the traditional *hatimah* of this benediction, "Who restores His divine presence to Zion", was also included, and phrases beseeching God to restore the Temple, "and rebuild it soon and magnify its glory" were included in the Festival *Musaf* service.

Of course, from the standpoint of the Orthodox, none of this spared the Hamburg Temple prayerbook condemnation. The 1819 *Gebetbuch* elicited a storm of protest from the Orthodox and a collection of Orthodox rabbinic responsa, entitled *Elleh Divrei ha-Berit*, savagely attacked the prayerbook for its deviations from received Jewish liturgical tradition.[9] Yet, from the viewpoint of Reform Judaism, the 1819 Hamburg Temple Prayer Book constituted a first attempt to compose a liturgy that would calibrate between the push of tradition and the pull of the present. The 1841 *Gebetbuch* constituted a second.

While the first Hamburg *siddur* was limited to services for the Sabbath and Festivals, the 1841 edition added a daily service as well as a Sabbath afternoon service (*Minhah*). Though it continued many of the practices and embodied many of the same sensibilities and concerns that had marked the 1819 *Gebetbuch*, this latter liturgy represented on the one hand, as Petuchowski phrased it, "a return to Tradition, and, on the other, an espousal of a more 'radical' Reform point of view".[10] For example, *P'sukei d'Zimrah*, (the Verses of Song), which had virtually disappeared in the first Hamburg prayerbook, were restored, in Hebrew, in the 1841 edition. In addition, the phrase, "O, may You cause a new light to shine upon Zion . . .", was reinserted in the 1841 liturgy. However, it was set in small type and placed in parentheses, and left untranslated. Similarly, the sentence, "Restore the sacrificial worship to Your sanctuary, and accept Israel's fire-offerings and their prayer with love and favour" was set in small type and placed in parentheses in the Hebrew text of that prayer. In addition, this Hebrew text did not appear in German translation in the 1841 prayerbook. Thus, a prayer that was omitted in the earlier edition was restored half-heartedly in the later one, while a prayer found in the first edition was inserted parenthetically and untranslated in the second.

The 1841 *Gebetbuch* also attempted to be more thoroughgoing in its elimination of passages referring to the physical restoration of the Jews to Palestine, as well as the centrality of Zion than had its predecessor. Thus, in the rendition of the *hatimah* for the *Hashkiveinu* prayer on the eve of the Sabbath, the 1841 *siddur* completely omitted the traditional conclusion, "Blessed be You, O God, Who spreads the tabernacle of peace over us, over Your people Israel, and over Jerusalem", and substituted in its place, "Gelobt seiest du, Gott, der du dein Volk Israel ewiglich beschuetzest" [Blessed are You, O God, who protects Your people Israel forever]. In addition, the *hatimah* of the first of the last three benedictions in the *Amidah*, "Who restores His divine presence to Zion was replaced by the

---

[9]For a description of the Orthodox responses as collected in *Elleh Divrei ha-Berit* to the 1819 Hamburg Reform rite, see David Ellenson, 'Traditional Reactions to Modern German Jewish Reform: The Paradigm of German Orthodoxy', in Daniel Frank and Oliver Leaman (eds.), *A History of Jewish Philosophy*, London 1996, pp. 734ff.

[10]Petuchowski, *Prayerbook Reform in Europe*, p. 54.

words, "Whom alone we serve in reverence". A note at the end of the 1841 edition of the Hamburg *Gebetbuch* cited a remark by Rashi upon *Berakhot* 11a, to justify this *hatimah* from the standpoint of Jewish tradition. Indeed, the production of such warrants from Jewish literature to legitimate the changes they introduced in their order of prayer was characteristic of the approach taken by the authors of these *siddurim* in both 1819 and 1841.[11] However, the authors of this prayerbook undoubtedly selected this conclusion to the prayer because its manifest content was more in accord with their religious sentiments than the one which featured Zion. The precedent undoubtedly would not have been selected had this not been so.

The universalistic and anti-nationalistic proclivities and views of the 1841 prayerbook are also evidenced in the intermediate benedictions its authors composed for the daily *Shemoneh Esreh*. Written in German, the manifest content of these Hamburg blessings departed radically from that of the traditional Ashkenazic rite. An analysis of two of them will suffice to illustrate the religious viewpoint that marked them. The eleventh benediction, *Kibbutz Galuyot* (The Ingathering of Exiles), which calls upon God to bring freedom to the people Israel and asks that all the Jews of the Diaspora be returned to the Land of Israel, was altered to assert that the banner of freedom be lifted up "for all who sigh in their servitude" and asked that God gather up not the "dispersed", but the "disowned" among the people Israel. In a similar universalistic vein, the next benediction, *Jerusalem*, abandoned its hope that God would rebuild Jerusalem and establish His divine dwelling, as well as the Davidic throne, there. Instead, the Hamburg edition of this blessing inserted the words of Isaiah 2:3, "For from Zion shall go forth Torah, and the word of God from Jerusalem", to obviate the particularistic thrust of the traditional prayer and to emphasise in its stead the universal mission of Jewish teaching.

In its composition of these intermediate blessings, the 1841 *Gebetbuch* continued the thrust evidenced in its predecessor of removing or muting passages that referred to the elimination and downfall of Israel's enemies. Thus, the benediction, *Malshinim* (Slanderers), asking that God's wrath be visited upon those who have slandered the Jewish people and those who are the enemies of God, was simply omitted. Similarly, in the Torah service, the 1841 prayerbook reaffirmed an alteration initiated in the 1819 *Gebetbuch*, and eliminated the passage from Numbers 10:35, "Arise, O God, and let Your foes be scattered, and let those who hate You flee from You". However, it went even further in this direction than the 1819 service had, as can be seen from an analysis of the 1841 edition of the *Ezrat Avoteinu* prayer. In this prayer, one traditional passage reads, "From Egypt You redeemed us, Lord our God, and from the house of bondage You liberated us. All their first-born You slew, but Your first-born You redeemed. You split the Red Sea, and You drowned the evil sinners. The beloved You brought across, and the water covered their foes, not one of them was left". While the authors of the 1819 Hamburg prayerbook kept these lines intact, the editors of the 1841 Hamburg *siddur*, cognizant of the hostility these lines displayed

[11]See footnote 7.

towards the enemies of Israel, felt these sentences to be inappropriate for the universalistic orientation that marked their community. The later prayerbook therefore muted the tone of this passage, and deleted the phrases, "All their first-born You slew, but Your first-born You redeemed", and "the water covered their foes, not one of them was left". In short, the Hamburg Temple prayerbook of 1841, while distinct in certain respects from the preceeding liturgy, continued the basic thrust and sentiments of the earlier *siddur*.

While the Hamburg Temple *Gebetbücher* were the works of an independent Reform congregation, the authors of these *siddurim* did not see themselves as promoting a radical disjunction with the past. They remained active members of the Hamburg Jewish community, and they were eager, as we have seen, to demonstrate their compliance with Jewish law. As Petuchowski has commented, "The farthest thing from their mind was the formation of a new Jewish sect ... The Judaism to which they wanted to bring liturgical reform was a Judaism based on Bible, Talmud, and Codes; and it was by an appeal to these accepted bases of Jewish life that they sought to justify their place *within* Judaism".[12] Nevertheless, the changes the Hamburg Temple Reform liturgists introduced into the traditional order of prayer elicited the wrath of the Orthodox in 1841, just as they had in 1819. Isaac Bernays, Orthodox rabbi of Hamburg, attacked this new Reform effort, and issued a *moda'ah*, a public pronouncement, declaring "that a Jew could no more recite his obligatory prayers from this new edition than the earlier prohibited old one", and he "cast aspersions on the motivations of its editors, using terms such as "frivolous" and "mischievous" to describe their work".[13] The Reformers decided to respond to Bernays, and in 1842 published a series of rabbinic responsa, *Theologische Gutachten*, to defend the Jewish character of their *siddur*. Among the respondents was Abraham Geiger, and it is to an analysis of his liturgical writings – both theoretical and applied – that we now turn.

GEIGER AND JEWISH LITURGY: THEORETICAL VIEWS AND PRACTICAL APPLICATIONS

In the *Theologische Gutachten*, Geiger offered a brief explanation of his own views on Jewish prayer in general and on the Hamburg *Gebetbuch* in particular. In this document Geiger defended the Hamburg Reformers from the onslaught of Bernays and said of the Hamburg *Gebetbuch*, "I can assert with full conviction that the ordering of the prayers does not contradict the laws of the Talmud and the rabbis as long as the essential prayers, 'Sh'ma' and its blessings, expressing the acceptance of the yoke of the kingdom of Heaven and the remembrance of the Exodus from Egypt, and the *Amidah* are contained therein". As the Hamburg rite contained all these elements, Geiger concluded that the public condemnation

---

[12]Petuchowski, *Prayerbook Reform in Europe*, pp. 33 and 98. The precise quotation is found on p. 98.
[13]Meyer, *Response to Modernity*, p. 117.

of the Hamburg prayerbook by Bernays was completely unfounded from the standpoint of the Jewish laws of public prayer.[14]

However, during that same year in another forum, Geiger displayed a rather critical attitude toward the liturgy of the Hamburg Temple, accusing it of displaying unwarranted inconsistencies in its application of Reform principles. He wrote in the *Allgemeine Zeitung des Judenthums*:

> I see no excuse for the fact that, in a period of 23 years, the leaders of the Temple have achieved nothing beyond a second edition of their prayer book which reflects the same lack of decisiveness as the first one did. Despite their avowed Liberal position ... they have done almost nothing for the proper advancement of those ideas of which ... the reforms in divine services are merely an outgrowth. .... The fact of the matter is that they are still beating about the bush today; they still refuse to speak out openly, and still persist in seeking to make the difference appear minute ... All that these gentleman can make of these things is just a number of paltry changes in a few isolated words.[15]

Geiger offered a much fuller explication of his attitudes on the topic in another work published that same year. Entitled *Der Hamburger Tempelstreit. Eine Zeitfrage*, the document contained more than eighty pages. In it, Geiger wrote a rather lengthy prologue describing the history of the development of Jewish prayer. In so doing, he indicated that Jewish worship had always been rather fluid and flexible, and that the reforms he would like to have seen introduced into the modern prayerbook possessed historical warrant.

After he had completed this preliminary historical survey, Geiger turned directly to the topic of the Hamburg Temple *Gebetbücher* themselves. He made note of all the reforms these prayerbooks were meant to address, and lauded the spirit of change that motivated their authors. However, he objected strenuously to the lack of consistency these prayerbooks displayed in the application of Reform principles and compiled a litany of charges that indicted these works for their failure to fulfill the Liberal liturgical promise their vision championed. A rehearsal of several of these charges will illustrate the nature of the critique Geiger offered. For example, both prayerbooks were inconsistent in the manifest content of the liturgy they presented. Each denied any desire for the restoration of the priesthood and sacrificial cult. Yet, at the same time, they maintained the rite of *duchenen* in *birkat kohanim*, thereby maintaining a priestly prerogative. Similarly, these prayerbooks did not eliminate – despite their avowed goal of doing so – all passages dealing with the sacrifices themselves, and there were remnants of such prayers in various places in both *siddurim*. Geiger also felt that the Hamburg *Gebetbuch* of 1841 represented, in many places, a retreat from the advances embodied in the earlier liturgy. The restoration of the passage, "May You cause a new light to shine upon Zion", was deemed unfortunate, since it reflected a Jewish national hope, and while Geiger approved the

---

[14] *Theologische Gutachten ueber das Gebetbuch nach dem Gebrauche des Neuen Israelitischen Tempelvereins in Hamburg*, Hamburg 1842, pp. 63ff.
[15] *Allgemeine Zeitung des Judenthums* (XXIII 29), pp. 345ff., as cited and translated in Max Wiener, *Abraham Geiger and Liberal Judaism: The Challenge of the Nineteenth Century*, Philadelphia 1962, pp. 93–94.

removal of the *hatimah*, "Who restores His divine presence to Zion", he questioned the retention of the passage immediately preceding: "May our eyes behold Your return to Zion in compassion." Furthermore, the editors' efforts to remove passages denigrating other peoples was surely praiseworthy. Nevertheless, they completely failed to articulate positively the great principle that prompted their removal – the universal mission assigned Israel by God. He asserted:

> The doctrine of the election of Israel echoed in the prayerbook should have made room for the idea of the mission of Israel, her acceptance of the belief in the one God and her task to preserve this belief and to bear this mission throughout history until that time when all mankind will be united in the acceptance of this belief.[16]

In short, the Hamburg Temple *Gebetbücher* were inconsistent in their incomplete attempts to compose a liturgy that embodied the integrity of Liberal Jewish belief.

While the Hamburg Temple prayerbooks were noble first attempts in this direction, more work needed to be done, and Geiger, in subsequent years, accepted the challenge of composing a Liberal Jewish liturgy, as well as the task of articulating the principles that such a liturgy had to embody. Foremost among these principles was the notion of Jewish mission, the belief that "the true Israelite testifies gladly to Israel's high vocation to carry the faith in the One and Holy God in all its purity to the world". This meant that "outgrown attitudes" which still appeared in Jewish prayer had to be eliminated, and a systematic reform of the prayer book had to be undertaken.[17]

In the preface to his 1854 prayerbook, Geiger defined the particular features of this modern liturgy. He stated:

> The lamentation about the lost national independence of Israel, the plea for the gathering of the dispersed in Palestine and the restoration of the cult and priests – all that is relegated to the background. Jerusalem and Zion are places whence instruction went forth, and to which holy memories are attached. But, on the whole, they are to be celebrated more as a spiritual idea, as the nursery of the Kingdom of God than as a certain geographical locale connected with a special divine providence for all times. Likewise, the hopeful look into the future is directed to the messianic kingdom as a time of the universal reign of the idea of God, of a strengthening of piety and righteousness among all men, but not as a time for the elevation of the *People* of Israel.[18]

In addition, Geiger wrote that the *siddur* should preserve its traditional character so that its links to Jewish history could be maintained. Thus, he favoured the retention of Hebrew as the primary language of Jewish public prayer. However, Geiger was also cognizant that most Jews in his day either did not know Hebrew at all, or "do not know it sufficiently to find edification in Hebrew prayer". Consequently, Geiger asserted that rather than a German translation of the Hebrew

---

[16]For all of the information contained in these paragraphs, see Abraham Geiger, *Der Hamburger Tempelstreit. Eine Zeitfrage*, Breslau 1842. For this particular quotation, see p. 47.
[17]See Abraham Geiger, 'Suggested Changes', in Gunther Plaut (ed.), *The Rise of Reform Judaism*, New York 1963, pp. 156ff.
[18]The Preface to the 1854 Geiger prayerbook appears in English translation in Petuchowski, *Prayerbook Reform in Europe*, pp. 150–152. The translation is found on those pages.

text, the German part should constitute "a completely new reworking of the Hebrew prayers in the German language".[19]

Fifteen years later, in 1869, Geiger published a *Denkschrift* in which he articulated in great detail the principles that had guided and would continue to direct him in the construction of his liturgy. As in 1854, he asserted that the prayerbook "should continue to express in a precise form its connection with the whole history of Judaism. Consequently, ... the worship service remains in Hebrew. The traditional Hebrew expression ... is, on the whole, to remain untouched". However, Geiger once again insisted that the Hebrew text not be translated literally. Rather, "the Hebrew text must be accompanied by a *German adaptation*" in keeping with contemporary sensibilities. In addition, Geiger declared that "religious *concepts* that have a temporal validity, but which have been displaced by a *progressively purer conception,* must not be retained in a one-sided and sharp accentuation". This meant that the Hebrew text, in certain instances, must be recast. Indeed, Geiger went on to specify precisely what he intended by this.[20]

Geiger asserted that anthropomorphic descriptions of the deity as commonly found in the *piyutim* had to be removed from the prayerbook, and that references to angelology were to be eliminated. The belief in immortality was not to emphasise the notion of physical resurrection, but was to include "the concept of spiritual continuity".[21] Finally, the universal mission of Israel as "the bearer and herald" of the doctrine "of truth and light" to all humankind had to find expression in the *siddur* and the "*national* aspect" of Jewish tradition "must recede into the background". As a result, any prayers which expressed a separation between Israel and the other peoples were to be eliminated, as were "any side glances at '*other peoples*' which possessed the "appearance of *overbearance*". The hope for the unification of all mankind dictated that a modern Liberal liturgy must purge all prayers of a national and superstitious character from the prayerbook. Thus, prayers that asked for the restoration of a Jewish State in Palestine, the building of a Temple in Jerusalem, and the return of the sacrificial cult, as well as those that expressed the hope for the ingathering of the dispersed were to be eliminated. In short, Geiger intended that a Reform *Gebetbuch* be cut from whole-cloth and he insisted that an authentic Liberal liturgy both display a complete integrity of principles and avoid the inconsistencies evidenced in the Hamburg prayerbooks. This was of the utmost importance and concern to him, and Geiger repeated *verbatim* the principles for the composition of a Liberal liturgy he had articulated the previous year in the preface to his 1870 *Gebetbuch*.[22]

For a period of three decades, Geiger displayed consistency in his theoretical approach to Jewish prayer. An analysis of the *Gebetbücher* he himself produced

[19]*ibid.*, p. 151.
[20]The Geiger *Denkschrift* is found in English translation in *ibid.*, pp. 165–167.
[21]As Jakob Petuchowski has pointed out in his 'Modern Misunderstandings of an Ancient Benediction', in J.J. Petuchowski and Ezra Fleisher (eds.), *Studies in Aggadah, Targum, and Jewish Liturgy in Memory of Joseph Heinemann,* Jerusalem 1981, pp. 45–46, European Liberal Jews were comfortable with and therefore stressed the "idea of Immortality ... at the expense of the belief in Resurrection." Geiger affirmed this belief in this part of his prayerbook.
[22]Petuchowski, *Prayerbook Reform in Europe*, pp. 165–170.

indicates that Geiger did create an unmistakably Liberal liturgy. However, an examination of his works also demonstrates that Geiger, like the Hamburg *Gebetbuch* authors of whom he had been so critical, did not apply the principles and notions he established for the writing of a Jewish prayerbook with absolute consistency. The same ambivalence that marked the liturgy of Hamburg characterised the prayerbooks of Geiger, especially the 1854 version upon which Joël constructed his own *siddur*.

In keeping with the principles he had established for the character of the Liberal *Gebetbuch*, Geiger consistently eliminated those passages from his prayerbooks that called for the restoration of the sacrificial cult. While, in his 1854 *siddur*, he retained the passage in the Sabbath *Musaf* service that began with the words, *Tikanta Shabbat*, Geiger changed its wording so as to purge all references to sacrifices contained in the traditional version of the prayer. Similarly, the 1854 prayerbook removed such elements from the *Mipnei Hataeinu* prayer for the Festival *Musaf* service. Yet, in light of his own ideological pronouncements, Geiger felt a problem still remained, and in his 1870 *Gebetbuch*, Geiger did not simply reformulate the manifest content of these two paragraphs in the Sabbath and Festival *Musaf* services, but removed these two paragraphs altogether. In addition, Geiger completely omitted the line, "Restore the sacrificial worship to Your sanctuary, and accept Israel's fire-offerings and their prayer with love and favour" from the first of the final three benedictions of the *Amidah*. In so doing, Geiger displayed a greater degree of consistency on this issue than did the Hamburg Temple prayerbooks. Other areas in the Geiger liturgy display this principled Reform approach to Jewish prayer.

In accord with his writings on the topic, Geiger, like the Hamburg Reformers, attempted to remove those passages which alluded to the centrality of Zion and that asked for Jewish national restoration in Palestine. While he retained the traditional formulae for the Sabbath *Shaharit kedushah*, Geiger resolved the problem of the paragraph beginning with the words, "From Your place, our King, You will appear", by removing those phrases from the prayer – "When will you reign in Zion" and "May You be exalted and sanctified in Jerusalem" – that he regarded as offensive. In a comparable vein he, like the Hamburg Temple prayerbook authors, removed the famous passage "And bring us in peace from the four corners of the earth, and cause us to walk upright into our land" altogether, and he, like them, did not include lines such as "And bring near our dispersed from among the nations" in his Festival liturgy. In the Torah service, Geiger retained the famous Hebrew proclamation of Isaiah 2:3: "For from Zion shall go forth Torah, and the word of God from Jerusalem" but rendered "teitzei" (shall go forth) in German in the past tense, as "ist ausgegangen" (went forth). All this accords with Geiger's notion that Zion was the place "whence instruction went forth, and to which holy memories are attached". However, Israel surely was not the "geographical locale connected with a special divine providence for all times".

As a result, Geiger also altered a number of the middle benedictions in the *Shemoneh Esreh* that embodied a nationalist ethos. For example, in the tenth and eleventh blessings of his 1854 daily *Amidah*, Geiger radically altered the traditional Hebrew text so as to eliminate the nationalistic hopes that these blessings classically expressed. In *Kibbutz Galuyot* (The Ingathering of the Exiles), Geiger offered the following Hebrew prayer, "Sound the great shofar for our freedom and save, O Lord, Your people, the remnant of Israel, in the four corners of the earth. Praised are You, O Lord, Who saves the remnant of Israel", in lieu of asking God to restore the Jewish people to Zion. The opening line of *Birkat Mishpat* (Justice), which traditionally states, "Restore our judges as before and our counselors as at the beginning", was changed to read, "Restore us to the joy of Your salvation and may a noble spirit sustain us". Geiger also amended the fourteenth benediction, *Jerusalem*, and omitted the classical phrase, "And rebuild it speedily in our day", so that it no longer called for the Holy City to be reconstructed.

Geiger was committed to innovations in the received Ashkenazic rite of German Jewry in other areas as well. Like his Hamburg counterparts, Geiger attempted to rid his *siddurim* of passages that expressed seemingly derogatory attitudes towards Gentiles. Thus, in the 1854 *Gebetbuch*, he substituted the phrase, "Who has made me to serve him" in place of, "Who has not made me a gentile". In addition, Geiger purged, as had the Hamburg *Gebetbücher*, the passage that asked that God avenge "the blood of Your servants that has been shed", as well as the prayer concerning the Sabbath that began, "You did not give it, O Lord our God, to the nations of the earth, nor did You make it the inheritance, our King, of the worshipers of graven idols. And in its rest the uncircumcised shall not abide . . .". Furthermore, in the *Aleinu*, he removed the words, "Who has not made us like the peoples of the lands, and has not given us a position like the families of the earth, since he did not let our portion be like theirs, nor our lot like that of the multitude" and substituted in its place, "Who has been revealed to our fathers, and Who informed them of His will. He established His covenant with them, and bestowed upon us His Torah as an inheritance". Finally, he altered the wording of *Birkat ha-Minim* (The Benediction Concerning Heretics) in the *Shemoneh Esreh* to read "Slander" (*malshinut*), instead of, "Slanderers" (*malshinim*), in his 1854 *siddur*, and he removed the phrase, "May all your enemies be cut down speedily" and reworded "May You speedily uproot, smash, cast down, and humble the wanton sinners" to state simply, "May You humble wantonness speedily". In 1870, Geiger reworded the prayer more positively to read, "And may those who stray return unto You". In so doing, Geiger sought to give positive expression to the hope that all humanity would one day be united in truth and integrity.

The universalistic thrust of the 1854 Geiger prayerbook is evident in other passages as well. In the *Birkhot ha-Shahar* (Morning Blessings), Geiger reworked the blessing which concludes, "Who bestows beneficent kindnesses to His people Israel" read, "Who bestows beneficent kindnesses upon His creatures", by substituting "His creatures" for "His people Israel". Indeed, this trend towards the inclusion of all humanity, and the rejection of Jewish particularity, is apparent throughout the prayerbook. Geiger constantly omitted the phrase, "From among all peoples", in his *siddurim*, including the *Kiddush* for Sabbaths and Festivals and the Torah blessings. To have included such a phrase would have displayed, in his view a "side glance at '*other peoples*', . . . an overbearance". He therefore altered the *Havdalah* benediction recited at the end of the Sabbath, omitting the words "between Israel and the nations", so that the prayer no longer proclaimed, as did the received rite, that God divided Israel from the nations.

This trend towards universalism found expression in other places in his *Gebet-bücher*. In both the *Sim Shalom* and *Shalom Rav* prayers for peace, the final benedictions of the morning and afternoon *Shemoneh Esreh*, Geiger retained the particularistic Hebrew texts of the prayers, texts that asked that God bestow peace upon Israel. However, in German translation, Geiger added the phrase "unter den Voelkern" so that the wish could be expressed that God bestow peace upon all humanity. Likewise, in the prayer for the New Month Geiger preserved the traditional Hebrew, which reads, "May the Holy One, Blessed be He, renew this month upon us and upon all His people, the Household of Israel", but refused to translate the words, "and upon all His people, the Household of Israel". Instead, he simply asserted "*uns*" (us). His conviction that the modern *siddur* had to purge itself of a noxious particularity and to articulate, in its stead, the ideal of Jewish mission found additional expression in his German phrase, "Who has chosen Israel for His teaching" (*der Israel zu seiner Lehre erkoren*), which he offered for the Hebrew statement, "Who has chosen His people Israel in love". As inheritors of the covenant, the Jews are reminded by the prayerbook that their task as Israel is to proclaim God's teachings to humankind.

As so many of these citations demonstrate, Geiger, like the Hamburg Reformers he had criticised, frequently maintained the Hebrew prayers of the traditional *siddur* even when he had difficulties with their manifest content. On other occasions, he, like the Reformers of Hamburg, employed translation as the vehicle whereby the ideals of Reform Judaism could find expression. Several last examples will illuminate how he did this. Like the Hamburg *Gebetbücher*, the 1854 Geiger prayerbook retained the word "go'el" (redeemer) in the Hebrew, though it offered, "Erlösung" (redemption) not "Erlöser" (redeemer) in German. Similarly, Geiger, like the Hamburg Temple Reformers whom he chastised, preserved the references to angelology contained in the Hebrew text of the *Kedushat d'Yotzer* located in the 1854 *Gebetbuch*, while, at the same time, offering a vernacular prayer that praised God as the creator of the natural world. In so doing, he obviated the literal meaning of the words. Geiger also retained those Hebrew phrases in the *Amidah* that spoke of "resurrection of the dead" (*Tehiyat ha-Meitim*) but did not translate them literally. Thus, the *hatimah* of the second benediction of the *Amidah*, "Who resurrects the dead" (*m'hayei ha-Meitim*) was translated as, "Who dispenses life here and beyond" – (*der Leben spendet hier und dort*).

The Geiger *Gebetbücher* displayed far-reaching Reform. Yet, like the authors of the Hamburg *Gebetbücher*, they were not absolute in their application of Reform principles – particularly in the 1854 edition of his liturgy. Geiger, in his 1854 prayerbook, included the Hebrew passages "May You cause a new light to shine upon Zion" and "May our eyes behold Your return to Zion in compassion". In addition, Geiger also printed the *hatimah*, "Who restores His divine presence to Zion", in his 1854 *siddur*, though the formula, "Whom alone we serve in reverence", was substituted in the 1870 prayerbook. Echoes of the approach adopted by the Reform editors in Hamburg can be heard here as well. Furthermore, Geiger, despite his own strictures, retained the *Musaf* service itself in both his prayerbooks. In this way, he displayed a sensibility akin to that of the Hamburg Reformers. Like them, Geiger also maintained the rite of *duchenen* in both his *siddurim*, thereby continuing, despite his own protests, elements of the priestly prerogatives. In addition, in his 1854 *Gebetbuch* Geiger, in keeping with Jewish tradition, stipulated that a Levite was to be the second man called to the reading of the Torah. Indeed, the structure and order of the actual services he composed demonstrates how traditional his practical approach was to Jewish public prayer. There are daily morning, afternoon, and evening services, including *Tahanun*, as well as Sabbath and Rosh Hodesh services. Prayers for Purim and Hanukah, as well as evening and morning services for Tisha b'Av are included. The services for the three pilgrimage festivals, in addition to the already-mentioned *Musaf* services for these days, contain the texts of the Torah readings for each holiday, both first and second days. In addition, there is a service for Simhat Torah, prayers for *Tal* (Dew) and *Geshem* (Rain) on Passover and Shemini Atzeret, and *Hoshanot*.

The Geiger prayerbooks, especially the 1854 liturgy, were no more consistent in their application of Reform principles than were the *Gebetbücher* of the Hamburg Temple that Geiger had so vociferously denounced. The 1854 *Gebetbuch* displayed the same departures from a principled Reform, as Geiger himself defined it, that the Hamburg Temple *Gebetbücher* had. In light of his strong views, it seems that Geiger failed to construct a comprehensive Reform liturgy that embodied a total fidelity to the ideals of Reform.

The spirit of compromise that marked the prayerbook creations of Geiger, as well as of the Hamburg Reformers who had preceded him, was the result of several factors. One was the view of Jewish communal unity that informed the authors of these Reform liturgies. These men had internalised an approach to Judaism that led them to seek attachment to the Jewish past, and their *siddurim* reflect the views of men who saw themselves as part of historical Jewish tradition. They aspired to be members of the larger Jewish community, and they rejected a sectarian posture. As Petuchowski has noted, "Geiger . . . twice refused to heed the call to the pulpit of the Berlin Reform Congregation", a separatist congregation that was "as radical in its Reform as Hamburg tended to be moderate." Instead Geiger, "the liturgical practicioner, . . . set out to lead whole Jewish communities, and not merely 'denominational' Reform groups".[23]

Again, this does not mean that either the *Gebetbücher* of Hamburg or those of Geiger did not reform elements in the traditional service that their authors regarded as atavistic. The prayerbooks composed by the Reform Jews of Hamburg, as well as those of Geiger, were written to reflect a redefinition of Jewishness in keeping with the position and ideals that marked the Jewish community in nineteenth century Germany. As this analysis reveals, Geiger did compose

[23] Jakob J. Petuchowski, 'Abraham Geiger: The Reform Jewish Liturgist', in Petuchowski (ed.), *New Perspectives on Abraham Geiger*, Cincinnati 1975, pp. 48–49.

a Reform *siddur*. On the level of manifest content, his *Gebetbücher* embodied significant departures from the Ashkenazic liturgical tradition that he had received.
Nevertheless, his was a reform of evolution, not revolution. From the perspective
of the Orthodox right, his *siddurim*, like those of Hamburg, were seen as radical
departures from the received Ashkenazic rite. At the same time, a radical
Reform left could condemn them as inconsistent and piecemeal.

   The existence of the *Einheitsgemeinde*, the unified Jewish political-communal
structure that obtained in Germany during the 1800s, also had a conserving
effect upon these Liberal liturgists. Rabbis like Geiger served venerable communities that were embedded in tradition, and they had to take into consideration
the sentiments and feelings, as well as religious commitments, of many. The
prayerbooks of Geiger, as well as those of the Hamburg Temple, reveal a Jewish
world caught between the tug of tradition and the pull of modernity. Manuel Joël
also participated in this arena. His specific resolution of the problem will reflect
how a more conservative Liberal Jew – one who identified with Positive-Historical Judaism as formulated by Zacharias Frankel – struggled with this dilemma.

THE RESPONSE OF MANUEL JOËL:
THE LITURGY OF A POSITIVE-HISTORICAL JEW

As Petuchowski has explained, "While Geiger sat in Frankfurt o. M. [*sic*], preparing the new edition of his prayerbook, his old congregation in Breslau had
entrusted his successor there, Manuel Joël, with the task of revising Geiger's
1854 prayerbook in a more traditionalist direction." As Joël himself testified in
his introduction to his *Israelitisches Gebetbuch*, "the erection of a community synagogue, one which, for the first time was built to be representative of the community as a whole", occasioned the "need" for this new liturgy to be written. While
Geiger was not altogether sanguine about this development, Joël, in his introduction to his *Israelitisches Gebetbuch*, wrote: "After Dr. Geiger had given the desired
approval to the board of the Breslau community, the further discussion of the
principles governing the new prayerbook was begun, and, after their determination, the undersigned rabbi was entrusted with the editorial work." In composing
his *siddur* for the entire community, Joël had to pay attention to those persons in
the community who, as he noted, had preserved the traditional Ashkenazic
liturgy "unchanged" in their "synagogues". At the same time, he was careful to
honour, both because of his own internalisation of certain values and norms as
well the prestige Geiger still commanded in the Breslau community, the
model the Geiger prayerbook provided. Indeed, Joël expressed the hope that,
"the many parts of it which have proved themselves through years of experience
would be preserved for us".[24] The Joël prayerbook thus cannot be understood
nor can his own distinctive stance be illuminated without reference to Geiger
and the 1854 Breslau *Gebetbuch* Geiger authored. Michael Meyer has summed it
up well when he writes, "[t]he lay leadership . . . charged Geiger's successor in

[24]Petuchowski, *Prayerbook Reform in Europe*, pp. 171–172.

Breslau, Manuel Joël, to come up with an acceptable compromise between the traditional prayerbook and Geiger's. Joël ... agreed to use Geiger's first edition as the basis, *retaining the fundamental ideological tendency with which he sympathized.* But he modified it somewhat in a traditional direction ...".[25]

Joël was undoubtedly more conservative than Geiger. In 1869, he described himself at a rabbinic synod as a person who was "rather inclined to retain than to destroy".[26] Yet, his sentiments and inclinations were not altogether different from those of Geiger. Indeed, as Meyer observed, Joël agreed to use the 1854 edition of the Geiger *Israelitisches Gebetbuch* precisely because he identified with its fundamental ideological tendency. Joël was a man who applauded the importance that modernity had placed upon the dignity of the individual. In antiquity, Joël observed, "the individual had no rights vis-à-vis the community. Our time is great because we emphasise individual more than communal tendencies". Yet, in a tone reminiscent of Zacharias Frankel, he maintained: "True greatness comes from the community." In constructing a prayerbook, Joël said, "On the one hand, we must express the freedom of the individual, but, on the other, especially as far as ritual is concerned, the individual must give expression not merely to that which moves him, but also to that which affects Israel and the total community".[27] In the effort to maintain a common worship service for all Jews, the autonomy of the individual, in the opinion of Joël, was not absolute. It had to be curbed, and a spirit of compromise had to prevail. Joël, like Geiger, sought to calibrate the proper response to this dilemma.

In the preface to his 1872 liturgy, Joël outlined the points that guided his response. Addressing himself to the Hebrew section of his liturgy, Joël, as a Positive-Historical Jew informed by the historicism that marked his trend in German Judaism, contended that "even the conservatives do not close their minds to the recognition that the removal of numerous prayers is not only religiously *permitted*, but religiously *commanded*". The historical development of Jewish tradition – including the liturgical one – was too apparent to be denied. At the same time, restoration, not just innovation, must mark the Jewish public prayerbook. Joël was concerned that, "through an unjustified and far too pedestrian evaluation, some prayers which undoubtedly have retained their ability to edify to this day were reckoned among the doubtful prayers". Prayerbook reform must therefore proceed cautiously.[28]

Joël insisted that two prayers were of fundamental importance – "The Confession of Faith (*Shema*) with its Blessings" and "The so-called *Tephillah* proper". With regard to the latter prayer, Joël observed that the formulae of the middle blessings in the *Amidah*, blessings dealing with the restoration of Zion and Jerusalem as well as the reinstitution of the sacrificial cult, were those that gave rise to controversy in the present-day community. Therefore, he suggested, as was

[25]Meyer, *Response to Modernity*, p. 187 (my italics).
[26]As quoted in Plaut, *The Rise of Reform Judaism*, p. 181.
[27]*ibid.*
[28]The citations and arguments in this paragraph are found in Petuchowski, *Prayerbook Reform in Europe*, p. 173.

already the custom in German Liberal prayer, that these benedictions should not be recited aloud, but only prayed silently. In this way, "there could be no objection to the retention of the old formulation by the side of the reformed one, which latter corresponds more to our views provided, of course, that the new formulation does not bear the stamp of arbitrariness, but likewise demonstrates the retention of that which is fundamental". Indeed, this was how Joël proposed to solve the dilemma of communal worship in a pluralistic setting where different members of the community held different attitudes and sensibilities towards prayer. As Petuchowski accurately describes it, Joël printed a "reformed" text of the controversial passages "in large print, and the German translation would refer to that 'reformed' version. But also, in small print and without translation, Joël would restore the traditional text, for the benefit of those congregants who were uncomprimisingly attached to it".[29] In addition, Joël declared, "For congregational purposes, I regarded as correct and appropriate the method of Geiger, i.e., to substitute a free paraphrase for a literal translation." In so doing, Joël claimed that he strove for fidelity to the Hebrew text and its spirit. Nevertheless, Joël confessed, "What appears to be faithful to one looks like being too free to another".[30] The task of navigating between the Scylla of tradition and the Charybdis of modernity was a formidable one. An analysis of the elements of his prayerbook reveals how Joël sought to accomplish this goal.

Like Geiger and the Hamburg Reformers, Joël often displayed a penchant in his liturgy for the Sephardic rite. For example, he retained the formula of *Menuha N'chonah* that Geiger had introduced into the Breslau rite for the Memorial service. Joël also sought to purge the prayerbook of those passages that presented Gentiles in a derogatory fashion that he found inappropriate and offensive to the spirit of the modern age as well as those phrases and sentences that needlessly distinguished between Israel and the nations. He substituted the phrase, "Who has made me an Israelite", for the traditional, "Who has not made me a gentile". Similarly, he removed the passage in the Sabbath *Shaharit* service that asserted that the "uncircumcised" could not enjoy Sabbath rest, and declared simply and positively, "And You have given it, O God, to Your people Israel". While he retained the controversial passages in the Hebrew text of the *Ezrat Avoteinu* that referred to the drowning of the Egyptians at the Red Sea, Joël, like Geiger in 1854, left them untranslated. Joël's wording for *Birkat ha-Minim* was somewhat different to Geiger's. However, his prayer conveyed the same meaning and he, again following Geiger, substituted "Slander" (*Malshinut*) for "Slanderers" (*Malshinim*) in the first word of the prayer. Joël elected to preserve the 1854 Hebrew text Geiger had produced for the *Aleinu* and, though his German translation of the prayer differed from that offered by Geiger, it conveyed a comparable meaning and emphasized that God had bestowed upon Israel "a holy teaching as an inheritance". The universal mission assigned Israel to disseminate this teaching meant that "noxious passages", like that found in the *Havdalah*

[29]*ibid.*, p. 171.
[30]*ibid.*, p. 175.

ceremony that distinguished Israel from the nations, had to be removed from the prayerbook, and the Joël *Gebetbuch*, like that of Geiger, did so.

Joël followed the model Geiger had established in other ways as well. He removed the passage prior to the recitation of the *Sh'ma* that asked God to restore the people of Israel to its land, and offered an alternative to the traditional *Kibbutz Galuyot* benediction in the *Amidah*. Instead of asking God "to gather us together from the four corners of the Earth", Joël composed a prayer that expressed the hope that "the voice of freedom and salvation would be heard in our tents". Joël asked that the "offspring of righteousness" and not "the offspring of David Your servant" flourish, and he provided an alternative for the benediction that asserted, "Restore our judges as at first . . .", with the words, "Justify us with Your judgments and guide us with Your counsel". In his prayer for Jerusalem, Joël praised God, "Who remembers Jerusalem and its ruins".

Joël's imitation of Geiger is also apparent in other prayers he composed. Like Geiger in 1854, Joël left the traditional Hebrew text of the first two blessings of the *Amidah* undisturbed. However, like Geiger, he used translation as a vehicle to obviate meanings he found disturbing. Thus, he retained the Hebrew word, "Go'el" (Redeemer) but translated it as *Erlösung* (Redemption). Furthermore, his German translation offered a spiritual understanding of *Tehiyat ha-Meitim*, and Joël refused to affirm the notion of bodily resurrection contained in the Hebrew. Finally, like Geiger, Joël retained the angelology of *Kedushat d'Yotzer* in Hebrew, but provided a German translation that neglected those elements of angelology and instead exclusively affirmed God as the creator and master of the universe.

In keeping with German Jewish liturgical tradition, Joël rewrote the middle benediction of the Sabath *Musaf* service. Instead of asking God to restore the sacrificial cult, Joël wrote, "May it be pleasing before You, O Lord our God, that You prepare our hearts to observe Your Sabbaths, and may You bring blessing upon our land and contentment within our borders, so that our heart will be open to Your service. And may the expression of our lips instead of the additional sacrifice of this Sabbath that our ancestors offered before You be pleasant unto You". In these brief lines, Joël displayed significant departures from the ideological content of the traditional liturgy. The sacrificial cult was reduced to an historical memory, and the prayer now focused on Germany, not *Eretz Yisrael*, as the focus of Jewish hopes and prayers.

Despite all the innovation present in the Joël prayerbook, his *siddur* also displayed some departures from a rigid Liberal tradition. For example, Joël, despite his apparent distaste for the priestly cult, retained, as Geiger had, the rite of *Duchenen* in his service. He restored the phrase, "When will You reign in Zion", to the *Kedushah* of the Sabbath *Shaharit* service, though he continued to omit the phrase, "May You be exalted and sanctified in Jerusalem Your city". Unlike Geiger, Joël retained the phrase, "from among all peoples", throughout his prayerbook, and while, as we have seen, he emphasised the notion of Jewish mission, he was more comfortable with Jewish particularity than was Geiger. His German translation of the lines, "And may You cause our eyes to behold Your return to Zion . . .", and, "Who restores His divine presence to Zion", was faithful to the Hebrew and, in the final benedictions of the *Amidah* in both morning and evening services, Joël felt free to emphasise in German translation, in a way that Geiger had not, that God had extended the teachings of peace to Israel – though, to be sure, the mission of Israel to spread those teachings to humanity is as apparent in the German rendition of the Joël prayer as it was in the Geiger prayerbook.

The spirit that marked the Joël prayerbook is perhaps best captured in an analysis of Joël's treatment of the line, "Cause a new light to shine upon Zion ...", Joël, as had Geiger in 1854, placed this line in the Hebrew text of his liturgy. However, unlike Geiger, he restored this prayer fully by translating it into German as well, rendering it in the words, "*So lass, o Gott, ein neues Licht auch Zion leuchten*". Nevertheless, Joël then felt constrained to add the phrase, "*und dieses Licht auch uns den Weg erhellen*" (and this light will also illumine the way for us). The particularity of the prayer was thereby muted, and the spirituality of the universal mission assigned Israel thereby highlighted. The Joël *Gebetbuch*, like the Geiger *siddurim*, was very much a product of the spirit that infused German *liberales Judentum*.

CONCLUDING CONSIDERATIONS

An analysis of the manifest content of the Geiger and Joël prayerbooks – as well as those of the Hamburg rites which preceded them – has revealed that a broad consensus of feeling and belief marked the leaders of German Liberal Judaism during the nineteenth century. Themes and innovations present in one *Gebetbuch* found expression in the others as well. This does not mean that these prayerbooks were identical. However, an assessment of these works unmistakably yields the conclusion that a common central European context informed these authors, and that similar sensibilities characterised the framers of these liturgies.

The *siddurim* of Geiger and Joël explain, in part, why separate Liberal Jewish religious denominations, akin to Reform and Conservative branches of Judaism in the United States, did not emerge in Germany at this time. Simply put, the ideological consensus and cultural proclivities that marked Joël and Geiger were simply too great to justify the creation of separate religious movements. The attitudes and principles, as well as applications, evidenced in the *Gebetbücher* of these men do not distinguish them sufficiently to speak of distinct Reform and Positive-Historical denominations. The differences that do distinguish these *siddurim* are, at best, ones of degree, not kind. Joël, like Geiger, embodied the ethos of *Liberales Judentum*. His Positive-Historical Judaism, as displayed in his *Gebetbuch*, represented a trend, not a distinct denomination, in German Liberal Judaism.

Of course, an analysis of other prayerbooks produced by other rabbis associated with the Positive-Historical trend in German Jewish religious life might well produce a different portrait of German religious denominationalism in general and Positive-Historical Judaism in particular. For example, *Das Gebetbuch der Israeliten*, published by Rabbi Michael Sachs of Berlin in 1855, represented a different sensibility and approach to Judaism and liturgy than was evidenced in the Joël *siddur*. Sachs was a preeminent spokesman for Positive-Historical Judaism in nineteenth-century Germany, and Joël had been his pupil and remained among his closest colleagues and friends in the years thereafter.[31] However, the Sachs *Gebetbuch*, unlike that of Joël, maintained the traditional Ashkenazic liturgy of German Jewry in its entirety. Indeed, the traditional nature of the Sachs *siddur* aroused the ire of Reform colleagues and his studies in liturgy as well as the translation he offered in his prayerbook exerted a profound influence on Orthodox as well as Liberal circles in Germany.[32]

The Sachs *Gebetbuch* possessed an aesthetic appearance, and provided a graceful German translation that marked its author as an individual embedded in and informed by contemporary central European culture. Nevertheless, Sachs consistently maintained the Hebrew text and his translation always rendered the Hebrew faithfully. Occasionally, passages concerning sacrifices at the beginning and end of various services were left untranslated, as were several other prayers such as *Y'kum Purkan* that asked divine blessing upon the heads of the Babylonian Jewish community. However, this was characteristic of other Orthodox liturgies of the day as well. Indeed, the only places where there was even a hint of apology on the part of Sachs for the traditional *siddur* were in two translations he provided concerning gentiles. In one, Sachs rendered, *"She'lo a'sani nochri"* (Who has not made me a gentile) with the gentler phrase, *"der mich nicht gemacht zum Nichtisraeliten"* (Who has not made me a non-Israelite). In a parallel vein, Sachs offered *Fremde* (the strangers) as the translation for *a'reilim* (the uncircumcised) in the Sabbath morning service.

The Sachs *Gebetbuch*, unlike that of Geiger or Joël, was thoroughly traditional. It was not part of the Liberal tradition of prayerbook reform that marked both the Reform and Positive-Historical trends in German *Liberales Judentum* during the nineteenth century. It provides a powerful and instructive counter-model to the *siddurim* of Geiger and Joël, and indicates that nineteenth-century Positive-Historical Judaism in Germany was not confined to a liberal expression. It had its conservative wing as well. The situation that obtained in German Positive-Historical Judaism foreshadowed developments that were to emerge in American Conservative Judaism – the heir to German Positive-Historical Judaism – during our century, where traditional and liberal wings of that movement have struggled for hegemony. Contemporary American Jewish intra-denominational differences thus have their parallels in the German situation of the past century.

---

[31]Rivka Horowitz includes Sachs among those contemporaries of Zacharias Frankel whose views were representative of the Positive-Historical School, in her book, *Zacharias Frankel and the Beginnings of Positive-Historical Judaism*, (Hebrew) Jerusalem 1984, pp. 185–194. For an account of the relationship between Sachs and Joël, see Lucas and Frank, *Michael Sachs*, pp. 98 and 118.

[32]See Lucas and Frank, *Michael Sachs*, pp. 115–116, for a description of the conflict and criticism the Sachs liturgy engendered among Reform circles of his day. For a discussion of the role that Sachs occupied in the formation of the modern German Orthodox service, see E.D. Goldschmidt, 'Studies on German-Jewish Liturgy by German-Jewish Scholars', in *LBI Year Book II* (1957), pp. 122–123.

This study, by allowing the Joël and Geiger *Gebetbücher* to provide foci for analysis, has contributed to an understanding of the nature and evolution of Jewish religious denominationalism in both nineteenth-century Germany and the modern era. At the same time, it points in the direction of further research. For while the Geiger and Joël *siddurim* testify to the state of nineteenth-century German *Liberales Judentum* and demonstrate that there was a Positive-Historical wing fully ensconced within its precincts, additional investigation into the *siddurim* of figures like Sachs will eventually provide a fuller understanding of the nature of German Liberal Judaism in general and its Positive-Historical wing in particular.

*Jewish Experiences in the Weimar Republic and
National-Socialist Germany*

Art Under Siege:
The Art Scholarship of Rachel Wischnitzer in Berlin, 1921–1938

BY KATHARINA S. FEIL

Throughout her life Rachel Wischnitzer tirelessly promoted the importance of Jewish Art. Born in 1885 in Minsk during the time of Czarist Russia, Rachel Bernstein-Wischnitzer grew up as the daughter of Russian upper middle class Jews who later on would have the privilege to move to St. Petersburg. Rachel died more than a century later in New York City where she, her husband Mark and son Leonard had found refuge in 1940. During her long and eventful life she had lived in nearly a dozen Central European cities before moving to New York City, meanwhile carving out her extraordinary career as a scholar of Jewish art. Rachel Wischnitzer took the quest of nationalist Russian Jews seriously and made it her task to reveal to her audience the complexity of the creative process linked to Jewish Art. By giving her people an identity that was steeped in its artistic heritage, Wischnitzer wished to strengthen the Jewish national consciousness.

According to nineteenth century nationalism a people had to have its own language, its own land and its own cultural heritage to be considered a nation. Wischnitzer's liefelong quest was based on precisely that pursuit which had dominated the intellectual climate during the formative years she spent as a young scholar in St. Petersburg. She maintained this vision during the years of forced emigration and persecution.

Wischnitzer's approach to the study of Jewish art was to insist that it was essential to look at the surrounding social milieu in which a given piece of art was created and then to contextualise that object. In this way she would uncover its meaning and its history and discover the reason for the shape it had been given. It was Wischnitzer's singular and farsighted contribution to point out the connections between Jewish and non-Jewish art as well as the ways in which Jewish art had influenced Christian Art. She did this without defensiveness or chauvinism. Wischnitzer's goal was to position Jewish Art among the art of other nations and to discover its historical and cultural context which had influenced its styles.

Whether living in St. Petersburg, Berlin or New York City, Wischnitzer never abandoned her mission and always contributed to the scholarly field she had created herself. Rooted among the Russian-Jewish intellectuals, Wischnitzer nevertheless left St. Petersburg for Berlin like hundreds of fellow Russians in

1921. She arrived with her husband Mark whom she had married in 1912 to establish a family and to play an active part in the local Jewish community.

WEIMAR BERLIN

Berlin during the 1920s represented as powerful a myth as New York City does today. It was a place of utmost talent and creativity, a place of decadence and despair – a city at the crossroads of the world. The twenties were a time when, during the inflation, food became a currency and when the desperate living situation, caused by the economic situation, turned the capital into Babylonic chaos. Above all, "Berlin in the 1920's represented a state of mind, a sense of freedom and exhilaration."[1] In Berlin, brightness and darkness ruled simultaneously. Berliners were not like other Germans, they were the New Yorkers of Central Europe.[2]

"If Paris became the political capital of Russia-in-exile in the early 1920s, Berlin became, beginning in the winter of 1921–1922, its cultural centre."[3] The Berlin in which the Wischnitzers decided to settle was a city on the verge of becoming the cultural centre of Russia-in-exile. Sociologically, Russian emigration in those years consisted of mainly two groups: the upper class and the intelligentsia.[4]

By the early twenties, a thriving Russian community had evolved, building up and running its own theaters, bookstores, shops, restaurants, employment agencies as well as establishing "three daily newspapers and five weeklies."[5] The most vibrant centres of intellectual exchange and creativity were the literary cafés where émigré writers and artists met regularly. In Berlin the Russian émigré community formed a world of its own. Vladimir Nabokov later recalled that no real communication existed between the native population and the Russian émigrés:

> I see myself, and thousands of other Russians, leading an odd but by no means unpleasant existence, in material indigence and intellectual luxury, among perfectly unimportant strangers, spectral Germans and Frenchmen in whose more or less illusory cities we, émigrés, happen to dwell.[6]

Within the Russian community, the Russian Jewish community was a growing element. Like thousands of other *Ostjuden* this community started to create its own literary clubs, societies and other support systems which, by 1920, were organised under the title *Verband der Ostjuden in Deutschland*. In the same year, a Union of Eastern Jewish artists, the *Ostjüdischer Künstlerbund*, was founded as well. The management of the Café Leon, one of the centres of Russian literary life, organised readings given by prominent Russian authors. Discussions about

[1]Otto Friedrich, *Before The Deluge: A Portrait of Berlin in the 1920's*, New York 1972, p. 8.
[2]*ibid.*, p. 6.
[3]Robert Williams, *Culture in Exile: Russian Emigrés in Germany, 1881–1941*, Ithaca – London 1972, p. 242.
[4]*ibid.*, p. 111.
[5]Friedrich, pp. 82, 83.
[6]*ibid.*, p. 87.

new forms of art and their mission within the modern world of Western Europe were common.[7] Russian Jewish artists sat in these cafés continuing to do what they had done in Russia: they discussed their "visions of a new and avant-garde Jewish art".[8] It is here that we encounter El Lissitzky and Issachar Ryback, two artists who had been much impressed by their discoveries of Jewish folk art traditions during one of the expeditions the Jewish Historical and Ethnographic Society had launched in 1916.

Berlin in the 1920s was not only the home for thousands of émigrés from the East, but also a major centre for book publishing. By 1900, German publishers operated the most advanced printing, typesetting, and distribution facilities. Berlin's publishing facilities would serve as a beacon to thousands of emigrants. Furthermore, post-war conditions in Germany were ideal for publishing since the cost of paper and typesetting was relatively low, a fact that made the city attractive to publishers from other European countries. *Russkaia Mysl* (Russian Thought), for example, an art journal originally published in Paris, was transferred to Berlin in the winter of 1921/1922 to escape the sudden rise in the cost of paper, printing and publishing which plagued France at that time. At that point, Berlin became "the most important single centre of Russian book publishing, including Petrograd and Moscow".[9]

RIMON/MILGROIM: JOURNAL OF ART AND LITERATURE
(1922–1924)

Both the non-Jewish and Jewish émigré communities of Berlin voiced their opinions by publishing journals, books and newspapers. Regardless of the language—Russian, Hebrew or Yiddish—the printing presses were available and prices "lower than anywhere else."[10] For the Jewish population such circumstances eventually led to a significant output of Hebrew and Yiddish literature. The *Farlag Yiddish, Wostok* (The East), the *Klal-Farlag*, a continuation of the *Folks-Farlag* of Kiev, *Rimon* (Pomegranate), a Jewish art and literature publishing company, the *Yiddisher Kultur Farlag* and the *Yiddisher Literarischer Farlag* were some of the Yiddish publishing houses created in or transferred to Berlin at that time. Hebrew publishing houses experienced similar developments. In 1922 the *Dvir* publishing house was moved to Berlin from Odessa, where it had been founded under the name of *Moriah*.[11]

During those years, Rachel and Mark Wischnitzer became the founders of *Rimon*, an international and multi-faceted publishing house based both in London and Berlin. Publications of the Rimon Publishing Company strove to

[7]Fritz Mierau (ed.), 'Introduction' to 'Zoo', in *Russen in Berlin 1918–1933. Eine kulturelle Begegnung*, Weinheim and Berlin 1987, pp. 259–271.

[8]Leo and Renate Fuks, 'Yiddish Publishing Activities in the Weimar Republic, 1920–1933', in *LBI Year Book XXXIII* (1988), p. 421.

[9]*ibid.*, pp. 132, 133.

[10]*ibid.*, p. 421.

[11]Delphine Bechtel, 'Les revues modernistes yiddish à Berlin et à Varsovie de 1922 à 1924. La quête d'une nouvelle Jérusalem?', in *Études Germaniques*, (April–June 1991), p. 168.

make known Jewish works of art and examine them from an art-critical as well as from a cultural-historical perspective. The idea of the creators was to awaken the interest of the Jewish public in its artistic heritage and thus create and educate an audience that was interested in learning about the connections between Jewish art and Jewish history.[12] Additional publications by the Rimon Publishing Company were books on Jewish art, art history, musicology, history and philosophy.[13] It was not crucial that the contributing authors be Jewish, but rather that the issues under discussion were of Jewish concern.

Apart from these publications of the Rimon Publishing Company, a journal of Jewish art appeared simultaneously in Hebrew and Yiddish. From 1922 to 1924, six issues of *Rimon/Milgroim* were published. It embraced the study of all art forms of all ages. Sculpture, painting, music as well as theatre were subject to discussion with special attention being given to the artistic productivity of the Jewish people. The editors had determined that each issue would include 25 to 30 coloured and/or black and white illustrations. Issues 1 and 2 were published in 1922, issues 3, 4 and 5 in 1923 and issue 6 in 1924. Contributions ranged from an art-historical discussion of Cézanne's work to obituaries of famous Jewish thinkers, theologians and editors.

Readers of *Rimon/Milgroim* were offered poetry by Jewish poets as well as an essay, for instance, on Walter Rathenau. The magazine published discussions concerning the art-historical meaning of the wall paintings in seventeenth and eighteenth century synagogues and contemporary works of Russian-Jewish artists. The hymns of Egyptian King Aknaton were as much of interest to its editors as the national aspect within Jewish music. Among the contributing authors were archaeologist Eliezer Lipa Sukenik, J. Katzenelson, the German art historian J. Meier-Graefe, the Jewish historian Simon Dubnow; the poets Chaim N. Bialik and Shmuel Yosef Agnon; Russian-Jewish artist Eliesser Lissitzky as well as the German-Jewish artist Hermann Struck.

Rimon/Milgroim clearly catered to a well-read and highly educated audience. The editors knew that *Rimon* readers were familiar with the hymns of King Aknaton and would enjoy reading them in Yiddish and Hebrew. *Rimon Milgroim*'s aim was to facilitate a Jewish view on world cultures. Consequently its editors featured Hebrew and Yiddish translations of Egyptian poetry, samples of Chinese paintings, a discussion of the works of sixteenth century German theologian Johannes Reuchlin as well as an essay on the contribution of nineteenth century French philosopher of art Hippolyte A. Taine. *Rimon/Milgroim* was created to present high culture to an educated Jewish audience and to bring culture into Jewish homes in their own language.

---

[12]Rachel Wischnitzer-Bernstein, 'Eine Selbst-Anzeige', in *Soncino-Blätter. Beiträge zur Kunde des jüdischen Buches*, vol. I, (1925–1926), pp. 95, 96.
[13]Rimon Publishers edited the following titles: Ch. N. Bialik, *Ktina Kolbo: Verses for the young;* Dr. M. Gaster, *The Ketubah;* Prof. F. Landsberger, *Impressionism and Expressionism;* Rachel Vischnitzer, *Joseph Ibn Hayyim: A Jewish Illuminator of the Fifteenth Century;* A. Z. Idelson, *The Music of the Orient;* Th. Mommsen, *Judaea and the Jews;* Dr. J. Klatzkin, *Hermann Cohen;* Prof. A. Kulischer, *Earl of Beaconsfield;* E. Keuchel, *Vladimir Soloviev.*

Many years later Rachel Wischnitzer would recall *Rimon/Milgroim*'s beginnings as follows:

> It so happened that Leopold A. Sev, a friend of ours from St. Petersburg, came to Berlin on a visit from Paris. He had been the editor of the St. Petersburg Russian language periodical *Novy Voskhod* (New Dawn). Our idea of publishing a magazine fascinated him. He enlisted the interest of Ilyia Paenson for our venture. Paenson was a Zionist, an admirer of Jewish literature and the arts, a business man with some means. That is how *Rimon* and *Milgroim* originated.[14]

Before publishing the first issue, the Wischnitzers decided to share responsibilities for the journal. Mark, along with others, was to be the journal's literary editor while Rachel, as its artistic editor, decided on the journal's visual appearance.

The editors of *Rimon/Milgroim* never formulated a manifesto but from a summarising description written by Rachel Wischnitzer it became obvious that she perceived the journal as a way to make clear to the world that a Jewish artistic heritage existed and was worth rediscovering.[15] It was her desire to publish the contents and explain the art-historical context of the multiple Hebrew manuscripts she had found in public and private collections. She was convinced of the importance of showing the "continuity of Jewish creativity, the cultural unity of Jews from all around the world, and, most importantly, the value of artistic creations which Jews did not know how to appreciate in the same way as they appreciated their literature".[16] Jews, according to Wischnitzer, had to become acquainted with their own artistic heritage. In 1953, during a public celebration of the journal's thirtieth anniversary held in New York City,[17] Wischnitzer recalled the particular interests and trends that shaped the image of the journal:

> We did not want the sophisticated Jewish reader in Germany or *blasé* reader in England, we wanted them too, of course, but in the first place we wanted people, the men and women who lived a genuine Jewish life, who could understand and were fond of Jewish poetry and a Jewish song. That is how we decided to publish our magazine in Hebrew and in Yiddish.
>
> With the language problem solved, we felt free to deal with any type of art, Jewish and non-Jewish. The Jewish reader needed a general art education to learn to compare, to judge, to evaluate. All too often Jewish art is dealt with as something isolated. We were a people among the peoples, a nation among the nations.[18]

Her vision was to find and educate an audience in search of its own artistic heritage.

Rimon Publishers produced, albeit for only two years, "the most beautiful and interesting journal of Jewish art that ever appeared and the like of which had never before been published for Jewish readers".[19] Combining a discussion of

[14] Rachel Wischnitzer, 'From My Archives', in *Journal of Jewish Art*, No. 6 (1979), p. 6.

[15] Wischnitzer-Bernstein, 'Eine Selbst-Anzeige', p. 95.

[16] *ibid.*, p. 96.

[17] In February 1953 the Congress of Jewish Culture and the Jewish Museum organised the thirtieth anniversary celebration of *Rimon/Milgroim* in New York City.

[18] Archive of Leonard Winchester (ALW): Unpublished speech by Rachel Wischnitzer-Bernstein given at the commemorative *Rimon/Milgroim* symposium, 7 February 1953.

[19] Fuks, p. 423.

new approaches to Jewish art, beautifully illustrated essays on Jewish as well as non-Jewish literature, the journal had been inspired not only by the Russian Jewish quest for a Jewish artistic heritage, but also by the German expressionist journals devoted to both art and literature.

Rimon/Milgroim was a product of its time. The combination of art and literature within one journal was a new concept found in other German expressionist journals such as Herwarth Walden's *Der Sturm* (1910–1933) which was based in Berlin, Franz Pfemfert's *Die Aktion* and Paul Westheim's *Das Kunstblatt,* as well as the Munich-based almanac *Der Blaue Reiter* (1912–1933), whose editors were the two artists Franz Marc and Vassily Kandinsky. Kandinsky and Marc had started publishing *Der Blaue Reiter* in 1912, using it as a platform for the current questions and discussions on Modern Art. *Der Sturm,* a weekly publication, informed its readers on the newest cultural developments and the arts. The intention was to capture its audience by an unprecedented union between avant-garde literature and graphic art.[20] In the case of *Der Sturm,* there is no doubt about the journal's success, both as a forum of literary Expressionism and as a most effective medium for the dissemination of expressionist, futurist and cubist art. *Die Aktion* (1912–1933) and *Das Kunstblatt* (1917–1933) were journals of the political left which linked the discussion of art to a broader political vision of reconciliation among European countries. With a mixture of politics, literature and art, these two journals tried to overcome the limits of nationalism and set the tone for a pacifist cosmopolitanism typical of a powerful strain in Weimar political culture.[21]

The emergence of German Expressionism itself was strongly linked to the political upheavals Germany had experienced between 1905 and 1920. Expressionism was by no means limited to the Fine Arts. The desire to follow an expressionist style was equally widespread in literature, stage design, dance, film and architecture.[22] The art and literature journals of the period thus functioned as one of the vehicles for the expressionist artistic impulse. For the Jewish context, this impulse meant a search for a new and modern approach to a Jewish culture in which the arts were intended to play a decisive role. Inspired by German Expressionism, *Rimon/Milgroim*'s agenda was not, however, limited to the expressionist art form. Its editors' aims were to deal with all kinds of art forms, those of the present (Impressionism, Expressionism, Constructivism) as well as those of the past (Gothic style, Baroque), stressing especially those styles in which Jewish art had appeared throughout the ages.[23] German Expressionism, with the art and literature journals it produced, provided a model for the dissemination of those ideas.

Rachel Wischnitzer helped determine the circle of readers both by setting the agenda and by deciding that both Hebrew and Yiddish would be the languages in

[20]Bernd Evers, 'Eine neue Kunstzeitschrift, wie wir sie brauchen', in *Europäische Moderne. Buch und Graphik aus Berliner Kunstverlagen 1890–1933*, Berlin 1989, p. 56.

[21]Peter Gay, *Weimar Culture: The Outsider As Insider*, New York 1968.

[22]Dietmar Elger, *Expressionism: A Revolution in German Art*, Cologne 1991, p. 8.

[23]Wischnitzer-Bernstein, 'Eine Selbst-Anzeige', p. 96.

which the journal should be published. She later explained this choice of language:

> We realised that German, the language of Goethe, Schiller and Moses Mendelssohn was, after World War I, no longer the unifying cultural vehicle of the Jewish intelligentsia. We wanted to reach out to Jewish groups in America and the growing Jewish community in Palestine.[24]

Thus Yiddish literature generally found its readers either in the United States or in Poland, or Palestine, not in Germany:

> The very factors that limited the marketplace for Yiddish publications in Germany also helped promote their production: inflation and hence cheap labor, an ample supply of journalists, scholars, and writers, and the financial support of the government for the Jewish community in Berlin during the worst years of inflation.[25]

By publishing the journals both in Yiddish and in Hebrew, the editors of *Rimon/Milgroim* were trying to reach the entire Ashkenazi Jewish world whose intelligentsia by then had been split into two ideological camps, namely the Yiddishists and the Hebraicists. During the first decades of the twentieth century, the Yiddish-speaking Jewish public had been growing. Both the Czernowitz Conference of 1908 and the Russian Revolution had been crucial events in the history of Yiddishism. In Czernowitz, Yiddish was declared to be the national language of the Jewish people. Additionally, Lenin's policy on ethnic minorities, and his view of Zionism as 'bourgeois nationalism,' led the Bolshevik government to declare Yiddish to be the only national language of the Jews, since it was the language of the Jewish 'working class'. Finally, those instrumental in the creation of the Versailles Treaty of 1920 guaranteed Yiddish the status of a minority language. Strengthened by these events, the community of Yiddish speaking Jews, by 1921, was growing and as such constituted an expanding group of potential subscribers.

Rimon/Milgroim was not the only Yiddish journal that was published during the twenties; other journals were published in Moscow, Berlin, New York and Poland.[26] Among the post-World War I Yiddish avant-garde groups, the *Shtrom* group of Moscow and the *Milgroim* group of Berlin were both active between 1922 and 1924. In New York, the *Inzikhistn* existed throughout the twenties and thirties, while the *Khalyastre* group of Poland published various journals between 1919 and 1924.

Eschewing a political vision, *Rimon/Milgroim* was criticised by other Jewish modernist journals like the Polish-Yiddish *Di Khalyastre*. While *Rimon/Milgroim* tried to uphold a scholarly neutrality in the ideological conflict between Yiddishists and Hebraicists, *Di Khalyastre*, in an expressionist vision of the apocalyptic state of the world, strove to help rebuild a secular Jewish life in Yiddish the disappearance of which its editors considered imminent. The message of the

---

[24]Rachel Wischnitzer, 'From My Archives', p. 7.
[25]Arthur Tilo Alt, 'The Berlin Milgroym Group And Modernism', in *Yiddish*, vol. VI, No. 1 (1985), p. 35.
[26]Seth Wolitz, '*Di Khalyastre*: The Yiddish Modernist Movement in Poland. An Overview', in *Yiddish*, vol. IV, No.3 (1981), p. 6.

Khalyastre group was clearly political, even anti-aesthetic.[27] The circle of writers and artists that formed the *Khalyastre* group was driven by the expressionist need to reconstruct cosmic disorder and understood itself to be explorers of a new Jewish life.[28] To them, *Rimon/Milgroim* represented an empty aestheticism that used "beauty as mere decoration";[29] they criticised the journal as offering an illusion of neutrality in its bi-linguality at a time when the issue of choosing either Hebrew or Yiddish was in itself a highly political and ideological choice. To them, *Rimon/Milgroim* had lost its avant-garde character and could, at best, be called a modernist publication.

Conceived by two middle-class academics, *Rimon/Milgroim* did not live up to the political expectations of the Polish Yiddishists. The journal's aestheticism and international aspiration differed from the radicalism of the *Khalyastre* group. The Wischnitzers meant to address a Jewish audience that looked for discussions on Jewish art and literature. Without proclaiming a political manifesto, *Rimon/Milgroim* was meant to redefine Jewish identity and widen the view of Jewish culture by providing scholarly essays along with poetry and decorative graphics.

Many German Jews were involved in the publication of expressionist art journals in Germany. One of them, Herwarth Walden (1878–1941), was the editor of the successful journal *Der Sturm* and an assimilated[30] German Jew himself. Walden, born Georg Lewin, had no interest in stressing Jewish culture and aimed his publication "at a broad German public".[31] Unlike Walden, the Wischnitzers specifically tried to address a Jewish audience by using the language of aestheticism and academia rather than the rhetoric of political radicalism. Their publication was part of a Jewish Renaissance movement closely linked to the discussion of art.[32]

Within this Jewish Renaissance movement, a movement that re-evaluated Jewishness, the journal *Ost und West* (1901–1923) was a very significant contribution which combined the discussion of nationalism and art. Aside from many Zionists (Martin Buber, Alfred Nossig, Max Nordau, Otto Warburg), non-Zionists such as Moritz Lazarus, Ludwig Geiger and Martin Phillipsohn were on the founding committee. Published in German, *Ost und West* addressed the assimilated German Jewish public and by combining the political and cultural debate, art criticism and literature, it became one of the most important documents of the Jewish Renaissance.[33] The journal was read by an

---

[27] *ibid.*, p. 16.

[28] *ibid.*, p. 5.

[29] Arthur Tilo Alt, 'The Berlin Milgroym Group And Modernism', p. 36.

[30] Assimilation is understood as "a process engaged in by a minority whose goal is fusion with the majority", Marion A. Kaplan, in 'Tradition and Transition: The Acculturation, Assimilation and Integration of Jews in Imperial Germany', in *LBI Yearbook XXVI*, (1982), p. 4.

[31] Lewin, 'Introduction', in *Europäische Moderne*, p. 12.

[32] Inka Bertz, *"Eine neue Kunst für ein altes Volk": Die Jüdische Renaissance in Berlin 1900 bis 1924, (Ausstellungsmagazin)* Berlin 1991.

[33] *ibid.*, p. 28.

estimated ten percent of German Jewry, its core audience being the Berlin *bourgeoisie*.[34]

During the twenties Rachel Wischnitzer emerged as a serious scholar of the history of Jewish art. As the discussion of her Berlin years will show, her scholarly contribution to the field of Jewish art was accompanied by her activism in the public sphere of museum work. While her work for *Rimon/Milgroim* occurred in co-operation with her husband, she nevertheless succeeded in sketching out her methodological approach in the few articles published in the journal. These articles need to be valued as Wischnitzer's early contributions to the field of Jewish art. During the years of *Rimon/Milgroim's* publication, Wischnitzer contributed seven articles,[35] three of which specifically discuss Jewish art, its history and the Jewish response to art in general. All of them appeared in either Hebrew or Yiddish and were translated for that purpose since Wischnitzer herself did not write Hebrew nor Yiddish.

In the first issue of *Milgroim*, Wischnitzer in 1922 published an article on *'Di neie kunst un mir'* (Modern Art and our Generation).[36] Inspired by the aforementioned Russian Jewish quest for Jewish art, Wischnitzer explored the different art forms which did, and those which did not, influence Jewish artists. She found that Modern Art, unlike Naturalism, had created "rhythms that reached the Jewish ear."[37] Surveying several periods within Jewish history, she identified the modern type of Jewish artist as the expressionist who has ecstatic characteristics, those that make him paint with "heart and soul".[38] Issachar Ryback, in her eyes, was such an artist. Painting the old synagogue of Dubrovna, he managed to bring out a certain pride that emerged from the structure of the building rather than stressing the sense of submission and fragility that could dominate any old building. Wischnitzer noticed the same sense of self-confidence in Ryback's depiction of an old Jew. Looking at this figure, she observed how Ryback tried to stress the dignity of Jewish tradition since he did not depict a submissive ghetto Jew eager to gain the viewer's sympathies, but rather self-confident and deeply rooted person. Wischnitzer saw that by using Expressionism, Ryback conveyed the Russian Jewish message of Jewish self-confidence in altering the image of submissiveness and stressing a Jewishness which contained cultural, national as well as religious elements.

Wischnitzer saw an art emerging, in which the "human being is again at the centre of the artist's interest."[39] The "New Ones", as Wischnitzer called them,

[34]David Brenner, 'Marketing Eastern Jewish Nationalism in the West: The Case of the Jewish Cultural Review Ost und West, Berlin 1901–1923', Paper delivered at a YIVO conference, 'Political, Religious and Cultural Responses to Modern Jewish Nationalism in Eastern European Jewry, 1897–1939', 14–16 November 1992.

[35]Rachel Wischnitzer, 'Modern Art and Our Generation', in *Rimon/Milgroim (R/M)*, 1 (1922); *idem*, 'Max Liebermann. On the occasion of his 75th anniversary', *R/M*, 2 (1922); *idem*, 'On Taine's Philosophy of Art', *R/M*, 3 (1923); *idem*, 'The Motive of Porch Ornamentation', *R/M*, 4 (1923); *idem*, 'Max Nordau as an Art Critic', *R/M*, 4 (1923) *idem*, 'David and Samson slaying the Lion', *R/M*, 5 (1923); *idem*, 'Emanuele Glicenstein', *R/M*, 6 (1924).

[36]Rachel Wischnitzer, 'Di Neie Kunst un Mir', in *Milgroim*, 1, Berlin 1922, pp. 2–7.

[37]*ibid.*, p. 2.

[38]*ibid.*, p. 7.

[39]*ibid.*

had received their first impulses from synagogue wall paintings. Involved in their art with heart and soul, this new generation of artists had created a "new kind of religious art".[40]

In their response to modernity, Wischnitzer thought, Russian Jewish artists did not abandon their traditions and religious values but stressed them. Their vision of modernity was linked to their national, religious and cultural identity as Jews, which to Wischnitzer explained why the artist's horizon was "filled with figures taken from mythology, folk legends and holy tales".[41] She found that modern art had helped Jewish artists to communicate with the non-Jewish world by sharing their vision of modern Jewish life. Modernity, so she maintained, had not uprooted the Jews but had supplied them with new tools which brought them closer to the non-Jewish world.

In her article on 'The Gate Motif in Book Ornamentation',[42] Wischnitzer showed how the motif of the gate had been used by Jewish and Christian illuminators throughout the ages. She sought to retrace the different shapes the gate-motif had adopted when being used for book illustrations by Jews and Christians alike. Throughout her career, Wischnitzer constructed her arguments to show how Christian and Jewish art had influenced one another. With her essay on the gate-motif, Wischnitzer started to establish a comparative history of Hebrew and Christian traditions of book illumination by using that particular motif to point out the differences found within the two theologically distinct, yet artistically related, traditions. The goal of this method was to make her readers understand how Christian illuminators were adopting and altering Jewish motifs for their purposes.

Beginning with a tenth-century Hebrew illuminated manuscript from Egypt—found in the St. Petersburg Imperial Library—that had been used as a commentary on the Second Book of Moses and depicted the desert tabernacle, Wischnitzer described the illumination as a mixture of illustrative and ornamental style. Commenting on other manuscripts from the same source and the same period, she noticed a trend towards a stylization of the objects and concluded that *Mizrach-menshen* (people from the East), meaning Jews, tended to create ornamental art.[43] According to her, early Christian manuscripts, found in tenth century Syria, adopted the architectural shape of the *Aron*-motif by framing a text with the form of an arch.[44] To Wischnitzer this proved that Christians had adopted and altered a motif taken from a Jewish context. Byzantine art changed the *Aron*-motif into that of a gate decorated with flowers and palm leaves and then had used it to frame a book page. In a fourteenth-century *Haggadah* from the British Museum, the gate motif regained its original meaning and became the frame of a text again. With the emergence of Naturalism during the second half of the nineteenth century, the strict frame provided by the gate-motif became

[40] *ibid.*
[41] *ibid.*
[42] *idem*, 'Der Toir-Motiv In Der Buch-Kunst', in *Milgroim*, 4, Berlin 1923, pp. 2–7.
[43] *ibid.*, p. 5.
[44] *ibid.*

superfluous and the text was separated from the illumination. Within the tradition of Hebrew illuminations, the gate-motif therefore lost its function at a certain point in time.

In the fifth issue of *Rimon/Milgroim,* Wischnitzer published an article on '*Der Leib-Bezwinger in der Jidisher Kunst*' (The Conqueror of Lions in Jewish Art).[45] Wischnitzer once more picked a specific motif, in this case that of the heroic fighter and the wild beast, and examined its appearance, shapes and context throughout art history. She found that the battle scenes between a heroic hunter and a monstrous animal were old and dated back to the beginnings of civilization. The Gilgamesh epic, a Babylonian legend from the second millennium BC, was one of the sources for such scenes. Wischnitzer identified the heroes of the Gilgamesh epic, Gilgamesh and Enkidu, as the forerunners of the biblical heroes David and Samson based on the fact that both Babylonian heroes were depicted with long hair, an image which later on had influenced the Samson legends. Further developing her argument, Wischnitzer pointed out that Hellenism too had copied the gestures found in the Gilgamesh epos. Hellenistic images of Daniel in the den of lions were similar to the triumphant gestures found in depictions of the Gilgamesh epos.

Throughout her argument, Wischnitzer tried to make clear how the depiction of David and Samson had developed differently when used by different theologies. Christian iconography used David as the conqueror of evil, while Jewish tradition attributes this role to Samson. Several Jewish manuscripts, a thirteenth century manuscript by Benjamin *ha Sofer*, the Leipzig *Mahzor*, the *Haggadot* of the eighteenth century and the Carpua *Mahzor* of 1700, showed Samson riding the lion stylising him into a popular hero who conquered with ease. During the Middle Ages, Jewish iconography had used Samson as a symbol of Israel's invincible power. In Christian iconography David was used as Jesus' counterpart. Symbolising victory over evil in the world he was perceived as the Hebrew forerunner of Jesus, who came into this world to conquer "evil".[46] In Christian iconography, David took Samson's role and became the conqueror of lions while in Hebrew manuscripts he took the role of a wise king or that of the young man playing the harp.

As a scholar of Jewish art and contributor to *Rimon/Milgroim,* Rachel Wischnitzer made a noteworthy contribution to a developing field of scholarship. By raising the issue of the interdependency between Christian and Jewish images, Wischnitzer addressed an issue which would be repeatedly discussed by art historians over the course of years.[47]

Before 1923, the subject of Jewish art in general and Hebrew illuminations in particular had not been totally ignored by Jewish scholars. David Kaufmann

---

[45]*idem,* 'Der Leib-Bezwinger In der Jidisher Kunst', in *Milgroim,* 5, Berlin 1923, pp. 1–4.

[46]*ibid.,* p. 4.

[47]The extent to which the issue of mutual dependency between the Jewish and Christian artistic traditions remains to be important becomes clear in a recently published volume which deals with the complex issue of borrowing and re-interpreting cultural symbols. See Heinz Schreckenberg and Kurt Schubert (eds.), *Jewish Historiography and Iconography in Early and Medieval Christianity,* Assen and Maastricht 1992.

(1852–1899), the renowned Hungarian Jewish scholar, had contributed to the field of history, medieval Jewish philosophy, history of religion and the history of Jewish art. Shortly before his death, in 1898, Kaufmann published his pioneering essay '*Zur Geschichte der Jüdischen Handschriften-Illustrationen*'.[48] In this essay Kaufmann directed most of his efforts at proving that, despite the general Jewish iconoclastic attitude, Jewish illuminators had decorated Hebrew manuscripts and had left behind a rich legacy. He pointed out that the scholarship on Jewish art had been neglected by Jews since they were widely under the wrong impression that Jewish art did not exist because of the prohibitive laws within Judaism. Kaufmann took his examples from all over Europe, thereby showing his readers ample evidence of illuminated Jewish texts. By doing so, he succeeded in displaying the richness and diversity of Jewish art. Interestingly, only towards the end of his essay did he widen the readers' perspective by noting that sometimes Christian illuminators were the artists who had illuminated Jewish texts.

In her articles Wischnitzer assumed the existence of a rich tradition of Jewish art and boldly pushed the agenda further. For her, it was important to see Jewish art in its cultural context. By doing so, Wischnitzer followed in the footsteps of the prominent Viennese art historian Josef Strzygowski (1862–1941), who in his two publications from the beginning of the twentieth century[49] suggested that "illuminated Christian manuscripts like the Ashburnham Pentateuch and the Alexandrian World Chronicle might be rooted in a hitherto undiscovered tradition of illustrated Jewish manuscripts".[50] The lack of artistic and literary evidence did not stop Strzygowski from formulating this propositon.

With her article on 'The Motif of the Gate in Book Ornamentation', Wischnitzer had proved that looking at Jewish art in a historical way meant seeing its impact on early Christian art. She therefore examined the wall panels used and tried to identify the different cultural influences that helped create new motifs. This was based on her conviction that Jewish art had existed throughout the ages and had been influenced by the cultures within which Jews had dwelled. Wischnitzer's *Rimon/Milgroim* articles foreshadowed her comparative approach that would perceive Jewish art as an art created not in isolation but as part of the different cultural settings in which Jews had lived throughout history and in its day the *Rimon/Milgroim* journal was "the first Yiddish magazine that had undertaken to give art a status beside literature in Jewish cultural life".[51]

---

[48] David Kaufmann, 'Zur Geschichte der Jüdischen Handschriften-Illustration', in David Heinrich Müller, Julius v. Schlosser (eds.), *Die Haggadah von Sarajewo. Eine Spanisch-Jüdische Bilderhandschrift des Mittelalters*, Wien 1898, pp. 255–312.

[49] Josef Strzygowski, *Orient oder Rom*, Leipzig 1901; *idem* and A. Bauer, *Eine Alexandrinische Weltchronik*, Vienna 1906.

[50] Joseph Gutmann, 'The Illustrated Jewish Manuscript in Antiquity: The Present State of the Question', ed. by Joseph Gutmann, *No Graven Images: Studies in Art And The Hebrew Bible*, New York 1971, p. 232.

[51] ALW: RW to Samuel Niger, 2 April 1952. On 7 February 1952, thirty years after the journal's publication in Berlin, the New York Jewish Museum together with the Congress of Jewish Culture organised a conference to commemorate the singular contribution made by the journal. Samuel Niger, who presided, spoke of the journal's significance for Jewish literature. Dr. Stephen Kayser, curator of Judaica at the New York Jewish Museum, evaluated the journal from the aesthetic point of view.

Left to right: Professor Wolfskehl (artist), Rachel Wischnitzer, Max Osborn (art critic), Professor Franz Landsberger (curator), Mrs Cassierer (secretary of the exhibition) and Mr Bato (artist) shortly before the opening of the Jewish Museum spring exhibition in April 1937.

Mark Wischnitzer, Dr. Alfred Klee and Rachel Wischnitzer in Berlin, March 1938, a month before Rachel Wischnitzer and her son Leonard left Germany.

Reproduced with the kind permission of Mr.Leonard Winchester

A deer hunt symbolising the persecution of the Jews from a fifteenth century *Haggadah*.

Landesbibliothek Darmstadt, cod. or. 8.

The fountain of youth from a fifteenth century *Haggadah*.

Landesbibliothek Darmstadt, cod. or. 8.

ולקחתם לכם ביום הראשון פרי עץ הדר כפות תמרים וענף עץ עבת
וערבי נחל ושמחתם לפני יהוה אלהיכם שבעת ימים

A circuit in the synagogue with the four species of Sukkot. The Hebrew beneath
is from the biblical command for the four species in Leviticus 33:40.

Copperplate, Josef Herz

VOLUNTARY CURATOR AT THE BERLIN JEWISH MUSEUM
1933–1938

The mere act of founding a museum needs to be understood as a significant move from the private to the public, a move that marks the democratisation of art. Furthermore, the public display of art for the Jewish community meant a conscious effort to show the Jewish cultural experience to interested citizens, Jews or non-Jews alike.[52] Through the public display of Jewish culture in a museum setting, Berlin Jews expressed their desire to be perceived as a culturally independent and identifiable part of German society. Those involved in the work of the museum wanted to reform their image as a group within German society, and make clear that they were confident enough to leave behind the traditional setting of the Jewish home and community. Their museum demanded the recognition of a Jewish cultural identity, which, as hindsight would have it, was in 1933 either an act of immense bravery or foolish naiveté. For Wischnitzer this was the logical step towards the political goal of attempting to demonstrate Jewish nationhood.

It was Karl Schwarz who, in 1932, named the art collection *Jüdisches Museum Sammlung der Jüdischen Gemeinde zu Berlin* (Jewish Museum Collection of the Berlin Jewish Community), thus anticipating that space for a museum would soon be found. An art historian by profession, Schwarz had been employed by the community in 1927 to take care of its art collection and by 1930 was appointed as its director. In January 1933 new rooms were rented at Oranienburger Strasse 31 and the museum was festively inaugurated. The works of art on exhibition were sculptures, paintings and ritual objects, as well as archeological artifacts from Palestine and a collection of ancient coins that had originally been in the possession of Albert Wolf, a Jewish collector from Dresden. Within its first year, the museum counted 13,000 visitors, who were "joyfully discovering Jewish art".[53]

The creation of the Berlin Jewish Museum needs to be perceived as an attempt to solve a problem European Jews faced after Emancipation, namely the dilemma of how to fill the vacuum created by modernity, which had led many Jews to leave their religious identity behind in the hope of being welcomed into European society. Modernity had brought urbanisation and secularisation as well as an upward social mobility to Jews during the nineteenth century. At the dawn of the twentieth century, European Jews were searching for a new self-definition beyond their religion and those dealing with Jewish art often found it in their cultural heritage. Furthermore, in the Germany of 1933 this search for a

---

Artists and contributors to the journal, such as Joseph Opatoshu and Emanuel Romano spoke about their work. Finally, the two editors, Rachel and Mark Wischnitzer related some episodes as insiders of the journal, pointed out the artistic goals of the undertaking and gave a picture of the cultural atmosphere of the period, ALW, Description of the symposium, undated.

[52] Richard Cohen, 'Self-Image Through Objects: Toward a Social History of Jewish Art Collecting and Jewish Museums', in *The Uses Of Tradition: Jewish Continuity In The Modern Era*, ed. by Jack Wertheimer, New York 1992, p. 205.

[53] Erna Stein, 'Ein Jahr Jüdisches Museum. 13.000 Besucher', in *Gemeindeblatt der jüdischen Gemeinde zu Berlin*, (9 February 1934), p. 3.

new self-image was a way of reacting to the political pressures which surrounded the Jewish population.

Before 1933, the year the museum opened, Berlin Jews had expressed their artistic heritage in different ways. In 1907, Jewish artists had exhibited modern painting and sculpture alongside Jewish ceremonial art and artifacts.[54] It was through this exhibit that the interest in and appreciation of Jewish art in Berlin was awakened and that the idea for the establishment of a Jewish museum began to take shape.[55]

During the same year the Dresden jeweller and collector Albert Wolf donated his Judaica collection to the Berlin community, which then was the largest German Jewish community. In 1927, after having been stored away for twenty years, the collection, consisting of coins, books, manuscripts, seals, ritual objects and portraits of famous Jews,[56] was exhibited in two rooms that were part of the administrative building of the Berlin Jewish community.

From the very beginning, education was a priority for the museum staff. Between 1917 and 1927, Moritz Stern, the community's head librarian, had been responsible for the art collection and Jewish students were brought to the exhibitions to learn about Jewish history. Later, under the guidance of Karl Schwarz, director of the art collection from October 1927 until 1935, the *Jüdischer Museumsverein* (Jewish Museum Society) was founded. In 1935, Wischnitzer delivered a paper to the *Museumsverein* on 'The Cherubim in Jewish Art', which gained her the reputation of being an "excellent specialist in Jewish art" who was able to enthrall her audience.[57] In 1936, Wischnitzer introduced the public to Jewish folk art in her lecture on 'The Significance of Torah Binders in Art History',[58] and became an avid supporter of the work of the *Museumsverein*.

At its core, the *Jüdischer Museumsverein* was committed to promoting the knowledge about Jewish cultural treasures, making them accessible to the public while maintaining that "Judaism itself did not belong in a museum".[59] The founders of the *Museumsverein* saw themselves facing a difficult task: to show that Judaism was a vital part of people's daily lives while inanimate Jewish art objects were used to support this opinion. The purpose of a Jewish museum was not to keep alive the memory of a lost tradition, but rather to help visitors see that the Jewish tradition and religion had developed throughout the ages and continued to exist in the present. This point is important since today's European Jewish Museums are mostly the cultural testimony of a destroyed, though once vital, Jewish community.

In the thirties, special attention was given to the way objects were displayed in the new rooms of the Berlin Jewish Museum. The exhibition rooms were arranged chronologically so that the visitor would follow the thread of Jewish

---

[54]*ibid.*, p. 234.
[55]Hermann Simon, *Das Berliner Jüdische Museum in der Oranienburger Straße. Geschichte einer zerstörten Kulturstätte, Stadtgeschichtliche Publikationen II*, Berlin 1983, p. 7.
[56]*ibid., p.* 9.
[57]Wischnitzer, 'The Cherubim in Jewish Art', in *Gemeindeblatt*, (17 November 1935).
[58]*idem*, 'The Significance of Torah Binders in Art History', *Gemeindeblatt*, (20 December 1936).
[59]*Jüdische Rundschau*, No. 95, 3 July 1929, p. 639.

history, starting with Jewish antiquity and continuing through the Middle Ages, the eighteenth and nineteenth centuries up to the present.[60] Importance was further given to housing the collection and to the acquisition of additional pieces which would embody the long and unbroken tradition and history of the Jewish people. In its goals and endeavors, the *Museumsverein* prepared the way for the founding of the Berlin Jewish Museum.

Ironically, the very year that marked the transformation of the art collection into a public Jewish institution coincided with Adolf Hitler's rise to power as chancellor of Nazi Germany. Like the *Jüdischer Kulturbund* the Museum's management was confronted with the difficult task of representing German Jewry while facing an increasingly repressive regime which persecuted its Jewish citizens.

Franz Landsberger, the museum's founding director, understandably promoted a mixed agenda: on the one hand, his work emphasised the Jewish heritage and supported a stronger self image among Jews, on the other hand, he felt cautious about "consciously strengthening"[61] that Jewishness in the arts. Written in 1935, his words reveal the inner conflict he must have experienced when organising the Jewish Museum while witnessing the rising power of Nazism. The interested Jewish public, meanwhile, turned to the Museum as a place where it could find a positive self-image and distraction from the Nazis' humiliating campaign against its religion and culture.[62]

Until 1938, Nazi politics suggested that the government favoured the cultural development of Jews within Germany, as long as they did not exhibit the traits that had been branded by the Nazis as despicable and specifically Jewish.[63] In 1936 Adolf Eichmann himself visited the Jewish Museum. Given a tour of the exhibition *"Unsere Ahnen"* by Wischnitzer. He discussed Jewish affairs with a level of expertise or at least familiarity with the appropriate terminology which, to a naive observer, might have suggested a true interest in and appreciation of Jewish culture. Later on Wischnitzer recalled that

> Dr. Alfred Klee and Heinrich Stahl, director of the Board of the Jewish Community, were present. I was showing Eichmann around. He said that American Jews who were Sefardi Jews are of a higher cultural standard than Ashkenazi Jews. Dr. Klee remarked that most American Jews are of Ashkenazi descent. Eichmann asked me about my husband's book *Juden in der Welt* (1935). He was up-to-date on Jewish affairs.[64]

Deceived by this illusory freedom to express themselves and by the Nazis' interest in Jewish affairs many Berlin Jews wholeheartedly embraced the idea of a cultural life of their own. To them an evening at the *Kulturbund* meant meeting as a community at a time when everything German society associated with that community was negative. Soon after the idea of the *Kulturbund* was beginning to

---

[60]Rachel Wischnitzer, 'Das jüdische Museum', in *Jüdische Rundschau*, No. 8, (27 January 1933).

[61]*ibid.*, p. 58.

[62]Franz Landsberger, 'Unser Museum. Rückblick auf 1935', in *Gemeindeblatt der jüdischen Gemeinde zu Berlin,* (5 January 1936), p. 18l.

[63]*ibid.*, p. 12.

[64]Wischnitzer, 'From My Archives', p. 11.

be advertised, the response among Berlin Jews was greater than anticipated. The first public evening, held at the synagogue on Prinzregentenstrasse – which included a choir, an orchestra and a welcoming speech – was attended by 2,500 Jews. Half of the audience joined the *Kulturbund* right away while 90 per cent of the rest joined within the next ten days.[65]

In the beginning, the activities of the *Kulturbund* were not censored. Only after the Cultural Leagues (*Kulturbünde*) had been active for a while did Hans Hinkel, a Nazi official in charge of cultural affairs, demand that their repertoire be exclusively Jewish and that non-Jewish German authors should not be used any more. For the theater managers, the problem now was to find Jewish plays and music for an audience that was much more interested in viewing internationally acclaimed theater pieces than seeing the plays of Yiddish authors such as Mendele Mocher Sforim and Sholem Aleichem. Berlin Jews would come to see famous artists not because they were Jewish but because they were internationally renowned. Cornered by Nazi politics, Berlin Jews were now forced to develop a taste for their own cultural heritage.

While some Berlin Jews were struggling to build up a Jewish cultural life, the German government was moving towards its politics of exclusion. Jewish cultural institutions, such as the *Kulturbund* and the Berlin Jewish Museum, were built on thin ice. They tried to further self-esteem by promoting Jewish culture, while being watched by Nazi officials who until 1935 accepted Jews as culturally active as long as they would behave "like a guest: restrained and inconspicuous".[66] The tone had obviously changed since 1933. Nazis, who then had claimed to protect the *Kulturbund* unconditionally had changed their position into one of imposing ever increasing restrictions and rules.

Unlike the *Kulturbund*, the Berlin Jewish Museum grew out of the endeavors of its own community members without government approval or support. While other Jewish communities around the country slowly disappeared through emigration, Berlin remained the last bastion of liberalism and a vital centre of Jewish life. Against all odds, Berlin Jews proudly exhibited their Jewish tradition and culture. They responded to Nazi politics in a particular way and Berlin seemed, for a short while, to provide the perfect platform. Known for its liberalism and tradition of tolerance, Berlin offered fertile ground for their cultural endeavours. The creation of a separate arena for Jewish cultural activities was a mixed blessing. As much as it gave them 'a place to be', Jews themselves felt that it confined them to a specifically Jewish niche within German society. Before they were forced into that niche, many Berlin Jews had lost their connection to the religious community and had enjoyed all the cultural stimulations the non-Jewish German society had to offer. Wischnitzer, both visionary and realist, understood that a Jewish cultural institution had to work hard to bring positive meaning and dignity to its audience. Many years later she recalled:

[65] Monika Richarz (ed.), *Jüdisches Leben in Deutschland. Selbstzeugnisse zur Sozialgeschichte 1918–1945*, Stuttgart 1982, p. 316.
[66] Volker Dahm, *Das Jüdische Buch Im Dritten Reich*, vol. I (*Die Ausschaltung der jüdischen Autoren*), Frankfurt a. Main 1979, p. 91.

Wagner, the great anti-Semite, had declared there was no such thing as Jewish music. In Europe, the church and cathedral were far more important to art historians than the synagogue. We had to restore dignity to Jewish art and architecture.[67]

In 1935, over two years after the opening of the Museum, both Karl Schwarz and Erna Stein, at that time Schwarz's assistant, left their positions. A new staff was appointed with Franz Landsberger as the Museum's director and curator and Rachel Wischnitzer-Bernstein[68] as its honorary research assistant and curator.[69] On 11 April 1935 the organ of the *Centralverein deutscher Staatsbürger jüdischen Glaubens* (C.V.) announced the change in leadership with the headline: "*Das Berliner Jüdische Museum unter neuer Leitung*".

Franz Landsberger, who had already been dismissed by the Nazis from his position as a professor of art history at the University of Breslau in 1935, came to Berlin in the same year and stayed as museum director for four years. In 1910 he had founded the *Verein für Jüdische Kunst* (Society for Jewish Art) in Breslau. Landsberger's interest in dealing with Jewish art was primarily academic. For him, the preservation, research and exhibition of Jewish art was directly connected to the larger investigation of art history which, in the middle of the eighteenth century, had been initiated by German archaeologist Winckelmann's *Geschichte der Kunst des Altertums*.[70] It was for the sake of scholarship, not for the sake of Jewish self-definition, that Landsberger researched the traditions of Jewish art.

The *Kommission der Kunstsammlung* of the Jewish Community in Berlin, of which Rachel Wischnitzer was a member, had decided to hire him only under the condition that Wischnitzer would be his assistant. Many years later Wischnitzer would recall the circumstances:

> In 1935 Schwarz and his assistant left for Israel [the Museum was founded in 1917] we arranged for Dr. Landsberger to become the curator. He had lost his professorship in Breslau. He was a friend of mine, I had published an article of his in the *Rimon*. My position was honorary. Landsberger was a thoroughly assimilated German and he got the position on the condition that I would advise him. He expanded the modern section, which was what he really could handle.[71]

This letter addresses two important issues, namely the museum's agenda and Wischnitzer's position within that institution. The concern voiced about Landsberger's degree of assimilation reveals that other issues were at stake for those in charge of the museum. Apart from exhibiting Jewish culture, the organisers of the museum were eager to represent the religious aspect of Judaism and thus were concerned to hire people who had not lost their connection to Jewish culture and religion. While Landsberger was perceived as

---

[67]Roberta Elliott, 'Centenarian thrives on her synagogue architecture work', in *The Jewish Week*, (24 May 1985).

[68]In the early years of her marriage Rachel Wischnitzer used her maiden name.

[69]ALW: Letter sent to Dr. Rachel Wischnitzer-Bernstein by the *Vorstand der Jüdischen Gemeinde*, 22 March 1935. Her title was *Wissenschaftlicher Beirat und Kustos im Ehrenamt*.

[70]Franz Landsberger, 'Das Wesen des Jüdischen Museumswesens', in *C.V.-Zeitung*, vol. XVI, No.1 (1937).

[71]Correspondence from the personal archives of Claire Richter Sherman, Washington (ACRS), letter from Rachel Wischnitzer to Claire Richter Sherman, 28 January 1978.

assimilated,[72] Wischnitzer was the acculturated[73] Jew and as such perceived as the guarantor of Jewishness. The board of directors was trying to secure the museum's religious and cultural authenticity by inviting Wischnitzer to become Landsberger's assistant.

Wischnitzer's family background was fairly traditional. Her father's "nationalistic *Haskalah* was manifested in his thorough knowledge of Hebrew and his observance of some traditional Jewish customs at home",[74] while her mother was versed in both the Jewish culture and the languages of Europe. With that kind of background and her own commitment to "things Jewish", Wischnitzer seemed steeped deeply enough in the Jewish tradition to appear as a fit counterpart to the assimilated Landsberger.

To Franz Landsberger the promotion of Jewish art seemed desirable. However, under the supervision of the Hinkel office, he had to be cautious not to overstress the importance and meaning of Jewish art.[75] To argue that Jewish art was a crucial cultural issue in 1935 was a highly political and risky statement which could have endangered the institution and with it the entire community. Oddly enough, a mere involvement in research on Jewish art was not perceived as a political statement. In those days, one still believed that scholarship could be objective, de-personalised and thus apolitical.

With Landsberger as director and Wischnitzer as honorary curator, the Museum had hired two highly qualified scholars. Weeks before she began her work, Wischnitzer was asked to catalogue the holdings so that on the day she started work "everything would be in order".[76] Her new position was discussed during a conversation with Alfred Klee, a board member of the local Jewish community. During this conversation, it was determined that Landsberger was to be in charge of the administration and within the collection would concentrate on 'Gemälde, Graphik und Archäologie' (paintings, graphics and archeological artifacts) while Wischnitzer was to be in charge of objects relating to 'Kultus und Ritual' (worship and ritual). Officially, Wischnitzer was asked to hold the position of curator, while adding to her title, if she so wished, the notation that it was an honorary position.[77]

Wischnitzer had been involved in the work of the Berlin Jewish community since 1927, the year in which she was elected to work in the *Kommission der Kunstsammlung*.[78] Although nothing is known about the nature of this work it shows that

[72]Assimilation is understood as "a process engaged in by a minority whose goal is fusion with the majority". See Marion A. Kaplan, 'Tradition and Transition: The Acculturation, Assimilation and Integration of Jews in Imperial Germany', in *LBI Yearbook XXVII*, (1982), p. 4.
[73]Acculturation is understood as "the acceptance of many of the customs and cultural patterns of the majority of society and the simultaneous commitment to the preservation of ethnic and/or religious distinctiveness". *ibid.*, p. 5.
[74]Bezalel Narkiss, 'Rachel Wischnitzer – Doyenne of Historians of Jewish Art', in *From Dura to Rembrandt: Studies in the History of Art*, Jerusalem 1990, p. 10.
[75]Franz Landsberger, *Einführung in die jüdische Kunst*, Berlin 1935, p. 58.
[76]ALW: Letter from Alfred Klee to Rachel Wischnitzer, 15 April 1935.
[77]ALW: Letter from the Board of directors of the Berlin Jewish Community to Rachel Wischnitzer, Berlin, 7 March 1935.
[78]ALW: Letter from Aron Sandler, Jewish Community Berlin, to Rachel Wischnitzer, 17 November 1927.

her commitment to the Jewish artistic heritage led her to cooperate with the Jewish community long before her actual work in the Jewish Museum began. During her years at the museum, Wischnitzer was responsible for two major historical exhibits, both dealing with outstanding Jewish individuals who lived during a period of historic transition. Her first exhibition focused on the Sephardi philosopher Don Isaac Abrabanel who lived at the time of the expulsion of the Jews from Iberia and their resettlement in Italy, Turkey, Holland and North Africa; the second focused on the Ashkenazi Rabbi Akiba Eger (the Younger), a man of great learning who was active during the Enlightenment, the Napoleonic Sanhedrin, the birth of Reform Judaism and Modern Orthodoxy.

A closer look at the two personalities clarifies what Wischnitzer was trying to accomplish. By choosing Don Isaac Abrabanel and Rabbi Akiba Eger, Wischnitzer had decided to focus on two prominent Jewish figures who, in their history and time, had dealt with their Jewish heritage in a positive fashion. As a curator Wischnitzer had immediate influence on what to show her audience and with her choices she sent a message to the Berlin Jewish community which contained elements of continuity and pride in the Jewish tradition. In June 1937, Abrabanel, statesman, philosopher, and biblical exegete, was remembered on the occasion of his 500th birthday. The catalogue listed the 123 objects on exhibit. This major cultural event was discussed throughout the local Jewish press. Max Osborn, a renowned Jewish art critic who had mainly written for the *Vossische Zeitung*, described the show as "a highly interesting, incredibly stimulating and instructive exhibit".[79] Osborn marvelled at how well the exhibit gave the visitor an impression of Abrabanel's historic reality.

By meticulously tracking down the family history, Rachel Wischnitzer had managed to recreate the world of the Abrabanels in front of the viewer's eyes. Kurt Pinthus in the *Israelitisches Familienblatt* affirmed that the exhibit's concept superseded everything previously written about Abrabanel by visually retracing his life in Portugal, Spain and Italy.[80] Besides paintings, Wischnitzer had accumulated rare books relating to the topic in an abundance never seen before which gave an impression of the knowledge, culture and wealth that characterised this Sephardi family.

The exhibit, which was widely recognised both inside and outside Germany,[81] can today be reconstructed through its catalogue. Written in 1937, at a time when the Gestapo had started to confiscate Jewish newspapers, Wischnitzer's catalogue was published as a matter-of-fact account of the objects that were exhibited, which serves as another example of the vigilance and caution with which Jews in Nazi Germany had to negotiate an increasingly oppressive system.

The issue of censorship under the Nazi government is a complicated issue. While the Jewish press was subjected to post-censorship, the activities launched by the Jewish *Kulturbünde* were censored by the above-mentioned Hinkel office.[82]

[79]Max Osborn, *Jüdisches Gemeindeblatt*, No. 24 (13 June 1937).
[80]Kurt Pinthus, *Israelitisches Familienblatt*, (17 June 1937).
[81]*Beiblatt, C.V.-Zeitung*, Nos. 3 and 4, (20 January 1938).
[82]Herbert Freeden, *The Jewish Press in the Third Reich*, transl. by William Templer, Providence – Oxford 1993, p. 9.

The publications of the Berlin Jewish Museum were sure to be affected by these pressures: however, the extent to which Jewish public institutions were censored still remains to be explored.

At this point a look at the exhibition catalogue itself is most instructive. Its introductory remarks, signed by Dr. Alfred Klee, a lawyer and member of the community's board, revealed the message the exhibit's organisers wished to send out to their audience, namely that Abrabanel was to be understood as a symbol of hope and encouragement for the Jews of Germany.[83] Wischnitzer's introduction followed Klee's words explaining her attempt to enter into the family's world that lay beyond the realm of books and learning. She suggested that this cultured and highly educated family, even after its expulsion from Spain, had excelled as the keeper of tradition, both of Spanish culture as well as of its Jewish religious heritage. Wischnitzer also insisted on including the lives of other family members within the show. Special attention was thus given to Benvenida Abrabanel, Isaac's niece, who, while living in Italy, became the governess of the Spanish princess Eleonora of Toledo, to whom she was requested to convey the values of Spanish culture.[84] Benvenida's example showed that Jews could function both as Jews and as representatives, teachers and even promoters of a non-Jewish culture. Wischnitzer possibly picked the example of a woman because she perceived her own role within the Jewish family and community as that of preserving Judaism.[85] The exhibit retraced Abrabanel's life starting with his work as a financial counsellor at the Portuguese court of King Alfonso V. Paintings and engravings of the king, the city of Lisbon and the local synagogue, as well as a document issued by the king, were instrumental in illustrating Abrabanel's years in Portugal. The new life in Spain, whence Abrabanel and his family emigrated from Portugal, was illustrated through images of cities such as Toledo and Granada, which then were vibrant centres of Jewish life. As one example, Wischnitzer chose to depict a room in the Alhambra where Isabella of Castille and Ferdinand II of Aragon signed the Edict of Expulsion of the Jews from Spain in 1492. Paintings of outstanding figures of the period, such as Columbus and the inquisitor, Torquemada, were part of the exhibit, as well as a carpet depicting the motif of the temple, showing yet another facet of that prosperous period in Jewish history. Furthermore, Abrabanel's Italian years were illustrated through portraits of contemporaries such as Eleonora of Toledo who had been portrayed by the Italian Renaissance painter Angiolo Bronzino, and a Titian portrait of Emperor Charles V. The places from which Wischnitzer retrieved the art used for this part of the exhibit reflect both her intense research as well as her connections within the art world. The Abrabanel exhibit borrowed art from the Prado in Madrid, the *Uffizi* and the *Pinacoteca Comunale* in Florence, the *Pinacoteca* in Perugia, a gallery in Modena, the University Library of Bologna

---

[83]'Introduction', Alfred Klee, in *Gedenkausstellung Don Jizchaq Abrabanel. Seine Welt. Sein Werk*, (Exhibition Catalogue, June 1937), p. 1.

[84]*ibid.*, p. 2, 3.

[85]Marion Kaplan, 'Priestess and Hausfrau: Women and Tradition in the German-Jewish Family', in *The Jewish Family: Myths and Reality*, Steven M. Cohen and Paula E. Hyman (eds.), New York – London 1986, pp. 188–212.

and the *Palatina* in Parma, the Library of the University of Cambridge, the Victoria and Albert Museum in London, the *Kunsthistorisches Museum* in Vienna as well as from various Berlin museums.[86]

To Wischnitzer, dealing with Jewish art always meant recreating the context in which it had been produced. Her articles published in *Rimon/Milgroim*, already showed this approach, which was then further exemplified by her work on the Abrabanel exhibit. The portrait of Emperor Charles V, for example, was intended to remind the visitor of his cooperation with and generous attitude towards the Jews of Naples. Jewish art, according to Rachel Wischnitzer, had to be viewed as closely connected to and influenced by the society in which it was conceived. Through Wischnitzer's approach, a visitor to the exhibit gained an impression of Abrabanel's intricate life experience. His Judaism was highlighted through the display of ritual objects such as Spanish Seder plates and amulets as well as the commentaries he had published. The exhibit's scope then opened up to the entire Abrabanel family by following their path to both Amsterdam and London. Visualising its complexity, Wischnitzer had researched the details necessary to depict a family tree, which was reproduced especially for the exhibit.

Wischnitzer's second exhibition commemorated a Jew who had been a spiritual leader of his community: Rabbi Akiba Eger. Mounted just a few months after Abrabanel in December of 1937 on the occasion of the one hundredth *Yahrzeit* of the Posen rabbi, the "last *Gaon* from Germany",[87] that exhibit was made possible through the cooperation between the Museum, the community library and the *Gesamtarchiv der Juden in Deutschland*. Rabbi Akiba Eger was historically and geographically closer to the German-Jewish audience than the Sephardi Abrabanel. In the introductory remarks to this catalogue, Alfred Klee once again expressed the hope that showing the life of a Jewish scholar and committed Jew could function as a model to German Jews.[88] By curating the Eger exhibit, Wischnitzer continued her effort to revive the lives of great Jewish personalities and scholars of the past.[89] For the Eger exhibit, Wischnitzer was able to locate objects that still were and had been in the possession of members of the Eger family and which represented different stages in Eger's professional and personal life. Some members of the family even attended the opening ceremony, which gained religious meaning from its timing and was celebrated as a candle-lit *Hanukkah* evening.

Displays included portraits of the most prominent Jewish thinkers of the Mendelssohn period, the reform movement and of the rabbinic authorities of the eighteenth and early nineteenth centuries. Books about and by Eger were shown as well, sometimes autographed and annotated by the author himself. Other objects included the rabbi's last will issued by the Posen court on 24 March 1837, as well as a miniature Bible from his library, his silver *Hanukkah* lamp, the

---

[86] It seems rather astonishing that in 1937 international loans of art works were still possible, especially for a Jewish institution in Germany.
[87] 'Introduction', Alfred Klee, in *Akiba Eger Ausstellung* (Exhibition Catalogue, Hanukka 1937).
[88] *ibid.*
[89] *Jüdisches Gemeindeblatt für Berlin* (5 December 1937).

spice box and *seder* cup he had used, a filigree box which had been presented to him by the community in which he was a rabbi, a silver cup in the shape of a deer which he had presented to his grandson Hirsch David Eger, and a series of autographs.

In the catalogue's introduction, Wischnitzer described Eger as the hero of his time and as symbolising the Jewish struggle to preserve its tradition while opening its hearts to the demands of Enlightenment. Through Wischnitzer's way of presentation, Eger, just like Abrabanel, emerged as the keeper of tradition, thus speaking to the need of German Jews to find a positive self image. By portraying these outstanding individuals in the Berlin Jewish Museum, Wischnitzer had found a way of spiritually uplifting members of the community. The exhibition reminded them of the power and pride they could experience by adhering to their culture.

Curating the exhibition, Wischnitzer divided the displayed material into four sections: the period of Enlightenment; changes within the structure of communal affairs; worship; attitudes and education; the ancient Jewish tradition and Rabbi Akiba Eger and his family. The first part was meant to introduce the main figures involved in the internal Jewish disputes that resulted from the Enlightenment. The second part dealt with the German, French and Italian communal response by showing the individual portraits of Jews whose struggle with the challenges of the Enlightenment had been extraordinary. The third section portrayed those who had responded in a religious conservative way. The most extensive section of the exhibit focused on the figure of Rabbi Akiba Eger. It is remarkable that in the Nazi-controlled Berlin of 1937 Wischnitzer managed to compile over eighty objects linked to Eger's life and religious practice.

Aside from the scholarly aspect of Rachel Wischnitzer's work there is a social aspect which needs to be considered. While Rachel Wischnitzer's contribution to the Jewish community was not exactly that of a social worker; her curatorial work nevertheless needs to be seen as her way of strengthening that community. Her unique contribution was the education of the Jewish public about its rich artistic heritage and history. In the *Jüdische Lehrhaus* she organised a workshop on 'The meaning of our religious art',[90] addressing an audience of Jewish teachers, leaders of youth groups, rabbis and Jewish women who felt that they were facing the new challenge of promoting Judaism at home.[91]

Conscious about the shift taking place within the Jewish community in the wake of an increasing number of emigrants, Wischnitzer in 1936 published an appeal to the community.[92] Well aware of forced auctions and confiscations of Jewish property by Nazi officials, she urged those who left Berlin to donate their art objects and educational aids to a Jewish organization that would channel the material to Palestine were it could be used in museums and schools. Raised to be

---

[90] ALW: Letter from *Jüdisches Lehrhaus Sekretariat* to Rachel Wischnitzer, Berlin, 23 September 1935.

[91] Ernst Simon, *Aufbau im Untergang. Jüdische Erwachsenenbildung im nationalsozialistioschen Deutschland als Geistiger Widerstand*, Tübingen 1959, pp. 55–65.

[92] Rachel Wischnitzer, '*Brauchen wir Kunst? Eine Sammlungs-Aktion für Palästina*', in *Jüdische Rundschau* (13 March 1936), p. 5.

sensitive to interpersonal behavior and social situations, Wischnitzer had her social antennae finely tuned and addressed an issue that had emerged in the wake of emigration. She was, like most women, closely connected to everyday life. Overhearing talk at the grocer's, visiting their children's schools and attending lectures and concerts, women often had a better sense than men about how desperate Jewish life in Germany was becoming.[93] Emigration would eventually also be the only viable solution for the Wischnitzers themselves. In view of the escalating political situation the Wischnitzers prepared for their emigration to the United States and transferred their son Leonard to a Berlin-based American School in 1937.[94]

Early on, Wischnitzer herself had experienced Nazi racism while doing research in a local University library. Besides her work at the Jewish Museum, Wischnitzer had started to catalogue and photograph the collection of Hebrew illuminated manuscripts in the Berlin *Staats- und Universitätsbibliothek*. Adolph Goldschmidt, professor at the Humboldt University supported her plans and saw the project as complementary to the already existing collection of Medieval and Renaissance miniatures. He was convinced that for those studying the decoration of Hebrew literature, such a collection would be a much desired resource.[95] For a while, Wischnitzer managed to get all the support she needed for her project. As late as 20 February 1933, the director of the library's manuscript collection, Karl Christ, promised her his cooperation on the "scientifically so desirable project".[96] However, as soon as the Nazis consolidated their power, Christ ceased to respond to Wischnitzer's requests to secure access to the collection and finally refused to support her research.[97]

The Wischnitzer family continued to stay in Berlin until 10 April 1938, the year in which German Jews, after the November Pogrom (*Kristallnacht*), had to realise that there was no place for them in Germany. The *Anschluß* of Austria in March of that year sent shock waves reverberating through the already unstable foundations of Jewish life under Nazi rule. After the registration of all Jewish property and assets was ordered in April, the increasingly frenzied tone in the official press could not be overlooked.[98] During the summer, the first attacks on synagogues had culminated in the destruction of the Nuremberg synagogue.[99]

In 1938, the Wischnitzer family emigrated to Paris, where they stayed until 1940, waiting for visas to continue their emigration to the United States. Wischnitzer's departure did not go unnoticed and was mentioned in various local Jewish newspapers and was marked by a festive farewell evening at the Berlin Jewish Museum. Recognised as "the ingenious art historian and thorough Hebraicist", Wischnitzer was forced to leave behind her work, having given

---

[93]Marion Kaplan, p. 200.
[94]Bezalel Narkiss, 'Priestess and Hausfrau', p. 21.
[95]ALW: Letter from Adolph Goldschmidt to Rachel Wischnitzer, Berlin, December 1932.
[96]ALW: Statement by Karl Christ (20 February 1933).
[97]Bezalel Narkiss, p. 20.
[98]Freeden, p. 93.
[99]*ibid.*

Berlin Jews a new appreciation of Jewish art and having helped them to reclaim a positive self-image.

This article will be followed in Year Book XLV by a further contribution on Rachel Wischnitzer's work. Editor.

Kurt Sabatzky: The C.V. Syndikus of the Jewish Community in Königsberg during the Weimar Republic

BY SABINE THIEM

In 1923 Kurt Sabatzky travelled to East Prussia to take up his appointment as *Syndikus* of the *Centralverein deutscher Staatsbürger jüdischen Glaubens* (C.V.) in Königsberg. The atmosphere of the area was that of a quasi-colonial,[1] impoverished province[2] increasingly Nationalist in political tendency and fearful of its isolation from the *Reich*[3] and of its proximity to strong neighbour states of the former Tsarist Empire.[4] The Jewish community in Königsberg shared these perceptions, going out of its way to receive money from Berlin to save "Germanness and Jewishness" in the East. The fact that the German-Jewish community presented itself as such was for functional reasons, yet this also appealed to a broader mentality, which may be what the Liberal community rabbi Reinhold Lewin termed "the peculiarity of our community" (Eigenart unserer Gemeinde).[5] However, scholars now generally view the Königsberg Jewish community as not essentially different from any large urban Jewish community in the *Reich*.[6] This would seem to be

---

[1] A 1927 guidebook opens with the words: "Königsberg ist heute die Hauptstadt einer Kolonie, der einzigen, die Deutschland besitzt." in *Fremdenführer durch Königsberg in Preußen*, reprinted Leer 1990, p. 28.

[2] Although the Reich lavished special development area programmes on the province, East Prussia remained a relatively poor part of Germany throughout the Weimar Republic.

[3] Kurt Sabatzky, *Meine Erinnerungen an den Nationalsozialismus*, typed manuscript, n.d. [1953] in the Leo Baeck Institute, New York (original manuscript in the Wiener Library, London), p. 4.

[4] This is what emerges from so many official brochures and the daily press. Cf. Hartmut Boockmann, *Ostpreußen und Westpreußen Deutsche Geschichte im Osten Europas, I*, Berlin 1992, pp. 403–407, for the many official brochures and daily press reports voicing these fears.

[5] Reinhold Lewin, 'Vier Jahre Königsberger Gemeindeblatt', in *Königsberger Jüdisches Gemeindeblatt* (henceforth *KJG*), 9 (1928), p. 118. Reinhold Lewin was born in Magdeburg in 1888. An army rabbi during the First World War, he succeeded the renowned rabbi Hermann Vogelstein who moved to Breslau in 1921. Lewin was Rabbi at the Königsberg Liberal New Synagogue until 1938 and then moved to Breslau as well. From there he was deported in 1942.

[6] Not much research has been devoted to the Königsberg Jewish community: Yoram K. Jacoby, *Jüdisches Leben in Königsberg/Pr. im 20. Jahrhundert*, Würzburg 1983, is valuable for factual information but focuses, despite its title, on Jewish institutions. A few articles aside, the most comprehensive work is for the time being Stefanie Schüler-Springorum, *Die jüdische Minderheit in Königsberg/Preußen, 1871–1945*, Göttingen 1996. In my M.A. thesis I take a different angle, describing the community on the basis of their own view (or representation) of themselves as seen in their newspaper. See Sabine Thiem, *Das Königsberger Jüdische Gemeindeblatt. Publizierte jüdische Identität in der Endphase der Weimarer Republik (1928–1933)*, Hamburg 1995 (typescript in the Wiener Library, London).

borne out by the outward appearance of this *Gemeinde* with its roughly 4,000 members,[7] its five different synagogues (the Liberal *Neue Synagoge* commanding the biggest congregation), and its various organisations and *Vereine*. The leading positions were occupied by the upper stratum of Königsberg Jewry: the professions, industrialists, merchants. At almost three hundred miles distance from Stettin, the nearest big city in Germany, Königsberg's Jewish community appeared to have been every bit as "German" as all the others. At the same time, contemporary self-perception and present-day scholarship are in agreement that the neighbouring countries of the Tsarist Empire – Warsaw, Vilnius and Riga are nearer than Stettin – had not only brought about economic and social contacts.[8] Jewish-Russian agents trading in agricultural and forestry products and holidaymakers at the seaside resorts on the East Prussian Baltic coast (where a synagogue functioned during the summer months) meant that *Ostjuden* were a common feature in pre-1914 Königsberg.

After war, revolution and civil war, this seems to have changed. Not only did the seaside synagogue have to be closed in 1922 due to falling Russian attendance,[9] trade with the new nation states and the socialist Soviet Union was now rearranged along new lines. As a result, the Eastern European Jewish presence in Weimar Königsberg is mostly called into question or denied outright – then as much as now.[10]

The Jewish population of Königsberg was partly descended from Eastern European immigrants who had then, in their own good time, become "assimilated". Moreover, there had been a wide range of welfare institutions in pre-1914 Königsberg catering for the medical needs of migrating *Ostjuden*.[11] After 1922 it was above all Kowno (Lithuanian) that came within the scope of welfare activities from Königsberg. There were close contacts with the Jewish community in the capital of the new Lithuanian state: Zionist youth groups organised exchange visits, liberal and conservative welfare institutions gave support to schools and orphanages or helped out in catastrophes. Still these contacts allowed only a limited number of people to see for themselves the men and

---

[7]4,049 members in 1925, equivalent to 1,4% of the total population of the town. N.A., 'Auf- und Abstieg der Königsberger Gemeinde', *KJG* 6 (1927), p. 79.

[8]The seasonal presence of migrant Jews from the Tsarist Empire lending to imperial Königsberg "the aspect of a Jewish town during summer" is commonplace in literature on the Königsberg Jews. Cf. Jacoby, pp. 9–10.

[9]*KJG* 6 (1931), pp. 80–81.

[10]Cf. statistics in Schüler-Springorum, p. 200–201. The ubiquitous *Ostjude*, imagined and imaginary, who loomed large in debates in Königsberg during the Weimar Republic, makes it irrelevant to call the concept of *Ostjude* into question as has been done since the 1980s. Stefanie Schüler-Springorum, for instance, rejects the term in discussing Königsberg as unhelpful in the light of modern studies of acculturation, undifferentiated as to geographical variety, and politically charged ("Hetzbegriff", p. 160). In the study of ideologies, however, there is no point in omitting a concept central to the men and women under discussion simply because it seems to make less sense to the scholar. When Königsberg Jews spoke of "*Ostjuden*" they did not imply any such differentiation. In the community's self-perception *Ostjude* served as a construct, as a metaphor.

[11]The *Bikur Chaulim*, founded in 1887, assumed the care for "unbemittelte[n] kranke[n] Israeliten aus Rußland..., die behufs ärztlicher Behandlung nach Königsberg kommen". 'Bikur Chaulim', *KJG* 1 (1925), p. 8.

women known as *"Ostjuden"*. As most East Prussians probably never ever left their province, and thus knew the *Korridor* and *Abtrennung* only from propaganda, so also to "German" Königsberg Jews, the '*Ostjude*' would have been considered something of a myth. And the myth was interpreted differently according to need and aim. The platform for doing so was the *Königsberger Jüdisches Gemeindeblatt*, the monthly paper started in 1924. Its editor, Reinhold Lewin, made a point of publishing contributions from the widest possible spectrum of Jewish politics, or so he claimed.[12] It is difficult to tell whether the editor, whose socio-economic position depended on the liberal synagogue, was indeed equally open to all sides. At least he can be credited with fairly high standards of publishing. Since the *Gemeindeblatt* was much more than an annotated calender of events, Lewin always allowed continuous debates to occupy a large section of the paper alongside *Verein* information and questions of religious practice. Furthermore, he included source texts from the community's history, matters of general "cultural" interest (e.g. articles on Shakespeare or George Eliot) and entire lectures given at Königsberg and East Prussian events. "To keep a high standard"[13] was Lewin's aim and pride.

The debates show that sympathy for or objection to *Ostjuden* had really much more to do with discussing one's own Jewishness. For instance, the Russian-born Shmaryah Levin, who had studied medicine at Königsberg and settled there, wrote to recall what the community owed to Eastern Europe and that it was indeed Eastern European in origin. He emphasised the fact that in the nineteenth century there had been opportunities for Jewish immigrants from Eastern Europe to achieve positions in the *Gemeinde* unthinkable in Berlin, and that the Königsberg community had then numbered many more Russian than "local" Jews,[14] interestingly subsuming non-*Ostjuden* as "local" even if they, like the bankers' family Marx for example, had originally come from the Rhineland. While Levin wrote an altogether edifying tale of industriousness, just reward and acceptance into the *Gemeinde*, there are other images of *Ostjuden* that are, however well-intentioned their authors claimed to be, indebted to an outright colonialist mentality. Lecturing to the *Israelitischer Frauenverein* in Marienwerder, Dr Löwenherz, former headmaster of a Hebrew grammar school in Lithuania, used these words to solicit sympathy for the distant neighbour:

> The *Ostjude* is amorphous only in appearance; he has different forms of social intercourse and conduct – strict, if often incomprehensible, to the West. Even his attitude towards religion is defined by life within a firm, well-organised [...] community; it is more immediate, more sanguine and with all strict obedience of the Law, it is far from doctrinal.[15]

In 1928 Kurt Schereschewsky, writing an article about a recent *Bar Kochba* tour around Lithuania, waxed enthusiastic with praise of the pious, honest *Ostjuden*,

---

[12]The only exception was the *Verband nationaldeutscher Juden* about which Lewin remarked sarcastically that its local branch "seems to have perished at some point". See 'Vier Jahre Königsberger Gemeindeblatt', *KJG* 9 (1928), p. 118.

[13]*ibid.*

[14]Shmarya Levin, 'Die Königsberger Judenheit vor vierzig Jahren', *KJG* 10 (1933), p. 115.

[15]Dr Löwenherz, 'Aus den Provinzgemeinden', *KJG* 3 (1930), pp. 47–48.

"Thank you, dear friends, for showing us what treasures are still *alive* in Judaism about which we *here*, in Germany, have only a dim idea!"[16]

From all these various reports readers learned less about *Ostjuden* than about Jewish life as recommended to them by the respective authors. The general debate was thus framed by the metaphoric use of Eastern versus Western Jewishness. On top of this, in a province that saw itself as having been saved from the Russian invaders only by a hair's breadth in 1914, any mention of their Eastern European connections was a particularly uncomfortable subject to many well-acculturated Liberal Jews.[17] Gerhard Birnbaum (son of the *Neue Synagoge* cantor Eduard Birnbaum who died in 1920) used his journey to Poland as an occasion to attack Zionism, portent of another quite more imminent danger from the East:

> Polish Zionist youth sympathises almost in its entirety with illegal Communist agitation, and most of the messengers who, in the Eastern regions, campaign for a Soviet Poland under Russian protection, are indeed Jewish.[18]

Birnbaum's attack was strongly rebuffed by the *Ostjüdisch* student groups in Königsberg, who attacked Birnbaum severely for his "potentially antisemitic arguments".[19] Birnbaum responded peacefully pointing out that this was a travelogue, not an academic treatise, stressing his own Eastern European origins, but justifying his right to criticise "his own camp" without being accused of heresy.[20]

Birnbaum constructs a double image of the *Ostjude*. On the one hand he knows the *Ostjudentum* he himself "stems from", thereby invalidating all criticism of his stand on the subject. On the other side he paints a two-headed Eastern European spectre that betrays the Fabian fears of a Social Democrat: "revolutionary, are-ligious and anti-religious youth hails Soviet Communism as the path to salvation".[21] Beyond the corridor in the *Reich*, *Ostjuden* were regarded as foreigners, possibly ancestors but certainly not close neighbours of the community. In "severed East Prussia" the continuous construction of the image of the *Ostjude* worked as a two-tier self-assertion in the face of a threateningly imminent East, even to non-Jewish Königsberg.

This was the situation awaiting Sabatzky when he alighted the platform at Königsberg (the station forecourt was described to visitors from the *Reich* as

---

[16]Kurt Schereschewsky, 'Unsere Fahrt nach Litauen', *KJG* 11 (1928), pp. 146–147. It is impossible to render the pathos-laden, archaising style of the original.

[17]The "Tannenberg myth" around the battleground in southern East Prussia where Field Marshal (and *Reichspräsident*-to-be) Hindenburg had stopped the invading Tsarist army in 1914 can hardly be over-estimated in its significance for post-war mentality in the province. As is discussed, this was to cause Sabatzky one of his biggest worries.

[18]Gerhard Birnbaum, 'Besuch bei den polnischen Juden', *KJG* 1 (1927), p. 3. Birnbaum was a journalist with the Social Democrat *Königsberger Volkszeitung*.

[19]'Einige Bemerkungen zu Herrn Birnbaums "Besuch bei den polnischen Juden" ', *KJG* 2 (1927), p. 16.

[20]G. Birnbaum, 'Replik auf die Entgegnungen aus den Kreisen der ostjüdisch Studierenden in Königsberg', *KJG* 2 (1927), pp. 16–17. Since both texts appeared in the February edition, Reinhold Lewin must have unfairly given the Liberal champion the opportunity to have his reply published immediately after the Zionist intervention.

[21]Birnbaum, *KJG* 1.

"unpleasant, almost a bit Russian"[22]) to assume office as C.V. *Syndikus*. He had not been born there nor did he have any affiliation with East Prussia. Sabatzky was about to meet a *Gemeinde* he would not immediately be able to reconcile with his previous experience. However, through his position in the C.V., Sabatzky was to become an important representative of the *Gemeinde*, including the Province Communities, and to defend it vigorously against antisemitic and National Socialist attacks right until 1933. His official, albeit not his private, voice found expression in his regular column in the *Königsberger Jüdisches Gemeindeblatt*, "Neues vom C.V.-Syndikat". Some of his personal views we know from his *Erinnerungen* (Memoirs), written in London in 1953. Apparently the *Erinnerungen* were written with two groups of readers in mind: Sabatzky's English hosts,[23] and future generations for whom the former C.V. lawyer – who had spent most of his life exposing Nazism – wished to describe the life of Jews in Magdeburg, Königsberg and Leipzig during the Weimar Republic and the Third *Reich*. Together with some few scattered remarks in other autobiographical recollections, the *Gemeindeblatt* and the memoirs constitute the main sources from which to view Sabatzky.[24]

Kurt Sabatzky was born in 1892 in Köslin, Pomerania. No information is available about his childhood and schooling, nor about precisely when and where he studied law. He had a sister, Edith, and a brother, Fritz; his parents were still living in Köslin in 1932.[25] Sabatzky saw action on the Western Front during the First World War, was buried alive in the rubble of a trench, and acquired a permanent heart and nervous disease from a gas attack. Returning to Berlin in November 1918 (it is with his recollection of being handed an antisemitic leaflet on leaving the station that he begins his *Erinnerungen*), he became a member of the *Deutsche Demokratische Partei* (DDP) and secretary of the party *Bezirk* organisation[26] before the end of the year. In January 1919 he fought "at night-time, after party duty, gun in hand, with the loyal regiment *Reichstag*, defending the *Anhalter Bahnhof* against the Communists".[27] In February 1920, during a meeting of the Jewish War Veterans Organisation (*Reichsbund jüdischer Frontsoldaten* – RjF), he found himself embroiled in the Kapp Putsch, taking up

---

[22] *Fremdenführer*, 1927, p. 28.

[23] Or at least those that could read German and used the Wiener Library – unless he was thinking of an English translation.

[24] It is interesting to compare both sources: the contemporary regular column read by Königsberg Jews, and the *Erinnerungen* written with hindsight and often about things he could (or would) not mention at the time. The memoirs are more personal also in the sense that their language is skilfully stylised for accessability and effect. Therefore, direct speech in the *Erinnerungen* must not be taken at face value (one can hardly imagine the Nazi *Gauleiter* Koch in a theatre foyer actually saying: "Excellenz, Sehen Sie den dahinten, das ist der Jude Sabatzky, Syndikus des Centralvereins deutscher Staatsbürger jüdischen Glaubens!" [p. 13])—which, nevertheless, does not diminish their basic facticity.

[25] *Erinnerungen*, p. 13. Unless otherwise stated, all biographical information on Sabatzky is from this source.

[26] The DPP, the only Weimar Liberal party not dominated by "National Liberalism", was continuously in office during the 1920s, mostly with the *Sozialdemokratische Partei Deutschlands* (SPD). From being the second strongest party in the 1919 and 1920 elections, its electorate dwindled steadily, until in 1930 the party was re-organised as the *Deutsche Staatspartei*, whereupon Sabatzky left.

[27] *Erinnerungen*, p. 1.

fighting again, albeit this time "only on street orator duty" ("im Straßenredner-Dienst"). Sabatzky recounts his activity as motivated by his democratic beliefs and by a marked sense of justice – a perfectly balanced depiction of Sabatzky defending the Republic against right-wing as well as left-wing extremism.

His commitment to the first German attempt at democracy aside, Sabatzky's main concern was to achieve normality and equality for German Jews. In 1920 he returned to Köslin, becoming editor of the *Kösliner Zeitung*, the DDP-connected regional newspaper. At the same time he founded the local section (*Ortsgruppe*) of the C.V. because "antisemitism is growing."[28] The C.V. offered Sabatzky a legal and legitimate opportunity to stand up to growing antisemitism (possibly even more recognisable in hindsight). At the C.V. *Hauptversammlung* in Berlin in November 1921 where Sabatzky represented the Köslin section, there was a call for "politicians"[29] to act as legal representatives in different parts of the *Reich*. Sabatzky was nominated and he accepted. From January to May 1922 he was trained as a political *Dezernent* in Berlin, then – probably in June – he was posted to Magdeburg, assuming responsibility for the C.V. *Syndikat* for the Prussian Province of Saxony. He stayed there for a year.

In 1923 Sabatzky was on his way to "that agrarian province of East Prussia, branched off from the Reich"[30] to live in Königsberg and act as the *Syndikus* of the C.V. provincial organisation. Furthermore he became a member of the *Vorstand* of the RjF and *Pressewart* of the Republican Club. Through his political commitments he was also able to establish himself socially. He worked strenuously for the *Gemeinde* in his capacity as C.V. *Syndikus*, taking part in many meetings and discussions in which he voiced his concerns regarding the dangers of National Socialism. He even attended NSDAP campaign assemblies, trying to counter prejudice with discussion and argument (*aufklären*). As did the C.V. everywhere, Sabatzky methodically opposed antisemitic slander and behaviour by legal means.

There was a private man behind the politician and *Syndikus*: there are brief references in his memoirs to his wife, Herta (a C.V. *Frauenverein* activist) and to the birth of his daughter, Ruth Maria, but the main drift of the memoirs is the opposition to National Socialism. A thumbnail sketch by his contemporary Max Fürst, however, reveals Sabatzky's activities from an altogether different angle:

> A certain Herr Sabatzki [*sic*] reigned in the C.V. office, a tiny, squat man ... The big time for general secretaries had yet to come. To be secretary of a *Verein*, was a foretaste of hell, as Herr Sabatzki [*sic*] assured us convincingly. He was a hurried nothing between the *Verein* dignitaries who all had their word to put in...[31]

As an additional forum for his activities Sabatzky made use of the *Königsberger Jüdisches Gemeindeblatt*. It is open to debate just how much Sabatzky himself was instrumental in its foundation, but there is strong reason to believe that it was to a

---

[28] *ibid.*

[29] *ibid.*, p. 2, possibly meaning legally trained men with a known interest in politics.

[30] *ibid.*, p. 4, "*abgezweigt*" (literally "branched off") has a connotation of "embezzled".

[31] Max Fürst, *Gefilte Fisch. Eine Jugend in Königsberg*, München 1973.

considerable extent his own brainchild. The newspaper's guiding spirit was, by his own account, its editor Reinhold Lewin. He was already working in the editorial office of the *Kameraden* newsletter in 1924 and was active in the C.V. and RjF, just like Sabatzky, who was three years his junior. Lewin's "outstanding command of rhetoric and his acute wit had quickly won him the esteem of the community", as Erwin Lichtenstein, then a Königsberg resident, put it.[32] However, when Lewin tried to set up a regular newspaper, he encountered some difficulties in the *Gemeindevorstand*. Objections to the project were plentiful: too few subjects, irregular contributions, insufficient funds. The main objection was that "divisions and dissent in our community will have a new object for dispute". Only when "one of the parties" threatened to start a newspaper on its own, was the problem solved.[33] This controversy left no trace in the institution's board and their minutes.[34] But Lewin had to accept an advisory council (*Beirat*, consisting of one member of each political group in the community institutions plus an expert on economic matters) with the final right of editorial decision. If nothing else, this settlement must have affected the way the paper reported on community politics. Lewin himself was to proclaim publicly his regret that his *Gemeindeblatt*, unlike others, did not report discussion in the institutions but only results, in "brief summary" and non-controversial form.[35] The Jewish community was careful to appear united and was wary of acknowledging dissent.

The *Königsberger Jüdisches Gemeindeblatt* first appeared on 1 September 1924. Its initial circulation was 1,400 rising to 1,920 by 1930. Lewin was the *Schriftleiter* (chief editor). It was a monthly newspaper of some 10 to 26 pages, distributed to the members of the community free of charge.[36] It supported itself through advertisements and donations. In 1929 the paper became the official newsletter of the East Prussian Federation of Synagogue Communities. To the editor and rabbi it represented a "*jüdisches Kulturgut*". Just what Kurt Sabatzky's part was in the making of the newspaper is a matter of speculation. He might have had similar ambitions as in Köslin where he himself edited a newspaper. It is probable that Lewin's allusion to the possible foundation of a party paper hinted to Sabatzky and the C.V. The fact is that, from the first, Sabatzky was prominent with his half page 'Bulletin of the C.V. Syndicate', which appeared just before the notices on *Vereine* and organisations. In addition he wrote a great number of articles on election results, C.V. events and RjF meetings. To Sabatzky this was ample space to promote his work – and he must have enjoyed

---

[32]Erwin Lichtenstein, *Bericht an meine Familie. Ein Leben zwischen Danzig und Israel*, Darmstadt 1985, p. 38.

[33]Reinhold Lewin, 'Vier Jahre Königsberger jüdisches Gemeindeblatt', *KJG* 9 (1928), pp. 117–119. This commemorative article is the only place where these difficulties were ever mentioned in the paper.

[34]"Any future historian of the Königsberg community will be very disappointed at how much the documents fail him on the founding of our newspaper." *ibid.*, p. 118. Lewin's report to the community was oral.

[35]The articles by the keeper of the minutes of the *Repräsentantenversammlung* were "proof-read" by its members three times before publication. *ibid.*, p. 119.

[36]There was a bad slump in circulation when postage costs were introduced for readers outside Königsberg.

his quasi-monopoly.[37] In 1928 he vehemently opposed plans to establish a special press office with the Prussian or the *Reich* C.V. organisation. He gave a detailed account of his own press work over the past years and then it was his turn to warn "taxpayers" of the "costly apparatus" and officials of "long journeys and heavy correspondence work" such a press office would entail. These arguments were similar to those levelled against the *Gemeindeblatt* four years previously. In short, it would be "superfluous", because the local syndics were already doing the job to everyone's satisfaction.[38] In the end, nothing came of the project. Sabatzky was left on his own with his task of supplying the non-Jewish press with refutations and corrected accounts.

For his own column, Sabatzky's most frequent theme was antisemitism and *völkisch* propaganda. "Enlightening" was his main concern when he pinpointed even the smallest antisemitic incident in Königsberg and East Prussia, named perpetrators, brought connections and backgrounds to light. In his court reports he often had to report lenient judges' reactions to "young lads' tomfoolery". But it was not only the heedless complicity of the non-Jewish milieu that gave Sabatzky food for thought. Even in his own circles his persistence did not only win him friends, as impatient reactions to his appeals for boycotting anti-Jewish businesses suggest: "We have no reason whatsoever to suspect the *Judenfeind* in every political opponent."[39]

Sabatzky's confrontations with the Nationalsozialistische Deutsche Arbeiterpartei (NSDAP) – the Königsberg party group was founded in 1925 – and Erich Koch, the *Gauleiter* (1927–1945), took a definite turn for the worse towards the end of the decade. Libel actions became a matter of course,[40] Sabatzky reporting the facts in the manner of a court report with himself (in the third person) as participant. What read objectively in the *Gemeindezeitung* took on a more dramatic tone in the *Erinnerungen*. More than once Sabatzky was physically threatened or assaulted at meetings, received threatening letters[41] and was insulted in theatres or restaurants. None of this ever filtered through in his *Gemeindeblatt* column – we cannot tell whether this was intentional or due to pressure from community dignitaries who feared that Nazi reactions might rebound on the *Gemeinde* as a whole.

Sabatzky did not confine his legal activity to Königsberg. He often toured the many small rural communities of East Prussia giving help and advice. He took legal action against slander, desecration and violent incidents; furthermore he was eager to enlighten the non-Jewish public by co-operating with their press. In his articles for these papers he was careful to make his point by supplying full

---

[37] In the *Erinnerungen* he complacently reports how his activities won him notoriety throughout the *Reich*. Cf. *Passim* and p. 31.

[38] Kurt Sabatzky, 'Brauchen wir eine amtliche jüdische Pressestelle?' *KJG* 10 (1928), pp. 133–134.

[39] Dr Rosenhain, 'Boykott', *KJG* 1 (1926), pp. 4–5. Rosenhain had been C.V. *Syndikus* before Sabatzky, so there is a chance that personal antagonism came into it.

[40] On one occasion Koch was sentenced to a fine of 400 RM for having written in the *Ostdeutscher Beobachter*, the NSDAP paper: "Herr Sabatzky, the *Königsberger Jüdisches Gemeindeblatt* and the *Königsberger Volkszeitung* [the SPD paper] lie and slander!" ('Neues vom C.V.-Syndikat', *KJG* 5 (1931), p. 73.

[41] Sabatzky complains that the Chief of Police, Tietze, did not take them seriously when Sabatzky submitted them for investigation (*Erinnerungen*, p. 17).

documentation, court decisions, outside expertise; even so, he found his contributions were not always welcome with editors. In a purported "ritual murder" case in Memelland, Sabatzky nearly bit off more than he could chew when he tried to stem the surge of popular anti-Judaism by attempting to publish the expert opinions of a Protestant theologian and a forensic doctor:

> I add an enlightening article to the expert's findings and ask the leading Memelland newspaper, the *Memeler Dampfboot* to print them. The editor-in-chief at first refuses. I make it plain that in that case I am going back into Germany to declare publicly that vast parts of the German population of Memelland are so culturally backward that they believe in tales of ritual murder. This helps. My article, complete with the two expert opinions, is published. Popular opinion is calming down. . .[42]

The antisemitic attacks were not just rooted amongst the general public. Sabatzky also had to cope with attacks from Monarchist officers and with National Socialist tendencies within the juridical system. His influential friends and acquaintances would stand by him if necessary, but with the rise of Nazism such support as there was tended to recede or simply become ineffectual.

A specially colourful example of public antisemitism was, to the C.V. as well as in Sabatzky's column, the exclusion of the Jewish speaker at the celebration for the inauguration of the Tannenberg Memorial in 1927. The massive monument commemorating the two battles of Tannenberg was heavily charged with political symbolism.[43] Paul von Hindenburg, in his twin function as victor of the battle of 1914 and as the contemporary *Reichspräsident*, was the guest of honour. To commemorate the battle, speakers for the three main denominations had been invited, including Lewin from Königsberg, former army rabbi, representing the Jewish community. All three speeches had been cleared and the programme for the day had been published. Shortly before the celebration, however, Lewin's speech was cancelled. C.V. representatives, in Königsberg as well as in Berlin, raised an outcry over this.

> Apparently the chairman of the Monument Committee [*Generalmajor a.D.* Kahns], himself a man with no prejudices, had meanwhile met with considerable resistance . . . The Committee attempted to justify the necessity of excluding the Jewish clergyman (*jüdischer Geistlicher*) from the service because of consideration for the venerable age of the President. The President, who would have to be standing for hours during the celebration, was to be spared the four minutes of the Rabbi's speech.[44]

Since the celebration was ostensibly a private function organised by the Monument Committee, the Jewish *Gemeinde* could not formally appeal to the authorities but had to comply. Lewin along with the RjF cancelled their participation in protest. Sabatzky supplied more details in his later recollection. "The committee, because of National Socialist and other interventions, decided" not

---

[42] *ibid.*, p. 14.

[43] The battles of 1410 between the Order of the Teutonic Knights and the King of Poland and, more recently, in 1914 between the German and the Russian armies. The whole thing had the eerie appearance of a Wagnerian *Ordensburg* stronghold against the hordes from the East. It was completely levelled after 1945.

[44] Dr Julius Brodnitz, 'Tannenberg', *C.V.-Zeitung*, 38 (1927), pp. 1–2.

to allow the rabbi to speak.[45] Before Lewin and the RjF finally announced their withdrawal, Sabatzky contacted the C.V. and the RjF in Berlin, where it had been ascertained that President Hindenburg had had nothing to do with the rabbi's exclusion:

> I inform the General of both this and the opinion of the central Jewish organisations. General Kahns lies to me, declaring he has orders to the contrary. On this we decide that neither the Rabbi nor the RjF are to participate in the celebration, and release, via the Wolffsches Telegraphen-Büro, a statement in the German press giving the reasons for our non-attendance. General Kahns accepts the charge of untruthfulness we have made in our release without reacting. We experience the satisfaction of seeing the entire German press – except for the Nazi papers and some few Right-wing publications, but including the *völkisch* "*Deutsche Zeitung*" – come out on our side and regret that Jewish war veterans have been slighted.[46]

Sabatzky describes in detail different currents within the army: "old Monarchist as well as young National-Socialist officers" such as army chaplain Müller (according to Sabatzky, "the pacemaker of National Socialism in the army"), taking issue with Republicans, among whom was *Oberst* Erich von Bonin, a man "of that civil courage so seldom found in Germans". It is typical of Sabatzky to use every opportunity to declare his own position:

> They call him "Red Bonin". He socialises in the Republican Club, founded by myself and Dr. Albrecht von Holtum, press adviser in the East Prussian *Oberpräsidium* (supreme provincial authority) and also in the *Reichsbanner*. Of course such contacts are no secrets to Koch for long. He terms Bonin, Holtum and myself a triumvirate secretly holding the whole of East Prussia in its sway – which is sadly not true. One particular editorial by Koch is headed: 'Oberst von Bonin, the friend of traitors and conscientious objectors' ... The [Nazi] newspaper was banned for a couple of days, Koch charged. And now something very strange happens regarding the *esprit de corps* of *Wehrmacht* officers. While the action for libel against Koch is still pending, army chaplain Müller, serving on the same staff corps and of course well aware of the case of Bonin versus Koch, is a character witness in another trial for libel against Koch. Müller receives [nothing but] a reprimand, after the Protestant *Feldprobst* had accorded him protection.[47]

The aforementioned Republican Club afforded Sabatzky the opportunity to come into contact with leading SPD politicians such as Braun and Severing. Once more, Sabatzky's warnings of National-Socialist danger fell on deaf ears:

> Both share the opinion widespread among East Prussian Social Democrats, namely that not the Nazis but the Communists represent the real threat to the State. As a Jewish representative I tended to see the dangers of National Socialism disproportionately large, which, given my point of view, they were perfectly able to understand![48]

---

[45] *Erinnerungen*, p. 7.

[46] *ibid.*, p. 8. Sabatzky's juridical prose can sometimes be hard to digest. His referring to the non-Jewish papers as "die deutsche Presse" is an interesting slip of the tongue, or pen, for a former C.V. syndic.

[47] *ibid.*, pp. 9–10.

[48] *ibid.*, p. 14. Otto Braun, born in Königsberg, was Prussian Prime Minister until 1932, Carl Severing was Minister of the Interior. For a comprehensive discussion of the attitude of leading democratic politicians in Prussia to Sabatzky and the C.V., see Arnold Paucker, *Der jüdische Abwehrkampf gegen*

The personal risk for Sabatzky in campaigning for the C.V. became ever geater: by his own account he was the single most prominent target for all NSDAP attacks in East Prussia. On several occasions, both in the *Gemeindeblatt* and in the *Erinnerungen*, Sabatzky describes how Koch hurled insults and made personal threats against him – at campaign meetings, in the NSDAP newspaper and in chance encounters – which became ever less veiled.[49] From 1931 on the NSDAP expanded its structure to give outstanding members impressive functions. Nazi groups began to permeate all sectors of public life: women's, pupils', students', teachers' and doctors' associations too. At the same time attacks on Jews and boycotts of Jewish-owned businesses were on the increase. In his column Sabatzky lost no opportunity to warn of these threats. When speaking in public as a C.V. representative, on the other hand, he sometimes sounded as though he were rather playing the whole issue down, even as late as 1932:

> It is erroneous to believe the Third *Reich* is imminent . . . however serious the situation may be, there is no reason for German Jews to despair. *Deutschtum* and *Judentum* have had harder times to overcome.[50]

This sounds more like the point of view taken by Sabatzky's C.V. superiors[51] than his own. Personally he must have felt badly under threat by then as he gave no more public lectures after 1932.[52] After the dissolution of the Braun/Severing government the same year he played an active part in the Social Democrats' election campaign, but he was feeling the strain of the continuous stream of threats. In the *Erinnerungen* Sabatzky recounts how he "disappeared" from Königsberg on election day (31st July), knowing his family was safe with his father-in-law in Greifenberg, Pomerania, seeming to have had a premonition about what was to happen:

> The day before the election I travel to my family, voting card in my pocket . . . I vote there and travel on westward that same afternoon to relax at Bad Neuenahr [Rhineland]. From Berlin I travel in a sleeping-car. The other person in my compartment is a Berlin Jew who remembers my name from my articles and reports in the *C.V.-Zeitung*. He says I should be happy to have come through the campaign unharmed, given the situation in East Prussia. . . At six o'clock in the evening, at the newsagent's stand on the Kurplatz in Bad Neuenahr, I spot the *Kölner Tageblatt* with a banner headline in very large letters: "Bloodshed in Nazi Terror in Königsberg".[53]

What Sabatzky read on the Kurplatz was a report of assaults in the night after the election, perpetrated by Nazis in Königsberg. The Communist MP Sauff had

Antisemitismus und Nationalsozialismus in den letzten Jahren der Weimarer Republik, Hamburg 1968, pp. 85ff. and pp. 265–266.

[49] On one occasion Koch shouted out through the lobby of an assembly room: "That one's first on the gallows as soon as we're on top!", *Erinnerungen*, p. 13.

[50] [Kurt] Sabatzky, 'Centralverein deutscher Staatsbürger jüdischen Glaubens', *KJG* 3 (1932), p. 35, retranslation into direct speech of his own report on 'What is the C.V. doing in the current situation?'

[51] See the articles (mostly about youth issues and community politics) by *Geheimrat* Prof. Dr. Bruno Falkenheim, head of the local C.V. and, from 1928, chairman of the *Gemeindevorstand*.

[52] Jacoby, *Jüdisches Leben*, p. 101. Sabatzky does not mention this decision (if such it was) either in his column or in the *Erinnerungen*.

[53] *Erinnerungen*, p. 19.

been shot dead through the head and several politicians and journalists severely injured. All of them were attacked in their homes. Sabatzky evidently had reason to believe that only his well-timed spa tour had saved him from a similar fate. His flat at 14 Kastanienallee had also been broken into in the early morning; the housekeeper had managed to chase away three or four young men.[54] "So precisely twelve hours before I read the news in the Cologne paper the Nazis had sought to put an end to my life!" Sabatzky's secretary, Else Ascher – "she is at first very upset and cries" – told him on the phone that the flat had been thoroughly searched. Sabatzky, comments on official reactions:

> The Königsberg police force was still essentially republican in outlook. This goes especially for the political police. And this was the reason why investigation of the assaults was taken out of the hands of the Königsberg police and given to a *Sonderkommando* of 100 members of a political branch of the *Kriminalpolizei* from Berlin, all of them Nazis, who saw it as their prime duty to obliterate all evidence.[55]

There was no way Sabatzky's safety could be guaranteed any longer. "At the urgent entreaty of my Königsberg friends", he exchanged positions with the C.V. syndic in Stettin for three months.

Within the Jewish community Sabatzky did not find much support. This is evident from a letter the Königsberg section of the C.V. addressed to the Berlin central office in March 1933, asking for the appointment of a new *Syndikus* – just a few day after Sabatzky himself, counselled by his friends in the police force, had left East Prussia for what he thought was only to be a temporary absence. Sabatzky's *Abwehrkampf* had apparently terrified many C.V. members: ". . .as a result of the psychological state of our co-religionists in the Province, Herr Sabatzky's activities would be all but paralysed because they are afraid to be seen together with Herr Sabatzky in any way."[56] There was not much he could do legally after the *Machtergreifung*, in Spring 1933. *Polizeipräsident* Berner (who had been appointed by the previous Papen government) was prepared, on being entreated by Sabatzky, to guarantee the safety of Jewish businessmen, but was unable to make good his promise. On 9th March 1933 the Rubinstein baker's shop was attacked with an incendiary bomb. Two days later, Berner personally warned Sabatzky he had better leave town:

> Both the *Polizeipräsident* and the *Hauptmann* of my local police force felt responsible for my own and my family's well-being. This is why they pressed me to leave Königsberg with my family before nightfall and get into safety, which was very clearly advisable after what had happened on 1st August [1932]. . . After a few days, by when tensions should have relaxed, I might return. – Actually I was never to see Königsberg again.[57]

---

[54] C.V. chairman Julius Brodnitz, in his appeal to the Prussian Ministry of the Interior for enhanced police protection, calls Sabatzky's absence "coincidental". Cf. Arnold Paucker, 'Der jüdische Abwehrkampf', in Werner E. Mosse and Arnold Paucker (eds.), *Entscheidungsjahr 1932*, Tübingen 1965, p. 237.

[55] *Erinnerungen*, p. 20. In his *Erinnerungen* he recalls how during his absence his wife, who had stayed in Königsberg, was "worn down" by anonymous telephone calls at night, which promptly ceased when he returned and answered the phone himself.

[56] Letter dated 24th March 1933, quoted from Schüler-Springorum, p. 298.

[57] *Erinnerungen*, p. 21.

That same night Sabatzky set out for Köslin with his family. Three days later there were several attacks in Königsberg on Jews and Left-wing politicians and journalists, with about twenty murdered.[58] Sabatzky's flight from Königsberg was not reported in the *Gemeindeblatt* with a single word.[59]

Sabatzky first went to Berlin and then to Leipzig, becoming the new C.V. *Syndikus* for the area organisation of *Mitteldeutschland*. He stayed on in Germany until 1939, trying to ease the predicament of Jews in his area through legal measures and personal intervention. "After the *Machtergreifung* I saw it as my foremost duty to give legal aid and counsel to the Jews and above all to find holes in the tightly-knit net of Party and *Gestapo* through which Jews might be able to escape."[60] On several occasions the *Gestapo* took him into custody and questioned him. He reports how in the course of one of these interrogations in Leipzig *Kriminalinspektor* Kuchmann, who had come "specially" from Berlin, bellowed at him: "And anyway, you're the notorious Sabatzky from Königsberg!"[61] Sabatzky escaped all those interrogations unharmed.

On 10th November 1938, Sabatzky was arrested in Dresden. He was transferred to the KZ Buchenwald but released after four weeks "due to my standing as a war veteran".[62] Sabatzky then liquidated the C.V. organisation at Leipzig and spent six weeks in Essen, acting as community syndic and *Reichsvertretung* director for the Rhineland-Palatinate. His family stayed in Leipzig, where during one of his visits Sabatzky and his wife were arrested by the *Gestapo*. They were given orders to leave Germany within six to eight weeks and not to take on any official duties during that time:

> I immediately went to see Otto Hirsch in Berlin, who telephoned the president of Bloomsbury House in London to get me a permit straight away ... We were immensely relieved when we touched down at London's Croydon Airport on 21st August 1939, ten days [*sic*] before war broke out.[63]

Sabatzky was interned on the Isle of Man for two months but then released after his wife had been able to give convincing evidence that Sabatzky had been active against Nazism for nearly twenty years. From 1945 he worked at the Wiener Library in London and organised a Jewish tracing service. He died in London in 1955.

In his *Erinnerungen* Sabatzky depicts himself as a preacher in the desert, gifted with a political vision superior even to the leading representatives of the democratic Prussian government. His writings from the 1920s and 1930s undoubtedly bear out this self-assessment. At first glance, his *Mitteilungen des C.V.-Syndikats* seem to make monotonous reading: ever the same warnings, ever the same sort of trial, ever the same subjects of civil and social equality. Many readers of the

---

[58] *ibid*. In Sabatzky's words the murdered were "linksgerichtete Arier".

[59] Yet the newspaper printed numerous articles on the "removal" (*Fortzug*) of prominent community members during 1933.

[60] *Erinnerungen*, p. 24.

[61] *ibid*., p. 31: "Und überhaupt sind Sie der berüchtigte Sabatzky aus Königsberg!"

[62] *ibid*., p. 41: "wegen meiner Eigenschaft als ehemaliger Frontkämpfer".

[63] *ibid*., p. 42, *permit* in the English original.

Gemeindeblatt may have retained just such an impression. But taken all in all, Sabatzky's column is the one consistent thread running through the ten years of the Jewish press in East Prussia – though within the Jewish community Sabatzky's warnings were probably not much heeded, sometimes sharply criticised, and his ultimate departure not too deeply regretted.

In Königsberg, more than elsewhere perhaps, the debate within the intellectual Jewish community was still about achieving civil and social equality and integration – sometimes, as shown, assuming the symbolic role of the imaginary *Ostjude*. Sabatzky, on the other hand, seems to have realised that Jewish existence in Germany was no longer under threat from the past, but from the future. That particular brand of modernity was something for which the Jewish middle class in the easternmost German city was definitely not prepared. More than to Jews west of the Polish Corridor, the *Reich* was the guarantor of their social existence, of their self-perception. More than others they had reason to cling to this orientation. This is why at the end they were unwilling to listen any longer to Sabatzky's sombre forecasts.

Polish and German Jews Between Hitler's Rise to Power and the Outbreak of the Second World War

BY YFAAT WEISS

I.

In the Middle Ages and at the beginning of the modern period, German and Polish Jews were part of the same social and spiritual environment.[1] The prevailing economic and linguistic links, the frequent occurrence of marriages between Jews in Germany and Poland, and the movement of students and rabbis between these areas, demonstrate that the Jews in these countries belonged to a single centre.[2] But economic prosperity, civic status, social prestige and the acculturation of the Jews in Germany, in the course of the nineteenth century and up to the end of the 1920s, generated a profound gulf between them and the Jews of Eastern Europe. Jewish life in Eastern Europe, particularly in those parts which were destined to become part of an independent Poland after the Treaty of Versailles, was difficult in the extreme, and very different from the ease and prosperity characteristic of Jewish life in Germany. The complex relationship between German and Eastern European Jews is well known. As Jews in Germany became increasingly attached to the state, their attachment to the Jewish community, and especially to Eastern European Jews, the *Ostjuden*, weakened. Eugen Fuchs, one of the heads of the *Centralverein deutscher Staatsbürger jüdischen Glaubens* (C.V.), stated in 1919: "We Western Jews ... are inseparable from our peoples ... In the East, things are different. The Polish, Galician, Lithuanian, Romanian Jews are nationalities."[3] His attitude was not significantly different from that of the German Zionist Franz Oppenheimer, who in 1910, when trying to explain the difference between Eastern and Western European Zionism, distinguished between *Stammesbewußtsein* and *Volksbewußtsein*.

> We Western Jews have ethnic consciousness ... Ethnic consciousness [is] a consciousness of joint sources, common blood, or at least of a former common nationality, a common history with its memories of suffering and joy, heroism and great needs.

---

[1]As defined by Jacob Katz: whether distant places belong together is determined by a link between their lifestyles and a common normative pattern. Jacob Katz, *Tradition and Crisis: Jewish Society at the End of the Middle Ages*, New York 1961, p. 6.
[2]See also Karl Erich Grözinger (ed.), *Die wirtschaftliche und kulturellen Beziehungen zwischen den jüdischen Gemeinden in Polen und Deutschland vom 16. bis zum 20. Jahrhundert*, Wiesbaden 1992.
[3]Kurt Stilschweig, *Die Juden Osteuropas in den Minderheitsverträgen*, Berlin 1936, p. 25.

Oppenheimer went on to assert:

> National consciousness, on the other hand, is motivated by the present: a common language, customs, economic and legal relations, etc., and spiritual culture. It is the mental reflection of the society in which and through which we live.

Oppenheimer stressed that Western European Jews did not need the kind of national identity which existed among Eastern European Jews.

> Their native countries had afforded asylum to them or their fathers. They gave them language, customs, wealth and education, political and as often as not, full or partial civic equality. It would be a wicked and unnatural man who could forget that.[4]

Like Oppenheimer, most Jews in Germany believed that what connected European Jewry was a common past, but they refused to recognise the possibility of a common present or future. In 1927 Ludwig Holländer, one of the heads of the C.V., wrote in an encyclopaedia entry:

> The Jews were once a people . . . Then, as a result also of historical developments, they lost the attribute of being a people with a state, because they overwhelmingly lost those elements which the science of politics requires for the concept of a people, namely: a common country, common language, common history, common culture and similarly oriented hopes of the future.[5]

Despite the denial of a common future, and hence also the denial of the existence of a common destiny, most German Jews were united in solidarity with the Eastern European Jews. Although it changed its character and form, this pattern, which originated in Jewish law, maintained its force across the transition to modern life, and found its expression in forms of Jewish diplomacy as well as in international Jewish aid activities.[6] Some right-wing German-Jewish groups, organised under Max Naumann in the *Verband nationaldeutscher Juden*, did not share this sentiment, waging a bitter struggle against Jewish migrants from Eastern Europe. The majority of organised German Jews, however, did not exhibit an overtly hostile attitude towards the *Ostjuden*, although they were concerned that the presence of the *Ostjuden* in Germany would increase antisemitism.[7] Active help was extended to the Eastern European Jews by numerous

---

[4]*Die Welt*, No. 7, 18 February 1910, transl. by Jehuda Reinharz, 'East European Jews in the Weltanschauung of German Zionists 1882–1914', in *Studies in Contemporary Jewry* I (1984), pp. 72–83.

[5]Ludwig Holländer, *Jüdisches Lexikon*, entry Central-Verein, columns 1289–1294, 1927.

[6]Jonathan Frankel, 'Assimilation and the Jews in Nineteenth-Century Europe: Toward a New Historiography?', in Jonathan Frankel and Steven J. Zipperstein (eds.), *Assimilation and Community: The Jews in Nineteenth Century Europe*, Cambridge 1992, pp. 1–37; Pierre Birnbaum and Ira Katznelson, 'Emancipation and the Liberal Offer', in *idem*, (eds.), *Paths of Emancipation: Jews, States, and Citizenship*, Princeton 1997, pp. 3–36; Daniel Gutwein, 'Jewish Diplomacy in the Nineteenth Century: The Beginning of Jewish Nationalism?', in Jehuda Reinharz, Gideon Shimoni and Yosef Salmon (eds.), *Jewish Nationalism and Politics: New Perspectives* [Hebrew], Jerusalem 1997, pp. 159–176.

[7]Much has been written about the relations between German and Eastern European Jews in Germany. For political relations, see Trude Maurer, *Ostjuden in Deutschland 1918–1933*, Hamburg 1986; Jack Wertheimer, *Unwelcome Strangers: East European Jews in Imperial Germany*, Oxford 1987; Shulamit Volkov, 'Die Dynamik der Dissimilation: Deutsche Juden und die ostjüdischen Einwanderer', in *Jüdisches Leben und Antisemitismus im 19. und 20. Jahrhundert*, Munich 1990, pp. 166–180; Ludger Heid, *Malocheemdash keine Mildtätigkeit. Ostjüdische Arbeiter in Deutschland 1914–1923*, Hildesheim 1995. For cultural relations, see Steven E. Aschheim, *Brothers and Strangers: The East European*

organisations, of which the main ones were the *Hilfsverein der deutschen Juden* and the Zionists. These two groups operated on entirely different premises: the former tried to help the hungry Jewish masses in Eastern Europe both materially and spiritually, to encourage changes in Eastern European Jewry's vocational structure, and to support mass emigration to the West. The latter placed their trust in Jewish settlement of Palestine as a permanent solution to the "Jewish Question". The activities of all the Jewish organisations in Germany towards their Eastern European co-religionists were characterised by paternalism and were not based on assumptions of equality. To the extent that there was any belief in the virtues of the Eastern European Jews, these were virtues of spirit, of Jewish culture and faith. During and after the First World War there prevailed in certain post-emancipationist Zionist circles a profound admiration for Eastern European Jewish culture, which was depicted – unlike the culture of the German Jews – as an authentic one.[8] But these advantages, ascribed to *Ostjuden* by a minority of German Jews, were insignificant in the face of their material inferiority. The political status and consciousness of Western Jews allowed them to stand side by side with Eastern European Jews in their struggle for political and economic equality.

Furthermore, German-Jewish assimilation became identified with assimilation of all Jews. Among Eastern European Jews, Germany became a kind of ideal of Jewish life in a foreign country. *Nathan der Weise*, Lessing and Mendelssohn became Jewish codewords for economic success and social recognition. The social integration of German Jews was admired and emulated. With America, Germany was undoubtedly the *goldeneh medina* for the Jews of Eastern Europe. This is how Germany appeared to Eastern European Jews, and this is how many of the German Jews perceived themselves and their status among Jews as a whole.

II.

German-Jewish self-confidence was based primarily on civic equality, attained as early as the last third of the nineteenth century. It was not only the date of recognition which separated the German and Polish Jews – Poland's Jews first gained civic equality in independent Poland after the First World War – but also the practical consolidation of formal rights. Poland was compelled to grant equality to minorities under the agreements which followed the Treaty of Versailles, a complex of events in which Western Jews played a key role.[9] In contrast, the

Jew in German and German-Jewish Consciousness, 1800–1923, Madison 1982; Sander I. Gilman, 'The Rediscovery of the Eastern Jews: German Jews in the East, 1890–1918', in David Bronsen (ed.), *Jews and Germans from 1860 to 1933: The Problematic Symbiosis*, Heidelberg 1979, pp. 338–365.

[8] Aschheim, *Brothers and Strangers*, pp. 100–120.

[9] Kurt Stilschweig, *Die Juden Osteuropas in den Minderheitenverträgen*, Berlin 1936, pp. 180ff; Oscar I. Janowsky, *The Jews and Minority Rights, 1898–1919*, Columbia 1933; Pawel Korzec, 'Polen und der Minderheitenschutzvertrag (1919–1934)', in *Zeitschrift für Ostforschung*, 24, (1975), pp. 515–555. On the role of German Jewry in the struggle for civic equality for Jews in Poland, see Steven Aschheim, 'Eastern Jews, German Jews and Germany's Ostpolitik in the First World War', in *LBI Yearbook XXVIII* (1983), pp. 351–365; Egmont Zechlin, *Die deutsche Politik und die Juden im Ersten Weltkrieg*, Göttingen 1969.

civic equality of Germany's Jews came about as a result of an ongoing process of legislation which was an integral part of the creation of the liberal nation-state, and their equality increasingly became a fact of daily life. The world economic crisis, the undermining of German democracy, and the rise of the Nazi Party at the end of the 1920s shook the confidence of German Jews and brought the first reconsideration of the relationship between the Jews of Poland and Germany. "We are undoubtedly facing very difficult times in Germany", wrote Dr Mark Wischnitzer, secretary of the *Hilfsverein der Deutschen Juden* in 1930.

> However, we have had a typical comment from a member of many years standing, who has read in the newspapers of the dreadful suffering in Poland, and who asks just how it is possible that help is no longer provided. He asks whether the suffering in Poland can in any way be compared with our own.[10]

The comparison between what was happening in Poland and what was happening in Germany aroused a storm of indignation. Many of the Jews in Germany rejected this comparison. The independent newspaper the *Israelitisches Familienblatt* commented on the involvement of Jews in Poland on behalf of Jews in Germany:

> It seems to us rather inappropriate when protest resolutions against Nazi petitions in the Prussian state parliament are drawn up by all possible bodies in Warsaw. The German Jews consider the drawing up of such resolutions by both official and unofficial bodies in Warsaw to be rather undesirable. As long as the suffering of the Jews in Poland is as extreme as it is now, the bodies in Warsaw should deal first with this suffering and refrain from undertaking what is undoubtedly an unintentional exoneration operation for Mr. Pilsudski's government. It is up to the German Jews themselves to make statements about their situation and to adopt the relief measures suitable for the circumstances.[11]

In mid-1932 the community newspaper in Breslau rejected an offer by a Jew in Lemberg to translate articles describing the situation of the Jews in Poland on the grounds that "there is no room at the moment for reports about the situation of the Jews in Poland and similar subjects".[12]

Under the impact of the national situation, Jews in Germany gradually realised that they could no longer ignore the impact of antisemitic trends in Germany on the Jews of Poland. At the end of 1932, the C.V.'s newspaper featured an article which described the implications of antisemitic riots in Poland, which had begun at the universities and spread to entire cities.[13] The newspaper concluded with a warning to German readers not to content themselves with expressing revulsion at similar events at German universities, but to actively combat these events in order to prevent the universities from being a

---

[10] Osobyi Archive Moscow, Speech by Dr Mark Wischnitzer in 1930, 1325/1/74.

[11] 'Unerwünschte Einmischung', in *Israelitisches Familienblatt*, 14 July 1932, quoted in Avraham Margaliot, 'The Political Reaction of the Jewish Institutions and Organizations in Germany to the Anti-Jewish Policy of the National Socialists, 1932–1935' [Hebrew], PhD diss., Hebrew University of Jerusalem 1971, p. 120.

[12] Zydowski Instytut Historyzny (Warsaw), Die Schriftleitung des Gemeindeblattes an Herrn O. Preminger am 1.4.1932, Synagogen Gemeinde zu Breslau, Akt. Nr. 88.

[13] *Centralverein Zeitung*, (9 December 1932).

source of violence across Germany. At the same time, the Zionist *Jüdische Rundschau* published, next to the leading article (a forecast of Hitler's rise to power and what could be expected as a result for the Jews), a detailed article about riots taking place against the Jews in Polish towns.[14] In the Zionist view, it was natural to report events in Poland and Germany side by side, because this was an endorsement of the classic Zionist argument about the distorted form of Jewish existence in the Diaspora.

III.

Until Hitler's rise to power, Germany acted as a centre for Jewish activity aimed towards Eastern Europe. The relative political freedom which characterised the Weimar Republic, the economic prosperity of the mid 1920s, the geographical proximity to Eastern Europe, and the linguistic closeness between German and Yiddish all encouraged this development. Yiddish newspapers and Yiddish literature were printed and published in Germany for a readership in Eastern Europe.[15] The Central European branches of a large number of organisations which were involved in providing support to the Jews of Eastern Europe, such as the American Jewish Joint Distribution Committee, ORT and ICA, had their offices in Berlin.[16] The political upheaval in Germany put an end to this extensive activity. Moreover, Germany, which had been a symbol of Jewish equality and a model of Jewish assimilation became overnight a state in which the existence of the Jews was not desired, and which discriminated and humiliated them at every turn.

In numerical terms the position of German Jews might seem of secondary importance compared with that of the Jews in Poland. But events in Germany decisively influenced the situation of the Jews in Eastern Europe a considerable time before the outbreak of the Second World War. "Let us not play down the size of the danger awaiting us. Hitler's success in the elections of March 5 should serve as a sharp warning to us. And let us know that 'our Hitlerists' won't be any gentler in their wars and victories than the ones in Germany", wrote a *Hehalutz* member in the movement's Polish magazine.[17] Hitler's victory in Germany and anti-Jewish policies there did indeed spill over into the countries of Eastern Europe and to Poland in particular.[18] Polish antisemitic right-wing circles were greatly influenced by Nazi policies toward Jews, despite their fear of Germany's increasing strength and the possibility that Germany would demand a revision of

[14] *Jüdische Rundschau* (6 December 1932), quoted in Avraham Margoliot, 'Political Reaction of Jewish Institutions', p. 108.

[15] Leo and Renate Fuks, 'Yiddish Publishing Activities in the Weimar Republic, 1920–1933', in *LBI Year Book XXXIII* (1988), pp. 417–434.

[16] S. Adler-Rodel, *Ostjuden in Deutschland 1880–1940. Zugleich eine Geschichte der Organisationen, die sie betreuten*, Tübingen 1959, pp. 103ff.

[17] Z. Rosenstein, 'Towards the Eighteenth Congress' [Hebrew], in *He-Atid* (the newspaper of the World Hehalutz Organization), Warsaw (5 May 1933).

[18] A comparison between German and Polish antisemitism between the wars is offered by William W. Hagen in 'Before the "Final Solution": Toward a Comparative Analysis of Political Anti-Semitism in Interwar Germany and Poland', in *Journal of Modern History*, vol. 68, No. II (June 1996), pp. 351–381.

its borders with Poland.[19] Many anti-Jewish initiatives in Poland were copied from Germany, including the ban on *shechita*, the struggle to introduce a *numerus clausus*,[20] and the introduction of separate benches for Jews at the universities, as well as isolated attempts to introduce racial laws in Poland.[21]

Under these conditions, Germany's Jews found themselves in the same position as their co-religionists in Poland. In practically every statement and initiative by international Jewish organisations German-Jewish and Polish-Jewish distress were referred to in the same breath. This was as true of the World Zionist Congress in 1933[22] as it was of the Canadian-Jewish Congress in 1934.[23] The World Jewish Conference, meeting in Geneva in August 1934, discussed not only the anti-German boycott movement and the status of the Jews in the Saarland were it to be taken over by the Germans, but at the same time also the danger to the continued application of the minorities treaty which Poland had adopted under the Versailles agreements.[24] Fundraising was also frequently carried out both for German and Polish Jewry.[25]

IV.

It has already been indicated that the traditional attitude of German Jewry toward the *Ostjuden* was paternalistic, based on the economic and political advantage of Germany's Jews compared with those of Poland. For the first time in centuries, German Jewry suddenly found itself competing with Polish Jewry for aid and support.[26] The dire world economic situation and the withdrawal of German Jewry from all Jewish philanthropic circles significantly reduced the financial

[19]Yosef Te'eni, 'Hitler's Rise to Power and the Influence of German Anti-semitism on the Situation of Poland's Jews between 1933 and 1939' [Hebrew], PhD diss., Hebrew University of Jerusalem 1980, pp. 56ff; Karol Gruenberg, 'The Atrocities against the Jews in the Third Reich as seen by the National-Democratic Press (1933–1939)', in *Polin*, vol. V (1990), pp. 103–113.

[20]An independent Polish initiative to introduce a *numerus clausus* at universities was rejected in 1923 because of League of Nations opposition and the contradiction between this legislation and the minorities treaty that Poland had signed at the end of the First World War. Initiatives to introduce a *numerus clausus* in the mid 1930s were partly German-inspired, as they were in Romania and Hungary.

[21]On Polish antisemitic policies, see Emanuel Meltzer, *No Way Out: The Politics of Polish Jewry 1935–1939*, Cincinnati 1997. On the link between antisemitic legislation in Germany and Poland, see Yfaat Weiss, 'Dokument. Das Gespräch zwischen Jerzy Potocki, Stephan Wise und Louis Lipsky am 31. März 1938', in *Arbeitsmigration und Flucht. Vertreibung und Arbeitskräfteregulierung im Zwischenkriegseuropa*. Beiträge zur nationalsozialistischen Gesundheits- und Sozialpolitik II (1993), pp. 205–212.

[22]'Der 18. Zionisten-Kongreß. Überblickreferat von Sokolow über die Lage der Juden in Europa (Rußland, Polen, Deutschland)', in *Jüdische Zeitung*, No. 34 (1 September 1933).

[23]Central Archive for the History of the Jewish People (Jerusalem), General call for participation in the Congress, 10 August 1934, Inv. 124 (21).

[24]Central Zionist Archive (Jerusalem), Nachum Goldmann, Rundschreiben an die Mitglieder des Exekutive-Comités, 18 July 1934, Lausanne. Provisorische Tagesordnung. A127/140.

[25]For example, fund-raising in the USA for the United Jewish Appeal under Felix Warburg, *Jüdische Zeitung*, No. 21 (7 June 1935).

[26]Zosa Szajkowski, 'Western Jewish Aid and Intercession for Polish Jewry, 1919–1939', in *Studies on Polish Jewry 1919–1939: The Interplay of Social, Economical and Political Factors in the Struggle of a Minority for its Existence*, New York 1974, pp. 150–241, 184ff.

resources during a period of growing need in Germany and Eastern Europe. The ORT bulletin reported that the organisation's activities in the vocational training fields in Germany were detracting from its activities in Poland.[27] Conversely, the C.V.'s newspaper expressed fear that émigré activity in Britain on behalf of Poland's Jews would detract from similar activities on behalf of Germany's Jews.[28] The *Hilfsverein*, which had operated for decades among German Jews on behalf of Eastern European Jews, drastically changed the nature of its activities, and began to act energetically in order to arrange the emigration of the Jews from Germany.[29] The American Jewish Joint Distribution Committee, the most important Jewish aid organisation which had traditionally helped Eastern European Jews, changed its agenda in 1933 and began, for the first time since its establishment, to aid Jews in Germany.[30]

German Jewry's transformation from a provider to a recipient of support is an event of decisive importance. Its impact on the consciousness of the German-Jewish establishment is reflected in the following extract from the 1936 annual activity report of the *Zentralausschuß für Hilfe und Aufbau*:

> It is very painful for Jews in Germany, who in previous years have so generously contributed to alleviating the suffering of our co-religionists, particularly in Eastern Europe, that they are no longer able to participate in this community assistance at a time when the crisis affecting the Jews in Eastern Europe has become more acute than ever before. The power of historical developments has turned us from a community which could give into a circle of people who are themselves dependent on assistance. We have tried and we shall continue to try to compensate for this difficult position by applying our own forces in order to shape our destiny in a positive fashion by combining and adapting to the utmost. But beyond this, the only thing we can do is to express the utmost gratitude for the assistance that we have found where our own forces were no longer adequate.[31]

Within the Zionist movement, too, conflicts erupted between the competing needs of German and Polish Jews. Apart from the struggle for financial support,[32] Jews in Germany and Poland – or, to be more precise, the Zionist Federations in those countries – competed for the distribution of entry permits to Palestine.[33] British Mandate policy was to restrict Jewish immigration to Palestine. The distribution of the limited permits made available by the British

---

[27]'The World ORT Organisation found it necessary to devote much of its financial strength to the problems of the German Jews, and as a result cannot support the Polish ORT work in measure with the great need that prevails in that country.' *People's ORT Federation Bulletin*, No. 6 (July 1934).

[28]'Aktionen zu Gunsten der polnischen Juden', in *Centralverein Zeitung*, No. 17 (23 April 1936).

[29]These changes did not escape the attention of the German authorities, as shown by the RSHA reports. Moscow, Politische Gliederung der Juden in Deutschland, 15 January 1936, RSHA, 500/1/430.

[30]Yfaat Weiss, 'Equal and More Equal: The American Jewish Joint Distribution Committee and Relief Efforts in Germany and Poland, 1933–1936' [Hebrew], in *Gal-Ed*, vols. XV–XVI (1997), pp. 111–145.

[31]Reconstructed Reichsvertretung Archive, Hebrew University of Jerusalem, Arbeitsbericht des Zentralausschusses für das Jahr 1936.

[32]Daniel Fraenkel, *On the Edge of the Abyss: Zionist Policy and the Flight of the German Jews 1933–1938* [Hebrew], Jerusalem 1994, p. 60.

[33]On the struggle for permits, see also Aviva Halamish, 'Immigration and Absorption Policy of the Zionist Organisation' [Hebrew], Diss., Tel Aviv 1995, pp. 257ff.

to the Jewish authorities was implemented by the Jewish Agency in accordance with changing needs in Palestine and in the Diaspora. From the beginnings of the Zionist movement, the numbers of German immigrants to Palestine had been low compared with the numbers of Jewish immigrants from Eastern Europe. Between 1920 and 1932, altogether 1,948 individuals emigrated to Palestine from Germany. In the six-monthly immigration quota at the end of 1932, Germany received 118 out of 4,500 permits.[34]

As the situation in Germany deteriorated and showed itself to be permanent, so the number of Jews seeking to emigrate grew. Because of the limited number of permits and the absence of alternative emigration channels, the 1930s were characterised by a demand for permits which was out of all proportion to the numbers of documents made available to the Zionist Movement. Under these circumstances, it was difficult to reach a solution which would satisfy all sides. Werner Senator, who had overall responsibility for dealing with the German-Jewish community in Palestine on behalf of the Jewish Agency in London, tried to alleviate the resentment of Polish Zionist activists who complained that "the German catastrophe was reverberating through the Jewish world and Palestine", while "the disaster of Polish Jewry and Jewish youth in Poland was not".[35]

An entirely different impression was received by the German emigration authorities.[36] To them it seemed that German Jews were being discriminated against in the distribution of permits, compared with Poland's Jews.[37] Poland's Jews were receiving more permits as labourers than were Germany's Jews, according to a German Emigration Office report, because "the Jews resident in Germany [could] not provide the Palestine Office with the proof that they were physically fit enough to be able to carry out agricultural work in Palestine in the same way as the fellow members of their race from Poland." The reason for this, according to the report, was the low level of *Hachsharah* in Germany.

The German emigration services appear to have been influenced in their evaluation by the German Zionists' belief that they were being discriminated against. British policy on immigration tightened and quotas were reduced at the end of 1936, sparking a debate about the immigration quota or Schedule. This schedule allowed 590 permits for Polish Jews, and 295 for German Jews.[38]

---

[34]Fraenkel, *On the Edge*, pp. 101, 105.

[35]House of Ghetto Fighters' Archive (Kibbutz Ghetto Fighters), conversation with Dr. Werner Senator in a meeting of the Hehalutz central committee 1936, Z8/1 of the Hehalutz Archive in Poland, File 18.

[36]The *öffentlichen deutschen Auswanderungsberatungsstellen* (public emigration-services) had already been established throughout Germany during the Weimar Republic. These institutions provided information to those wishing to emigrate. Although it was a state enterprise, the emigration service's employees were members of the *Zentrumspartei* and they were not members of the National-Socialist Party. See Doron Niederland, 'German Jews Emigrants or Refugees? Emigration Patterns between the Two World Wars' [Hebrew], Diss., Hebrew University of Jerusalem 1988, pp. 11f.

[37]Staatsarchiv Hamburg, Reichsstelle für das Auswanderungswesen, Berlin, Stand der Auswanderungsbewegung im 1. Kalendervierteljahr 1935, Auswanderungsamt I, Akt Nr. II A 3a, Band 1.

[38]Central Zionist Archive, Eliahu Dobkin, Immigration Department, Jewish Agency Circular No. 2115/227, 10 December 1936, File S6/3643.

Eliahu Dobkin, head of the Jewish Agency's Immigration Department, replied to a complaint voiced by the German Immigrants Association:

> We do not see ourselves bound by any obligation concerning a fixed percentage for German immigrants. The same applies to every other country ... We consider very strange any arguments about "discrimination" against German immigrants during the distribution of the Schedule. As you know, over the last three years we have given preference to the immigration of Germany's Jews over that of Jews from other countries.[39]

Werner Senator replied in a similar vein to the Palestine Office in Berlin:

> It is obvious to us that this number of permits cannot satisfy the demands for immigration which exist in Germany and among its refugees, but this sort of thing has also happened to other countries. If you look at the situation in Poland and the number of permits allocated for it, you will see that we had no way of doing for you more than what has been done.[40]

Many years later, when Dr Franz Mayer, head of the Palestine Office in Berlin, was asked about the distribution of permits between Germany and Poland, he replied:

> I am undoubtedly not objective, but given the urgency of the German situation in these years ... the number did seem to me to be low. On the other hand, I realised that prior to 1933 the German Jews provided a simply extraordinarily low number of *olim*; and that it is perhaps possible that for this reason the Jewish Agency earmarked only a very small number of permits for Germany.[41]

Under the pressure of events, it was undoubtedly difficult to recognise the Polish Zionists' right on a "first-come" basis, but it was increasingly acknowledged that the emigration of German Jews could not be examined separately from, or in competition with, the emigration of Eastern European Jews. In reaction to the White Paper published by Britain at the end of 1937, the Zionist Federation in Germany called for the gates to be opened in the name of the Jews of Germany and Eastern Europe jointly.[42] Likewise, the *Reichsvertretung* made a point of reducing the expectations of those applying to it by stressing that what it was able to do did not depend exclusively on its own wishes and the work of the emigration organisations, but rather on other countries' willingness to open their gates to émigrés from Germany as well as from Eastern Europe.[43]

---

[39] *ibid.*, Dobkin to the German Immigrants Association, Jerusalem Section, 14 December 1936. Germany's Jews actually received 30%–40% during the period immediately following Hitler's rise to power, but by the autumn of 1934 the percentage had already dropped to 17%. Fraenkel, *On the Edge*, p. 120.

[40] Central Zionist Archive, Werner Senator to the Palestine Office in Berlin, 27 December 1936, File S6/3643.

[41] Oral Documentation Institute, Institute for Contemporary Jewry, Hebrew University of Jerusalem, Testimony of Franz Mayer, p. 19.

[42] 'Das neue Weißbuch', in *C.V.-Zeitung* (13 January 1938).

[43] *Jüdisches Gemeindeblatt für den Bezirk der Synagogengemeinde Aachen*, vol. 12 (1 February 1938).

V.

In recent Hitler-Germany neither the wildest agitation by ministers nor the open incitements to pogroms by the highest representatives of government are successful. The population – in the broadest sense of the word – remains aloof to incitements to pogroms. When the government needs a pogrom it has to send in its loyal servants of the Hitler party ... A completely different situation is presented to us in Poland. The government fights weakly against pogroms, undetermined, not active and strong enough. Pogroms there were not incited actively "from above," but rose "from below" through the broad masses, the intelligentsia, small proprietors, peasants, the uprooted, and the outcast of their class.[44]

It is difficult to determine whether the Jews' situation was worse in the mid 1930s in Germany or Poland. The economic situation of the Jews in Poland was undoubtedly worse than in Germany, and many were starving. Physical intimidation and injuries were also more widespread in Poland than in Germany. In the wake of his visit to Poland in the summer of 1936, Ben-Gurion believed that "the disastrous situation of Polish Jewry proper, a permanent pogrom situation – in political, physical, economic and moral terms – perhaps far worse than that in Germany – dulls the emotions".[45]

Dobkin wrote in his diary at the end of 1936:

It is difficult to describe the oppressive feeling, particularly for somebody who comes [to Germany] from outside. When I was in Lvov, I saw them beating Jews in the streets. The day I arrived in Bialystok, the pogrom happened in Wysokie-Mazowieckie, and nevertheless the atmosphere in Poland cannot be compared with the feeling of utterly depressing helplessness and humiliation felt by the Jew [in Germany], and to the special "Jewish" feeling there is added further the atmosphere which is suffused with preparations for war: practically every third man in the street is in uniform.[46]

This description identified one of the quintessential differences between the Jews' situation in Germany and in Poland. While Poland's Jews, for most of the 1930s, enjoyed formal equality before the law and were able to operate an active self-defence system, possibilities for Germany's Jews were extremely limited. Unlike German Jewry, Polish Jewry had faith in a tradition of separate Jewish political activism, which had evolved over generations and had received official parliamentary expression in the "minorities bloc".[47] It is true, however, that Polish Jewry failed to overcome internal differences of opinion and to establish a united central framework in striking contrast to German Jewry, which managed to set up the *Reichsvertretung* as early as 1933.[48] It is possible that the roots of this

[44] Jacob Lestchinsky, *Erev Horban: Of Jewish Life in Poland 1935–1937* [Yiddish], Buenos Aires 1951, p. 134.

[45] Quoted in Fraenkel, *On the Edge*, p. 240.

[46] Israel Labour Party Archive, Lavon Institute, Tel Aviv, File III-38-43-12, Germany diary, Berlin, 18 October 1936, p. 1.

[47] Moshe Landau, *The Jews as a National Minority in Poland, 1918–1928* [Hebrew], Zalman Shazar Centre, Jerusalem 1986.

[48] Azriel Hildesheimer, *The Central Organization of German Jews in the Years 1933–1945: Its Legal and Political Status and its Position in the Jewish Community* [Hebrew], Jerusalem 1982; Max Grünewald, 'Der

failure lay in the fact that in Poland there was a more deeply-rooted tradition of contrasts between different Jewish and class outlooks but, despite the division of their political strength, Poland's Jews waged an unrelenting struggle against antisemitic initiatives in Poland, many of which were imported from Germany.

A striking example of the difference between the nature of Polish Jewry's struggle and that of German Jewry is the campaign against the ban on *shechita*. The anti-*shechita* law in Germany was one of the first pieces of legislation passed by the Nazis. As early as March 1933 a number of the German states authorised the slaughter of warm-blooded animals only after they had been stunned, and on 21 April 1933 the law was extended to the entire *Reich*.[49] Apart from reactions and correspondence among ultra-Orthodox Jews, it is difficult to identify opposition from Jews in Germany. The public controversy about *shechita* in Poland erupted in mid-1935, and the law prohibiting it was passed by the country's parliament, the *Sejm*, in March 1936.[50] The ramifications of the law were extremely severe in all senses: Poland's Jews were more punctilious about *kashrut* than were the Jews in Germany. When the law was enacted in Germany three years earlier, the ultra-Orthodox Jews had been able to import meat from Poland, and hence the ban on *shechita* in Poland meant the elimination of sources of kosher meat for the Jews of Germany and Poland alike. In addition, the number of Jewish families who made a living from the kosher meat industry was considerable: it has been estimated that some 60,000 directly derived their livelihood from it.[51] In their struggle for *shechita*, Poland's Jews made widespread use of their right to vote, of the parliamentary system, and of public opinion.[52] Jewish representatives in the *Sejm* took steps to renew the alliance with the representatives of the Ukrainian minority, who co-operated in opposing the law. In parallel with all these external efforts, there was widespread mobilisation among the Jewish public, expressed in protest rallies and the proclamation of mass fasts.

Poland's Jews waged similar struggles against attacks on Jews at the universities, against the imposition of separate benches for students, and against the attempt to restrict the proportion of Jews in higher education.[53] This obstinate struggle included debates in the *Sejm*, enlisting the support of Polish intellectuals, as well as physical resistance and defence by Jewish students at the universities. In the long run, the campaign failed: the absolute number of Jewish students, as well as the Jewish proportion of the total student body, dropped from one year to the next. In 1925, Jews made up 25% of the total student body at Poland's universities. In 1935 the figure dropped to 14.8%; in 1937–1938 it was 10% while in

Anfang der Reichsvertretung', in Robert Weltsch (ed.), *Deutsches Judentum. Aufstieg und Krise. Gestalten, Ideen, Werke*, Stuttgart 1963, pp. 315–325.

[49]Joseph Walk (ed.), *Das Sonderrecht für die Juden im NS-Staat. Eine Sammlung der gesetzlichen Maßnahmen und Richtlinien – Inhalt und Bedeutung*, Heidelberg–Karlsruhe, 1981, pp. 5, 15.

[50]On the parliamentary debate in Poland, see Joseph Gitman, 'The Jews and Jewish Problems in the Parliament, 1919–1939', Diss., Yale University 1963, pp. 114ff.

[51]Meltzer, *No Way Out*, p. 86.

[52]*ibid.*, pp. 86ff.

[53]*ibid.*, pp. 74ff.

1938–1939 it sank to around 8.2%.[54] Nevertheless, the very fact that the struggle was waged testifies to the difference in political reaction in Poland and Germany. Germany's Jews undertook no struggle whatsoever against their isolation in the universities or against the legislation which instituted a *numerus clausus* in universities and in higher education generally. As far as German Jews were concerned, the struggle for higher education took the form of establishing a Jewish education system in Germany, and efforts to arrange the emigration of its young people.

A further, final example is the struggle against the expulsion of Jewish pedlars from markets. Jealousy and economic competition, which were frequently the grounds for hatred and persecution of the Jews, were reflected throughout Germany and Poland in local initiatives by both groups and individuals to expel Jewish pedlars from markets and restrict their economic activities. In Germany most of the Jewish pedlars were of foreign origin. Apart from the central body's limited activity, which focused primarily on legal advice for the victims, most of the struggle was waged by the foreign consulates, particularly Poland's, in order to protect the economic status of their citizens in Germany and to prevent their return to their countries of origin.[55] In Poland, in contrast, Jewish organisations, led by the *Bund*, waged an active struggle in which they made use of weapons and self-defence, in order to protect the pedlars and the whole of the threatened Jewish public.[56]

Throughout the 1930s, the Jews of Poland were aware of the danger confronting them as a result of the antisemitic legislation imported into Poland from Germany. In their struggle against these influences, they made use of their formal rights, such as participation in elections and representation in parliament, as well as public opinion. They waged an active fight on all fronts, and did not flinch from physical defence and armed struggle. Nevertheless, unlike the Jews of Germany, Polish Jews did not manage to set up a central organisation to represent their interests, and the resulting fragmentation undoubtedly weakened their ability to react. The *modus operandi* adopted by Poland's Jews – the search for parliamentary political partners, recruiting the intelligentsia, attempting to influence the Jewish voter, and extensive information campaigns – were very similar to German Jewry's political activities in its heyday. In contrast, German Jewry found itself at the beginning of 1933 dispossessed of its political rights, so that the legal means of struggle available to it were extremely limited. Lacking a militant tradition, and in the absence of conditions conducive to an underground struggle, Germany's Jews focused their energies on improving the conditions of their lives among the constant reality of discrimination and humiliation.

---

[54]The figures are taken from the *Encyclopaedia Ha-Ivrit*.

[55]Yfaat Weiss, 'Ostjuden' in Deutschland als Freiwild. Die nationalsozialistische Außenpolitik zwischen Ideologie und Wirklichkeit', in *Tel Aviver Jahrbuch für deutsche Geschichte*, vol. XXIII (1994), pp. 215ff.

[56]Leonard Rowe, 'Jewish Self-Defence: A Response to Violence', in Fishman (ed.), *Studies on Polish Jewry*, pp. 105–149, 117ff.

VI.

The historic role of Western Jewry had been to mobilise public opinion to protect Eastern European Jewry from riots. In this way the Jews of Romania attained their rights at the Congress of Vienna in 1870; in this way mass emigration took place during the Czarist period; and in this way the rights of the national minorities were consolidated in the new states which came about in Central and Eastern Europe in the wake of the Treaty of Versailles. The 1930s were characterised by a kind of role reversal: now it was Polish Jews, both inside and outside Poland, who were campaigning to stir world opinion concerning events in Germany and the status of the Jews in the Third *Reich*.

In April 1933 a congress of Jewish communal organisations was held in Poland to discuss the situation of Germany's Jews.[57] The congress issued a protest against the exclusion of the Jews from the German economy. It emphasised that emigration, particularly to Palestine, was the main solution to the problem of Germany's Jews, and called upon the other countries to open their gates. Lastly, it demanded that Germany allow freedom of religion, referring in particular to the ban on *shechita*. This call represented an ironic twist of fate, and could have been drawn up some twenty years earlier by Germany's Jews on behalf of their co-religionists in Tsarist Russia.

In the same month, a delegation of the Jewish Students Union in Poland refused to take part in the International Students Congress, which was supposed to meet in 1933 at Ettel near Munich,[58] after Warsaw and Danzig had been judged unsuitable locations in light of the political atmosphere prevailing in Poland.[59] Assemblies to express solidarity and calls of support initiated by Polish Jews on behalf of the Jews in Germany after 1933 encompassed broad sectors of the Jewish public both inside and outside Poland. At the end of 1933, the executive board of the Organisation of Polish Rabbis called upon all rabbis to refer in their Sabbath sermons to the situation of the Jews in Germany, and to appeal to believers to express their willingness to make sacrifices by contributing to the spontaneous fundraising appeals on behalf of German Jewry.[60] In Paris, too, a meeting was held of representatives of Eastern European Jewish community organisations in France, which called upon the Eastern European Jews living in France to raise at least a million French francs to benefit Germany's Jews.[61]

Some suspicion might have trickled through the considerable solidarity manifested in this way that the massive focus on events in Germany was tending for a while to distract attention from events in Poland itself. In a semi-ironic tone the C.V.'s newspaper described the great interest shown by Jews in Poland in the

[57]'Kongreß der jüdischen Gemeinden und Organisationen Polens in Warschau', in *Jüdische Zeitung*, No. 17 (28 April 1933).
[58]Osobyi Archive Moscow, Alexander Teich (Jüdischer Hochschulausschuß, Vienna) to Dr Walter Kotsching (International Studenten-Service, Geneva), 25 April 1933, 1230/1/21.
[59]*ibid.*, Alexander Teich to Leo Steining, 15 June 1932.
[60]*Jüdische Zeitung*, No. 21 (2 June 1933).
[61]*Ibid.*, No. 4 (28 January 1934).

situation in Germany.[62] According to the article, the news coverage of developments in Germany occupied an entire page in the Jewish newspapers in Poland. Furthermore, it might have seemed that at least until the signing of the non-aggression pact between Poland and Germany in 1934, there was a tendency to think that criticism of the situation of Jews in Germany was likely to please the Polish authorities. The board of the Federation of Polish Jews in America issued a proclamation supporting the defence of the rights of Jews in Germany. In the same context the board referred to events in Poland, declaring

> that anti-Jewish discrimination in Poland did not represent the will of the Polish people or of Polish authorities, and they thanked the Warsaw government for its "splendid efforts" on behalf of Jewish refugees from Germany.[63]

In 1933 Vladimir (Ze'ev) Jabotinsky, the leader of the Zionist Revisionist movement, put forward an argument to the effect that Polish-Jewish protests against Hitlerism derived from the desire to please the Polish master.[64] Jabotinsky's argument was not entirely correct. Poland's Jews steadfastly maintained their support for German Jewry after the agreement between Poland and Germany had been signed. Jewish aid committees were active throughout Poland up to 1935.[65] Their activities were not limited to dealing with the Jewish refugees from Germany in Poland, but also included organising mass rallies against German anti-Jewish policies. At the end of 1934 the Jewish Congress, meeting in Warsaw, discussed the persecution of the Jews in Germany. The Congress called on world Jewry and the whole of civilised, freedom-loving humanity to engage in a defensive operation against the unprecedented infringement of fundamental human rights.[66] A year later, the situation of the Jews in Germany was a central issue at the World Congress of Polish Jews Outside Poland. Many of the Congress participants drew comparisons between the Jews' situation in Poland and in Germany, and the Polish representative even argued that the situation of Poland's Jews in Germany was "paradise" compared with their situation in Poland proper.[67] The World Organisation of Polish Jews Outside Poland was active on behalf of the Polish Jews in Germany, and demanded that the Polish government should also take action.[68]

---

[62]'Ein Streifzug durch die Nachbarschaft', in *C.V.-Zeitung*, No. 26 (28 June 1934).

[63]'Hail Senator's Stand Against Nazis' Bias', *New York Times* (12 June 1933).

[64]*He-Atid*, No. 144 (30 May 1933).

[65]Although these committees operated throughout Poland, the only surviving documentation is of the activities of the Cracow Aid Committee. Zydowaski Instytut Historyczny, Warsaw, Komitet Pomocy Uchodzcom z Niemic, Krakowie.

[66]Das politische Archiv des Auswärtigen Amtes (Bonn), Rundfunksender Luxemburg; German Embassy, Warsaw, to Foreign Office, Berlin, 21 January 1936, R100210.

[67]Das politische Archiv des Auswärtigen Amtes (Bonn), German Consulate General of Belgium to the Foreign Office, 26 August 1937, R99458.

[68]Bundesarchiv Abteilung Potsdam, Zidovska Telegrafny Agentura Prag, III Jg., No. 62 212, 16 September 1935, Reichsministerium für Volksaufklärung und Propaganda No. 1158.

VII.

International Jewish efforts on behalf of the Jews in Germany culminated in the boycott movement against German products initiated by Jewish organisations in many countries. As part of these efforts, Polish-Jewish activities were of supreme importance.[69] Jews played a key role in Polish commercial life, and the geographical proximity of Poland and Germany, and German businessmen's willingness to adapt German products to the conditions of the Polish market, helped to turn Germany into a prime source of goods imported into Poland. According to Polish statistics, in 1932 German imports into Poland made up around a fifth of all of imports. Exports to Poland totalled just 1.6% of total German exports. In terms of principle, however, the boycott of German products in Poland was of immense significance.

When the boycott movement was first organised in Poland, Jewish economic organisations, and in particular the Jewish Traders' Association, played a key role, and in an effective operation managed to recruit broad sectors of the Jewish public into boycotting German goods. The boycott was preceded by a prolonged search for alternative sources of German products, in order to avoid shortages and to prevent commercial competitors from gaining a foothold in the market. In mid-1934 the Jewish boycott included some 200 local committees, which organised anti-German publicity, monitored German merchandise in Poland, and instituted legal proceedings against boycott breakers.[70] During the operation of the boycott from 1933 to 1935, the value of German imports into Poland dropped from 173 million zloty in 1932 to 146 million in 1933, and to 108 million in 1934,[71] during a period when Poland's overall imports increased. The Jewish boycott movement undoubtedly deserves the credit for this achievement.

The boycott movement in Poland operated as an interest group in all respects. In the framework of the United Jewish Committee for the Struggle against the Persecution of the Jews in Germany, the Jewish Boycott Committee and the United Jewish Committee for the Aid of Refugees from Germany operated side by side.[72] Meetings, fund-raising drives, reports and circulars were examples of modern political and secular action. But the boycott committees' activities were not entirely devoid of unique indications of traditional Judaism, and particularly of its Polish form. Thus, for example, some committee meetings were held in synagogues.[73] Major efforts were made to recruit rabbis to support the boycott movement, in the hope that their appeals not to buy German products would have a far-reaching effect on the general Jewish

---

[69] On the boycott movement in Poland, see Emanuel Meltzer, 'The Jewish Anti-German Economic Boycott in Poland 1933–1934' [Hebrew], in *Galed* VI (1983), pp. 149–166.

[70] On the organisation and operation of these committees, see the report by Wolkowicz (Vereinigtes Comité Warschau) to the World Jewish Conference in Geneva, 20–23 August 1934, Central Zionist Archive A127/140.

[71] Meltzer, *The Economic Boycott*, p. 157.

[72] *ibid.*, p. 153.

[73] Politisches Archiv des Auswärtigen Amtes, (Bonn), German Embassy in Warsaw to the Foreign Ministry, 22 April 1935, R 99532.

populace.[74] Above all, the legal proceedings, sentences and fines imposed on boycott-breakers indicate the existence of internal Jewish jurisdictional frameworks, the existence of which would have been inconceivable in Western countries.[75] Perhaps the most telling evidence of the intensity of traditional patterns in Poland is the initiative of the Jewish representatives from Poland at the Jewish Boycott Committee in London in 1934 to impose segregation and excommunication sanctions on those Jews who breached the anti-German boycott.[76] The Polish representatives' demands that the names of such individuals be published in a list, and that they be prevented from participating in Jewish social and economic organisations or in community leadership have the character of both excommunication and sanction – customary measures in traditional Jewish communities.

Despite the fact that the boycott movement was established for the sake of the Jews in Germany, it was impossible to prevent a clash of interests between the Jews of Germany and Poland in this matter. As soon as the boycott movement began, the Nazi authorities brought pressure to bear on the Jewish leadership in Germany and induced it to take action to reduce the movement's activities. In this connection, for example, the head of the German Zionist Association, Kurt Blumenfeld, reported on his efforts to prevent mass rallies in Poland by approaching the Jewish leaders in Cracow, Warsaw and Lvov.[77] There is no doubt that Germany's Jews were afraid of a backlash from the Jewish boycott of German goods, fearing an intensification of the German boycott of German-Jewish businesses. The clash of interests actually intensified with the signing of the Transfer Agreement between bodies connected with the Jewish Agency and Nazi Germany. The agreement, which was intended to save part of German Jews' assets and at the same time to support the settlement enterprise in Palestine, adversely affected the boycott movement both in terms of principle and in practical terms.[78] It was hard to convince the Polish Jews to fight the Nazis in the economic sphere while Zionism had commercial ties with Nazi Germany. Welkowicz, a Boycott Committee representative from Poland, raised this issue at the meeting of the World Boycott Congress in London in 1934,[79] but it would appear that Congress members were willing to distinguish between the boycott movement and the Transfer Agreement.[80]

The matter was raised again at the Nineteenth Zionist Congress in September 1935. Meir Grossman of the Jewish State Party explained the reasons for his

---

[74]The report on these efforts to the Foreign Ministry stressed the great influence of rabbis in Poland, in contrast to the situation in the West, where rabbis did not enjoy such authority. Politisches Archiv des Auswärtigen Amtes (Bonn), Anschrift zu J. No. 831/34, R 99532.

[75]*ibid*; Central Zionist Archive L13/32; Meltzer, *The Economic Boycott*, p. 159.

[76]Politisches Archiv des Auswärtigen Amtes (Bonn), German Embassy in Warsaw to the Foreign Office, 27 November 1934, R 99532.

[77]Bundesarchiv (Koblenz), Blumenfeld to Oberregierungsrat Sommerfeldt, Prussian Ministry of the Interior, 27 March 1933, R43II/600.

[78]The German authorities were aware of, and interested in, this adverse effect. Meltzer, *The Economic Boycott*, p. 152.

[79]Central Zionist Archive, A127/140.

[80]Meltzer, *The Economic Boycott*, p. 162.

opposition to the Transfer Agreement, stressing that it was "unheard of that after two years of dreadful persecutions, of increased boycotts, and after efforts to acquire the sympathy of the non-Jewish world for the boycott operation, this proposal is now put forward ... that the [Zionist] Executive should act as an agency for German industry".[81] Dr Emil Schmoreck of the General Zionists B group argued that Congress should refuse to ratify the Transfer Agreement on the grounds that "when we consider things from the point of view of the transfer, we should have the courage and the consistency to utterly oppose the imposition of a boycott against German goods. The Jewish world", he added, "will not understand this dual morality. And since the entire people is convinced that the boycott is not vital, it is my opinion that the Zionist Organisation should not get involved with this matter. And if any individual or institution wishes to do something immoral, please do not impose this on the Congress".[82] His reasoning failed. The dominant position was that of Golda Myerson (later Meir) of the Palestine Labour faction, who stated in the debate that "war on Hitler's Germany does not mean war on the Jews ... There was a time", she added, "when we reacted to the Jewish people's suffering only with cries and protests. The only bright spot in the current calamity is that apart from cries and protests, we now also have actual possibilities for doing something real to save hundreds of Jews ... The Zionist movement has matured to a point where it thinks that transfer in the present situation is something which is absolutely vital, and it is prepared to take the responsibility for this". The Transfer Agreement was ratified by the Zionist Congress with 169 votes for, twelve against and seventeen abstentions.

In the dire economic situation facing Poland's Jews, many of them found it hard to grasp why the sums raised from fines of boycott-breakers should be transferred not to them but to German refugees.[83] It was incomparably more difficult to convince them to adopt anti-Nazi economic resolutions when in Germany there was economic co-operation between the regime and the Zionists. In addition to the economic issues, there was a Transfer Agreement which was problematic not merely from the point of view of principle. This agreement, the Jewish leaders feared, could jeopardise the position of the Jews in Eastern European countries. In a letter to Nahum Goldmann, Yizhak Gruenbaum voiced vehement criticism of the agreement:

> In respect of the transfer, also, differences of opinion have been found between us [Gruenbaum and Ben-Gurion]. As far as the situation is concerned, the Germans require the transfer operations to be expanded. Ben-Gurion, who agrees whole-heart-

---

[81] Nineteenth Zionist Congress and Fourth Session of the Jewish Agency Council, Lucerne, 20 August–6 September 1935, stenographic record, Jerusalem, pp. 440ff.

[82] German propaganda was fed an inaccurate report according to which Schmurck argued that "it will be possible to maintain the boycott movement in Poland, it being linked to major financial losses, while the Zionist Executive is making statements about its willingness to act as an agency for German products". Bundesarchiv (Potsdam), Zidovska Telegrafny Agentura Prag, III Jg., No. 203, 5 September 1935, Reichsministerium für Volksaufklärung und Propaganda No. 1158.

[83] Politisches Archiv des Auswärtigen Amtes (Bonn), German Embassy in Warsaw to the Foreign Office, 22 April 1935, R 99532.

edly with them, nevertheless does not want to ignore the Congress resolutions. He is, however, prepared to be adamant in insisting on this demand and convene the Executive so we can debate the issue and take a decision. It came to an argument about principles, and I insisted on the disaster that this expansion would cause to the Jews of all countries which would observe what Hitler is doing and see that he has actually managed to expel the Jews and harness them to the chariot of German industry and trade.[84]

Gruenbaum argued that the fight against Hitler should not be abandoned, but that its influence should be considered in the wider European context. As he stressed elsewhere in the same letter:

A war must also be waged against Hitler's government, and this war in Palestine has been stopped. Should we really not protest against the thoughts of making Germany a member of the League of Nations again? Should we really not demand that Germany sign undertakings to comply with the treaty on minorities after it has proclaimed that the Jews are a national minority? I am of course aware that the conditions are not the best and most convenient ones for running such a campaign, but this does not discharge us from it. And I have no doubts whatsoever that the very demand will force Germany to cut back its restrictive legislation. Flight and arrangements for an exodus can only increase it, and also make the countries of Eastern and Central Europe try similarly to get rid of their Jews. In Poland it would appear that this is beginning: terror is on the rise again.

Gruenbaum's position clearly reflects the conflict of interests that became clear between German and Polish Jews in their opposition to Nazism. The boycott of Jewish businesses in Germany on the one hand, and the stringent German currency laws on the other, put the Jews in Germany in a very difficult economic position and made it very hard for them to leave the country. Under these circumstances it was natural that someone would try to take action in order to reduce the Jewish economic boycott in the hope that, in parallel, there would occur an easing of the boycott of Jews in Germany. It was also natural that the Jews in Germany would support the Transfer Agreement, because this enabled many of them to save their property and emigrate to Palestine. From the Polish-Jewish perspective, things looked completely different. The following appeared in an appeal for the Jewish boycott in Poland:

German National Socialism has started a war against the entire Jewish people, which it has conducted in the course of the three and half years that it has been in power with an unprecedented ruthlessness and cruelty ... Besides this, German National Socialism has generated an unheard-of cruelty and inflammatory propaganda campaign against all of Jewry through literature and agitation ... with the purpose of poisoning all the people of this world with racial hatred and hostility to the Jews.[85]

The boycott movement was intended to signify publicly that world Jewry would not acquiesce in what was happening in Germany, and as a matter of principle would fight all manifestations of antisemitism wherever they occurred. Polish Jewry's leadership grasped the calamitous significance of Nazism in Germany for Jews in general and for Polish Jews in particular, and consequently rejected

---

[84]Central Zionist Archive, Gruenbaum to Goldmann, 2 July 1935, L22/201.
[85]Central Zionist Archive, Resolution in favour of boycott [Yiddish, n.d.], A127/149.

the idea of reaching understandings with Nazi Germany. In this sense it assumed the task of an uncompromising struggle with Nazism.

VIII.

David Carnovsky, a lumber merchant from Congress Poland and a holder of *Mitnagged* views, wished to leave home:

> Not only did he want to abandon the town that had so disgraced him, but all of Poland, which was steeped in darkness and ignorance. For a long time he had been drawn to Berlin – the city in which the sainted Moses Mendelssohn had once lived and from which he had spread the light across the world. From early childhood, when David Carnovsky had studied German from Mendelssohn's Pentateuch, he had been drawn to that land across the border that was the source of all greatness, knowledge, and light.[86]

I.J. Singer sends his hero to the longed-for land, to live there valiantly until the collapse of German liberalism and the rise of Nazism, eventually finding himself a refugee towards the end of his life with his family in America. This Germany, which for David Carnovsky as for many Polish Jews, had been a symbol of Jewish progress in the Diaspora, during the 1930s became a symbol for antisemitism and the persecution of Jews.

On the eve of Hitler's rise to power, many German Jews denied any common destiny between themselves and the Jews in Poland. Reality proved the German Jews wrong: within a short time they found themselves ostracised, humiliated and excluded from all areas of life. Gradually many of them began to acknowledge the change in their status. The shift from provider to recipient of support was a particularly difficult one. The political conditions in Germany, the loss of civil rights, and the absence of a public domain; German Jewry's demographic structure; and the absence of a militant tradition among German Jews made it difficult for them to run an active self-defence struggle. It was the Jews in Poland who joined in the struggle against antisemitism, whether in its traditional Polish form, its German variant, or as a German import into Poland. It was they who campaigned to enlist the world's public opinion, as well as that of the international Jewish institutions, just as Western Jews had done in the struggle against anti-Jewish policies in Eastern Europe. Their struggle did not always coincide with the aspirations of German Jewry or the views of Zionists. Unlike the Jews of Germany, many of Poland's Jews came to realise that the fate of German Jewry was bound to impact on the fate of Polish Jewry. In those years their fear focused on the possible influence of anti-Jewish Nazi policy on the policy of the Polish government (and also the Romanian, Hungarian and Lithuanian governments). The dimensions of the calamity that was to befall both German and Polish Jewry exceeded the worst fears of both.

---

[86]I.J. Singer, *The Family Carnovsky*, New York 1988, p. 7, transl., (first published in Yiddish, 1943).

Jewish Refugees and Displaced Persons

"Jewish Refugees Should be Welcomed and Assisted here!"[1] Shanghai: Exile and Return

BY BARBARA GELDERMANN

As the melting pot of Eastern and Western culture in the 1920s and 1930s, Shanghai became China's most socio-economically developed city. The resulting openness turned it into a destination for adventurers and emigrants worldwide, despite attempted counter measures by the city council. At the same time, it was also a city open to its hinterland, a refuge for people who wanted to escape to the physical and legal security of the International Settlement.[2] The cosmopolitan city of Shanghai become one of the last refuges from Nazi persecution with the arrival of the first European refugees in the mid 1930s. Unable to find sanctuary anywhere else in the world, this group of refugees was obliged to adapt to the Chinese life-style more than any other earlier group of foreigners. They did not conform to the then prevalent Chinese picture of foreigners. In contrast to the British, Americans and French, many Jewish refugees lived in the suburb of Hongkew alongside its Chinese inhabitants crowded into a very limited area. Their living conditions were equally as bad as that of the Chinese. As Jonathan Spence has pointed out: "Many Jews were reduced to performing 'coolie' labour for local Chinese or eating in the soup kitchens that local charities kept going, and nearly all suffered from malnutrition."[3] These Westerners were the antithesis of the Chinese perception of the material superiority of the west. What was the relationship the Chinese had with these foreigners who were not better off than the majority of the Chinese? Did the Chinese just regard them as a few more thousand people adding to the millions that had fled to Shanghai since the outbreak of the war?[4]

ESCAPE FROM EUROPE

As the situation became desperate for Jews after November 1938, two main sanctuaries came into focus as last resorts: countries in Latin America (Paraguay and

[1] See article in *China Weekly Review* (4 February 1939), p. 1.
I would like to thank Joachim Augstein for translating my article.
[2] Fritz Osterhammel, *China und die Weltgesellschaft. Vom 16. Jahrhundert bis in unsere Zeit,* München 1989, p. 248.
[3] Jonathan D. Spence, *The search for modern China,* New York 1990, p. 475.
[4] At this point I would like to thank Sonja Mühlberger and Martin Beutler for their support. Both of them spent part of their childhood in Shanghai as refugees. I would also like to thank Christiane Hoss and Georg Armbrüster of the Active Museum Berlin who were a permanent and helpful source of information.

Ecuador for example) and Shanghai. Shanghai was the predominant destination; despite Japanese occupation, this port town with its international settlements neither demanded any entry visas nor limited the influx of foreigners in any way. The usual route to Shanghai was by sea passage with the Italian company Lloyd Tristino. When Italy entered the war in June 1940 the Trans-Siberian Railway became the last means of transport to Shanghai for those fleeing persecution or death at the hands of the Nazis. Later, there was enforced shipment to Shanghai on the so-called *Judenschiffe*.

A daughter of Jewish refugees born in Shanghai in 1939, Sonja Mühlberger, described the flight of her parents:

> Like many others, my father was arrested during the night of *Kristallnacht*, November 1938, and incarcerated in the Dachau concentration camp. My mother, who was still young then, showed much inner strength and courage. From the Jewish Community in Frankfurt she learnt that it was possible to secure refuge in China and that refugees travelling to Shanghai required no visas. She then arranged some sort of forms and applications and successfully enabled my father's release by producing these forms and promising to leave Germany, having herself been detained by the Gestapo for two days in the process. A passage on a ship was secured with the help of a school friend my father had made who worked in a travel agency.[5]

It was different for those who were expelled by the Nazis and had to take the *Judenschiffe* that went from Hamburg to Shanghai. Travel agencies chartered ships for the *Gestapo*, for example the *Usamaro* in April 1939. According to a communication from the *Verband der Deutschen Reeder* to the city council of Hamburg on 8 July 1939, "[F]or the transport of refugees from Hamburg to Shanghai, a Vienna travel agency chartered the *Usamaro* from the German-Africa Line in the spring of 1939."[6] And in April 1939 the *Reich* Commissioner for Emigration reported:

> The steamship *Usamaro* of German-Africa Line took a large number of Jews to Shanghai. For large scale accommodation ship space intended for baggage and children play areas was utilised. The accommodation and furnishings for the 104 passengers, though simple, were clean and thought out with care.[7]

Together with his family, Martin Beutler was one of the passengers. His father, Gustav Beutler – a tobacco retailer from Merseburg – was arrested on 10 November 1938 and taken to Buchenwald. He was released nearly five weeks later on condition that he leave the country as soon as possible. In February 1939 he was arrested again and imprisoned in Halle. Martin Beutler, only five years old at the time, has to rely on the accounts of family members as to what followed. The *Gestapo* escorted his father from Halle prison to Hamburg.[8] In the

---

[5] Unpublished manuscript: Report by Sonja Mühlberger, Berlin, 17 March 1993, p. 1.

[6] Staatsarchiv (StA) Hamburg Bestand: Verband der Deutschen Reeder, Schreiben an die Gemeindeverwaltung der Hansestadt Hamburg. Verwaltung für Handel Schiffahrt und Gewerbe vom 8. Juli 1939.

[7] StA Hamburg: Deputation für Handel Schiffahrt und Gewerbe. Reichskommissar des Auswanderungswesens: Spezialakten XXI A12 No. 14, vol. VI: Monatsbericht an den Reichsminister des Inneren vom 25. Mai 1939.

[8] See also Jacob Toury, 'Ein Aspekt zur Endlösung', in Ursula Bittner (ed.) *Das Unrechtsregime* vol.I, Hamburg 1986, pp. 176–196, note 77: "... Der Autor des Berichts teilte nämlich weiter mit, daß die

meantime, Martin and his mother were also taken to Hamburg and the family was reunited at the harbour. Gustav Beutler's passport bears a departure stamp for 25 April 1939. Interestingly, the passport was issued in Merseburg on 22 April while Gustav Beutler was still in prison. The *Reichsanzeiger* and the *Preußische Staatsanzeiger*[9] published a decree depriving the Beutler family of German citizenship.[10]

Many Jews left for Shanghai after their applications for emigration to other countries had not been granted in time. The Eisfelder family had first tried to obtain visas for Australia. After waiting several months their request was denied and they had to decide on another country: "Now we had to move and act quickly, with very little time left before our passports expired. With every door shut to us, Shanghai remained the only place."[11] For the majority of the refugees Shanghai was the last option. Most of them had very little knowledge about what Shanghai would be like. They thought of it as a wild and exotic place where it would be difficult to survive. This view was based on émigré reports published in 1937 in the *Aufbau* which emphasised, "Shanghai has all the disadvantages of an overseas colony and a large city on the United States and none of their advantages".[12]

From 1938 onwards an increasing amount of information about life in Shanghai was published. Details varied widely. In a letter in the *Gemeindeblatt der Jüdischen Gemeinde* in the summer of 1938, emigration to Shanghai was strongly recommended. The writer claimed that there was enough food and work for those who could speak English, although he also revealed some misgivings.[13] The article by Fritz I. Friedlaender, published in the *Jüdischen Nachrichtenblatt* in 1939, described in greater detail the advantages and disadvantages of Shanghai. His advice to refugees was:

> It is not with the intention of discouraging, but out of regard for our people, and to safeguard them from bitter disillusionment, that one has to point out that it would be best for anyone emigrating here, not to bring with them emotional and spiritual expectations. In other words, it is best to abandon the civilized European norms. Nevertheless it would be wrong to warn against emigrating to Shanghai when there are no other opportunities for emigration.[14]

After 10 November 1938, the discouraging news from Shanghai that repeatedly made its way to Europe hardly deterred anyone who obtained passage from

Entlassenen (hier handelt es sich um Entlassungen aus Buchenwald, A. d. V.) »sogar an die Grenze oder auf die Auswanderungsschiffe gebracht«, d.h. von der Gestapo begleitet wurden."

[9] *Reichsanzeiger*, No. 24 (29 January 1940). See Michael Hepp (ed.), *Die Ausbürgerung deutscher Staatsangehöriger 1933–1945 nach den im Reichsanzeiger veröffentlichten Listen*, Munich–New York–London–Paris 1985, p. 271.

[10] Unpublished manuscript. Interview with Martin Beutler, 5 March 1997.

[11] Horst P. Eisfelder, *Chinese Exile: My years in Shanghai and Nanking (Nanjing), 1938 to 1947*, n.p. December 1996, p. 5.

[12] Max Ludwig Berges, 'Jüdische Emigranten in Shanghai', in *Aufbau* (1 October 1937), p. 7.

[13] 'Existenzmöglichkeiten in Shanghai', in *Gemeindeblatt der jüdischen Gemeinde Berlin* (19 June 1938), p. 5.

[14] Fritz Israel Friedlaender, 'Juden in Shanghai', in *Jüdisches Nachrichtenblatt* (8 August 1939), p. 2.

going to China. Émigrés did not have high expectations, but hoped rather to be able to enter a foreign country with the minimum of bureaucratic fuss. Reports from former refugees describe the difficult living conditions more as a struggle for survival than assimilation. "To survive, in any way possible, was the overwhelming drive of these people."[15]

LEADING AUTHORITIES IN SHANGHAI

At this time there were still two colonial political systems in Shanghai. The French Concession, founded in 1849, was still governed by the Consul General. In the International Settlement, which had existed since 1843, there were official representatives from the foreign powers, for example from the United States and Britain. They did not participate in the administration; however, they had the right to defend their nations' territory by armed force if necessary. The Chinese part of the city was under the control of the city council of Greater Shanghai until the outbreak of the Sino-Japanese war in 1937. Its mayor had to report directly to the government in Nanking. After the Japanese invasion a Chinese puppet administration was installed.[16] The weight of political influences reflected the population strength of the various ethnic groups. In 1930 there were 50,000 foreigners in Shanghai, 27,000 of whom lived in the International Settlement; another 12,000 lived in the French Concession and the rest in the adjoining streets. The number of Chinese living in the settlements amounted to 970,000, and another 1,5 million lived in the other quarters of the city.[17] In the French Concession the police authority was in the hands of the French police, whereas in the International Settlement authority was excercised by the Shanghai Municipal Police. After the spring of 1938, the Japanese demanded more power within the Shanghai Municipal Police. After their successful attacks on Shanghai at the end of 1937 they had won control of the districts of Hongkew and Yangtzepoo, which formerly belonged to the International Settlement. Finally, the Japanese Naval Landing Party took over the policing duties in these districts. In the wake of the Japanese invasion of the International Settlement on 8 December 1941, Japanese military administration was instituted. The refugees from Western Europe who landed in Hongkew and mainly settled there were those most concerned by the events in the International Settlement after 1938. For many of them the German Consulate remained the main authority to resort to.

[15] Alfred Dreifuß, 'Shanghai – Eine Emigration am Rande', in *Kunst und Literatur im antifaschistischen Exil 1933–1945, vol. III: Exil in den USA*, Leipzig 1975, pp. 447–517, here p. 449. Also on this subject see Alfred Dreifuß, *Ensemblespiel des Lebens. Erinnerungen eines Theatermanns*, Berlin 1985; Hugo Burkhard, *Tanz mal Jude! Von Dachau nach Shanghai. Meine Erlebnisse in den Konzentrationslagern Dachau, Buchenwald, Getto Shanghai, 1933–1938*, Nürnberg 1968; Ernest G. Heppner, *Shanghai Refugee: A memoir of the World War II Jewish Ghetto*, Lincoln 1994.

[16] See Shanghai Municipal Council (SMC), Report for the year 1938 and budget for the year 1939, Shanghai 1939, p. 117.

[17] See Richard Feetham, *Report of the Hon. Richard Feetham, C.M.G. Judge of the Supreme Court of the Union of South Africa to the Shanghai Municipal Council*, vol. III, Shanghai 1931, p. 55.

Conditions for refugees in communal homes were very basic.

Café Barcelona in Shanghai

Jewish refugees selling their belongings in a Shanghai market.

Refugee doctors served the local population.

China Daily Tribune

German Language Supplement

Die aktuelle Tageszeitung

696/5 Tongshan Road   Tel. 52414

EASTERN - THEATER

" Die Dreigroschenoper "

Ein Spiel in 3 Akten (9 Bildern)

von JOHN GAY   Text BERT BRECHT
                Musik KURT WEILL

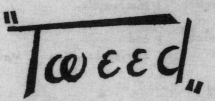
By courtesy of the Leo Baeck Institute Inc., 129 East 73rd Street, New York, NY 10021

JEWISH REFUGEES AND GERMAN REPRESENTATIVES IN SHANGHAI

The outbreak of the Sino-Japanese war endangered the position of foreigners in China. The International Settlement in Shanghai remained relatively untouched until December 1941. Finally, in January 1943, all the signatory powers renounced their extra-territorial rights.

Caught up in a web of changing rulers the Jewish refugees were unrepresented and thus lacked protection. Although privileged compared to the Chinese, among the foreigners they were at a disadvantage and dependent on the benevolence of the Japanese. The unsolved question of their citizenship became the dominant threat. In the German Reich and in Austria they had been second-class citizens. Following their expulsion, their documentation unmistakably branded them as Jews. In Shanghai they were at first safe from the immediate clutches of the German government. But, with the *Elfte Verordnung zum Reichsbürgergesetz* on 25 November 1941, the refugees were dealt the next blow. The new amendment formally deprived them of German citizenship. In practice, they had already lost it long before. Now "stateless", they were offered neither support nor diplomatic protection by their home country. Instead, they were under permanent surveillance by the German consulate. With the increase of foreign refugees even the British and Japanese representatives turned to the German consulate asking for measures to tackle the refugee problem. The German embassy sent regular reports to the foreign ministry in Berlin. One such detailed report on '*Judentum in Shanghai*' was sent to the foreign ministry on 11 January 1940 by the head of the Consulate General, Martin Fischer. In it he showed himself knowledgeable about the situation. Looking into the future he observed:

> How the community of emigrated Jews will develop in the future is not possible at the present time to surmise. One can only conjecture what the future aims will be considering their present desire for self-administration, but these are all worries which will have to be solved later in Shanghai. What matters for Germany at the moment is to be freed of a large number of Jews, who would be able to draw away from Europe more of their racial kind.[18]

Official German efforts to promote anti-semitism abroad were not likely to succeed in China according to the German Consulate:

> The Chinese look upon them [the Jews] merely as representatives of the 'white race' and exponents of the country whose nationality they possess. Since the activities of the foreigners in China are limited to few areas and so in practice is concentrated in the districts where foreigners may live it follows that any increase of foreigners of whatever race does not threaten the Chinese further because the overpopulation of

---

[18]Bundesarchiv (B.A.) Berlin: Deutsche Botschaft in China 2329, Bericht des Deutschen Generalkonsulat an das Auswärtige Amt, Berlin, von Martin Fischer: 'Judentum in Shanghai' vom 11. Januar 1940.

the areas available to the foreigners is bound to lead to inreasing competitive struggles between them.[19]

The municipal police in the International Settlement had been in close contact with the German institutions as early as November 1933.[20] The inauguration of the *Zentralstelle für jüdische Auswanderung* in Vienna under the directorship of Adolf Eichmann was publicly announced on 20 August 1938, just a few days after the International Committee for Granting Relief to European Refugees (I.C.) had been founded in Shanghai.[21] Paul Komor acted as the honorary secretary of the I.C. He was the mediator between the municipal police, the German Consulate General and the refugees.[22] In the beginning the relief committee collected data concerning the refugees. This fell into the hands of the German Consulate General. The work of the I.C. reflects the conflicting position of the refugees alongside the other foreigners living in Shanghai. On the one hand, due to their origin, the refugees belonged to the party of the "white colonial masters", on the other, they were a burden since they had been expelled from their countries of origin and were poverty-stricken. Their uncertain existence was also underlined in the fact that the advantages of extra-territoriality – the right of nations to administer justice in their own consular lawcourts – did not apply to them.

THE COURTS OF ARBITRATION

The German Reich did not hold any extra-territorial rights in China. Since 1921 the First Special District Court whose members were *de jure* installed by the national government in Chungking was responsible for the Germans in China. The Second Special District Court, which came under control of the Wang Ching-wei government during the war, administered the French Concession. The Jewish refugees were not granted any extra-territorial rights in either of these courts. They actually viewed this as favourable for them.

> It is practically only for Russian, Soviet Russian, White Russian immigrants, and for us Germans – which also means for the immigrants mostly from Germany – that Chinese law courts have jurisiction. The Chinese Courts have behaved in a sympathetic way in dealing with these immigrants. They have never made any differences in their dealings with those immigrants subject to them.[23]

Refugees could also resort to the courts of arbitration set up after 1939 by the Jews in Shanghai primarily to settle disputes of civil law.[24] Questions about the

[19]B.A. Berlin: Deutsche Botschaft in China 2329, Schreiben des Generalkonsulats Shanghai, das Bezug nimmt zum Transport jüdischer Auswanderer nach Shanghai mit einem Schiff der Woermann Linie vom 20. März 1939.

[20]D.S. Pitts: 'Germans of the Jewish faith who have recently arrived in Shanghai'. Shanghai Municipal Police Report (11 November 1933). Washington: National Archives. RG 263, D 5422 (A).

[21]See *North China Herald* (24 August 1938), p. 327.

[22]See B.A. Berlin: Deutsche Botschaft in China 2329, Anlage zu Shanghai-Bericht vom 25. März 1939): Central European Jews – Arrival in Shanghai (18 March 1939) p. 1; Alfred Dreifuss, *Shanghai. Eine Emigration am Rande*. Berlin 1985.

[23]Victor Sternberg, 'Die Rechtsverhältnisse der Emigranten', in Ossi Lewin (ed.), *Almanac-Shanghai 1946/4*, Shanghai 1947, p. 98.

[24]*ibid.*, p. 99; Norbert Freundlich, 'Das Schiedsgericht für europäische Emigranten in Shanghai', in *Shanghai Jewish Chronicle, Sondernummer, 'Ein Jahr Aufbau'* (March 1940).

jurisdiction of those courts were raised by a Chinese lawyer, Tsai, who argued that these courts impaired the rights of Chinese courts. This conflict very clearly showed the disparity between refugees being privileged and merely being tolerated.[25] The conflict about competences intensified when the courts of arbitration ruled out appeals to the Chinese courts.

At first, neither the Chinese national government nor the embassies of the United States and Britain tried to solve the conflict. After growing public pressure and negotiations with the Association of Chinese Lawyers the competences of the arbitration courts were limited. The Chinese did not resent the creation of these courts as such, but rather their infringing on Chinese rights. The courts of arbitration were not highly valued among the refugees until 1942. Only when they became a part of the Jewish Community in 1942 did their importance grow. The Japanese authorities transferred some political power to this originally religious institution.[26]

SHANGHAI'S CONDUCT TOWARDS THE INFLUX OF REFUGEES

On 31 May 1933 the China League for Civil Rights, under the leadership of Sun Yat-sen (Soon Ching Ling) and other leading Chinese intellectuals,[27] submitted a note of protest to the German Consular General in Shanghai, R.C.W. Behrend. This note was handed over with the request to pass it on to the Legation in Peking. The China League for Civil Rights listed specific abuses: German violence towards Jews and intellectuals, the oppression of the free press, as well as other violations of human rights. This note of protest was published in both Chinese and English newspapers throughout China and caused a commotion at the German embassy.[28] Just one day earlier, on 12 May 1933, the Shanghai Zionist Association had also submitted a note of protest to the German Consulate General in Shanghai.[29]

The opinions and reactions of the international community to the refugees in Shanghai are reflected in countless press articles published between 1937 and 1941. A particular concern repeatedly raised was the problem of accommodating the refugees. The tenor of the press was that Shanghai's capacities were not sufficient to provide for the refugees from Western Europe in addition to the Chinese refugees.

The press also debated the violations of human rights in Nazi Germany. Dis-

---

[25]A. Jovishoff, 'Jewish Refugee Committee Declared Infringing On Chinese Sovereignty', in *China Weekly Review* (2 December 1939), pp. 25–26; 'New refugee court investigated', in *North China Herald* (13 December 1939).

[26]David Kranzler, *Japanese, Nazis and Jews: The Jewish Refugee Community of Shanghai, 1938–1945*, New York 1976, p. 533.

[27]Among those were Cai Yuanpei, Lin Yutang and Lu Xun.

[28]See B.A. Deutsche Botschaft in China 2325. This file contains the letters to the German legation in Beijing as well as press articles from *The Peiping Chronicle* and *The North China Daily News* (20 May 1933); *Deutsche Shanghai Zeitung* (16 May 1933).

[29]*ibid.* Unfortunately, there are almost no additional sources that could reveal more information about the Chinese reaction towards the refugee problem.

cussion in the international press included an article, 'Concentration Camp Torments: Jewish Refugees from Germany and Austria describe Experience; Cruel Punishments', in the *North China Daily News (NCDN)* on 25 November 1938. The article describes the arrival of Jewish immigrants reporting brutal treatment in German concentration camps. After the publication of this article the German Consulate was able to secure a rebuttal, an indication of the powerful influence of Germany at that time. Surprisingly, not only the Germans but also the president of the International Jewish Committee, Paul Komor, pleaded with refugees not to give interviews to the press fearing adverse repercussions from the German authorities in Shanghai.[30] But the German influence in Shanghai was not strong enough to suppress the manifold and critical reports altogether. Numerous Jewish refugees continued to publish reports of their own experiences.

Although the majority of the English-speaking press was in favour of accommodating the refugees and claimed it was an act of humanity, it also acknowledged the difficulty of providing for and integrating these immigrants in addition to all of the Chinese refugees.[31] The influx of refugees also raised the concern of the international city council. This was reflected by an article – 'Limitation of the European Jewish Refugees May be Instituted by the Council' – published in the *Shanghai Times* on 24 December 1938.[32] "It was learnt here yesterday that the Shanghai Municipal Council may have taken steps to limit the arrival of European Jewish immigrants in this port in order to keep the situation from getting out of control."[33]

After August 1939 the international and the French administrations, in accordance with the Japanese, demanded special permits for European refugees in order to stop immigration. Every adult had to prove that they were in possession of US\$400, every child US\$100, or a contract for work with a Shanghai citizen had to be presented. Close family ties could also be claimed for entry into Shanghai.[34] The permits were only required for the well-off areas of the settlement. They were not necessary for the districts north of Soochow Creek. Due to the restrictions of the city council and the outbreak of the war in September 1939, the entry of refugees dwindled; there were no new arrivals after emigration from the German Reich was prohibited on 23 October 1941.

INCORPORATION OR NON-INTEGRATION?

When they entered, the European refugees could not but help being struck how foreign their new land was. The sub-tropical climate and the colourful street-life

---

[30]See B.A., Deutsche Botschaft in China 2329.

[31]See 'Hitler presents Shanghai with another relief problem', in *The China Weekly Review* (24 December 1938) pp. 108–109; 'Hitler's gift to Shanghai. Jewish Refugees', in *Oriental Affairs* (March 1939), p. 153; 'Refugee Problem', in *North China Herald* (5 May 1939).

[32]See *The Shanghai Times* (24 December 1938).

[33]*ibid.*

[34]See Shanghai Municipal Archives: Secretariat, S.M.C. U1–4–2972: Shanghai Municipal Council, 22 October 1939. 'Entry of European Refugees'.

were a strong contrast to their lost homes. For many refugees the encounter with rickshaw-drivers was their first intense impression of the locals. In the *Gelbe Post* Storfer wrote: "Worried about his own future the new arrival, whom the stormy times have tossed as if shipwrecked to these shores, must regard with astonishment and shock the overburdened labourers in the harbour."[35] Did this foreshadow their own fate? In what respect would their lives be different from those of the Chinese labourers? With only ten *Reichsmark*, which was all that most of them possessed when they arrived in Shanghai, it was almost impossible to build up a new existence. The extent to which they were integrated into the economy of the country they settled in was the first visible indicator that the refugees had settled down.[36]

The first refugees to Shanghai after 1933 could still find accommodation in the traditional foreigners' districts. When their numbers increased, the overspill was housed provisionally and inexpensively on the borders of these districts outside the international trade zones. From the summer of 1938 onward, a growing number of persecuted people from the German Reich crammed into Shanghai's Japanese occupied eastern and northern districts alongside countless Chinese refugees.[37] Those refugees who had been able to provide for themselves in the beginning did so by selling their belongings, received money through friends and relatives abroad or were entitled to claim a HICEM cheque.[38] Most of those who were financially secure did not report to the aid committees. But the majority of refugees were looked after by such committees which provided accommodation and advice.

The people entering this new world had to fight poverty and to recover from the experiences of persecution and maltreatment. Julius Rudolphs graphically describes this:

> By June [1939], 1,000 more refugees had come to Shanghai and the number of those who had found jobs or had opened their own business totalled 680. There were probably 500 more who did not need to ask the committee for assistance and who were able to start work after they arrived ... Among these thousands of jobless were many with shiftless or criminal natures, lazy people who preferred to live in idleness ... However the numbers of idlers and swindlers was small. The overwhelming majority of the newcomers were in earnest search of work. Unfortunately, many of those who had suffered in the terrible concentration camps of Germany were unable to get a new start. Many of them had lost their self confidence and were suffering from an inferiority complex.[39]

---

[35] Adolf Josef Storfer, 'Hut ab vor dem Kuli!', in *Die Gelbe Post*, 1. Jhg., vol.I (1 May 1939), p. 2.

[36] See Herbert Strauss, 'The Immigration and Acculturation of the German Jew in the United States of America', in *LBI Year Book XVI* (1971), pp. 63–94.

[37] Sebastian Steiner, 'Als erste Emigrantenfamilie in Hongkew', in *Shanghai Jewish Chronicle* (März 1940).

[38] See Kranzler. p. 85ff, p. 127ff.

[39] Julius Rudolph, 'Psychology of the Newcomers to Shanghai', in *The China Weekly Review* (2 September 1939), p. 11.

The number of refugees depending on public welfare was considerable because they had lost all their cultural, material and spiritual roots. Most of them were too impoverished to pay for clothes, housing or food.

Welfare in Shanghai was not organised by the city authorities but was completely in the hands of private individuals, with all the associated advantages and disadvantages.[40] The two most important charities were the International Committee for Granting Relief to European Refugees (I.C.) headed by Sir Victor Sassoon, and the Committee for the Assistance of European Jewish Refugees in Shanghai presided over by Dr. Kurt Marx. The I.C., among other things, granted credit for setting up business. It established contacts with consular authorities and local administration and also organised a children's milk fund. A report in the *North China Herald* from 5 May 1939 shows that the growing number of refugees led to increasing calls for donations: "In speaking of the financial problem, Sir Victor said that all the work was being done on a monthly budget of $90,000, which amount is regularly received from London, New York and Egypt, whilst other contributions amount to anywhere between $5,000 and $10,000."[41] When private donations no longer sufficed, Jewish aid organisations abroad agreed to assist. Among these organisations, the American Jewish Joint Distribution Committee (the "Joint") was remarkable. A network of welfare institutions for education, medical service and judicial advice was set up and administered by the refugees themselves. At first, the refugees without any means could only be accommodated in the homes at the Embankment Building and on Washing Road. When these homes became full, another home was opened on Ward Road. At the end of 1939 there were six homes and two hospitals, all of them north of Soochow Creek.[42]

The refugees tried to make their environment reminiscent of their homes in Europe. Not only were the devastations of two wars evident in the districts north of Soochow Creek, but so too was their reconstruction by a group of people willing to make it their new home. Beside "Little Tokyo" and "Little Moscow", a "Little Vienna" and a "Little Berlin" came into existence. Until May 1943, when the refugees were forced into a special district by the Japanese, some of them had been able to afford houses in the better parts of the city south of Soochow Creek. Almost half of the lawyers resided in the International Settlement as well as two-thirds of the doctors. There were many suppliers of fashion accessories in the French Concession. Doctors and ladies' clothes shops could mainly be found on Bubbling Well Road and women's tailors and textile shops on Avenue Joffre.[43]

Those able to still work in the professions they had learnt and live in the districts preferred by foreigners amounted to only a small number. The struggle for survival forced the majority to take on unusual jobs. Sonja Mühlberger reports

---

[40]See SMC Report for 1939, p. 174; report for 1940, p. 199.

[41]'The Premises for the Jewish refugees. No Accommodation for 800 Arriving on Monday; 20,000 Expected before End of Year', in *North China Herald* (12 May 1939), p. 282.

[42]Kranzler, p. 129; SMC Reports 1939–1942.

[43]See *Emigranten Adressbuch für Shanghai. Mit einem Anhang Branchen-Register*, Shanghai 1939.

on her father's attempt at finding a job: "My father tried like most immigrants to find work of some kind. Later on, like others, he found work with a Chinese employer selling eggs. As a result he learnt to speak Chinese well, including the Shanghai dialect."[44] Mühlberger's job exemplifies some of the unusual paths to employment the refugees took in order to build up their own modest existence. Life primarily took place in the main business area of East Seward Road where a modern block of businesses had been built and in Chusan Road with its restaurants and cafés.[45] A great number of refugees worked and lived in the lanes off Tongshan Road and Point Road. In spite of the rigorous Japanese restrictions against Chinese people who wanted to move into this area, there were about 280,000 Chinese living there in 1939. When the restrictions were eased, the numbers increased even more. The Japanese were permanently present in these areas. The day after the outbreak of the Pacific War the Japanese occupied the whole of Shanghai, thereby cutting off all international contact. Money from abroad could no longer be received, and the resulting lack of resources put the refugees' existence in danger. In 1942 more refugees than ever before were dependent on provisions in welfare homes.[46]

The relationship between the Western European refugees and the rest of the international community in Shanghai was not only determined by the situation of the rich merchants. The European refugees were also in direct competition with refugees from Russia who had been stranded in Shanghai twenty years earlier. Among both groups there were doctors, clerks, pedlars and musicians as well as shorthand typists, shop assistants and fashion salon owners.[47] According to a report published in the *North China Daily News* in Spring 1939 these people lived together peacefully. The reporter found thriving Russian and German-Jewish businesses in Hongkew that served their respective customers. But only the Chinese retailers supplied reasonably priced cigarettes and changed money.[48] According to the refugees, the Chinese competitors were a bigger problem. The low prices of their handicrafts and services made even the cheapest European products look expensive.

The European refugees had difficulty adapting to the lower standard of living in China.[49] In many cases their new existence meant living and working in one room, as was customary for the Chinese. In this way, the basic living conditions of the Chinese and the majority of the European refugees did not differ much. For many refugees working as pedlars provided an important source of income just as it already did for many of the poor Chinese. The life which evolved for refugees in Hongkew was coloured by the local living conditions and widespread poverty. The Chinese merchants who did not always understand their new customers' habits were a part of everyday life: "Now and then the midday quiet was inter-

---

[44]Mühlberger, p. 2.
[45]See Wolfgang Fischer, 'Broadway- Geflüster', in *Acht-Uhr-Abendblatt* (8 December 1940).
[46]See SMC Report 1942, p. 80.
[47]See 'In the Russian Colony', in *North China Herald* (26 October 1938), p. 17.
[48]See 'Russian, Jewish Refugees. Hongkew sees opening of new establishments daily; confidence reigns among shop-keepers', in *North China Herald* (10 May 1939), p. 238.
[49]Kranzler, p. 543f.

rupted by tradespeople offering their wares half in Chinese and half in German."[50] Sonja Mühlberger provides an interesting picture of relationships with Chinese neighbours:

> In the lane behind our house there existed a balloon factory belonging to a Chinese. I was allowed to visit it as I played with the two children of the owner. We generally had little contact with the Chinese population. My father enjoyed good relations with his employer and my mother did her shopping in the Chinese market. Beyond this we watched each other, we were tolerated, we came in contact and, when necessary, spoke with a Chinese.[51]

The refugees regarded their environment as a temporary arrangement that was only meant to last for the duration of the war. Building up a new existence was unthinkable under the impoverished circumstances experienced by most of them.

The time for integration was very limited, for even after 1945 the government of sovereign China only offered the refugees very little opportunity to choose Shanghai as their future home. Chiang Kai-shek's party, the *Kuomintang*, and the communists were fighting a civil war against each other. They were, however, united in the aim of ultimately eliminating foreign influence. Neither before nor after 1949 did the Chinese authorities enable the thousands of refugees to lead an independent existence. The refugees remained excluded from participation in the revolutionary process of their host country, and at the end of their exile in Shanghai it seemed as though they had never been there.

By 1943 the Japanese occupation in 1941 of the whole of Shanghai led to severe changes in the lives of the refugees which had been built up under such difficult circumstances. After the Japanese had abolished extra-territoriality for all foreigners they published a proclamation in the Shanghai press on 18 February 1943 in Chinese, German, English and Russian concerning the erection of a special district for "stateless refugees".[52] The term "stateless refugees" shows distinctly that the measures of the Japanese were intended to harm those refugees who had had to leave their home countries because of Nazi banishment and persecution. The proclamation, moreover, only concerned refugees who arrived after 1937. The specification of that year suggests that it referred especially to Jewish refugees, since they were the only group of people arriving in vast numbers after 1937. In an article published in the *Shanghai Times* the borders of the district are given as follows: "The designated area is bordered on the west by the line connection Chaoufoong, Muirhead and Dent Roads; on the east by Yangtzepoo Creek; on the south by the line connection East Seward, Muirhead and Wayside Roads and on the north by the boundary of the International Settlement."[53] In May 1943 the resettlement had almost been completed. Half of the refugees had to give up their lodgings and businesses in order to move into

---

[50]Kurt Lewin, 'Shanghaier Bilderbogen', in *Shanghai Herald* (14 April 1946), p. 3.

[51]Mühlberger, p. 4.

[52]'Proclamation Concerning Restriction of Residence and Business of Stateless Refugees', *Shanghai Times* (18 February 1943); Institut für Zeitgeschichte, München:Nachlaß (NL) Ludwig Lazarus, Sammlung (Slg) Lazarus, No. ED 207, vol. II.

[53]*Shanghai Times* (18 February 1943); Shanghai Municipal Archives, SMC collection: World War II, No. U 1–4–1826.

the area of the guarded "ghetto". The district was partly secured by barbed wire. Inside the restricted area the refugees had to provide for themselves. This presented enormous difficulty because they were excluded from earning a living in the other parts of Shanghai. The proclamation limited freedom of movement. Posts and patrols inside and outside ensured that nobody could leave without permission. The special district was governed by the Japanese military administration, the Bureau for Stateless Refugee Affairs. Those who wanted to leave the restricted area had to have a special pass. In order to acquire such a pass one had to face being interviewed by the Japanese officer Ghoya who proclaimed himself "King of the Jews" and proved to be a wayward tyrant.

THE WAR IS OVER. WHERE DO WE GO NOW?

In September 1945, Chiang Kai-Shek's National Chinese army[54] and American troops occupied Shanghai. The ghetto was dissolved and freedom of movement was restored. The foreigners, however, had lost their extra-territorial rights. China became a sovereign nation again. The refugees faced the questions of whether to return, emigrate somewhere else or settle finally in their country of exile. In fact, many of them wished to stay at first. At the end of their exile, they shied away from emigrating to yet another country and having to start all over again; many were old or ill. However, the situation for the refugees soon worsened when, on 27 November 1945, the Chinese government issued a decree demanding the repatriation of all Germans. The term "Germans" explicitly included Austrians and Jews. Legally this equated German-Jews with hostile aliens. For Germans without visas and passports there was only a limited chance of being granted the right to reside in China from the Chinese point of view; since the conditions no longer existed which had led to the flight of the refugees, there was no reason why they should not return.[55]

The Chinese military governors and the merchants soon remembered their previous good cooperation with German merchants and military advisors.[56] These Germans were at first interned but this did not last very long. Convictions for espionage and collaboration were made subject to an American court. The Americans, however, did not prosecute these crimes with zeal. In 1947, war criminals sentenced in the trial against the *Büro Erhard* were granted *habeas corpus* by the Court of Appeal in Washington D.C. and released, and those who were still in custody were also released.[57] The refugees did not fare so well. Three quarters of them could not earn enough money to make a living.[58] On the basis of human

---

[54]The National Chinese army were the followers of Chiang Kai-shek who set up a "Nationalist" government in 1928, and fought against warlords, the Japanese and the Communists for control of China over the next 20 years.

[55]See 'Die Lage der jüdischen Refugees', in *The Jewish Voice of Far East,* vol.VI, No. 60 (December 1945), p. 1; 'Camps for Jews', in *China Weekly Review* (22 December 1945), p. 55.

[56]See Klaus Mehnert, *Ein Deutscher in der Welt,* Stuttgart 1981, p. 320ff.

[57]Fritz van Briessen, 'Deutsche Institutionen und Persönlichkeiten in China', in Machetzki, Rüdiger (ed.), *Deutsch-chinesische Beziehungen: Ein Handbuch,* Hamburg 1982, p. 37ff.

[58]See 'Mr Siegel über die Lage der Shanghaier Refugees', in *The Shanghai Herald: German language supplement* (14/15 March 1946), p. 3.

rights they appealed against the repatriation decree and emphasised their enmity to the Japanese, their incarceration in the special district and their subsequent liberation by the Chinese. Like the Chinese, they claimed they had lost homes and businesses.[59] While at first they hoped to remain in China, the attitude of the Chinese authorities and their inability to integrate forced them to rethink their future:

> It seemed quite reasonable to suppose even in 1945 that at least a large number would find a permanent home in China. As a result of events later on that expectation had to be revised. It is now clear that the only possible solution of the problem was the complete evacuation of these immigrants.[60]

The most popular countries for emigration were the United States, Australia and also Palestine. Few wanted to return to Germany.[61] As stateless refugees their wishes could not be fulfilled easily. They needed an organisation that would attend to their desire to settle in another country. The refugee community was headed by the Council of Delegates consisting of representatives from charity organisations, religious groups and the different *Landsmannschaften*. The Council of Delegates was supported by the internationally renowned aid organisation United Nations Relief and Rehabilitation Administration (UNRRA). Together with the American Jewish Joint Distribution Committee (the "Joint") it took care of the refugees' subsistence for which no government felt responsible. The tasks of these organisations ranged from providing food to organising emigration. UNRRA mainly took care of the refugees' return or further migration and the "Joint" provided food.[62]

The emigration movement lasted until the 1950s. One of the biggest obstacles facing the refugees were newly enacted immigration quotas in many desirable countries for immigration, such as the United States and Australia, which prevented their entry. For instance, Poland was assigned a very low quota so that refugees of Polish origin had almost no chance of entering America. Furthermore, transportation to the new country was also difficult for emigrants to organise.

Besides the American Jewish Joint Distribution Committee there was also the *Gemeinschaft der Demokratischen Deutschen in Shanghai* (later called Association of Refugees from Germany), founded in 1945, which supported people who wanted to emigrate, especially those who wanted to return to Germany. The Association repeatedly published appeals for support in Germany. In a letter published in *Der Weg* in 1948, they emphasised the intention of 2,500 refugees to return.[63] Sonja Mühlberger's father was also involved with this association. Her family wanted to return to Germany to help build up a new Germany:

---

[59]'Petition an das Ministerium des Äußeren in China', in *Shanghai Journal. Die neue Zeit* (17 January 1946), p. 1.

[60]'Der Joint in Shanghai', in *Almanac Shanghai*, 1947, p. 89.

[61]A. Schwarz, 'Auch wir wollen leben. Die Frage nach Weiterwanderung', in *The Shanghai Herald: German language suppplement* (April 1946), p. 6.

[62]'Der Joint', in *Almanac*, p. 89.

[63]See Georg Armbrüster, 'Auswege. Das Ende des Exils in Shanghai', in *1945: Jetzt wohin? -Exil und Rückkehr... nach Berlin? Ausstellungskatalog*. Berlin 1995, p. 234f.

My parents, shortly after their arrival in Shanghai in April 1939, belonged to the small group of active illegal anti-fascists. They led courses in which Johannes (Hans) König, Walter Czollek, Berthold Manasse, Jacob (Peneira) and Annemarie Fass, Genia and Günter Nobel, Max Lewinsohn amongst others participated. After the liberation by the Americans in 1945 they contributed significantly to the formation of the Association of Democratic Germany in Shanghai. It was governed by immigrants from different social groups and beliefs including Germans who had previously entered Shanghai (before the forced emigration of the Jews.) [64]

Understandably enough only a minority of the refugees, wanted to return to Germany. Those who did return faced harsh criticism:

Most of the immigrants expressed great reservation against returning to a country which had trampled on their human dignity, which had murdered their relatives and friend ... I cannot forget how when I was a child adult Germans would shout abuse and even spat at me ... [65]

A small anti-facist group returned to Germany together. They went to the Soviet sector in order to build a new democratic state. Gustav Beutler, who had been on the board of the Association of Refugees from Germany and who helped to organise the return to Germany, and his son Martin Beutler were among those who went to live in the Soviet sector. In order to return they needed a document from Germany certifying that there was work and accommodation available for them. In Gustav Beutler's case, the document was sent by a former political friend who had meanwhile become mayor of Leuna.

Between 1946 and 1950, the majority of re-emigrants settled in Israel, Australia or the United States. The exodus of refugees accelerated when the communists conquered southern China in 1949. On 20 August 1954 the New York *Aufbau* reported that there were still 800 Jews living in Shanghai, most of them either very old or invalids. In 1958 evacuation was completed. UNRRA managed to charter the American troopship *Marine Lynx* in order to send 650 returnees to Naples. 295 of these travelled on by special train to Berlin.[66] On 21 August 1947, the Berlin *Wochenschau der Augenzeuge* reported their arrival at Görlitzer Bahnhof:

Speaker: German citizens who had been persecuted because of their Jewish religion and escaped to China have returned to their home. They have left Shanghai where they lived for nine years to start a new life in Berlin. Only some of them have found members of their families or friends. They know that here they have to bear the deprivations and difficulties of the postwar time. The fact that they have returned of their own free will therefore makes all the greater an impression on us.

A returned refugee: We could have stayed in China but we longed for our *Heimat*.

Another refugee: I left for Shanghai in 1940 and have now returned so that at 84 years of age I can end my days here with my children.[67]

The deputy mayor of Berlin, Dr. Ferdinand Friedensburg, said in his welcome speech that the people of Berlin were empty-handed but he could assure them

---

[64]Mühlberger, p. 5.

[65]*ibid.*, p. 4.

[66]See Armbrüster, p. 247; 'Zwischen Shanghai und Berlin. Die Ankunft der 295 Rückkehrer', in *Der Weg* (29. August 1947), p. 3–4.

[67]Text from weekly newsreel "Der Augenzeuge" No.68, 1947.

that the city council would do everything it could to help, he hoped that they would assist in the re-education of German people, and that anti-semitism would cease to exist. The returned emigrants soon learnt the opposite from relatives describing their own experiences.[68] In the former Soviet sector as well as in West Germany, return and reintegration proved to be a long and strenuous process for the returning Jews.

For the Jews who returned from Shanghai to live in West Berlin or in the Federal Republic it was difficult to obtain official acknowledgement that the time spent in the Shanghai 'ghetto' had been a form of imprisoment entitling them to restitution. Between 1949 and 1956, administrations and law courts concerned with compensation claims did not decide on this issue unanimously. Several expert opinions were solicited and handed in by the general secretary of the *Zentralrat der Juden*, Henrik George van Dam, on 23 January 1951. Among them were statements from US citizens who had participated in the 1946 trials against war criminals in Shanghai. One of them, H.E. Klepetar, the official interpreter, stated "[t]here can be no doubt that the Hongkew Plan was thought up by the Germans".[69] A statement by the former German Consul General, Fritz Wiedemann, also reaffirms the same notion: "I have no doubt that the internment of the Jews in the Shanghai Ghetto can be traced back to the insistence of the German authorities."[70] Wiedemann was not supported by his former colleagues. They stated that the refugees had not been limited in their freedom of movement.[71] They also denied any Nazi-German influence on the Japanese in their decision to deprive them of their freedom of movement. A testimony given on 8 May 1953[72] by the judge Dr. Robert Michaelis, who had also survived in exile in Shanghai and who had been the president of *Vereinigung mitteleuropäischer Rechtsanwälte*, refutes the evidence given by the former diplomats:

> No doubt one can find many Germans and Japanese who know nothing about these things just as millions of Germans never knew about the gassing of the Jews. Nor can it be denied that the majority of Germans in Shanghai committed no injustices and that some behaved very helpfully and humanely ... but that does not alter my findings that, unfortunately, the majority of German diplomats cooperated with the unjust regime of the Nazi state.[73]

In the end, the testimony by Dr. Michaelis was successful. He emphasised the evidence given by one witness, Kordt. Jewish refugees were deprived of their freedom because they had been deprived of their German citizenship in 1941.[74] In 1957 it was the Federal Court's final ruling that did justice to the

---

[68] See 'Zwischen Shanghai und Berlin', in *Der Weg*, p. 4.

[69] See Institut für Zeitgeschichte, München, NL Lazarus, Slg. Lazarus, vol. IV, letter from H.G. van Dam, 23 January 1951.

[70] *ibid.*, added statement by Fritz Wiedemann, former Consul General, 22 January 1951.

[71] See circular St.15.: Conference of ministers for reparation, Branch office in the Ministry of Justice, Stuttgart, 28 November 1951, signed by Otto Küster. NL.Lazarus, vol. IV.

[72] See N. L. Lazarus, vol. IV, expertise by Dr. Robert Michaelis, 8 May 1953.

[73] *ibid.*

[74] See Christiane Hoss, 'Kein sorgenfreies Leben', in *Leben im Wartesaal. Exil in Shanghai 1938–1947. Ausstellungskatalog.* Berlin 1997, pp. 100–119.

refugees accepting that the loss of freedom constituted imprisonment and though undertaken by a foreign state was made possible by the loss of protection by the German state or the loss of German citizenship.[75] The further issue of whether these measures were taken in consequence of German influence on the Japanese authorities remained, however, disputed.[76]

[75]H.G. van Dam und Heinz Loos, *Bundesentschädigungsgesetz (BEG) Kommentar*, Berlin – Frankfurt am Main 1957, p. 248ff.
[76]In 1960 this question was again referred to in a legal case. See BEG § 43, paragraph 1, sentence 2: "Für die Errichtung des Sperrbezirks in Shanghai-Hongkew hat eine nicht nur unwesentliche Mitveranlassung von ns-deutschen Stellen vorgelegen.", *Neue Juristische. Wochenschau. Supplement: Rechtsprechung zu Wiedergutm.-recht*, 1960 Heft 11, pp. 506–508, here p. 508.

Experiences of Survival

BY EVA KOLINSKY

The National-Socialist policy of persecuting Jews and excluding them from civil society culminated in the system of deportations, incarceration, slave labour and genocide which the perpetrators and many historians have referred to as the "Final Solution". As historiography shifted from chronicling the policy and process of "exterminating Jews" to showing how individuals were driven to their death and the dehumanisation endured by those who survived, the terms "Holocaust" or "Shoah" replaced the Nazi phrase.[1] The recast terminology aimed at articulating the uniqueness of the persecution and mass murder of the Jews and also at reversing the perception of Jews as nameless victims devoid of a personal history worth telling.

While the research agenda on the implementation of the Holocaust and the motives of the perpetrators is by no means closed,[2] the focus on the persecuted as individuals is arguably more effective in communicating the enormity and inhumanity of what happened.[3] In *The Holocaust: The Jewish Tragedy*, Martin Gilbert links a painstaking account of deportations and camps with personal testimony of individuals caught up in the killing machine.[4] Studies by Wolfgang Benz and Monika Richarz show that Jews who lived in Germany and were exposed to the same policies of exclusion felt their impact in very different, personal ways.[5] Jonathan Webber and David S. Wyman conclude that the destruction of life and communities in the Holocaust shifted the centre of Jewish culture from Europe to the United States and Israel,[6] while Jews' perceptions of

[1] Michael M. Marrus, *The Holocaust in History*. London 1988, pp. 3ff.

[2] Thus, Daniel Goldhagen, in *Hitler's Willing Executioners: Ordinary Germans and the Holocaust,* London 1996, attempts to explain the Holocaust as a consequence of a specifically German type of eliminationist antisemitism; the controversy following the book's publication highlighted that there is no consensus about the origins, implementation or impact of the Holocaust.

[3] This point is developed in detail, with reference to schoolbook historiography, in Eva Kolinsky, 'Remembering Auschwitz. A Survey of Recent Textbooks for the Teaching of History in German Schools', in *Yad Vashem Studies* XXII, 1992, pp. 287–307; *idem*, 'Geschichte gegen den Strom. Zur Darstellung des Holocaust in neuen Schulgeschichtsbüchern', in *Internationale Schulbuchforschung*, vol. XIII, No. 2, 1991, pp. 121–146.

[4] Martin Gilbert, *The Holocaust: The Jewish Tragedy*, London 1986; Ronald J. Berger, *Constructing a Collective Memory of the Holocaust: A Life History of Two Brothers' Survival*, Colorado 1995.

[5] Wolfgang Benz (ed.), *Juden in Deutschland 1933–1945*, Munich 1989; Monika Richarz (ed.), *Bürger auf Widerruf. Lebenszeugnisse deutscher Juden 1780–1945*, Munich 1989 (Publication of the Leo Baeck Institute); see also Avraham Barkai, Paul Mendes-Flohr and Steven M. Lowenstein, *Deutsch-jüdische Geschichte in der Neuzeit*, vol. IV: 1918–1945, Munich 1997 (Publication of the Leo Baeck Institute).

[6] Jonathan Webber (ed.), *Jewish Identities in the New Europe*, London–Washington 1994; David S. Wyman and Charles H. Rosenzweig (eds.), *The World Reacts to the Holocaust*, Baltimore–London 1996.

identity became individualised, mirroring "the experience as citizens of the countries in which they lived".[7]

The Holocaust "has different meanings for different Jews".[8] Autobiographical accounts and oral testimony reveal valuable details of survival in the camps, during the "selections" and on the Death marches. They narrate what only those who were there can know[9] and demonstrate that there were no predictable rules of fair treatment or survival. This very unpredictability turned survival itself into a personal achievement, the Holocaust experience into an individual experience. Although it was a "shared experience" at the level of policy, organisation and process, for the individuals caught in the Holocaust personality traits and coincidences became the crucial resource of survival.[10] As literature on the Holocaust and its impact, memoirs and oral testimony are potent sources for exposing its abnormality.[11]

Liberation, which should have marked the beginning of a return to normal life, became for most survivors merely the beginning of an extended interim. Early accounts highlighted the plight of Holocaust survivors detained as Displaced Persons in overcrowded, unsanitary and guarded camps. Their common purpose was to persuade the public – notably the American public – that Displaced Persons should be helped either by relaxing the immigration rules to the US or by creating a Jewish state in Palestine in which they could settle.[12] More recent studies added historical documentation and archival sources to show how policy stalemates and intransigence on immigration trapped most Displaced Persons in Germany for at least three years.[13] The jumble of improvisation, inertia and obstructive regulations as Allied occupation forces and military government, German local authorities and burgomasters, UNRRA (United Nations

[7]Webber, p. 5.

[8]John Bornemann and Jeffrey M. Peck, *Sojourners: The Return of German Jews and the Question of Identity*, Lincoln and London 1995, p. 23.

[9]H.G. Adler, *Theresienstadt 1941–1945. Das Antlitz einer Zwangsgemeinschaft*, Tübingen 1960, p. 214, argues that only those who lived through it can write about the Holocaust.

[10]Ronald J. Berger, *Constructing a Collective Memory of the Holocaust: A Life History of Two Brothers' Survival*, Colorado 1995; also Lawrence L. Langer, *Holocaust Testimonies: The Ruins of Memory*. New Haven and London 1991.

[11]Berger, p. 13.

[12]See, for example, Zorag Warhaftig, 'Where shall they go?' in *Jewish Affairs*, vol. I, No. 7 (1 May 1946), pp. 3–19; Francesca M. Wilson, *Aftermath*, London 1947; Koppel S. Pinson, 'Jewish Life in Liberated Germany', in *Jewish Social Studies*, vol. IX, 1947, pp. 101–126; Jane Perry and Clark Carey, *The Role of Uprooted People in European Recovery: An International Committee Report*, Washington 1948; Joseph Noia, *Two Years with Displaced Persons*, London 1948; Philip S. Bernstein, 'Displaced Persons', in *American Jewish Yearbook*, vol. XLIX, 1947–1948, pp. 520–532; *The DP Story: Memo to America*, Final Report of the United States Displaced Persons Commission, Washington 1952; Henry B.M. Murphy, *Flight and Resettlement*, Unesco Report, Geneva 1955.

[13]Kurt R. Grossmann, *The Jewish DP Problem: Its Origins and Liquidation*, New York 1961; Leonard Dinnerstein, *America and the Survivors of the Holocaust*, New York 1982; idem, 'German Attitudes towards Jewish Displaced Persons, 1945–1950', in Hans L. Trefousse (ed.), *Germany and America: Essays on the Problem of International Relations and Immigration*, New York 1980; Wolfgang Jacobmeyer, *Vom Zwangsarbeiter zum heimatlosen Ausländer. Die Displaced Persons in Westdeutschland 1945–1951*, Göttingen 1985; Angelika Königseder and Juliane Wetzel, *Lebensmut im Wartesaal. Die jüdischen DPs (Displaced Persons) im Nachkriegsdeutschland*, Frankfurt am Main 1994; Mark Wyman, *DP. Europe's Displaced Persons, 1945–1951*. London–Toronto 1989, 2nd edn. 1998.

Relief and Rehabilitation) and other aid organisations tried to follow their respective agendas often failed to address the needs of Holocaust survivors.[14]

While studies of policy tend to attribute a collective identity to "the saved remnants", portrayals of life in the camps present a more vivid picture of the individuals involved, their experiences during the Holocaust, and their determination to build a future. Often, army chaplains and rabbis were the first people Jewish survivors met after liberation and their accounts name individuals, tell their stories and leave the reader in no doubt that proffering effective help to those who needed it often meant breaking rules and risking disciplinary action.[15] Margaret Myers's study records how Displaced Persons married and had children; sought education, training and employment; and made use of black market opportunities in a bid to rebuild an everyday life for themselves, even in the interim between liberation and resettlement.[16]

Drawing on oral testimony[17] – much of it published here for the first time – and accounts written by individuals who were closely involved in assisting survivors to regain a sense of self-worth, this paper explores the meaning of liberation for individual survivors and records their efforts to rebuild their sense of personal and Jewish identity. Although Zionism and religious Orthodoxy vied for dominance and both enjoyed a considerable following, there was no corporate project that could explain how the experience of Holocaust survival should manifest itself other than in making the Holocaust itself the core of a multifaceted and individualised Jewish identity.

LIBERATION RECALLED

In April 1945, Ruth Borsos was liberated by the French Army from an internment camp near the Swiss border. She had arrived there by train from Bergen-Belsen concentration camp, one of a group of Jews who were to be exchanged for

---

[14]Cilly Kugelmann, 'The Identity and Ideology of Jewish Displaced Persons', in Michal Bodemann (ed.), *Jews, Germans, Memory: Reconstructions of Jewish Life in Germany*, Ann Arbor 1996, pp. 65ff. In his review of the book in *Patterns of Prejudice*, vol. XXXII, No. 1, 1997, Rodney Livingstone notes: "The obtuseness of some of the liberators beggars belief." (p. 71). For an excellent discussion of conditions in the US Zone, see Constantin Goschler, 'The Attitude towards Jews in Bavaria after the Second World War', in *LBI Year Book XXXVI* (1991), pp. 443ff; also Ronald Webster, 'American Relief and Jews in Germany' in *LBI Year Book XXXVIII* (1993), pp. 293ff.

[15]See, for example, George Vida, *From Doom to Dawn: A Jewish Chaplain's Story of Displaced Persons*, New York 1967; Louis Barish, *Rabbis in Uniform*, New York 1970; Alex Grobman, 'American Jewish Chaplains and the Remnants of European Jewry', Ph.D. Diss., Hebrew University of Jerusalem, n.d.; for the work of Jewish Advisors, see Judah Nadich, *Eisenhower and the Jews*, New York 1953; Louis L. Kaplain and Theodor Schuchat, *Justice – Not Charity: A Biography of Harry Greenstein*, New York 1967; and Abraham S. Hyman, *The Undefeated*, Jerusalem 1993.

[16]Some of the most powerful accounts are written by authors who knew life in a Jewish DP camp personally, e.g. Simon Schochet, *Feldafing*, Vancouver 1983; Major Irving Heymont, *Among the Survivors of the Holocaust in 1945*, Cincinnati 1982. For excellent discussions of the hopes of and obstacles to normalisation see also Margaret Myers, 'Jewish Displaced Persons in the US Zone', in *LBI Year Book XLII* (1997), pp. 303ff; Monika Richarz, 'Jews in Today's Germany', in *LBI Year Book XXX* (1985), pp. 265ff.

[17]United States Holocaust Memorial Museum (USHMM), Oral History Collection.

Germans by the Red Cross, but whose hopes of freedom were dashed when the deal was called off. Although the Jews from Belsen had been deloused before their departure and received some food on the journey, most looked so emaciated and ragged that the border guards refused them entry into Switzerland. Saved only by the bomb damage of the railway system from being deported back to Belsen, Ruth remembers her liberation and the impatient hope of a new beginning she felt at the time: "Liberation was unbelievable ... It was so unbelievable that we should suddenly have our freedom again."[18] Having survived flight from Germany to Holland in 1938 and imprisonment in Westerbork and Bergen-Belsen from 1943, she "wanted to already arrive somewhere"[19] as soon as she was free. It was to take another three years before she saw "a new beginning"[20] in the United States.

Survival of the Holocaust was totally unpredictable. Alice Cahane was just fifteen years old in June 1944 when she was deported from Budapest to Auschwitz and from there to Guben, a sub-camp of Gross-Rosen in Prussia, to work in an ammunition factory. She had managed to stay with her sister "on the same selection" leaving Auschwitz by pleading with the SS woman in charge that it was her birthday and she should be allowed to go as well. From Guben, in February 1945 both girls were put on a Death march to Bergen-Belsen "in the middle of winter, without socks, without underwear, without coat; just a blanket we had to wrap around us".[21] During a brief rest, the sisters and a friend managed to hide in a barn and had a first taste of freedom when they heard the SS men and their transport move away: "There is no way to explain what it is, freedom – at that moment, that you don't hear the voices any more, that you know they went away and now you are somehow – your plot worked. You are free!"[22] A group of Italian prisoners of war sheltered the girls, shared their food with them and even entertained them with songs. Freedom was short-lived, however. The SS rounded them up on the following day but did not shoot them. Forced to rejoin the original transport, Alice Cahane was taken to Bergen-Belsen. It was "hell on earth. Nothing ever in literature could compare to anything what Bergen-Belsen was ... When we arrived, the dead were not carried away anymore ... [People] were crying, they were begging. It was hell. Day and night. You couldn't escape the crying".[23] By the time Bergen-Belsen was liberated by the British on 15 April 1945 "we were already dazed". After her escape, Alice had felt elated; now she expected evidence of change. "I say to Edith: 'What does it mean: liberation? I don't understand the word. What's liberation? What does it mean?' She said: 'Free. Repeat it: free. We are free.' So I told her: 'But then I have to go and find

---

[18]Ruth Moser Borsos, Oral Testimony, Transcript of interview held on 3 July 1990, USHMM, RG 50, 'Oral History', 030*035, p. 23.

[19]*ibid.*, p. 26.

[20]*ibid.*, p. 27.

[21]Alice Cahane, Oral Testimony, Transcript of interview held on 4 December 1990, USHMM, RG 50, 'Oral History', 030*051, p. 24. Readers should bear in mind that the oral testimony quoted here and subsequently was given in English by non-native speakers of English who were much affected by the process. Hence the idiosyncrasies of grammar and syntax.

[22]*ibid.*, p. 26.

[23]*ibid.*, p. 32.

us clean clothes. We are full of lice. We are full of this vermin all around our bodies.' "[24] She found some SS uniform parts and boots in a storeroom but she was too weak to put them on and had them taken from her by others. Some days later Edith, already ill with typhus, died from dysentery after eating canned hash given to her by a well-meaning British soldier. Alice, herself ill with typhus and "every illness there was",[25] was nursed back to health in Sweden, one of a group of young Holocaust survivors taken there by the Swedish Red Cross and cared for in hospitals and families until they could be resettled.

Charles Bruml was also liberated in Bergen-Belsen. He had been deported in December 1941 from Prague to Theresienstadt, and from there to Auschwitz in January 1942 for slave labour in the Buna works. On 18 January 1945 he was death-marched for two days without food, proper shoes or clothing to Gleiwitz in Upper Silesia. In order to escape the "pandemonium there, because nobody knew what was happening",[26] he attached himself to a group that was taken out by train. They travelled for ten days without food or water. "On the train, they were dying ... They were often killing each other, because they thought somebody was dying already. They took his shoes. The situation was horrible ... Every day was so horrible that you don't recall the day before."[27] On arrival at Mauthausen, the transport was denied entry and taken to Dora-Nordhausen in central Germany. Here, Charles Bruml hid in a haystack to avoid a transport to Ellrich, a sub-camp of Buchenwald known to be an SS extermination camp and was moved instead to another SS-camp and from there on one of the last transports to Bergen-Belsen. "There were already inscriptions that it is under the Red Cross, but the SS was still there ... They ... they could ... could shoot." Liberation for Charles Bruml was just another stage in his struggle for survival. "Finally we saw the English who came in. And they put in charge – because there were very few people with tanks – they put the SS in charge, but the Hungarian SS."[28] Yet the change of regime allowed him to escape into a nearby forest and obtain food, a coat and a radio from local farmers "who knew this was the end".[29] Ordered back to the camp – the British enforced a quarantine to curtail the typhus epidemic – he secured a job with the camp administration, first in the clothing warehouse and then as supervisor in the kitchen, before returning to his native Prague.[30]

Bruml was still able to walk when his liberators arrived, but many, after years of hardship and incarceration, were desperately ill by the time they were found.

[24] *ibid.*, p. 33.
[25] *ibid.*, p. 38.
[26] Charles Bruml, Oral Testimony, Transcript of interview held on 9 February 1990, USHMM, RG 50, 'Oral History', 030*042 , p.22.
[27] *ibid.*, pp. 23–24.
[28] *ibid.*, p. 29. In *Belsen: The Liberation of a Concentration Camp*, London 1998, Joanne Reilly confirms Bruml's recollections: "The Hungarian guards ... had remained at the camp as part of the original truce" (p. 37) and continued to use force: "An incident in which several internees were shot dead by Hungarian guards over a few potatoes, happening as it did *after* liberation, was incomprehensible to the survivors" (p. 82).
[29] Charles Bruml, p. 29.
[30] *ibid.*, p.30.

In the last months of the war the situation degenerated to one of total neglect, starvation and lack of water, and the collapse even of the inadequate sanitation provisions that had existed before. Although the gas chambers had ceased to operate, 500,000 Jews perished between January and April–May 1945. Many who had survived the Holocaust were struck down by illnesses they had contracted during their incarceration, or died after eating food which was too rich and too plentiful for their shrunken stomachs. Visitors to the liberated concentration camps of Buchenwald, Dachau and Bergen-Belsen noted the shuffling gait of those who could walk, their skeletal figures and ashen skin. Helen Goldkind recalled the moment when British soldiers first entered the hut where she was lying: "They opened up these barracks. And then they opened up, you know, they were just staring at us. We stared at them. We didn't know what to make out. We didn't know it was the liberation army. We just didn't know."[31]

SCARRED, NOT BROKEN

In 1946, the psychologist David Pablo Boder conducted interviews with eight Holocaust survivors. The survey, published in 1949, attempted to record the impact of the Holocaust on personality and behaviour. Boder's "traumatic index" lists twelve events which may occur singly or in a small number and disrupt the personal balance of the adult or child involved. Holocaust survivors, however, experienced most or all of these in their treatment at the hands of the National Socialists and the system of persecution, dehumanisation and annihilation instituted in Germany and Nazi-occupied Europe. Experiences inventoried by Boder as traumatic include insufficient food, clothing and shelter; lack of means and facilities for personal and community hygiene; chronic overtaxing of physical and mental endurance; seizure of personal property; blocking of the habits of reading, writing and worship; abolition of traditions of dignity and decency between the sexes, in treatment of the sick and in disposal of the dead; lack of medical and dental care and wanton mutilation for purposes of alleged medical research; and brutal punishment for trivial infringements of camp rules, and group punishments for alleged offences perpetrated by unidentified persons.[32] After liberation, survivors had to rebuild their sense of individuality, personal dignity and cultural identity, and find themselves a place in society.

Telling her story after more than forty years, Alice Cahane still remembered when she regained her sense of personal dignity: she was just about to return to Hungary, where her father had survived, when a distant acquaintance of her family who had befriended her in Stockholm insisted that, as a young lady, she could not travel without a hat: "And so we went into a place and found a brown little chapeau. I put it on and bashfully said: 'That's perfect. Thank you.' And that little hat was my dignity. He gave me back my dignity."[33]

[31] Helen Goldkind, Oral Testimony, Transcript of interview held on 16 January 1990, USHMM, RG 50, 'Oral History', 030*083, p.19.
[32] David Pablo Boder, *I Did Not Interview The Dead*, Urbana 1949, p. xix.
[33] Cahane, p. 40.

Recording experiences from a group of some 700 young concentration camp survivors who were brought to Britain after August 1945 for a two-year programme of rehabilitation approved by the government and funded by the Jewish charity the Central British Fund, Martin Gilbert tells of their excitement at having clean sheets and even a little room after years without privacy or personal comfort in ghettos and camps.[34] The scars of the past, however, were slower to heal. At meal times, those nearest to the serving dishes or bread basket grabbed as much as they could and hid it under the table for fear that no further food would be distributed, while those who did not receive any food flew into a rage. Many had survived by grabbing food when it was available while the Death marches or train transports without food or water lay only a few months behind them.[35] When Irving Heymont took over as commander of the Displaced Persons camps at Landsberg in September 1945 he proposed to establish a central mess to stop residents from eating in their rooms and hoarding food in unsanitary conditions. In a letter to his wife he aired his misgivings: "A central mess hall is in direct opposition to re-establishment of family life – it runs contrary to the privacy and dignity of a family. Requiring all people to eat the same food at the same time certainly does not foster any personal sense of independence or freedom. Yet, there does not seem to be any other solution to the sanitary problem."[36]

At a mental health symposium held in 1955 under the auspices of UNESCO, one of the papers explained the complex relationship of Holocaust survivors to food after their history of starvation: "Bread was something that they clutched to their bodies, and later, when they were recovering, it was something they threw about and wasted ... It was to destroy, to deny this power which it (bread) had over them that they wasted and dirtied it, and one cannot regard such behaviour as reprehensible when one knows the circumstances."[37]

Regaining a sense of personal dignity exposed the extent of humiliation that had gone before. Most survivors were denied eating utensils. When Hana Bruml was deported to Auschwitz from Theresienstadt, where she had worked as a nurse, one of the first things that struck her was that "everybody slurped like an animal. You were being made into an animal".[38] The spoon she managed to pull from a storage sack allowed her to defy some of the "dehumanisation" intended for her: "So I pulled it out; so I was already more civilised. I had a spoon ... It was part of becoming less than human when you have to slurp like a dog."[39] For Martha Glass, who had been deported from Hamburg to Theresienstadt in 1942, her sense of dignity was linked to fighting the lice which infested and killed so

---

[34]Martin Gilbert, *The Boys. Triumph over Adversity: The Story of 732 Young Concentration Camp Survivors*, London 1996, p. 248.

[35]*ibid.*, p. 297.

[36]Irving Heymont, *Among the Survivors of the Holocaust – 1945*, p. 16.

[37]Louise Pinsky, 'The Children', in Henry B. Murphy, *Flight and Resettlement*, Unesco Report, Geneva 1955, p. 55.

[38]Hana Bruml, Oral Testimony, Transcript of interview held on 27 February 1990, USHMM, RG 50, 'Oral History', 030*043, p. 37.

[39]*ibid.*, p. 37.

many others.[40] Hana Bruml remembers that finding her first louse was "an absolute downer",[41] sapping for a time her will to survive.

In reconstructing a sense of personal worth after liberation, "the importance of clothes cannot be overestimated".[42] Martin Gilbert shows that the only time serious tensions broke out among "The Boys" concerned the distribution of clothing. The young survivors had handed over without protest the clothes in which they had travelled; the supervisors did not think they were hygienic enough for the new environment and feared the spread of disease. Replacements, however, were late to arrive and when they eventually did, several days later, there were not enough outer garments to go around and those there were varied in quality. Only when everyone was allowed to choose a new suit from Burton's did jealousies subside a little. After their prolonged deprivation, "The Boys" turned into immaculate dressers, eager to assume an outward appearance that made them part of society and allowed room for their individuality.

In Germany's Displaced Persons camps, a somewhat different survivors' culture emerged. Simon Schochet report from Feldafing, the first exclusively Jewish camp in Germany, a distinctive DP style of fashion:

> You can recognise a DP at a glance on the streets of Munich or any other German city. He dresses differently so as not to be mistaken for a German. The shoes are of the greatest importance. The most favoured are the highly-glossed black leather riding boots which were worn in the past by officers in the Central European armies. They look most elegant when worn with riding pants, but are worn with long pants tucked inside at the ankle, G.I. fashion. Coats are three-quarter length, cut military-style, and made of used American army blankets or German army coats which have been dyed blue. Jackets are long with narrow lapels. Shirts of every colour in the rainbow (white is conspicuously absent) are topped with wide, splashy American ties. Hats of infinite variety usually conform to the nationality of the wearer ... Outside his camp the DP carries his proverbial briefcase, containing cigarettes and foodstuffs such as coffee and tea. These are for exchange purposes only, and the briefcase rather than a weapon rounds out the military uniform of the DP army man. The ladies also favour high black boots but their coats, although cut from the same fabric, suggest a more feminine militancy. Sometimes they are adorned with fur pieces.[43]

Yet Schochet also recalls that those who had not managed to focus on a new beginning would still be wearing concentration camp uniforms months after liberation. And would sit passively in the camp or by the side of the lake while others tried to regain some form of normality through employment or by trading scarce goods such as cigarettes and coffee from their food parcels for everyday luxuries like soap, underwear or shoes, of which they had been deprived for so long. In his attempt to boost morale in Landsberg and to get residents more actively involved in running the camp, commander Irving Heymont delivered a pep talk which linked reprimand with compassion. It was, he confided to his wife, well received by his audience:

[40]Martha Glass, *Jeder Tag in Theresin ist ein Geschenk. Die Theresienstädter Tagebücher einer Hamburger Jüdin, 1943–1945*, ed. by Barbara Müller-Wesemann, Hamburg 1996, p. 68.
[41]Hana Bruml, p. 47.
[42]Gilbert, *The Boys*, p. 302.
[43]Schochet, p. 165.

Cleanliness comes only with work ... I know better than to accuse you of laziness. Under the Germans, work meant death for you. The harder you worked, the weaker you got on the few hundred calories you were fed. Every bit of work you did strengthened your oppressor. Even now you are reluctant to do any work in the camp. You think – "why work in the camp. We will not be here forever" ... All of that is true. But now is the time to relearn the habits of work and industry. Now is the time to relearn how to be self-respecting civilised persons. No man can ask you to forget what you and your families have been through. However, you can't live in the shadow of the past forever.[44]

IN SEARCH OF HOME

As soon as they had recovered their physical strength, survivors began to look for their families. "That's the only thing you had on your mind", remembers Abraham Levent.[45] He was liberated, aged twenty-one, on 30 April 1945, when the Americans some days earlier stumbled across one of the deportation trains that had left Dachau, with neither food and water nor a definite destination.

> The minute the train opened you see all the dead falling out. Only young people could have survived. And after this me and one more guy we went over there. We took our little strength and we says: "we're gonna walk to a town" ... I remember it like now. We came to a house with a German woman inside, and she saw us and started running. She ran away. We walked in that house. What a beautiful house. All kinds of china with closets with clothes. First thing I did, I took off my things. I took out a shirt and put on a shirt. This is the first time in three, four years that I had a shirt on my back.[46]

When the woman returned they asked for food. "She gave us some food." Then they left the house to set out and find their families. Abraham Levent and his friend were picked up by American soldiers and among the first to be taken to the DP camp at Feldafing. Using this as a base, they and many others like them wandered from camp to camp to inquire whether anyone they knew had survived. "And any place you went you saw hundreds and hundreds of little pieces of paper written down with names in case somebody saw somebody."[47]

Beno Helmer was liberated by the Americans in Ludwigslust, near Berlin, after Auschwitz, a Krupp labour camp, Buchenwald and so many camps afterwards that he could not remember their names nor how long he had been in them. As soon as he had eaten some soup from an Allied field kitchen, he decided to start walking. Since his friend Monyele had a sister in France before the war, the two boys, both sixteen years old at the time, decided to walk to France. On their way they met an American soldier who offered to take them to Paris in his jeep, only "he took us to a detention camp".[48] His friend agreed to stay and make his way to

[44]Heymont, letter dated 28 September 1945, pp. 27–28.

[45]Abraham Levent, Oral Testimony, Transcript of interview held on 20 October 1989, USHMM, RG 50, 'Oral History', 030*130, p. 42.

[46]*ibid.*, p. 41.

[47]*ibid.*, p. 44.

[48]Beno Helmer, Oral Testimony, Transcript of interview held on 25 June 1990, USHMM, RG 50, 'Oral History', 030*093, p. 37.

Paris from there, while Beno pretended to be Polish ("they didn't expect me not to be Polish. I spoke Polish")[49] and joined a group of Polish forced labourers in the hope of returning to his hometown of Teplice in the Sudetenland. After being press-ganged into the Russian army ("Our job was looting")[50] he escaped and joined another transport of former slave labourers to Prague, where he fell ill and was hospitalised for three weeks. Finally, he reached Teplice: "I was the only Jew who came back. There was nobody left in the whole city."[51] The family home was occupied by a German, but the Czech government helped him find an apartment and set up a business. Once Russian influence asserted itself more forcefully, "life became unbearable",[52] and he returned to Germany before emigrating to the United States.

Eva Stock was a young woman of twenty-six who had been working as a slave labourer, with her mother and one sister, in a number of factories and camps before being held outside Berlin after "days and days transferring from place to place without food".[53] On 20 April 1945, Hitler's birthday, the barracks where she was locked in with 1,100 women were hit by bombs. Only fifty women survived the bombing. They were helped by Italian prisoners of war as the Russians arrived to liberate them. "And there was still fire. Just as we were already starting to eat, the Russians gave us ... food. ... we started to go home ... Again we had to walk. No trains, no transportation. Nothing. I managed to put my mother [who had been injured in the bomb attack] on a horse and wagon, and we walked. We walked by day and night. And my sister, she got a bicycle. We were walking a lot and didn't know anybody."[54] As soon as they reached the Polish border they encountered hostility. Although Eva Stock remained in Poland for several months and married there, she illegally crossed the border back to Germany in 1947. "It was easier. We were less afraid then of the Germans than the Poles."[55]

Renata Laqueur returned to Holland from Bergen-Belsen. Her parents and younger sister had been spared deportation and continued to live in the family home; one brother survived because his mother pretended that he was her love-child with a German; and her older sister died from typhus and malnutrition in Bergen-Belsen. Laqueur herself came close to death through typhus after liberation: "I wanted to live. I wanted to go home. Only not to die now. I had coped for too long to die like this. I wanted to pull through."[56] In July 1945 she was well enough to be taken to a DP camp near Amsterdam with her husband, who had been in Bergen-Belsen with her and whom she had nursed to health from near death in the camp. Going home, however, revealed the gulf that now separated her from people who had led normal lives. When she telephoned home on 22 July

[49]*ibid.*, p. 38.
[50]*ibid.*, p. 39.
[51]*ibid.*, p. 43.
[52]*ibid.*, p. 44.
[53]Eva Stock, Oral Testimony, Transcript of interview held on 26 July 1989, USHMM, RG 50, 'Oral History', 030*225, p. 28.
[54]*ibid.*, p. 35–36.
[55]*ibid.*, p. 42.
[56]Renata Laqueur, *Schreiben im KZ. Tagebücher 1940–1945*, Hanover 1991, p. 22.

1945 she was told that everything was fine there. Four days later, she returned home to a family of strangers.

> On 26 July 1945 I sat in my long brown trousers which I had worn for years and a brown Hitler youth shirt which I had managed to get in Tröbitz at home on the large settee. Paul [her husband] asked whether they kept his flute and his books. I asked whether my sister had some clothes for me. A conversation did not develop.[57]

The concentration camp experience had left Laqueur in need of re-education:

> I had become too perfect in "organising" things. In the camp and after liberation I had taken whatever I could get, I was an expert thief, liar and cheat. In this topsy-turvy world the well brought-up daughter from a good home had to live by the law of survival, and I am proud that I managed and survived because of it.[58]

After her liberation, Laqueur and her husband tried to start a normal life by having children but several miscarriages and a stillbirth shattered both their hopes and their marriage.[59]

NEW BEGINNINGS

Marriage and starting a family became a hallmark of a new beginning after survival. "Even as they continued to hope for news of relatives, Jewish survivors began to create new families for themselves ... The DPs were re-establishing Jewish life and community at the most fundamental level, that of the family."[60] Jacob Biber and his wife were among the first couples to get married and have a child in Föhrenwald DP camp.[61] Liberated near the Swiss border on 1 May 1945 from one of the deportation trains that had left Dachau, Ernest Landau, who had lived in Vienna before the Holocaust, became one of the earliest residents of the DP camp at Feldafing. Here he played a leading role in breaking "the concentration camp habit of self-neglect" by suggesting that all but the sick should be given employment in exchange for their rations and by helping to set up the Central Committee for Liberated Jews, which was to become the major voice of Jewish survivors in the US Zone of Occupation. He also was among the first in Feldafing to get married. All camp residents were invited to the wedding and there was wine for everyone. Looking back after fifty years he recalled how a German informed him at the time that the Munich firm Dallmayr, which had counted Hitler and other high-ranking Nazis among its customers, held vaults filled with wine and delicatessen. Ernest Landau and a group of friends went there to help themselves. After the currency reform in June 1948, Dallmayr sent him a bill totalling DM 70,000. The American Joint Distribution Committee (AJDC)

[57]*ibid.*, pp. 22–23.
[58]*ibid.*, p. 25.
[59]Renata Laqueur, Oral Testimony, Transcript of Interview held on 16 July 1995, USHMM, RG 50, 'Oral History', 030*370, p. 84.
[60]Margarete L. Myers, 'Jewish Displaced Persons in the US Zone' in *LBI Year Book XLII* (1997), p. 306.
[61]Jacob Biber, *Risen from the Ashes: A Story of Jewish Displaced Persons in the Aftermath of World War II*, San Bernadino 1990, pp. 36, 47.

agreed to pay Dallmayr DM 7,000 "since the transaction had taken place in *Reichsmark* times".[62] By 1947, Jewish DP camps averaged 600 births per month, three times more than the year before. One in three Jewish women between the ages of eighteen and forty-five were either pregnant or nursing. A spokesman for the AJDC concluded: "There was an overwhelming desire of Displaced Persons to propagate and perpetuate their line."[63]

Abraham Levent was also taken to Feldafing after his liberation and recalled how intently survivors rebuilt their lives. "And after a while you start – even right after the liberation – people start to make committees, to start learning, to make a newspaper. All kinds of little things show to you that's how fast the people – the Jewish people – are raising up from the ashes and right away they start building up a home."[64]

John Komski married shortly after liberation. He had been on the first transport to Auschwitz ("the last number in our transport was 784 or 785. I was 564")[65] in the slave-labour contingent that was forced to build Auschwitz, and was one of the few to escape, only to be recaptured and imprisoned in another string of camps.[66] He arrived in Dachau from Hersbruck near Nuremberg, a sub-camp of Flossenbürg, in April 1945 after a Death march of twenty days, five of them without food or water, which just 2,000 of the 10,000 who had set out survived.[67] After his liberation, he contracted typhus and remained in hospital in Dachau for two months. On his recovery, he went on a day trip to Garmisch to visit Germany's highest mountain, the Zugspitze. There he met a former fellow prisoner from Auschwitz and Buchenwald who had reached the United States and become an American soldier. The soldier encouraged him to apply for a visa, and Komski also met his future wife, a fellow survivor who worked in the administration of the local DP camp. They married and moved into a house reserved for DPs in Garmisch, where Komski worked in the camp office before emigrating: "So I went to the United States but ... nobody cared for the poor displaced people who had come."[68] In the early 1950s, he returned to Germany.

For Martha Glass, family and future took a somewhat different turn. She was already in her sixties when she was deported with her husband from Hamburg to Theresienstadt in 1942. One of her adult daughters had managed to escape to Spain and later gained entry to the United States; the other lived in Berlin and enjoyed the precarious protection against persecution and deportation afforded by the Nazis to Jews in mixed marriages. Glass's husband succumbed to the constant under-nourishment, overcrowding and abysmal sanitary conditions that prevailed in Theresienstadt and which have often been obscured by its

[62]'Landau, Ernest', in Michael Brenner, *Juden in Deutschland nach dem Holocaust 1945–1950*, Munich 1996, pp. 126–127.
[63]*Stars and Stripes*, 1 September 1947.
[64]Levent, p. 43.
[65]John Komski, Oral Testimony, Transcript of interview held on 7 June 1990, USHMM, RG 50, 'Oral History', 030*115, p. 10.
[66]*ibid.*, pp. 12–14.
[67]*ibid.*, p. 40.
[68]*ibid.*, p. 46.

Nazi-projected image as a model ghetto. She survived, as she recorded in her concentration camp diary, only because some food parcels from her daughters got through and helped her to fight the worst effects of malnutrition. In her determination to keep going, Glass clung to as normal a life as possible. She and her friends who had not yet died or been deported would celebrate birthdays, write witty poems for special occasions and retain a meticulous regime of personal care and hygiene.[69] After liberation, Glass was stranded in Theresienstadt without a word or parcel from either of her daughters, one of 6,000 German Jews who remained there with nowhere to go.[70] Those with relatives in other countries who did not want to live in Germany were moved to a DP camp in Deggendorf until they emigrated. The others were left without help until "their" city sent transport. Glass finally left on 8 August after someone in her office happened to mention that her daughter in Berlin had contacted the camp and authorised her return. Just before climbing onto the open truck that was to take her home, she also received word from her other daughter who had found refuge in the United States. She left Berlin after two years to join her daughter in the United States. Since her diary does not cover these years, we do not know what she thought of Germany after the Holocaust and can only guess at her reasons for emigrating. The editor of her diaries suggested that Glass may have been looking for more material security than Berlin could offer at the time. "It was probably the massive shortage of food in post-war Germany which influenced this decision. In her daily life, food continued to be of very great importance. The years of starvation in Theresienstadt had left her with a trauma."[71]

Gerty Spiess had been deported to Theresienstadt from Munich but had nobody to request her return. When a transport from her hometown finally arrived in August, she felt no excitement or sense of future. In her memoir *My Years in Theresienstadt*, she recalled:

> And then, on a late summer evening – the Russians had been there a long time – someone woke me up, shook me and yelled in my ear: "[The transport from] Munich is here!" All the time I had grumbled: almost all cities had already sent their vehicles. A few days ago it had been Frankfurt. Only from Berlin, Hamburg and Munich there was no sign. Well, good, now it was time. And it did not hurt and did no harm – I was dead.[72]

On the morning of her departure she got up, her belongings packed, to make her way to the Munich convoy and found it already full. "All the others had fought for their places, they had stayed awake all night. No more room for me. There I stood with another companion and a very old married couple. There simply was no room for the four of us."[73] Someone pushed them onto the

---

[69]Martha Glass, *Jeder Tag in Theresin ist ein Geschenk. Die Theresienstädter Tagebücher einer Hamburger Jüdin 1943–1945*, Hamburg 1996.
[70]Czechoslovakia, where Theresienstadt was then situated, insisted that the camp be emptied of the remaining residents by 17 August 1945.
[71]Barbara Müller-Wesemann, 'Einleitung', in Glass, p. 58.
[72]Gerty Spies, *My Years in Theresienstadt: How One Woman Survived the Holocaust*, New York 1997, pp. 185–186.
[73]*ibid.*, p. 187.

luggage trailer, where they crouched in the open between shifting suitcases: "I was on my way."[74]

For Spies, settling in Munich was comfortless. On the way there, "they told us to take off the yellow Jewish star".[75] She could not bear to return to the house in which she had lived before her imprisonment and which was now occupied by other people. Instead, she took a stroll in Munich's English Garden. Here, the signs banning Jews had been taken down and Jews were no longer forbidden to sit on park benches.[76] It was then that she felt she had come home but could not shake off the horrific experience of Theresienstadt and the Holocaust. "To leave Theresienstadt – my dream for three years, a dream of an eternity! How did it happen that a dream stopped being a dream? But in reality, we left ourselves behind, in an almost inconceivable hurry we distanced ourselves from the world into which fate had thrust us, a world to whose terrors and sufferings habit shackled us."[77] A stranger in this world in which people who denounced her in the past were still alive and now tried to greet her, she found a new sense of purpose: to ensure that the dead are not forgotten. "I continued to write. My existence had a new mission."[78]

CHOICE AND BELONGING

Persecution, imprisonment and the Holocaust nullified choice and the right to difference: "My choices were taken away", Renata Laqueur recalls. "Whether I wanted to go to the park or to the movies or take a streetcar or buy something not before three in the afternoon and not in a certain store. Not having choice, and it gets worse when they imprison you, because you have no choices."[79] Sevek Finkelstein, who was just thirteen years old when he was marched out of Buchenwald on 5 April 1945, also remembers that the absence of choice and the absence of rights went together: "We had given up long ago caring much about anything. We knew that the American army was just a few miles away but as far as I was concerned they, the Americans, could be back in Washington, it had no effect on me. I think that by then I was just a robot doing the next thing to stay alive. I had no will-power or choices of my own. Later on it was always strange to hear Americans talk of choices."[80]

Liberation presented choices and created new divides. As camp populations celebrated their liberation, Jewish survivors faced the first question of identity: should they join national groups and celebrate their deliverance as Czechs, Poles, French, Hungarians, Dutch, Belgians or Italians – to cite just a few of the nationalities found among Holocaust survivors. And what about German Jews? Were they to hoist a German flag as their symbol of belonging? In concentration

---

[74]*ibid.*, p. 188.
[75]*ibid.*, p. 190.
[76]*ibid.*, p. 192.
[77]*ibid.*, p. 188.
[78]*ibid.*, p. 193.
[79]Laqueur, Oral Testimony, p. 32.
[80]Quoted in Gilbert, *The Boys*, pp. 219–220.

camps with active political groups among the survivors, such as Buchenwald and Dachau, liberation celebrations drowned in a sea of flags. German Jews were not alone in being excluded from this sense of reborn identity. In general, Jews could only join the national groups if they disregarded their Jewishness in favour of the country in which they were born and whose passport they had carried. Yet most had become stateless as a result of Nazi decrees or because the territories they came from had changed hands. With the emergence of the Soviet bloc in Eastern Europe, countries in which Jews had lived in the past, disappeared.

Even more important was the personal sense of belonging. How could Jewish survivors identify with a place where no one was left, where their families and communities had been destroyed, and where local populations remained hostile? Again and again, survivors who struggled to make their way back home to Hungary, Poland or Romania were not welcomed as returnees. When Agnes Vogel and her mother returned to Hungary from forced labour in Floridsdorf, a sub-camp of Mauthausen in an industrial district of Vienna, the homecoming "was not pleasant. We were walking down the street. The people, instead of saying 'Well, how nice to have you here', said, 'Oh, why did you come back? You were supposed to die'. So after that, I soon left".[81]

Prospects for a new beginning after liberation were directly linked to national belonging. In April 1945, over 340 liaison officers were attached to the Allied armies of occupation in order to assist their own nationals who were found in Germany as prisoners of war or Displaced Persons. France alone employed eighty-nine such liaison officers in a concerted effort at rescue and repatriation.[82] Jews had no such assistance. Since the military did not recognise Jews as a national group and regarded liaison officers as representatives of a foreign government, the appointment of Jewish liaison officers was deemed impossible.

In addition to liaison officers, soldiers of all nationalities scoured Displaced Persons camps to find their own nationals and take them home. On 16 April, SHAEF (Supreme Headquarters Allied Expeditionary Forces) had issued a directive that prominent survivors should be identified and taken out of the camps without delay. Reporting on the week ending 30 April 1945, Colonel Fierst of the US War Department noted: "Instructions have been issued to repatriate important liberated political and racial personages immediately."[83] One of the beneficiaries of these instructions on "distinguished nationals" was Leo Baeck, former rabbi in Berlin and a leading member of the Jewish Council in Theresienstadt.[84] He was whisked away in an American jeep days after the camp was liberated while ordinary survivors were left.

---

[81] Agnes Vogel, Oral Testimony, Transcript of interview held on 14 July 1989, USHMM, RG 50, 'Oral History', 030*239, p. 13.

[82] SHAEF list of liaison officers, dated 27 May 1945. NA (National Archives of the United States of America, Suitland, MD), RG (Record Group) 331/52, G-5/2726/4.

[83] H. A. Fierst, Memorandum for the Chief, Economics and Relief Branch. Highlights of the Weekly Report No. 30, dated 30 April 1945, on SHAEF Displaced Persons Activities, 11 May 1945. NA, RG 165/829/SHAEF Reports.

[84] Cable from SHAEF Main to G-5 Branch of 12th and 21st Army, dated 23 May 1945, stating that "distinguished nationals" had been moved first from concentration camps, NA, RG 331/56/G-5/ 2852, Racial and Political Prisoners.

In Buchenwald, Abraham Ahubia, a Jewish Holocaust survivor, aired his disappointment and sense of abandonment in his diary on 20 April 1945, nine days after liberation:

> The Frenchmen and the Belgians are going *home*. Yes indeed, they are going *home*, to their relatives, families, and neighbours. They go to those whom they love and who return their love. They are returning to their former lives. And I – where will I go? Where shall I seek my home? Where shall I find my family and relatives? I have neither.[85]

In May 1945, a request to appoint a Jewish liaison officer had been channelled through the British Division of the Allied Control Commission and turned down by the Displaced Persons Branch at SHAEF on the grounds that "the problems of Jewish Displaced Persons are similar to those of other stateless and those other Displaced Persons persecuted by reason of race, religion of political affiliation".[86] On 9 May, Congressman Emmanuel Celler of New York began to coordinate an initiative aimed at recognising that Jews faced special problems of support and rehabilitation after the Holocaust, and that repatriation was not an option. Gradually, the US War Department concurred with the proposal that a Jewish advisor should be appointed, but disagreement continued as to his functions. The military argued that any special adviser should be attached to the United Nations Relief Organisation and should assist with welfare provisions, while UNRRA remained inactive, claiming that "the final decision was up to the military authorities".[87]

The stalemate continued until August 1945 when Judah Nadich, who had been attached as chaplain to SHAEF headquarters in Paris, was asked by General Eisenhower to act as his personal adviser on Jewish affairs.[88] From October 1945 the post of Jewish Adviser was held by eminent civilians who were given honorary military ranks and remained affiliated directly to the office of the Commander-in-Chief and Military Governor in the US Zone. The last incumbent, Harry Greenstein, served until October 1949 and the office was finally wound up in December by Abraham Hyman, who had been deputy to every Jewish Adviser since August 1946.[89]

Creating the office of personal Jewish Adviser to the Military Governor and Supreme Commander in the US Zone constituted a breakthrough. It meant that there was a guardian of Jewish concerns near the centre of power who could scrutinise the regulations and practices employed in running Displaced Persons camps and in caring for Jews who lived out of camp or in Jewish communities. One of the first anomalies to be rectified concerned Jews living out of camp.

[85]Quoted in Judith Tydor Baumel, *Kibbutz Buchenwald. Survivors and Pioneers*, New Brunswick 1997, p. 19.
[86]Displaced Persons Branch, PW & DP Division, Control Commission, Germany, 28 April 1945 to Col A.H. Moffet, jr. DP -Branch G-5 Div., SHAEF (Main) and SHAEF G-5 Division, Displaced Persons Branch to Control Commission British Element, Attn. Lt. Col. L.W. Charley, OBE, 10 May 1945. NA, RG 331/56/G-5/2846, Persecuted Persons.
[87]Col. Dayton Frost, Memo for the Record, 26 July 1945, NA, RG 165/842/ Special Jewish Representative.
[88]Nadich, pp. 29–30.
[89]Hyman, pp. 309 ff.

Military personnel had interpreted the directives to provide food, accommodation, clothing and medical care to DPs in camps as meaning that persons who were displaced, or who had been persecuted but did not live in a camp, were not entitled to support. Successive Jewish Advisers played an important role in creating understanding for Jewish needs and Jewish culture among military and civilian policy-makers, camp directors and rank and file soldiers. Since other zones of occupation and military governments failed to endorse the activities of the Jewish Adviser or create an equivalent office,[90] their impact was confined to the US Zone, which became something like a haven for Jewish survivors in the interim between liberation and resettlement.

HELP AFTER LIBERATION

The role of the Jewish Adviser in voicing the interests of survivors at the policy level cannot be overestimated. But a single adviser could not be as active and visible as several dozen liaison officers. He could do no more than inspect some of the DP camps, meet some of their residents, and gain an overview. He could not give advice or practical help to individuals. Before commencing his duties, Judah Nadich went on two intensive fact-finding tours. He also used his access to the British zone of occupation with a guest to take David Ben-Gurion with him. Ben-Gurion wanted to address Holocaust survivors, win their support for Zionist ideals, and instil in them the desire to settle in Palestine. During his tour of Germany in October 1945, he went to Bergen-Belsen after visiting several DP camps in the US Zone.[91] In Landsberg DP camp, Ben-Gurion's presence coincided with the first elections to the self-governing body, which also marked the emergence of Jewish political groups. On 22 October 1945 Irving Heymont, the camp commander, wrote to his wife: "To the people of the camp, he is God. It seems that he represents all their hopes of getting to Palestine. The first I knew of Mr. Ben-Gurion's coming was when we noticed the people streaming out to line the street leading from Munich. They were carrying flowers and hastily improvised banners and signs. The camp itself blossomed out with decorations of all sorts. Never had we seen such energy displayed in the camp. I don't think that a visit by President Truman could cause as much excitement."[92] Boleslaw Brodecki, a survivor from Warsaw, who had been liberated by the Russians in Leitmeritz near Theresienstadt and who lived in Landsberg, recalls less exuberantly that "Ben-Gurion was wearing a dirty shirt".[93]

What was needed was hands-on help in the camps. Zvi Asaria, then called

[90]Norman Bentwich reports that following US authorisation for the appointment of a Jewish Adviser to serve at the headquarters of the military and civil government in Germany, the British appointed Colonel Robert Solomon, who "did a splendid job until his death in 1948". Norman Bentwich, *They Found Refuge*, London 1956, p. 144. The London-based office lacked the hands-on involvement of its US-Zone counterpart, however. No successor was appointed after Solomon's death.

[91]Nadich, p. 230.

[92]Heymont, pp. 65–66.

[93]Boleslaw Brodecki, Oral Testimony, Transcript of interview held on 18 September 1989, USHMM, RG 50, 'Oral History', 030*040, p. 42.

Hermann Helfgott, a Jewish army chaplain from Yugoslavia who had been a prisoner of war in Germany when he was liberated, assigned himself to Bergen-Belsen, where he and his French colleague Rabbi Goldfinger began to bury the dead and aid the survivors. When Ben-Gurion toured the camp on 24 and 25 October 1945, Asaria accompanied him:

> On Friday night he visited two groups of the 'Noar Chaluzi Meuchad', the united pioneer youth, listened attentively and made notes in his little notebook. The following day he went into the death camp with Rabbi Helfgott who filled him in on the details. They went to the crematoria and he again made notes. Standing in front of the mass graves he asked how the dead had been treated. Then he visited the children's block. When he heard that these were children who had only been saved by a miracle, he was very moved. It seemed as if he had only understood the depth of the Jewish tragedy at this moment. This time he took no notes and tears flowed from his eyes.[94]

Help for Jews seemed particularly scarce. In Bergen-Belsen, Rabbi Helfgott noted that many nations had sent helpers – former Yugoslav prisoners of war brought food for fellow Yugoslavs, while the Red Cross had recruited medical students – but no Jews had come.[95] In his frustration he remonstrated with Colonel Hartmann, one of the two British army chaplains in Belsen whose main task seemed to consist of sending reports back to London:

> Where is the Jewish help? Where are the brothers from England and America? Don't tell me that they are not allowed to come here! When the English and Americans find just one of their nationals, they immediately fly him home. And those without British or American citizenship – are they just left to die? True, there are collections of clothes and foodstuff. But why do they not send a rescue team of a thousand or may be a couple of hundred people in order to really help their brothers?[96]

Dr. Zalman Grinberg, a medical doctor and himself a Holocaust survivor, set up a hospital in St. Ottilien for liberated fellow prisoners who had been close to death on a deportation train from Dachau. Despite the objections of the monks, Dr. Grinberg had taken over some outlying houses belonging to the monastery for his patients. (The main part of the building was used as a hospital for German officers.) Since St. Ottilien had not been established by the military, it was not recognised as a DP camp and its residents were not provided with food or medicine for several months. In July 1945, two months after the DP hospital was created, UNRRA responded to Dr. Grinberg's plea for help by sending a team to investigate. Robert Hilliard, then a soldier in the US army, remembered:

> They examined the situation minutely: the living conditions, the medical resources and care, the food needs and availability, the scarcity of clothing. They talked to dozens of patients, ascertaining their psychological as well as physical needs. Before they left they guaranteed Dr. Grinberg that help would be on the way. Help did come six months later, in January 1946, when the worst was already over.[97]

---

[94] Asaria, p. 121.
[95] *ibid.*, p. 109.
[96] *ibid.*, p. 112.
[97] Robert L. Hilliard, *Surviving the Americans: The Continued Struggle of Jews After Liberation. A Memoir*, New York 1997, pp. 194–195.

Experiences with Jewish aid organisations were much the same. The AJDC sent a team to St. Ottilien on 15 July 1945. It was headed by Eli Rock, the newly appointed director of the AJDC in the US Zone who left after several days with a promise that help was imminent. Instead of help, the director of operations in Europe, Harold Trobe, arrived from Paris to explain that the US military authorities were preventing help from getting through. Some time later, a representative of the AJDC's office in Paris visited St. Ottilien. Hilliard comments: "When he departed, he was more to the point than his predecessors, flatly telling Dr. Grinberg not to expect any help from the AJDC. He gave no reason. The AJDC was true to its word."[98] It was not before late 1945, over half a year after liberation, that the AJDC was able to build up an effective aid organisation in support of Holocaust survivors in Germany. It then played a crucial role in upgrading their food rations, as well as in providing clothes, books, educational materials and religious articles. Yet, it always remained critically short of qualified Jewish social workers to help in Germany's DP camps.

After liberation, the all-important helpers were courageous individuals who happened to be Jewish and who happened to find themselves in a place or position where they could assist Holocaust survivors. Robert Hilliard must be counted among these unsung heroes. Together with his friend Ed Herman, he broke a good many rules about using army facilities during his time as a soldier to bring food to St. Ottilien when no other provisions were made. He had come to St. Ottilien to report on its "liberation concert" for his army paper, *The 2nd Wing Eagle*. This is how he described the event:

> They were without food, without clothing, without medical aid.... Four hundred of them, the remnants of millions. Four hundred of them, sick starving, ragged, dying, on this late spring day in Bavaria, on this afternoon of May 27, 1945. And what were they doing? They were giving a concert! ... A liberation concert at which most of the liberated people were too weak to stand. A liberation concert at which most of the people still could not believe they were free.[99]

When no help was forthcoming for St. Ottilien, he and Ed Herman sent more than a thousand letters to family, friends and their local communities in the United States begging for clothing and food to help the survivors through the winter. They even persuaded the Protestant army chaplain, Claude Bond, to act as a postbox, since Displaced Persons were not allowed to receive parcels and GIs could not solicit charity donations. Theirs was a strongly worded letter.

> Friends:
> The Jews of Europe are a dying race. Even now after the defeat of Hitler and Nazism, they are slowly being exterminated from the face of the earth. *You are to blame* ... These words may be strong – but they are meant to be – for there is nothing too strong or too bitter if it will prevent the destruction of the human race. We understand that there are many things that you do not know; that you would be only too willing to help if you knew the facts, if you knew the actual situation of the Jewish people in Germany

[98]*ibid.*, p. 106.
[99]*ibid.*, p. 9.

today. That is the purpose of this letter. To let you know what the Jews have suffered, what they are suffering and what you can – and must – do to help.[100]

Ed Herman's brother Leonard made sure that a copy of the letter reached his local Congressman, news agencies and political leaders in the United States. It may even have reached the president. The two GIs were instructed in no uncertain terms by their commanding general to send no more letters. Once parcels with food and clothing began to arrive in October 1945, after having been held up in New York harbour for about two months, the acute hardship suffered by Jewish survivors in St. Ottilien came to an end. There was even enough to share with other Jewish camps in the region.

Many more individuals defied red tape, senseless military restrictions and practical difficulties to improve the conditions for Jews after their survival. Rabbi Abraham Klausner, an army chaplain on special assignment to a military hospital unit in Dachau, played a leading role in setting up the Central Committee for Liberated Jews in Bavaria, which gave Jews a public voice and an institutional framework for educational and cultural renewal. He was also the first to compile lists of names to help survivors trace their families.[101] In Buchenwald, Rabbi Herschel Schacter enabled a group of young survivors to take over a farm and set up a kibbutz. Having tried repeatedly to interest Jewish welfare workers – Buchenwald was the first DP camp to have its own AJDC worker – he noted with regret that "official Jewish agencies and bodies let the survivors down".[102] David Bergman is one of many who remembered with affection the special care given by Allied soldiers to survivors even though the war had not yet ended. In his case, American soldiers saved his life by supplying him with potatoes and carrots for three weeks when he would not eat any other food.[103]

In the south-western region of the US Zone, Albert A. Hutler found himself in charge of the Displaced Persons branch. In letters to his family, he aired his concern that the military government, and especially the military police, seemed to be soft on Germans and harsh on DPs:

> There are some that believe their job is to assist Germans in the reconstruction and rehabilitation of their country. These feel that their job is to make the DP as uncomfortable as possible, and I might say they succeed. Take one of our brilliant officers: he had the military police raiding homes and taking DPs out of their homes and leading them to the camp. I fought that for a week all the way up from the major to the general and finally won the battle. There have even been cases of taking a woman out of her house and leaving her little baby behind ... I made an appeal to the general that asked him what on earth we were fighting for.[104]

When the French asked him whether he could do anything for a group of Jews about to be sent to a large Polish camp, he requisitioned Schloss Langenzell, a

[100]*ibid.*, pp. 137–141.

[101]*ibid.*, pp. 36–39.

[102]Quoted in Baumel, p. 23.

[103]David Bergman, Oral Testimony, Transcript of interview held on 18 July 1990, USHMM, RG 50, 'Oral History', 030*020, p. 33.

[104]Albert A. Hutler, USHMM RG 19, 'Rescue, Refugees, Displaced Persons', Folder 028.26, Albert A. Hutler letters, 15 May 1945.

moated castle near Heidelberg where "the people get plenty of care, rest, relaxation and time to recover. They also draw a special diet".[105] On 25 June 1945 he informed his wife that "our experimental camp for broken minds and bodies had its official opening" and described the festivities:

> Two hundred and nineteen people let God know that their faith had been answered. ... They danced, and there was joy in their eyes. They ate the food, the cakes they had made. One of their number read a poem of gratitude to the allies ... We will nurse these shadows back to normal. We must help them forget a little of the past. The last six years cannot ever be erased from their minds and hearts. It is our hope that Schloss Langenzell will push a little of the horrible pictures from their minds.[106]

IN SEARCH OF RESETTLEMENT

The Jewish Brigade brought help of a different kind. Made up of Jewish soldiers from Palestine who had fought in Italy, the Brigade sought permission from the British army to spend time in Germany immediately after liberation. Individually or in groups, soldiers of the Jewish Brigade visited Jews in Displaced Persons camps. Emissaries of Palestine and its Jewish settlement of 600,000, the soldiers of the Jewish Brigade became torchbearers of Zionism in the DP camps, embodying the hope that Jews could have a homeland of their own and that Holocaust survivors could and should play a key role in building it. In many cases, the soldiers of the Jewish Brigade were the only Jews from the outside world who had personal contact with survivors. The young, in particular, who were impatient to leave for Palestine and who set up kibbutzim and similar groupings to acquire agricultural skills or engage in fitness training, felt inspired in their Zionist resolve by the presence of Jewish Brigade soldiers. They, in turn, were struck by the courage and determination of the survivors they encountered. After visiting Kibbutz Buchenwald, a young farming collective run by DPs, Jewish Brigade members from Givat Brenner wrote in the kibbutz diary: "May the flames of sorrow and torture produce a new generations, hardened by the Nazi hell fires and able to begin a new life, a life of free activity and work, a socially just life, the life of the rejuvenated Hebrew culture which is developing in our country."[107] Schools used books and teachers provided by the *Yishuv*, and Jewish history and Hebrew headed the syllabus. Vocational training focused specifically on trades, farming and skills thought to be useful in Palestine.

Most survivors felt, like Helen Goldkind, that "we did not know what we want";[108] none knew where to go but had no wish to stay in Germany. After his liberation from Theresienstadt, Abe Malnik, with no hope of finding members of his family alive in his native Kovno, joined a kibbutz near Lodz. From there he operated as a courier for the *Brichah*, helping Jews to cross illegally into Italy on their way to Palestine. Although caught by the British, he escaped to the

[105]Hutler, letter to his wife, 23 June 1945.
[106]Hutler, letter to his wife, 25 June 1945.
[107]Quoted in Asaria, p. 136.
[108]Goldkind, p. 23.

American zone, settled in Landsberg and trained as a car mechanic in preparation for Palestine. While waiting for permission to leave, he also registered to go to America. "So the HIAS [Hebrew Immigration Aid Society] called me first with America."[109]

Perec Zylberberg met soldiers from the Jewish Brigade when he was recuperating in Theresienstadt and remembers their impact. "There were people ready to persuade you to go to Palestine for settlement. Quite a few local Jewish ex-prisoners were joining the campaign to direct us to the Middle East. How was one to choose? There were not many open avenues to take, except to go back to your country of origin. Almost all other routes outward were fraught with danger, prohibition and real hassle."[110] The route home, of course, was also barred, and Perec Zylberberg came to England. When "The Boys" assembled in Landsberg, local Zionists tried to prevent them from leaving and forced them to depart from nearby Föhrenwald instead.[111]

While liberation removed the immediate threat of violence, hunger and maltreatment, it did not promise resettlement. "Where shall they go?" asked Zorach Warhaftig a year after the war ended, listing all the restrictions and special conditions that barred Jews from finding refuge and a new home in Europe, North and South America, Australia or New Zealand.[112] During the Holocaust, pleas that governments should wave their immigration restrictions and accept Jews fleeing for their lives met with very limited success; in the immediate aftermath of the Holocaust, the barriers remained. Although President Truman's Executive Order of 22 December 1945 stipulated that immigration quotas should be fully utilised and former victims of Nazi persecution be given priority, it took until May 1946 for the first ship to set sail to the United States, while tardy administration and a shortage of shipping space produced waiting lists of two years or longer even after visas had been issued. When US immigration legislation was finally amended in 1948 to admit 200,000 Displaced Persons over and above national quotas, it applied only to persons who had been registered in the US Zone before 22 December 1945. Since the majority of Jewish survivors could not meet this deadline, either because they had been moving across Germany and Europe in search of their families or because they had fled Eastern Europe at a later stage, the 1948 legislation favoured Protestant and Catholic Displaced Persons and placed Jews at a disadvantage. Balts, many of whom had entered Germany as auxiliary SS or voluntary workers, were deemed particularly promising immigrants to the United States because they seemed suited to the farm work envisaged for newcomers. It took another two years for United States immigration legislation to be amended to admit some 400,000 Displaced Persons and thus make a substantial contribution to providing a destination for Holocaust survivors.[113]

[109]Abe Malnik, Oral Testimony, Transcript of interview held on 10 May 1990, USHMM, RG 50, 'Oral History', 030*145, p. 41.

[110]Quoted in Gilbert, p. 261.

[111]*ibid.*, p. 321.

[112]Zorag Warhaftig, 'Where shall they go?' in *Jewish Affairs*, vol. I, No. 7, 1 May 1946.

[113]For a detailed analysis of Jewish immigration to the US, see Leonard Dinnerstein, *America and the Survivors of the Holocaust*; statistical overviews in *American Jewish Yearbook*, vol. XLVII (1945–1946),

Although countries such as France and Sweden offered temporary visas with few restrictions, the general picture after liberation was that Jews were trapped in Germany. Even entry into Palestine remained restricted since the British authorities issued only 1,500 Palestine certificates per month. Within a year of liberation, some 40,000 who had tried to reach Palestine without certificates had been captured by the British and interned in Cyprus. In September 1947, the *Exodus*, with over 4,400 Holocaust survivors on board, was impounded off Haifa and its passengers forcibly returned to internment in camps in the British Zone of Germany. Only the creation of the State of Israel in May 1948 removed immigration restrictions and offered Jewish survivors a chance of resettlement. Yet even then obstacles remained as the United Nations attempted to define all men between the ages of eighteen and thirty-five as "fighting personnel" who required special clearance before they could enter Israel. To overcome this obstacle, the United States interpreted the restriction as applying only to active members of a fighting force, a status not normally held by Jewish DPs of any age.[114]

In Germany, the Jewish *Wochenblatt* published something resembling an order to enlist: "The State of Israel calls upon all young people between the ages of 17 and 35, including childless married people, to volunteer immediately for the Jewish army in the land of Israel. The Central People's Service [*Volksdienst*] Committee in the British Zone, which is recognised by the Jewish Agency and all Jewish organisations and institutions, hereby orders all Jewish men in this age group to register immediately."[115] Posters urged: "Your brothers in Israel are giving their blood for you and your freedom. Will you remain passive?"[116]

Given the challenge of national renewal, remaining in Germany no longer seemed justified unless the individuals were too broken to leave and had lost the ability to lead independent lives. The "sojourners"[117] were referred to as "hard core". Harry Greenstein, the last Jewish Advisor to the military government to serve in Germany, estimated their number at 2,700 in 1948 but had to revise this figure to 15,000 when the DP camps were about to close in 1949.[118]

For their Jewish residents, these camps had become home and their closure generated fear and protests. Even in 1945, Irving Heymont had observed that survivors were afraid of moving: when Landsberg, a former military compound without private facilities, became overcrowded, he tried to persuade residents to transfer to Föhrenwald where families lived in their own homes and in a village setting. Despite the better conditions, the dread of transport to yet another camp

---

pp. 650ff; vol. XLVIII (1946–1947) pp. 610ff; vol. XLIX (1947–1948), pp. 520ff; and United States Displaced Persons Committee, *The DP Story.*

[114]Department of the Army. Civil Administration Division, cable dated 27 August 1948, to Eucom and Omgus; NA, RG 165/845/2.

[115]*Jüdisches Wochenblatt*, 23 May 1948, quoted in Asaria, p. 171.

[116]Quoted in Asaria, p. 170.

[117]Borneman and Peck, p. 8.

[118]*Stars and Stripes*, European edn., 19 September 1949. From a peak of sixty-four camps in 1946, Jewish camps were to be reduced to five by June 1950; see NA RG 165/827/Closure of DP Camps. The process of closure took until December 1950 and one Jewish camp, the village of Föhrenwald in Bavaria, remained until 1957.

persisted.[119] Heymont allowed his charges to take their time and find the confidence to move. Four years on, personal objections were submerged in the anti-Communist climate which had turned post-war Germany from an enemy country into a bulwark of the West against the East. A press release from the office of the US High Commissioner stated bluntly: "To accelerate the long planned absorption of the DPs in the German economy, and to provide space and permit repair and rehabilitation of kasernes in time to care for additional troops which are to be sent to Germany to strengthen Western European defences, US. High Commissioner John J. McCloy has directed the evacuation of ... former *Wehrmacht* kasernes and installations in the US Zone now occupied by Displaced Persons."[120]

BLUEPRINTS AND COINCIDENCES

As they overcame illness and recovered their physical strength, survivors regained a sense of dignity and self-esteem although many remained tormented by fears that there would be no food tomorrow and that apparently well-meaning authorities of today might again turn against them without cause. When they were liberated, few Holocaust survivors knew what was to become of them, where they would live or how they would live as Jews. Others had a more explicit agenda for survivors and there was no shortage of blueprints of what Jewish identity should consist of and which choices Holocaust survivors should make.

The Zionist agenda assumed that Jews would wait in camps for resettlement in Palestine, a potent reminder to policy-makers that the issue of a Jewish homeland needed to be addressed and restrictions lifted. During his visit to Germany in October 1945, Ben-Gurion proposed that all Jews should be moved from Germany to an enclave in Italy to intensify pressure on world leaders to set up a Jewish State. In the event, Judge Simon Rifkind, who had recently taken over as Jewish Advisor from Judah Nadich, objected to the plan and persuaded General Clay to reject it.[121] Arguably more effective in advancing the Zionist case may have been Clay's testimony before the United Nations sub-committee on Palestine that "Jewish DPs cannot be absorbed into the German economy without a revival of anti-Semitism".[122]

An anti-Zionist agenda also existed, although it was less prominent. In his account of his time as Jewish chaplain in the US Army, George Vida accuses the chairman of the Anglo-American Commission of Inquiry into the Future of Palestine, Judge Hutcheson, of bias against the Zionist project. Vida was acting

---

[119]Heymont, letter to his wife, 29 September 1945, p. 24.

[120]Office of the US High Commissioner For Germany (HICOG) Press Release, Frankfurt/Main, 6 October 1950, NA, RG/165/827/Closure of the Camps; Ronald Webster, in 'American Relief and Jews in Germany, 1945–1960. Diverging Perspectives', in *LBI Year Book XXXVIII* (1993), pp. 310 ff., shows that the AJDC came to regard DPs who remained in Germany and resisted resettlement as black marketeers and criminals.

[121]Hyman, pp. 92–95. Detailed records on the work of Judge Simon Rifkind in the papers of Col. Dayton Frost, US War Department, NA, RG 165/850/4, File Judge Rifkind.

[122]*Stars and Stripes*, 14 August 1947.

as an interpreter to the Commission at the time and had assumed that its chairman was to lead a fact finding mission to determine whether a Jewish homeland in Palestine was wanted and could be established. He was shocked to find minds made up before any questions were asked: "Judge Hutcheson ... expressed the opinion that we Jews should look upon ourselves as Jews by religion only, and we should eliminate all 'Jewish nationalism' from our minds. I was deeply shaken by the argument of a man who was to judge the right of DPs to rebuild their lives in Palestine ... I replied: 'You mean that we Jews had a right to die as Jews but we have no right to live as Jews?' "[123]

Orthodox groups defined identity in religious terms and made a considerable effort to make Orthodox institutions and practices obligatory among survivors. In the early months of severe shortages, one such group offered to supply kosher food but only on condition that all recipients adhered to *kashrut*. In the camps, Orthodox groups soon established a strong presence and laid claim to represent Jewish culture as a whole. In Landsberg, Irving Heymont witnessed their resolve as well as their limited impact:

> In dealing with the Orthodox group, I am particularly careful. I have been cautioned many times not to do anything that could be interpreted as interfering with religious practices ... I am baffled at the thinking of the Orthodox group. Perhaps their way of thinking is a form of fanaticism, engendered by their terrible sufferings on account of their religion, that keeps them from compromising with reality. The great majority of people in the camp are Jews primarily because of being born into a cultural group. Some had tried to flee their background only to be pushed back by the Nazis. Strict Orthodoxy fails to attract most of them.[124]

The *Vaad Hatzala*, a strictly Orthodox organisation based in the US, was one of the first to commence welfare work in occupied Germany. Devoted to creating an Orthodox Jewish culture among Holocaust survivors, the *Vaad* supplied prayer books, shawls and other articles for religious practice, equipped and ran kosher kitchens in DP camps as well as in twenty-four German communities, and established ritual baths for women. In 1947, a rabbinical convention brought together fifty-nine rabbis from all over Germany. The *Vaad* founded fourteen rabbinical seminaries with 1,515 students, fifty-nine religious schools with over 3,000 places for boys, and sixteen schools for girls. In 1947 and 1948, there were more Orthodox institutions of Jewish culture in Germany than ever before.[125]

Most Jews inside and outside the DP camps regarded the freedom to practice their religion as a central facet of their reconstructed identity. Neither Orthodoxy nor a specific facet of Jewish observance dominated their agenda. They wanted to express their sense of belonging in their own way. This might entail drawing on their home background·and the meaning of Jewish identity they had absorbed before the Holocaust; it might mean adopting practices which they had learned after their liberation from other survivors, army chaplains or representatives of religious groups working in the DP camps. Jewish religious

[123]Vida, p. 73; Dinnerstein, *America and the Survivors of the Holocaust*, pp. 73 ff.
[124]Heymont, p. 84.
[125]Vaad Hatzala, *Germany 1948: Pictorial Review*, n.p., 1948.

identity after liberation was multifaceted. How individuals defined their own Jewishness depended as much on coincidence and circumstances as their survival and their experiences since liberation had done.

When Rabbi Abraham Klausner conducted the first Jewish service in Dachau after liberation, those attending relished the freedom to express their Jewishness in public and without fear. They were not concerned about versions of Jewishness. Even secular Jews and Zionists participated in this liberation service and perceived it as a powerful symbol of belonging. A similar spirit prevailed when Rabbi Hans Neuhaus and Rabbi Judah Nadich jointly conducted the first High Holy Day services in Frankfurt's main synagogue. Hans Neuhaus had just returned from imprisonment in Theresienstadt, Judah Nadich had come to Frankfurt as Jewish Advisor, and the synagogue in the Freiherr-von-Steinstrasse still bore the scars of its destruction in 1938. Two thousand people attended – US soldiers stationed in the area, Jews living in Frankfurt and its region and Jewish DPs from nearby camps. As a congregation they did not adhere to the same interpretation of Jewish religious observance but as Jews they articulated their common culture through the medium of religion.

After the Holocaust, Jews in Germany rebuilt their identity not as a corporate but as a private enterprise. There was no direction applicable to all, no inevitable decision about where to settle or how to regain self-esteem, identity and family. Hana Bruml recorded in her oral testimony that Holocaust survival had been, "coincidences all along".[126] There was no common formula, no predictable event or circumstance to defy death and gain life. This personal and individual experience of survival generated a personal and individual approach to reconstructing life and identity after liberation. While blueprints and agendas offered guidance and suggested pathways of normalisation, individuals took them up or ignored them, depending on the coincidences in their lives and their way of coping after their experience of survival.

[126]Hana Bruml, p. 19.

A Case Study

Mischling *Deserters from the* Wehrmacht

BY STEVEN R. WELCH

On 23 July 1944, the naval gunner Anton Mayer, who had been sentenced to death for desertion by a naval court three days earlier, penned a four-page letter to Admiral Dönitz, Commander-in-Chief of the German Navy. Mayer pleaded to be given the chance to redeem himself by being dispatched immediately to the front. His letter concluded with the following passage:

> I beg you to believe me when I say that I was always a good German; in earlier years I constantly suffered under the persecution which afflicted us as Germans in Romania. I was proud of my Germanness and in my work as a language teacher I passed on German culture and German values! I ask you, Herr Admiral, to consider the fact that I am the only son of my elderly parents who sacrificed everything for my studies. I am their sole support in their old age and my disgraceful end would also mean their death! I beg you, Herr Admiral, to allow me the chance to prove myself under the most difficult circumstances! Long live our great Führer! Long live Greater Germany![1]

As was the case for thousands of other German soldiers sentenced to death for desertion during the Second World War, Mayer's request fell on deaf ears. On 21 August 1944 he was beheaded in the prison of Brandenburg-Havel west of Berlin. There was nothing particularly remarkable about this method of execution. Although beheading had originally been reserved for executing those soldiers whose crimes were deemed especially heinous and dishonourable by the military leadership – as opposed to the usual, more honourable method of death by firing squad – by 1944 the guillotine had become an increasingly common way of executing convicted soldiers. What makes Anton Mayer's case remarkable and worthy of examination is the fact of his "racial" status. In the grotesque racist terminology of the Third Reich Anton Mayer was a "first-degree *Mischling*" – a "half-Jew".[2] He thus belonged to those 200,000 or more individuals who found themselves uncomfortably stranded in the racial no-man's land carved out by the Nazis to separate "Aryans" on one side from "*Volljuden*" ("full-Jews") on the other. Descent rather than religious affiliation was the criterion according to which individuals were assigned their place in this racial topography.

Before examining in more detail the tragic case of Anton Mayer and seven other *Mischlinge* who deserted from the German military forces in the Second

---

[1]Letter of 23 July 1944 in Bundesarchiv Zentralnachweisstelle (hereafter BA-ZNS) RM123-35944.
[2]In this article it has been necessary to make frequent reference to a number of distasteful Nazi racial terms. These should be regarded as *termini technici* of the Third Reich; their use does not reflect any endorsement of the misconceptions upon which they are based.

World War, it is first necessary to provide some historical background and context in order to understand and evaluate their cases. The first part of this article surveys the bizarre topography of that National Socialist no-man's land inhabited by the *Mischlinge* and chronicles their treatment by the German military. The second part analyses the case studies of eight *Mischling* soldiers who deserted from Hitler's army between 1940 and 1943 and were court-martialled and punished by the military justice system.

MISCHLINGE AND THE GERMAN MILITARY

. At the outset it is necessary to make two general points. First, as John A. S. Grenville has rightly emphasised, "in reality there was in fact no group of '*Mischlinge*' ... it was a national socialist fiction".[3] But, in the Third Reich fictions, however widely divorced from fact, generated their own dangerous and often lethal reality, and the history of the *Mischlinge* provides a sobering example of this. By inventing the category of *Mischling*, by fabricating in effect a new "racial" group where in fact none existed, the Nazis forced into existence a new "community of fate" which encompassed an otherwise widely diverse group of individuals who in nearly all respects were indistinguishable from the rest of the German population.[4] The *Mischling* label, however, served to stigmatise and sever this group from their fellow Germans and transformed them into targets of discrimination and persecution by the Nazi state.

Second, it is also important to stress that when discussing *Mischlinge* in the *Wehrmacht* one is not dealing with "Jewish" soldiers. Some of the recent confusion on this point may be due to an uncritical acceptance of the Nazi terms "Jewish *Mischlinge*" and "half-Jews".[5] The distinction between Jews as racially defined by the Nazis and Jews understood as members of the Jewish faith needs to be kept in mind. As the figures from the racial census taken on 17 May 1939 indicate, the overwhelming majority of the *Mischlinge*, some 88 per cent, was Christian or did not belong to any particular faith.[6] Less than seven per cent of the *Mischlinge* in Germany in 1939 listed their religious affiliation as Jewish. Males of military age from this small group would have been considered as so-called "*Geltungsjuden*". Under Nazi law *Geltungsjuden* were treated as "full-Jews" and therefore were excluded from military service.[7] The *Mischling* soldiers in the

[3] John A. S. Grenville, 'Die "Endlösung" und die "Judenmischlinge" im Dritten Reich', in Ursula Büttner (ed.), *Das Unrechtsregime. Internationale Forschung über den Nationalsozialismus*, Hamburg 1986, vol. II, p. 95.

[4] On the issue of *Mischlinge* forming a *Schicksalsgemeinschaft*, see Werner Cohn, 'Bearers of a Common Fate? The "Non-Aryan" Christian "Fate-Comrades" of the Paulus-Bund, 1933-1939', in *LBI Year Book XXXIII* (1988), pp. 327–366.

[5] See Günter Schubert, 'Hitlers "jüdische" Soldaten. Ein Defizit der Holocaustforschung oder nur ein Medienereignis?' in *Jahrbuch für Antisemitismusforschung*, 7 (1998), pp. 307–321.

[6] Jeremy Noakes, 'The Development of Nazi Policy towards German-Jewish Mischlinge 1933–1945', in *LBI Year Book XXXIV* (1989), p. 294. The figures are for Germany, excluding Austria.

[7] The term "*Geltungsjude*" also applied to those "half-Jews" who were married to Jewish spouses. By September 1942 a small number of *Geltungsjuden*, some 339, had been reclassifed as "*Mischlinge* of the

Wehrmacht were therefore almost without exception Christians.[8] It is therefore quite misleading and inaccurate to refer to them as Jewish soldiers.

Over the course of the Third *Reich* Nazi policy towards the *Mischlinge* was often erratic, ambivalent and contradictory. The self-created "problem" of the *Mischlinge* proved to be one of the thorniest and most intractable for the racial planners of the Third *Reich*. From the Nazi perspective, the *Mischlinge* were not Jews, nor were they Germans. They were a troublesome "third race" whose very existence marred the simplistic binary divisions between "us" and "them", between racial comrade and racial other which were so central a feature of the Nazi world view. The attempts by the regime to bring recalcitrant reality into line with its racist world view resulted in a policy which fluctuated and changed direction depending on circumstances, competition among various interests – the bureaucrats of the Interior Ministry, the representatives of the *Wehrmacht*, the SS and the Nazi Party all advocated different approaches to the *Mischling* issue at various times – and last but not least the shifting moods of the *Führer*. As Jeremy Noakes has noted, with respect to policy on *Mischlinge* "Hitler's own caution and uncertainty ... produced a stream of contradictory and confusing impulses".[9] As the following survey shows, the same pattern of contradiction and confusion can also be discerned in Nazi policy towards *Mischlinge* in the *Wehrmacht*.

During the first two-and-a-half years of the Nazi regime a fundamental racial distinction was drawn between "Aryans" and "non-Aryans"; those who were later to be labelled as *Mischlinge* were originally consigned to the latter category.[10] Recognition of *Mischlinge* as a separate group came about in 1935, as a result of the infamous Nuremberg Laws issued in September of that year.[11] The First Regulation to the Reich Citizenship Law of 14 November 1935, singled out for discrimination those individuals considered to be of "mixed Jewish blood".[12] In general terms, "*Mischlinge* of the first degree" were persons who des-

---

first degree". See Bernhard Lösener, 'Als Rassereferent im Reichsministerium des Innern', in *Viertel-jahrshefte für Zeitgeschichte*, 9 (1961), p. 310.

[8] In the 1939 census some nine per cent of respondents either supplied no information or were classified as "believers in God" or "without faith". Male *Mischlinge* from these groups would, of course, have been liable for military service. Noakes, 'Nazi Policy', p. 294.

[9] Noakes, 'Nazi Policy', p. 354.

[10] For an overview of the origins of the term *Mischlinge* see Annegret Ehmann, 'From Colonial Racism to Nazi Population Policy: The Role of the So-Called Mischlinge', in Michael Berenbaum and Abraham J. Peck (eds.), *The Holocaust and History: The Known, the Unknown, the Disputed, and the Reexamined*, Bloomington 1998, pp. 115–133.

[11] See Jeremy Noakes, 'Wohin gehören die "Judenmischlinge"? Die Entstehung der ersten Durchführungsverordnungen zu den Nürnberger Gesetzen', in U. Büttner (ed.), pp. 69–89.

[12] An English translation of the Regulation can be found in Benjamin Sax and Dieter Kuntz (eds.), *Inside Hitler's Germany*, Lexington 1992, pp. 404–406. Categorisation as a *Mischling* could be affected by certain additional criteria. Raul Hilberg has provided a convenient summary of the Nazi legal definitions of *Mischlinge*: "(1) any person who descended from two Jewish grandparents (half-Jewish), but who (a) did not adhere (or adhered no longer) to the Jewish religion on September 15, 1935, and who did not join it at any subsequent time, *and* (b) was not married (or was married no longer) to a Jewish person on September 15, 1935, and who did not marry such a person at any subsequent time (such half-Jews were called *Mischlinge* of the first degree), and (2)

cended from two Jewish grandparents, while *"Mischlinge* of the second degree" had just one Jewish grandparent. There are widely varying estimates of just how many *Mischlinge* there were in Germany at the time of the Nuremberg racial decrees, but recent studies have suggested that the number was around 200,000.[13] It remains unclear just how many of the *Mischlinge* were males of military age. During the preparations for the reintroduction of compulsory military service in 1935, Major Hossbach, Hitler's *Wehrmacht* Adjutant, asked the Reich Ministry of the Interior to supply statistics concerning the number of Jews and *Mischlinge* eligible for military service. According to the Ministry's response there were 308,000, of whom approximately 150,000 were *Mischlinge*.[14] As Jeremy Noakes has commented, this figure appears to have been "grossly exaggerated".[15] The estimate provided in late 1935 by Dr. Bernhard Lösener, the desk officer for racial affairs in the Interior Ministry, of some 45,000 "half-Jewish" men of military age in Germany, seems much more plausible.[16] The existence of this relatively substantial pool of potential soldiers may well have been one of the factors which motivated the *Wehrmacht* and the Nazi leadership to create a special category for "half-Jews", thus preserving them for future use as soldiers for the *Führer*.

Well before the introduction of the Nuremberg race laws in 1935, the German military had moved to purge its ranks of "non-Aryans".[17] In July 1933 the *Reichswehr* closed its ranks to "non-Aryan" applicants and also ordered that in future all soldiers' brides must be of Aryan ancestry.[18] In compliance with the Aryan paragraph of April 1933, the military dismissed its "non-Aryan" officers and soldiers following an order issued on 28 February 1934 by the Minister of Defence, General Werner von Blomberg.[19] Under the

---

any person descended from one Jewish grandparent (*Mischling* of the second degree)." Cited in Raul Hilberg, *The Destruction of the European Jews*, New York 1985, vol. I, p. 72.

[13]On the various estimates of the *Mischling* population in Germany see Saul Friedländer, *Nazi Germany and the Jews*, New York 1997, pp. 150–151. For a further discussion of the statistical information on the number of *Mischlinge* see John A. S. Grenville, 'Neglected Holocaust Victims. The Mischlinge, the Jüdischversippte, and the Gypsies', in Berenbaum and Peck (eds.), pp. 319–320.

[14]Noakes, 'Nazi Policy ', p. 301.

[15]Noakes, *ibid*.

[16]Cited in Hilberg, p. 71. Hilberg's reference is to an affidavit prepared by Lösener in February 1948 during the war crimes trials at Nuremberg. In Lösener's 1950 document describing his activities in the Interior Ministry, he indicates that during the discussions leading up to the drafting of the First Regulation to the *Reich* Citizenship Law of 14 November 1935, he argued that exclusion of the "half-Jews" from the military would mean the "loss of approximately 2 divisions of soldiers", an estimate which would involve about 35,000 men. See Bernhard Lösener, p. 280.

[17]For a brief account of the purge process see Manfred Messerschmidt, 'Juden im preußisch-deutschen Heer' in *Deutsche Jüdische Soldaten 1914–1945*, edited by the Militärgeschichtliches Forschungsamt, Freiburg 1982, pp. 112–118.

[18]Rudolf Absolon, *Die Wehrmacht im Dritten Reich*, Boppard am Rhein 1969, vol. I, p. 154.

[19]Order of 28 February 1934 concerning the application of paragraph 3 (Aryan paragraph) of the Law for the Restoration of the Professional Civil Service of 7 April 1933 to the soldiers of the *Reichswehr*, reprinted in Klaus-Jürgen Müller, *Armee und Drittes Reich, 1933–1939: Darstellung und Dokumentation*, Paderborn 1987, p. 183. Jewish soldiers who were veterans of the First World War had initially been allowed to remain in the army. An estimated 100,000 German Jews served in the First World War; about 12,000 were killed, just under 30,000 were decorated, and 2,000 became officers. As

prevailing definition of "non-Aryan", this order applied to any officer or soldier who had even one Jewish parent or grandparent – it thus applied not only to full Jews but also to men who would after 1935 be categorised as *Mischlinge*. Veterans who had fought in the First World War – *Frontkämpfer* – were, however, exempted from the purge. Those "non-Aryan" soldiers who did not qualify for such an exemption were expelled from the military on grounds of "being unfit for duty".[20] The initial purging of "non-Aryans" from the 100,000-man army involved a relatively small number of soldiers and officers, perhaps no more than 70.[21]

In spring 1935, when Hitler reinstituted compulsory military service, a new conscription law came into effect. Paragraph 15 of that law stipulated that "Aryan descent is a precondition for active military service".[22] A subsequent ordinance issued in late May 1935 defined as "non-Aryan" anyone who had even one Jewish parent or grandparent; it thus excluded from active military service young men who would subsequently be classified as *"Mischlinge* of the first and second degree" following the introduction of the Nuremberg race laws later that same year.[23] At the same time, the ordinance also stated that "non-Aryans" could petition for acceptance into active military service, thus leaving open the possibility that exceptions to the harsh exclusory policy might be approved.[24]

After the Nuremberg Laws were issued in late 1935, it became necessary for the military to revise its own definitions of "non-Aryans" in order to bring them in line with the legal norms the regime had established. As a result, the revamped conscription law of June 1936 distinguished between Jews and *Mischlinge*. The former were categorically excluded from military service: "A Jew cannot carry out active military service".[25] All *Mischlinge*, by contrast, were required to serve in the German military. *"Mischlinge* of the first degree", or "half-Jews", were, however, prohibited from being promoted to the status of non-commissioned officer.[26] Such advancement would put them in a position of command over Aryans, obviously an unacceptable situation from the racist point of view

---

Müller points out, the purge process was in part a response by the military leadership to attacks on its ideological reliability levelled by Nazi Party members. Müller, *Armee und Drittes Reich*, pp. 57–61.

[20] See Rolf Vogel, *Ein Stück von uns: Deutsche Juden in deutschen Armeen 1813–1976. Eine Dokumentation*, Mainz 1977, p. 222.

[21] See the 'Endgültige Zusammenstellung der Zahl der durch die Einführung des Arierparagraphen betroffenen Soldaten der Reichswehr from June 1934' reproduced in Klaus-Jürgen Müller, *Das Heer und Hitler. Armee und nationalsozialistisches Regime 1933–1940*, Stuttgart 1969, p. 598.

[22] Military Service Law of 21 May 1935 in Absolon, *Wehrmacht im Dritten Reich*, vol. III, p. 353.

[23] Verordnung über die Musterung und Aushebung 1935, excerpt reprinted in Vogel, p. 232.

[24] *ibid*. See also the 'Verordnung über die Zulassung von Nichtariern zum aktiven Wehrdienst vom 25. Juli 1935' in Absolon, *Wehrmacht im Dritten Reich*, vol. III, p. 384–387, which outlines the petitioning procedures for "non-Aryans".

[25] Revised text of paragraph 15 of the Military Service Law, dated 26 June 1936 in Absolon, *Wehrmacht im Dritten Reich*, vol. III, p. 354.

[26] For a contemporary overview of the legal stipulations regarding the military status of Jews and *Mischlinge* see Theo München, 'Die Stellung der Blutsfremden im deutschen Wehrrecht', in *Zeitschrift für Wehrrecht*, 5 (1941), p. 505f.

endorsed by the Nazi Party.[27] "Quarter-Jews" enjoyed a slightly greater degree of equality with their Aryan comrades and could in exceptional cases become non-commissioned officers. Helmut Krüger, a "half-Jew" born in 1913, commented in his memoirs that Mischlinge greeted the 1936 law with relief: "Many Mischlinge of military age between 18 and 25 joyfully volunteered for the Labour Service or the military in the belief that after fulfilling their 'duty of honour to the German people' they might anticipate some additional mitigation [of pressure] in their professional lives and above all more protection for their Jewish parent".[28] These hopes for better treatment in return for service to the Nazi fatherland were, however, sadly misplaced as the events of the coming years were to demonstrate.

Even before the outbreak of the war in September 1939, there were troubling signs that the already limited tolerance of the regime for "non-Aryans" was contracting. In January soldiers who had voluntarily signed on for long terms of service and whose wives were "racially" Jewish were dismissed from the army.[29] A few weeks later dismissal was also the fate of civilian employees and workers for the military whose wives were "racially" Jewish.[30] The dismissals paralleled the accelerating oppression of Jews heralded by the Kristallnacht pogrom of November 1938.

During the first six months of the war Mischlinge fought alongside their Aryan comrades in the Blitzkrieg against Poland as well as in the Sitzkrieg in the West. Many were promoted and decorated for bravery; Helmut Krüger, for example, became a corporal and squad leader and was later awarded the Iron Cross, second class.[31] But towards the end of 1939 or in early January 1940 Hitler evidently began to contemplate the adoption of a different policy towards Mischling soldiers. A directive from the Armed Forces High Command dated 16 January 1940 stated that Hitler had called for a listing of all "Mischlinge of first and second degree" in the Wehrmacht.[32] This "census" of Mischlinge was to be completed by 15 March 1940. Towards the end of March meetings were held by a number of officials to discuss the situation of Mischlinge in the military; presumably the results of the report ordered in January provided a basis for these discussions. Werner Blankenburg of the Führer Chancellery sent a letter to Hitler's army adjutant, Major Engel, on 28 March 1940, in which he outlined certain problems associated with the presence of Mischlinge in the military and suggested that "half-Jews" should be excluded from the

---

[27]On 13 May 1936 Hitler had ordered that Wehrmacht officers and non-commissioned officers be chosen "in accordance with the most demanding racial criteria". Cited by Jürgen Förster, 'Wehrmacht, Krieg und Holocaust', in Rolf-Dieter Müller and Hans-Erich Volkmann (eds.), Die Wehrmacht. Mythos und Realität, Munich 1999, p. 4.

[28]Helmut Krüger, Der halbe Stern. Leben als deutsch-jüdischer 'Mischling' im Dritten Reich, Berlin 1993, pp. 73–74. It needs to be always borne in mind that the so-called Mischlinge who were called "half" or "quarter" Jews by Nazi definition could not be Jews by religion; most of them were Christians, some may not have had any religious affiliation.

[29]Erlass dated 20 January 1939. BA-ZNS Sammlung Juden.

[30]Erlass from 2 March 1939. BA-ZNS Sammlung jüdische Mischlinge.

[31]Krüger, pp. 66–68.

[32]OKW 1i20/204/40 AWA/J (Ic) published in the Heeres-Verordnungsblatt Teil C, 1940, p. 42.

Wehrmacht.[33] Blankenburg's letter apparently provided the occasion for the formulation of a new policy towards *Mischlinge* which was communicated in a
secret Armed Forces High Command (*Oberkommando der Wehrmacht*, hereafter
OKW) directive of 8 April 1940. In this directive issued on the eve of the
German occupation of Denmark and the invasion of Norway, Hitler ordered
that all "half-Jewish" soldiers and all soldiers married to "racial" Jews or to
"half-Jews" be immediately dismissed from all branches of the *Wehrmacht*[34]
(refer to document 1 at the end of this article). The order did allow for exceptions "in special cases". Soldiers or their commanders could submit petitions to
the OKW requesting that individual "half-Jews" be permitted to remain in the
military. "Quarter-Jews" were not expelled from military service nor were
"half-Jewish" officers who had previously been declared by Hitler to be of
"German blood" (*deutschblütig*).[35] In exceptional cases "quarter-Jews" could
be promoted to positions of authority. But such promotion was also subject to
Hitler's express approval.

Hitler's secret order appears to have had little immediate impact. Some units
apparently did not hear about the order; in others commanders, preoccupied
with the upcoming military actions in the West, simply ignored it. Only after
the conclusion of the campaign against France did the new policy begin to take
effect, with thousands of "half-Jewish" soldiers or soldiers married to "racial"
Jews or "half-Jews" being dismissed from the *Wehrmacht.*[36] In the face of these
mass dismissals hundreds of soldiers submitted petitions requesting that they be
granted exceptional status and be allowed to remain in the military. An army
communication of August 1940 which acknowledged the surge of petitions trig-
gered by the purge order complained that most of the supporting documentation
supplied by the individual units was far too general in content and failed to apply
sufficiently strict criteria in sorting out those soldiers who deserved to be considered for exceptional treatment. In particular, it was noted that the selection and
preparation of petitions "required a special understanding for the significance of
the principles of racial law". Units were instructed in future to submit petitions
only in cases where exceptional acts of military bravery could be demonstrated.
Good conduct, above-average performance and even decoration with the Iron
Cross were not sufficient grounds for granting exemption from Hitler's dismissal
order.[37]

By 30 June 1942, 1,005 first-degree *Mischlinge* or soldiers married to Jews or
"half-Jews" had submitted petitions to enlist, remain in or re-enlist in the *Wehr-*

---

[33]On the meetings and Blankenburg's letter see Noakes, 'Nazi Policy', p. 331.

[34]OKW Az 12i 10-20J (Ic) Nr. 524/40 geh. 8 April 1940. The text can also be found in Absolon, *Wehrmacht im Dritten Reich*, vol. V, p. 149.

[35]A list with the names of 77 officers who were *Mischlinge* or whose wives were *Mischlinge* can be found
in BA-ZNS Sammlung jüdische Mischlinge. The list is mentioned in Sigrid Lekebusch, *Not und Verfolgung der Christen jüdischer Herkunft im Rheinland*, Köln 1995, p. 122. On the recent controversy surrounding the "discovery" of this list by the American historian Bryan Rigg and the subsequent
media attention devoted to it, see Schubert, pp. 307–308.

[36]The exact number dismissed is unclear, but according to contemporary records some 25,000 men
would have been affected. See Noakes, 'Nazi Policy', p. 331, esp. footnote 127.

[37]Allgemeine Heeres-Mitteilung 1940, Ziff. 849, dated 7 August 1940, cited in Krüger, pp. 75–76.

macht; 250 (25 per cent) of the requests were granted.[38] The fact that the final decision in every case was made personally by Hitler – despite the multitude of pressing problems which he faced as Germany's supreme warlord – is a dramatic demonstration of just how seriously he regarded the racial issue. Hitler's approval seems to have depended primarily on his assessment of a petitioner's physical appearance (photographs were an essential part of the application), on whether the applicant had demonstrated bravery in action or had given distinguished service to the Party.[39] Those soldiers who received Hitler's approval were issued a document which authorised them to remain in the *Wehrmacht* (refer to document 3 at the end of this article). But many *Mischling* soldiers remained in the *Wehrmacht* without the protection of such an authorisation. In September 1940 the Army High Command (*Oberkommando des Heeres*, hereafter OKH) complained that "again and again cases have come to the attention of the OKH in which Jewish *Mischlinge* of the first degree (50%) or soldiers married to such Jewish *Mischlinge* are still in active military service in violation of the order ... of 20.4.40".[40] The OKH insisted that all soldiers be required to sign a declaration attesting to their racial status and those who were found to be "first-degree *Mischlinge*" be dismissed immediately (refer to documents 2a, b, c at the end of this article).

It seems quite likely that from autumn 1940 on many "half-Jews" signed false Aryan declarations in order to avoid being expelled from the military (see the case of Werner K. described below, for example). Many others, as will become clear from the case studies below, unaware of their status as "first-degree *Mischlinge*", also signed declarations affirming that they were of German blood and stayed with their army units. Their true status would only come to light when they later sought permission to marry – and were thus required to submit documented proof of their Aryan ancestry – or for some other reason came to the attention of the Nazi bureaucracy which policed racial purity in the Third Reich. Evidence seems to show that the lower echelons of the military were not particularly concerned with the issue and did not invest much time or effort in enforcing the ban on "half-Jews". The Aryan declarations were filed away with other papers and no follow-up investigations took place to test their validity. Some "half-Jewish" soldiers confided in their commanders and were protected.[41]

In any event, an undetermined number of "first-degree *Mischlinge*", but most

---

[38] Figures from the Führer Chancellery in a report of 28 October 1943 cited by Noakes, 'Nazi Policy', p. 336. Some 238 "second-degree *Mischlinge*" or those married to them had submitted petitions requesting promotion; 207 (87 per cent) of those requests were approved. One case in which a *Mischling* was granted permission to remain in the *Wehrmacht* is mentioned by Nathan Stoltzfus in his book *Resistance of the Heart: Intermarriage and the Rosenstrasse Protest in Nazi Germany*, New York 1996, p. 122.

[39] An airforce communication (Merkblatt 99) dated 26 February 1942 sets out a precise list of necessary supporting material for *Mischling* applications. These included: a certified photograph, service record, evaluation by the most recent military superior with special emphasis on bravery in action and any decorations earned, information about any special services to the Party, and information about the occupation and address of the soldier's parents. BA-ZNS Sammlung jüdische Mischlinge.

[40] Allgemeine Heeres-Mitteilung 1940, Ziff. 1041, dated 18 September 1940, cited in Krüger, p. 76.

[41] Vogel, pp. 266–271. See also the case of Werner K. described below.

likely several thousand, remained in the German military despite Hitler's order for their dismissal. Helmut Krüger, who was awarded the Iron Cross, second class, was not expelled until April 1941. His brother Answald continued to serve in the army until the summer of 1942, by which time he had been wounded in Russia and, like his older brother, had been decorated with the Iron Cross.[42] Fritz Lichtenberg, "a first-degree *Mischling*", was drafted in September 1939, fought on the Eastern front, was wounded and awarded the Iron Cross, second class, in 1942. Although his racial status was known to the members of his unit and his commanding officer from at least early 1942, he was not dismissed until June 1943.[43] Some "*Mischlinge* of the first degree" undoubtedly sought to remain in the military as a way of protecting themselves or their Jewish family members; many others, most likely the great majority, sought to remain because they considered themselves first and foremost Germans, no different from their Ayran comrades-in-arms.[44] By performing bravely on the battlefield "first-degree *Mischlinge*" believed – erroneously, as it turned out – that they could prove their loyalty and utility to the Nazi regime and thus pave the way for recognition and acceptance in German society once the war was over.

In the summer of 1941 official policy concerning "half-Jews" underwent a subtle shift. The first hints of this shift can be detected in the minutes of a meeting of the army leadership in Zossen on 4 June 1941, at which field commanders were informed by General Bodewin Keitel, Chief of the Army Personnel Office, that "at the moment the *Aryan paragraph* is being handled in a liberal manner (*wird mit grossem Wohlwollen behandelt*). In so far as cases exist, this should be utilised".[45] As the notes taken by participants at the meeting indicate, Keitel was referring to the possible equalisation or "Aryanisation" (*Arisierung*) of *Mischlinge* in the military. One set of notes records that in the upcoming campaign "Aryanisation as a result of proving worth in the face of the enemy will be 100% approved, eg. for officers with a Jewish grandmother important with respect to the children".[46] It remains unclear from these brief notes whether the promised "Aryanisation" would extend not just to officers but to ordinary *Mischling* soldiers as well.[47] Precisely

---

[42]Krüger, p. 71.

[43]See Fritz Lichtenberg's account of his war years in Carl Schüddekopf, *Krieg: Erzählungen aus dem Schweigen. Deutsche Soldaten über den Zweiten Weltkrieg*, Reinbek 1997, pp. 99–124. Lichtenberg's Jewish father died in a Jewish hospital in Cologne in 1940; his Jewish uncle was deported first to Theresienstadt and then to Auschwitz where he was gassed. Lichtenberg testifies eloquently about the fear and anxiety he experienced as a result of his *Mischling* status during his years in the *Wehrmacht*.

[44]Fritz Lichtenberg noted that when he informed his parents that he had been drafted in September 1939 they responded, "You are actually going to become a soldier. Thank God, now nothing more can happen to us!"; Schüddekopf, p. 102. Werner Goldberg, a first-degree *Mischling* who had the distinction of being pictured in a Berlin newspaper in 1939 as "The Ideal German Soldier", described his membership in the *Wehrmacht* in the following terms: "I had reached this safe shore, where I could say to myself, 'Nothing can happen to me now'." Quoted from Stoltzfus, p. 113.

[45]Besprechungsnotizen, p. 15, of the 17th Army, Bundesarchiv Militärarchiv Freiburg, (hereafter BA-MA), BA-MA RH20-17/23. Emphasis in original.

[46]Notes of the Zossen discussion in BA-MA RH21-3/v.46.

[47]The discussion notes of the Chief of Staff of the 18th Army make no specific reference to officers and simply record that "*Aryanisation* will be dealt with more favourably in cases of bravery in the face of the enemy (*Bewährung vor dem Feinde*)". BA-MA RH 20-18/71, p. 87. Emphasis in original.

why the army leadership chose to adopt such a position on the eve of launching Operation Barbarossa is uncertain. But perhaps they were responding to indications that Hitler's own standpoint was shifting slightly.

Evidence of such a shift is provided in the introductory comments from an OKW meeting held on 10 July 1941 in Berlin to discuss policy regarding Jewish *Mischlinge*. Lieutenant-Commander Frey of the OKW (who was responsible for processing petitions from *Mischlinge*) chaired the meeting and noted:

> The Führer has indicated that he wishes to show that he is not ungrateful towards *Mischlinge* who have fought and bled for the Third Reich and wishes to avoid [a situation] in which after the war front fighters (possibly with war decorations) express publicly at home and abroad their anger and discontent. It is also intended that 25% *Mischlinge*, who exhibit certain characteristics, may be treated after the war like those of German blood.[48]

The minutes then outlined a policy change affecting some of the "*Mischlinge* of the first degree" who had been expelled from the military since April 1940: "50% Mischlinge *who have already served in the new Wehrmacht* but were discharged, *may* upon petition be recalled, *provided they have won war citations of the Third Reich*".[49] Every case for recall had to be submitted to Armed Forces High Command, which would then pass on the request to Hitler who reserved the final decision for himself.

The proposals endorsed at this meeting, with some minor alterations, were issued six days later and distributed throughout the army.[50] The new order began by stating that all "half-Jews" or soldiers married to Jews or "half-Jews" were to be expelled on grounds of "being unfit for duty". This was immediately followed, however, by the statement that exceptions could be made in certain special cases. "Half-Jews" who were still in the army as well as those who had already been dismissed were eligible to apply to remain in or rejoin the army if they had demonstrated extraordinary bravery and had been awarded the Iron Cross or a similar battle citation.

What prompted such a policy change on Hitler's part? The episode can perhaps be understood as a product of Hitler's often ambivalent and sometimes contradictory approach to the *Mischling* issue. Noakes has observed, "Hitler's attitude towards the question of *Mischlinge* in the *Wehrmacht* appears to have been marked by sharp fluctuations of mood over the years".[51] The policy shift of July 1941, which represented a partial reversal of the 1940 expulsion order, would appear to be a prime example of such a mood swing. Hitler's alleged

---

[48] Aktenvermerk detailing a meeting of OKW section I, (Ic) held in Berlin on 10 July 1941. BA-ZNS Sammlung jüdische Mischlinge. Rudolf Absolon summarises the outcome of this meeting in *Wehrgesetz und Wehrdienst 1935–1945*, Boppard am Rhein 1960, p. 119.

[49] Aktenvermerk detailing a meeting of OKW section I, (Ic), 10 July 1941. BA-ZNS Sammlung jüdische Mischlinge. Emphasis in original.

[50] OKH Nr. 6840/41 g PA 2 (Ic) 16 July 1941 (reproduced in Vogel, pp. 259–262). An airforce communication (*Merkblatt* 99) dated 26 February 1942 also followed the general policy proposals outlined at the July 1941 meeting. A copy of this *Merkblatt* can be found reproduced as document 88 in Lekebusch, pp. 371–374.

[51] Noakes, 'Nazi Policy', p. 333.

concern about appearing ungrateful towards soldiers who had fought and bled for the fatherland, even if those soldiers were *Mischlinge*, should also not simply be dismissed out of hand. Hitler's glorification of soldierly sacrifice was a central feature of his fascist value system, and on occasion his admiration for the combat soldier and his sense of what constituted soldierly honour could come into conflict with his fervently held views on the racial issue. Noakes provides a telling example of this in his description of Hitler's response following the French campaign of 1940 when he was informed that several "half-Jews" had been deco-rated for bravery (although they technically should have been expelled from the army before the campaign began) and had then submitted petitions asking to be racially regraded. According to Philipp Bouhler, the head of the Führer Chancel-lery, Hitler at that time expressed the following view:

> These people have, albeit by chance, performed meritorious service for the Greater German *Reich* and the National Socialist State. They have been publicly decorated for it. Second class treatment of these soldiers is unworthy of the National Socialist State. They must, therefore, as soon as possible be declared to be of German blood.[52]

Hitler's method of reconciling the two conflicting values – honouring the heroic conduct of the soldiers and at the same time upholding Nazi racist principles – was to declare the *Mischling* heroes to be of German blood. His decision in 1941 to allow a small number of "half-Jews" who had already demonstrated bravery in action and had been decorated, the opportunity to reapply for service in the military must be seen in this light. Those "half-Jews" who were allowed to remain in or rejoin the *Wehrmacht* were required to demonstrate their worthiness in combat. On 4 August 1941, the OKH issued the following order:

> On 2.8.41 the Führer and Supreme Commander of the Wehrmacht ordered that those Jewish Mischlinge who were permitted by him as a result of the clemency process to remain in or rejoin active military service ... be sent *immediately* to *combat units* since on the basis of the *conduct in the face of the enemy* by these Mischlinge a decision will be made after the conclusion of the war concerning their equalisation with German-blooded persons. Those eligible officers, non-commissioned officers and soldiers are, *at the earliest opportunity*, to be sent with marching battalions to the *Eastern front.*[53]

The Eastern front offered an ideal testing site where *Mischlinge* could prove their worthiness and, by virtue of their combat prowess, earn the right at the end of the war to be declared to be of German blood. This was a solution to the *Mischling* "problem" which was fully in line with fascist ideology: combat would determine who would qualify for full membership in the postwar National-Socialist *Volks-gemeinschaft*.[54] The wording of the order seems to extend this possibility to "first-degree *Mischlinge*"; they, after all, were the ones who had been required to appeal

---

[52]*ibid.*, p. 332.

[53]OKH Br. 7486/41 PA 2 (I/Ic) 4th August 1941, BA-ZNS Sammlung jüdische Mischlinge. Emphasis in original.

[54]Conduct in combat and not necessarily survival was the key to equalisation, as this comment from the OKW from September 1943 indicates: "According to the Führer's wish, Jewish *Mischlinge* of the first or second degree who have been killed in action or have been severely disabled can be declared equivalent to persons of German blood". Quoted in Noakes, 'Nazi Policy', p. 335.

to Hitler in order to remain in or re-enter the military.[55] A select and tiny group of "*Mischlinge* of the first degree" were *in theory* being offered the possibility of equalisation after the war, should they prove themselves under the horrendous conditions of combat on the Eastern front. In the context of subsequent policy towards "first-degree *Mischlinge*", however, the potential equalisation proffered in August 1941 appears as nothing more than a fleeting and hollow promise. Noakes has argued, given the tendency of policy from 1942 onwards, that extermination and not equalisation would have been the more likely postwar fate of "half-Jews".[56]

By spring 1942 Hitler's attitude towards the "first-degree *Mischlinge*" had shifted back again into a more hostile mode. At the *Wolfsschanze* on 10 May 1942, Hitler expressed his dissatisfaction with the numerous exceptions allowed by the *Wehrmacht* with regard to "half-Jews".[57] On 1 July 1942, he stated, "our people does itself damage when it allows *Mischlinge* to serve in the military and thereby opens up for them the possibilities for equalisation with those of German blood".[58] From the summer of 1942 onwards, policy towards "*Mischlinge* of the first degree" became harsher. Hitler's private secretary and head of the Party Chancellery, Martin Bormann, issued a Circular to party members in July 1942 which announced that the *Führer* wished to see "the most exacting standards" applied in the judgment of "half-Jews". Bormann sarcastically chided his party underlings for their gullibility towards "half-Jews" who made claims that they had been "party members from the earliest days of the NSDAP or [that] the true father was not the Jewish husband of their mother, but a golden-haired Aryan, etc".[59] Bormann directed that only in exceptional cases would "*Mischlinge* of the first degree" be allowed in the *Wehrmacht*. Proof of earlier membership in the Party was not sufficient; only "half-Jews" who had been Party members and had suffered severe wounds or long incarceration could be considered for military service. The *Führer*, he added, would personally judge the merits of each individual case.

On 25 September 1942 the Armed Forces High Command issued an order calling for the dismissal of all "half-Jews" still in the military.[60] Exceptions were made only for "half-Jewish" officers who had earlier been declared to be of German blood and for the roughly two 250 "half-Jews" who had up to that point been granted permission by Hitler to serve in the *Wehrmacht*. The same order also announced that no more petitions from "half-Jews" requesting to remain in or rejoin the *Wehrmacht* would be accepted and all pending petitions should be rejected.

---

[55]There is evidence that at various times Hitler endorsed the idea that "half Jews" could qualify for equalisation. The authorisation allowing first-degree *Mischling* Rüdiger von B. to remain in the army (see document 3) explicitly held open this possibility. See also the quotation cited in the previous footnote.

[56]Noakes, 'Nazi Policy', p. 354.

[57]Henry Picker (ed.), *Hitlers Tischgespräche im Führerhauptquartier*, Stuttgart 1976, p. 277.

[58]*ibid.*, p. 400.

[59]Rundschreiben Nr. 91/42, NSDAP Partei-Kanzlei, 3 July 1942, BA-ZNS, Sammlung Zeittafel

[60]Absolon, *Wehrgesetz und Wehrdienst*, p. 119.

Even after the 1942 order for the dismissal of all "first-degree *Mischlinge*" from the *Wehrmacht*, "half-Jewish" soldiers or ex-soldiers continued to petition to remain in or be reinstated in the military; and, despite Hitler's order, these petitions continued to be processed.[61] But the number of petitions which received Hitler's approval declined drastically from the levels of 1940 and 1941. As was noted above, prior to the end of June 1942 twenty-five per cent of petitions by "first-degree *Mischlinge*" had been approved; between 30 June 1942 and 30 September 1943 the approval rate plummeted to barely two per cent (30 out of 1,427).[62] In a letter from May 1943 to the father of a "first-degree *Mischling*", a Nazi party functionary replied to the father's request that his son be granted permission to serve in the military by noting that "in view of the existing provisions of the OKW there is no prospect of success for such a petition".[63] According to a lengthy memorandum prepared for the NSDAP Party Chancellery in early 1944, the processing of such petitions still continued to require a substantial amount of time. But after noting that the petition of a "half-Jew" who had been a distinguished member of the Nazi Party and had even served several years in prison as a result of his party activities had been rejected, the memorandum concluded that "it can therefore be assumed that today exceptional treatment of first-degree *Mischlinge* is simply no longer possible".[64]

Those "*Mischlinge* of the first degree" who were dismissed from military service returned to civilian life. Some were able to start or resume university study or vocational training or find jobs in industry. The presence of healthy young males of military age on the home front was often regarded with suspicion, and *Mischlinge* in some cases became targets of public criticism which labelled them as shirkers who were unfairly avoiding the sacrifices demanded of other young German men.[65] Such public discontent, as well as the unquenchable demand for labour, prompted Nazi authorities in autumn of 1944 to order all male "first-degree *Mischlinge*" to report for labour service with the Organisation Todt (OT).[66] Fritz Lichtenberg, who since his dismissal in June 1943 had completed his engineering degree in Karlsruhe and then taken a position as an engineer with I. G. Farben in Frankfurt-Hoechst, received an order to report for duty with the OT in January 1945. "Three times I was ordered to report to the OT, three times I ignored it. I was afraid and at the same time unbelievably careless".[67] Lichtenberg succeeded in avoiding service in the OT and a threatened arrest by the *Gestapo*; he remained in Frankfurt until it was occupied by the

---

[61] Noakes, 'Nazi Policy', p. 335.

[62] Figures from the Führer Chancellery in a report of 28 October 1943 cited by Noakes, 'Nazi Policy', p. 336.

[63] Letter from *Kreisgeschäftsführer* Klein dated 21 May 1943, Institut für Zeitgeschichte, MA 139, frame 305097.

[64] 'Denkschrift der Parteikanzlei über die Behandlung von Mischlingen', March 1944, in Helmut Heiber (ed.), *Akten der Partei-Kanzlei der NSDAP*, Munich 1983–1985, vol. I, 10700382-427, quotation from frame 10700419.

[65] Werner Goldberg, for example, recalls being repeatedly questioned about why he was not on the front, Stoltzfus, p. 118.

[66] Noakes, 'Nazi Policy', p. 351.

[67] Lichtenberg, in Schüddekopf, p. 121.

Americans. In contrast, Helmut and Answald Krüger, along with "a large contingent of Mischlinge of the first degree", were transported in early January 1945 to the forced labour camp of Miltitz-Roitzschen where they worked on the construction of large subterranean factories in which synthetic fuels were to be produced.[68]

As the war entered its final phase in late 1944, the Army Personnel office issued new guidelines based on an "expression of the Führer's will" which ordered the dismissal of all "half-Jewish" officers and officers married to "half-Jewish" wives, including those who had been declared "of German blood" as well as those who had otherwise received permission from the *Führer* to remain in active military service.[69] On 28 November 1944, the Armed Forces Command, in response to a request from the Security Police, ordered that any "half-Jews" still discovered to be serving in the military were to be expelled. Local authorities were to be notified in advance so that the "half-Jews" could "be picked up without delay" by the *Gestapo*.[70] This marked the culminating point of the uneven and erratic purging campaign against "first-degree *Mischlinge*" which had begun in 1940. "Second-degree *Mischlinge*" – and those few "first-degree *Mischlinge*" who had either been granted permission by Hitler to serve or who had managed somehow to conceal their racial identity or otherwise evade detection – continued to serve in the ranks of the *Wehrmacht* until the bitter end in May 1945.

Case Studies of Mischling Deserters

While the sample of eight cases surveyed below is certainly too small to be considered as representative, the cases are individually quite interesting, and they do provide insights into how the *Wehrmacht* viewed *Mischlinge* in general and how certain German military judges chose to deal with the issue of Jewish ancestry in specific cases involving *Mischling* deserters. They also offer concrete examples of many key aspects of the operation of the military justice system – court-martial procedure, the practice of retrials, the confirmation process, and the variety of forms of implementing punishment – which affected not only *Mischling* deserters but deserters in general.

Before we turn to the individual case studies, a few observations should be offered about the nature of the source materials on which they are based. The stories told below are drawn from the court-martial records of cases tried before six different courts. In some cases the files are quite extensive, in others they are only fragmentary. Most of the details about the soldiers' backgrounds and the events of their desertions are taken from the verdicts which the military judges prepared as part of the sentencing procedure. Additional information has been gleaned from interrogation records, clemency pleas, statements, memos and trial transcripts,

[68]Krüger, p. 101.
[69]Heerespersonalamt Nr. 13 640/44 g Ag P 2/3b, 26 October 1944, BA-ZNS Sammlung jüdische Mischlinge.
[70]OKW Az. 1 i 20.12 NSF W/4 (J) Ib, dated 28 November 1944, BA-ZNS Sammlung jüdische Mischlinge.

where these are still to be found in the case files. All of these sources were produced by the persecutors and therefore reflect their views and were shaped according to their objectives. As historian Günther Fahle has noted, "military court-martial files are documents of the rulers (*Herrschaftsquellen*) which provide more information about the case from the perspective of the judges linked to the National Socialist system than about the mind and motivational structure of the victim".[71]

The voices of the persecuted, when they can be heard at all, have been filtered through the police and judicial apparatus of the Third Reich. The following passage from a letter which a deserter unsuccessfully attempted to smuggle out of a military prison in 1943 offers a defendant's perspective of the intimidating atmosphere which prevailed at a court-martial and reflects the very uneven power relationship which inhibited the defendants from presenting their side of the story: "In court people don't get much of a say, above all the common soldiers have none at all. The judges are very high-ranking officers; a person is completely powerless. The only salvation is a good lawyer but they demand an enormous amount of money".[72] It is therefore often extremely difficult to discern the motives which might have been at work in the individual cases of desertion. Expressions of loyalty to the regime and support for the *Führer*, such as those voiced in Anton Mayer's clemency plea to Admiral Dönitz cited at the outset of this article, did not necessarily represent the genuine feelings of the soldiers. Faced with execution or the prospect of long prison sentences under brutal conditions, it is hardly surprising that soldiers would proclaim loyalty as part of a last-ditch attempt to save their lives or reduce their sentences. Their statements need to be read against this background and evaluated within the context of their prosecution by a military justice system which was more preoccupied with making a contribution to "maintaining military discipline" than in protecting the rights of the individual defendant. Such statements cannot simply be taken at face value. One must attempt to read between the lines, draw possible connections between disparate pieces of information, and indulge in a certain amount of speculation. But in the end even these speculations must rely largely on the materials assembled by the prosecution.

The stories below therefore must lean heavily on the narratives supplied in the courts-martial documents, especially the multi-page verdicts which lay out the facts of the case and offer the judge's reasoning for the sentence. The judge, of course, was principally concerned to provide a description of the circumstances of the case and the act of desertion which supplied a formal and legal grounding to justify his sentencing of the accused.[73] Those facts which were significant for

---

[71]Günther Fahle, 'Pfade zur Geschichte ungehorsamer Soldaten in der Ems-Jade Region. Kategorien, Quellen, Zugänge' in Fietje Ausländer (ed.) *Verräter oder Vorbilder? Deserteure und ungehorsame Soldaten im Nationalsozialismus*, Bremen 1990, p. 188.

[72]Letter from navy gunner Jakob Peters to his wife, dated 22 May 1943, in BA-ZNS RM 123-542 (6089). Peters was sentenced to death for desertion and was executed on 31 July 1943.

[73]For a discussion of some of the methodological issues involved in the use of court verdicts from the Third *Reich* see Michael Stolleis and Dieter Simon, 'Vorurteile und Werturteile der rechtshistorischen Forschung zum Nationalsozialismus' in *NS-Recht in historischer Perspektive*, edited by the

the judge's decision received mention. But those facts which did not comfortably fit into the narrative might well be left out. In reconstructing the events of a particular desertion there was a strong tendency for judges to ignore those parts of the story which might raise doubts about the guilt of the accused. Contradictory, ambivalent and potentially exonerating evidence was often set aside in favour of a streamlined, logically coherent account which supported the judge's conclusion.

The crime of desertion was considered to be the most serious military offence which could be committed by a soldier, a transgression which posed a severe threat to the discipline and combat capability of the armed forces. Hitler and the *Wehrmacht* leadership were particularly concerned to avoid a repeat of the high rate of desertions which had afflicted the German army in the last phases of the First World War.[74] The alleged laxity of the military justice system was blamed for the upsurge of desertion, and Hitler and other right-wing critics were determined to ensure that in the next war courts-martial would enforce military discipline against deserters with absolute severity. As Hitler insisted in *Mein Kampf*:

> If you want to hold weak, wavering or actually cowardly fellows to their duty, there has at all times been only one possibility: The deserter must know that his desertion brings with it the very thing he wants to escape. At the front one *may* die; as a deserter one *must* die. Only by such a Draconian threat against any attempt at desertion can a deterring effect be obtained, not only for the individual, but for the whole army.[75]

Paragraph 69 of the Military Penal Code defined desertion in the following terms: "Anyone who leaves or absents himself from his unit or post with the intention of permanently avoiding his obligation to serve in the *Wehrmacht* or of obtaining the dissolution of his employment contract will be punished for desertion".[76] The Special Wartime Military Penal Code (*Kriegssonderstrafrechtsverordnung*, hereafter KSSVO), which was completed in August 1938 and put into effect at the outbreak of the war, stipulated that desertion was to be punished with the death penalty, or with life imprisonment or a term of up to fifteen years imprisonment.[77] From the very beginning of the war German military judges proved to be very responsive to Hitler's desire that deserters be punished severely. Between the end of August 1939 and the beginning of April 1940, 275 death sentences against soldiers were confirmed (135 of those for desertion) and 228 of these sentences were executed, an execution rate of eighty-three per

---

Institut für Zeitgeschichte, Munich 1981, pp. 13–51. An abridged English translation is now available: 'Biases and Value Judgments in the Study of National Socialist Legal History', in Michael Stolleis, *The Law under the Swastika*, Chicago 1998, pp. 25–39.

[74] On German desertion in World War One see Christoph Jahr, *Gewöhnliche Soldaten. Desertion und Deserteure im deutschen und britischen Heer 1914–1918*, Göttingen 1998.

[75] Adolf Hitler, *Mein Kampf*, translated by Ralph Manheim, Boston 1943, p. 524.

[76] *Militärstrafgesetzbuch* with commentary by Erich Schwinge, 6th edition, n.p. 1944, p. 185.

[77] *Kriegssonderstrafrechtsverordnung*, revised version of paragraph 70 of the Military Penal Code, reprinted in Rudolf Absolon, *Das Wehrmachtstrafrecht im 2. Weltkrieg*, Kornelimünster 1958, p. 49.

cent.[78] Within the first six months of the war German military judges had imposed more death sentences than their predecessors had during all of the First World War, and almost five times as many German soldiers had been executed as had been between 1914 and 1918. That such a high number of death sentences was imposed during a period in which there was, following the Polish campaign, relatively little military action reinforces the impression that the military justice system was engaged in a policy of extreme harshness towards deserters.[79]

On 14 April 1940, just six days after issuing the order purging "half-Jews" from the ranks of the *Wehrmacht*, Hitler promulgated a set of specific guidelines for punishment of deserters. Since the guidelines became a central element in the *Wehrmacht* policy on punishment of deserters and were frequently cited in courts-martial verdicts against deserters, including some of the *Mischling* deserters whose cases are reviewed below, it is worthwhile to quote them in their entirety.

> I. The death penalty is required if the perpetrator acted out of fear of personal danger or if, after consideration of the special conditions of the individual case, the death penalty is imperative in order to maintain discipline. The death penalty is in general appropriate in cases of repeat or joint desertion and in cases of flight or attempted flight abroad. The same applies when the perpetrator has a considerable previous criminal record or engages in criminal activity during desertion.
> II. In all other cases of desertion it must be determined whether, in consideration of the overall circumstances, the death penalty or imprisonment is appropriate. A prison sentence will generally be considered as sufficient atonement if youthful thoughtlessness, incorrect official treatment, difficult domestic circumstances or other non-dishonourable motives were the primary determinants for the perpetrator.
> III. These principles also apply to those cases in which escape from a penal institution is regarded as desertion.[80]

The 1940 guidelines, which remained in effect throughout the rest of the war, had the effect of reinforcing the already marked tendency of military judges to impose the death penalty on deserters. Fritz Wüllner has estimated that during the Second World War approximately 40,000 German soldiers were convicted of desertion; of these, some 22,000 to 25,000 were sentenced to death and an estimated 16,000 to 18,000 of the death sentences were carried out.[81] By contrast, the British executed no deserters (the death penalty for desertion was abolished

---

[78]Figures from the Wehrmachtkriminalstatistik in BA-MA RH14/64, pp. 1, 7, and 18. If one applies the overall execution rate to the desertion cases, it would mean that 112 deserters were executed during the first six months of the war.

[79]The harshness also extended beyond the ranks of the *Wehrmacht*. The figures cited above do not include death sentences imposed by military courts on civilians. A memo dated 20 November 1939 from the OKW to Admiral Bastian, President of Germany's highest military court, the *Reichskriegsgericht* (RKG), noted that between the outbreak of the war and 18 November 1939 military courts had handed down 120 death sentences against Poles. RKG records in BA-MA RKG microfilm M1001.

[80]Guidelines of the Führer and Supreme Commander of the Armed Forces for Determining the Penalty for Desertion issued by Hitler on 14 April 1940. BA-MA RH14/22, p. 193.

[81]Fritz Wüllner, *Die NS-Militärjustiz und das Elend der Geschichtsschreibung. Ein grundlegender Forschungsbericht*, Baden-Baden 1997 (2nd edition), pp. 446 and 476.

in 1930) and the Americans only one over the course of the war.[82] As these figures indicate, the number of death sentences imposed on deserters by the German military justice system in World War Two was of a completely different magnitude from that of the military courts of the Western Allies and also presents a stark contrast with the relatively lenient and humane performance of the German military courts in World War One.[83] What Manfred Messerschmidt has described as the "total change in German law theory and practice" in the Third Reich resulted in a staggering harvest of death in the ranks of *Wehrmacht* soldiers convicted of desertion by the military courts.[84] Among those soldiers who were subjected to this harsh brand of military justice were a small group whose special characteristic was their racial status as "first-degree *Mischlinge*" and in the following their cases are presented in chronological order based on the date of sentencing.

1. Paul A.[85]

Paul A. was born in Berlin in 1913.[86] As the ancestry certificate supplied by the *Reichsstelle für Sippenforschung* (*Reich* Office for Family Research) in November 1940 indicated, Paul A. was officially considered a "Jewish *Mischling* with two racially Jewish grandparents" (refer to document 4 at the end of this article). His paternal grandmother was Jewish and had married a German who had earlier converted to Judaism. Under the Nuremberg Laws this meant that the grandfather, although "of German blood", counted as a "full Jew". According to the Nazi racial classification system Paul A. was therefore a "half-Jew".[87] As the hand-sketched genealogical chart included in his court-martial file shows, Paul A.'s own parents were both Christians, however, and he himself, although never christened or confirmed, had received Christian religious instruction and was raised in a Christian home environment (refer to document 5 at the end of this article).

   Paul A. had experienced a difficult youth and never learned any specific trade. Throughout the 1930s he was dependent on welfare support, and he proved incapable of holding a steady job. His extended periods of unemployment brought him to the attention of the authorities. He was quickly relegated to the ranks of the "work shirkers", a category included among the "asocials" con-

---

[82] Figures for Great Britain and the U.S.A. from Manfred Messerschmidt and Fritz Wüllner, *Die Wehr-machtjustiz im Dienste des Nationalsozialismus. Zerstörung einer Legende*, Baden-Baden 1987, pp. 29–30.

[83] In the First World War only eighteen German soldiers were executed for desertion; the British executed 269 deserters. See Jahr, p. 18.

[84] Manfred Messerschmidt, 'German Military Law in the Second World War', in Wilhelm Deist (ed.), *The German Military in the Age of Total War*, Leamington Spa 1985, p. 324.

[85] In accordance with privacy stipulations the surnames of those individuals whose wartime fates remain unclear are not given. The names of those who were executed are given in full.

[86] Information from the court-martial file BA-ZNS RW55/160.

[87] Paul A. was an example of a *Mischling* who was 'by blood' (*blutsmäßig*) only a "quarter-Jew", since he had three "German-blooded" grandparents; according to the provisions of the Nuremberg laws, however, he was "on paper" (*papiermäßig*) a "half-Jew". The same is true of Kurt Schinek, whose case is discussed below.

demned by the Nazis as parasites on society. From late 1937 until his military call-up in December 1939, he was consigned to a workhouse in Lichtenberg near Berlin. On at least one occasion in July 1938 he escaped from the workhouse but returned voluntarily just two days later. A district mayor of Berlin in early 1940 specifically labelled Paul A. as an "asocial".

Paul A. was ordered to appear at a collection point in Berlin near Schlesischer Bahnhof on the morning of 1 December 1939 in order to begin his military service. Although sent on his way from the workhouse at 5.30 a.m., he failed to appear at the scheduled time at the collection point. His excuse, as recorded in the court documents, was that his clothes were in such a state of disrepair that he was ashamed to appear in them in front of his comrades. His attempts to find a new set of clothes made him late. He was then beset by fear of what punishment might be in store for him. According to his testimony, a soldier had told him that anyone who reported late for his military call-up was automatically charged with desertion and immediately executed.

Paul A. wandered through Berlin for a few days, spent some nights in the men's hostel in Greifswalder Straße and finally checked into a Catholic shelter. He dutifully registered his new address with the police on 11 December. A few weeks later, on 5 January, the police used this information to locate and arrest him. One month later *Oberstabsarzt* Schmidt prepared a medical opinion in which he labelled Paul A. "a work-shy young man of limited capacity but nevertheless quite cunning" and concluded that he was of sound mind and therefore should be held fully responsible for his actions.

The main issue at the trial was whether Paul A. was guilty of desertion or had simply gone absent without leave. The prosecutor had requested a sentence of five years imprisonment for desertion. The judge, Dr. Vanselow, concluded that there was no substantial proof of Paul A.'s intention to desert.[88] The fact that he registered with the police and made no attempt to go underground was cited to support this conclusion. No genuine deserter would behave in such a fashion, the judge argued. Paul A. was convicted of the lesser charge of being absent without leave. Vanselow insisted nevertheless that a stiff penalty be called for given the length of Paul A.'s absence (five weeks) and above all in view of the obviously asocial behaviour of the defendant. Borrowing freely from the medical opinion in formulating his verdict, Vanselow stated that "the determining factor [for the jail sentence of three years] was the fact that the defendant is a work-shy but cunning young man who is a worthless member of human society. The defendant feels most comfortable when he can live at public expense or on the charity of others without having to work". Vaneslow then drew attention to Paul A.'s

---

[88]The charge of subversion (*Wehrkraftzersetzung*), which was applied to those men who refused to report for military service, was ignored by the judge who saw no evidence in Paul A.'s behaviour that he was seeking to avoid his military obligation. If a conscript failed to report and attempted to hide he was charged with desertion; if he failed to report but stayed at home where he could easily be apprehended he was charged with evading the draft which fell under the category of subversion. In the early stages of the war members of the Jehovah's Witnesses were the principal victims singled out for persecution on the charge of subversion. See Detlef Garbe, *Zwischen Widerstand und Martyrium: Die Zeugen Jehovas im Dritten Reich*, Munich 1993.

"racial inferiority as a Jewish *Mischling*", which the judge concluded "may well have contributed to this conduct". Paul A.'s *Mischling* status was thus explicitly acknowledged as a factor in the judge's sentencing deliberations.

The sentence was confirmed on 14 December 1940 with the stipulation that Paul A. be sent to an army penal camp (*Straflager*) for the purpose of "education". Following the general practice outlined in paragraph 104 of the KSSVO, the time Paul A. spent in the convict camp would not count towards serving his sentence; this would only begin after the war was over. Paul A.'s sentence was in effect for three years *plus* the duration of the war. In the terminology of the *Wehrmacht* justice system Paul A. was to be kept in "penal custody" (*Strafverwahrung*) for as long as the war lasted. In an evaluation written by his company commander in the convict camp, Paul A.'s conduct was rated as "good", his soldierly bearing as "mediocre"; his chief failings were cited as "neglect of duty" and a "non-military attitude" (*wehrunwillig*). The report concluded by specifically noting: "as half-Jew unserviceable for the troops". Paul A.'s racial status disqualified him from the dubious privilege of being sent to a probationary unit in order to "rehabilitate" himself through extraordinary bravery on the front. The commander recommended instead that he begin serving his jail sentence. Paul A.'s ultimate fate is not disclosed in the existing records; the last available information indicated that he was still alive in May 1944.

2. Heinz Schmidt

Heinz Schmidt was born in Nuremberg in 1917 as the illegitimate son of a Jewish father named Stern.[89] His Aryan mother later married, and Heinz was adopted by his stepfather. According to the Nuremberg racial classification system Heinz Schmidt was a "first-degree *Mischling*".

Schmidt attended secondary school but did not go on to learn a trade. In December 1938 he joined the army. As a civilian Schmidt had a clean record, but he evidently had great trouble adjusting to military life and quickly acquired a reputation as a problem soldier, a fact reflected in a record of eleven disciplinary punishments and one court-martial in 1940 which led to a sentence of three months in jail. In early May 1940 Heinz Schmidt was dispatched to a so-called Special Detachment (*Feldsonderabteilung*), a unit specifically designed to deal with soldiers who were considered to present disciplinary problems.[90] According to a directive issued in November 1940, "maladjusted" soldiers ("psychopaths", "troublemakers" and those considered "lazy, slack, dirty, insubordinate, refractory, anti-social, asocial, unfeeling, unstable, dishonest") were the target group for the specific brand of education which was dispensed in the Special Detach-

---

[89]BA-ZNS RW55/7224.
[90]See Hans-Peter Klausch, "'Erziehungsmänner" und "Wehrunwürdige" Die Sonder- und Bewährungseinheiten der *Wehrmacht*' in Norbert Haase and Gerhard Paul (eds.) *Die anderen Soldaten*, Frankfurt 1995, pp. 66–82; Hans-Peter Klausch, *Die Bewährungstruppe 500. Stellung und Funktion der Bewährungstruppe 500 im System von NS-Wehrrecht, NS-Militärjustiz und Wehrmachtstrafvollzug. Darstellung und Dokumentation*, Bremen 1995, pp. 19–40; Fritz Wüllner, *Die NS-Justiz*, pp. 659–667.

ments.[91] After three to six months under a harsh regimen of ten to fourteen hours of hard labour daily at eighty per cent of normal rations these problem soldiers would either be returned to regular units if their re-education was deemed successful or expelled from the military and sent to prisons or concentration camps. Hans-Peter Klausch has estimated that over the course of the war some 10,000 "maladjusted" soldiers were funnelled through the Special Detachments, with perhaps ninety per cent being returned to the regular forces.[92]

In autumn 1940 Schmidt had the bad luck to find himself in Special Detachment A stationed in occupied France. This detachment had a particularly poor reputation due to the brutality of its supervisory personnel. Upon arrival in the unit soldiers had their hair shorn, their insignia ripped from their uniforms and were forced to don prisoners' garb. Beatings and floggings with leather whips were part of the everyday disciplinary routine. One measure of how harsh the treatment must have been can be garnered from the fact that several desperate soldiers (ten over a seven-week period in 1940 according to court records) attempted to flee the unit, even though they, like all those consigned to Special Detachments, had been "given special notice that desertion and similar dishonourable offences will be punished by death".[93]

In October 1940 Heinz Schmidt was nearing the end of his six-month period of disciplinary education. He was informed that because of a run-in with one of his superiors he would not be going back to a regular unit but instead would be court-martialled and sent to the military prison in Germersheim in south-western Germany. Schmidt, along with two other soldiers who faced the same grim prospect of imprisonment in Germersheim, twenty-one year-old Günther Reinhardt and twenty-five year-old Friedrich Glöde, decided to desert. On 11 October 1940 the three escaped at night from their quarters near Laon and fled into the French countryside.

The escapees found shelter with a series of French farmers and were able to avoid recapture by the German field police. They burned their paybooks and army documents and put on civilian clothes. In December, using forged papers which identified them as Alsatians, they succeeded in travelling to Germany. A month later they returned to the area around Laon where they carried out a series of thefts from *Wehrmacht* facilities. They earned money by selling at least thirty sets of forged identification papers useful for crossing the demarcation line. After 242 days of freedom Schmidt and his companions were finally arrested on 10 June 1941.

Their case was tried before the Court of the Commander of Greater Paris, a court which seems to have been particularly harsh in its treatment of deserters. Of the 41 deserter cases for which records from this court still exist, 35 resulted in death sentences (85 per cent) and 28 of these (80 per cent) were carried out.

[91] Heeres-Sanitätsinspekteur, AZ B 49a 12 Beih. SIn/WiG (I), Nr. 1177/40, Berlin, dated 5 November 1940, quoted from Manfred Messerschmidt, *Die Wehrmacht im NS-Staat. Zeit der Indoktrination*, Hamburg 1969, p. 385.

[92] Klausch, "'Erziehungsmänner'", p. 71.

[93] Chef HRüst u. BdE 54 10 AHA/Ag/40 dated 9 January 1940, quoted from Klausch, "'Erziehungsmänner'", p. 70.

These statistics were considerably higher than those of many other stationary courts and were more on a par with death sentences passed by military courts with front-line units. On 3 October 1941 the court found all three men guilty of desertion and sentenced them to fifteen years in prison. The judge did not impose the death penalty because he found that their desertion was caused by the "undignified, disgraceful, dishonourable treatment" which they had received in Special Detachment A. In making this argument he could refer to Hitler's guidelines which specifically singled out "incorrect official treatment" as a sufficient reason for imposing a prison sentence rather than the death penalty.

This, however, was not the end of the matter. Once a military court had sentenced a defendant to death or to a prison term of more than one year the decision had to be referred to the responsible divisional commander (or in the case of a city or district, to the commander of the garrison). A senior military judge had to draft a legal opinion commenting on the case and indicating whether the sentence should be confirmed or disapproved. If the commander confirmed the sentence, it became legal and binding. If the sentence was disapproved, another court-martial had to be convened and the matter retried. The military leadership in the Third Reich, thus, had the final say in determining how deserters (and soldiers found guilty of other serious offences) would be punished. If a commander felt that a sentence was too lenient, he could refuse confirmation and explicitly indicate that the punishment should be increased. In desertion cases in which the original court-martial had imposed a prison sentence, it was not unusual for commanders to state in their disapproval decisions that they considered the death penalty to be the only appropriate punishment. Theoretically, an individual case could be retried any number of times until the commander was satisfied with the decision and gave his confirmation.[94]

In Heinz Schmidt's case the senior military judge who wrote the legal opinion for the confirmation process did not agree with the verdict and recommended to the *Gerichtsherr* (the commander with confirming authority) that the sentence be rejected and the case retried in front of another judge. He specifically noted that in this case he considered the death penalty as the only appropriate punishment. Heinz Schmidt's second trial took place on 16 December 1941, again in the Court of the Commander of Greater Paris, but with a different military judge presiding. Rejecting all of the mitigating circumstances mentioned in part II of Hitler's sentencing guidelines for deserters, judge Baecker instead focused on part I and imposed the death sentence because the defendants had carried out a joint desertion and had engaged in criminal activity during their desertion. Castigating

[94] In the more than 1600 desertion cases on which I have gathered data, there were 128 instances in which a retrial was ordered. Ninety of these deserters were retried once, thirty-three retried twice and four were retried three times before their sentences were finally confirmed. The Anton Mayer case, discussed below, is one of the rare cases which was tried four times before being resolved to the satisfaction of the military authorities. Those deserters who were subjected to a second, third or even fourth retrial faced bleak prospects. Only four soldiers came away with lesser sentences, while 108, or ninety per cent, had their sentences increased. Thirty of these had the length of their prison terms increased and seventy-eight saw their original prison terms replaced by death sentences. Forty-six of these death sentences were subsequently carried out.

Schmidt, Reinhardt and Glöde as "parasites", judge Baecker complained that they had "separated themselves from the *Volksgemeinschaft* and in a relatively short period of time degenerated into marauders and dangerous, fully unscrupulous habitual criminals". All three, in Baecker's judgement, therefore deserved death.

After the second court-martial the legal opinion called for confirmation, and the presiding judge and the two associate judges all voted against recommending clemency.[95] Schmidt's sentence was confirmed on 20 December and two days later he, Reinhardt and Glöde were executed by firing squad at Fort Mont Valérien outside Paris.

In Schmidt's case his racial status was noted by the court but seems to have exercised no discernible impact on the sentencing. Because the court-martial file contains neither the trial transcript nor any of the supporting documentation, it is impossible to tell if the fact that Schmidt was a *Mischling* played any significant role in the preparation or prosecution of his case. There is no way of knowing if Schmidt ever signed an Aryan declaration. At the time he was sent to the Special Detachment, in May 1940, "first-degree *Mischlinge*" were in theory supposed to have been expelled from the army following Hitler's purge order of the previous month.

As a "troublemaker" with a long disciplinary record who had engaged in further criminal activity during his long period of desertion, Schmidt neatly fitted the profile of the "perpetrator type" which the military jurists commonly associated with deserters. The use of the term "parasite" in the verdict made it quite clear that the judge regarded Schmidt and his co-defendants as "degenerate personalities" who represented a threat to the vaunted *Volks- und Wehrgemeinschaft*. The fact that Schmidt had escaped from a Special Detachment made it highly likely that he would receive the death penalty, regardless of the presence of any other factor including his racial background. The *Wehrmacht* leadership was fully convinced that only the most severe punishment could achieve the necessary deterrent effect on those "maladjusted" members of its special disciplinary units. That was certainly the main reason why the prison term imposed by the original court-martial was overturned. In Schmidt's case the military leadership's self-perceived need for *Abschreckung* (deterrence) took priority over the issue of *Abstammung* (ancestry).

3. Kurt Aschkenasi

Born in Vienna in 1919, Kurt Aschkenasi was the son of a chauffeur.[96] His father was a "full-Jew", his mother Aryan. Until he was ten, Aschkenasi was raised in the Jewish faith; in 1929 he was baptised a Catholic. After completing four years

---

[95]German courts-martial had three judges: a presiding judge who was a professional lawyer with the legal qualifications of a judge, and two *Beisitzer*, one normally a staff officer and the other a soldier of the same rank as the accused.

[96]Copy of the verdict found in the Military History Archive in Prague, Entscheidungen des Reichskriegsgerichts, Leitz-Ordner with verdicts from 1942, No. 155.

in a *Realschule*, Aschkenasi learned the trade of car mechanic and began his apprenticeship in 1935. That same year he was found guilty of car theft and served a six-and-a-half month sentence. In 1937 he was again convicted of the same crime and spent thirteen months in jail until his release in early March 1938. Aschkenasi then returned to his apprenticeship but on 14 June 1938, during the so-called "June action", he was taken into protective custody as part of the Nazi campaign against asocials and Jews who had previous criminal records.[97] Aschkenasi was sent first to Dachau and then to Buchenwald where, according to the court, he "was looked upon as a full-Jew". Released from the concentration camp in June 1939, Aschkenasi briefly returned to his work as a car mechanic before being drafted into the *Wehrmacht* on 30 August 1939. Shortly after joining his first unit in Mödling-Vorderbrühl he attempted suicide, in the words of the court, "because he was treated as a Jew". After his recovery Aschkenasi continued to have difficulty adjusting to military life. During the first four months of 1940 he incurred four disciplinary punishments. His conduct was described as "poor", and his commander, employing terms often associated with "Jewish" behaviour, characterised him as cunning, under-handed and insincere (*durchtriebener, unaufrichtiger und hinterhältiger Charakter*).

Granted a short leave in mid-April 1940, Aschkenasi returned home to Vienna. On the last day of his leave he discovered, hidden between two books, a notification that his father had been convicted by a military court on 5 March 1940 of giving a false declaration and of *Rassenschande*; he had been sentenced to four years in prison and dispatched to the Esterwegen military concentration camp in Emsland. Robert Aschkenasi was a First World War veteran who some months prior to the outbreak of war in September 1939 had petitioned *Wehrmacht* authorities for a special dispensation to allow him to serve again in the military despite the fact that he was a Jew. This petition was denied. But after the outbreak of the war Robert Aschkenasi was nevertheless mistakenly called up as a sergeant in the air force. In November 1939 he falsely declared that he had no Jewish ancestry. In January 1940 this deception was discovered and he was arrested and then court-martialled.

Afraid that the same fate might be in store for him, Kurt Aschkenasi decided to desert. Although he returned to his unit at the end of his leave, he left just two days later on 29 April 1940 and headed back to Vienna where he stayed with his Italian girlfriend. Together they attempted to cross the border into Italy at the beginning of May but failed and returned again to Vienna. Aschkenasi then tried to cross into Hungary alone but this also failed. Using false papers he finally succeeded in crossing into Yugoslavia in May 1940. After being interrogated by Yugoslav authorities – to whom he apparently gave false information concerning a German chemical wonder weapon which could inflict death within two seconds – he was released and allowed to work as a truck driver for several months in Uzice.

In January 1941 Aschkenasi made a failed attempt to return to Germany and in the aftermath was jailed by the Yugoslavs on suspicion of engaging in espio-

---

[97]See Wolfgang Ayass, '*Asoziale' im Nationalsozialismus*. Stuttgart 1995, pp. 147–165.

nage for Germany. He escaped from jail in mid-March and remained in hiding until he encountered invading German troops near the Romanian border on 14 April 1941. Claiming to be a non-commissioned officer named von Nemetz, he provided aid and advice to the German troops and supposedly also captured and turned over to the German field police a Serbian woman guilty of having carried out an attack on a *Wehrmacht* officer. Aschkenasi then forged some travel documents and attempted to make his way to Vienna. He was arrested by Hungarian police in Budapest while trying to sell some sheets of paper carrying the stamp of the German Consulate in Zagreb. He was handed over to the German authorities on 27 April 1941.

Aschkenasi was tried in front of the highest German military court, the *Reichskriegsgericht* (RKG), in Berlin in March 1942 on charges of desertion and treasonable communication of false information.[98] Aschkenasi did not challenge the desertion charge but denied having made treasonous statements. Since the court-martial file containing the supporting documentation and the trial transcript appear to have been destroyed in the latter stages of the war, it is impossible to know to what extent the court carried out inquiries about Aschkenasi's *Mischling* status or what role, if any, his racial status played in the prosecutor's preparation of the charges. Although the verdict clearly notes that Aschkenasi's primary motivation for desertion was his fear that he might be punished, as his father had been, because of false statements about his racial ancestry, the judges made no specific reference to Aschkenasi's *Mischling* status in the section explaining their reasons for his sentence nor did they, in contrast to the case of Paul A. discussed above, attempt to identify his racial background as a factor contributing to his crimes. The judges, however, berated Aschkenasi as being a "morally unstable and thoroughly criminally predisposed person" and insisted that he deserved no leniency. Citing the 1940 *Führer* guidelines on the punishment of deserters, the court asserted that Aschkenasi's flight abroad and criminal activity during his desertion necessitated the imposition of the death penalty. The sentence was confirmed by Admiral Bastian, the President of the RKG, on 18 April 1942, and Kurt Aschkenasi was executed less than a month later on 13 May.

4. Werner K.

Werner K. was the illegitimate son of a German mother and a Jewish father and was accordingly classified as a "half-Jew".[99] At the time of his birth in 1910 his mother was married to an Aryan husband, and according to his later account he never met his Jewish father. Werner K. was brought up by Christian foster

---

[98]On the Reichskriegsgericht see Norbert Haase, *Das Reichskriegsgericht und der Widerstand gegen die nationalsozialistische Herrschaft*, Berlin 1993; Manfred Messerschmidt, 'Zur Rechtsprechung des Reichskriegsgerichts' in Wolfram Wette (ed.), *Was damals Recht war ... NS-Militär- und Strafjustiz im Vernichtungskrieg*, Essen, 1996, pp. 14–46; Fritz Wüllner, 'Die Judikatur des Reichskriegsgerichts in der Gesamtunrechtsbilanz der Wehrmachtgerichtsbarkeit', Sonderdruck, 1994.
[99]BA-ZNS RW55/1589.

parents and only after he turned eighteen did he re-establish contact with his mother. After completing elementary school he became a painter with Siemens. When the depression hit Germany he was unemployed for several years. Sometime in 1930 he became a member of the Nazi party and the SA, and he remained in both organisations until he was expelled in 1934 because of his Jewish background.

In June 1939 he was conscripted. He participated in the invasion of Poland, the German campaigns in the West against Belgium and France, the invasion of Yugoslavia, and the opening weeks of Operation Barbarossa in Russia. In August or September 1940 he signed a declaration claiming he was Aryan. As he stated in interrogations prior to his trial, "I really wanted to remain a soldier and therefore I hid my background". Werner K. noted that his comrades had often teased him about his Jewish-sounding last name but he consistently denied that he had any Jewish ancestry. The psychological stress must have been considerable, however, and Werner K. decided at one point to confide his secret to one of his superior officers who responded with a promise to protect him. The death of this officer in Russia may well have been one of the factors which contributed to Werner K.'s growing sense of insecurity which preceded his decision to desert.

In July 1941 Werner K. contracted dysentery and was sent to hospital for treatment. During his convalescent leave in Berlin in August of that year he met a woman and became engaged. In late October or early November his fiancée became pregnant and from that point on Werner K. seems to have become increasingly concerned to arrange their marriage. Given his *Mischling* status this was a fraught enterprise, and Werner K. ran the very real risk that by applying for a marriage certificate his racial status would become known and he would be expelled from the army and court-martialled for the false Aryan declaration he had signed in 1940. While mulling over these considerations, he was reassigned to his unit on the Eastern Front during the harsh and desperate winter of 1941–1942. In February 1942 two of his closest comrades were wounded, one mortally, and, according to his later testimony, as a result of these traumatic events he "thought a lot about the whole thing and wondered what might happen later if I were also wounded". Coupled with these concerns were his continuing worries about his fiancée as well as his fears that he "would later be treated as a second-class person" because of his Jewish ancestry. All of these concerns probably contributed to his decision to desert his unit on 22 February 1942 and to attempt to return to his fiancée in Berlin. In a statement made two months later, on the day he was arrested, Werner K. stated he deserted "since in my opinion I didn't need to be a soldier since my father M. was a Jew. I was expelled from the Party about six years ago for that reason. I've enjoyed being a soldier up to now but having thought a lot about my future prospects in the light of my background, I decided to leave my unit". Werner K. travelled via Riga and Königsberg back to Berlin, arriving about one month after having left his unit. Upon his arrival in Berlin he purchased a military decoration (*Panzersturmabzeichen*) and wore it on his uniform even though he was not entitled to do so. He stayed with his fiancée until he was arrested in a local tavern on 22 April.

Werner K. was tried before the largest stationary military court in Germany, the Court of the Berlin *Kommandatur*, on 6 July 1942.[100] The prosecutor in the case, military judge Dr. Schulz, asked that K. be given four years in prison for desertion, unauthorised wearing of insignia and giving a false declaration. In a verdict which was not distinguished by its logic, judge Grimsinski rejected Werner K.'s explanation that he had falsely claimed Aryan ancestry because he wanted to remain a soldier. The desire to remain a soldier qualified as an ethical motive, according to the judge; yet Werner K. had deserted from the front lines in February 1942 at a time of intensely cold temperatures. This, the judge reasoned, revealed that Werner K. really did not want to remain a soldier. Invoking the racial stereotype of the deceptive Jew, Grimsinski went on to argue that "this deliberate pretence of noble motives in order to attain egoistic advantage in the well-known manner of Jewish business practices calls for a harsher sentence". The judge also noted that the defendant's "insolent conduct" during the trial as well as his previous criminal record necessitated imposing a more severe punishment. Yet in spite of his obvious disdain for the *Mischling* defendant, Grimsinski in the end sentenced Werner K. to only four years in prison for desertion plus an additional nine months on the other two charges. Werner K. was in many respects very fortunate to have received what was in effect a relatively light sentence. The average prison sentence handed down by the Berlin court for desertion was just over nine years, and nearly fifty per cent of the soldiers court-martialled there for desertion received the death penalty.[101]

On 25 July 1942 Werner K.'s sentence was confirmed. While in the military jail in Berlin-Tegel awaiting transfer to the Emsland concentration camp, Werner K. wrote a clemency plea in which he asked for the opportunity to redeem himself through service in a probationary battalion on the front. He cited his previous membership in the party and the SA and his participation in the military campaigns on both the Eastern and Western fronts. The reason he had hidden his *Mischling* status, he claimed, was so that he could continue to serve Germany and the *Führer*. He made a clear attempt to distance himself from his Jewish background: "My mother, who is a pure Aryan, was seduced as a young girl by a Jew who pretended to be a Dane. I was born from this unholy relationship. Following this shameful act the Jew abandoned my mother and the child he had produced . . . Since I do not in the least look like a Jew or have any Jewish characteristics, I request that I be granted clemency". Werner K.'s plea was rejected and he was sent to Aschendorfermoor camp in Emsland on 27 August 1942. The following year he was part of a contingent of convicted ex-soldiers who were dispatched from Emsland to work in Norway. In January

[100]See Norbert Haase, *Fahnenflucht in der Deutschen Wehrmacht 1939–1945. Eine historische Untersuchung unter besonderer Berücksichtigung der vom Gericht der Wehrmachtkommandantur Berlin ausgesprochenen Todesurteile.* Magisterarbeit am Fachbereich 1 der Technischen Universität Berlin, Berlin 1986, esp. pp. 100–102 (copy in BA-ZNS); and Wüllner, *Die NS-Militärjustiz*, p. 111.

[101]The statistics are based on 319 cases. They include all of the existing wartime desertion court-martial records of the *Wehrmachtkommandantur* Berlin in the BA-ZNS (286) plus information on an additional 33 cases found in other files in the BA-ZNS, in the BA-MA Freiburg and in the records of the Deutsche Dienststelle, Berlin.

1945 Werner K. filed a renewed request to be allowed to serve on the front. His request was again denied and his *Mischling* status was explicitly cited as the reason for his rejection. Werner K. survived the war.

5. *Kurt Schinek*

As in the cases of Werner K. and Günther M. (below), the desertion of Kurt Schinek involved difficulties related to his frustrated attempts as a *Mischling* to obtain permission to marry.[102] Schinek's paternal grandfather was Jewish and his grandmother an Aryan who had converted to Judaism. His father was therefore "by blood" a "half-Jew", but since he practised the Jewish faith he was considered to be a "full-Jew" in terms of the Nazi race laws. Kurt Schinek's official status was that of a "first-degree *Mischling*", although, as he and his fiancée were at pains to insist in their interrogations, "by blood" he was a "*Mischling* of the second degree".[103]

Born in Hamburg in 1918, Schinek was baptised as a Protestant, and after his parents separated in 1925 he was raised by his mother, who earned her living as a cleaning lady. After attending elementary school Schinek spent three years at the *Höhere Handelsschule* in Hamburg but left before he had gained a finishing certificate. During these three years, from 1930 to 1933, Schinek was an active member of the Hitler Youth and enthusiastically supported the party by distributing election fliers and by hanging posters around Hamburg. According to Schinek he voluntarily left the Hitler Youth in 1933 because too many former Communists were joining its ranks. In 1935 he began working on ships, first as a page and later as a steward with the HAPAG shipping firm. In 1938 he fathered an illegitimate child. The following year he fulfilled his labour service obligation and then went to work in an armaments factory in Hamburg. In January 1940 he was conscripted for military service in the navy. Schinek attempted to marry the mother of his illegitimate child a week before his induction day, but permission to marry her was denied. The registrar informed him that as the son of a Jew he could not marry an Aryan without special permission. Schinek's mother urged him not to lodge an application because this would endanger his father who had not registered himself with the authorities as a Jew. Schinek acquiesced in his mother's request and broke off his relationship with his fiancée.

Schinek was inducted into the navy on 14 January 1940 and served with various naval artillery units in Germany and Denmark. There is no indication that he was ever ordered to sign the required Aryan declaration and he made no mention of any concern about or even knowledge of Hitler's order of April 1940 calling for the dismissal of all "first-degree *Mischlinge*". Schinek's superiors rated his military skills as "adequate" and his conduct as "good" to "very good" and

---

[102]BA-ZNS SCH 1837 and Strafakten der StA b.d. LG Hamburg 11/ Js P 933/42 (Rep. Nr. 4231/ 1943)

[103]Schinek's classification as a "*Mischling* of the first degree" provides an example of one of the anomalies resulting from the use of religion to define who was considered a full Jew. On this point see Noakes, 'Nazi Policy', pp. 314–315.

praised his efforts to carry out his orders to the best of his ability. He did however suffer two disciplinary punishments for guard duty infractions and was sentenced in March 1940 to fourteen days close arrest for being absent without leave.

In late 1940 Schinek fell in love with Thea L., then a nineteen-year-old girl who worked as a shorthand typist in Hamburg. Schinek wanted to marry Thea L. but was convinced that, as in 1940, he would be denied permission because of his *Mischling* status.[104] He also hesitated to apply to the authorities for permission since, in his words, "I thought that I would endanger my father if my ancestry were carefully scrutinised. I wanted to avoid this under all circumstances". Following the heavy British bombing raids against Hamburg at the end of July 1942, Schinek received permission to call his mother in order to find out if his parents had survived the firestorm unleashed by "Operation Gomorrah". Although his mother told him that both she and her father were fine, Schinek falsely informed his commander that his father had been badly injured and he then requested leave to go to Hamburg.[105]

Schinek was granted leave from first to fifth August, and he spent this time in Hamburg with Thea L. On 4 August he sent a telegram to his unit requesting an additional two days leave. Two days later he forged and sent a telegram with the signature "Dr. Crone" which falsely stated that his father had died and that he needed additional leave in order to attend the funeral. On 10 August he sent a third telegram, this time claiming to be a lawyer named "Bügel", in which he requested two more days in order to settle the matter of his father's will. Before receiving a response to this last telegram, Schinek and his fiancée, who had withdrawn 500 RM from her savings account, had left Hamburg and travelled to Flensburg. Their intention was to cross the border into Denmark, where they evidently believed they would be free to marry and settle down. After spending two nights in Flensburg, however, they returned to Hamburg where they stayed for two nights in a hotel. On 15 August the two of them boarded a midnight train for Freiburg and along the way Thea L. purchased tickets from Freiburg to Weil, a station near the Swiss border. They planned to cross into Switzerland, get married and seek work. At the train station in Weil both were arrested when Schinek was caught trying to evade a checkpoint manned by SS personnel.

Schinek's court-martial took place in Copenhagen on 2 October 1942 before the Court of the Navy Commander of Denmark. At the trial he confessed to

---

[104]Schinek's sense that his chances to gain permission to marry his Aryan fiancée were negligible was quite correct. Although paragraph 16 of the First Supplementary Decree of the Law for the Protection of German Blood and German Honour of 14 November 1935 allowed "*Mischlinge* of the first degree" to apply for exemptions from the marriage restrictions stipulated in the Decree, in practice such exemptions were almost never granted. Lösener notes that of the many thousands of applications lodged between 1935 and 3 March 1942 (after which applications were no longer accepted) only about a dozen were approved, an outcome which Lösener correctly termed 'a pathetic [rate of] success'; Lösener, p. 285. For a description of the application procedures see Noakes, 'Nazi Policy', pp. 315–18.

[105]This is the version of the story from Schinek's court-martial. In the later trial of Thea L. on charges of aiding an act of desertion, the court argued that Thea L., as part of a prearranged plan to swindle leave for her fiancé, had sent a telegram to Schinek telling him that his father had been badly injured in the bombing.

having forged the telegrams and also admitted that in Flensburg he had decided
to desert the *Wehrmacht* and flee to Switzerland since that appeared to be the only
way he could arrange to marry his fiancée. The presiding judge, von Tabouillot,
sentenced Schinek to death for desertion, noting that the *Führer*'s guidelines
called for death in cases where the soldier attempted to flee abroad (refer to
document 6 at the end of this section). The judge chastised Schinek for allowing
"personal considerations" to take precedence over his military oath of loyalty
and commented that permission for him to marry Thea L. would "undoubtedly
have been granted since his father was a veteran of the world war".[106] He dismissed Schinek's concerns about endangering his father and asserted that
through his conduct Schinek had failed to honour his obligations to the community and had in fact given support to his father's criminal activity (failing to
register and to wear the yellow Star of David). In addition to the death sentence
the judge, for good measure, also imposed a jail sentence of three years for falsifying documents and for subversion (attaining leave by lying to his superior officer
constituted an act of subversion or *Wehrkraftzersetzung*).

Kurt Schinek's sentence was confirmed on 15 October 1942. Pleas for
clemency by his fiancée and his mother were ignored by the Naval Commander
in Denmark, and on 23 October Schinek was executed by firing squad in
Hansted, Denmark.

Thea L. was tried before a civil court in Hamburg on 8 March 1943 on the
charge of aiding an act of desertion. By that time nearly seven months had
passed since her arrest, and it had been over four months since her fiancé had
been executed. She had in the meantime become engaged to another man
whom she was to marry two days before her trial commenced. Given these circumstances it is perhaps not surprising that she sought to distance herself from
Schinek and minimise her own role in the affair. She argued that she had been
under Schinek's influence, and she sought to portray their relationship in
slightly different terms than she had at the time of her arrest. For example, in
her initial interrogation by the *Gestapo* in August 1942 she had stated that she
had first learned of Schinek's racial status during his leave in the first week of
August and that this knowledge made no difference to her and did not alter her
decision to marry him. In her pre-trial interrogation in January 1943, however,
the knowledge of Schinek's *Mischling* status was evaluated somewhat differently:
"my fiancé first told me during this leave that he was a *Mischling*. If I had known
this before, we probably would not have become engaged". Thea L.'s mother
also claimed not to have known that Schinek was a "first-degree *Mischling*" and
stated that she would not have agreed to the engagement if she had known.

District Court Judge Bayer found Thea L. guilty of having provided material
support to Schinek by giving him 500 RM from her savings which enabled him to
pay for their trips to Flensburg and to Weil. But he also faulted her for providing
psychological support to Schinek by travelling with him and by failing to urge
him to fulfil his soldierly duty and return to his unit. "As a German woman she

---

[106]Given the extraordinarily low number of marriage permissions actually granted between 1935 and
1942 (see note 104) the judge's claim was extremely dubious.

had to know the duties of a soldier just as well as Schinek himself." The court concluded that the defendant bore "a considerable share of the guilt for the death of Schinek". Thea L. was sentenced to one year in jail.

6. Kurt M. and Ivan L.

In July 1943, three weeks prior to his eighteenth birthday, Kurt M. was conscripted by the *Wehrmacht*.[107] Born in Nuremberg, he was raised as a Protestant by his mother Cornelia, a baptised "full-Jew" who had been born in Budapest in 1890 and moved to Nuremberg in 1924, where she married Kurt M.'s father, an Aryan who ran a photographic shop. Kurt M. was accordingly a "half-Jew", but he was ignorant of his racial status until the information surfaced following his conviction for desertion in late 1943.

On 12 September 1943 Kurt M.'s unit was on its way to deployment in Serbia when the train stopped near Agram in Croatia. Kurt M. left the train, claiming that he was not feeling well, and stayed with his aunt in Agram. He reported to the German military authorities for the next few days and was repeatedly told to rejoin his unit. But Kurt M. remained in Agram with his relatives. After telling his Croatian cousin, Ivan L., about his fears of being punished for his absence, his cousin advised Kurt M. to stay with him. Ivan L. provided Kurt M. with a set of civilian clothes, burned his uniform and army paybook, secured some false identification papers and found him a job as an apprentice in Agram where he worked for several weeks. Kurt M. was arrested by three SS troops on 12 November 1943, after having been absent without leave for 55 days.

At his first interrogation Kurt M. lied and claimed to be a Croatian named Anton Kuletin. In the second round of questioning he admitted that he was not Kuletin but continued to hide his true identity. Only after his cousin Ivan L., who had been arrested on a charge of aiding an act of desertion, revealed M.'s true identity did Kurt M. acknowledge his previous lies and confess the facts concerning his absence.

Kurt M. and Ivan L. were tried together before the court of the Field *Kommandatur* 725 on 21 December 1943. The prosecutor called for the death penalty for Kurt M. and a prison term of ten years for his cousin. Kurt M. denied that he had intended to desert. Ivan L. argued that he had simply tried to help his "lost" younger cousin as best he could. He recognised that he had made a mistake by hiding Kurt M. but he had felt unable to turn him in to authorities once he learned that a death sentence for desertion was the likely penalty. Basing his judgment on Hitler's 1940 guidelines, military judge Dr. Frind refused to accept the notion of "youthful thoughtlessness" as a mitigating element and argued instead that Kurt M. had acted out of fear of personal danger. The court sentenced Kurt M. to death and Ivan L. to eight years in prison.

The cousins' racial status was not known to the court and therefore was not an issue at the trial. The sentences against the two defendants were confirmed on 21 December, with Ivan L.'s sentence being reduced by the *Gerichtsherr* from eight

[107]BA-ZNS Feldkommandantur 725/44.

years in prison (*Zuchthaus*) to four years in jail (*Gefängnis*). Eight days later the *Sicherheitsdienst* (hereafter SD) office in Agram notified the military authorities that a confidential agent there had informed them that Ivan L. was of Jewish origin.

Acting on this new information so generously supplied by the SD, the military justice section of the OKH instructed the court of the Field *Kommandatur* 725 "to interrogate the convicted individual [Kurt M.] about whether he is a half-Jew. Should this be the case, a new statement is to be obtained from the *Gerichtsherr* and the file is to be forwarded to the *Oberstkriegsgerichtsrat* with the Military Commander Southeast, who will be requested to obtain a new statement from the Military Commander". The clear implication was that if Kurt M. was a "first-degree *Mischling*" this was a factor which needed to be taken into account in the statements prepared for the clemency procedure which would determine whether the death sentence would be executed, suspended or possibly changed to a lesser punishment. A definite determination of Kurt M.'s racial status was not made until mid-March 1944 after the SD had carried out an investigation in Agram, and both Kurt M. and Ivan L. had been questioned about the racial backgrounds of their respective mothers. The SD report, drawing on records from the police files as well as the marriage register of the church of St. Peter in Agram, concluded that both Kurt M. and Ivan L. were "first-degree *Mischlinge*" (refer to document 7 at the end of this article). When questioned in February 1944, Kurt M. responded that he had no idea at all that his mother and her three siblings were Jewish. He could not explain how it had been possible for him to provide an Aryan certificate which years before had allowed him to remain in the Hitler Youth. There is no indication whether he ever signed an Aryan declaration when he joined the army. Ivan L. confirmed that his mother and Kurt M.'s mother were sisters but refused to provide any further information.

The *Gerichtsherr*, Generalmajor Hotzy, then submitted the following statement on the case:

> In my opinion both convicted men – M. and L. – deserve the harshest punishment. The convicted L., whose half-Jewish ancestry was not known at the time, has however had his sentence mitigated to a mild punishment of four years in jail. In his crafty way he managed to keep quiet about his ancestry, which was undoubtedly known to him, and to obtain references attesting to a pro-German attitude [L. had been a Humboldt fellow in Berlin in 1935–1936 and spoke fluent German]. But as long as the lenient punishment against him retains its legality, it is my opinion that a pardon of the convicted M. cannot be denied. L. is the principal who most energetically pressed for and encouraged the desertion of the younger and much less perceptive M. As he himself stated, he 'in a certain sense terrorised' M. 'in all of his actions from the outset' ... In these circumstances I consider the mitigation of the sentence of the convicted M. to a prison term, despite his half-Jewish ancestry, as of necessity appropriate. Execution of the sentence in a convict detachment ... cannot be considered since as a half-Jew M. is forbidden to remain in the *Wehrmacht*.[108]

---

[108]*ibid., Stellungnahme*, dated 5 April 1944.

Hotzy's argument that, given the relatively lenient treatment accorded to L., Kurt M.'s death sentence would have to be mitigated, was accepted by the military justice section of the OKH. On 17 June 1944 Kurt M.'s death sentence was changed to a twelve-year prison term, and in October he was sent to Börgermoor, one of the concentration camps in Emsland. Kurt M. survived the war.

The military justice section in the OKH, however, dealt more harshly with the civilian *Mischling* Ivan L., who had initially been sent to Graz in February 1944 to begin serving his sentence. On 12 July 1944 the OKH justice section notified the Military Commander Southeast that "the sentence against L. has been annulled because the penalty imposed on him is indefensibly lenient. L. is – as has subsequently become known – a half-Jew. His conduct deserves death. In view of the ordered transfer to the SD a new trial and sentencing can be dispensed with. The SD should be notified at the time of the transfer about the facts of the case". Rather than waste time and resources on another court-martial in order to achieve the outcome it desired, the OKH simply relied on the SD to do the job in its own fashion. Ivan L.'s transfer to the SD on 7 September 1944 was therefore tantamount to a death sentence.

The case of Kurt M. and Ivan L. is instructive because it demonstrates that racial policy considerations could intrude into the operation of the military justice system even after the completion of the formal court-martial procedure. When the *Mischling* status of the two convicted individuals emerged it was regarded as significant enough to require a re-evaluation of the sentences which had been imposed. In Kurt M.'s case, his *Mischling* status, as Hotzy's statement indicates, seemed to offer a further reason to apply the death penalty. Yet some rather formalistic legal considerations ultimately worked in his favour – "despite" his "half-Jewish" ancestry. Ivan L., perhaps because he was a Croatian civilian rather than a (former) German soldier like Kurt M., was not so fortunate, and the military justice authorities showed little hesitation in over-turning his supposedly legally binding sentence in order to hand him over to the SD.

7. Anton Mayer

Anton Mayer, whose clemency plea to Admiral Dönitz was quoted at the beginning of this article, should never have been in the *Wehrmacht*.[109] At the time of his call-up (via the German embassy in Budapest) in January 1942, "half-Jews" were barred from serving in the military. Born in Budapest in 1911, Mayer was the son of an Austrian father and a Jewish Hungarian mother. Rather than reveal that he was a "half-Jew", however, and thus endanger himself and his parents, Mayer told officials at the German embassy that he was of Aryan descent. In

[109]BA-ZNS RM123-35944. Mayer's case is also briefly referred to by Manfred Messerschmidt, 'Deutsche Militärgerichtsbarkeit im Zweiten Weltkrieg' in Adalbert Podlech, Helmut Simon, and Hans-Jochen Vogel (eds.), *Die Freiheit des Anderen. Festschrift für Martin Hirsch*, Baden-Baden 1981, pp. 131–132.

breach of procedure, he was never asked by the military authorities to fill out the standard Aryan declaration required of all soldiers.

Mayer served during 1942 as an army interpreter in France. His unit commander praised his intelligence but noted that "as a soldier [he is] too soft" and that his attitude towards the Third *Reich* was less than enthusiastic. He had no previous criminal record in civilian life and had had only one minor brush with the military discipline system when he received three days confinement to quarters for lying about the whereabouts of his boots.

On home leave in Bucharest with his parents in December 1942, Mayer became ill and did not depart on time for his return to France. After overstaying his leave by three weeks he finally boarded a train headed for France via Vienna on 12 January 1943. He disembarked, however, in Budapest and visited his fiancée and various friends and relatives. He stayed in Budapest and passed himself off as a German interpreter stationed in the harbour. Five months later, on 22 June 1943, he was arrested on a city street by a military police patrol. Mayer attempted to run away but was quickly recaptured. Two days later he suffered serious injuries when he jumped out of a fourth floor window of the military jail in an attempt to escape by way of the roof of a neighbouring house. His interrogation and trial were pushed back while he recovered from his injuries.

At the time of his arrest, Anton Mayer admitted that he was a *Mischling*, and so from the outset of his court-martial the racial issue became a central factor in the deliberations. The military court contacted the German authorities in Romania and requested a copy of his mother's birth certificate in order to verify that she was in fact a "full Jew". The court also discovered that there was no Aryan declaration from Mayer on file with the military authorities in Budapest or with his unit. This saved him from a possible additional charge of having made a false declaration.

In his pre-trial interrogations Mayer claimed that once he had overstayed his leave he had not returned to his unit out of fear of the punishment he was bound to incur. "I didn't really give any further thought to my future fate, in particular to the issue of rejoining the army." In response to the question whether he had intended to desert, Mayer said he could give no satisfactory answer and went on to comment: "Two thoughts continually went through my head: one, that I should permanently escape from military service; the other, that I should turn myself in. Both thoughts constantly struggled within me without either winning the upper hand." Throughout all of the subsequent court-martial proceedings Mayer never admitted any intention to desert. He argued at one point that he feared being punished more severely for his absence without leave because he was a "half-Jew" and therefore did not dare to return to his unit. But at the time of his desertion the German military authorities had no knowledge of his racial background. This became known to them only after Mayer himself revealed it to them following his arrest.[110]

---

[110]Mayer explained that he had revealed his "half-Jewish" background because he believed it might help to exonerate him. Perhaps he was hoping that if his background were known the military would simply dismiss him rather than court-martial him for desertion.

Mayer's fear of punishment once he had overstayed his leave was quite understandable and justified given the harsh punishments which were commonly meted out for desertion and for being absent without leave. Just why he overstayed his leave in December, however, remains unclear. Mayer admitted in court that his illness at the end of December had not been so severe that he could not have returned on time to his unit, and he had failed to consult either a military or a civilian doctor. One is left to speculate that he decided at some point in December or even January – perhaps as a result of conversations with his parents or friends, or after seeing his fiancée in early January – not to return to his unit. Perhaps his failure to leave Bucharest on time was due simply to his desire to see his fiancée in Budapest since he had missed seeing her when he travelled through that city on his way home in December. Or perhaps he had already decided weeks or months before that he would use his leave as an opportunity to turn his back on the navy. Or perhaps, as his comments in his interrogations seem to hint, he never really "decided" to desert at all, but let himself be driven along by events, partially paralysed by a mixture of indecisiveness and fear. The available records do not permit any resolution of this issue.

From the perspective of the military justice system, Mayer's motives were in any event only of secondary importance. The primary concern was to determine not *why* but *whether* he had deserted, that is, whether he had sought to separate himself permanently from the navy. What his precise motivation might have been was a matter that did not demand definitive clarification. Mayer's defence counsel at his first two trials in Vienna, Dr. Karl Postl, advanced a clever defence, arguing that since Mayer was a "half-Jew" and was therefore not allowed to serve in the military, he could not fulfil the subjective condition of intending to withdraw permanently from military service. Since he could at any time, simply by pointing out his racial status, immediately effect his release from military service, why would he take the much more dangerous method of desertion? Postl called on the court to regard his client's actions as a case of the less serious offence of absence without leave. Postl's approach unfortunately was undermined by Mayer himself, who stated quite explicitly at both his first and second trials that he was unaware that he would have been dismissed from the military if his racial status was known.

The military judges who dealt with Mayer's case found little difficulty in deciding that he was guilty of desertion. They were persuaded by the length of his absence (over five months) and by his failure to contact any military office during that time that he had indeed deserted. The fact that he had continued to wear his military uniform in Budapest was interpreted not as an indication of his intention to return at some point to military service, but rather as a clever tactic to protect him from police scrutiny and enable him to make social contacts which would aid him in prolonging his desertion.

Anton Mayer's court-martial was, nevertheless, no simple matter. His status as a "first-degree *Mischling*" proved to be a serious complicating factor when it came to determining the appropriate punishment. During 1944 he was, in fact, subjected to four court-martial proceedings on the charge of desertion. Multiple trials proved necessary because the naval Commander refused after each of the first three trials to confirm the prison sentences which had been handed down, insisting that the death penalty was required.

In each of the first three trials Mayer's status as a *Mischling* ironically worked to his advantage. At his first trial in Vienna in January 1944, the judge argued that "since he is a Jewish *Mischling*, first degree, this does not qualify as a crime worthy of death. If the actual situation had been known, the defendant would not have become a soldier". Mayer was therefore sentenced to ten years in prison. In the confirmation process this reasoning was sharply attacked in the legal opinion supplied by the military judge attached to the Commander of Naval Operations West: "the fact that the defendant is a Jewish *Mischling*, first degree, is in no way sufficient to justify a more lenient judgment". Very much in line with prevailing practice, he argued that death was the only appropriate penalty. The Commander endorsed this view and called for a second trial in Vienna.

In the second trial in March 1944 the military prosecutor, taking his cue from the obvious wishes of his superiors, called for the death penalty. The judge, however, suggested that part of the blame fell on the military officials who failed to secure an Aryan declaration from Mayer as they were required to do. He argued that since "half-Jews" had been dismissed from the military by Hitler's order in 1940, this case of desertion was different from other desertion cases. A sentence of fifteen years in prison was deemed appropriate. Admiral Warzecha of the Naval High Command, however, refused confirmation and ordered a new trial in Berlin.

In the third trial held in June 1944, the judge adopted the same line of reasoning that had been presented at the first trial: "Although the weight of the defendant's guilt makes the death penalty appear appropriate, the court could not decide to apply it since the defendant would not have been used in military service if his *Mischling* status had been known to the military office responsible for his induction." The legal section of Naval Supreme Command found this argument no more convincing now than it had in January. It again rejected the verdict, insisting that "it cannot be permitted that [the defendant] is given preferential treatment compared with soldiers of German blood on the grounds that he is a *Mischling*". In order to avoid such an "unsatisfactory outcome" Mayer was ordered to stand trial yet again.

We have no evidence to indicate just how this continuous series of courts-martial affected Anton Mayer, but it seems safe to assume that the psychological stress must have been most severe. After his first three sentences were rejected as too lenient (although fifteen years imprisonment was, in practice, the maximum prison sentence imposed for desertion), he must have sensed that his chances for survival were very slim indeed. Brought before a court-martial for the fourth time on 20 July 1944, the day of the failed assassination attempt on Hitler, Mayer was finally sentenced to death. The judge now dutifully echoed the line of his military superiors: "to give him preferential treatment because he is a *Mischling* would be an injustice to soldiers of German blood". At last, the naval leadership had achieved its goal of having Mayer's desertion punished with death. In doing so it had also defended the "principle" that *Mischling* status could not be invoked as a way for "half-Jewish" deserters to gain "preferential treatment" over

Aryan deserters. On 5 August the death sentence was confirmed and sixteen days later, at 10.56 a.m. (the exact time meticulously noted by the court clerk) on 23 August 1944, Anton Mayer was beheaded. His father in Bucharest was notified four days after the execution (refer to document 8 at the end of this article). The terse note contained the standard reminder that since his son's death had been dishonourable "the placing of death notices or obituaries in newspapers, magazines, etc. is forbidden".

8. Günther M.

Born in 1910 in Upper Silesia, Günther M. was the illegitimate son of a Jewish banker from Breslau and a German bookkeeper and was therefore a "first-degree *Mischling*".[111] A baptised Catholic and raised exclusively by his mother, he grew up completely ignorant of his paternal ancestry. After elementary school Günther M. trained as a dental technician but soon abandoned this occupation and became a business clerk. After moving to Berlin he opened his own grocery store in 1931 in a northern suburb which was described in the court verdict as "a communist-infected area". Günther M. soon found himself embroiled in political confrontations with his "red" neighbours thanks to his active championing of nationalistic and right-wing politics. At the age of seventeen he had joined the *Jungstahlhelm* and he actively participated in its various marches and rallies. He also served as a contact man between the *Stahlhelm* and the SA, a role which caused the local communists to brand him a "Nazi dog". Günther M.'s activities included street battles with his political enemies and as a result of one of his more violent scuffles with Red Front fighters he had a severely scarred chin. When the *Stahlhelm* merged with the NSDAP Günther M. was not accepted into the party because he failed to supply the necessary Aryan certificate. His mother succeeded, in the words of the court verdict, in "shrouding his ancestry in a veil of mystery" and Günther M. was not to discover the truth about his father until 1942.

Günther M. volunteered for the army and was called up at the end of April 1940. He participated in the campaigns in France and Russia, was promoted to corporal in October 1942, and was decorated with the *Ostmedaille* in August of that year. In November 1942 he received leave in order to return to Berlin to marry his pregnant fiancée. It was in the process of assembling the necessary documentation for his marriage that Günther M. finally found out from his mother his true background. According to M., the shock was profound; his *Mischling* status destroyed his marriage plans – his fiancée immediately ended their relationship – and undermined his future in the *Wehrmacht*. Günther M. decided not to return to his unit because he was afraid he would lose face with his comrades "with whom he had been in agreement in rejecting Jewry".

In his desperation Günther M. sought help from an acquaintance who referred him to a man who claimed to have connections with the German Army High

[111]BA-ZNS RW55/3843.

Command. For 1500 *Reichsmark* this man promised to arrange to obtain clemency for Günther M. from the *Führer*. Günther M. paid the money but it soon became clear that he had been the victim of fraud and extortion and that no clemency from the Führer was going to be forthcoming. Even if such a clemency plea had been lodged, as the statistics cited earlier in this article make clear, by 1943 only a minuscule two per cent of petitions to the *Führer* by "first-degree *Mischlinge*" were being approved; so in any case Günther M.'s chances of salvaging his army career were extremely slim.

. By now, Günther M. had long since overstayed his leave and he was being hunted by the police as a deserter. But he succeeded in evading arrest for almost twenty-one months. He stayed with his mother or in the flat of another family friend for the first eleven months. Then he moved in with his new fiancée, a divorced woman who was soon expecting a child from him, and he managed to remain undetected for an additional ten months. On 23 September 1944 he was finally found by accident and arrested during a routine police inspection in the apartment building of his fiancée.

Given the length of Günther M.'s desertion one might well have expected him to receive the death penalty as punishment. But in the trial before the Court of the *Kommandatur* Berlin in late November 1944, *Oberstabsrichter* Dr. Werner Friedrich Arnold found that M.'s earlier commitment to the "national movement" in the final years of the Weimar Republic, the fact that he had no previous criminal record, that he had volunteered for military service and had a strong military record including promotion and decoration all spoke against against the imposition of the death sentence. The judge even put a fairly positive interpretation on the link between M.'s racial status and his desertion: "the court is of the view that for the defendant the special circumstances of his ancestry rather than any dishonourable motives principally determined his decision to desert". Günther M.'s "soldierly attitude" counted for more in the eyes of the court than his racial background. He was given a prison sentence of eight years for desertion plus an additional six months on charges of falsifying documents and unauthorised wearing of an insignia.

Military judge Rieder in his legal opinion prepared for the *Gerichtsherr* noted that M.'s nearly two-year desertion really called for the death penalty. But he immediately added that "since the defendant, as a half-Jew, should have been expelled from military service anyway, I consider the penalty imposed to be defensible". He suggested that Günther M. be sent to a concentration camp. In Günther M.'s case, then, his *Mischling* status appears to have ironically worked to his advantage. As Rieder's remarks make clear, it provided a sufficient reason to justify a prison sentence rather than the death penalty and thus obviated the need for a retrial. Here the contrast to the reasoning applied in the case of Anton Mayer is glaringly apparent. In Mayer's case the naval leadership was clearly intent on imposing the death penalty and would not countenance the use of his *Mischling* status as a way of avoiding that outcome. In Günther M.'s case his racial status was advanced as a reason why the death penalty, though considered appropriate, was in fact unnecessary.

But racial status did have an impact on the execution of Günther M.'s punishment. With his love of the military life and his nationalistic dedication to the cause of the Reich, Günther M. would have liked nothing better than to return to combat on the front. But as a "first-degree *Mischling*" in late 1944 this was impossible. Instead he was turned over to the *Gestapo* and dispatched to the concentration camp in Buchenwald in January 1945. M. was one of over eight hundred court-martialled soldiers who were sent to Buchenwald between autumn 1944 and March 1945 as part of a programme codenamed "*Zwischenhaft* II".[112] These men were considered "unusable" as soldiers but their labour power could still be exploited.[113] Because of his *Mischling* status Günther M. was regarded as "unusable" for anything but hard labour. Most of the convicted soldiers at Buchenwald were assigned to work under horrendous conditions on the production of the V-2 rocket in Dora-Mittelbau.[114] Whether M. survived his ordeal in the concentration camp is unknown.

CONCLUSION

Ironies and paradoxes pervade the story of Jewish *Mischlinge* in the Third Reich, as is typically the case with groups posed uneasily along the fault lines of society. The uncertain, changing, ambiguous treatment of *Mischlinge* by the *Wehrmacht* outlined in the first part of this article accurately mirrored the shifting and often confused policy towards *Mischlinge* in the *Reich* at large and reflected the Nazi regime's own difficulties in finding a solution to a "problem" of its own invention. The case studies of *Mischling* deserters provide us with one narrow but nevertheless revealing lens through which to examine this tragic and disturbing dimension of the terrible reality of Hitler's racial state.

For most of the eight soldiers whose cases have been reviewed here their connections with the German Jewish community were tenuous or non-existent. Only two or possibly three of the soldiers (Kurt Aschkenasi and Anton Mayer and perhaps Kurt Schinek) seem to have had contact with a Jewish parent. At least five, and probably six, of the eight soldiers were raised as Christians, and another (Kurt Aschkenasi) became Christian at age ten. Four of the soldiers (Werner K., Kurt Schinek, Günther M. and Kurt M.) appear to have known nothing about their Jewish background during their childhood and youth and only found out about it after they were eighteen or older and were required to provide proof of their Aryan ancestry.[115] These men were thus socialised within Christian

---

[112]After Heinrich Himmler was appointed as head of the reserve army on 20 July 1944 (an action planned before the assassination attempt on Hitler) he introduced a new scheme for executing punishments and this included turning convicted soldiers over to the Gestapo for work in concentration camps. Those designated for "*Zwischenhaft* I" were sent to Mauthausen, those for "*Zwischenhaft* II" to Buchenwald. See Klausch, *Die Bewährungstruppe 500*, pp. 256–261.

[113]The term is contained in the OKH directive from 17 July 1944, quoted in Messerschmidt and Wüllner, *Die Wehrmachtjustiz*, p. 116.

[114]*ibid.*, p. 260.

[115]In addition, the cases of Werner K. and Günther M. are good examples of the "typical hard case" mentioned by Noakes in his description of the petition process for *Mischlinge*: "somene who was illegitimate, had never seen his Jewish parent and had been brought up solely by his Aryan one"; see Noakes, 'Nazi Policy', p. 332.

German society and undoubtedly considered themselves to be equal and fully legitimate members of the German nation whose values and prejudices they shared. The sense of shared values could even extend to anti-Semitism as the case of Günther M. demonstrates. The same might also have been true of Werner K. who for four years was a member of the NSDAP and the SA; and if he did not already hold antisemitic views before 1934 it is not hard to imagine that he might have developed them given that his *Mischling* background first put an end to his party membership and later destroyed the military career of which he was so proud. On the basis of the evidence supplied in the court-martial files of these eight soldiers it appears that most of them thought of themselves as Germans who shared a common history and set of values with their fellow citizens. Their stigmatisation as members of a "mixed race" who presented a threat to the German *Volksgemeinschaft* must have been perceived by them as a bewildering and unjustified act of exclusion. (Kurt Aschkenasi might be the lone exception. Aschkenasi's treatment "as a Jew" in Dachau and Buchenwald following his round-up in the "June action" of 1938 might well have brought home to him his marginal, endangered status.)

In at least four of the cases surveyed the soldier's *Mischling* status was a factor, and perhaps the main factor, motivating his desertion. Anxiety about their future prospects in the face of the regime's increasingly harsh and discriminatory policy towards *Mischlinge* certainly afflicted Werner K. and Günther M. and played the key role in their decisions to desert. Upon discovering that his Jewish father had been sent to a concentration camp in Emsland and fearing a similar fate if his racial status were discovered, Kurt Aschkenasi also opted to desert. Kurt Schinek, Werner K. and Günther M. all had to confront the reality that their racial status made it impossible for them to fulfil their desire to marry; for Schinek desertion and flight abroad appeared to offer the only opportunity for him to circumvent the prohibition against his planned marriage. In Anton Mayer's case, it is unclear if considerations of his *Mischling* status entered into his decision to desert but by his own admission his fear that as a "half-Jew" he would suffer harsher punishment if he returned to his unit convinced him to prolong his desertion.

The court-martial outcomes in the cases examined here reveal that five of the seven soldiers convicted of desertion (Paul A., it will be recalled, was convicted of being absent without leave) were given the death penalty and in four cases the penalty was executed. This rather closely parallels the outcome pattern for *Wehrmacht* deserters as a whole. Wüllner has calculated that between one-half and two-thirds of soldiers convicted of desertion were given the death penalty and of those some two-thirds to three-quarters were executed.[116] The three *Mischling* deserters who ended up with prison terms received sentences averaging eight years. This too was quite in line with the average of 8.8 years for deserters as a whole.[117] In terms of sentencing outcomes, therefore, there does not appear to

---

[116]Wüllner, *Die NS-Militärjustiz*, pp. 446, 476.

[117]The average is based on a sample of 556 prison sentences for desertion imposed by army and navy courts-martial over the entire course of the war. The sample is based on cases drawn from the

be any discrepancy between these *Mischling* cases and the punishments meted out to non-*Mischling* deserters.

Is it fair to conclude, then, as Otto Schweling and Erich Schwinge do in their history of German military justice in the Second World War, that *Mischlinge* "were not disadvantaged" in the German military justice system?[118] In the extremely brief two-page section which they devote to "treatment of Jews", Schweling and Schwinge, both former military judges during the Third Reich, refer to only one case against a *Mischling* who was court-martialled for being absent without leave from the *Organisation Todt*. They emphasise that the verdict contains no mention of the defendant's *Mischling* status and this seems to provide them with sufficient grounds to make the confident assertion that *Mischlinge* were not disadvantaged. But as the case studies examined here make clear, in some instances (Paul A., Anton Mayer, Ivan L. and Werner K.) *Mischlinge were* very definitely disadvantaged, and their racial background *did* have an impact on their punishment. The cursory treatment of the issue in the apologetic account by Schwelling and Schwinge gives a distorted and simplistic view of what was a much more complex and problematic aspect of the functioning of the military justice system in the Third Reich.[119]

As the cases of Günther M., Paul A., Kurt M. and Werner K. all demonstrate, those convicted "first-degree *Mischlinge*" who had the good fortune to escape a death sentence were treated differently after their court-martialling from other military convicts in one crucial respect: because of their racial status they were prohibited from being sent back to the front in so-called convict battalions. Service in such battalions theoretically offered the opportunity of "rehabilitation" and possible reintegration into the regular army (although in practice rehabilitation very rarely happened). Since after April 1940 "half-Jews" – except with special permission from the *Führer* – were denied the right to serve in the military, they were also considered unsuitable for the convict battalions. Here the twisted logic of the Nazi racial state actually worked to the advantage of the *Mischlinge*, since the death rate in the convict battalions was almost certainly higher than in the Emsland camps in Germany. Ironically, then, racially-based discrimination against these convicted *Mischlinge* enhanced their likelihood of survival.

---

courts-martial files housed in the German Federal Archives branch in Kornelimünster, from cases which came before the *Reichskriegsgericht* held in the Military Historical Archive in Prague, from cases found in the records of the Hessian State Archive in Wiesbaden, and documents in the Deutsche Dienststelle in Berlin.

[118] Otto Peter Schweling, *Die deutsche Militärjustiz in der Zeit des Nationalsozialismus*, 2nd edn., edited by Erich Schwinge, Marburg 1978, p. 342.

[119] On the controversy surrounding the refusal of the Institut für Zeitgeschichte to publish the Schweling/Schwinge book see Karl-Dietrich Erdmann, 'Zeitgeschichte, Militärjustiz und Völkerrecht. Zu einer aktuellen Kontroverse', *Geschichte in Wissenschaft und Unterricht*, 30 (1979), pp. 129–139. Two critical reviews of the Schweling/Schwinge book are provided by Michael Stolleis, '"Hart, aber gerecht". Die Wehrmachtjustiz im Dienst des Nationalsozialismus', in *Recht im Unrecht. Studien zur Rechtsgeschichte des Nationalsozialismus*, Frankfurt 1994, pp. 221–232, and David H. Kitterman, 'The Justice of the Wehrmacht Legal System: Servant or Opponent of National Socialism?' *Central European History*, 24 (1991), pp. 450–462.

The handful of desertion cases surveyed here do not provide a sufficient empirical basis for firm generalisations about the treatment of *Mischlinge* who were prosecuted by the military justice system. A much larger sample would have to be assembled in order to arrive at solid conclusions. But four tentative conclusions can nevertheless be suggested; future research will be needed to validate or qualify them.

First, the issue of racial status was a factor which at least some judges took into account in rendering their verdicts, but the treatment of *Mischling* deserters was by no means uniform. Some judges appear to have been able to ignore the racial dimension in *Mischling* deserter cases and render judgment according to the same – harsh – criteria they applied to "non-*Mischling*" defendants. But others, as we have seen, allowed the racial issue to intrude into the judicial process and influence their treatment of the defendant. In the verdicts handed down in two of the case studies examined here the judges invoked crude Jewish stereotypes or made denigrating remarks about the racial inferiority of the defendant. Denigration and humiliation of defendants by military judges, it must be added, seems to have been quite a common practice. Judges in deserter cases often castigated defendants as "worthless", "inferior", "parasitical", "psychopathic" and "asocial"; a defendant's *Mischling* status simply gave some judges another opportunity to deprecate him.

Secondly, apart from the verdicts themselves, racist expressions and antisemitic attitudes also crop up in the supporting documents – legal opinions, statements from *Gerichtsherren* and memos – included in court-martial case files. There has long been evidence of the racist and antisemitic views of some members of the *Wehrmacht* leadership, of the junior officer corps and of significant numbers of ordinary soldiers.[120] The expression of these views in court-martial files simply underlines the prevalence of such attitudes and indicates that racism and anti-Semitism also infected the military justice system.

Thirdly, the files also demonstrate quite clearly that the military justice system co-operated with local Nazi party functionaries and with the SS and SD in exchanging information about "half-Jewish" soldiers and in tracking down racial information about parents and relatives. The lines of communication were open, and the officials of the military justice system availed themselves of the services of party organisations and Himmler's SS. There was no firewall protecting a "clean" and "honourable" military justice system from the rest of the Nazi regime and its institutions.

Finally, we can conclude that by identifying *Mischling* deserters as such, assigning them a special status and denying them the opportunity for "rehabilitation" (however illusory that opportunity might have been in reality) the *Wehrmacht* leadership and the military justice system helped to underwrite and sustain the

---

[120]On the antisemitism of the *Wehrmacht* leadership see *Deutsche Jüdische Soldaten 1914–1945*, edited by the Militärgeschichtlichen Forschungsamt, Freiburg 1982, and relevant documents in Vogel, *Stück*; on the junior officers see Omer Bartov, *The Eastern Front 1941–1945: German Troops and the Barbarisation of Warfare*, London 1985; on the attitudes of regular troops see , Walter Manoschek, (ed.), *Es gibt nur eines für das Judentum: Vernichtung. Das Judenbild in deutschen Soldatenbriefen 1939–1944*, Hamburg 1995.

racial policies of the Third Reich. In its treatment of *Mischling* deserters the military justice system functioned as a culpable partner in the racial purging policies of the Nazi regime.

Oberkommando der Wehrmacht

Az. 12i 10—20J (Ic)

Nr. 524/40 geh.

Berlin, den 8 April 1940

Geheim!

Betr.: Behandlung jüdischer Mischlinge in der Wehrmacht

Der Führer und Oberste Befehlshaber der Wehrmacht hat nachstehende Entscheidung getroffen:

1. 50%ige jüdische Mischlinge oder Männer, die mit 50%igen jüdischen Mischlingen oder Jüdinnen verheiratet sind, sind je nach Lebensalter (§§ 10 und 11 des WG) der Ersatzreserve II bzw. der Landwehr II zu überschreiben, jedoch mit dem jeweiligen Zusatz »n. z. v.« (nicht zu verwenden), um sie von den übrigen Wehrpflichtigen dieser Kategorien grundsätzlich zu unterscheiden.

Ausgenommen bleiben hiervon die Offiziere, die auf Grund der Führerentscheidung (OKW — WZ (II)/J — Nr. 651/39 vom 13. 3. 39) in der Friedenswehrmacht verblieben sind.

In besonders gelagerten Fällen behält sich der Führer Ausnahmen vor, die über OKW zu beantragen sind.

2. 25%ige Mischlinge und Wehrmachtangehörige, die mit 25%igen Mischlingen verheiratet sind, verbleiben in der Wehrmacht und können während des Krieges ausnahmsweise befördert und als Vorgesetzte verwendet werden, wenn eine besondere Bewährung erwiesen ist.

Außerdem können ehemalige Unteroffiziere, Beamte und Offiziere, die 25%ige Mischlinge sind, oder solche, die mit 25%igen Mischlingen verheiratet sind, bei ausreichender Begründung während des Krieges in der Wehrmacht verwendet werden.

Jeder Beförderungs- bzw. Wiedereinstellungsantrag ist dem Führer über OKW zur Entscheidung vorzulegen.

Um beschleunigte Durchführung der angeordneten Maßnahmen sicherzustellen, wird um umgehende Bekanntgabe vorstehender Verfügung gebeten.

Die Verfügungen OKW Nr. 190/40 J (I c) vom 16. 1. 40 und OKW Nr. 280/40 J (I c) vom 20. 1. 40, letztere mit Ausnahme der für Freimaurer geltenden Bestimmungen, werden hiermit aufgehoben.

Der Chef des Oberkommandos der Wehrmacht

Keitel

Document 1. Copy of Hitler's secret order of 8 April 1940 which ordered the dismissal of all "half-Jews" from the Wehrmacht. (Source: BA-ZNS RW55/1589)

(Ort) (Datum)

Erklärung

(Beim Truppenteil auszufüllen)

Nach sorgfältiger Prüfung der mir zur Verfugung stehenden Unterlagen erkläre ich pflichtgemäß, daß ich — meine Ehefrau — ....%/iger jüdischer Mischling bin.

Über den Begriff jüdischer Mischling in diesem Zusammenhang bin ich durch meinen Disziplinar-vorgesetzten belehrt worden.

Mir ist bekannt, daß ich Strafverfolgung zu gewärtigen habe, falls sich die Erklärung als unrichtig erweisen sollte.

Mir ist eröffnet worden, daß ich, falls ich durch unrichtige Angaben meine Vorgesetzten täuschte in der Absicht, mich der Erfüllung des Wehrdienstes zu entziehen, wegen Zersetzung der Wehrkraft mit den höchsten Strafen, unter Umständen mit dem Tode bestraft werden kann.

(Unterschrift mit Vornamen)

Nichtzutreffendes ist zu streichen.

(Nach der Entlassung durch die zuständige Wehrersatzdienststelle auszufüllen)

(Ort und Datum)

Die Richtigkeit der vorstehenden Angaben ist durch Nachprüfung der Geburts- bzw. Taufurkunden bis zu den Großeltern einschließlich festgestellt.

(Name, Dienstgrad und Dienststelle,

Document 2a. Aryan declaration forms. All soldiers were required to fill out a declaration. Form A (above) required soldiers to indicate whether they or their wives were of German blood or were *Mischlinge*. A *Mischling* would have to stipulate which category he belonged to: 25% or 50% Jewish *Mischling*. Form B (overleaf), used by the navy, required sailors to declare both that they were of German blood and had no previous criminal record. Form C (overleaf) makes no mention of the terms Jewish *Mischling* or Jew. Interestingly, it warns soldiers that if they make a false declaration of their racial ancestry – in other words if they falsely declare themselves to be *Mischlinge* – in order to avoid military service they may be prosecuted and sentenced to death for subversion. (Sources: BA-ZNS RW55/1589 and BA-ZNS Sammlung Juden)

Erklärung
über deutſchblütige Abſtammung
und polizeiliche oder gerichtliche Strafen.

I. Mir ſind nach ſorgfältiger Prüfung keine Umſtände bekannt, die die Annahme rechtfertigen könnten, daß ich jüdiſcher Miſchling oder Jude bin. Ueber die Begriffe des jüdiſchen Miſchlings und des Juden bin ich unterrichtet worden.

II. Ich verſichere, daß ich gerichtlich nicht vorbeſtraft bin oder gegen mich ein Verfahren wegen einer ſtrafbaren Handlung nicht eingeleitet iſt.

Mir iſt bekannt, daß ich mich ſtrafbar mache, falls dieſe Erklärung unrichtig iſt."

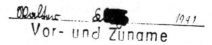

1941

Vor- und Zuname

Document 2b.

Erklärung.

Nach sorgfältiger Prüfung der mir zur Verfügung stehenden Unterlagen erkläre ich pflichtgemäß, daß ich und meine Frau deutschblütig sind.

Über den Begriff „deutschblütig" in diesem Zusammenhang bin ich durch meine Disziplinarvorgesetzten belehrt worden. Mir ist bekannt, daß ich Strafverfolgung zu gewärtigen habe, falls sich die Erklärung als unrichtig erweisen sollte. Mir ist eröffnet worden, daß ich, falls ich durch unrichtige Angaben meine Vorgesetzten täusche in der Absicht, mich der Erfüllung des Wehrdienstes zu entziehen, wegen Zersetzung der Wehrkraft mit den höchsten Strafen, unter Umständen mit dem Tode bestraft werden kann.

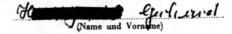

(Name und Vorname)

A. G. D. DRUCK, MINDEN I. W.

Document 2c.

**Der Führer und Oberste Befehlshaber
der Wehrmacht**

Jch genehmige, daß der Oberfüsilier

Rüdiger von B ▬▬▬▬▬

weiter im aktiven Wehrdienst verbleiben und zum

Vorgesetzten befördert werden kann.

Nach Abschluß des Krieges werde ich bei

voller Bewährung über die Deutschblütigkeit mit allen

daraus sich ergebenden Rechten und Pflichten

entscheiden.

Berchtesgaden, den 29. November 1940.

gez. Adolf H i t l e r .

Für die Richtigkeit der Abschrift:

Berchtesgaden, den 29.11.1940.

Hauptmann und Adjutant der
Wehrmacht beim Führer.

Document 3. Copy of an authorisation from Hitler allowing *Mischling* Rüdiger von B. to remain in the army stating that he is eligible to be considered for promotion. (Source: BA-ZNS Sammlung jüdische Mischlinge)

**Der Direktor
der Reichsstelle für Sippenforschung**

Akten-Z.: I⁴ (X) u 24197 Dr.Br/No.

<small>Es wird gebeten, dieses Geschäftszeichen bei
weiterem Schreiben anzugeben.</small>

Berlin NW 7, den 16. November 1940
Schiffbauerdamm 26
Fernsprecher: 42 33 83
Drahtanschrift: Reichssippenforschung

Abstammungsbescheid

Paul A ▮▮▮▮▮▮▮▮▮▮

in Berlin,

geboren zu Berlin   am 10.5.1913,

– – – – – – gilt als jüdischer Mischling – – – – – –

mit zwei der Rasse nach volljüdischen Großelternteilen

im Sinne der Ersten Verordnung zum Reichsbürgergesetz vom 14. November 1935
(RGBl. I S. 1333).

Die Abstammung wurde hier nachgeprüft.

Gründe:

Der Großvater väterlicherseits, August Theodor Julius
B a a s e (geb. zu Danzig am 5.3.1834), war deutschblütig. Er
wurde jedoch im Jahre 1858 unter dem Namen Israel A ▮▮▮▮▮▮
▮▮▮▮▮ in das Judentum aufgenommen und hat bis zu seinem Tode
(gest. zu Danzig am 26.11.1884) der jüdischen Religionsgemeinschaft
angehört. Er gilt infolgedessen ohne weiteres als volljüdischer
Großelternteil des Prüflings.

Israel A ▮▮▮▮▮▮▮▮ heiratete zu Danzig am
31.7.1865 die Jüdin Mirjam (Maria) B l u m e n t h a l (geb.
zu Danzig am 23.9.1837).

Die Großeltern mütterlicherseits des Prüflings waren
deutschblütig.

Sonach ergibt sich die oben festgestellte rassische Einordnung des Prüflings.

In Vertretung:
gez. Dr. K n o s t

Kriegsgerichtsrat.

X 220 / 7 40 / 5000 C / 0667

Document 4. Ancestry Notice for Paul A. issued by the Reich Office for Family Research declaring him to be a "first-degree *Mischling*". (Source: BA-ZNS RW55/160)

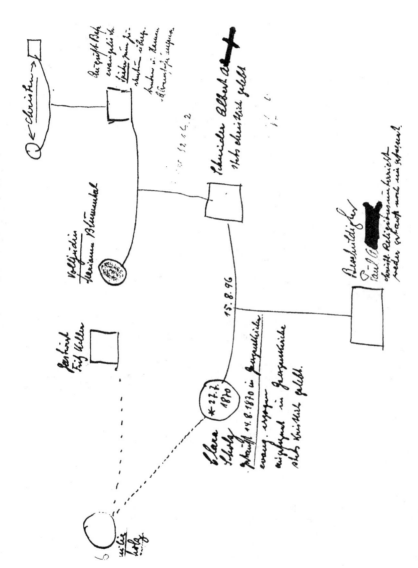

Document 5. Hand-sketched genealogical chart for Paul A. included in his court-martial file. The chart provides a clear example of the conflation of racial and religious categories in the Nazi classification system. Paul A.'s racial status is determined on the basis of the religious affiliations of the previous two generations. (Source: BA-ZNS RW55/160)

Gericht des
Marinebefehlshabers Dänemark.
J.II.172/42.

F e l d u r t e i l
im Namen des Deutschen Volkes.

In der Strafsache gegen den Mar.Artl.Kurt S c h i n e k
vom Kommando 1.Marine Flak Abteilung 814
wegen Fahnenflucht
hat ein am 2.Oktober 1942 in Kopenhagen
auf Befehl des Gerichtsherrn und Marinebefehlshabers Dänemark
zusammengetretenes Feldkriegsgericht,
an dem teilgenommen haben:

           Als Richter:
1. Marinekriegsgerichtsrat Dr.von Tabouillot,
              Verhandlungsleiter,
2. Korv.Kapt.Dämmrich,
3. Verw.Gefr.Bähr,

        als Vertreter der Anklage:
Marinekriegsgerichtsrat Dr.Bohnenkamp,

        als Urkundsbeamter der Geschäftsstelle:
Marinehilfsjustizinspektor Hässler,
für Recht erkannt:
              "Der Angeklagte wird wegen Fahnenflucht im Felde
              zum Tode und wegen fortgesetzter Zersetzung der
              Wehrkraft in Tateinheit mit fortgesetzter Urkunde
              fälschung zu 3 - drei - Jahren Gefängnis verurtei
              Gleichzeitig wird auf Wehrunwürdigkeit wie auf
              Verlust der bürgerlichen Ehrenrechte auf Lebens-
              zeit erkannt."

                                        Gründe:

Document 6. Court-martial verdict dated 2 October 1942 which sentenced Kurt Schinek
to death for desertion. (Source: BA-ZNS SCH 1837)

DER KOMMANDEUR
der Sicherheitspolizei und des SD Agram
E. K. 4

N/ -Tgb. Nr. 2512/43-IV

Agram, den 5. März 1944.

> Gericht der
> Feldkommandantur 725
> Eingeg: 6. III. 1944
> Anlagen: 1

An das
Gericht der Feldkommandantur 725
in A g r a m.

Betr.: Jüdische Herkunft des Grenadiers Kurt Emanuel Josef
M ▬▬▬ und des Ivan L ▬▬▬.

Vorg.: Hiesig. Schr.v.29.12.43 - Nr.2512/43, dort. Schr.v. 8.2.,
19.2. und 28.2.44 - Nr.St.L.365.

Anlage: 1 Stammbaum.

Durch V-Personen wurde die hiesige Dienststelle darauf aufmerksam
gemacht, dass Ivan L ▬▬▬ jüdischer Herkunft ist. Die hierauf
getätigten Ermittlungen ergaben, dass die Grossmutter des Ivan
L ▬▬▬ und Mutter der Dora L ▬▬▬ geb. Conrid - die Ilka
C o n r i d, geb. Rosenstolz - im hiesigen amtlichen Polizeimel-
deregister als Jüdin registriert ist.Im Eheregister der Kirche
Sv. Petar zu Agram (VI/Seite 42/Nr.49) wurde bei der Eheschliessung
der Dora C o n r i d mit dem Dr. Richard L ▬▬▬ die Eintragung
gefunden, dass die Eltern der Dora C., und zwar der Kaufmann
Emanuel C o n r i d und die Ilka Conrid geb. Rosenstolz, Juden
sind. Ferner konnte im Polizeimeldregister der Stadt Agram festgestellt werden, dass die Brüder der Dora L ▬▬▬ geb. Conrid, t
und zwar Artur und Adam C o n r i d, dort unter den getauften Juden geführt werden.
Durch die Ermittlungen ist erwiesen, dass es sich bei der Dora
L ▬▬▬ geb. Conrid, der Mutter des Ivan L ▬▬▬, um eine
getaufte Volljüdin handelt. Demnach ist auch ihre Schwester Nelly
M ▬▬▬ geb. Conrid, die Mutter des Kurt Emanuel Josef M ▬▬▬
eine Volljüdin. Die beiden Verurteilten sind daher als jüdische
Mischlinge I. Grades anzusehn.
Eine Abschrift des hier aufgrund der amtlichen Eintragungen zu-
sammengestellten Stammbaumes wird diesem Schreiben beigefügt.-

Durch Meldungen von V-Personen und durch hier getätigte Verneh-
mungen ist offensichtlich, dass Ivan L ▬▬▬ keineswegs der
Deutschenfreund ist, als der er sich ausgibt. L. hat verschie-
dentlich Äusserungen darüber fallen lassen, dass er die Sieges-

Document 7. Memo from the Commander of the Security Police and the SD in Agram providing the military court of the Field *Kommandantur* 725 with information on the Jewish ancestry of Kurt M. and Ivan L. (Source: BA-ZNS FK725 No. 44)

138

Gericht der Kriegsmarine
Berlin
RHJ. II 54/44

(1) Berlin-Charlottenburg, den 25.8.194⁴
Messedamm 4.

Ruf: 99 6281
App.   240

An
den Techniker
Herrn Robert M a y e r,
B u k a r e s t
Stefan cel Mare No. 63.

       Das gegen Ihren Sohn, den Mar.Artl.Gefr.Anton
M a ye r, wegen der von ihm begangenen Straftat am
20.7.1944 vom Kriegsgericht auf Todesstrafe erkannte
Urteil ist nach Bestäti ung durch den zuständigen
Gerichtsherrn am 21. August 1944 vollstreckt worden.

       Die Bestattung erfolgte in Brandenburg/Havel.

       Todesanzeigen oder Nachrufe in Zeitungen,
Zeitschriften und dergl. sind verboten.

                   Auf Befehl:

                   Marinejustizinspektor

Document 8. Notice sent to Anton Mayer's father informing him of his son's execution on 21 August 1944, with the warning that no public announcements of the death were permitted. (Source: BA-ZNS RW123/35944)

Kaufmann Kohler

This portrait of Kaufmann Kohler should have accompanied Jacob Haberman's article 'Kaufmann Kohler and his Teacher Samson Raphael Hirsch' in *LBI Year Book XLIII*, pp.73-102. We regret its omission.

By courtesy of the Jacob Rader Marcus Center of the American Jewish Archives, Cincinnati

Publications on German-speaking Jewry

A Selected and Annotated Bibliography of Books and Articles 1998

Compiled by

BARBARA SUCHY and ANNETTE PRINGLE

The Bibliography is supported by grants from:

Robert Gavron Charitable Trust

Sheldon and Suzanne Nash Fund

The Rayne Trust

Robert Bosch Stiftung

Wissenschaftsfonds der
Deutschen Genossenschaftsbank

Leo Baeck Institute
4 Devonshire Street
London W1N 2BH

CONTENTS

BIBLIOGRAPHY 1998

Includes books and articles published in 1998 as well as some supplementary books and articles published in 1996 and 1997 and not yet listed in the previous two bibliographies.

Owing to the wealth of studies on the history of German-speaking Jewry and antisemitism which appeared in 1998, Section VII (Participation in Cultural and Public Life) and Section IV B (Post-1945/Education and Teaching. Memorials) had to be curtailed.

Preference has been given to entering as many publications as possible and, to this end, cross-references have been cut somewhat. All titles are, however, fully indexed: names, places, periodicals, titles (in some cases), subjects.

Communal and regional histories are listed either in Section I B (Communal and Regional History), or in Section III (The Nazi Period), depending on their main focus.

Autobiographies and memoirs are listed either in section III (The Nazi Period), or in Section VIII (Autobiography, Memoirs, Letters), again depending on their main focus.

(B.S.)

I. HISTORY

A. General

35897. Aschheim, Steven E.: *German history and German Jewry: boundaries, junctions and interdependence.* [In]: Leo Baeck Institute Year Book XLIII, London, 1998. Pp. 315–322, footnotes.

35898. Bacharach, Zwi: *The traumatic encounter between Jews and Germans in the Weimar period.* [In]: Daniel Carpi; Jubilee volume. A collection of studies on the history of the Jewish people presented to Daniel Carpi on his 70th birthday by his colleagues and students. Tel Aviv: Tel-Aviv Univ., 1996. Pp. 211–221. [In Hebrew.]

35899. Barkai, Avraham: *The Jews of Germany.* Jerusalem: Ministry of Education, Culture and Sport. Information Centre; Leo Baeck Institute, 1996. 79 pp. [In Hebrew, title transl.]

35900. Barkai, Avraham: *Hoffnung und Untergang. Studien zur deutsch-jüdischen Geschichte des 19. und 20. Jahrhunderts.* Mit einer Einführung von Ursula Büttner. Hamburg: Christians, 1998. 290 pp., notes. (Hamburger Beiträge zur Sozial- und Zeitgeschichte; Darstellungen, Bd. 36.) [Cont. 11 previously publ. essays, some transl. from Hebrew and English, (titles partly abbr.): Zur Einführung (Ursula Büttner, 1–14). Die deutschen Juden in der Zeit der Industrialisierung (15–34). Die Juden in Deutschland am Beginn der Industrialisierung (35–63). Juden, Judentum und die Entwicklung des Kapitalismus (63–74). Auswanderung als Emanzipationsersatz? (75–94). Die Juden als sozioökonomische Minderheitsgruppe in der Weimarer Republik (95–110). Zwischen Deutschtum und Judentum. Richtungskämpfe im Centralverein deutscher Staatsbürger jüdischen Glaubens, 1919–1933 (111–140). Zur politischen Biographie von Leo Baeck 1933–1945 (141–166). Das deutsche Interesse am Haavara-Transfer 1933–1939 (167–196). Deutschsprachige Juden in osteuropäischen Ghettos (197–224). "Zwischen Ost und West". Deutsche Juden im Ghetto Lodz (225–274). Regierungsmechanismen im Dritten Reich und die "Genesis der Endlösung" (275–288).]

35901. Battenberg, J. Friedrich: *Rosheim, Josel von (ca. 1778–1554).* [In]: Theologische Realenzyklopädie. In Gemeinschaft mit Horst Balz [et al.] hrsg. von Gerhard Müller. Bd. XXIX, Religionspsychologie – Samaritaner. Berlin; New York, 1998. Pp. 424–427, bibl.

35902. BERKOWITZ, MICHAEL: *Robert S. Wistrich and European Jewish history: straddling the public and scholarly spheres.* [In]: Journal of Modern History, Vol. 70, No. 1, Chicago, March 1998. Pp. 119–136, footnotes. [Review article of W.'s oeuvre in the context of modern European and modern Jewish history.]

35903. BLUMENTHAL, MICHAEL W.: *The invisible wall. Germans and Jews.* A personal exploration. Washington, DC: Counterpoint, 1998. XIV, 444 pp., illus. [Retraces the experiences of his ancestors, putting them in the larger context of German history and, especially, in the context of the history of German antisemitism.] [Cf.: "In the end, it had become a wall of death (Isabel Loudig) [in]: Aufbau, Vol. 64, No. 23, New York, Nov. 6, 1998, p. 14. "Jews in Germany are cautious and watchful"; head of Berlin Jewish Museum on German Jewry (Lori Eppstein) [in]: Aufbau, Vol. 64, No. 24, New York, Nov. 20, 1998. Explaining the inexplicable (Ronald Stent) [in]: AJR Information, Vol. 53, No. 10, London, Oct. 1998, p. 4.] [M.B., b. 1926 in Oranienburg, emigr. in 1941 to Shanghai, in 1947 to the US, manager, Treasury Secretary under President Carter, at present director of the new Jewish Museum in Berlin.]

35904. BORCHERS, SUSANNE: *Jüdisches Frauenleben im Mittelalter. Die Texte des Sefer Chasidim.* Frankfurt am Main; New York: Lang, 1998. 300 pp., footnotes, bibl. (284–293), index (subjects and names). (Judentum und Umwelt, Bd. 68.) Zugl.: Köln, Univ., Diss, 1998. [Incl. transl. of selected texts relevant to the topic.]

35905. BORUT, JACOB/HEILBRONNER, ODED: *Leaving the walls or anomalous activity: the Catholic and Jewish rural bourgeoisie in Germany.* [In]: Comparative Studies in Society and History, Vol. 40, No. 3, Cambridge, July 1998. Pp. 475–502, footnotes. [A comparison of Jewish and Catholic patterns of political and social behaviour in Western and Southern Germany after 1871.]

35906. BRENNER, MICHAEL/PENSLAR, DEREK J., eds.: *In search of Jewish community: Jewish identities in Germany and Austria, 1918–1933.* Bloomington: Indiana Univ. Press, 1998. XV, 251 pp., notes. [Cont. (titles abbr.): German Jews between fulfillment and disillusion: the individual and the community (Shulamit Volkov, 1–14). Religious ferment in Weimar liberal Judaism (Michael A. Meyer, 15–35). Gemeindeorthodoxie in Weimar Germany: the approaches of Nehemiah Anton Nobel and Isak Unna (David Ellenson, 36–55). Jewish youth in Weimar Germany (Michael Brenner, 56–73). Ideological controversies inside the Centralverein (Avraham Barkai, 74–91). Was there a Zionist subculture in Weimar Germany? (Jacob Borut, 92–114). Bundists in Vienna and the varieties of Jewish experience in the Austrian First Republic (Jack Jacobs, 115–133). Jewish ethnicity in a new nation state (Marsha L. Rozenblit, 134–153). Jewish university women in Germany and Austria (Harriet Pass Freidenreich, 154–175). The crisis of the Jewish family in Weimar Germany (Sharon Gillerman, 176–199). Correctional education and family breakdown in German Jewish families (Claudia Prestel, 200–222). Decline and survival of rural Jewish communities (Steven M. Lowenstein, 223–242).]

35907. DAVIS, NATALIE ZEMON: *Lebensgänge. Glikl. Zwi Hirsch. Martin Guerre. Ad me ipsum.* Aus dem Amerik. von Wolfgang Kaiser. Berlin: Wagenbach, 1998. 124 pp. (Kleine kulturwissenschaftliche Bibliothek, Bd. 61.) [Incl. the essay: Noch einmal 'Religion und Kapitalismus'? Jüdische Kaufmannskultur im siebzehnten Jahrhundert (7–40; deals with the memoirs of Glückel von Hameln and the life story of Zwi Hirsch Aschkenasi written in Hebrew by his son Jacob Emden. Incl. a critical analysis of Werner Sombart's 'Die Juden und das Wirtschaftsleben').]

35908. FRIEDRICH, MARTIN: *Juden und Frauen – Objekte "bürgerlicher Verbesserung" im Zeitalter der Aufklärung.* [In]: Zeitschrift für Religions- und Geistesgeschichte, Jg. 50, H. 2, Leiden, 1998. Pp. 156–168, footnotes. [On Christian Wilhelm Dohm and Theodor Gottlieb von Hippel.]

35909. FRIESEL, EVYATAR: *Jewish and German-Jewish historical views: problems of a new synthesis.* [In]: Leo Baeck Institute Year Book XLIII, London, 1998. Pp. 323–335, footnotes.

35910. GAMM, HANS-JOCHEN: *Das Judentum*. Aktualisierte Neuauflage. Frankfurt am Main; New York: Campus, 1998. 190 pp., tabs., maps. (Reihe Campus. Einführungen.) [First publ. 1961; numerous further edns.]

35911. GERHARDT, DIETRICH: *Süßkind von Trimberg*. Berichtigungen zu einer Erinnerung. Frankfurt am Main; New York, 1997. 394 pp., illus., bibl. (335–376), Beilage: XI pp. [Deals mainly with the discussions of Germanists, among them antisemites, about the medieval poet and the meaning of his poems; also on fiction about him.] [Cf.: Fremd im Hermelin. Der rätselhafte Süßkind von Trimberg (Hans-Herbert Räkel) [in]: 'FAZ', Nr. 122, Frankfurt am Main, 29. Mai 1999, Beilage, p. V.]

35912. *Die Geschichte der Juden im Rheinland und in Westfalen*. Hrsg. von Michael Zimmermann. Mit Beiträgen von Diethard Aschoff [et al.]. Köln: Kohlhammer, 1998. 329 pp., notes, bibl. (313–318), index (persons, places, 319–328). [Incl.: Die Juden in Antike und Mittelalter (Diethard Aschoff, 15–78). Von der Frühen Neuzeit bis zur Judenemanzipation (Suzanne Zittartz, 79–140). Von der rechtlichen Gleichstellung bis zum Genozid (Yvonne Rieker/ Michael Zimmermann, 141–259). Jüdische Geschichte in Nordrhein-Westfalen (Micha Guttmann, 260–310).]

35913. GOSEWINKEL, DIETER: *"Unerwünschte Elemente"* – Einwanderung und Einbürgerung von Juden in Deutschland 1848–1933. [In]: Tel Aviver Jahrbuch für deutsche Geschichte, Bd. 27, 1998, Gerlingen, 1998. Pp. 71–106, footnotes.

35914. GOTZMANN, ANDREAS: *The dissociation of religion and law in nineteenth-century German-Jewish education*. [In]: Leo Baeck Institute Year Book XLIII, London, 1998. Pp. 103–126, footnotes.

35915. GREEN, NANCY L., ed.: *Jewish workers in the modern diaspora*. Ed. by Nancy L. Green with the collaboration of Patrick Altman, Edgardo Bilsky, David Cesarani, David Feldman, Ludger Heid, Selma Leydesdorff, Daniel Soyer, Jack Wertheimer. Berkeley, CA; London: Univ. of California Press, 1998. VII, 256 pp., bibl. (239–246), index. [Book is based on a comparative approach to Jewish workers around the world; cont. annot. docs. related to the sections: 1. Daily life and work. 2. Societies, organisations, and schools. 3. Politics and ideology. 4. Culture and identities. Incl. Germany.]

35916. GRUPP, PETER: *Juden, Antisemitismus und jüdische Fragen im Auswärtigen Amt in der Zeit des Kaiserreichs und der Weimarer Republik*. Eine erste Annäherung. [In]: Zeitschrift für Geschichtswissenschaft, Jg. 46, H. 3, Berlin, 1998. Pp. 237–248, footnotes. [Deals also with Jews in the Diplomatic Service.]

35917. HAASIS, HELLMUT G.: *Joseph Süß Oppenheimer, genannt Jud Süß*. Finanzier, Freidenker, Justizopfer. Reinbek: Rowohlt, 1998. 479 pp., illus., bibl. notes, index (467–477). [Cf.: Besprechung (Peter Fuchs) [in]: Historische Zeitschrift, Bd. 268, H. 3, München, Juni 1999, pp. 775–777. Bespr. (J. Friedrich Battenberg) [in]: Archiv für hess. Geschichte und Altertumskunde, N.F., Bd. 56, Neustadt an der Aisch, 1998, pp. 464–466. Besprechung (Gudrun Emberger) [in]: Zeitschrift für Württembergische Landesgeschichte, Jg. 58, Stuttgart, 1999, pp. 437–441. Schon im Titel ein Faux-pas: Wie Lion Feuchtwanger Geschichtslegenden übernahm (Jürgen Elsässer) [in]: Israelitisches Wochenblatt, Nr. 14, Basel, 3. April 1998, p. 27.]

35918. HERZOG, ANDREAS: *Zum Bild des "Ostjudentums" in der "westjüdischen" Publizistik der ersten Jahrzehnte des 20. Jahrhunderts*. [In]: Forschungsstelle Judentum, Mitteilungen und Beiträge 14, Leipzig, April 1998. Pp. 26–49, footnotes.

35919. HOLLENDER, ELISABETH/BERZBACH, ULRICH: *Einige Anmerkungen zu biblischer Sprache und Motiven in Piyyutim aus der Kreuzzugszeit*. [In]: Frankfurter Judaistische Beiträge, 25, Frankfurt am Main, Dez. 1998. Pp. 63–74, footnotes. [On the Hebrew reports of the Rhineland persecutions.]

35920. Hopp, Andrea: *Das Jahr 1929: Erinnerung und Selbstverständnis im deutschen Judentum.* [In]: Trumah 7, Berlin, 1998. Pp. 113–134, footnotes.

35921. *Integrazione e identità. L'esperienza ebraico in Germania e Italia dall'Illuminismo al fascismo.* A cura di Mario Toscano. Milano: Franco Angeli, 1998. 267 pp., footnotes. (Studi e ricerche storiche, 1573.) [Cont.: Prefazione (Werner E. Mosse/Dan V. Segre/Mario Toscano, 7–10). Introduzione (ed.). Lei è ebreo? È solo una domanda (Claudio Magris, 23–31). Verso la modernità: l'esperienza ebraica in Europa dagli inizi dell'emancipazione (Reinhard Rürup, 32–48). Sulla presenza ebraica nell'economia italiana. Note metodologiche (Giulio Sapelli, 51–66). Gli ebrei nell'economia tedesca: industrie, banche e commercio (Werner E. Mosse, 67–72). Un profilo sociale degli ebrei tedeschi 1850–1933 (Monika Richarz, 73–83). L'emancipazione degli ebrei in Italia (Dan V. Segre, 84–113). Gli ebrei e la construzione della nazione in Germania (1815–1918) (Peter Pulzer, 114–132). Riforme religiose e tendenze secolari nella vita degli ebrei tedeschi. Un programma di ricerca (David Sorkin, 133–151). Qualche riflessione sulla "mancata Riforma" (Alberto Cavaglion, 152–166). Le Chiese, gli ebrei e la società moderna: l'Italia (Renato Moro, 167–182). Chiese, ebrei e società moderna (Werner Jochmann, 183–183). L'antisemitismo nella società moderna: continuità e discontinuità (Helmut Berding, 194–209). L'uguaglianza senza diversità: Stato, società e questione ebraica nell'Italia liberale (Mario Toscano, 210–235). Razzismo e nazionalismo in Europa (George L. Mosse, 236–243). I profughi ebrei in Italia (1933–1945) (Klaus Voigt, 244–267).] [Papers presented at a conference in Rome, organised by the London Leo Baeck Institute in co-operation with the Goethe-Institut, the Centro Sistema Bibliotecario and the Unione Comunità Ebraiche Italiane in Rome, Nov. 15–18, 1993. English and German contribs. transl. into Italian by Marina Astrologo.]

35922. *Jewish history and Jewish memory: essays in honor of Yosef Hayim Yerushalmi.* Ed. by Elisheva Carlebach, John M. Efron, David N. Myers. Hanover, NH; London: Univ. Press of New England, for Brandeis Univ. Press, 1998. XV, 462 pp., notes, bibl. (works of Yerushalmi, 457–459). [Incl. chaps. (titles abbr.): The Regensburg expulsion in Josel of Rosheim's 'Sefer ha-miknah' (Elisheva Carlebach, 40–53). The Mainz anonymous: historiographic perspectives (Robert Chazan, 54–69). 'Besamim Rosh' and the invention of pre-emancipation Jewish culture (Talya Fishman, 70–88). The rise and fall of the Italian Jewish model in Germany: from Haskalah to Reform, 1780–1820 (Lois C. Dubin, 271–295). The conventional lies about Jewish doctors (John M. Efron, 296–310; deals also with anti-Jewish attitudes). Myths of origin and myths of belonging in nineteenth-century Bohemia (Hillel J. Kieval, 348–368). Between Haskalah and Kabbalah: Peter Beer's history of Jewish sects (Michael Brenner, 389–404). The autobiography of Rabbi Jacob Emden (1697–1776) (Jacob J. Schacter, 428–452).]

35923. *Juden im Wilhelminischen Deutschland 1890–1914.* Ein Sammelband. Hrsg. von Werner E. Mosse unter Mitwirkung von Arnold Paucker. 2., durchgesehene Auflage. Tübingen: Mohr Siebeck, 1998. XIV, 786 pp., footnotes, bibl. (705–754), indexes (persons; subjects, 757–782). (Schriftenreihe wissenschaftlicher Abhandlungen des Leo-Baeck-Instituts, 33.) [Incl.: Vorwort zur zweiten Auflage (Werner E. Mosse, VI-VII). For first edn. and complete listing of essays see No. 13387/YB XXII.]

35924. *Die Juden und die jüdischen Gemeinden Preußens in amtlichen Enquêten des Vormärz.* Enquête des Ministeriums des Innern und der Polizei über die Rechtsverhältnisse der Juden in den preußischen Provinzen 1842–1843. Enquête des Ministeriums der geistlichen, Unterrichts- und Medizinal-Angelegenheiten über die Kultus-, Schul- und Rechtsverhältnisse der jüdischen Gemeinden in den preußischen Provinzen 1843–1845. Bearb. und hrsg. von Manfred Jehle. Mit einem Beitrag von Herbert A. Strauss. München: Saur, 1998. 4 vols. XCIII, 1671 pp., footnotes. (Einzelveröffentlichungen der Historischen Kommission zu Berlin, Bd. 82/1–4.) [Teil 1 cont. (titles partly abbr.): Bilder von Juden und vom Judentum in der Entwicklung der Gesetzgebung Preußens im Vormärz (Herbert A. Strauss, XXIX-LVIII, footnotes). Die Enqueten der preußischen Regierung zu den Verhältnissen der Juden und der jüdischen Gemeinden, 1842–1845. Einleitung zur Edition (Manfred Jehle, LIX-XCIII). Ministerium des Innern: Berlin, Provinzen Brandenburg, Preußen, Pommern, Posen, Schlesien, Sachsen, Westfalen (3–444). Teil 2 cont.: Ministerium des Innern: Rheinprovinz (445–548). Ministerium der geistlichen Angelegenheiten. Berlin, Provinzen Brandenburg, Preußen, Pommern (551–827). Teil 3 cont.: Ministerium der geistlichen Angelegenheiten: Provinzen Posen, Schlesien, Sachsen, Westfalen (829–1258). Teil 4 cont.: Ministerium der geistlichen Angelegenheiten: Rheinprovinz (1259–1504). Verzeichnis der gedruckten Quellen, Gesetzessammlungen, Repertorien, Nachschlagewerke (1505–1533). Literaturverzeichnis (1534–1598). Indexes (names; places, 1599–1671).]

35925. *Jüdisches Leben in der Weimarer Republik/Jews in the Weimar Republic* Hrsg. von Wolfgang Benz, Arnold Paucker und Peter Pulzer. Tübingen: Mohr Siebeck, 1998. VI, 288 pp., footnotes, index. (Schriftenreihe wissenschaftlicher Abhandlungen des Leo-Baeck-Instituts, 57.) [Papers presented at a conference in Oxford in 1995, organised by the London Leo Baeck Institute and the Berlin Zentrum für Antisemitismusforschung. Cont.: Einleitung (Wolfgang Benz, 1–6). Essays are arranged under the following sections: I. *Juden in der Politik/Jews in politics;* cont.: Zwischen Abwehrkampf und Wählermobilisierung. Juden und die Landtagswahlen in Baden 1929 (Martin Liepach, 9–23). "Er ist ein Rätsel geblieben". Oskar Cohn – Politiker, Parlamentarier, Poale-Zionist (Ludger Heid, 25–48). Bernhard Weiß – a Jewish public servant in the last years of the Weimar Republic (Werner T. Angress, 49–63). Industriefinanzierung in Deutschland. Die Bedeutung jüdischer Privatbankhäuser in der Weimarer Republik (Keith Ulrich, 65–86). II. *Juden in der Gesellschaft/Jews in society;* cont.: Jüdische Wissenschaftler in Weimar: Marginalität, Identität und Innovation (Klaus Fischer, 89–116). "Bin Ich doch ein Israelit, ehre Ich auch den Bischof mit – village and small-town Jews within the social spheres in Western German communities during the Weimar Republic (Jacob Borut, 117–133). The "new Jewish woman" in Weimar Germany (Claudia Prestel, 135–155). III. *Antisemitismus und Gruppenbeziehungen/ Antisemitism and group relations;* cont.: Legally citizens: Jewish exclusion from the Weimar polity (Anthony Kauders, 159–172). "Der Miterlebende weiß nichts". Alltagsantisemitismus als zeitgenössische Erfahrung und spätere Erinnerung (1919–1933) (Werner Bergmann/Juliane Wetzel, 173–196). Mingling, marrying and distancing: Jewish integration in Wilheminian Breslau and its erosion in early Weimar Germany (Till van Rahden, 197–222). IV. *Das Geistesleben/The life of the mind;* cont.: The 'Kriegserlebnis' and Jewish consciousness (Paul Mendes-Flohr, 225–237). Jiddische Zeitungen und Zeitschriften im Berlin der Weimarer Republik (Marion Neiss, 239–251). Aporien der jüdischen Identität. Literatur und Judentum in der Zeitschrift 'Der Jude' von Martin Buber (Silvia Cresti, 253–267). V. *Conclusion;* cont.: Between hope and fear: Jews and the Weimar Republic (Peter Pulzer, 271– 279).]

35926. KOLLATZ, THOMAS: *Fascination and discomfort: the ambivalent image of the Netherlands in the Jewish-German press in the 1830s and 1840s.* [In]: Studia Rosenthaliana. Vol. 32, No. 1, Amsterdam 1998. Pp. 43–66, footnotes. [Incl. list of periodicals.]

35927. LINDNER, ERIK: *Deutsche Juden in der Revolution von 1848/49. Barrikadenkämpfer, radikale Demo-kraten, gemäßigte Parlamentarier und Monarchisten.* [In]: "der schlimmste Punkt in der Provinz". Demokratische Revolution 1848/49 in Trier und Umgebung. Katalog-Handbuch. Hrsg. von Elisabeth Dühr. Trier: Selbstverl. des Städt. Museums Simeonstift Trier, 1998. Pp. 622–642, illus., notes. [Also in this book: Karl Marx und die Trier'sche Zeitung (Heinz Monz, 539–540, illus.).]

35928. *Medizinische Bildung und Judentum.* Hrsg. von Albrecht Scholz und Caris-Petra Heidel. Dresden: ddp goldenbogen, 1998. 96 pp., illus., notes, tabs. [Incl.: Soziale Voraussetzungen des Medizinstudiums von Juden im 18. und 19. Jahrhundert (Monika Richarz, 6–14). Aufstieg auf Zeit. Jüdische Ärzte und Heilkundige in westfälischen Städten bis zur Mitte des 16. Jahrhunderts (Kay Peter Jankrift, 15–19). Jüdische Apotheker im Deutschen Reich (Frank Leimkugel, 20–28). Die Traubes: Geschichte und Leistungen einer jüdischen Ärzte-und Naturwissenschaftlerfamilie in Berlin (Peter Schneck, 47–56). Die Arztfamilie Straßmann in Berlin (Manfred Stürzbecher, 57–67). Suizidalität bei den Juden – Folge der Assimilation? (Susanne Hahn, 68–75). Aufstieg durch Bildung? Das Schicksal der Jüdinnen unter den ersten russischen Ärztinnen (Ingrid Kästner, 76–83). Jüdische Ärzte im Spannungsfeld zwischen nationaler Identität und wissenschaftler Akkulturation (Klaus Hödl, 88–96). Incl. also an article on Russian antisemitism (Natalija Decker, 84–87).]

35929. MEIRING, KERSTIN: *Die christlich-jüdische Mischehe in Deutschland 1840–1933.* Hamburg: Dölling und Galitz, 1998. 237 pp., notes (143–208), bibl. (207–234), indexes (persons; places, 235–237). (Studien zur jüdischen Geschichte, Bd. 4.) Zugl.: Bielefeld, Univ., Diss., 1995. [Cf.: Besprechung (Trude Maurer) [in]: Aschkenas, Jg. 9, H. 1, Wien, 1999, pp. 265–266.]

35930. MEYER, MICHAEL A./BRENNER, MICHAEL: *Deutsch-jüdische Geschichte in der Neuzeit.* Zwei Vorträge. Frankfurt am Main: Freunde und Förderer des Leo Baeck Instituts e.V., 1998. 23 pp. (LBI Information; Sonderheft.) [Cont.: Vorwort (Georg Heuberger, 3). Juden – Deutsche – Juden. Wandlungen des deutschen Judentums in der Neuzeit (Michael A. Meyer, 5–16). Deutsch-jüdische Geschichte nach 1945 – nur ein Epilog? (Michael Brenner, 17–23).]

——— MEYER, MICHAEL A.: *Juden – Deutsche – Juden. Wandlungen des deutschen Judentums in der Neuzeit.* [See in No. 36147.]

35931. MEYER, MICHAEL A.: *Juden–Deutsche–Juden.* Wandlungen des deutschen Judentums in der Neuzeit. [In]: Aufbau, Jg. 64, No. 20, pp. 16–17; No. 21, p. 15; No. 22, p. 20, New York, Sept.-Oct. 1998. [Lecture delivered in Munich in Nov. 1997.]

35932. MUTIUS, HANS-GEORG VON: *Kritische Anmerkungen zu Elisabeth Hollender: Zwei hebräische Klagedichtungen aus der Zeit nach dem Zweiten Kreuzzug.* [In]: Aschkenas, Jg. 8, 1998, H. 2, Wien, 1999. Pp. 477–492, footnotes. [Essay is followed by a reply: Stellungnahme zur Kritik von Hans-Georg von Mutius (Elisabeth Hollender, 493–500). For Hollender's previous article see No. 33653/YB XLII.]

35933. NASH, STANLEY, ed.: *Between history and literature: studies in honor of Isaac Barzilay.* Tel-Aviv: Hakibbutz Hameuchad, 1997. 358; 218 pp. [In Hebrew and English.] [Incl. (in Hebrew): Permutations of the messianic idea among the Jews of Germany (Shlomo Eidelberg, 25–54; 17th and 18th cent.). Salomon Maimon: the book of Maimon's life written by himself (Menucha Gilboa, 75–99). Maimonides and Elisha ben Abuyah as archetypes in modern Hebrew literature (challenge or symptom?) (Yehuda Friedlander, 271–290; incl. German Haskalah literature). The Trier unit of the lengthy Hebrew First-Crusade narrative (Robert Chazan, 37–49; in Engl.).]

35934. NIEDERLAND, DORON: *German Jews – emigrants or refugees? Emigration patterns between the two World Wars.* Jerusalem: Magnes Press, Hebrew University, 1996. 257 pp. [In Hebrew.]

35935. NIEDERLAND, DORON: *Leaving Germany – emigration patterns of Jews and non-Jews during the Weimar period.* [In]: Tel Aviver Jahrbuch für deutsche Geschichte, Bd. 27, 1998, Gerlingen, 1998. Pp. 169–194, footnotes.

35936. PULZER, PETER: *A minority in a democracy, the Jews in the Weimar Republic.* The Leo Baeck Memorial Lecture delivered on Nov. 11 in London. London: The B'nai Brith Leo Baeck Lodge, Leo Baeck Hall, No. 11, 1998. 1 issue.

35937. RÜRUP, REINHARD: *Der Fortschritt und seine Grenzen. Die Revolution von 1848 und die europäischen Juden.* [In]: Dieter Dowe [et al.], eds.: Europa 1848. Revolution und Reform. Bonn: Dietz Nachf., 1998. Pp. 985–1005, footnotes. [Also, by the same author: Revolution und Volksbewegung: 1848/49 im Kontext der deutschen Geschichte (in): Gewerkschaftliche Monatshefte, Jg. 49, H. 4, Köln, 1998. Pp. 208–221; incl. the emancipation of the Jews.]

35938. SCHATZKER, CHAIM: *Jewish youth in Germany between Judaism and Germanism 1870–1945.* Jerusalem: Zalman Shazar Center for Jewish History, 1998. 315 pp. [In Hebrew.] [Cf.: Besprechung (Barbara Schäfer) [in]: Frankfurter Judaistische Beiträge, 25, Frankfurt am Main, Dez. 1998, pp. 191–196.]

——— SCHOEPS, JULIUS H.: *Das Gewaltsyndrom. Verformungen und Brüche im deutsch-jüdischen Verhältnis.* [See No. 36438.]

35939. SHOHAM, CHAIM: *In the shadow of the Berlin Enlightenment.* Tel-Aviv: Hakibbutz Hameuchad, 1996. 233 pp. [In Hebrew.] [On the beginning of the Jewish Enlightenment in 18th-century Germany.]

35940. TENENBAUM, KATJA: *Wahrheit und Geschichte des jüdischen Volkes im Urteil der Aufklärung.* [In]: Judentum und Moderne in Frankreich und Italien. Hrsg. von Christoph Miething. Tübingen: Niemeyer, 1998. Pp. 244–253. [On Moses Mendelssohn and Rousseau.]

35941. TOCH, MICHAEL: *Die Juden im mittelalterlichen Reich.* München: Oldenbourg, 1998. X, 185 pp., bibl. (143–176), index (177–185). (Enzyklopädie deutscher Geschichte, Bd. 44.) [Cont. the sections: I. Enzyklopädischer Überblick. II. Grundprobleme und Tendenzen der Forschung. III. Quellen und Literatur.] [Cf.: Besprechung (Johannes Heil) [in]: Zeitschrift für Geschichtswissenschaft, Jg. 47, H. 3, Berlin, 1999, pp. 266–267.]

35942. ZIMMERMANN, AKIVA: *'Loyal Guardian of Zion'. An orthodox Jewish bi-weekly in mid-19th century Germany.* [In Hebrew, with English summary]. [In]: Qesher, No. 19, Tel-Aviv, May 1996. Pp. 131–134. [On 'Der Treue Zions-Wächter'.]

35943. ZUSMAN, JACOB: *Fragments of the Jerusalem Talmud – an Ashkenazic ms.* Towards a solution of the riddle 'Sefer Yerushalmi'. [In Hebrew, title transl.] [In]: Kobez al-Yad, No. 12, Jerusalem, 1994. Pp. 1–120. [Pp. 25–120 cont. the texts of the fragments found in the libraries of Trier, Munich and Darmstadt.]

35944. ZWEIG, ARNOLD: *Bilanz der deutschen Judenheit 1933: ein Versuch.* [Bd.-Bearb.: Thomas Taterka]. Berlin: Aufbau, 1998. 441 pp. (Berliner Ausgabe/Arnold Zweig: 3, Essays, 3,2.) [Orig. publ. 1934 in Amsterdam (Querido).] [Cf.: Arnold Zweig und die Liebe zur Gerechtigkeit. Ein verwundeter Intellektueller, ein Jude ohne Thora, ein bedeutender Schriftsteller voller Makel – und Teil der deutschen Literaturgeschichte (Fritz J. Raddatz) [in]: Die Zeit, Nr. 5, Hamburg, 28. Jan. 1999, pp. 39–40.]

Linguistics/Western Yiddish

35945. ALTHAUS, HANS PETER: *Melech/Mélac.* [In]: Jiddistik-Mitteilungen, Nr. 20, Trier, Nov. 1998. Pp. 1–22, notes.

——— BÖNING, ADALBERT: *Ein Brief des Jakob Falk, eines um 1810 von Altena nach England ausgewanderten Juden, an seine Geschwister in der alten Heimat (9. Januar 1820).* [See No. 35957.]

35946. EGGERS, ECKHARD: *Sprachwandel und Sprachmischung im Jiddischen.* Frankfurt am Main; New York: Lang, 1998. 494 pp., footnotes, tabs., maps, ibl. (461–494). [Cf.: Review (Marion Aptroot) [in]: Aschkenas, Jg. 8, H. 2, Wien, 1998, pp. 553–554.]

35947. GIRTLER, ROLAND: *Rotwelsch. Die alte Sprache der Gauner, Dirnen und Vagabunden.* Wien: Böhlau, 1998. 255 pp., bibl., index. [Refers also to the Hebrew and Yiddish components.]

——— HAARSCHER, ANDRÉ-MARC: *Les juifs du Comté de Hanau-Lichtenberg entre le quatorzième siècle et la fin de L'Ancien Régime.* [See No. 36086.]

35948. KEIM, HEINRICH: *Jiddische Sprachelemente in Marktsprache und Mundart der Niederhessen.* [In]: Jahrbuch '97 [des Landkreises Kassel], Kassel, 1996. Pp. 33–37.

35949. KLEINE, ANE: *Parallelisierung von Maks Vaynraykh (1973): geshikhte fun der yidisher shprakh und der englischen Übersetzung Max Weinreich: History of the Yiddish Language (1980).* [Issue title of] Jiddistik Mitteilungen, Sonderheft, Trier, Nov. 1998. 1 issue, 32 pp., tabs.

——— KRANHOLD, KARINA: *Jiddische Kinderliteratur.* [See in No. 36653.]

35950. LIPSKER, AVIDOV/BAMBERGER, JOSEPH: *Rabbi Amram's coffin.* [In]: Chulyot, No. 4, Haifa, Summer 1997. Pp. 121–140. [In Hebrew, with English summary.] [On a story from the Yiddish 'Maasse Bukh' (Basle, 1602).]

35951. LIPSKER, AVIDOV: *The mirror in which Rabbi Simon the Great of Mainz did not see clearly.* [In]: Chulyot, No. 3, Haifa, Spring 1996. Pp. 33–57. [In Hebrew, with English summary.] [English title not identical with the Hebrew. On a story from the Yiddish 'Maasse Bukh' (Basle, 1602).]

35952. REERSHEMIUS, GERTRUD: *Biographisches Erzählen auf Jiddisch.* Grammatische und diskursanalytische Untersuchungen. Tübingen: Niemeyer, 1997. 423 pp., footnotes. (Beihefte zum Language and culture atlas of Ashkenazic Jewry, Bd. 2.) [Deals also briefly with the origins and characteristics of Western Yiddish.]

35953. SCHUPPENER, GEORG: *Jüdisch-deutsche Identifikation – Reflexionen zu einem judendeutschen Kaiserwahllied des 17. Jahrhunderts.* [In]: Volker Hertl [et al.], eds.: Sprache und Kommunikation im Kulturkontext. Beiträge zum Ehrenkolloquium aus Anlaß des 60. Geburtstages von Gotthard Lerchner. Frankfurt am Main; New York, 1998. (Leipziger Arbeiten zur Sprach- und Kommunikationsgeschichte, Bd. 4.). Pp. 33–46, notes, bibl. [On a poem of 23 verses written in Western Yiddish on the occasion of the election of Leopold I. in 1658; this is part of the Wagenseil collection at the Ratsbibliothek in Leipzig; incl. the text written in Hebrew letters).]

35954. TIMM, ERIKA: *Die Bibelübersetzungssprache als Faktor der Auseinanderentwicklung des jiddischen und des deutschen Wortschatzes.* [In]: Sprache und Identität im Judentum [see No. 36627]. Pp. 91–110.

———— TURNIANSKY, CHAVA: *Yiddish literature in Frankfurt am Main.* [See in No. 35999.]

B. Communal and Regional History

1. Germany

35955. AHRWEILER. WARNECKE, HANS, ed.: *Zeugnisse jüdischen Lebens im Kreis Ahrweiler.* Bad Neuenahr-Ahrweiler: ARE Buchhandlung, 1998. 171 pp., illus., lists, notes. [Contribs. on Ahrweiler, Bad Breisig, Dernau, Gelsdorf, Königsfeld, Dedenbach, Schalkenbach, Bad Neuenahr, Niederzissen, Remagen and Sinzig. Incl. the cemeteries in this area.]

35956. ALDENHOVEN (Kreis Jülich). BERS, GÜNTER, ed.: *Aldenhoven. Neue Aspekte der Ortsgeschichte.* Jülich: Joseph-Kuhl-Ges. für die Gesch. der Stadt Jülich und des Jülicher Landes, 1996. 1 vol. [Incl. chap. dealing with the Jews of Aldenhoven in mid-19th cent. (Werner Pankoke, 148–164).]

35957. ALTENA. BÖNING, ADALBERT: *Ein Brief des Jakob Falk, eines um 1810 von Altena nach England ausgewanderten Juden, an seine Geschwister in der alten Heimat (9. Januar 1820).* [In]: Der Märker, Jg. 47, H. 2, Lüdenscheid, 1998. Pp. 71–76, facsims., notes. [Incl. transcription of letter written in Hebrew letters.]

———— ALTONA. [See also HAMBURG.]

35958. ALTONA. DICK, JUTTA: *Freundinnen. Rahel de Castro, Ludmilla Assing, Ottilie Assing.* [In]: Menora 1997, Bodenheim, 1997. Pp. 181–198. [Based on letters found in the Varnhagen collection in Cracow, written by three women from Altona, of whom Ottilie A. emigr. 1853 to the US and Ludmilla A. lived in Florence.]

35959. ALTONA. HINNENBERG, ULLA: *Die Kehille: Geschichte und Geschichten der Altonaer jüdischen Gemeinde.* Ein Buch über Altona. [Hrsg.: Stadtteilarchiv Ottensen]. [Hamburg-Altona]: Dingwort, 1996 [?]. 288 pp., illus., bibl. (Stadtbilder.)

35960. ALTONA. Lehmann, Dora: *Erinnerungen einer Altonaerin: 1866–1946.* Hrsg. vom Joseph-Carlebach-Institut, Israel. Hamburg: Dölling und Galitz, 1998. 148 pp., illus.

——— ALTONA. Zürn, Gaby: *Tod und Judentum in der Zeit der Aufklärung am Beispiel des jüdischen Begräbniswesens in Altona.* [See in No. 36643.]

35961. ALTONA-HAMBURG-WANDSBEK. Rohrbacher, Stefan: *Die Drei Gemeinden Altona, Hamburg, Wandsbek zur Zeit der Glikl.* [In]: Aschkenas, Jg. 8, H. 1, Wien, 1998. Pp. 105–124, footnotes.

35962. BAD VILBEL. Ritscher, Berta: *Geschichte der Vilbeler Juden.* Von der Integration zur Deportation. Hrsg. vom Bad Vilbeler Verein für Geschichte und Heimatpflege e.V. im Auftrag des Magistrats der Stadt Vilbel unter Mitarbeit der Jüdischen Gemeinde Bad Vilbel e.V. Bad Vilbel [Bad Vilbeler Verein für Gesch. und Heimatpflege e.V., Rathaus], 1998. 357, LXXXVIII pp., illus., facsims., docs., plan, footnotes, bibl., index (places, names, subjects, XLI-LXXXVIII). [Incl.: Zum Werdegang des Projektes "Geschichte der Juden in Vilbel". Book covers the period from the mid-17th cent. to the present; incl. the cemetery, 125 family biographies, arranged alphabetically.]

——— BADEN. Liepach, Martin: *Zwischen Abwehrkampf und Wählermobilisierung. Juden und die Landtagswahl in Baden 1929.* [See in No. 35925.]

35963. BAMBERG. Walther, Karl Klaus: *"Kolleg und vertrauter Freund des großen Mendelssohn". Aspekte jüdischen Lebens in Bamberg am Anfang des 19. Jahrhunderts.* [In]: Menora 1998, Bodenheim, 1998. Pp. 349–360.

——— BAVARIA. [See also No. 36044.]

35964. BAVARIA. *Theodor Harburger*: Die Inventarisierung jüdischer Kunst- und Kulturdenkmäler in Bayern. Hrsg. von den Central Archives for the History of the Jewish People, Jerusalem und dem Jüdischen Museum Franken – Fürth & Schnaittach. Fürth; Schnaittach: [Jüd. Museum Franken], 1998. 3 vols., 799 pp., illus. [Vol. 1 cont. 2 articles by Theodor Harburger and four contribs. on Th. H., his life and his photographic collection by Hadassah Assouline, Joel S. Fishman, Bernhard Purin and Annette Weber; also Engl. summaries, bibl. and indexes. Vols. 2 and 3 cont. 850 photographs of synagogues, cemeteries and ritual objects made by Th.H. between 1926 and 1932 at 28 different locations; incl. his descriptions as well as annotations by the eds.] [Th.H., 1887 – 1949, art historian, emigr. in 1933 from Munich to Palestine.] [Cf.: Besprechung (Saskia Rohde) [in]: Aschkenas, Jg. 9. H. 1, Wien, 1999, pp. 191–193. Die Photosammlung Theodor Harburger: ein Gedenkbuch (Jim G. Tobias) [in]: Aufbau, Vol. 64, No. 23, New York, Nov. 6, 1998, p. 5.]

35965. BAYREUTH. Gothart, Josef: *Was der jüdische Friedhof Bayreuths uns zu sagen hat.* [In]: Archiv für Geschichte von Oberfranken, Bd. 78, Bayreuth, 1998. Pp. 457–470, illus.

35966. BEDBURG (ERFT). *Juden in Bedburg an der Erft. Spurenfragmente einer Minderheit.* Dokumentiert von Gerd Friedt unter Mitarbeit und mit einem Beitrag von Achim Jaeger. München: Gerd Friedt, 1998. [Privately printed]. 217 pp., illus., facsims., bibl, indexes. [Incl. the Nazi period. Available at the Bibliothek Germania Judaica, Cologne.]

——— BERLIN. [See also in No. 35928.]

35967. BERLIN. Alexander, Gabriel E.: *Berlin Jewry and their community during the Weimar Republic (1919–1933).* Jerusalem: Hebrew Univ. of Jerusalem, 1995. 364, XXXVIII pp. (Diss.) [In Hebrew, with English summary.]

35968. BERLIN. Asai, K.: *'Geborgensein' und 'Ausgesetztsein'. Walter Benjamins Berlin.* [In]: Doitsu Bungaku, H. 101, Tokyo, Herbst 1998. Pp. 35–45, footnotes. [With Engl. summary.]

35969. BERLIN. Ehrenfreund, Jacques: *Mémoires et intégration; conscience historique et rapport au passé des Juifs berlinois sous le second Reich.* Jerusalem: Hebrew Univ. of Jerusalem, 1997. VII, 419, 21 pp. (Diss.) [With Hebrew summary.]

——— BERLIN. *Intermezzo Berlin. Wiener in Berlin 1890–1933.* [See No. 36749.]

35970. BERLIN. Kojima, H.: *Die Großstadt Berlin und Alfred Döblin.* [In]: Doitsu Bungaku, H. 101, Tokyo, Herbst 1998. Pp. 46–54, footnotes. [With Engl. summary.]

35971. BERLIN. Neiss, Marion: *Jiddische Presse in Berlin zu Beginn der 20er Jahre. Die Kritik am deutschen Judentum in den Wochenblättern "Der Freitag" und der "Der Misrach-Jud".* [In]: Jahrbuch für Antisemitismusforschung 7, Frankfurt am Main; New York, 1998. Pp. 226–240, notes.

——— BERLIN. Neiss, Marion: *Jiddische Zeitungen und Zeitschriften im Berlin der Weimarer Republik.* [See in No. 35925.]

35972. BERLIN. Yamaguchi, Y.: *Berlin im Roman "Eine jüdische Mutter" von Gertrud Kolmar.* [In]: Doitsu Bungaku, H. 101, Tokyo, Herbst 1998. Pp. 55–64, footnotes. [With Engl. summary.]

35973. BERLIN-HOHENSCHÖNHAUSEN. Friedrich, Thomas/Wolf, Frank: *Jüdische Einwohner Hohenschönhausens. Ein biographischer Spaziergang über den Jüdischen Friedhof Berlin-Weißensee.* Berlin: Verein "Biographische Forschungen und Sozialgeschichte e.V.", 1998. 31 pp., illus., plan. (Biographische Forschungen und Sozialgeschichte, H. 3.)

35974. BINSWANGEN. *Alte Synagoge Binswangen.* Eine Gedenkschrift. Hrsg.: Landkreis Dillingen. Dillingen: Eigenverlag Landkreis Dillingen, 1996. 60 pp., illus. [Incl. contribs. on the history of the Jews of Binswangen/Bavaria (Reinhard H. Seitz), on the synagogue (Peter Fassl), on the restoration of the synagogue (Egon Georg Kunz) and on Isaac Hirsch Gunzenhausen, rabbi in Binswangen 1821–1881.]

35975. BONN. Brocke, Michael/Bondy, Dan: *Der alte jüdische Friedhof Bonn-Schwarzrheindorf. 1623–1956. Bildlich-textliche Dokumentation.* Köln: Rheinland-Verl.; Bonn: Habelt, 1998. 593 pp., illus., bibl., indexes, plan. (Arbeitsheft der Rheinischen Denkmalpflege Nr. 50.) [Documents and annotates all inscriptions, with German transl.]

35976. BRAUNSCHWEIG. Friedrichs, Nelli H.: *Erinnerungen aus meinem Leben in Braunschweig, 1912–1937.* Hrsg.: Stadt Braunschweig, Der Oberstadtdirektor. 3., erw. Aufl. Braunschweig: Stadtarchiv, 1998. 51 pp., illus. (Kleine Schriften/Stadtarchiv und Öffentliche Bücherei Braunschweig, 32.)

35977. BREISACH. Blum, Hans David: *Juden in Breisach. Von den Anfängen bis zur Schoáh.* Bd. 1: 12.–19. Jahrhundert. Hrsg. von Erhard Roy Wiehn. Konstanz: Hartung-Gorre, 1998. 263 pp., illus., facsims., docs., footnotes, tabs., lists. [Incl. list of Nazi victims.]

35978. BRESLAU. Nick, Dagmar: *Jüdisches Wirken in Breslau.* Eingeholte Erinnerung: Der Alte Asch und die Bauers. Würzburg: Bergstadtverlag W.G. Korn, 1998. 219 pp., illus., notes (203–210), index. [Deals with the author's ancestors, among them the Breslau physician Sigismund Asch, active in the 1848 Revolution; the manufacturer Albert Bauer; and his daughter, the writer and philanthropist Lina Morgenstern.]

35979. BRESLAU. Rahden, Til van: *Die Grenze vor Ort – Einbürgerung und Ausweisung ausländischer Juden in Breslau 1860–1918.* [In]: Tel Aviver Jahrbuch für deutsche Geschichte, Bd. 27, 1998, Gerlingen, 1998. Pp. 47–69, footnotes.

——— BRESLAU. Rahden, Til van: *Mingling, marrying and distancing: Jewish intergration in Wilhelminian Breslau and its erosion in early Weimar Germany.* [See in No. 35925.]

35980. BÜHL. Mohr, Günther: *Unruhen gegen den Amtsdespoten. Exzesse gegen Juden. Aufbrüche zur Revolution in der ländlichen Amtsstadt Bühl.* [In]: Die Ortenau, Jg. 78, Offenburg/Baden, 1998. Pp. 245–274, facsims., notes.

35981. BUSENBERG. Weber, Otmar: *Der jüdische Friedhof Busenberg: die zentrale Begräbnisstätte der Juden im Wasgau.* [Hrsg.: Ges. für Christl.-Jüd. Zusammenarbeit Pfalz, Landau]. Landau: Ges. für Christl.-Jüd. Zusammenarbeit Pfalz, 1998. 368 pp., illus., map, bibl. (351–366). [Place of publ. on title page also given as: Busenberg/Pfalz; Dahn.]

35982. CHEMNITZ. Richter, Tilo: *Erich Mendelsohns Kaufhaus Schocken: jüdische Kulturgeschichte in Chemnitz.* Hrsg. vom Evang. Forum Chemnitz. Leipzig: Passage-Verl., 1998. 120 pp., illus., bibl.

35983. COLOGNE. Schütte, Sven: *Der Almemor der Kölner Synagoge um 1270/80 – Gotische Kleinarchitektur aus der Kölner Dombauhütte.* Befund, Rekonstruktion und Umfeld. [In]: Colonia Romanica. Jahrbuch des Fördervereins Romanische Kirchen Köln e.V., Bd. XIII, Köln, 1998. Pp. 188–215, illus., plans, notes.

35984. DESSAU. *1. Dessauer Gespräche. Gesellschaft – Religion – Wissenschaft – Kultur.* Ins Leben gerufen von Eveline Goodman-Thau in Verbindung mit der Robert Bosch Stiftung. [In]: Zwischen Wörlitz und Mosigkau. H. 50, Hrsg. vom Museum für Stadtgeschichte Dessau, Dessau, 1998. (Dessau-Wörlitz-Beiträge VIII.) 1 issue, illus., plans, notes. [Cont.: Religion in der Moderne – zur Neubestimmung des Verhältnisses von Ethos und Aufklärung (Eveline Goodman-Thau, 3–10). Fürst Franz und die anhalt-dessauischen Juden: "Von der Dessauer Gemeinde ging die Emanzipation der deutschen Juden aus" (Erhard Hirsch, 11–15). Aus der Dessauer Judenschaft um 1800 (Andreas R. Riem (1749–1807), 16–18). Baron Moritz von Cohn (1812–1900): Privat- und Hofbankier in Dessau und Berlin (Erik Lindner, 19–22). Zwischen Synagoge und Herzoglichem Hoftheater. Kurt Weill: Kindheit und Jugendjahre (Jürgen Schebera, 23–29). Die Dr. Nathan-Meyer-Stiftung Dessau und die Entstehung einer städtischen Kunstsammlung in Dessau (Günter Ziegler, 30–37). Katalog (38–49; listing objets d'art acquired with the financial help of the "Stiftung"). Die Dessauer Synagoge. Eine architekturhistorische Betrachtung (Andreas Butter, 50–63). Jüdische Studierende am Bauhaus (Margret Kentgens-Craig (64–66).]

——— DORTMUND. *Benno Elkan. Ein jüdischer Künstler aus Dortmund.* [See No. 36813.]

35985. DORTMUND. *Biographien bedeutender Dortmunder.* Menschen in, aus und für Dortmund. Hrsg. von Hans Bohrmann im Auftrag des Hist. Vereins für Dortmund und die Grafschaft Mark e.V. Red.: Helga Köhler und Hans Bohrmann. Bd. 2. Essen: Klartext, 1998. 160 pp., ports. [Incl. contribs. on Paul Walter Jacob (70–72; actor, theatre director); Charlotte (Lotte) Temming (116–118; writer); Felix Wolfes (151–153; composer, conductor).]

35986. DRESDEN. Friedrichs, Christopher R.: *Jüdische Jugend im Biedermeier. Ein unbekanntes Tagebuch aus Dresden, 1833–1837.* Leipzig: Simon-Dubnow-Institut für jüdische Geschichte und Kultur e.V., 1998. 22 pp., footnotes. [Incl.: Vorwort (Stefi Jersch-Wenzel/Andreas Reinke, 3–4). Deals with Louis Lesser's diary (90 per cent of which was written in English). Ms. was discovered in Canada.]

35987. DRESDEN. Künzl, Hannelore: *Die Synagoge in Dresden von Gottfried Semper.* [In]: Trumah 7, 1998. Pp. 147–160, footnotes, illus.

35988. DRESDEN. Lässig, Simone: *Juden und Mäzenatentum in Deutschland. Religiöses Ethos, kompensierendes Minderheitsverhalten oder genuine Bürgerlichkeit?* [In]: Zeitschrift für Geschichtswissenschaft, Jg. 46, H. 3, Berlin, 1998. Pp. 211–236, footnotes. [On the Dresden banking family Arnhold.]

——— DRESDEN. Lässig, Simone: *Nationalsozialistische "Judenpolitik" und jüdische Selbstbehauptung vor dem Novemberpogrom. Das Beispiel der Dresdner Bankiersfamilie Arnhold.* [See No. 36238.]

35989. DÜSSELDORF. *Juden in Düsseldorf: Ein fotografisches Erinnerungsbuch mit Arbeiten von Marcus Kiel/Jews in Düsseldorf: A fotografic memor book with works by Marcus Kiel.* Vorwort/preface: Hans-Heinrich Grosse-Brockhoff. [Konzeption und Red.: Angela Genger. Kurzerl.: Angela Genger in Zusammenarbeit mit Hildegard Jakobs.] Düsseldorf: Mahn- und Gedenkstätte Düsseldorf, 1998. 224 pp., ports. [All texts in German and English. Incl.: The Jewish presence in Düsseldorf and the Lower Rhine Region (Angela Genger, 7–13; only in English, for German orig. article see in No. 34763/YB XLIII). Hundert Portraits/Hundred portraits (14–215; with biogr. annotations).]

——— DÜSSELDORF. Schwarz, Egbert F.: *Zur Geschichte der Gebrüder Schöndorff AG (1890–1933).* [See No. 36942.]

35990. DUISBURG. Heid, Ludger: *Jüdische Arbeiterfürsorgeämter im rheinisch-westfälischen Industriegebiet 1919–1927.* [In]: Duisburger Forschungen, Bd. 43, Duisburg, 1997. Pp. 287–310.

35991. EAST PRUSSIA. Kabus, Ronny: *Juden in Ostpreußen.* [Hrsg. vom Ostpreußischen Landesmuseum, Lüneburg]. Husum: Druck- und Verlagsges., 1998. 202 pp., illus. [Publ. to accompany an exhibition with the same title in Lüneburg in the Ostpreußisches Landesmuseum, Nov. 21, 1998 – March 3, 1999.]

35992. EIFEL. Linder, Christian: *Der tote Friedhof von Drove. Auf den Spuren Heinrich Bölls in der Eifel.* [In]: Jahrbuch des Eifelvereins, Düren 1998. Pp. 107–115, illus. [On the Jewish cemetery and Böll's interest and research in this matter in the early 1980s.]

35993. EINBECK. Bertram, Frank [et al.]: *Verloren, aber nicht vergessen: jüdisches Leben in Einbeck.* Oldenburg: Isensee, 1998. 150 pp., illus., bibl. (Studien zur Einbecker Geschichte, Bd. 15.)

35994. ELSOFF. Hüster, Kurt: *Christen und Juden in Elsoff.* [In]: Wittgenstein, Blätter des Wittgensteiner Heimatvereins, Bd. 61, H. 3, Bad Laasphe, 1997. Pp. 109–114.

35995. ERFURT. Weiß, Ulman: *Habet Erbarmen mit meiner armen Jüden-Seele!: Judentaufen im kurmainzischen Erfurt.* [In]: Pietismus und Neuzeit, Jg. 21, Göttingen, 1996. Pp. 299–318.

35996. FRANCONIA. August, Tom: *Eine Gemeinde, in der sich's leben läßt! Jüdisches Leben in einem fränkischen Dorf.* [In]: Jüdischer Almanach 1999 des Leo Baeck Instituts, Frankfurt am Main, 1998. Pp. 24–32, notes. [Transl. from English by Dorthe Seifert. Deals with Schopfloch.]

35997. FRANCONIA. Ebner, Robert: *Jüdische Schulen und Bildungseinrichtungen in Franken in der ersten Hälfte des 19. Jahrhunderts.* [In]: Jahrbuch für fränkische Landesforschung, 58, Neustadt/Aisch, 1998. Pp. 349–370, footnotes. [Incl. curricula of Jewish schools. See also in No. 36044.]

35998. FRANCONIA. Knörlein, Georg: *Jüdisches Leben im Forchheimer Land.* Haigerloch: Medien und Dialog Schubert, 1998. 18 pp., illus.

——— FRANKFURT am Main. Elon, Amos: *Der erste Rothschild. Biographie eines Frankfurter Juden.* [See No. 36928.]

35999. FRANKFURT am Main. *Jüdische Kultur in Frankfurt am Main von den Anfängen bis zur Gegenwart.* Ein internationales Symposium der Johann Wolfgang Goethe-Universität Frankfurt am Main und des Franz Rosenzweig Research Center for German-Jewish Literature and Cultural History Jerusalem. Hrsg. von Karl E. Grözinger. Wiesbaden: Harrassowitz, 1998. XIII, 422 pp., illus., facsims., tabs., bibl. notes, index. (Jüdische Kultur, Bd. 1.) [Essays are arranged under the sections: *Geschichte – Gesellschaft – Wirtschaft*; cont.: Alltagsleben in der Frankfurter Judengasse im 17. und 18. Jahrhundert (Marianne Awerbuch, 1–24). Wirtschaft und Geldwesen der Juden Frankfurts im Spätmittelalter und in der Frühen Neuzeit (Michael Toch, 25–46). Jüdische Handwerker und Kleinhändler im Frankfurt des 18. und 19. Jahrhunderts (Uri R. Kaufmann, 47–72). Gabriel Riessers Plädoyer für die Gleichberechtigung. Das demokratische Prinzip und die Rolle der Juden in der 48er Revolution und in der Frankfurter Paulskirche (Julius H. Schoeps, 73–81). Die Rothschilds – ein

Mythos und seine Nachwirkungen (Frederic Morton, 83–90). *Religion und Ethik*; cont.: Besonderheiten des alten Frankfurter Synagogengesangs (Mordechai Breuer, 91–100). Jüdische Religion und Kultur in Frankfurt am Main im 16. und 17. Jahrhundert – Yuzpa Hahn und sein 'Yosifmez (Chava Fraenkel-Goldschmidt, 101–121). On Rabbi Zvi Hirsh Koidanover's Sefer Qav Ha-Yashar (Moshe Idel, 123–134; on the kabbalistic musar book Qav, printed in 1705 in Hebrew in Frankfurt am Main where rabbi K. lived during the later part of his life). R. Nathan Adler and the Frankfurt Pietists. Pietist groups in Eastern and Central Europe during the eighteenth century (Rachel Elior, 135–177). Legenden aus dem Frankfurt des 18. Jahrhunderts (Karl E. Grözinger, 179–205). Religious trends and tensions – Orthodoxy and reform in Frankfurt in the 19th and 20th centuries (Robert Liberles, 207–216). The "Freies Jüdisches Lehrhaus" of Frankfurt (Paul Mendes-Flohr, 217–229). *Literatur und Druckwesen*; cont.: Hebrew printing by and for Frankfurt Jews – to 1800 (Herbert C. Zafren, 231–271). Yiddish literature in Frankfurt am Main (Chava Turniansky, 273–288). Architektur und Kunst; cont.: Synagogenarchitektur in Frankfurt am Main (Salomon Korn, 287–319; from the 12th – 20th cent.). Moritz Daniel Oppenheim und die Tradition des Kultgerätes aus der Frankfurter Judengasse (Annette Weber, 321–344). Jüdische Malerei des 18. und 19. Jahrhunderts in Frankfurt am Main (Hannelore Künzl, 345–353). *Wissenschaft und Kultur in der Verfolgung*; cont.: Max Horkheimer und die "Zeitschrift für Sozialforschung" (Alfred Schmidt, 355–372; on the periodical founded in 1932, from Nov. 1933 until 1937 publ. in Paris). Musik als Form geistigen Widerstandes. Jüdische Musikerinnen und Musiker von 1933 bis 1945 (Joachim Carlos Martini, 373–407.]

36000. FÜRTH. JÜDISCHES MUSEUM FRANKEN. PURIN, BERNHARD: *"... ein Schatzkästlein alter jüdischer Geschichte". Die Sammlung Gundelfinger im Jüdischen Museum Franken.* With an English summary. Fürth: Jüdisches Museum Franken, 1998. 40 pp., illus. [Incl. English summary.] [Werner Gundelfinger, born 1921 in Fürth, emigr. during the Nazi period to Switzerland, in his later life returned to Fürth and donated his collection of religious objects to the museum, incl. some pieces from the family of his wife: Suzanne G. née Freud, born in Stuhlweissenburg (= Szekesfehérvár, Hungary).]

36001. FULDA. HOPPE, HEINZ-JÜRGEN: *Das jüdische Fulda. Ein historischer Stadtrundgang.* Mit einem Geleitwort von Wolfgang Hamberger. Hünfeld: Rhön-Verl., [1998?]. 64 pp., bibl.

36002. GERA. SIMSOHN, WERNER: *Juden in Gera.* 2. Jüdische Familiengeschichten. Hrsg. von Erhard Roy Wiehn. Konstanz: Hartung-Gorre, 1998. 334 pp., illus., facsims., bibl., index. [For Vol. 1 see No. 34778/YB XLIII.]

36003. GERNSBACH. PATZER, GEORG/KUHNER, TANJA: *"... denn sie lieben sich" oder Der Versuch des jüdischen Händlers Simon Kaufmann, eine Christin zu heiraten.* [In]: Aschkenas, Jg. 8, H. 1, Wien, 1998. Pp. 193–197, footnotes. [On an incident in Gernsbach, Grand Duchy of Baden, 1810.]

36004. GIESSEN. ALTARAS, THEA: *Stätten der Juden in Gießen: Von den Anfängen bis heute.* Königsstein/Ts.: Langewiesche; Köster, 1998. 80 pp., illus., facsims. (Die blauen Bücher.)

36005. GOLDBACH. HEEG-ENGELHART, INGRID: *Die jüdische Gemeinde in Goldbach von ihren Anfängen bis 1942.* [In]: Markt Goldbach. Geschichte und Gegenwart. Hrsg.: Markt Goldbach. Goldbach 1998. Pp. 226–257. [Goldbach: near Aschaffenburg.]

——— HAMBURG. [See also ALTONA.]

36006. HAMBURG. HINRICHSEN, TORKILD/KAUFMANN, GERHARD, eds.: *Schatten: jüdische Kultur in Altona und Hamburg.* [Anläßlich der Ausstellung "Schatten" – Jüdische Kultur in Altona und Hamburg" im Altonaer Museum 20.5.1998 – 27.9.1998 hrsg. für das Altonaer Museum]. Hamburg: Dölling und Galitz, 1998. 150 pp., illus., facsims., bibl. [Incl. personal memoirs by Miriam Gillis-Carlebach; also on the collection of Dr. Max Salzberg.]

36007. HAMBURG. JAEGER, ROLAND: *"Block & Hochfeld". Die Architekten des Deutschlandhauses. Bauten und Projekte in Hamburg 1921–1938. Exil in Los Angeles.* Berlin: Gebr. Mann, 1996. 247

pp., illus. [On life and work of Fritz Block and Ernst Hochfeld, who emigr. in 1938 to the US.]

36008. HAMBURG. Kürschner-Pelkmann, Frank: *Jüdisches Leben in Hamburg*. Ein Stadtführer. Mit Fotografien von Thomas Nagel. Hamburg: Dölling und Galitz, 1997. 191 pp., illus.

36009. HAMBURG. Liedtke, Rainer: *Jewish welfare in Hamburg and Manchester, 1850–1914*. Oxford: Clarendon Press; New York: Oxford Univ. Press, 1998. VI, 266 pp., illus., gloss., footnotes, bibl. (245–258). (Oxford historical monographs.) [Orig. Ph.D. thesis, Oxford Univ., 1995.]

36010. HAMBURG. Studemund-Halévy, Michael: *Sephardische Bücher und Bibliotheken in Hamburg*. [In]: Menora 1997, Bodenheim, 1997. Pp. 150–180, notes.

36011. HAMBURG. Wallenborn, Hiltrud: *"Portugiesische Nation" und "hochdeutsche Juden"*. *Die Hamburger sephardische Gemeinde und die Ansiedlung von aschkenasischen Juden im Hamburger Raum*. [In]: Menora 1997, Bodenheim, 1997. Pp. 121–149, notes. [On the period before 1669.]

36012. HANOVER. Jürgens, Wilhelm: *Jüdische Vereine und Stiftungen im Erziehungswesen in Hannover im 19. Jahrhundert*. [In]: Menora 1997, Bodenheim, 1997. Pp. 313–341, notes.

36013. HANOVER. Schulze, Peter: *Beiträge zur Geschichte der Juden in Hannover*. Hannover: Landeshauptstadt Hannover, 1998. 222 pp., illus., map, plan, index, footnotes. (Hannoversche Studien, Bd. 6.) [Cont. 11 previously publ. essays dealing with general aspects of the history of Jews in Hanover; incl. also the "Landrabbinat", youth and sports movement, historical Torah (Ark) curtains, the Berliner family, the author Werner Kraft.]

36014. HANOVER. Voigt-Deutsch, Elfriede: *"... ärgerte ich mich der Trägheit, die mich abhielt, nach Hannover hinüber zu fahren ..."*. *Johannes Brahms, Joseph Joachim und Hannover*. [In]: Hannoversche Geschichtsblätter, Bd. 52, Hannover, 1998. Pp. 297–328, illus., bibl. [Deals a.o. with J.J.'s musical career incl. his time in Hanover, where between 1853 and 1865 he was first concert-master, then later musical director.]

36015. HECHINGEN. Werner, Otto: *Rabbiner Dr. S. Samuel Mayer und die Hohenzollern*. [In]: Zeitschrift für Hohenzollerische Geschichte. Bd. 34 – Bd. 120 der ganzen Reihe, Sigmaringen, 1998. Pp. 133–169, ports., footnotes. [S.S.M., 1807 Hechingen – 1875 Hechingen, Reform rabbi and lawyer in Hechingen 1834–1875.]

36016. HEMER (Westphalia). Stopsack, Hans-Hermann, ed.: *Juden in Hemer. Spuren ihres Lebens*. Autoren: Wilhelm Gröne [et al.]. Hrsg.: Verband für die Volkshochschule Menden-Hemer-Balve. Menden/Hemer, 1998. 224 pp., illus., tabs. [From the 17th to 20th cent.]

36017. HESSE. Friedman, Jonathan C.: *The lion and the star: Gentile-Jewish relations in three Hessian communities, 1919–1945*. Lexington: The Univ. Press of Kentucky, 1998. X, 292 pp. tabs., maps, notes (187–270), bibl. (271–283). [On Frankfurt, Giessen, Geisenheim.]

36018. HESSE. Gölzenleuchter, Franz: *Sie verbrennen alle Gotteshäuser im Lande*. Psalm 74,8. Jüdische Spuren im Rhein-Lahn-Kreis – Jahrzehnte danach. Limburg: F. Gölzenleuchter (Schulplatz 9), 1998. 128 pp., illus., notes, bibl.

36019. HESSE. Heinemann, Hartmut: *Die jüdischen Friedhöfe in Hessen*. [In]: Denkmalpflege in Hessen, H. 2, Wiesbaden, 1997. Pp. 32–41, illus., plan, maps., bibl. [Incl. a list of 344 cemeteries.]

36020. HESSE. Lotze, Siegfried: *Der Vormärz und die Revolution 1848 in den Reinhardswalddörfern*. [In]: Jahrbuch '99 [des Lankreises Kassel], Kassel, 1998. Pp. 28–32, notes. [Incl. the participation of Jews.]

36021. HESSE. Zink, Wolfgang Se'ev: *"... das Zerbrechen eines Weinfläschchens bei der Trauung, im Bereich der Synagoge, ist gänzlich untersagt"*. Die jüdischen Gemeinden im Großherzogtum Hessen 1815–1848 zwischen traditioneller Frömmigkeit und neuen Gottesdienstidealen.

[In]: Archiv für hessische Geschichte und Altertumskunde, N.F., Bd. 56, Neustadt an der Aisch, 1998. Pp. 117–144, notes.

36022. HESSISCH-OLDENDORF. Hoffmann, Erik: *Jüdische Nachbarn in Hessisch Oldendorf.* Ihre 600jährige Geschichte in der schaumburgischen/hessischen/preußischen Kleinstadt. Hameln: Niemeyer Buchverl., 1998. 95 pp., illus., facs., docs., tabs., bibl., index.

36023. HILCHENBACH. Dietermann, Klaus: *Familie Levi Holländer. Ein Schicksal aus Hilchenbach.* Hrsg. von der Ges. für Christl.-Jüd. Zusammenarbeit Siegerland e.V. Siegen: Ges. für Christl.-Jüd. Zusammenarbeit e.V., 1998. 40 pp., illus., docs.

36024. HÖCHBERG. Flade, Roland: *Lehrer, Sportler, Zeitungsgründer. Die Höchberger Juden und die Israelitische Präparandenschule.* Würzburg: Schöningh, 1998. 128 pp., illus. bibl. (Schriften des Stadtarchivs Würzburg, H. 12.) [Deals also with the Sonnemann family and esp. with the banker, publisher and founder of the 'Frankfurter Zeitung', Leopold Sonnemann, a former student of the Höchberg school for students from Orthodox families founded by rabbi Lazarus Ottensoser in 1861.]

36025. HOFGEISMAR. Burmeister, Helmut: *Die Ausschreitungen von 1848 in Hofgeismar.* Anmerkungen zur Stadtgeschichte und ihrer Quelle. [In]: Jahrbuch '99 [des Landkreises Kassel], 1998. Pp. 33–35, notes. [Deals with the Jews in Hofgeismar in the context of revolutionary riots.]

36026. HOLZMINDEN. Kieckbusch, Klaus: *Von Juden und Christen in Holzminden 1557 – 1945.* Ein Geschichts- und Gedenkbuch. Holzminden: Verl. Jörg Mitzkat, 1998. 624 pp., illus., facsims., notes (583–599), bibl. (599–606), indexes (persons; places, 607–624).

36027. INGELHEIM. Meyer, Hans-Georg/Mentgen, Gerd: *Sie sind mitten unter uns. Zur Geschichte der Juden in Ingelheim.* Hrsg.: Deutsch-Isr. Freundeskreis Ingelheim e.V. Ingelheim: [Gebr. Kügler], 1998. 684 pp., illus., facsims., appendix (docs., lists, 593–670), index (671–684). [Incl. the cemetery, Nazi period.]

36028. JENA. Kirsche, Brigitta: *Juden in Jena: eine Spurensuche.* Hrsg.: Jenaer Arbeitskreis Judentum. Jena: Glaux, 1998. 199 pp., illus.

36029. JÜCHEN. *Ausgegrenzt, ausgeliefert, ausgelöscht, überlebt? Jüdische Schicksale in Jüchen zwischen Spenrath und Damm.* Horb am Neckar: Verl. Geiger, 1998. 300 pp., illus., footnotes. (Geschichte der Gemeinde Jüchen, Bd. 4.) [Incl.: Jüchen und die Juden (Heinz Spelthahn, 8–14). Jüchen und der Holocaust nach 1945 (Peter Giesen, 15–25). Gedanken zu einem Jüchener Holocaust-Mahnmal (Michael Wolf, 26–27). Schicksale antijüdisch Verfolgter (1933–1945) aus dem Gebiet der heutigen Gemeinde Jüchen (Thomas Wolf, 28–210, bibl., index of persons & places, 172–210). Jüdisches Leben in der Bürgermeisterei Bedburdyck (Dieter Ohlmann, 211–241). Der Kindesmord in Neuenhoven und das Judenpogrom von 1834 (Hans Georg Kirchhoff, 242–271, docs.). Statut der Synagogengemeinde Jüchen vom 4. Juli 1858 (Ariane Rhöse/Thomas Wolf, 272–300).]

36030. JÜLICH. Bers, Günter: *Personenstandsbeurkundungen für jüdische Einwohner der Stadt Jülich 1798–1808.* [In]: Neue Beiträge zur Jülicher Geschichte. Bd. 9, Jülich, 1998. Pp. 145–156, footnotes.

36031. KAMEN. *Spuren jüdischen Lebens in Kamen von 1900 – 1945: "Zukunft ohne Vergessen".* [Hrsg.]: Hermann-Ehlers-Gesamtschule Kamen. Bearb.: Brigitte Lüchtemeier [et al.]. Engl. Übers.: Chris Beck. Werne: Regio-Verl., 1998. 139 pp., illus., facsims. [German and English texts.]

36032. KLEIN-KROTZENBURG (Hesse). Ritter, Thorwald: *Die Synagoge der jüdischen Gemeinde von Klein-Krotzenburg.* Frankfurt am Main: bLoch-Verl., Verl. für Zeitgeschichte, 1997. 42 pp., illus., graphs. [Klein-Krotzenburg: near Frankfurt am Main.]

36033. KÖNIGSBACH. *Spuren jüdischen Lebens in Königsbach*. Eine Einführung. Hrsg. von der Gemeinde Königsbach-Stein. Von Joachim Mehne/Dieter Wolf und Schülerinnen und Schülern der Arbeitsgemeinschaft "Spurensuche" des Lise-Meitner-Gymnasiums Königsbach. Königsbach-Stein: L.-Meitner-Gymnasium, 1998. 80 pp., facsims.

36034. KRONACH. Brod, Walter M.: *Das Medizinstudium des Leonhard Seeligsberg aus Kronach an den Universitäten Würzburg und München, 1827–1833*. [In]: Würzburger medizinhistorische Mitteilungen, Bd. 17, Würzburg, 1998. Pp. 105–111, footnotes, facsims. [L.S., physician, general practitioner in Kronach from 1835 on.]

36035. LADENBURG. Zieher, Jürgen: *"Die Gemeinde galt als Mustergemeinde im Musterländle"*. *Jüdisches Leben in Ladenburg von 1291 bis 1945*. [In]: Hansjörg Probst, Hrsg.: Ladenburg. Aus 900 Jahren Stadtgeschichte. Ubstadt-Weiher, Verl. für Regionalkultur, 1998. Pp. 671–719, illus., facsims., notes.

36036. LAUPHEIM. Adams, Myrah/Schönhagen, Benigna: *Jüdisches Laupheim: ein Gang durch die Stadt*. Haigerloch: Medien und Dialog, 1998. 33 pp., illus.

36037. LAUPHEIM. Hüttenmeister, Nathanja: *Der jüdische Friedhof Laupheim*. Eine Dokumentation. Laupheim: Stadt Laupheim, Verkehrs- und Verschönerungsverein Laupheim e.V., 1998. 599 pp., illus., docs., maps, indexes, bibl. [Incl. chaps. on the history of the Jews of Laupheim and the cemetery. Documents all gravestones, many with photos; inscriptions in Hebrew and German with annotations. An appendix cont. family trees of 13 families.]

36038. LEIPZIG. Kempter, Klaus: *Adolf Jellinek und die jüdische Emanzipation. Der Prediger der Leipziger jüdischen Gemeinde in der Revolution 1848/49*. [In]: Aschkenas, Jg. 8, H. 1, Wien, 1998. Pp. 179–191, footnotes.

——— LEIPZIG. Wassermann, Henry: *"Der Habilitand hat sich stets durchaus unjüdisch bescheiden gehabt ..."*. *Zur Geschichte der Judaistik an der Leipziger Universität*. [See No. 36618.]

36039. LEMGO. Pohlmann, Klaus: *Der jüdische Hoffaktor Samuel Goldschmidt aus Frankfurt und seine Familie in Lemgo (1670–1750)*. [At head of title: "... an gute Örter und Plätze ..."]. Detmold: Ges. für Christl.-Jüd. Zusammenarbeit in Lippe e.V., 1998. 178 pp., illus., docs., bibl., index. (Panu Derech, Bd. 15.)

36040. LOWER SAXONY. *Jüdischer Glaube – Jüdisches Leben. Juden und Judentum in Stadt und Universität Göttingen*. Hrsg. von Elmar Mittler und Berndt Schaller. Göttingen: Wallstein, 1996. 152 pp., illus., facsims., docs. [Catalogue of an exhibition held under the same title in Göttingen in 1996. Covers the history of the Jews in Göttingen and Southern Lower Saxony.] [Cf.: Besprechung (Herbert Reyer) [in]: Hildesheimer Jahrbuch für Stadt und Stift Hildesheim, Bd. 69, Hildesheim, 1997, pp. 273–275.]

36041. LUDWIGSBURG. Hahn, Joachim: *Die Entstehung der israelitischen Gemeinde in Ludwigsburg in der ersten Hälfte des 19. Jahrhunderts*. [In]: Ludwigsburger Geschichtsblätter, H. 52, Ludwigsburg, 1998. Pp. 47–66, notes, illus., facsims.

36042. LUDWIGSBURG. Hahn, Joachim: *Jüdisches Leben in Ludwigsburg*. Geschichte, Quellen und Dokumentation. Hrsg. von der Stadt Ludwigsburg – Stadtarchiv – und vom Hist. Verein für Stadt und Kreis Ludwigsburg e.V. Karlsruhe: Braun, 1998. 783 pp., illus., facsims., docs., bibl. (741–762), index (places, 763–780). [Incl. Nazi period, list of Nazi victims, cemeteries, restitution and commemoration.]

36043. MECKLENBURG. Bernhardt, Hans-Michael: *Bewegung und Beharrung. Studien zur Emanzipationsgeschichte der Juden im Großherzogtum Mecklenburg-Schwerin 1813–1869*. Hannover: Verl. Hahnsche Buchhandlung, 1998. XII, 374 pp., illus., facsims., maps., tabs., footnotes, docs., bibl. (314–337), indexes. (Forschungen zur Geschichte der Juden: Abt. A, Abhandlungen, Bd. 7.) Zugl.: Berlin, Techn. Univ., Diss., 1996.

36044. MILTENBERG. *Die mittelalterliche Synagoge in Miltenberg/Main*. [Issue title of]: Frankenland, Zeitschrift für fränkische Landeskunde und Kulturpflege, Jg. 50, H. 4, Würzburg, Aug. 1998. 1 issue, illus., facsims., notes. [Incl. papers presented at a symposium in Miltenberg, April 30 – June 1, 1998: Die mittelalterliche Synagoge in Miltenberg (Bernhard Purin, 213–217). Die mittelalterliche Synagoge in Miltenberg. Ergebnisse der Bauuntersuchung (Gerd Kieser/Thomas Schicker, 218–234). Kulturhändler zwischen den Welten. Juden in der mittelalterlichen Gesellschaft Bayerns (Christoph Daxelmüller, 235–251). "In der Juden Schul" – die mittelalterliche Synagoge als Gotteshaus, Amtsraum und Brennpunkt sozialen Lebens (Martha Keil, 252–260). Neues Leben in alten Mauern? Museale Nutzung mittelalterlicher Synagogen (Saskia Rhode, 261–273). Abschlußdiskussion (Hermann Neubert, 274–275). Also in this issue: Maßnahmen zur Verbesserung des jüdischen Schulwesens. Johann Baptist Grasers (1766–1841) Reformansätze (Robert Ebner, 276–281; on Graser's 'Das Judenthum und seine Reform', publ. 1828 in Bayreuth.]

36045. MÜHLHAUSEN. Liesenberg, Carsten: *Zur Geschichte der Juden in Mühlhausen und Nordthüringen und die Mühlhäuser Synagoge*. [Hrsg.: Mühlhäuser Museen in Zus.-arbeit mit dem Mühlhäuser Geschichts- und Denkmalpflegeverein]. Mühlhausen: Mühlhäuser Museen, 1998. 128 pp., illus., bibl. facsims. (Mühlhäuser Beiträge: Sonderheft, 11.)

36046. MÜNSTER. Möllenhoff, Gisela/Schlautmann-Overmeyer: *Jüdische Familien in Münster 1918–1945*. Bd. 2. Abhandlungen und Dokumente 1. 1918–1935. Im Auftrag der Stadt Münster hrsg. von Franz-Josef Jakobi, Susanne Freund, Andreas Determann, Diethard Aschoff. Münster: Westf. Dampfboot, 1998. 584 pp., illus., facs., tabs., docs., notes, bibl. (553–574). [For vol. 1 see No. 32601/YB XLI.]

36047. MUNICH. Maier, Dieter G.: *Otto Neuburger (1890–1956). Der Lebensweg eines Münchener Arbeitsamtleiters*. [In]: 1999. Zeitschrift für Sozialgeschichte des 20. und 21. Jahrhunderts, Jg. 13, H. 2, Hamburg, Sept. 1998. Pp. 72–99, footnotes. [O.N., Jan. 14, 1890 Munich – Dec. 21, 1956 Washington, DC, emigr. in 1936 to the US.]

36048. NASSAU. Zink, Wolfgang Se'ev: *"diese kalten Bäder ... sind von den verderblichsten Folgen für die Gesundheit der Frauen". 'Mikvot' im Herzogtum Nassau um 1840*. Die "Judenbäder" zwischen traditionellem Religionsgesetz und staatlichen Hygienevorschriften. [In]: Denkmalpflege in Hessen, H. 2, Wiesbaden, 1997. Pp. 42–49, illus., notes.

36049. NAUMBURG (Hesse). *"... da'war ich zu Hause". Synagogengemeinde Naumburg 1503–1938*. Hrsg. von Volker Knöppel und dem Magistrat der Stadt Naumburg. Hofgeismar/ Naumburg: Verein für hessische Geschichte und Landeskunde e.V. Kassel 1834 – Zweigverein Hofgeismar, 1998. 140 pp., illus., facsims., bibl. (135–138). (Die Geschichte unserer Heimat, Bd. 29; Jahrbuch des Geschichtsvereins Naumburg, Nr. 13.) [Also on Jews in Heimarshausen, Elben, Altenstädt, Altendorf. Incl.: Alphabetisches Einwohnerverzeichnis der Synagogengemeinde Naumburg 1503–1938 (98–134).]

———— NEUSTETTIN. *Der Prozeß um den Brand der Synagoge in Neustettin*. Antisemitismus in Deutschland ausgangs des 19. Jahrhunderts. Bearb. von Gerd Hoffmann. Mit einer Einführungsbibliographie und biobibliographischen Anmerkungen zu Ernst Henrici, Hermann Makower, Erich Sello. [See No. 37087.]

36050. NIEDERMEISER. Beck, Brigitte: *Die Geschichte der jüdischen Bevölkerung von Niedermeiser*. [In]: Jahrbuch '98 [des Landkreises Kassel]'. Kassel, 1997. Pp. 131–138, notes. [Incl. the Nazi period.]

36051. NORDHORN (EMSLAND). Naber, Gerhard: *Salomon de Vries – und "seine" Synagoge*. [In]: Bentheimer Jahrbuch 1999, Bad Bentheim, 1998. (Das Bentheimer Land, Bd. 145). Pp. 271–283, illus., facsims., bibl.

———— NORTH-RHINE WESTPHALIA. *Die Geschichte der Juden im Rheinland und in Westfalen*. Hrsg. von Michael Zimmermann. Mit Beiträgen von Diethard Aschoff [et al.]. [See No. 35912.]

36052. NUREMBERG. *Mitten in Nürnberg. Jüdische Firmen, Freiberufler und Institutionen am Vorabend des Nationalsozialismus.* Hrsg. von Michael Diefenbacher und Wiltrud Fischer-Pache. bearb. von Gerhard Jochem. Nürnberg: Stadtarchiv Nürnberg, 1998. IX, 110 pp., illus., lists, tabs., indexes (subjects, names, streets). (Quellen zur Geschichte und Kultur der Stadt Nürnberg, Bd. 28.) [Incl.: Zur Entwicklung jüdischen Lebens in Nürnberg 1850–1933 (1–22).]

36053. NUREMBERG. Tobias, Jim G.: *Orte der Erinnerung und der Verfolgung.* Ein Stadtführer. Hrsg. vom Bildungszentrum der Stadt Nürnberg und dem Stadtarchiv Nürnberg. Nürnberg: BZ Stadt Nürnberg, 1998. 76 pp., illus. (BZ-Materialien, Bd. 5.) [Covers 500 years of Jewish life in Nuremberg.]

36054. OFFENBURG. Wiehn, Erhard Roy, ed.: *Aus der Heimat verjagt. Zur Geschichte der Familie Neu.* Jüdische Schicksale aus Offenburg und Südbaden 1874–1998. [Dr. Erwin Neu zum 90. Geburtstag am 31. Mai 1998 sowie seiner Familie und der Jüdischen Gemeinde Offenburg gewidmet.] Vorwort von Erwin Neu. Konstanz: Hartung-Gorre, 1998. 252 pp., illus.

36055. ORTENAU. Stude, Jürgen: *"Freiheit, Gleichheit, – aber d'Jude min umbracht si.". Die Ortenauer Juden im Vormärz und in der Badischen Revolution 1948/49.* [In]: Die Ortenau, Jg. 78, Offenburg/Baden, 1998. Pp. 616–635, notes.

36056. OTTERSTADT. Kukatzki, Bernhard: *"Die Otterstadter Judengemeinde eine der ältesten, älter als die Speyerer ist". Zur Geschichte der israelitischen Kultusgemeinde Otterstadt-Waldsee 1684–1940.* Schifferstadt: [Privately printed], 1998. 23 [3] pp., illus., facsims., index.

36057. PALATINATE. Kukatzki, Bernhard: *Jüdische Kultuseinrichtungen in der Verbandsgemeinde Winnweiler.* Synagogen, Friedhöfe, Ritualbäder in Börrstadt, Breunigweiler, Imsbach, Münchweiler a.d. Alsenz, Steinbach a. Donnersberg, Winnweiler. Mannheim: [Privately printed], 1998. 26 [unpag.] pp., illus., facsims., index.

36058. PALATINATE. *Sachor. Beiträge zur jüdischen Geschichte und zur Gedenkstättenarbeit in Rheinland-Pfalz.* Jg. 8, H. 15 & 16. Bad Kreuznach, 1998. 2 issues, illus., facsims., notes, index. [H. 15 (82 pp.) incl. contribs. on the Jews of Göllheim, Landau-Arzheim, Rülzheim, Trier, Hoppstädten, Diez by Bernhard Kukatzki, Berthold Schnabel, Karl Geeck, Heinz Monz, Patrick Willems, Christoph te Kampe. H. 16 (74 pp.) incl. contribs. (partly focussing on the November Pogrom) on the Jews of Bingen, Bad Sobernheim, Kirchberg by Beate Goetz, Hans-Eberhard Berkemann, Chanan Peled, Hans-Werner Zierner, Gustav Schellack. Both issues incl. also contribs. on projects, exhibitions, cemeteries and memorials. Selected essays are listed according to subject.]

36059. PALATINATE. Swiaczny, Frank: *Räumliche Aspekte des Modernisierungsprozesses der jüdischen Bevölkerung in der Pfalz und in Nordbaden dargestellt am Beispiel der ökonomischen Aktivitäten in der Tabakbranche.* [In]: Badische Heimat, H. 2, Konstanz, Juni 1998. Pp. 239–247, notes.

—— POSEN. Labuda, Adam S.: *Ein Posener Itinerar zu Kantorowicz.* [See in No. 36867.]

—— PRUSSIA. [See also No. 35924.]

36060. PRUSSIA. Nowak, Kurt: *Judenpolitik in Preußen.* Eine Verfügung Friedrich Wilhelms III. aus dem Jahr 1821. Leipzig: Verl. der Sächs. Akad. der Wiss. zu Leipzig, 1998. 31 pp., footnotes, facsims., illus. (Sitzungsberichte der sächs. Akademie der Wiss. zu Leipzig; Philologisch-historische Klasse, Bd. 136, H. 3.)

36061. REICHELSHEIM (Odenwald). Grünewald, Reinhard: *Gegen das Vergessen: Juden in Reichelsheim.* [Hrsg. im Auftrag des Gemeindevorstands der Gemeinde Reichelsheim]. Lindenfels: Suin, 1998. 328 pp., illus.

36062. RHINELAND. Friedt, Gerd: *Ergänzende Darstellung zur Geschichte der Juden in den Orten Büsdorf, Fliesteden und Glessen.* [In]: Geschichte in Bergheim. Jahrbuch des Bergheimer Geschichtsvereins e.V., Bd. 7, Köln, 1998. Pp. 177–197, list, tabs., notes. [Büsdorf et al.: located in the Rhineland, near Cologne.]

36063. RHINELAND. *Petitionen und Barrikaden. Rheinische Revolutionen 1848/49.* Bearb. von Ingeborg Schnelling-Reinicke in Verbindung mit Eberhard Illner, hrsg. von Ottfried Dascher u. Everhard Kleinertz. Münster: Aschendorff, 1998. 512 pp., illus., facsims., bibl. (482–496), index (persons, places, subjects, 499–512). [Incl: Karl Marx (Ingeborg Schnelling-Reinicke, 172–174), Moses Hess (Ingeborg Schnelling-Reinicke, 176–178). Zwischen Emanzipation und Antisemitismus. Juden und Judenfrage in der nördlichen Rheinprovinz (Uwe Zuber, 292–296), Sophie von Hatzfeldt und Ferdinand Lassalle (Britta Stein, 326–328).

36064. ROTENBURG an der FULDA. NUHN, HEINRICH: *"Hier geht es wieder drüber und drunter – mit Äxten die ganze Nacht".* Rotenburg 1848 – Schauplatz antijüdischer Ausschreitungen. [In]: Zeitschrift des Vereins für hessische Geschichte und Landeskunde, Bd. 103, Kassel, 1998. Pp. 173–192, notes.

36065. ROTTWEIL. HECHT, WINFRIED: *Jüdisches Rottweil: Einladung zu einem Rundgang.* Haigerloch: Medien und Dialog, 1998. 17 pp., illus.

36066. SACHSEN-ANHALT. BRÜLLS, HOLGER: *Synagogen in Sachsen-Anhalt.* [Hrsg. vom Landesamt für Denkmalpflege Sachsen-Anhalt]. Berlin: Verl. für Bauwesen, 1998. 276 pp., illus., facsims., bibl. (Arbeitsberichte des Landesamtes für Denkmalpflege Sachsen-Anhalt, 3.)

36067. SACHSEN-ANHALT. *Wegweiser durch das jüdische Sachsen-Anhalt.* Im Auftrag der Moses Mendelssohn Akademie hrsg. von Jutta Dick und Marina Sassenberg. Potsdam: Verlag für Berlin-Brandenburg. 1998. 461 pp., illus., bibl. (397–417), gloss., index (persons, places). (Beiträge zur Gesch. und Kultur der Juden in Brandenburg, Mecklenburg-Vorpommern, Sachsen-Anhalt, Sachsen und Thüringen, Bd. 3.) [Incl. articles on 14 towns and 18 essays on people related to these towns; also on synagogues and cemeteries.]

36068. SALZUFLEN (BAD). MEYER, FRANZ [et al.]: *Jüdisches Leben in Bad Salzuflen und Schötmar 1918–1945.* Detmold: Ges. für Christl.-Jüd. Zusammenarbeit in Lippe, 1998. 94 pp., illus., facsims., notes. (Panu Derech – Bereitet den Weg, 16.) [Cont. contribs. by Ansgar Becker, Franz Meyer and Stefan Wiesekopsieker; incl. November Pogrom, list of deportees.]

36069. SCHIFFERSTADT. KUKATZKI, BERNHARD: *"Durchgehends ruhige, friedliebende und ehrbare Leute". Die jüdische Kultusgemeinde 1662–1940.* [In]: Schifferstadt. Geschichte und Geschichten. Hrsg. von der Stadt Schifferstadt. [Red.: Bernhard Kukatzki und Matthias Spindler]. Schifferstadt: Stadt Schifferstadt, 1998. Pp. 701–724, illus., notes.

36070. SCHLESWIG-HOLSTEIN. HARCK, OLE, ed.: *Jüdische Vergangenheit – jüdische Zukunft.* Mit Beiträgen von Hildegard Harck [et al.]. Kiel: Landeszentrale für Politische Bildung Schleswig Holstein, 1998. 117 pp., illus. (Gegenwartsfragen, 80.)

——— SCHLESWIG-HOLSTEIN. PAUL, GERHARD/GILLIS-CARLÉBACH, MIRIAM, eds.: *Menora und Hakenkreuz. Zur Geschichte der Juden in und aus Schleswig-Holstein, Lübeck und Altona (1918–1998).* [See No. 36435.]

36071. SCHWABEN. ULLMANN, SABINE: *Kontakte und Konflikte zwischen Landjuden und Christen in Schwaben während des 17. und zu Anfang des 18. Jahrhunderts.* [In]: Ehrkonzepte in der Frühen Neuzeit. Identitäten und Abgrenzungen. Hrsg. von Sibylle Backmann [et al.]. Berlin: Akademie Verl., 1998. (Colloquia Augustana, Bd. 8.) Pp. 288–315, footnotes.

36072. SIEGEN. DIETERMANN, KLAUS: *Jüdisches Leben in Stadt und Land Siegen.* Hrsg. von der Ges. für Christl.-Jüd. Zusammenarbeit Siegerland e.V. Siegen: Ges. für Christl.-Jüd. Zusammenarbeit 1998. 160 pp., illus., docs.

36073. THURINGIA. NOTHNAGEL, HANS, ed.: *Juden in Südthüringen, geschützt und gejagt: eine Sammlung jüdischer Lokalchroniken in sechs Bänden.* Bd. 1: Über jüdisches Leben und Erbepflege im Evangelischen Kirchenkreis "Henneberger Land". Bd. 2: Juden in den ehemaligen Residenzstädten Römhild, Hildburghausen und in deren Umfeld. Suhl: Verl. Buchhaus Suhl, 1998. 2 vols., 252 pp., illus.; 135 pp., illus., graphs.

36074.　TRIER. Spies, Gerty: *Meine Jugend in Trier.* Mit Einleitung und Erläuterungen von
Günther Franz. Gerty Spies, geb. Gumprich. Die aus Trier stammende jüdische Schriftstellerin starb im 100. Lebensjahr. [In]: Kurtrierisches Jahrbuch, Jg. 38, Trier, 1998. Pp. 219–
237, illus., facsims., footnotes. [Part of her memoirs, first publ. in 1984 in: 'Drei Jahre Theresienstadt', see No. 21187/YB XXX.] [Also in this issue: Gerty Spies – ein Jahrhundert-Leben
(Sigfrid Gauch, 239–243, illus.).] [G.S., née Gertrud Gumprich, Jan. 13, 1897 Trier – Oct.,
10, 1997 Munich; further data see 35894/YB XLIII.]

36075.　ULM. Adams, Myrah/Maihoefer, Christof: *Jüdisches Ulm: Schauplätze und Spuren.* Haigerloch: Medien und Dialog Schubert, 1998. 34 pp., illus.

36076.　WALLHAUSEN-MICHELBACH. Kaufmann, Uri R.: *Die Synagogen-Ablege in Wallhausen-
Michelbach.* Fragen zur jüdischen Kultur Württembergisch-Frankens. [In]: Württember-
gisch Franken, Bd. 82, Schwäbisch Hall, 1998. Pp. 143–156.

36077.　WEIMAR. Müller, Erika/Stein, Harry: *Jüdische Familien in Weimar: vom 19. Jahrhundert
bis 1945; ihre Verfolgung und Vernichtung.* Mit einem Beitrag von Ricklef Münich. [Hrsg. vom
Stadtmuseum Weimar]. Weimar: Stadtmuseum, 1998. 227 pp., illus. (Weimarer Schriften,
H. 55.)

36078.　WESTERWALD. Jösch, Joachim [et al.], eds.: *Juden im Westerwald: Leben, Leiden und
Gedenken.* Ein Wegweiser zur Spurensuche. Unter Mitarbeit von Stefan Aßmann [et al.].
Quirnbach: Stukemeier-Kommunikation, 1998. 355 pp., illus., map, bibl. (Werkstatt-
Beiträge zum Westerwald, Nr. 6.)

36079.　WESTPHALIA. Birkmann, Günter/Stratmann, Hartmut: *Bedenke vor wem du stehst. 300
Synagogen und ihre Geschichte in Westfalen und Lippe.* Unter Mitarbeit von Thomas Kohlpott
und Dieter Obst. Essen: Klartext, 1998. 310 pp., illus., bibl. (270–293), notes (295–300),
indexes (persons, places), gloss. [Incl. chap. on rabbis.]

————　WESTPHALIA. Jankrift, Kay Peter: *Aufstieg auf Zeit. Jüdische Ärzte und Heilkundige in
westfälischen Städten bis zur Mitte des 16. Jahrhunderts.* [See in No. 35928.]

36080.　WESTPHALIA. Linnemeier, Bernd-Wilhelm/Kosche, Rosemarie: *"Darum, meine lieben
Söhne, gedenkt, daß es Gott der Allmächtige so mit uns haben will, daß wir so zerstreut sind . . .".* Jüdische
Privatkorrespondenzen des mittleren 16. Jahrhunderts aus dem nordöstlichen Westfalen.
[In]: Aschkenas, Jg. 8, 1998, H. 2, Wien, 1999. Pp. 275–324, footnotes.

36081.　WESTPHALIA. Menneken, Kirsten/Zupancic, Andrea, ed.: *Jüdisches Leben in Westfalen.*
Eine Ausstellung der Gesellschaft für christl.-jüd. Zusammenarbeit Dortmund e.V. in Koo-
peration mit dem Museum für Kunst und Kulturgeschichte Dortmund [et al.]. Essen:
Klartext, 1998. 175 pp., illus., facsims., margin notes. [Incl.: Juden im mittelalterlichen
Westfalen (Thomas Schilp, 13–22). Das Judenbild in der christlichen Ikonographie des Mittelalters (Andrea Zupancic, 23–37). Ein schwerer Neubeginn – westfälische Juden zwischen
Reformation und Dreißigjährigem Krieg (Diethard Aschoff, 38–48). Das westfälische Land-
und Kleinstadtjudentum in der Frühen Neuzeit (Jörg Deventer, 49–56). Jüdische Kultge-
genstände aus westfälischen Gemeinden des 18. und 19. Jahrhundert (Annette Weber, 57–
74). Von der Aufklärung zur Emanzipation (Arno Herzig, 75–90). Jüdisches Schul- und
Ausbildungswesen in Westfalen im 19. Jahrhundert (Susanne Freund, 91–98). Westfälisches
Judentum zwischen Reform und Orthodoxie im 19. Jahrhundert (Thomas Kollatz, 99–108).
"Ihr kennt die Frauen nicht . . ." (Kirsten Menneken, 109–122). Zwischen tödlichem Zorn
und vereinnahmender Liebe. Streiflichter aus Westfalen zum Verhältnis der Christen zu den
Juden zwischen 1850 und 1933 (Günter Birkmann, 123–131). Arbeit und Alltag ostjüdischer
Arbeiter im rheinisch-westfälischen Industriegebiet (Ludger Heid, 132–141). Der Novem-
berpogrom 1938 (Rita Thalmann, 142–155). Nach dem Sturm. Begegnung in der Heimat
(Jenny Aloni, 156–157). Jüdische Gemeinden nach 1945 (Benno Reicher, 158–168).]

36082.　WESTPHALIA. Minninger, Monika: *Ostwestfälische Juden zwischen Emanzipation, Kultusre-
form und Revolution.* [In]: Eine Region im Aufbruch. Die Revolution von 1848/49 in Ostwest-

falen-Lippe. Hrsg. von Reinhard Vogelsang und Rolf Westheider. Bielefeld: Verl. für Regionalgesch., 1998. Pp. 159–190, footnotes.

36083. WESTPHALIA. Pracht, Elfi: *Jüdisches Kulturerbe in Nordrhein-Westfalen. Teil III: Regierungsbezirk Detmold.* (Beiträge zu den Bau- und Kunstdenkmälern von Westfalen. Bd. 1.1) Köln: Bachem, 1998. 545 pp., bibl. (503–522), index (places), illus., 6 maps (attached).

36084. WORMS. Reuter, Fritz: *Prof. Dr. Hugo Sinzheimer – Vater des deutschen Arbeitsrechts. Zugleich ein Beitrag zur Geschichte der Familien Sinzheimer und Buschhoff und ihres Hauses Wilhelm-Leuschner-Straße 26 in Worms.* [In]: Sachor. Beiträge zur jüdischen Geschichte und zur Gedenkstättenarbeit in Rheinland-Pfalz, Jg. 8, Heft 15, Bad Kreuznach 1998. Pp. 45–48, bibl. notes.

36085. WÜRZBURG. Dettelbacher, Werner: *Die jüdische Ärztin Sara und ihre Tätigkeit in Würzburg (1419).* [In]: Würzburger medizinhistorische Mitteilungen, Bd. 17, Würzburg, 1998. Pp. 101–103, footnotes, bibl.

1a. Alsace

36086. HANAU-LICHTENBERG. Haarscher, André-Marc: *Les juifs du Comté de Hanau-Lichtenberg entre le quatorzième siècle et la fin de l'Ancien Régime.* Strasbourg: Societé Savante d'Alsace; Librairie Gangloff, 1997. 269 pp., illus., docs., gloss., index. (Collection Recherches et Documents, 57.) [Incl. a preface by Freddy Raphael. Also on the Jews in Pfaffenhofen, Ingweiler, and Neuweiler. Incl. docs. in German, French, Western Yiddish and Hebrew.]

36087. METZ. Miskimin, Patricia Behre: *Jews and Christians in the market-place: the politics of kosher meat in Metz.* [In]: The Journal of European Economic History, Vol. 26, Rome, No. 1, Spring, 1997. Pp. 147–155, footnotes. [On 17th-cent. Metz.]

36088. Raphael, Freddy: *Une singulière présence des Juifs en Alsace. La construction d'un oubli.* [in]: Archives Juives, No. 31/1, 1er semestre, Paris, 1998. Pp. 39–51, notes. [On rural Jewry in Wintzenheim, Turckheim, Weltolsheim.]

36089. STRASBOURG. Weyl, Robert/Weyl, Martine: *La fresque de la cour du bain des juifs à Strasbourg.* [In]: Revue des études juives, T. 157, No. 3–4, Louvain, juillet-déc., 1998. Pp. 371–378, footnotes, illus.

2. Austria

36090. Amann, Klaus/Wagner, Karl, eds.: *Autobiographien in der österreichischen Literatur. Von Franz Grillparzer bis Thomas Bernhard.* Innsbruck: Studien-Verl., 1998. 272 pp., notes. (Schriftenreihe des Instituts für Österreichkunde, Bd. 3.) [Papers presented at a conference in St. Pölten, Nov. 1990. Selected essays: Das gerettete Ich. Impressionismus und Autobiographie (Konstanze Fliedl, 75–92; deals mainly with Arthur Schnitzler's autobiography). Gestalten und Figuren als Elemente der Zeit- und Lebensgeschichte: Canettis autobiographische Bücher (Alfred Doppler, 113–124). Überlebenserinnerungen. Zu den Autobiographien von Günther Anders, Jean Améry und Hilde Spiel (Konrad Paul Liessmann, 203–216).]

36091. Brook-Shephard, Gordon: *The Austrians: a thousand-year odyssey.* London: HarperCollins; New York: Carroll & Graf, 1997. XXIV, 483 pp., illus., map, notes. [Incl. antisemitism (incl. Nazi and post-war); also on the Jewish contrib. to Austrian culture.]

36092. BURGENLAND. Glück, Israel A.: *Kindheit in Lackenbach. Jüdische Geschichte im Burgenland.* Hrsg. von Erhard Roy Wiehn. Konstanz: Hartung-Gorre, 1998. 84 pp., illus. [Memoirs; author, b. 1921 in Vienna, an Auschwitz survivor, recollects his holidays with his grandparents in Lackenbach. Lives in Israel.]

36093. HÖDL, SABINE: *Eine Suche nach jüdischen Zeugnissen in einer Zeit ohne Juden. Zur Geschichte der Juden in Niederösterreich von 1420 bis 1555.* [In]: Mitteilungen des Österreichischen Staatsarchivs, Nr. 45, Wien, 1997. Pp. 271–296, footnotes.

36094. KARNIEL, JOSEPH: *A listing of articles on Orthodox Jewry in Austria published in the Austrian Orthodox Jewish press 1918–1938.* Ramat-Gan: Bar-Ilan Univ., 1996. 471 pp. [In Hebrew.] [Incl. contrib. on the Orthodox Jewish press in Austria (11–46). The rest of book consists of index of articles.]

36095. KEIL, MARTHA/LAPPIN, ELEONORE, eds.: *Studien zur Geschichte der Juden in Österreich.* Bodenheim: Philo, 1997. 222 pp., notes. [Cont. (some titles abbr.): Regesten zur Geschichte der Juden in Österreich im Mittelalter (Eveline Brugger et al., 1–8). Juden in Grenzgemeinden: Wiener Neustadt und Ödenburg im Spätmittelalter (Martha Keil, 9–34). Studien zur Judenfeindschaft in Österreich von 1496 bis 1620 (Sabine Hödl, 35–64). Antisemitismus und die Literaturpolitik des politischen Katholizismus in Wien 1880–1933 (Bettina Walzer, 65–80). Jüdische Gemeinden in Galizien und der Bukowina (Michael John/Albert Lichtblau, 81–122). Die Entwicklung der Jüdischen Gemeinde in Neunkirchen/NÖ im 19. und 20. Jahrhundert (Gerhard Milchram, 123–140). Ungarisch-jüdische Zwangsarbeiter in Österreich 1944/45 (Eleonore Lappin, 141–168). Auf den Spuren der Todesmärsche ungarischer Juden durch Österreich nach Mauthausen im April 1945 (Günther Burczik, 169–204). Die Wiener jüdische Gemeinde und der Antisemitismus nach 1945 (Evelyn Adunka, 205–222).]

———— REICHMANN, EVA, ed.: *Habsburger Aporien? Geisteshaltungen und Lebenskonzepte in der multinationalen Literatur der Habsburger Monarchie.* [See No. 36634.]

36096. SHANES, JOSHUA: *Yiddish and Jewish Diaspora Nationalism.* [In]: Monatshefte für deutschsprachige Literatur und Kultur, Vol. 90, No. 2, Madison, WI, 1998. Pp. 178–188. [Deals also with the struggle for the recognition of Yiddish as a legitimate language in Austria-Hungary.]

36097. ST. PÖLTEN. LIND, CHRISTOPH: *". . . es gab so nette Leute dort": die zerstörte jüdische Gemeinde St. Pölten.* Unter Mitarbeit von Matthias Lackenberger. St. Pölten: NP-Buchverl., 1998. 312 pp., illus. (Jüdische Gemeinden, 1.)

36098. STRONG, GEORGE V.: *Seedtime for Fascism: the disintegration of Austrian political culture, 1867–1918.* Armonk, NY: Sharpe (distrib. in UK by Eurospan), 1998. 214 pp., illus., map, notes, bibl. (199–207). [Incl. Jewish life in Austria; Zionism; Austrian antisemitism.]

36099. TERLAU, WILHELM: *Österreichischer Patriotismus und jüdische Solidarität. Die 'Selbstwehr' – eine zionistische Zeitung im Ersten Weltkrieg.* [In]: Jüdischer Almanach 1999 des Leo Baeck Instituts, Frankfurt am Main, 1998. Pp. 42–56, port., notes.

36100. VIENNA. ARBEL, MORDECHAI: *The Sephardi community in Vienna.* [In]: Pe'amim, No. 69, Jerusalem, Fall 1996. Pp. 95–114. [In Hebrew, with English summary.] [Deals with the period from 1736 to the community's liquidation by the Nazis.]

36101. VIENNA. DALINGER, BRIGITTE: *"Verloschene Sterne". Geschichte des jüdischen Theaters in Wien.* Wien: Picus, 1998. 312 pp., illus., notes (230–279), bibl. (280–301), indexes (persons; titles (302–311). [On Yiddish and other Jewish theatres, cabarets; incl. an alphabetical list of actors, singers, playwrights, dramatists (with short biographies, 196–227).]

36102. VIENNA. GOLLER, PETER: *'Ein starkes Stück. Versuchte Habilitation eines kommunistischen Juden . . .'.* Universitäten im Lichte politischer und rechtlicher Willkür am Beispiel des Habilitationsverfahrens von Karl Horovitz (1892–1958) an der Wiener Universität 1923–1925. [In]: Jahrbuch 1998 [des Dokumentationsarchivs des österreichischen Widerstandes]. Wien, 1998. Pp. 111–134, docs., footnotes. [K.H., physicist, from 1925 in the US, where he died 1958.]

36103. VIENNA. Jüdisches Museum der Stadt Wien. Glück, Alexander: *Das Jüdische Museum der Stadt Wien und seine Bibliothek.* [In]: Aus dem Antiquariat, [Beilage zum] Börsenblatt für den Deutschen Buchhandel, Jg. 165, Nr. 77, Frankfurt am Main, 25. Sept. 1998. Pp. A 651–A 654, illus.

36104. VIENNA. *Jüdische Brigittenau: auf den Spuren einer verschwundenen Kultur.* Katalog der gleichnamigen Ausstellung der Gebietsbetreuung Brigittenau, 5.-28. Nov. 1997/Gebietsbetreuung Brigittenau, Stadterneuerung im Auftr. der Stadt Wien. Wien: Gebietsbetreuung Brigittenau, 1997. 87 pp., illus.

36105. VIENNA. *Neudeggergasse 12. Die Synagoge in der Josefstadt. Die verlorene Nachbarschaft.* Eine Ausstellung im Bezirksmuseum Josefstadt vom 7. Okt. bis 18. Nov. 1998. Mit Beiträgen von Elfriede Faber [et al.]. Wien: Bezirksmuseum Josefstadt, 1998. 95 pp.

3. Central Europe

36106. BOHEMIA. Plaggenborg, Stefan: *Maria Theresia und die böhmischen Juden.* [In]: Bohemia, Bd. 39, H. 1, München, 1998. Pp. 1–16, footnotes. [Incl. English and French abstracts (236, 241). Deals with the eviction of Jews from Bohemia and the subsequent lifting of the ban.]

36107. CZECHOSLOVAKIA. Mueller, Daniel: *Manfred Georg and the Mucačevo 'Jüdische Revue' (1936–1938).* [In Hebrew, with English summary.] [In]: Qesher, No. 21, Tel-Aviv, May 1997. Pp. 91–100.

36108. CZERNOWITZ. Corbea-Hoisie, Andrei, ed.: *Czernowitz. Jüdisches Städtebild.* Mit Fotografien von Guido Baselgia und Renata Erich. Frankfurt am Main: Jüdischer Verlag, 1998. 320 pp., illus., bibl. [An anthology of texts from the 18th to the 20th cent. Incl.: Czernowitz. Bilder einer jüdischen Geschichte (ed., 7–32, notes).] [Cf.: Jerusalem am Pruth. Czernowitz als Literaturstadt (Andreas Breitenstein) [in]: 'NZZ', Nr. 158, Zürich, 11./12. Juli 1998, p. 68.]

36109. CZERNOWITZ. *"Czernowitz is gewen an alte, jidische schtat...".* Überlebende berichten. [Hrsg.: Heinrich Böll-Stiftung, Berlin; Elieser Steinbarg-Kulturgesellschaft, Czernowitz]. Czernowitz: Molodyj Bukowynez, 1998. 120 pp. [Also publ. in Russian; cont. interviews conducted in 1996 with students from the Osteuropa-Institut, FU Berlin.]

36110. HUNGARY. Peri, Anat: *Jewish settlements in Hungary under the Habsburgs (1686–1747).* [In]: Zion, Vol. 63, No. 3, Jerusalem, 1998. Pp. 319–350. [In Hebrew, with English summary.]

36111. PRAGUE. Goldberg, Sylvie Anne: *Crossing the Jabbok: illness and death in Ashkenazi Judaism in sixteenth- through nineteenth-century Prague.* Transl. by Carol Cosman. Berkeley, CA: Univ. of California Press, 1997. XVIII, 303 pp., illus. [First publ. in French in 1989. Cf.: Review (Joseph Shatzmiller) [in]: Journal of the History of Medicine, Vol. 53, No. 1, Oxford, Jan. 1998, pp. 187–189.]

36112. PRAGUE. Petersen, Heidemarie: *Die Rechtsstellung der Judengemeinden von Krakau und Prag um 1500. Beispiele jüdischer Existenz in Ostmitteleuropa.* [In]: Zeitschrift für Ostmitteleuropa-Forschung, Jg. 46, Marburg, 1997. Pp. 63–77, footnotes. [Incl. Engl. summary.]

4. Switzerland

36113. AARGAU. Bollag, Michy: *Wo nicht nur Gräber Zeugen sind.* Aus der Geschichte der Judendörfer Endingen-Lengnau. [In]: Israelitisches Wochenblatt, Jg. 98, Nr. 20, Zürich, 15. Mai 1998. Pp. 11–14, illus.

36114. BASLE. KURY, PATRICK: *"Man akzeptierte uns nicht, man tolerierte uns!" Ostjudenemigration nach Basel 1890–1930.* Hrsg.: Schweizerischer Israelitischer Gemeindebund. Basel: Helbing & Lichtenhahn, 1998. 151 pp., footnotes. (Beiträge zur Gesch. und Kultur der Juden in der Schweiz, Vol. 7.) Zugl.: Basel: Univ., Lizentiatsarbeit.

36115. HOCHREITER, WALTER: *Sport unter dem Davidstern: die Geschichte des jüdischen Sports in der Schweiz.* Basel: F. Reinhardt, 1998. 86 pp., illus.

———— *Schweizer auf Bewährung. Klara Obermüller im Gespräch mit Sigi Feigel.* [See No. 36817.]

36116. ZURICH. HUSER BUGMANN, KARIN: *Schtetl an der Sihl. Einwanderung, Leben und Alltag der Ostjuden in Zürich 1880–1939.* Zürich: Chronos, 1998. 303 pp., illus., facsims., graphs, tabs., notes (239–262), bibl., index. (Veröff. des Archivs für Zeitgeschichte des Inst. für Geschichte der ETH Zürich, Bd. 2.)

C. Various Countries

———— ALTER, PETER, ed.: *Out of the Third Reich: refugee historians in post-war Britain.* [See No. 36735.]

36117. BAADER, MARIA T.: *From "the priestess of the home" to "the rabbi's brilliant daughter". Concepts of Jewish womanhood and progressive Germanness in 'Die Deborah' and the 'American Israelite', 1854–1900.* [In]: Leo Baeck Institute Year Book XLIII, London, 1998. Pp. 47–72, footnotes. [On two American-Jewish periodicals mainly aimed at immigrants from German-speaking countries.]

36118. BEAR, JOHN J.: *Witness for a generation.* Santa Barbara, CA: Fithian Press, 1997. 127 pp., illus. [J.B., b. 1917 in Breslau, lawyer, gives an account of his experiences in Nazi Germany, his emigr. to Peru and Bolivia and impressions of life there, and his subsequent life in the US.]

36119. *Cleveland and its Germans.* Transl. from German, and with a preface and introd. by Steven Rowan. Cleveland, OH: The Western Reserve Historical Society; Columbus: Ohio State Univ. Press, 1998. XX, 185 pp., illus. [First edn. in English; orig. publ. under the title: 'Cleveland und sein Deutschtum' by the German-American Biographical Publ. Co. in Cleveland (1907). Deals also with the large German-Jewish community.]

36120. DOHRN, VERENA: *Die erste Bildungsreform für Juden im Russischen Reich in ihrer Bedeutung für die Juden in Liv- und in Kurland.* [In]: Aschkenas, Jg. 8, H. 2, Wien, 1999. Pp. 325–352, footnotes. [Incl. German-Jewish teachers.]

36121. EXILE. AURES, INGE: *Komm, sieh die Welt mit meinen Augen: Ehe-Paare im Exil.* Ein Vergleich der weiblichen mit den männlichen Perspektiven in Exilautobiographien. Ann Arbor, MI: UMI, 1997. VII, 424 pp. Zugl.: Nashville, TE, Univ., Diss., 1997. [Focuses on Carl Zuckmayer and Alice Herdan-Zuckmayer, Gottfried and Brigitte Bermann Fischer.]

36122. EXILE. EMBACHER, HELGA/STAUBMANN, HELMUT: *Österreichische Kulturschaffende im Exil: das Beispiel Herbert Zipper und Trudl Zipper-Dubsky.* Innsbruck: Inst. für Soziologie, 1996. 95 pp., illus. (Forschungsbericht/Inst. für Soziologie, Sozial- und Wirtschaftswiss. Fak., Univ. Innsbruck, Nr. 49.) [Based on an interview with Herbert Zipper in the US.]

36123. EXILE. *Exil in Mexiko.* [Issue title of] Mit der Ziehharmonika, Jg. 15, Nr. 1/Doppelnummer. Wien, März 1998. 1 issue. [Incl. contribs. by/on Lenka Reinerová, Christian Kloyber (on Mexico as a country of refuge after the 'Anschluß'), Gerhard Drekonja-Kornat (on Mexico and its protest against the 'Anschluß'), Marie Frischauf-Pappenheim, Leo and Friedrich Katz, Edith Blaschitz, Wolfgang Kießling (on Leo Katz), Anton Pelinka (on Stephen Sam Kalmar), Marta Marková (on Alice Rühle-Gerstel), Renata von Hanffstengel (on German-speaking Jewish émigrés in Mexico), Gerhard Scheit (on Austrian musicians in Mexico), Marcus B. Patka (on Austrian musicians in Mexico), Thomas B. Schumann (on Paul Mayer), Bruno Frei (on Anna Seghers).]

36124. EXILE. *Filmexil*. Eine Publikation der Stiftung Deutsche Kinemathek. Berlin 1998. No. 10, May; No. 11, Nov. 1998., 68 pp; 85 pp., bibl. [Cont. articles and biogr. details on many German-Jewish film directors, producers, composers and musicians; incl. Kurt Weill, Paul Dessau, Helmar Lerski.]

36125. EXILE. JAEGER, ROLAND: *"Luxus-Bändchen" des Exils: Die 'Pazifische Presse'*. [In]: Aus dem Antiquariat, [Beilage zum] Börsenblatt für den Deutschen Buchhandel, Nr. 11, Frankfurt am Main, 27. Nov. 1998. Pp. A 766–A 777, illus., notes. [On the private press in Los Angeles, established in 1942 by Ernst Gottlieb and Felix Guggenheim, who up to 1948 publ. eleven luxury edns. of émigré authors from Los Angeles.]

36126. GRASSL, GARY C.: *Joachim Gans of Prague: the first Jew in English America*. [In]: American Jewish History, Vol. 86, No. 2, Baltimore, MD, June 1998. Pp. 195–217, footnotes. [J.G., German-speaking Jew from Prague, metallurgist, relative of the astronomer David Gans, reached America on one of Raleigh's ships in 1585.]

36127. GREENBERG, MARK I.: *Becoming Southern: the Jews of Savannah, Georgia, 1830–70*. [In]: American Jewish History, Vol. 86, No. 1, Baltimore, MD, March 1998. Pp. 55–75, footnotes. [Incl. Jews from Germany, the largest group; also discusses German Jews as slave owners.]

36128. GUROCK, JEFFREY S., ed.: *American Jewish life, 1920–1990*. New York; London: Routledge, 1998. XV, 370 pp., illus., tabs., footnotes. (American Jewish history, Vol. 4.) [Incl. chaps.: The German-Jewish community of Washington-Heights (Steven M. Lowenstein, 51–60). The impact of Holocaust survivors on American society: a socio-cultural portrait (William B. Helmreich, 61–74).]

36129. GUROCK, JEFFREY S., ed.: *Central European Jews in America, 1840–1880: migration and advancement*. New York; London: Routledge, 1998. XVI, 389 pp., illus., tabs., footnotes. (American Jewish history, Vol. 2.) [Selected essays (titles abbr.): Jewish 48ers in America (B.W. Korn, 1–18). German-Jewish mass emigration: 1820–1880 (Rudolf Glanz, 19–36). German-Jewish migrations, 1830–1910 (Avraham Barkai, 37–55). Neiman-Marcus (Don M. Coerver and Linda B. Hall, 119–132). The case of the Lehmans and the Seligmans (Elliot Ashkenazi, 133–148). German-Jewish financiers in 19th-century New York (Barry E. Supple, 167–201). New York's German-Jewish investment bankers (V.P. Carosso, 203–224). The early Jews of Columbus, Ohio, 1850–1880 (M.L. Raphael, 225–242). A sociological portrait of German-Jewish immigrants in Boston: 1845–1861 (Stephen G. Mostov, 243–274). Jewish race and German soul in 19th-century America (Stanley Nadel, 305–425).]

36130. *A history of Austrian immigration to Canada*. Ed. by Frederick Engelmann [et al.]. Ottawa: Carleton Univ. Press. 1996. 199 pp. [Incl. essays by Gabrielle Tyrnauer and Anna M. Pichler dealing with Jewish emigrants from Austria and Canadian refugee policy.]

36131. JOSEPHS, JEREMY/BECHHÖFER, SUSI: *Rosas Tochter. Bericht über eine wiedergefundene Kindheit*. Aus dem Engl. von Michael Hofmann. München: Piper, 1998. 190 pp., illus. [Orig. publ. in 1996, see No. 33900/YB XLII; on twin sisters from Munich, who went to the UK in 1939 with a Kindertransport; on their life in Wales and on the search to uncover their true origins.]

36132. MATTHÄUS, JÜRGEN: *German Judenpolitik in Lithuania during the First World War*. [In]: Leo Baeck Institute Year Book XLIII, London, 1998. Pp. 155–174, map, footnotes.

———   RADEST, HOWARD B.: *Felix Adler. An ethical culture*. [See No. 36768.]

———   SAINT SAUVEUR-HENN, ANNE, ed.: *Zweimal verjagt. Die deutschsprachige Emigration und der Fluchtweg Frankreich – Lateinamerika 1933–1945*. [See No. 36742.]

36133. SCHNEIDER, BRONKA: *Exile: a memoir of 1939*. Ed. with forewords by Erika Bourguignon and Barbara Hill Rigney. Columbus: Ohio State Univ. Press, 1998. XXI, 132 pp., illus., bibl. [Memoirs of author and her husband who went to Britain in 1939 from Austria and spent the first year as housekeeper and butler in a castle in Scotland. Incl. a commentary, providing historical and political background, written by the author's niece, E. Bourguignon (101–132).]

36134. *Shalom Trieste. Gli itinerari dell'ebraismo.* Trieste: Comune di Trieste, 1998. 449 (2) pp., illus., notes, bibl. notes. [A collection of 40 essays, most of them dealing with the Jews of Trieste during the Habsburg era. Publ. on the occasion of an exhibition held in Trieste, July 31 – Nov. 8, 1998. Ed. and coordinated by Laura Oretti. Incl. introd. by Roberto Damiani. Essays are arranged under the following sections: I. Famiglie ebraiche a Trieste 1814–1914 (11–322). II. L'ebraismo di Svevo (323–346). III. Miniere di carbone di famiglie ebraiche nel Carso (347–360). Artisti triestini di origine ebraica (361–449).]

36135. SPITZER, LEO: *"Hotel Bolivia": the culture of memory in a refuge from Nazism.* New York: Hill & Wang, 1998. XX, 234 pp., illus. [Incl. Jewish refugees in Bolivia from Germany and Austria.]

36136. STUIBER, IRENE: *Die Initiatoren und Initiatorinnen von "German Educationalist Reconstruction". Eine gruppenbiographische Studie.* [In]: Exil. Forschung, Erkenntnisse, Ergebnisse, Jg. 18, Nr. 1, Frankfurt am Main, 1998. Pp. 48–60, notes. [Deals with a London-based exile org.]

36137. *Die vergessenen Juden in den baltischen Staaten.* Ein Symposium vom 4. bis 7. Juli 1997 in Hannover. Im Auftrag der Buber-Rosenzweig-Stiftung hrsg. von Ansgar Koschel und Helker Pflug. [Issue title of] Galut Nordost, Zeitschrift für jüdisch-baltische Kultur und Geschichte, Sonderheft 2. Köln, 1998. 1 issue, 198 pp. [Essays are arranged under the following sections: 1. *Aktuelles Gedenken* (contribs. by Eckhard von Nordheim, Guntis Ulmanis, Niels Hansen, Jaan Kross, 13–32). 2. *Beiträge zur Geschichte*; cont. (some titles abbr.): Zur Kulturgeschichte der Juden im Baltikum (Verena Dohrn, 33–50). Aspekte jüdischen Lebens in Estland bis 1940 (Helker Pflug, 51–60). Mike Rabinowitz, ein Memeler Jude (Ulla Lachauer, 61–68). Das Ghetto von Wilna (Roswitha Dasch, 69–76). Die vergessenen Juden in Riga (Alexander Bergmann, 77–84). Die Deportation deutscher Juden nach Riga (Herbert Obenaus, 85–98). Janis Lipke. Judenretter in Riga (Alexander Bergmann, 97–100). Der Umgang mit Tätern und Widerstandskämpfern im Nachkriegs-Deutschland, ein lehrreiches Exempel (Joachim Perels, 101–124). 3. *Heutige Probleme und zukünftige Aufgaben* (incl. 8 essays).]

36138. VOGEL, CAROLE GARBUNY: *Oswego, New York: wartime haven for Jewish refugees.* [In]: Avotaynu, Vol. XIV, No. 4, Teaneck, NJ, Winter 1998. Pp. 46–49, illus. [On the author's parents, refugees from Vienna and Berlin, who spent some time in the detention camp Oswego.]

36139. WOJAK, IRMTRUD: *"Wir, Deutschland, Chile, Palästina" – Die deutsch-jüdische Jugendbewegung 'Kidma' in Chile 1939–1949.* [In]: Tel Aviver Jahrbuch für deutsche Geschichte, Bd. 27, 1998, Gerlingen, 1998. Pp. 321–352.

II. RESEARCH AND BIBLIOGRAPHY

A. Libraries and Institutes

36140. DEUTSCHE ZENTRALSTELLE FÜR GENEALOGIE, LEIPZIG. JUDE, RENATE: *Die jüdischen Personenstandsunterlagen in der Deutschen Zentralstelle für Genealogie in Leipzig.* [In]: Genealogie, Jg. 47, Bd. 24, H. 1–2, Neustadt/Aisch, 1998. Pp. 4–18, lists [Part 1]. H. 3–4. Pp. 106–120 [Part 2].

36141. GERMANIA JUDAICA, KÖLNER BIBLIOTHEK ZUR GESCHICHTE DES DEUTSCHEN JUDENTUMS e.V.: *Arbeitsinformationen über Studienprojekte auf dem Gebiet der Geschichte des deutschen Judentums und des Antisemitismus.* Ausgabe 17. Red.: Annette Haller. Köln: Germania Judaica, 1998. 177 pp., indexes (authors; places, 166–177).] [Incl.: Vorwort (Annette Haller). This issue lists 771 projects carried out mainly in Germany, the US and Israel.]

36142. GERMANIA JUDAICA, KÖLNER BIBLIOTHEK ZUR GESCHICHTE DES DEUTSCHEN JUDENTUMS E.V.: *Die Kölner Bibliothek zur Geschichte des deutschen Judentums, Germania Judaica e.V.* [In]: "Zuhause in Köln . . .": jüdisches Leben 1945 bis heute [see No. 36510]. Pp. 161–166. [Teil 1: Die Anfänge (Jutta Bohnke-Kollwitz). Teil 2: Die Entwicklung 1979–1998 (Annette Haller).]

36143. HOCHSCHULE FÜR JÜDISCHE STUDIEN, HEIDELBERG. *Trumah 7.* Zeitschrift der Hochschule für Jüdische Studien Heidelberg. Hrsg. von der Hochschule für Jüdische Studien Heidelberg. Red.: Michael Graetz, Daniel Krochmalnik [et al.]. Koord.: Ursula Beitz. Berlin: Metropol, 1998. 184 pp., footnotes. [Essays in this issue mainly deal with Jews in Eastern Europe; incl. also book reviews. Essays pertaining to the history of German-speaking Jewry are listed according to subject.]

36144. INSTITUT FÜR DEUTSCHE GESCHICHTE, UNIVERSITÄT TEL AVIV. *Tel Aviver Jahrbuch für deutsche Geschichte.* Bd. 27 [with the issue title] Historische Migrationsforschung. Hrsg. im Auftrag des Instituts für deutsche Geschichte von Dan Diner. Gerlingen: Bleicher, 1998. 543 pp., footnotes. [Contribs. relevant to the history of German-speaking Jews are listed according to subject.]

36145. INSTITUT FÜR DIE GESCHICHTE DER JUDEN IN ÖSTERREICH, ST. PÖLTEN [IN VERBINDUNG MIT DEM] DEUTSCHEN KOORDINIERUNGSRAT DER GESELLSCHAFTEN FÜR CHRISTLICH-JÜDISCHE ZUSAMMENARBEIT]. *Aschkenas. Zeitschrift für Geschichte und Kultur der Juden.* Hrsg.: Friedrich Battenberg, Hans Otto Horch, Markus J. Wenninger. Red.: Till Schicketanz. Wien: Böhlau, 1998. Jg. 8, H. 1 & 2. IX, 637 pp., footnotes, index (persons, subjects, 609–633). [H. 1 cont.: Aufsätze (7–177). Kleinere Beiträge (179–198). Rezensionen und Buchanzeigen (199–264). Projektberichte und Veranstaltungshinweise (265–273). H. 2 (publ. 1999) cont.: Aufsätze (275–476). Kleinere Beiträge (477–524). Forschungs- und Literaturberichte (525–544). Rezensionen und Buchanzeigen (545–602). Projektberichte und Veranstaltungshinweise (602–608). Individual contribs. are listed according to subject.]

——— LEO BAECK INSTITUTE. GRUBEL, FRED: *Schreib das auf eine Tafel die mit ihnen bleibt. Jüdisches Leben im 20. Jahrhundert.* [See No. 36995.]

——— LEO BAECK INSTITUTE. SPIVEY, NIGEL: *For ordinary mortals: the birth of the Phaidon Press and the rebirth of "aura".* [See No. 36860.]

36146. LEO BAECK INSTITUTE. *Jüdischer Almanach 1999/5759 des Leo Baeck Instituts.* Hrsg. von Jakob Hessing und Alfred Bodenheimer. Frankfurt am Main: Jüd. Verlag, 1998. 182 pp., illus., notes. [Incl.: Zu diesem Almanach (eds., 7). Contribs. on Primo Levi (Zvi Jagendorf), women who settled in Palestine before 1880 (Margalit Shilo) and Amos Oz (Ruth Achlama). Further articles pertinent to German-Jewish history are listed according to subject. See also No. 36697.]

36147. LEO BAECK INSTITUTE. *LBI Information.* Nachrichten aus den Leo Baeck Instituten in Jerusalem, London, New York und der Wissenschaftlichen Arbeitsgemeinschaft des LBI in Deutschland. Sonderheft. Hrsg. von den Freunden und Förderern des LBI e.V. in Frankfurt/Main. Frankfurt am Main: Privately printed, 1998. 23 pp. [Incl.: Vorwort (Georg Heuberger, 3). Juden – Deutsche – Juden. Wandlungen des deutschen Judentums in der Neuzeit (Michael A. Meyer, 5–16). Deutsch-jüdische Geschichte nach 1945 – nur ein Epilog? (Michael Brenner, 17–23). See also No. 35930.]

36148. LEO BAECK INSTITUTE. *Leo Baeck Institute Year Book 1998.* Vol. XLIII. Ed.: J.A.S. Grenville, assoc. ed.: Julius Carlebach, assist. eds.: Shayla Walmsley, Gabriele Rahaman. London: Secker & Warburg, 1998. X, 518 pp., frontis., illus., footnotes, bibl. (351–500), general index (505–518). [Cont.: Preface (eds., IX-X). Essays are arranged under the sections: I. Religion and Jewish teaching. II. Antisemitism before National Socialism. III. Jews and the Fatherland in the twentieth century. IV. Persecution and rescue under National Socialism. V. The debate about German-Jewish relationships continued. VI. Memoir. Individual contribs. are listed according to subject.]

—— Leo Baeck Institute, New York. *Stammbaum.* [See No. 36656.]

36149. Leo Baeck Institute, London. *Report of activities 1998.* London: Leo Baeck Institute, June/ July 1998. 27 pp. [On LBI publications, seminars, conferences, conference proceedings and general activities.]

36150. Moses Mendelssohn Zentrum für europäisch-jüdische Studien. *Menora. Jahrbuch für deutsch-jüdische Geschichte 1998 & 1999.* Im Auftrag des Moses Mendelssohn Zentrums für europäisch-jüdische Studien hrsg. von Julius H. Schoeps, Karl E. Grözinger und Gert Mattenklott. Bodenheim: Philo, 1997 & 1998. 2 vols. (414 & 410 pp., notes, index). [Selected contribs. are listed according to subject.]

—— Moses Mendelssohn Zentrum für europäisch-jüdische Studien, Potsdam. *Archiv der Erinnerung. Interviews mit Überlebenden der Shoah.* 2 vols. [See Nos. 36172 & 36173.]

36151. Staatsbibliothek Preussischer Kulturbesitz, Berlin. Becker, Peter Jörg: *Das Archiv Martin und Bernd H. Breslauer in der Staatsbibliothek zu Berlin.* [In]: Jahrbuch Preußischer Kulturbesitz, Bd. XXXIV, Berlin, 1998. Pp. 383–393, illus., ports. [Collection was given to the Staatsbibliothek in Sept. 1997.] [M.B., antiquarian in Berlin, emigr. to the UK in 1937, transferred his antiquarian book trade in 1977 from London to New York.] [Also on this topic: Die Staatsbibliothek und das Antiquariat Breslauer (Regina Mahlke) (in): Mitteilungen Staatsbibliothek zu Berlin – Preußischer Kulturbesitz, N.F. 7, H. 1, Berlin, 1998. Pp. 102–111, illus., notes.]

36152. Zentrum für Antisemitismusforschung, Berlin. Kreuter, Marie-Luise: *Rettung von Juden im nationalsozialistischen Deutschland 1933–1945.* Ein Dokumentationsprojekt mit Datenbank am Zentrum für Antisemitismusforschung der Technischen Universität Berlin. [In]: Zeitschrift für Geschichtswissenschaft, Jg. 46, H. 5, Berlin, 1998. Pp. 445–449.

36153. Zentrum für Antisemitismusforschung, Berlin. *Jahrbuch für Antisemitismusforschung 7.* Hrsg. von Wolfgang Benz für das Zentrum für Antisemitismusforschung der Technischen Universität Berlin. Red.: Werner Bergmann, Johannes Heil. Geschäftsführende Redakteurin: Juliane Wetzel. Frankfurt am Main; New York: Campus, 1998. 367 pp., illus., notes. [Incl.: Vorwort (Wolfgang Benz, 9–12). Incl. six essays on antisemitism and the Holocaust in Slovakia, one on racism in Hungary after 1989; review essays. Contribs. pertaining to antisemitism in German-speaking countries are listed according to subject.]

B. Bibliographies, Catalogues and Reference Books

—— *Archiv der Erinnerung. Interviews mit Überlebenden der Shoah.* Bd. II: Kommentierter Katalog. [See No. 36173.]

36154. Cohen, Susan Sarah, ed.: *Antisemitism: an annotated bibliography.* Vol. 7–9. [Publ. by The Vidal Sassoon International Center for the Study of Antisemitism, the Hebrew Univ. of Jerusalem.] München: Saur, 1998. 3 vols., LXI, 394; XII, 395–930; XII, 931–1449 pp., index (authors, subjects). [The 3 vols. cont. 4270 entries of works on antisemitism publ. between 1991 and 1993; for earlier vols. see No. 24162/YB XXXIII; No. 29261/YB XXXVIII; No. 31686/YB XL; No. 34948/YB XLIII.]

36155. Cosner, Shaaron/Cosner, Victoria: *Women under the Third Reich: a biographical dictionary.* Westport, CT: The Greenwood Press, 1998. XVII, 203 pp., illus., ports., appendixes. [Incl. Jewish resistance; hidden children, rescuers.]

36156. *Demokratische Wege.* Deutsche Lebensläufe aus fünf Jahrhunderten. Hrsg. von Manfred Asendorf und Rolf von Bockel. Stuttgart: Metzler, 1997. XI, 747 pp., indexes. [Cont. ca. 300 alphabetically arranged biographies, more than 80 of them of Jews.]

36157. *The German minority census of 1939*. An introduction and register. Compiled by Thomas Kent Edlund. Teaneck, NJ: Avotaynu, 1996. VIII, 56 pp., tabs. (Avotaynu monograph series.) [Cont. register indexing documents of the May 1939 census of the "non purely Aryan population" microfilmed in 1991 under a contract between the Geneal. Soc. of Utah and the Bundesarchiv Potsdam. Microfilms (292 16 mm reels) are available at the Bundesarchiv, Potsdam, The Family History Library, Salt Lake City, and the US Holocaust Mem. Museum, Washington, DC.]

36158. GUGGENHEIMER, EVA H./GUGGENHEIMER, HEINRICH W.: *Etymologisches Lexikon der jüdischen Familiennamen*. München; New Providence, RI: Saur, 1996. XLI, 522 pp. [Revised and augmented German transl. of No. 29010/YB XXXVIII.] [Cf.: Besprechung (Manuel Aicher) [in]: Archiv für Familiengeschichtsforschung, Jg. 1, H. 2, Limburg, 1997. Pp. 137–140.]

36159. *Handbuch der deutschsprachigen Emigration 1933–1945*. Hrsg. von Klaus-Dieter Krohn, Patrik von zur Mühlen, Gerhard Paul und Lutz Winckler unter redaktioneller Mitarbeit von Elisabeth Kohlhaas in Zusammenarbeit mit der Gesellschaft für Exilforschung. Darmstadt: Primus, 1998. XIII, 1356 cols., bibl. notes, bibl. (1225–1240), indexes (persons, institutions, places (1249–1352).] [Incl.: Geleitwort (Rita Süssmuth, IX). Contribs. are arranged under the sections: I. *Anlässe, Rahmenbedingungen und lebensweltliche Aspekte.* II. *Zufluchtsländer: Arbeits- und Lebensbedingungen im Exil.* III. *Politisches Exil und Widerstand aus dem Exil.* IV. *Wissenschaftsemigration.* V. *Literarisches und künstlerisches Exil.* VI. *Rückkehr aus dem Exil und seine Rezeptionsgeschichte.*] [Cf.: Besprechung (Simone Barck) [in]: Mittelweg 36, Jg. 8, H. 3, Hamburg, 1999, pp. 49–53.]

——— LADWIG-WINTERS, SIMONE: *Anwalt ohne Recht. Das Schicksal jüdischer Rechtsanwälte in Berlin nach 1933.* [See No. 36201.]

36160. *Lexikon deutsch-jüdischer Autoren.* Bd. 6. Dore – Fein. Redaktionelle Leitung: Renate Heuer. Unter Mitarbeit von Andrea Boelke-Fabian [et al.]. München; New Providence: Saur, 1998. LVIII, 562 pp. (Archiv Bibliographia Judaica.)

36161. MADDEN, PAUL: *Adolf Hitler and the Nazi epoch.* An annotated bibliography: English-language works on the origins, nature, and structure of the Nazi state. Lanham, MD: Scarecrow Press; Pasadena, CA: Salem Press, 1998. XIII, 741 pp. [Incl. entries on racial policies, concentrations camps, refugees.]

36162. *Neues Lexikon des Judentums.* Hrsg. von Julius H. Schoeps. [Überarb. Neuausgabe.] Gütersloh: Bertelsmann Lexikon Verlag, 1998. 896 pp., illus., maps. [Revised and augmented edn., first publ. in 1992, see No. 29266/YB XXXVIII; incl. a new essay: Deutsch-jüdische Gedenkkultur nach dem Holocaust (Salomon Korn, 283–287).]

36163. *Publications on German-speaking Jewry.* A selected and annotated bibliography of books and articles 1997. Compiled by Barbara Suchy and Annette Pringle. [In]: Leo Baeck Institute Year Book XLIII, London, 1998. Pp. 351–500, index (names, places, periodicals, subjects, 469–500).

36164. SCHMITZ-BERNING, CORNELIA: *Vokabular des Nationalsozialismus.* Berlin, New York: de Gruyter, 1998. XLI, 710 pp., footnotes, bibl. (XVII-XLI). [Incl. entries related to Jews, Judaism and racial ideology.]

36165. WINKELMANN, ANNETTE, ed.: *Directory of Jewish studies in Europe.* Oxford: European Association for Jewish Studies, 1998. XI, 254 pp., notes.

36166. *Women writers in German-speaking countries: a bio-bibliographical critical sourcebook.* Ed. by Elke P. Frederiksen and Elizabeth G. Ametsbichler. Westport, CT: Greenwood Press, 1998. XXXIII, 561 pp., notes, bibl. (505–517), index (names, titles, subjects). [Incl. numerous German-Jewish women writers from all periods.]

——— WROCKLAGE, UTE: *Fotografie und Holocaust.* Annotierte Bibliographie. [See No. 36487.]

36167. WUTTKE, DIETER: *Aby M. Warburg-Bibliographie 1866 bis 1995. Werk und Wirkung.* Mit Annotationen. Baden-Baden: Valentin Koerner, 1998. XXIV, 511 pp., illus. (Bibliotheca bibliographica Aureliana, 163.)

III. THE NAZI PERIOD

A. General

36168. ALEXANDRE, MICHEL: *Der Judenmord. Deutsche und Österreicher berichten.* Köln: vgs, 1998. 208 pp., illus., ports., chronol., index. [Based on 38 interviews with non-Jews, most of whom were eye-witnesses to Nazi persecution and annihilation of Jews. Book was publ. in connection with a WDR television documentary of the same title.]

36169. ANDERSON, MARK M., ed.: *Hitler's exiles: personal stories of the flight from Nazi Germany to America.* New York: New Press, 1998. XIV, 354 pp., chronol. [Anthology of personal accounts, incl. Marta Appel, Hannah Arendt, Alfred Döblin, Lion Feuchtwanger, Käte Frankenthal, Peter Gay, Alfred Kantorowicz, Ludwig Marcuse, Alfred Polgar, Ernst Toller, Carl Zuckmayer, Stefan Zweig.]

36170. ANDREE, HANS: *"Schwabacher Judenlettern". Funktionalisierte Schrift-Bilder.* [In]: Mittelweg 36, Jg. 7, H. 3, Hamburg, 1998. Pp. 70–91, illus., footnotes. [Also on the antisemitic aspects in the propagation of different types in Nazi Germany.]

36171. ANGERER, CHRISTIAN: *"Wir haben ja im Grunde nichts als die Erinnerung". Ruth Klügers 'weiter leben' im Kontext der neueren KZ-Literatur.* [In]: Sprachkunst. Beiträge zur Literaturwissenschaft, Jg. 29, Halbband 1, Wien, 1998. Pp. 61–83, footnotes. [On R.K.'s autobiography 'weiter leben'; see No. 29395/XXXVIII.]

36172. *Archiv der Erinnerung. Interviews mit Überlebenden der Shoah.* Bd. I: *Videographierte Lebenserzählungen und ihre Interpretationen.* Im Auftrag des Moses Mendelssohn Zentrums für europäisch-jüdische Studien hrsg. von Cathy Gelbin, Eva Lezzi, Geoffrey H. Hartman, Julius H. Schoeps. Potsdam: Verl. für Berlin-Brandenburg, 1998. 476 pp., footnotes, bibl. (445–463). (Beiträge zur Gesch. und Kultur der Juden in Brandenburg, Mecklenburg-Vorpommern, Sachsen-Anhalt, Sachsen und Thüringen, Bd. 4.) [Cont.: Vorwort (Geoffrey H. Hartman/ Julius H. Schoeps, 9–11). Das Wort der Verfolgten (Gerhard Schoenberner, 13–17). Projektvorstellung und Einleitung (Cathy Gelbin/Eva Lezzi, 19–38). Teil I: *Allgemein-theoretische Betrachtungen zu videographierten Interviews mit Überlebenden der Shoah* (41–191; six contribs. by Geoffrey H. Hartman, Dori Laub/Daniel Podell, Karen Remmler, Stefanie Brauer, Barbara Krahé, Dieter Heger). Teil II: *Biographische Analysen*; cont.: Narrativer Prozeß und Subjektkonstitution in Überlebensgeschichten (Maximilian Preisler, 195–230). Kommunist – Deutscher – Jude: Eine politische Biographie (Sonja Miltenberger, 231–264). Zwischen Verfolgung und Anpassung: Die Lebensgeschichte eines ehemaligen "jüdischen Mischlings" (Cathy Gelbin, 256–298). Prozesse der sozialen Ausgrenzung von Kindern und Jugendlichen (Eva Lezzi/Angela S. Reinhard, 299–328). Der Beitrag von mündlichen Quellen für die Aufarbeitung von Lokalgeschichte. Dargestellt am Beispiel des Interviews mit Egon K. aus Rathenow (Irene Diekmann, 329–353). Teil III: *Die Auseinandersetzung mit der Shoah im sechsten Jahrzehnt nach der Befreiung*; cont.: Leben und älter werden in Deutschland: Alltagserfahrung und Erinnerungsformen (Eva Lezzi, 357–396). "Damit das Wissen lebendig bleibt". Zum Selbstverständnis der Zweiten Generation in der Bundesrepublik lebender Juden (Matthias Cohn, 397–418). Fragen aus dem Off: Die Interviewerinnen und Interviewer (Stefanie Brauer/Andrés Nader/Dori Laub, 419–443).]

36173. *Archiv der Erinnerung. Interviews mit Überlebenden der Shoah.* Bd. II: *Kommentierter Katalog.* Im Auftrag des Moses Mendelssohn Zentrums für europäisch-jüdische Studien bearb. und hrsg. von Sonja Miltenberger. Potsdam: Verl. für Berlin-Brandenburg, 1998. 262 pp., indexes (223–262; persons, places, subjects). (Beiträge zur Gesch. und Kultur der Juden in Brandenburg, Mecklenburg-Vorpommern, Sachsen-Anhalt, Sachsen und Thüringen, Bd.

4.) [Incl. summaries of ca. 80 interviews with people born between 1910 and 1950; also excerpts from 3 interviews.]

36174. ARIELI-HOROWITZ, DANA: *The Jew as 'destroyer of culture' in National Socialist ideology*. [In]: Patterns of Prejudice, Vol. 32, No. 1, London, Jan. 1998. Pp. 51–67, footnotes.

36175. AUSCHWITZ. DURLACHER, GERHARD: *The search: the Birkenau boys*. Transl. by Susan Massotty. London: Serpent's Tail, 1998. 182 pp. [Orig. publ. in Dutch in 1991. Author b. in Baden-Baden in 1928, fled to Holland, was eventually sent to an Auschwitz labour camp where he was in a group of 89 young prisoners. After his return to Holland he tracked down his fellow survivors and organised a reunion in Israel in 1990.]

36176. AUSCHWITZ. KATZ, ADAM: *The closure of Auschwitz but not its end: alterity, testimony and (post)modernity*. [In]: History & Memory, Vol. 10, No. 1, Bloomington, IN, Fall 1998. Pp. 59–98, notes.

36177. AUSCHWITZ. LAKS, SZYMON: *Musik in Auschwitz*. Aus dem Poln. von Mirka und Karlheinz Machel. Hrsg. und mit einem Nachwort versehen von Andreas Knapp. Düsseldorf: Droste, 1998. 160 pp. (Schriftenreihe des Fritz Bauer Instituts, Bd. 15.) [Deals also with German-Jewish prisoners.]

36178. AUSCHWITZ. PELT, ROBERT-JAN VAN/DWORK, DEBÓRAH: *Auschwitz. Von 1270 bis heute*. Aus dem Engl. von Klaus Rupprecht. Zürich: Pendo, 1998. 469 pp., illus., facsims., tabs., maps, notes (421–454), bibl., indexes. [For orig. edn. publ. in 1996 see No. 33952/YB XLII.]

36179. AUSTRALIA. PALMER, GLEN: *Reluctant refuge: unaccompanied refugee and evacuee children in Australia 1933–1935*. East Roseville, NSW: Kangaroo Press, 1997. 240 pp., illus., ports., facsims., tabs., notes, lists of names, bibl. (226–234). [Incl. chap.: Children from Germany (deals also with Jewish children from Germany and Austria).]

——— AUSTRIA [See also VIENNA.]

36180. AUSTRIA. FLANNER, KARL: *Die Wiener Neustädter Synagoge in der Pogromnacht 1938*. Wiener Neustadt: Verein Museum und Archiv für Arbeit und Industrie im Viertel unter dem Wienerwald, 1998. 8 pp. (Dokumentation des "Industrieviertel-Museums" Wiener Neustadt 1998/83.)

36181. AUSTRIA. LEBENSAFT, ELISABETH/MENTSCHL, CHRISTOPH: *". . . und aufregend war das Leben von uns allen . . ."*. *Vertreibung, Exil und Rückkehr des Rechtsanwalts Friedrich Schnek*. Eine Spurensuche. Wien: Öst. Akademie der Wissenschaften, 1997. 80 pp., frontis., bibl., index. (Österreichisches Biographisches Lexikon – Schriftenreihe, 3.) [Incl. also short biographies of Georg Bergman, Hans Escher, Johann Wolfgang Laszky.]

36182. AUSTRIA. LEBENSAFT, ELISABETH/MENTSCHL, CHRISTOPH: *Vom Service de Prestation zur Alien Labour Company. Ein Beitrag österreichischer Flüchtlinge im Kampf gegen NS-Deutschland, dargestellt nach britischen Quellen*. [In]: Mitteilungen des Österreichischen Staatsarchivs, Nr. 46, Wien, 1998. Pp. 89–105, footnotes, docs.

36183. AUSTRIA. NEUGEBAUER, WOLFGANG: *"Anschluß" 1938 – Einschätzungen und Auswirkungen*. [In]: Mit der Ziehharmonika, Jg. 15, Nr. 1, Wien, 1998. Pp. 5–8, illus., bibl. [Also in this issue: 'Darr Jud muß weg und sein Gerschtl bleibt da.' Die "wilden Arisierungen der Anschlußtage" am Beispiel von Briefen an "Reichskommissar" Bürckel (Gloria Sultano, 8–10, notes.]

36184. AUSTRIA. *Niemals vergessen! Judenverfolgung in Linz*. Zum Gedenken an die Ereignisse vom 9. November 1938. Mit Beiträgen von Franz Dobusch [et al.]. Linz: Stadt Linz, Kulturamt und Volkshochschule, 1998. 16 pp.

36185. AUSTRIA. SCHWARZ, PETER: *Tulln ist judenrein! Die Geschichte der Tullner Juden und ihr Schicksal 1938–1945.* [In]: Jahrbuch 1998 des Dokumentationsarchivs des österreichischen Widerstandes (DÖW). Wien, 1998. Pp. 95–102, footnotes.

36186. AUSTRIA. *Women in Austria.* Ed. by Günter Bischof [et al.]. New Brunswick, NJ: Transaction Books, 1998. 309 pp., notes. (Contemporary Austrian studies, Vol. 6.) [Selected essays: Middle class, liberal, intellectual, female and Jewish: the expulsion of "female rationality" from Austria (Helga Embacher, 5–15). Austrian women in the anti-Nazi resistance movement in Belgian exile (Erika Thurner, 28–40). Daniel Jonah Goldhagen, Hitler's willing executioners (Christopher R. Jackson, 269–278). Also chaps. on Neo-Nazism and Right-wing politicians in contemporary Austria.]

36187. AUSTRIA. *Wo ist dein Bruder? Novemberpogrom 1938 in Kärnten.* Dokumente und Berichte. Mit Beiträgen von Werner Wintersteiner [et al.]. [In]: Alpen-Adria-Alternativ, Nr. 4, Villach, 1998. Pp. 1–24.

36188. AYALON, MOSHE: *"Gegenwaertige Situation": report on the living conditions of the Jews in Germany. A document and commentary.* [In]: Leo Baeck Institute Year Book XLIII, London, 1998. Pp. 271–285, footnotes. [Incl. reprint of doc. from the Central Zionist Archives, Jerusalem, written by Dr. Julius Seligsohn, member of the executive of the Reichsvereinigung der Juden in Deutschland.]

——— BARKAI, AVRAHAM: *Hoffnung und Untergang. Studien zur deutsch-jüdischen Geschichte des 19. und 20. Jahrhunderts.* Mit einer Einführung von Ursula Büttner. [See No. 35900.]

36189. BARTOV, OMER: *Defining enemies, making victims: Germans, Jews, and the Holocaust.* [In]: American Historical Review, Vol. 103, No. 3, Washington, DC, June 1998. Pp. 771–816, illus., footnotes. [On the self-perceptions of Germans and Jews, with special reference to German attitudes in W.W.I, the Third Reich and FRG; and on attitudes (Jewish and German) to real and perceived enemies in the past and present. Responses to this article and the author's reply in Vol. 103, No. 4, Oct. 1998: Imagined enemies, real victims, Bartov's transcendent Holocaust (Paul B. Miller, 1178–1181). Two regimes of memory (Samuel Moyn, 1182–1186). Genocide, barbaric others, and the violence of categories, a response to Omer Bartov (Vinay Lal, 1187–1190). Reply (Omer Bartov, 1191–1194).]

36190. BAUMEL, JUDITH TYDOR: *Double jeopardy: gender and the Holocaust.* London, Portland, OR: Vallentine Mitchell, 1998. XV, 292 pp., gloss., notes, bibl. (263–284). (Parkes-Wiener series on Jewish studies.) [Deals with the two-fold danger facing Jewish women during the Nazi persecution and i.a. their role in the resistance.]

36191. BAYREUTH. PAULUS, HELMUT: *Die "Reichskristallnacht" und die Judenverfolgung in der Gauhauptstadt Bayreuth.* [In]: Archiv für Geschichte von Oberfranken, Bd. 78, Bayreuth, 1998. Pp. 403–455, illus., facsims., footnotes, bibl. [Based on criminal proceedings held between 1947 and 1949.]

36192. BECKMAN, MORRIS: *The Jewish Brigade: an army with two masters 1944–1945.* Staplehurst: Spellmount, 1998. XVI, 159 pp., illus., ports., facsims., map, appendixes. [On the Jewish Brigade, which served as part of the British Army in World War II, and which cont. a large number of German Jews.]

36193. BENZ, WOLFGANG: *Auswandern aus Deutschland. Einwandern in Palästina.* [In]: Fünfzig Jahre Israel: Vision und Wirklichkeit [see No. 37043]. Pp. 42–51.

36194. BENZ, WOLFGANG/WETZEL, JULIANE, eds.: *Solidarität und Hilfe für Juden während der NS-Zeit.* Regionalstudien II. Ukraine, Frankreich, Böhmen und Mähren, Österreich, Lettland, Litauen, Estland. Berlin: Metropol, 1998. 330 pp., footnotes, indexes (persons, places, 309–329). (Reihe Solidarität und Hilfe, Bd. 2.) [Incl. contribs. by Silke Ammerschubert, Frank Golczewski, Eugenia Gurin-Loov, Angelika Königseder, Ruth Kibelka, Livia Rothkirchen and Margers Vestermanis.]

36195. BERGEN-BELSEN. RAHE, THOMAS: *Jüdische Waisenkinder im Konzentrationslager Bergen-Belsen.* [In]: Dachauer Hefte, Jg. 14, H. 14, München, 1998. Pp. 31–49, notes.

36196. BERGEN-BELSEN. RAHE, THOMAS: *Rabbiner im Konzentrationslager Bergen-Belsen.* [In]: Menora 1998, Bodenheim, 1998. Pp. 121–152, notes.

36197. BERGMANN, MARTIN S./JUCOVY, MILTON E./KESTENBERG, JUDITH S., eds.: *Kinder der Opfer – Kinder der Täter. Psychonalyse und Holocaust.* Aus dem Amerikan. von Elisabeth Vorspohl. Frankfurt am Main: Fischer Taschenbuch Verlag, 1998. 425 pp. [Paperback edn. of No. 32769/YB XLI.]

36198. BERGHOFF, HARTMUT: *Zwischen Verdrängung und Aufarbeitung. Die bundesdeutsche Gesellschaft und ihre nationalsozialistische Vergangenheit in den Fünfziger Jahren.* [In]: Geschichte in Wissenschaft und Unterricht, Jg. 49, H. 2, Stuttgart, 1998. Pp. 96–114, footnotes. [Abstract on p. 78.]

36199. BERLIN. *Albert Speers Neugestaltung der Reichshauptstadt auf Kosten der Berliner Juden.* [Issue title of]: Bulletin für Faschismus- und Weltkriegsforschung, H. 10, Berlin, 1998. 1 issue. [Incl.: Die Neugestaltung Berlins als Reichshauptstadt – auf Kosten der Berliner Juden 1938 bis 1942 (Susanne Willems, 3–22, footnotes).]

36200. BERLIN. GAY, PETER: *My German question: Growing up in Nazi Berlin.* New Haven, CT: Yale Univ. Press, 1998. XII, 208 pp., illus., ports., facsims., map. [Memoirs focus on the period 1933–1939, also describe first post-war visit to Germany.] [Cf.: A historian rethinks his past (Henry Regensteiner) [in]: Midstream, Vol. 45, No. 1, New York, Jan. 1999, pp. 47–48. Enduring a hell in the making. Peter Gay's reflections on his boyhood in Germany (Marion Kaplan) [in]: Aufbau, Vo. 64, No. 22, New York, Oct. 23, pp. 12–13, illus. Ohne Anklage, ohne Selbstmitleid, ohne Klischee. Die Erinnerungen des Historikers Peter Gay (Hartmut Jäckel) [in]: 'FAZ', Nr. 281, Frankfurt am Main, 3. Dez. 1998, p. 10. See also: My German question (Peter Gay) [in]: American Scholar, Vol. 67, No. 4, Washington, DC, Autumn 1998.] [P.G. (orig. Fröhlich), b. 1923 in Berlin, historian, emigr. 1939 to Cuba, 1941 to the US. Lives in Yale.]

——— BERLIN. *Konflikte aus der Geschichte.* [See No. 36493.]

36201. BERLIN. LADWIG-WINTERS, SIMONE: *Anwalt ohne Recht. Das Schicksal jüdischer Rechtsanwälte in Berlin nach 1933.* [Hrsg.: Rechtsanwaltkammer Berlin]. Berlin: be.bra verl., 1998. 239 pp., illus., ports., notes (228–234), bibl. (235–238). [Incl.: Biographisches Verzeichnis der Berliner Rechtsanwälte jüdischer Herkunft (89–225; documents the biogr. data of 1,785 persons.]

36202. BERLIN. RICHIE, ALEXANDRA: *Faust's metropolis: a history of Berlin.* London: HarperCollins; New York: Carroll & Graf, 1998. XXVIII, 1139 pp., illus., maps, notes (892–1104). [Incl. pre-Nazi Jewish life in Berlin, the Nazi period, persecution of Jews and the Holocaust.]

36203. BERLIN. SCHRÖDER, NINA: *Hitlers unbeugsame Gegnerinnen: der Frauenaufstand in der Rosen-straße.* München: Heyne, 1998. 310 pp., illus., bibl. Orig.-Ausg.

36204. BERLIN-FRIEDRICHSHAIN. *Die Friedrichshainer Opfer des Holocaust. Ein Gedenkbuch.* Zusammengestellt von einer Projektgruppe beim Kulturring in Berlin e.V. Berlin: Kultur-ring in Berlin, 1998. 165 pp.

36205. BERLIN-HELLERSDORF. *Verfolgung und Widerstand in Berlin-Hellersdorf 1933–1945.* [Hrsg. von der Bezirkschronik Berlin-Hellersdorf und dem Heimatverein Hellersdorf, Kaulsdorf, Mahlsdorf e.V. Red.: Ursula Adam/Sabine Kadow]. Berlin-Hellersdorf: Heimatverein Hel-lersdorf [et al.], [1998]. 58 pp., illus. (Hellersdorfer Heimathefte, 8.)

36206. BERLIN-HOHENSCHÖNHAUSEN. *Juden in Hohenschönhausen.* Eine Spurensuche. Berlin: [Biographische Forschungen und Sozialgeschichte e.V.], 1998. 103 pp., illus., facsims. (Bio-graphische Forschungen und Sozialgeschichte e.V., H. 5.) [Cont. contribs. by Christa

Hübner, Bärbel Ruben, Frank Wolf. Deals mainly with the Nazi period, incl. survival in hiding.]

36207. BERLIN-HOHENSCHÖNHAUSEN. *Victor Aronstein.* Gedenkschrift zu seinem 100. Geburtstag am 1. November 1996. [Text.: Thomas Friedrich et al.]. Hrsg.: Verein "Biographische Forschungen und Sozialgeschichte e.V.". Berlin: [Privately printed], 1996. 96 pp., illus., facsims., notes, bibl. [On a physician, who lived in Berlin-Hohenschönhausen from 1933 until his deportation in Nov. 1941.]

36208. BERLIN-SPANDAU. Simonsohn, Gerhard: *Leben im Schatten wachsenden Unheils: Kindheit und Jugend in Spandau 1925–1945.* Hrsg. vom Kreis der Freunde und Förderer des Heimatmuseums Spandau, Heimatkundliche Vereinigung 1954, e.V. Spandau: Kreis der Freunde und Förderer des Heimatmuseums Spandau, 1998. 70 pp., illus.

36209. BERLIN-WEDDING. *Am Wedding haben sie gelebt: Lebenswege jüdischer Bürgerinnen und Bürger.* Hrsg.: Berliner Geschichtswerkstatt. Projektgruppe: Annegret Bühler [et al.]. Berlin: Metropol, 1998. 248 pp., illus. [Covers the years 1930–1950.]

36210. *Betrifft: "Aktion 3". Deutsche verwerten jüdische Nachbarn.* Dokumente zur Arisierung ausgewählt und kommentiert von Wolfgang Dreßen. Berlin: Aufbau, 1998. 256 pp., facsims., docs., notes. [Catalogue book of exhibition held in Düsseldorf, Oct. 1998 – Jan. 1999. Incl. 129 docs. from the Oberfinanzdirektion Köln.] [Cf.: Besprechung (Elke Kimmel) [in]: Zeitschrift für Geschichtswissenschaft, Jg. 47, H. 6, Berlin, 1999, pp. 567–568.]

36211. Blank, Ralf: *"… aus Holland stammende Judenmöbel". Die "Heimatfront" und der Holocaust.* [In]: Beiträge zur Gesch. Dortmunds und der Grafschaft Mark, Bd. 89, Dortmund, 1998. Pp. 263–290, footnotes, illus., facsims., docs. [On the dissipation and auctioning off of Jewish property in the Rhine-Ruhr region.]

36212. Blend, Martha: *Ich kam als Kind: Erinnerungen.* Aus dem Engl. von Karin Hanta. Wien: Picus, 1998. 236 pp. (Österreichische Exilbibliothek.) [Orig. title 'A child alone', publ. 1995; see No. 32785/YB XLI.]

36213. BREITENAU. Krause-Vilmar, Dietfrid: *Das Konzentrationslager Breitenau. Ein staatliches Schutzhaftlager 1933/34.* Marburg: Schüren, 1997. 318 pp., illus., facsims., footnotes. (Nationalsozialismus in Nordhessen, Bd. 18.) [Breitenau: part of Guxhagen, Hesse; incl. Jewish prisoners.]

36214. Breitman, Richard: *Official secrets: what the Nazis planned, what the British and Americans knew.* New York: Hill and Wang, 1998. VIII, 325 pp., notes (247–309). [Incl. knowledge of the extermination of Jews.] [Cf.: 'Tell them we're dying' (Niall Ferguson) [in]: The Observer, London, Jan. 24, 1999, p. 12. Could Britain have done more? (Norman Stone) [in]: Sunday Times, London, Jan. 24, 1999, p.6. Enigma of survival (John Keegan) [in]: The Daily Telegraph, London, April 17, 1999, p. A2.]

36215. BREMEN. Davids, Wiebke/Marssolek, Inge, eds.: *"Man hängt immer zwischen Himmel und Erde…". Jüdische Emigrantinnen und Emigranten (1933–45) aus Bremen berichten.* Bremen: Staatsarchiv Bremen, 1997. 237 pp., illus. (Kleine Schriften des Staatsarchivs Bremen, H. 28.)

36216. BREMEN. Decke, Bettina: *"Du mußt raus hier!". Lottie Abraham-Levy: Eine Jugend in Bremen.* Bremen: Donat, 1998. 163 pp., illus., bibl.

——— BREMEN. Schleier, Bettina: *Das Umzugsgut jüdischer Auswanderer – von der Enteignung zur Rückerstattung.* [See No. 36530.]

36217. BUCHENWALD. Kralovitz, Rolf: *Ten zero ninety in Buchenwald: a Jewish prisoner tells his story.* Köln: Walter Meckauer Kreis, 1998. 78 pp., illus., ports., facsims., plans. [For German edn. see No. 33984/YB XLII.]

36218. BUCHENWALD. Kreissler, Felix: *Österreicher in Buchenwald*. Vortrag in Weimar aus Anlaß des 'Symposiums 60 Jahre Buchenwald', 3. – 5. Oktober 1997. [In]: Jahrbuch 1998 des Dokumentationsarchivs des österr. Widerstandes, Wien, 1998. Pp. 30–45. [Incl. resistance.]

36219. Büttner, Ursula/Greschat, Martin: *Die verlassenen Kinder der Kirche. Der Umgang mit Christen jüdischer Herkunft im "Dritten Reich"*. Göttingen: Vandenhoeck & Ruprecht, 1998. 151 pp., footnotes, index. (Sammlung Vandenhoeck.) [Cont.: Von der Kirche verlassen: Die deutschen Protestanten und die Verfolgung der Juden und Christen jüdischer Herkunft im "Dritten Reich" (Ursula Büttner, 15–69). "Gegen den Gott der Deutschen". Marga Meusels Kampf für die Rettung der Juden (Martin Greschat, 70–85). Friedrich Weißler. Ein Jurist der Bekennenden Kirche im Widerstand gegen Hitler (Martin Greschat, 86–122). "Wohl dem, der auf die Seite der Leidenden gehört". Der Untergang des Dichters Jochen Klepper mit seinen jüdisch-christlichen Angehörigen (Ursula Büttner, 123–149).] [Cf.: Besprechung (Kurt Schilde) [in]: Zeitschrift für Geschichtswissenschaft, Jg. 47, H. 3, Berlin, 1999, pp. 282–283.]

36220. CHANNEL ISLANDS. Cohen, Frederick E.: *The Jews in the Channel Islands during the German occupation, 1940–1945*. London: Institute of Contemporary History, in association with the Jersey Jewish Congregation, 1998. 128 pp., illus., ports., facsims., maps, docs. [Some few of the Channel Islands' Jews were either German-born or German nationals. Also incl. paper on Jewish forced labourers who were transported to the Channel Islands during the German occupation.]

36221. Charles, Marion: *Leben vor und nach den Novemberpogromen von 1938*. Erinnerungen einer Jüdin, die nach dem Krieg nach Deutschland zurückkehrte. [In]: Neue Zürcher Zeitung, Nr. 254, Zürich, 14./15. Nov. 1998. P. 83. [Author emigr. from Berlin with a Kindertransport to the UK while her mother survived in hiding; lives in Badenweiler.]

36222. CHURCH. *Dimensions: a Journal of Holocaust Studies*, Vol. 12, No. 2 [with the issue title]: *The churches and the Holocaust: a reconsideration*. New York: Anti-Defamation League, 1998. 1 issue, illus., ports., notes. [Cont. (titles abbr.): Introd.: a suppressed history. 'We remember': reaction and analysis (John F. Morley, 3–9). The Vatican and the Holocaust: putting 'We remember' in context (John T. Pawlikowski, 11–16). Creative interfaith dialogue (Leon Kenicki, 17–22). A consideration of Christianity and the Holocaust (Michael Dobkowski, 23–26). The role of the churches (Victoria J. Barnett, 27–30). Collusion, resistance, silence: Protestants and the Holocaust (Doris L. Bergen, 31–36). The churches and the Holocaust era: bringing history to students (Karen Friedman, 37–38).]

36223. CHURCH. *Holocaust Scholars write to the Vatican*. Ed. by Harry James Cargas. Foreword by Eugene J. Fisher. Westport, CT: Greenwood Press, 1998. XV, 156 pp., notes, bibl. (143–148). [Essays on the role of the Catholic Church and the Vatican during the Nazi years, and the lack of response to the persecution of the Jews.]

36224. CHURCH. Meister-Karanikas, Ralf: *Die Thüringer evangelische Kirche und "die Judenfrage"*. Notizen zur Epoche 1933–1945. [In]: Thüringer Gratwanderungen. Beiträge zur fünfundsiebzigjährigen Geschichte der evangelischen Landeskirche Thüringens. Hrsg. von Thomas A. Seidel [et al.]. Leipzig: Ev. Verlagsanstalt, 1998. (Herbergen der Christenheit, Jahrbuch für deutsche Kirchengeschichte, Sonderband 3.). Pp. 111–123, footnotes.

36225. CHURCH. Phayer, Michael: *Pope Pius XII, the Holocaust, and the Cold War*. [In]: Holocaust and Genocide Studies, Vol. 12, No. 2, Oxford, Fall 1998. Pp. 233–256, notes. [Deals with the recent statement by the Vatican regarding the churches' role in the Holocaust, as well as the allegations of Vatican involvement in the post-war escape of war criminals.] [Cf.: Jews fault Vatican's Holocaust study [in]: The Christian Century, Vol. 115, No. 10, Chicago, April 1, 1998, pp. 337–339.]

36226. CHURCH. Thoma, Clemens: *Kommentar zum Dokument "Wir erinnern uns"*. [In]: Freiburger Rundbrief, N.F., Jg. 5, H. 3, Freiburg, 1998. Pp. 161–167. [Examines critically the Vatican's document about the annihilation of European Jewry, publ. March 16, 1998. This document is printed on pp. 167–177 in this issue.]

36227. CLENDINNEN, INGA: *Reading the Holocaust.* New York; Cambridge: Cambridge Univ. Press, 1998. 250 pp., illus., notes (208–233), bibl. (234–246). [Australian anthropologist develops a new way of interpreting and understanding both victims and perpetrators. Incl. a chap. on the Holocaust represented in art and literature.]

36228. COLOGNE. HOBERG, INGE: *Der Dom so nah und doch so fern.* Das Leben eines Mädchens im Versteck und auf der Flucht. Köln: Emons, 1998. 160 pp., illus. (Köln Bibliothek, 1.) [Author, b. 1930 in Cologne, went into hiding with her Jewish mother.]

36229. *Confronting the Holocaust: a mandate for the 21st century.* Ed. by G. Jan Colijn and Marcia Sachs Littell. Lanham, MD; Oxford: Univ. Press of America, 1997. XXII, 178 pp., notes. (Studies in the Shoah, Vol. XIX.) [Part one of the papers given at the 26th 'Annual scholar's conference on the Holocaust and the German churches', held in Philadelphia. Incl. (titles abbr.): Australian response to refugees from Nazism before World War II (Paul R. Bartrop, 63–80). "Liberal democracy – the end of history" or Carl Schmitt redivivus? The need for an anamnestic culture for Germany after Auschwitz (Jürgen Manemann, 81–90). Post Holocaust Jewish German dialogue: face to face Hubert Locke, Abraham Peck and Gottfried Wagner (133–144).]

36230. *Confronting the Holocaust: a mandate for the 21st century. Part two.* Ed. by Stephen C. Feinstein [et al.]. Lanham, MD; Oxford: Univ. Press of America, 1998. XX, 313 pp., notes. (Studies in the Shoah, Vol. XX.) [Part 2 of the papers given at the 26th 'Annual scholar's conference on the Holocaust and the German churches', held in Philadelphia. Incl. (titles abbr.): The German Catholic Church's response to National Socialism (Kevin Spicer, 71–88). The Auschwitz convent controversy (Susan E. Nowak, 109–122). Julius Streicher and Nazi medievalism (Frederick M. Schweitzer, 123–136). The Jewish identity of Jewish children during the Holocaust (Leora Saposnik, 137–168). Why did Hitler permit a Jewish hospital to function throughout the war? (Gerda Haas, 183–192).]

—————— COSNER, SHAARON/COSNER, VICTORIA: *Women under the Third Reich: a biographical dictionary.* [See No. 36155.]

36231. CZECHOSLOVAKIA. KÁRNÝ, MIROSLAV/KEMPER, RAIMUND/KÁRNÁ, MARGITA, eds.: *Theresienstädter Studien und Dokumente 1997.* Prag: Stiftung Theresienstädter Initiative; Academia, 1997. 360 pp., illus., facsims., tabs., notes, index (352–359). [Selected contribs. (some titles abbr.): Die Zentralstelle für jüdische Auswanderung in Prag. Genesis und Tätigkeit bis zum Anfang des Jahres 1940 (Jaroslava Milotová, 7–30). Zwei unbekannte Berichte aus dem besetzten Prag über die Lage der jüdischen Bevölkerung im Protektorat (Stanislav Kokoska, 31–49; cont. secret reports of the Prague Jewish community written in Aug. and Oct. 1939.). Erfassung der jüdischen Bevölkerung des Protektorats (Alena Hájková, 50–62). Die Emigration der Juden aus den böhmischen Ländern 1938–1941 (Bohumil Cern, 63–85). Das Schicksal der Juden im Sudetengau im Licht der erhaltenen Quellen (Ludomír Kocourek, 86–104). Die demographische Struktur der israelitischen Kultusgemeinden in Nordböhmen in den Jahren 1945–1949 (Zlatuse Kukánová/Lenka Matusiková, 105–117). Further contribs. are listed according to subject.]

36232. CZECHOSLOVAKIA. NIZNANSKY, EDUARD/SLNEKOVÁ, VERONIKA: *Die Deportationen der Juden in der Zeit des autonomen Landes Slowakei am 4./5.11.1938.* [In]: Bohemia, Bd. 39, H. 1, München, 1998. Pp. 33–51, footnotes. [Engl. summary on p. 237, French on p. 242.]

36233. DACHAU. NEUGEBAUER, WOLFGANG: *Der erste Österreichertransport in das KZ Dachau 1938.* [In]: Dachauer Hefte, Jg. 14, H. 14, München, 1998. Pp. 17–30, footnotes. [On a group of 150 leading Austrian personalities, among them numerous Jews, who were deported to Dachau in April 1938, after the "Anschluß".]

36234. DESSAU. *Verfolgt . . . vertrieben . . . Erinnerungen ehemaliger jüdischer Bürger aus Dessau.* Zusammengestellt von Eva-Maria Herz-Michl und Dagmar Marbert. Dessau: Moses Mendelssohn Gesellschaft e.V., 1998. 122 pp., illus., facsims. (Schriftenreihe der Moses-Mendelssohn-Gesellschaft e.V., Nr. 6.) [Personal recollections of former Dessauers from Australia, Great Britain, France, Israel, USA and Germany.]

36235. DORTMUND. SCHMALHAUSEN, BERND: *Dr. Rolf Bischofswerder: Leben und Sterben eines jüdischen Arztes aus Dortmund.* Bottrop: Verl. P. Pomp, 1998. 104 pp., illus., bibl. [On a young physician and his wife, deported to Riga in 1941.]

36236. DOUMA, EVA: *Deutsche Anwälte zwischen Demokratie und Diktatur 1930–1955.* Frankfurt am Main: Fischer Taschenbuch Verlag, 1998. 232 pp., tabs., notes (167–196), bibl. (199–211), index. (Die Zeit des Nationalsozialismus.) Orig.-Ausg. [Deals also with Jewish lawyers.]

36237. DRESDEN. HAASE, NORBERT/JERSCH-WENZEL, STEFI/SIMON, HERMANN, eds.: *Die Erinnerung hat ein Gesicht.* Fotografien und Dokumente zur nationalsozialistischen Judenverfolgung in Dresden 1933–1945. Bearb. von Marcus Gryglewski. Leipzig: Kiepenheuer, 1998. 223 pp., illus., facsims., footnotes, bibl. (Schriftenreihe der Stiftung Sächsische Gedenkstätten zur Erinnerung an die Opfer politischer Gewaltherrschaft, Bd. 4.) [Incl.: Geleitwort (Ignatz Bubis, 7–8). Die Erinnerung hat ein Gesicht. Anmerkungen zu einem Filmdokument (eds., 9–18; on a film made in Nov. 1942 in the ghetto of Dresden-Hellerberg). Zur Geschichte der nationalsozialistischen Judenverfolgung in Dresden 1933–1945 (Marcus Gryglewski, 87–150). Chronologie zur nationalsozialistischen Judenverfolgung in Dresden 1933–1945 (151–181). Bearb. und erg. Dokumentation der Deportationsliste (184–211; cont. 293 names of Jews deported in March 1943 from Hellerberg to Auschwitz).]

36238. DRESDEN. LÄSSIG, SIMONE: *Nationalsozialistische "Judenpolitik" und jüdische Selbstbehauptung vor dem Novemberpogrom. Das Beispiel der Dresdner Bankiersfamilie Arnhold.* [In]: Reiner Pommerin, ed.: Dresden unterm Hakenkreuz. Köln: Böhlau, 1998. (Dresdner Historische Studien, Bd. 3.). Pp. 129–191, footnotes, family tree. [Deals also with the pre-Nazi history of the Arnhold family. Incl. the 'aryanisation' of 'Gebr. Arnhold'. See also No. 35988.]

36239. DÜSSELDORF. DÜWELL, KURT [et al.], eds.: *Vertreibung jüdischer Künstler und Wissenschaftler aus Düsseldorf 1933–1945.* Düsseldorf: Droste, 1998. 244 pp., illus., notes. (Eine Veröff. des Hist. Seminars der H.-Heine-Univ. Düsseldorf und der Mahn- und Gedenkstätte Düsseldorf.) [Cont.: Einführung (Kurt Düwell, Angela Genger, Kerstin Griese, Falk Wiesemann, 7–13). Emigration aus Deutschland. Vertreibung jüdischer Künstler und Wissenschaftler 1933–1945 (Wolfgang Benz, 15–28). Jüdische Maler und Bildhauer in der Düsseldorfer Kunstszene (Annette Baumeister/Sigrid Kleinbongartz, 29–46). "... bluten wir nicht? ... lachen wir nicht?" Jüdische Theaterkünstler in Düsseldorf und im Exil (Winfried Meiszies, 47–66; mainly on Hermann Greid, Leon Askin, Fritz Valk, Gustav Lindemann). Der Bühnenbildner und Grafiker Fritz Lewy (1893–1950) (Birgit Bernard, 67–96). Jüdische Musiker, Komponisten und Musikwissenschaftler in Düsseldorf und in der Emigration. Fünf Portraitskizzen (Barbara Suchy, 97–140; on Jascha Horenstein, Hanns Walter David, Klaus Glücksmann/Israel Gihon, Gerhard Herz, Otto Joachim). Ossip K. Flechtheim und John H. Herz – fast parallele Lebensläufe. Zwei Freunde aus Düsseldorf auf der Flucht vor dem Nationalsozialismus (Kurt Düwell, 141–156). Ossip K. Flechtheim (1909–1998). Wissenschaftler und Aktivist (John H. Herz, 157–164; see also No. 36820). Der Mediävist Wilhelm Levison (1876–1947) (Rudolf Schieffer, 165–176). Jüdische Ärztinnen und Ärzte in Düsseldorf und in der Emigration (Kerstin Griese, Wolfgang Woelk, 177–206). Adolf Sindler (1899–1965): Kinderarzt und aktiver Zionist in Düsseldorf und Haifa (Falk Wiesemann, 177–206). "... gab es jetzt die Möglichkeit der Rückkehr". Entscheidungen nach 1945 (Cordula Lissner, 227–242).]

36240. ELIAS, RUTH: *Triumph of hope: from Theresienstadt and Auschwitz to Israel.* Transl. by Margot Bettauer Dembo. New York; Chicester: John Wiley, 1998. X, 274 pp., illus., ports., map. [For orig. German edn. see No. 25296/YB XXXIV.]

36241 FAUPEL, RAINER/ESCHEN, *Klaus: Gesetzliches Unrecht in der Zeit des Nationalsozialismus: vor 60 Jahren Erlaß der Nürnberger Gesetze.* Baden-Baden: Nomos-Verl.-ges., 1997. 71 pp. (Veröffentlichungen der Potsdamer Juristischen Gesellschaft, 3.)

———— FEDERN, ERNST: *Versuche zur Psychologie des Terrors: Material zum Leben und Werk von Ernst Federn.* Hrsg. von Roland Kaufhold. [See No. 36816.]

36242. FELDMAN, GERALD D.: *Flüchtlinge mit leeren Taschen.* Wie die deutschen Juden im Dritten Reich um ihre Versicherungsvermögen gebracht wurden. [In]: 'FAZ', Nr. 260, Frankfurt am Main, 9. Nov. 1998. P. 52.

36243. FELLBACH. *Fellbach: Juden in Fellbach und Waiblingen 1933–1945.* [Red.: Ralf Beckmann]. Hrsg. von den Städten Fellbach und Waiblingen. Fellbach: Stadt Fellbach; Waiblingen: Stadt Waiblingen, 1998. 211 pp., illus., facsims., map, bibl. (Fellbacher Hefte, 6; Waiblinger Hefte zum Nationalsozialismus, 1.)

36244. FILM. CONFINO, ALON: *Edgar Reitz's 'Heimat' and German nationhood: film, memory and understanding of the past.* [In]: German History, Vol. 16, No. 2, London, 1998. Pp. 185–208, footnotes. [Expresses the view that Reitz's film was designed to obscure the Holocaust and hide behind the mantle of memory. Also incl. discussion of the "Historians' Debate".]

36245. FILM. *Film und Holocaust* [issue title of]: Medien & Zeit, Jg. 12, H. 3, Wien, 1997. Pp. 4–51. [Incl. three contribs.]

36246. FILM. LACAPRA, DOMINICK: *History and memory after Auschwitz.* Ithaca: Cornell Univ. Press, 1998. IX, 214 pp., illus., notes. [Lanzmann's film 'Shoah' is used to illustrate the author's analysis of history and memory.]

36247. FILM. PALOWSKI, FRANCISZEK: *Witness: the making of Schindler's List: behind the scenes of an epic film.* Transl. from the Polish by Roberg G. and Anna Ware. London, Secaucus, NJ: Orion, 1998. XIX, 198 pp., illus., ports.

36248. FILM. SKLAR, ROBERT: *'Schindler's List's' Holocaust.* [In]: Dimensions, Vol. 11, No. 2, New York, 1997. Pp. 23–28, illus., ports. [Discusses the representation of the Holocaust in film, and compares Spielberg's film to Lanzmann's 'Shoah'.]

36249. FILM. STARGARDT, UTE: *'Rassenpolitik' in National Socialist cinema.* [In]: Shofar, Vol. 16, No. 3, West Lafayette, IN, Spring 1998. Pp. 1–27, footnotes.

36250. FILM. STEINER, GERTRUD: *Comedian Harmonists: ein Film über die Auswirkungen nationalsozialistischer Kulturpolitik.* [In]: Modern Austrian Literature, Vol. 31, Nos. 3/4, Riverside, CA, 1998. Pp. 212–224, notes. [Discusses the recent German film 'Comedian Harmonists' about the popular singing sextet of the 20s and 30s whose Jewish members were driven into exile.]

36251. FINAL SOLUTION. BAUER, YEHUDA: *Von Stalingrad zur "Stunde Null".* [In]: Menora 1998, Bodenheim, 1998. Pp. 100–120. [Based on a lecture given in 1997 at the Einstein-Forum, Berlin. Deals with the extermination of the European Jews 1943–1945.]

36252. FINAL SOLUTION. BROWNING, CHRISTOPHER R.: *Der Weg zur "Endlösung". Entscheidungen und Täter.* Aus dem Amerik. von Jürgen P. Krause. Bonn: Dietz Nachf., 1998. 231 pp., notes (189–222), index (226–229). [A collection of eight essays publ. between 1986–1996. For orig. publ. most of them see No. 29309/YB XXXVIII. The last two deal critically with Daniel Goldhagen's 'Hitler's willing executioners'.] [Cf.: Christopher Brownings wegweisende Beiträge zur Erklärung des Holocaust (Dieter Pohl) [in]: Die Zeit, Nr. 36, Hamburg, 27. Aug. 1998, p. 40. Wider die Eindimensionalität. Die Arbeitsweisen zweier Historiker im Konflikt (Frauke Hamann) [in]: Das Parlament, Nr. 26, Bonn, 25. Juni 1999, p. 17.]

36253. FINAL SOLUTION. GERHARDT, UTA: *Charismatische Herrschaft und Massenmord im Nationalsozialismus. Eine soziologische These zum Thema der freiwilligen Verbrechen an Juden.* [In]: Geschichte und Gesellschaft, Jg. 24, Göttingen, 1998. Pp. 503–538, footnotes.

36254. FINAL SOLUTION. GERLACH, CHRISTIAN: *The Wannsee Conference, the fate of German Jews, and Hitler's decision in principle to exterminate all European Jews*. [In]: The Journal of Modern History, Vol. 70, No. 4, Chicago, Dec. 1998. Pp. 759–812, footnotes.

36255. FINAL SOLUTION. GRAML, HERMANN: *Ist Hitlers "Anweisung" zur Ausrottung der europäischen Judenheit endlich gefunden?* Zu den Thesen von Christian Gerlach. [In]: Jahrbuch für Antisemitismusforschung 7, Frankfurt am Main; New York, 1998. Pp. 352–362, notes. [Refers to Gerlach's article 'Die Wannsee-Konferenz, das Schicksal der deutschen Juden und Hitlers Grundsatzentscheidung, alle Juden Europas zu ermorden', see in No. 35020/YB XLIII.]

36256. FINAL SOLUTION. HEINSOHN, GUNNAR: *Why was the Holocaust different from all other genocides?* [Hrsg.: Raphael-Lemkin-Institut für Xenophobie- und Genozidforschung, Univ. Bremen, Fachbreich 11, Human- und Gesundheitswiss.]. Bremen: Raphael-Lemkin-Inst., 1998. 90 pp. (Schriftenreihe des Raphael-Lemkin-Inst., Nr. 7.)

36257. FINAL SOLUTION. HERBERT, ULRICH, ed.: *Nationalsozialistische Vernichtungspolitik 1939–1945*. Neue Forschungen und Kontroversen. Mit Beiträgen von Götz Aly [et al.]. Frankfurt am Main: Fischer Taschenbuch Verlag, 1998. 332 pp., footnotes. (Die Zeit des Nationalsozialismus.) Orig.-Ausg. [Cont.: Vorwort (ed., 7–8). Vernichtungspolitik. Neue Antworten und Fragen zur Geschichte des "Holocaust" (Ulrich Herbert, 9–66). "Judenumsiedlung". Überlegungen zur politischen Vorgeschichte des Holocaust (Götz Aly, 67–97). Die Ermordung der Juden im Generalgouvernement (Dieter Pohl, 98–121). Judenpolitik und Judenmord im Distrikt Galizien, 1941–1942 (Thomas Sandkühler, 122–147). Die Debatte über die Täter des Holocaust (Christopher R. Browning, 148–169). Die deutsche Militärverwaltung in Paris und die Deportation der französischen Juden (Ulrich Herbert, 170–208). Die Vernichtung der Juden in Serbien (Walter Manoschek, 209–234). Die nationalsozialistische "Lösung der Zigeunerfrage" (Michael Zimmermann, 235–262). Deutsche Wirtschaftsinteressen, Besatzungspolitik und der Mord an den Juden in Weißrußland, 1941–1943 (Christian Gerlach, 263–291). Der Krieg und die Ermordung der litauischen Juden (Christoph Dieckmann, 292–329).]

—— FINAL SOLUTION. RIEGNER, GERHART: *Ne jamais désespérer. Soixante années au service du peuple juif et des droits de l'homme*. [See No. 37007.]

36258. FISCHLER, HERSCH: *Das Totengold der europäischen Juden und die deutschen Großbanken*. [In]: 1999. Zeitschrift für Sozialgeschichte des 20. und 21. Jahrhunderts. Jg. 13, H. 1, Hamburg, März 1998. Pp. 146–173, footnotes.

36259. *Fondation Auschwitz: Bulletin trimestriel*. No. spécial 59 [with the issue title]: *Études sur le témoignage audiovisuel des victimes des crimes et génocides nazis/Studies on the audio-visual testimony of victims of the Nazi crimes and genocides*. No. 1. Bruxelles, juin/june 1998. 1 issue. 187 pp. [Selected contribs.: For a study of the audiovisual testimony of survivors from the Nazi concentration and extermination camps (Geoffrey Hartman/Yannis Thanassekos, 7–14; text also in French). The contribution of oral history to historical research (Nathan Beyrak, 15–20). Reflections on the 'education' of child victims of the Holocaust who survived (Sydney Bolkovsky, 27–32). Les témoignages audiovisuels de l'holocauste. Rendre à l'histoire les visages de la mémoire (James Young, 83–102). Shaping public and private memory. Holocaust testimonies, interviews and documentaries (Joanne Weiner Rudof, 123–130). The contribution of Holocaust audio-visual testimony to remembrance, learning and hope (Roger Simon, 141–152).]

36260. *Fondation Auschwitz: Bulletin trimestriel*. No. 61 [with the issue title]: *Études sur le témoignage audiovisuel des victimes des crimes et génocides nazis/Studies on the audio-visual testimony of victims of the Nazi crimes and genocides*. 1 issue, 138 pp. Bruxelles, déc./dec. 1998. 1 issue, 138 pp. [Selected essays: "Victims' competitions"? (Alexander von Plato, 7–14). The survivor search for "meaning" (Sydney Bolkovsky, 15–22). Les adolescents dans les camps d'extermination (Josette Zarka, 23–34). Verfolgte Kinder: Erlebnisweisen und Erzählstrukturen (Eva Lezzi, 35–61). The tellable and the hearable: survivor guilt in narrative context (Henry Greenspan, 65–72).]

36261. FORCED LABOUR. Herbert, Ulrich: *Zwangsarbeiter im "Dritten Reich" – ein Überblick.* [In]: Klaus Barwig [et al.], eds.: Entschädigung für NS-Zwangsarbeit. Rechtliche, historische und politische Aspekte. Baden-Baden: Nomos, 1998. Pp. 17–32, footnotes. [Deals also with German Jews.]

36262. FORCED LABOUR. Herbert/Ulrich/Plocki, Melanie von: *"Es geht um Unrecht und die Wiedergutmachung von Unrecht".* Der Historiker Ulrich Herbert über Zwangsarbeit in Nazi-Deutschland. [In]: Aufbau, Vol. 64, No. 17, New York, Aug. 14, 1998. Pp. 1–3, illus. [An interview with U.H.; refers also to Jews in forced labour.]

36263. FRANCE. Caron, Vicki: *The Antisemitic revival in France in the 1930s: the socioeconomic dimension reconsidered.* [In]: The Journal of Modern History, Vol. 70, No. 1, Chicago, 1998. Pp. 24–73, footnotes. [Deals also with the refugees from Germany.]

36264. FRANCE. Gausmann, Angelika: *Deutschsprachige bildende Künstler im Internierungs- und Deportationslager Les Milles von 1939 bis 1942.* Paderborn: Möllmann, 1997. 144 pp., 96 pp. [illus., unpag.], footnotes, bibl. Zugl.: Paderborn, Univ., Diss., 1995. [Incl. Jewish artists.]

36265. FRANCE. Klein, Anne: *Conscience, conflict and politics: the rescue of political refugees from Southern France to the United States, 1940–1942.* [In]: Leo Baeck Institute Year Book XLIII, London, 1998. Pp. 287–311, illus., facsims., footnotes. [On Varian Fry and the Emergency Rescue Committee in Marseille. Also on Varian Fry: "Impelled by the myth of rescue" (Guy Stern) [in]: Aufbau, Vol. 64, No. 1, New York, Jan. 2, 1998, p. 12.]

——— FRANCE. Saint Sauveur-Henn, Anne, ed.: *Zweimal verjagt. Die deutschsprachige Emigration und der Fluchtweg Frankreich – Lateinamerika 1933–1945.* [See No. 36742.]

36266. FRANCE. Sanary-sur-Mer. *Deutsche Literatur im Exil.* Mit 136 Abbildungen. Bearb. von Heinke Wunderlich [et al.] Stuttgart: Metzler, 1996. X, 294 pp., ports., illus., facsims., footnotes, bibl., index. (Heinrich-Heine-Inst. Düsseldorf, Archiv, Bibliothek, Museum, Bd. 5.) [Incl.: Vorwort (Joseph A. Kruse/Hans Wißkirchen, IX-X). Sanary-sur-Mer. Deutsche Literatur im Exil (Heinke Wunderlich, 1–70; on the life of the exiled writers). Autorenporträts (Stefanie Menke/Heinke Wunderlich/Gisela Klemt, 71–259; short biographies, incl. many German- and Austrian-Jewish refugees). Also a contrib. on the non-Jewish artist Eva Hermann.]

36267. FRANK, ANNE. Benz, Wolfgang: *Deutscher Mythos. Warum sich Anne Franks Tagebuch so besonders gut als Betroffenheitstext eignet.* [In]: Die Zeit, Nr. 37, Hamburg, 3. Sept. 1998. P. 45–46.

36268. FRANK, ANNE. De Costa, Denise: *Anne Frank and Etty Hillesum: inscribing spirituality and sexuality.* Transl. by Mischa F.C. Hoyinck and Robert E. Chesal. New Brunswick, NJ: Rutgers Univ. Press, 1998. XII, 275 pp., illus., facsims., notes (243–260), bibl. (261–272). [Author explores the significance of sex and gender differences in the construction of history, using the writings of Frank and Hillesum as examples.]

36269. FRANK, ANNE. *Anne Frank in the world: essays and reflections.* Ed. and with introd. by Carol Rittner. Armonk, NY: M.E. Sharpe, 1998. XXXI, 133 pp., chronol., notes, bibl. (117–119), selec. videography (119–120). [Collection of essays by scholars, clergy, teachers and writers.]

36270. FRANK, ANNE. Loewy, Hanno: *Das gerettete Kind. Die "Universalisierung" der Anne Frank.* [In]: Deutsche Nachkriegsliteratur und der Holocaust [see No. 36760.]. Pp. 19–42.

36271. FRANK, ANNE. Maarsen, Jacqueline van: *My friend Anne Frank.* Transl. from the Dutch by Debra F. Onkenhout. New York: Vantage Press, 1997. 80 pp., illus. [For German edn. see No. 35032/YB XLIII.]

36272. FRANK, ANNE. Müller, Melissa: *Das Mädchen Anne Frank.* Die Biographie. Mit einem Nachwort von Miep Gies. München: Claassen, 1998. 447 pp., illus. [Engl. edn.: Anne

Frank: the biography. Transl. by Rita and Robert Kimber. With a note by Miep Gies. New York: Holt, 1998; London: Bloomsbury Publ., 1999. XVII, 330 pp., illus., geneal. tab.] [Cf.: Flatterndes Vögelchen mit Frischkäse. Sentimentalisierung einer Legende: Anne Frank in einer Biographie, die zuviel und zuwenig weiß (Hermann Kurzke) [in]: 'FAZ', Nr. 255, Frankfurt am Main, 3. Nov. 1998, p. L 6. Notate ohne Notizen (Claus-Henning Bachmann) [in]: Aufbau, Vol. 64, No. 22, New York, Oct. 23, 1998, p. 9.]

36273. FRANKFURT am Main. AYALON, MOSHE: *The end of a Jewish children's institution in Frankfurt am Main.* [In]: Dappim le-Cheker Tekufat ha-Shoah, Vol. 13, Haifa, 1996. Pp. 243–258. [In Hebrew, title transl.] [On the Flörsheim-Sichel Foundation.]

36274. FREEMAN, JOSEPH: *The road to hell: recollections of the Nazi death march.* Ed. by Donald Schwarz. St. Paul, MN: Paragon House, 1998. 110 pp., illus., map, gloss., notes. [Author's recollection of the march from Camp Spaichingen to Füssen.]

36275. FRIEDBERG. *Keine Volksgenossen. Politische, religiöse und rassische Verfolgung in Friedberg zwischen 1933 und 1945.* [Issue title of] Wetterauer Geschichtsblätter. Beiträge zur Geschichte und Landeskunde, Bd. 42, Teil II. Friedberg (Hessen): Verl. der Bindernagelschen Buchhandlung, 1998. 232 pp., notes. (Studien und Erinnerungen zur Geschichte der Wetterau zwischen Machtergreifung und Wiederaufbau, hrsg. von Michael Keller.) [Incl.: "Ein Gefühl der Ungezwungenheit zu vermitteln, das ich nicht erwartet hätte". 50. Jahrestag der Deportation jüdischer Bürgerinnen und Bürger aus Friedberg vom 17.-20. September 1992. Reden, Ansprachen, Zeitzeugenberichte, Briefe, zusammengestellt von Michael Keller und Ulrike Bonarius (151–68). Also a chap. dealing with a Jewish family from Dorheim (Karl Vetter, 67–79).]

36276. FRIEDLÄNDER, SAUL: *Das Dritte Reich und die Juden.* Erster Band. *Die Jahre der Verfolgung 1933–1939.* Aus dem Engl. übers. von Martin Pfeiffer. München: Beck, 1998. 458 pp., notes (361–421), bibl. (422–444), index (445–458). [For orig. publ. see No. 35037/YB XLIII. A Hebrew edn., transl. from the English edn. by Athalia Silber, was publ. in 1997: Nazi Germany and the Jews; the years of persecution, 1933–1939. Tel-Aviv: Am Oved, 1997. 525 pp.] [Selected reviews: Besprechung (Y. Michal Bodemann) [in]: Mittelweg 36, Jg. 7, H. 6, Hamburg, 1998, pp. 49–53. Besprechung (Tobias Brinkmann) [in]: Zeitschrift für Geschichtswissenschaft, Jg. 47, H. 2, Berlin, 1999, pp. 189–190. Stillschweigendes Einverständnis. Saul Friedländers großes Buch über die Verfolgung der Juden in Deutschland zwischen 1933 und 1939 (Volker Ullrich) [in]: Die Zeit, Nr. 14, Hamburg, 26. März 1998, p. 24. Besprechung (Aram Mattioli) [in]: Schweizerische Zeitschrift für Geschichte, Vol. 48, Basel, 1998, pp. 431–434.]

36277. FRIEDLÄNDER, SAUL: *Von den Ursachen der Gefühllosigkeit.* Mitwisserschaft, Mittäterschaft, Gleichgültigkeit: wie gewöhnlich war der gewöhnliche Antisemitismus? [In]: 'FAZ', Nr. 232, Frankfurt am Main, 7. Okt. 1998. P. 44.

36278. FRIEDMANN, RONALD: *Exil auf Mauritius: 1940 bis 1945. Report einer "demokratischen" Deportation jüdischer Flüchtlinge.* Berlin: Ed. Ost, 1998. 192 pp., illus., bibl. (168–172). (Weiße Reihe.) [On the sending of refugees from Palestine to internment in Mauritius by the British authorities.]

36279. FRIESDORF. MOLL, HELMUT: *Der Friesdorfer Pädagogik-Professor Hans Karl Rosenberg – von den Nationalsozialisten seelisch zermürbt.* [In]: Godesberger Heimatblätter, H. 36, Bad Godesberg, 1998. Pp. 63–67, illus. [On a Catholic writer and teacher, son of a Jewish father (1891 – 1942).]

36280. GALL, LOTHAR: *A man for all seasons? Hermann Josef Abs im Dritten Reich.* [In]: Zeitschrift für Unternehmensgeschichte, Jg. 43, Nr. 2, Stuttgart, 1998. Pp. 123–175, footnotes. [With Engl. abstract. Discusses also to what extent Abs can be held responsible for the 'aryanisation' of companies owned by Jews, the crimes of IG-Farben and the gold-trade; also on his personal relations with, and occasional help for, Jews.] [Also on this topic: *Das Deutsche Bank-Geheimnis. Deutschland hat sich von seinem Chefbankier ein falsches Bild gemacht.* Dossier (Andrea Böhm/

Thomas Kleine-Brockhoff/Stefan Willeke) [in]: Die Zeit, Nr. 34, Hamburg, 13. Aug. 1998. Pp. 11–14.]

36281. GELBIN, CATHY/LEZZI, EVA: *Literarische Verarbeitung der Mutter-Tochter-Beziehung: Elisabeth Langgässer und Cordelia Edvardson.* Anmerkungen zu einem nicht stattgefundenen Gespräch. [In]: Zeitschrift für deutsche Philologie, Bd. 117, Berlin, 1998. 565–615, footnotes. [First part of article is entitled: "Es war zwar mein Kind, aber die Rassenschranke fiel zwischen uns". Elisabeth Langgässer und die Mutter-Tochter-Beziehung (Cathy Gelbin, 565–596); second part is entitled: "Gebranntes Kind sucht das Feuer". Über die Zerstörung von Kindheit und Mutterschaft durch Auschwitz (Eva Lezzi, 597–615).] [For data C. Edvardson and 'Gebranntes Kind sucht das Feuer', see No. 23251/YB XXXII.]

36282. GELNHAUSEN. *Zur Geschichte der Juden in Gelnhausen während der nationalsozialistischen Verfolgung.* Ein Stadtrundgang. Hrsg.: Gelnhäuser Hist. Gesellschaft (GHG) e.V. Red.: F. Coy [et al.]. Hanau: CoCon-Verl., 1996. 31 pp., illus., facsims.

36283. GERLACH, CHRISTIAN: *Krieg, Ernährung, Völkermord.* Forschungen zur deutschen Vernichtungspolitik im Zweiten Weltkrieg. Hamburg: Hamburger Ed., 1998. 307 pp.

——— *The German minority census of 1939.* An introduction and register. Compiled by Thomas Kent Edlund. [See No. 36157.]

36284. GEROLSTEIN (EIFEL). THORMANN, KARL: *Die Odysse des Fritz Walbaum. Ein Leben zwischen Tradition und Emigration.* [In]: Jahrbuch des Eifelvereins 1998. Düren, 1998. Pp. 116–121, illus., bibl. notes. [On Dr. Fritz Walbaum, a doctor in Gerolstein since 1884, and his son Fritz (1884 Gerolstein – 1974 San Francisco, CA), an engineer, who fled in 1933 from Gerolstein to Switzerland, later via several countries in 1947 to the US.]

36285. *Geschichten vom Überleben: Frauentagebücher aus der NS-Zeit.* Hrsg. von Barbara Bronnen. München: Beck, 1998. 250 pp. Originalausgabe (Beck'sche Reihe, 1264.) [Excerpts from diaries; incl. German-Jewish women.]

36286. GÖPPINGER, HORST/HILLER, GERHARD: *Der Untergang des jüdischen Verlages I. Heß im Dritten Reich.* [In]: Steuer und Wirtschaft, NF 28 (Bd. 75), Nr. 1, Heidelberg, Feb. 1998. Pp. 81–91, footnotes. [On Isak Heß (1787 Lauchheim – 1866 Ellwangen) and his publ. comp., since 1905 in Stuttgart and since 1922 publ. 'Steuer und Wirtschaft'; also on the 'aryanisation' and the fate of the Jewish editors and authors.]

36287. GÖTTINGEN. REITER, RAIMOND: *Denunziationen im "Dritten Reich" im Kreis Göttingen.* [In]: Göttinger Jahrbuch, Bd. 46, Göttingen, 1998. Pp. 127–137, footnotes. [Incl. denunciations of Jews.]

36288. GOLDHAGEN DEBATE. BECKER, ULRIKE: *Goldhagen und die deutsche Linke oder die Gegenwart des Holocaust.* Berlin: Elefanten-Press, [1997]. 192 pp., bibl. (Antifa-Edition.)

36289. GOLDHAGEN DEBATE. BERMAN, RUSSELL A.: *An imagined community: Germany according to Goldhagen.* [In]: The German Quarterly, Vol. 71, No. 1, Cherry Hill, NJ, Winter 1998. Pp. 63–67.

36290. GOLDHAGEN DEBATE. BINNER, R., [et al.]: *Wiens schuld? De impact van Daniel Goldhagen op het holocaustdebat.* Houten: van Reemst, 1997. 263 pp.

36291. GOLDHAGEN DEBATE. BIRN, RUTH BETTINA/RIEß, VOLKER: *Das Goldhagen-Phänomen oder: 50 Jahre danach.* [In]: Geschichte in Wissenschaft und Unterricht, Jg. 49, H. 2, Stuttgart, 1998. Pp. 80–95, footnotes. [Abstract on p. 78.]

36292. GOLDHAGEN DEBATE. BIRN, RUTH BETTINA: *Ruth Bettina Birn answers Goldhagen.* [In]: German Politics and Society, Vol. 16, No. 2, Berkeley, CA, Summer 1998. Pp. 69–87, notes. [Also in this issue: Daniel Jonah Goldhagen comments on Birn (Daniel J. Goldhagen, 88–93, notes).]

36293. GOLDHAGEN DEBATE. Cattaruzza, Marina: *A discussion of D.J. Goldhagen's Hitler's willing executioner's.* [sic] [In]: Storia della Storiografia, No. 33, Milano, 1998. Pp. 97–107, footnotes.

36294. GOLDHAGEN DEBATE. Finkelstein, Norman G./Birn, Ruth Bettina: *A nation on trial: the Goldhagen thesis and historical truth.* Foreword by Istvan Deak. New York: Metropolitan Books; Hildesheim: Claassen, 1998. 148 pp., 191 pp. [Cf.: Book reopens 'all Germans are guilty' row (Ed Vulliamy) [in]: The Observer, London, Jan. 18, 1998, p. 12.]

36295. GOLDHAGEN DEBATE. Finkelstein, Norman G./Birn, Ruth Bettina: *Eine Nation auf dem Prüfstand. Die Goldhagen-These und die historische Wahrheit.* Aus dem Amerik. von Bernd Leineweber. Mit einer Einl. von Hans Mommsen. Hildesheim: Claassen, 1998, 192 pp. [German edn. of No. 36294. Cont.: Einleitung (Hans Mommsen, 9–22). Daniel Gold-hagens "Wahnsinnsthese": Hitlers willige Vollstrecker – eine Kritik (Norman G. Finkel-stein, 23–136). Eine neue Sicht des Holocaust (Ruth Bettina Birn, 137–192).] [Cf.: Besprechung (Franziska Werners) [in]: Mittelweg 36, Jg. 7, H. 3, Hamburg, 1998, pp. 38–43.]

36296. GOLDHAGEN DEBATE. *Goldhagen, the Germans and the Holocaust: twelve scholars discuss 'Hitler's Willing Executioners' and its implications.* [In]: Gesher, No. 134, Jerusalem, Winter 1996–97. Pp. 7–39. [In Hebrew.] [The participants were: Leni Yahil, Shlomo Aronson, Y. Michal Bodemann, Omer Bartov, Ralph Giordano, Yaacov Lozowick, Deborah Lipstadt, Asher Cohen, Andrei Markovits, Abraham Peck, Konrad Kwiet, Frank Stern.]

36297. GOLDHAGEN DEBATE. Heil, Johannes/Erb, Rainer, eds.: *Geschichtswissenschaft und Öffentlichkeit. Der Streit um Daniel J. Goldhagen.* Frankfurt am Main: Fischer Taschenbuch Verlag, 1998. 349 pp., notes. [Cont.: Vorwort (Wolfgang Benz, 9–15). Klage und Analyse im Widerstreit. Eine Einführung (eds., 16–26). Das Goldhagen-Phänomen (Raul Hilberg, 27–37). Nachgelesen. Goldhagen und seine Quellen (Ruth Bettina Birn/Volker Rieß, 38–62). Die Elimination wissenschaftlicher Unterscheidungsfähigkeit. Goldhagens Begriff des "eliminatorischen Antisemitismus" – eine Überprüfung (Olaf Blaschke, 63–92). Warum werden deutsche Historiker nicht gelesen? (Christof Dipper, 93–109). Die Kritiker-Falle: Wie man in Verdacht geraten kann. Goldhagen und der Funktionalismus (Bernd-A. Rusinek, 110–130). Im falschen System. Die Goldhagen-Debatte in Wissenschaft und Öffentlichkeit (Werner Bergmann, 131–147). Ein Ritterschlag zum Lehrmeister? Die Apo-theose des Daniel J. Goldhagen in der Laudatio von Jürgen Habermas (Uffa Jensen, 148–166). Im Bann der Bilder. Goldhagens virtuelle Täter und die deutsche Öffentlichkeit (Habbo Knoch, 167–183). Archetypen und der deutsch-jüdische Dialog (Steven E. Aschheim, 184–201). Die Goldhagen-Rezeption in den USA (Jane Caplan, 202–217). Die Goldhagen-Rezeption in den Niederlanden, in Frankreich und Italien (Juliane Wetzel, 218–234). "Goldhagen gegen rechts verteidigen und von links kritisieren". Die deutsche Linke in der Goldhagen-Debatte (Thomas Haury, 235–260). "Meine Geschichte – deine Geschichte". Oder: Das Verfügen über Geschichte und ihre Deutung (Marianne Kröger, 261–278). Künstler in Schuldgefühlen. "Denkmal für die ermordeten Juden Europas" (Hans-Ernst Mittig, 279–294). Streitkulturen und Gefühlslagen. Die Goldhagen-Debatte und der Streit um die Wehrmachtausstellung (Angelika Königseder, 295–311). Die Tagebü-cher Victor Klemperers und ihre Wirkung in der deutschen Öffentlichkeit (Alexandra Przy-rembel, 312–327). Vagabundierende Normalisierung. Gedanken zur politischen Historisierung des Nationalsozialismus (Harald Schmid, 328–343).]

36298. GOLDHAGEN DEBATE. Jahoda, Gustav: *"Ordinary Germans" before Hitler: a critique of the Goldhagen thesis.* [In]: The Journal of Interdisciplinary History, Vol. 29, No. 1, Cambridge, MA, Summer 1998. Pp. 69–88, footnotes. [Review article.]

36299. GOLDHAGEN DEBATE. Kautz, Fred: *Goldhagen und die "hürnen Sewfriedte".* Die Holo-caust-Forschung im Sperrfeuer der Flakhelfer. Berlin: Argument, 1998. 133 pp., footnotes, bibl. (119–133). [Incl. Nachwort (Helmut Dahmer, 115–118). Polemical discussion of the reaction of Hans Mommsen, Hans-Ulrich Wehler and Eberhard Jäckel on Goldhagen's book; incl. also a chap. on Ruth Bettina Birn.]

36300. GOLDHAGEN DEBATE. LEGENDRE, PIERRE: *La Brèche. Remarques sur la dimension institu-tionnelle de la Shoah.* [In]: Rechtshistorisches Journal, 17, Frankfurt am Main, 1998. Pp. 226–233, footnotes.

36301. GOLDHAGEN DEBATE. PETERSEN, JENS: *Holocaust und Goldhagen-Debatte in Italien.* [In]: Quellen und Forschungen aus italienischen Archiven und Bibliotheken, Bd. 77, Tübingen, 1997. Pp. 489–496, footnotes. [Incl. Italian abstract.]

36302. GOLDHAGEN DEBATE. PINTO-DUSCHINSKY, MICHAEL: *Wehler on Hitler's willing execu-tioners: a comment.* [In]: German History, Vol. 16, No. 3, Oxford, 1998. Pp. 397–411, notes. [Reply to Hans-Ulrich Wehler's critical review of Goldhagen's book, see No. 35069/YB XLIII.]

36303. GOLDHAGEN DEBATE. SCHMID, HARALD: *Vom "Henker" zum "Wunderheiler". Gerechtigkeit für Goldhagen?* [In]: Menora 1997, Bodenheim, 1997. Pp. 16–52, notes. [On the reception of G.'s book in Germany.]

36304. GOLDHAGEN DEBATE. SCHOEPS, JULIUS H.: *Deutschland, Goldhagen und die kollektive Erin-nerung.* Eine Debatte, die nach wie vor die Gemüter erregt. [In]: Das Gewaltsyndrom. Ver-formungen und Brüche im deutsch-jüdischen Verhältnis [see No. 36438]. Pp. 99–108. [Enlarged and revised lecture given at the universities of Jerusalem, Beer Sheva and Haifa.]

36305. GOLDHAGEN DEBATE. SHANDLEY, ROBERT R., ed.: *Unwilling Germans?: the Goldhagen debate.* Essays transl. by Jeremiah Riemer. Minneapolis, MN: Univ. of Minnesota Press, 1998. X, 295 pp.

36306. GOLDHAGEN DEBATE. VOLKOV, SHULAMIT: *A propos Goldhagen; antisemitism in German his-toriography revisit*ed. [In]: Zmanim, No. 59, Tel-Aviv, Summer 1997. Pp. 18–27. [In Hebrew.]

36307. GOLDHAGEN DEBATE. WAGNER, IRMGARD: *Geschichtsschreibung und Psychoanalyse. Zur Frage der Positionalität in der Goldhagen-Debatte.* [In]: Dimensionen der Historik. Geschichtsthe-orie, Wissenschaftsgeschichte und Geschichtskultur heute. Jörn Rüsen zum 60. Geburtstag. Hrsg. von Horst Walter Blanke [et al.]. Köln: Böhlau, 1998. Pp. 415–425, footnotes.

36308. GOLDHAGEN DEBATE. *Yad Vashem Studies* Vol. XXVI. Jerusalem, 1998. 1 issue. [Incl. 4 contribs. (two of them reprinted) dealing with Daniel J. Goldhagen's book and the ensuing debate: German historians face Goldhagen (Avraham Barkai, 295–328, footnotes). Goldha-gen – his critics and his contribution (Yisrael Gutman, 329–364, footnotes). The universe of death and torment (Götz Aly, 365–376). The Goldhagen phenomenon (Raul Hilberg, 377–386).]

36309. GOLDSCHMIDT, GERSON: *Am seidenen Faden.* Zürich: My Tours, Guggenheim, 1997. 166 pp., illus. [Memoirs dealing with the author's emigration in 1933 from Lübeck to Belgium, later to France and his escape to Switzerland in 1942. Lives in Antwerpen.]

36310. GREAT BRITAIN. GOTTLIEB, AMY ZAHL: *Men of vision: Anglo-Jewry's aid to victims of the Nazi regime, 1933–1945.* London: Weidenfeld and Nicolson, 1998. XIV, 258 pp., facsims., notes (207–250). [Incl. chaps. on the various aid organisations and their activities to rescue Jews from Germany, Austria and other European countries, such as the Central British Fund for German Jewry, the Jewish Refugees Committee, the Academic Assistance Council. Also several chaps. on aid to children, such as the Kindertransports and rescue of children from concentration camps.] [Cf.: Review (David Mauer) [in]: AJR Information, Vol. LIII, No. 11, London, Nov. 1998, p. 4.]

36311. GREAT BRITAIN. GRIFFITH, RICHARD: *Patriotism perverted: Captain Ramsay, the Right Club and British antisemitism 1939–40.* London: Constable, 1998. XI, 372 pp., illus., appendix, notes (315–340), bibl. (341–350). [Incl. pro-Nazi attitudes and antisemitism which reflected on refugee policies, also affecting German Jews.]

36312. GREBENSTEIN. Dorhs, Michael: *Nachbarn, die keiner mehr kennt.* Schicksale jüdischer Familien aus Grebenstein nach 1933. [In]: Jahrbuch '98 [des Landkreises Kassel]. Kassel, 1998. Pp. 119–130, ports., facsims., notes.

36313. Greenspan, Henry: *On listening to Holocaust survivors: recounting and life history.* Foreword by Robert Coles. Westport, CT: Praeger, 1998. XX, 199 pp., notes (173–186), bibl. (187–192). [Based on twenty years of interviews with the same core group of survivors, incl. German Jews.]

36314. Gruner, Wolf: *Der Deutsche Gemeindetag und die Koordinierung antijüdischer Kommunalpolitik. Zum Marktverbot für jüdische Händler und zur "Verwertung" jüdischen Eigentums.* [In]: Archiv für Kommunalwissenschaften, 37. Jg., Bd. 2, Stuttgart, 1998. Pp. 261–291, footnotes. [Incl. German and English abstract.]

36315. GURS. Schneider, Hansjörg: *Kabarett als Lebenshilfe. Peter Pan alias Alfred Nathan im Camp de Gurs.* [In]: Zeitschrift für Germanistik, N.F., Jg. VII, H. 3, Frankfurt am Main, 1997. Pp. 617–623, notes. [A.N., 1909 Berlin – 1976 Berlin (East), escaped from Gurs to Spain in late 1942, returned to East Berlin in 1957.]

36316. Gurock, Jeffrey S., ed.: *America, American Jews, and the Holocaust.* New York; London: Routledge, 1998. XIV, 486 pp., illus., facsims., tabs., appendixes, notes. (American Jewish history, Vol. 7.) [Selected contribs. (titles abbr.): Who shall bear the guilt for the Holocaust (Henry L. Feingold, 1–22). The State Department, the Labor Department, and the German Jewish immigration, 1930– 1940 (A.M. Kraut, R. Breitman and Th.W. Imhoof, 23–56). The St. Louis tragedy (I.F. Gellman, 57–70). The United States and the persecution of the Jews in Germany, 1933–1939 (S. Spear, 71– 98). American Jewish leaders and the emerging Nazi threat (1928 – Jan., 1933) (S. Shafir, 99–134). The prelude to Nazism: The German-American press and the Jews, 1919–1933 (D.G. Singer, 223– 238). Why Auschwitz was not bombed (D.S. Wyman, 279–300). A new deal for refugees: the promise and reality of Oswego (S. Lowenstein, 301–318).]

36317. Hachmeister, Lutz: *Der Gegnerforscher. Die Karriere des SS-Führers Franz Alfred Six.* München: Beck, 1998. 414 pp., illus., notes (343–385), bibl. (387–404), index (405–414). [Examines also Six's role as a leading functionary in the SD resp. in the RSHA (Sicherheitsdienst des Reichsführers SS/Reichssicherheitshauptamt) in its anti-Jewish policy.]

36318. Häntzschel, Hiltrud: *Remigration – kein Thema. Das Verschwinden der weiblichen Elite nach 1933 und die Folgen.* [In]: Exil, Forschung, Erkenntnisse, Ergebnisse, Jg. 18, Nr. 1, Frankfurt am Main, 1998. Pp. 17–25.

36319. HAMBURG. Bajohr, Frank: *The beneficiaries of "Aryanization": Hamburg as a case study.* [In]: Yad Vashem Studies, Vol. XXVI, Jerusalem, 1998. Pp. 173–202, footnotes.

36320. HAMBURG. Lorenz, Ina: *Verfolgung und Gottvertrauen. Briefe einer Hamburger jüdisch-orthodoxen Familie im "Dritten Reich".* Unter Mitarbeit von Birgitta Bohn-Strauss. Hamburg: Dölling und Galitz, 1998. 187 pp., illus., facsims., notes, bibl., gloss., geneal., index. (Studien zur jüdischen Geschichte, Bd. 5.) [Incl. 99 letters written by Benjamin Jakob Perlmann and his wife Elsa between 1932 and 1942 when they were deported to Auschwitz.]

36321. HANAU. Pfeifer, Monika/Kingreen, Monica: *Hanauer Juden 1933–1945. Entrechtung, Verfolgung, Deportation.* Hrsg.: Ev. Arbeitskreis "Christen – Juden" Hanau in Zusammenarbeit mit der Stadt Hanau. Hanau: CoCon-Verlag, 1998. 143 pp., illus., facsims., notes, bibl.

36322. Henderson, Jennifer: *Against all odds: the story of Kurt Pick.* London: Radcliffe Press, 1998. 203 pp., illus., ports., map. [K.P., b. 1912 in Austria, emigr. to Brussels in 1938, between 1942–1944 survived in hiding, emigr. 1948 to England.]

36323. Heppner, Ernest G.: *Fluchtort Shanghai: Erinnerungen 1938–1948.* Aus dem Amerik. von Roberto de Hollanda. Bonn: Weidel, 1998. 282 pp., illus. [For orig. edn. and data see No. 30624/YB XXXIX.]

36324. HERLEM, DIDIER: *Eine "Mischehe" im Dritten Reich. Eva und Victor Klemperer.* [Aus dem Franz. von Christine Alonzo.] [In]: Mittelweg 36, Jg. 7, H. 4, Hamburg, 1998. Pp. 82–91. [Also in this issue: Wär' sie doch ein Stück von mir. Eva Klemperer in Victor Klemperers Tagebüchern (Gaby Zipfel, 65–81).]

36325. HERZ-KESTRANEK, MIGUEL/ARNBOM, MARIE-THERESE: *... also hab ich nur mich selbst! Stefan Herz-Kestranek – Stationen eines großbürgerlichen Emigranten 1938 bis 1945.* Wien: Böhlau, 1998. 228 pp., illus. [Deals with the author's father, his flight from Vienna in 1938 and his subsequent life in Uruguay; based on his letters.] [Cf.: "... also hab ich nur mich selbst! Stefan Herz-Kestranek – Stationen eines grossbürgerlichen Emigranten 1938 bis 1945 (Michaela Ronzoni) [in]: Illustrierte Neue Welt, Wien, Aug./Sept. 1997.]

36326. HESDÖRFFER, HEINZ: *Bekannte traf man viele ... Aufzeichnungen eines deutschen Juden aus dem Winter 1945/46.* Zürich: Chronos, 1998. 229 pp., frontis., illus., facsims. [H.H., b. 1923 in Bad Kreuznach, went in 1939 with a Kindertransport to the Netherlands, deported to Westerbork, Theresienstadt, Auschwitz, Sachsenhausen. Memoirs were written in Brussels after liberation. Emigr. 1947 to South Africa, lives in Johannesburg.]

36327. HESSE. *Handbuch der hessischen Geschichte.* In Verbindung mit Helmut Berding [et al.] hrsg. von Walter Heinemeyer. Vierter Bd.: *Hessen im Deutschen Bund und im neuen Deutschen Reich (1806) 1815 bis 1945.* Zweiter Teilband: *Die hessischen Staaten bis 1945.* 1. Lieferung. Marburg: Elwert, 1998. 419 pp., footnotes, tabs. (Veröffentlichungen der Historischen Kommission für Hessen, 63.) [Incl. Preussische Provinz Hessen-Nassau 1866–1944/45 (Thomas Klein, 213–419; with the section: Das Schicksal der jüdischen Bevölkerung (399–407).]

36328. HEUSS, ANJA: *Das Schicksal der jüdischen Kunstsammlung von Ismar Littmann.* Ein neuer Fall von Kunstraub wirft grundsätzliche Fragen auf. [In]: 'NZZ', Nr. 188, Zürich, 17. Aug. 1998. P. 23. [On I.L., a Breslau lawyer (1934 suicide) and the fate of his collection of Expressionist paintings.]

36329. HILDESHEIM. REYER, HERBERT: *Die Verfolgung und Vernichtung der Hildesheimer Juden im "Dritten Reich".* Anmerkungen zum heutigen Forschungsstand. [In]: Hildesheimer Jahrbuch für Stadt und Stift Hildesheim, Bd. 69, Hildesheim, 1997. Pp. 225–240, footnotes. [Incl. list of 103 Nazi victims.]

36330. HILZINGER, SONJA: *"Das Wort der Stummen". Deutsch-jüdische Lyrik in Nazi-Deutschland.* [In]: Menora 1998, Bodenheim, 1998. Pp. 70–99, notes.

36331. HISTORIOGRAPHY. FRIEDLÄNDER, SAUL: *Writing the history of the Shoa: some major dilemmas.* [In]: Dimensionen der Historik. Geschichtstheorie, Wissenschaftsgeschichte und Geschichtskultur heute. Jörn Rüsen zum 60. Geburtstag. Hrsg. von Horst Walter Blanke [et al.]. Köln: Weimar, 1998. Pp. 407–417, footnotes.

36332. HISTORIOGRAPHY. SCHUBERT, GÜNTER: *Hitlers "jüdische Soldaten". Ein Defizit der Holocaustforschung oder nur ein Medienereignis?* [In]: Jahrbuch für Antisemitismusforschung 8, Frankfurt am Main; New York, 1998. Pp. 307–321, notes. [Examines critically Bryan Rigg's publ. research findings on soldiers of partly Jewish descent serving in Hitler's army for periods of time during World War II.]

36333. HISTORIOGRAPHY. SEIBEL, WOLFGANG: *Staatsstruktur und Massenmord. Was kann eine historisch-vergleichende Institutionenanalyse zur Erforschung des Holocaust beitragen?* [In]: Geschichte und Gesellschaft, Jg. 24, Göttingen, 1998. Pp. 539–569, footnotes.

36334. HISTORIOGRAPHY & HISTORIANS' DEBATE. SACHS, DAN: *Historiography and national identity: the new historians in Israel and the "historians' debate" in Germany.* [In]: Theoria u-Vikoret, Vol. 8, Tel-Aviv, Summer 1996. Pp. 73–89. [In Hebrew, title transl.]

36335. HISTORIOGRAPHY & HISTORIANS' DEBATE. ZIMMERMANN, MOSHE: *Historians' debates: the German experience and the Israeli experiment.* [In]: Theoria u-Vikoret, No. 8, Tel-Aviv, Summer 1996. Pp. 91–103. [In Hebrew, title transl.]

36336. HITLER, ADOLF. KERSHAW, IAN: *Hitler. 1889–1936: hubris.* London: Allen Lane, 1998. IX, 845 pp., illus., ports., facsims., gloss., notes (597–766), bibl. (767–797). [German edn.: Hitler 1889 – 1936. Aus dem Engl. von Jürgen Peter Krause und Jörg W. Rademacher. Stuttgart: Deutsche Verlags-Anstalt, 1998. 972 pp., illus., notes (751–923), bibl. (925–958), index.] [Cf.: Working toward the Führer (Gordon A. Craig) [in]: New York Review of Books, Vol. 46, No. 5, New York, March 18, 1999, pp. 32–35, illus., port. His path to power (Robert Harris) [in]: The Sunday Times, London, Sept. 13, 1998. Wir haben ihn uns engagiert. Die Biographie Adolf Hitlers als Geschichte seiner Macht: Ian Kershaw entzaubert die Dämonie des Willens und zeigt, wie Deutschland sich seinen Vollstrecker schuf (Frank Schirrmacher) [in]: 'FAZ', Nr. 231, Frankfurt am Main, 6. Okt. 1998, p. L 29. "Dem Führer entgegenarbeiten". Ian Kershaw porträtiert Hitler im Kontext (Norbert Frei) [in]: 'NZZ', Nr. 231, Zürich, 6. Okt. 1998, p. B 21.]

36337. HITLER, ADOLF. NELKEN, MICHAEL: *Hitler unmasked: the romance of racism and suicide.* Glastonbury, CT: Darkside Press, 1997. 276 pp., illus., maps, notes, bibl. (259–263). [Deals with the psychological origins of Nazism as seen through Hitler's life. Incl. chap.: The Holocaust as strategy.]

36338. HITLER, ADOLF. ROSENBAUM, RON: *Explaining Hitler: the search for the origins of his evil.* New York: Random House; London: Macmillan, 1998. XLVI, 444 pp., illus., notes (397–424). [Attempt to explain Hitler by reviewing theories of other scholars such as Alan Bullock, Hugh Trevor Roper, Claude Lanzmann, Emil Fackenheim, George Steiner, Lucy Dawidowicz, Daniel Goldhagen, several of whom are interviewed.] [Cf.: Making of a monster (Ian Kershaw) [in]: The Guardian, London, July 18, 1998. Can evil lie in an individual personality? (Hyam Maccoby) [in]: The Jewish Chronicle, London, Aug. 7, 1998, p. 26. Where's the medical proof of his missing testicle? (George Steiner) [in]: The Observer, London, July 12, 1998. A nice pleasant youth (John Gross) [in]: New York Review of Books, Vol. 45, No. 20, New York, Dec. 17, 1998, pp. 12–17, illus.]

36339. HOCHNEUKIRCH. RÖTTGER, RÜDIGER: *Davon haben wir nichts gewußt. Jüdische Schicksale aus Hochneukirch/Rheinland 1933–1945.* Düsseldorf: DTP Druck & Display, [1998]. 190 pp., illus., facsims. [Book presents the results of a school project enlarged by the author.]

36340. HOHENLIMBURG. *Hohenlimburg unterm Hakenkreuz.* Beiträge zur Geschichte einer Kleinstadt im Dritten Reich. Hrsg. im Auftrag des Hagener Geschichtsvereins von Hermann Zabel. Essen: Klartext, 1998. 508 pp., illus., bibl. (478–504). (Beiträge zur Förderung des christlich-jüdischen Dialogs, Bd. 17.) [Incl. chap.: Die Zerstörung der jüdischen Gemeinde (345–381).]

——— HOLOCAUST. [See also FINAL SOLUTION.]

36341. HOLOCAUST. EAGAN, JENNIFER L.: *Philosophers and the Holocaust: mediating public disputes.* [In]: International Studies in Philosophy, Vol. 29, No. 1, New York, 1997. Pp. 9–17, notes.

36342. HOLOCAUST. FISCHEL, JACK R.: *The Holocaust.* Westport, CT; London: Greenwood Press, 1998. XXXVII, 196 pp., illus., chronol., gloss., appendixes, bibl. (183–188). (Guides to historic events of the twentieth century.) [Incl. biographies of major perpetrators, also chaps. on Hitler and the Jews; the Nazi racial state; Genocide; the Final Solution; resistance.]

36343. HOLOCAUST. *The Holocaust and History: the known, the unknown, the disputed, and the reexamined.* Ed. by Michael Berenbaum and Abraham J. Peck. Bloomington: Indiana Univ. Press; Washington, DC: United States Holocaust Memorial Museum, 1998. IX, 836 pp., notes. [Cont. the following sections (titles abbr.): Part 1: Probing the Holocaust (contribs. by R. Hilberg, Y. Bauer, E. Jäckel, M.R. Marrus). Part 2: Antisemitism and racism in Nazi ideology (contribs. by D. Bankier, St. T. Katz, W.Z. Bacharach, O. Bartov). Part 3: The politics of racial health and science (contribs. by B. Müller-Hill, A. Ehmann, St. Kühl). Part 4: The Nazi state (contribs. by Ch. W. Sydnor, R. Breitman, P. Hayes, H. Mommsen, F.H. Littell). Part 5: "Ordinary men" (contribs. by H. Friedlander, C. R. Browning, J. Förster, G. Meershoek, D.J. Goldhagen). Part 6: Ideology, exclusion, and coercion (contribs. by J.A.S. Grenville, H.G. Gallagher, G. Grau, R. Lautmann, R. Kesting). Part 7: concentration camps (contribs. by F. Piper, S. Milton, E. Raim, G. J. Horwitz). Part 8: The axis, the allies, and the neutrals (contribs. by R.L. Braham, M. Michaelis, J. Ancel, G.L., Weinberg, S.S. Zuccotti, L. London, P.A. Levine, M.A. Epstein, J.T. Pawlikowski, D.I. Bergen). Part 9: Jewish leadership, Jewish resistance (contribs. by Y. Arad, R.I. Cohen, A. Rayski, L. Rothkirchen). Part 10: The rescuers (contribs. by N. Tec, E. Fogelman, S.P. Oliner). Part 11: The survivor experience (contribs. by J. Giere, Th. Albrich, D. Ofer, W.B. Helmreich, L. Eitinger, D. Porat, D. Laub with M. Allard).

36344. HOLOCAUST. Margalit, Avishai/Motzkin, Gabriel: *The uniqueness of the Holocaust.* [In]: Philosophy & Public Affairs, Vol. 25, Baltimore, MD, Winter 1996. Pp. 65–83, footnotes. [Discusses the uniqueness of the Germans, of the Jews and of the process of extermination.]

36345. HOLOCAUST. O'Kane, Rosemary H.T.: *Modernity, the Holocaust and politics.* [In]: Economy and Society, Vol. 26, No. 1, London, Feb. 1, 1997. Pp. 43–61, notes. [Discusses Zygmunt Bauman's claim that the potential for a Holocaust exists in all modern societies; for Bauman's book 'Modernity and the Holocaust' see No. 27283/YB XXXVI.]

36346. HOLOCAUST DENIAL. Finkielkraut, Alain: *The future of a negation: reflections on the question of Genocide.* Transl. from the French by Mary Byrd Kelly. Introd. by Richard J. Golson. Lincoln: Univ. of Nebraska Press, 1998. XXXIV, 146 pp., notes (125–142). [Deals with Holocaust denial by the Left, disguised as anti-Zionism.]

36347. HUNGARY. *The Nazis' last victims: the Holocaust in Hungary.* Ed. by Randolph L. Braham with Scott Miller. Foreword by Michael Berenbaum. Detroit, MI: Wayne State Univ. Press, 1998. 200 pp., illus., maps, index of persons. [8 essays, first presented at the commemoration of the 50th anniversary in May 1994 of the deportation of Hungarian Jewry. Publ. in association with the US Holocaust Memorial Museum, Washington, DC.]

36348. HUNGARY. Reuveni, Sari: *The circumstances which facilitated and prevented rescue of Hungarian Jewry.* [In]: Dappim le-Cheker Tekufat ha-Shoah, Vol. 14, Haifa, 1997. Pp. 313–325. [In Hebrew, title transl.]

36349. ICELAND. Eggerz, Solveig: *Jews flee from Nazis to Iceland.* [In]: Midstream, Vol. 44, No. 3, New York, April 1998. Pp. 20–22. [Discusses Iceland's hostile, racist policies towards the mainly German-Jewish refugees.]

36350. IRELAND. Keogh, Dermot: *Jews in 20th-century Ireland: refugees, anti-semitism and the Holocaust.* Cork: Cork Univ. Press, 1998. XV, 336 pp., illus., ports., tabs., map, notes (245–301), bibl. (303–320). [Deals with hostile Irish policy towards refugees from Nazi Germany on the eve of the 2nd World War. Incl. chaps: Irish refugee policy, antisemitism and the approach of the Second World War (115–152). Ireland, the Second World War and the Holocaust (153–198).]

36351. ITALY. Sarfatti, Michele: *Fascist Italy and German Jews in South-Eastern France in July 1943.* [In]: Journal of Modern Italian Studies, Vol. 3, No. 3, London, Fall, 1998. Pp. 318–328. [Incl. one German and two Italian documents, transl. into English.]

36352. Jäger, Gudrun: *Ins Kulturghetto verdrängt. Kurt Pinthus als Literaturkritiker und Publizist 1933–1938.* [In]: Jüdischer Almanach 1999 des Leo Baeck Instituts, Frankfurt am Main, 1998. Pp. 57–72, illus.

——— *Jüdisches Kinderleben im Spiegel jüdischer Kinderbücher.* [See No. 36653.]

36353. KAISER, REINHARD: *Königskinder. Eine wahre Liebe.* Frankfurt am Main: Schöffling & Co., 1996. 128 pp., illus. [Incl. letters of the Jewish geologist Rudolf Kaufmann, expelled from Greifswald University in 1933, who emigr. to Italy, returned to Germany, later escaped to the Soviet Union, where he was shot during the war. Letters were addressed to a Swedish woman.]

36354. KAPLAN, MARION: *Between dignity and despair: Jewish life in Nazi Germany.* New York: Oxford Univ. Press, 1998. XII, 290 pp., illus., tabs., notes (239–263), bibl. (265–274). [Focuses on the daily life of Jewish women and families (incl. "mixed" families), children and youth, November Pogrom, forced labour, deportations and life in hiding.]

36355. KEMPTER, KLAUS: *Ein Rechtsprofessor im Konflikt mit der NS-Rassengesetzgebung: der Fall Walter Jellinek.* [In]: Zeitschrift für Geschichtswissenschaft, Jg. 46, H. 4, Berlin, 1998. Pp. 305–319, footnotes. [Deals with W.J. (1885 – 1955), Protestant professor of law at Heidelberg Univ., who went to considerable pains to fight his classification as a 'non-Aryan'. See also No. 36750.]

36356. KIRSCHGENS, STEFAN: *Wege durch das Niemandsland. Dokumentation und Analyse der Hilfe für Flüchtlinge im deutsch-belgisch-niederländischen Grenzland in den Jahren 1933 bis 1945.* Köln: Rhein-land-Verl., 1998. 353 pp. (Mit-Menschlichkeit, 3.) Zugl.: Aachen, Techn. Hochsch., Diss., 1997.

36357. KLÜGER, LEO: *Lache, denn morgen bist du tot.* Eine Geschichte vom Überleben. Aus dem Schwed. von Verena Reichel. München: Piper, 1998. 362 pp., illus. [Personal recollections of an Austrian Jew who survived Auschwitz.]

36358. KOCH, ERIC: *Hilmar und Odette: zwei Leben in Deutschland.* Aus dem Eng. übertr. und bearb. von Matthias Reichelt. Gerlingen: Bleicher, 1998. 239 pp., illus. [For orig. edn. and details see No. 32910/YB XLI.]

36359. KÖPER, CARMEN RENATE: *Wer war Sonja Okun?* [In]: Jüdischer Almanach 1999 des Leo Baeck Instituts, Frankfurt am Main, 1998. Pp. 118–134, illus. [On a young woman who moved in Berlin theatre circles and worked for the Youth Aliya until she was deported to Theresienstadt in 1943 and to Auschwitz in 1944.]

36360. KOHN, PAVEL: *Jude und politisch unzuverlässig.* Erfahrungen eines Holocaust-Überlebenden in der Tschechoslowakei. [In]: Dachauer Hefte, Jg. 14, H. 14, München. 1998. Pp. 67–76. [P.K., b. Oct. 14, 1929 in Prague, son of a German-speaking father, writer, journalist, deported to Theresienstadt in 1942, later to Auschwitz. After liberation returned to Prague, fled to West Germany in 1967.]

36361. KOPPEL, GERT: *Untergetaucht. Eine Flucht aus Deutschland.* Würzburg: Arena, 1997. 238 pp., illus., facsims., footnotes, geneal. [Incl.: Nachwort (Malte Dahrendorf, 224–228).] [Memoirs of author, b. 1927 in Hamburg, who survived with his sister in hiding in Belgium and later emigr. to Ecuador. Now lives in California.]

36362. KOS, MARTA: *Frauenschicksale in Konzentrationslagern.* [Aus dem Tschech. von Ottilie Slálkova et al.]. Wien: Passagen-Verl., 1998. 223 pp. (Passagen Zeitgeschehen.) [Based on the author's dissertation written in 1948 at Prague Univ.; incl. 60 case studies.] [M. Kos-Robés, 1919 Slany – 1989 Vienna, psychologist, children's therapist, 1942–1945 imprisoned in Theresienstadt and Auschwitz, emigr. 1949 from Czechoslovakia to Austria.]

36363. KRAUSS, MARITA: *Grenze und Grenzwahrnehmung bei Emigranten der NS-Zeit.* [In]: Andreas Gestrich/Marita Krauss, eds.: Migration und Grenze. Stuttgart: Steiner, 1998. (Stuttgarter Beiträge zur historischen Migrationsforschung, Bd. 4). Pp. 61–82, footnotes. [Incl. English summary on p. 82.]

36364. KREFELD. *Gymnasium am Moltkeplatz Krefeld. Leben mit Erinnerungen – Zum Gedenken.* [Doku-mentation erstellt von Renate Starck.] Krefeld: Gymnasium am Moltkeplatz, 1998. 109 pp., illus., facsims. [Documentary based on a school project; incl. recollections and letters of Jews from Krefeld.]

36365. KREFT, GERALD: *"Ich habe Angst, ich darf es mir aber nicht merken lassen"*. *Zu den Tagebüchern (1933–1945) des "Mischlings 1. Grades" Professor Dr. med. Max Flesch-Thebesius (1889–1983)*. [In]: Medizinhistorisches Journal, Bd. 33, H. 3/4, Jena, 1998. Pp. 323–347, footnotes.

36366. LEAPMAN, MICHAEL, ed.: *Witnesses to war: eight true-life stories of Nazi persecution*. New York; London: Viking, 1998. 128 pp., illus., ports., facsims., maps, plans. [Incl. account by a German Jew from Munich; also stories of Jewish children from Alsace Lorraine; one chap. deals with Anne Frank.]

36367. LEE, STEPHEN J.: *Hitler and Nazi Germany*. London; New York: Routledge, 1998. XI, 129 pp., tabs., gloss., notes, bibl. (111–117). [Incl. chap.: Race, the Holocaust and the Jewish response (81–96).]

36368. LEZZI, EVA: *Verfolgte Kinder. Erlebnisweisen und Erzählstrukturen.* [In]: Menora 1998, Bodenheim, 1998. Pp. 181–223.

36369. LINGEN (Lower Saxony). SCHERGER, GERTRUD ANNE: *Verfolgt und ermordet. Leidenswege jüdischer Bürger in der Emigration, im Ghetto und in den Konzentrationslagern.* Beitrag zur Verfolgungsgeschichte der Juden aus dem Raum Lingen. [Hrsg.: Arbeitskreis Judentum – Christentum Lingen u. der Pax-Christi-Gruppe Lingen]. Lingen: Burgtor, 1998. 122 pp., illus.

36370. LONGERICH, PETER: *Politik der Vernichtung*. Eine Gesamtdarstellung der nationalsozialistischen Judenverfolgung. München: Piper, 1998. 772 pp., notes (589–731), bibl. (732–755), indexes (names; places). [Cf.: Besprechung (Klaus-Peter Friedrich) [in]: Aschkenas, Jg. 9. H. 1, Wien, 1999, pp. 278–279. Stufen des Terrors. Peter Longerichs Gesamtdarstellung der Judenverfolgung im "Dritten Reich" (Dieter Pohl) [in]: Die Zeit, Nr. 50, Hamburg, 3. Dez. 1998, p. 19.]

36371. LORENTZ, DAGMAR C.G.: *In search of the criminal – in search of the crime: Holocaust literature and films as crime fiction*. [In]: Modern Austrian Literature, Vol. 31, Nos. 3/4, Riverside, CA, 1998. Pp. 35–48, notes. [Deals with the way some modern Austrian-Jewish authors try to present Nazi crimes in terms of traditional detective fiction.]

36372. LÜBECK. JASHEK, RICHARD J.: *Die Geschichte meines Lebens*. Jürgen Jaschek. Wie ein zwölfjähriger jüdischer Junge aus Lübeck und Bad Schwartau die Konzentrationslager überlebte. Aus dem Amerik. übers. von Martin Harnisch [et al.]. Hrsg. vom Schulverein der Geschwister-Prenski-Schule. Lübeck: Schulverein der Geschw.-Prenski-Schule, 1998. 69 pp., illus. [Born 1929 in Lübeck, the author was deported to Riga in Dec. 1941.]

36373. MEIMBRESSEN/HESSE. GUDENBERG, EBERHARD WOLFF VON: *Erinnerungen an die untergegangene jüdische Gemeinde von Meimbressen.* [In]: Jahrbuch '97 [des Landkreises Kassel], Kassel, 1996. Pp. 38–40. [Also in this issue: Gegen das Vergessen (Ernst Klein, 30–32).]

36374. MERZ, KONRAD: *Berliner, Amsterdamer und ach – Jude auch.* Memoiren aus neunzig Jahren. Bocholt: Achterland-Verlagscompagnie, 1998. 192 pp., bibl. K.M. (189–192). [Incl.: Nachwort oder: Humor in der Tragödie (Ekhard Haack, 170–188).] [K.M., b. April 2, 1908 in Berlin, German-language exile writer (pseud.: Kurt Lehmann), physiotherapist, emigr. in 1934 to The Netherlands, where he survived in hiding. Lives in Amsterdam.]

———— MEXICO. *Exil in Mexiko.* [See No. 36122.]

36375. MICHMAN, DAN: *"Judenräte" und "Judenvereinigungen" unter nationalsozialistischer Herrschaft.* Aufbau und Anwendung eines verwaltungsmäßigen Konzepts. [In]: Zeitschrift für Geschichtswissenschaft, Jg. 46, H. 4, Berlin, 1998. Pp. 293–304, footnotes.

36376. MILCHMAN, ALAN/ROSENBERG, ALAN, eds.: *Postmodernism and the Holocaust*. Amsterdam; Atlanta, GA: Edition Rodopi, 1998. VII, 325 pp., notes. [Cont. 16 chaps. on different philosophical aspects of intepreting the Holocaust. Discusses a.o. the writings of Hannah Arendt, Emil Fackenheim, Martin Heidegger.]

36377. MINDEN. BRANDON, EDITH: *Ein Mindener Bürger. Hermann Bradtmüller und Familie.* Minden, Königstraße. Hrsg. vom Kulturamt der Stadt Minden in Zusammenarbeit mit Edith Brandon aus London. Minden: [Privately printed], 1994. 20 pp., frontis. [Personal recollections dealing with the decent and courageous behaviour of the author's uncle, a non-Jew, during the Nazi era.]

36378. MINDEN. *60 Jahre Reichspogromnacht in Minden.* [Red.: Heinrich Winter]. Minden: Ges. für Christl.-Jüd. Zusammenarbeit Minden e.V., [1998]. [Documents the "Informations- und Demonstrationsgang durch Mindens Innenstadt", organised by high school students to commemorate the November Pogrom.]

36379. *Mit den Augen eines Kindes.* Children in the Holocaust. Children in Exile. Children under Fascism. Hrsg. von Viktoria Hertling. Amsterdam; Atlanta, GA: Rodopi, 1998. 317 pp., footnotes. (Amsterdamer Publikationen zur Sprache und Literatur, 134.) [Incl. abstracts (303–317). Contribs. (selected, titles partly abbr.) are arranged under the following sections: *ZeitzeugInnen*; cont.: Interview with Sonia Levitin (SNCAT-Reno, 18–25; TV interview Oct. 2, 1996). Gespräch mit Stella Müller-Madej über ihr Buch 'Das Mädchen von der Schindler Liste' (Jörg Thunecke, 26–45). Eine Medaille aus Hildesheim (Guy Stern, 46–50; on a visit to the author's home town in 1970). *Traumatische Erfahrungen*; cont.: Formen, Tendenzen, Darstellungsweisen: Wie Kinder den Holocaust erlebten und wie sie ihre Erfahrungen als Erwachsene darstellten (Barbara Bauer, 51–85). Children and fairy tales in exile, war and the Holocaust (Donald Haase, 86–99). Five children's formative years in Third Reich camps (Deborah Vietor-Engländer, 100–110). *Schreibende im Versteck und im Exil*; incl.: Anne Frank, the writer (Laureen Nussbaum, 111–122). *Kinderbücher exilierter Schriftsteller und Texte für jüngere LeserInnen*; cont.: S.O.S. Schweiz. Emigranten schreiben Kinderbücher (Tamara S. Evans, 164–178). Ansätze und Strategien zur didaktischen Vermittlung des Themas Holocaust (Sigrid Thielking, 179–191). *Lebens- und Überlebensstrategien*; cont.: Leben und Werk von Robert L. Kahn (Klaus Beckschulte, 207–219). Exile or emigration: what shall we tell the children? Exil oder Auswanderung: was sagen wir den Kindern? (Hanna Papanek, 220–236; author, daughter of non-Jewish Social Democratic parents, who went into exile in 1934, contrasts her own experience with that of Ludwig Greve, her Jewish childhood friend). *Erinnerung und Erinnerungsverzerrungen*; incl.: Sieben Fragen an einen kleinen Text von Anna Seghers (Jochen Vogt, 237–251). Trennungen und Trennungsängste im Werk von Irmgard Keun (Eva-Maria Siegel, 252–271). Kinderwelten im Nationalsozialismus als Thema in Film und Literatur (Waltraud Strickhausen, 272–302).]

—— MOMMSEN, HANS: *Der Weg zum Völkermord an den europäischen Juden.* [See in No. 37041.]

36380. MORGENSTERN, SOMA: *Flucht in Frankreich.* Ein Romanbericht. Hrsg. und mit einem Nachwort von Ingolf Schulte. Lüneburg: zu Klampen, 1998. 431 pp., footnotes. (Soma Morgenstern; Werke in Einzelbänden.) [Incl.: Nachwort des Herausgebers (365–423, footnotes; on the situation of Jewish refugees in France with special reference to M.'s years in exile between 1938 and 1941. M.'s hitherto unpubl. autobiographical book, written as a novel, deals with his internment in France and his flight from a camp in Audierne (Finistère) to Marseille and Casablanca.] [Cf.: Kaffeehaus des Schreckens. Als Wien emigrierte: Soma Morgensterns "Flucht in Frankreich" (Susanne Klingenstein) [in]: 'FAZ', Nr. 40, Frankfurt am Main, 17. Feb. 1999, p. 46. Endstation Sehnsucht (Michael Kohtes) [in]: Die Zeit, Nr. 11, Hamburg, 11. März 1999, p. 47.]

36381. MOYN, SAMUEL: *Judaism against paganism: Emmanuel Levinas's response to Heidegger and Nazism in the 1930s.* [In]: History & Memory, Vol. 10, No. 1, Tel Aviv, Spring 1998. Pp. 25–58, notes.

36382. MUNICH. KRAUSS, MARITA: *Familiengeschichte als Zeitgeschichte. Die jüdischen Familien Bernheimer, Feuchtwanger und Rosenfeld in Nationalsozialismus und Nachkriegszeit.* [In]: Archiv für Familiengeschichtsforschung, Jg. 1, H. 3, Limburg, 1997. Pp. 162–176. [Incl. Engl. and French abstracts.]

36383. MUNICH. LARGE, DAVID CLAY: *Hitlers München*. Aufstieg und Fall der Hauptstadt der Bewegung. Aus dem Engl. von Karl Heinz Siber. München: Beck, 1998. 515 pp., illus., maps, notes (460–493), bibl., index. [On the city's history, its political climate and the Nazi movement from the beginning of the 20th cent. to the end of World War II; incl. numerous references to antisemitism and persecution of Jews. For orig. American edn. see No. 34828/ YB XLIII.]

36384. NETHERLANDS. FLIM, B.J.: *Omdat hun hart sprak. Geschiedenis van die georganiseerde hulp aan Joodse kinderen in Nederland, 1942–1945.* Kampen: Kok, 1996. 1 vol. [Deals with four resistance groups involved in rescuing children, finding addresses for them to hide and sometimes maintaining contact between the children and parents in hiding.]

36385. NETHERLANDS. MICHMAN, DAN: *Preparing for occupation? A Nazi Sicherheitsdienst document of Spring 1939 on the Jews of Holland.* [In]: Studia Rosenthaliana, Vol. 32, No. 2, Amsterdam 1998. Pp. 173–189, footnotes, docs.

36386. NIEHUSS, MERITH: *Eheschließung im Nationalsozialismus.* [In]: Frauen in der Geschichte des Rechts. Von der Frühen Neuzeit bis zur Gegenwart. Hrsg. von Ute Gerhard. München: Beck, 1997. Pp. 851–870, footnotes. [Deals also with "mixed marriages" (861–870).]

36387. NIEWYK, DONALD L., ed.: *Fresh wounds: early narratives of Holocaust survival.* Chapel Hill: Univ. of North Carolina Press, 1998. 414 pp., gloss., notes, bibl. (405–408). [Incl. 36 interviews with Holocaust survivors conducted by Russian-born American psychologist David P. Boder in 1946 in DP-camps across Europe; among them five interviews with German-Jewish survivors.]

36388. NOVEMBER POGROM. ESCHELBACHER, MAX: *Der zehnte November 1938.* Mit einer Einleitung "Rabbiner Max Eschelbacher und der Novemberpogrom in Düsseldorf" von Falk Wiesemann. Essen: Klartext, 1998. 79 pp., illus., notes. [New edn. of memoirs written after M.E.'s arrival in London in 1939; incl. new introduction (7–26). For first edn. see No. 25400/YB XXXIV.]

36389. NOVEMBER POGROM. JONCA, KAROL: *"Noc Krysztalowa". I casus Herschela Grynszpana.* Wroclaw: Wydawnistwo Uniwerzytetu Wroclawskiego, 1998. 403 pp., illus., docs., bibl., index. [In Polish, incl. German summary (385–390); on the November Pogrom, also on the fate of Herschel Grynszpan.]

36390. NOVEMBER POGROM. *Die Nacht, als die Synagogen brannten.* Texte und Materialien zum Novemberpogrom 1938. Hrsg.: LpB, Landeszentrale für Politische Bildung Baden-Württemberg, Fachreferat Lehrerfortbildung. Zsgst., bearb. und kommentiert von Myrah Adams [et al.]. Stuttgart: LpB, 1998. 93 pp., illus., bibl.

36391. NOVEMBER POGROM. REICHMANN, HANS: *Deutscher Bürger und verfolgter Jude. Novemberpogrom und KZ Sachsenhausen 1937 bis 1939.* Bearbeitet von Michael Wildt. München: Oldenbourg, 1998. 293 pp., footnotes, bibl. (285–288), index (289–293). (Biographische Quellen zur Zeitgeschichte, Bd. 21.) [Incl.: Einleitung & Zur Edition (Michael Wildt, 1–42).] [First, complete publ. of memoirs, written after the author's arrival in London in spring 1939.] [H.R., March 3, 1900 Hohensalza – May 24, 1964 Wiesbaden, lawyer, legal adviser and secretary of the Centralverein, emigr. to Great Britain in March 1939.]

36392. NÜRTINGEN. WERNER, MANUEL: *Juden in Nürtingen in der Zeit des Nationalsozialismus.* Nürtingen/Frickenhausen: Verlag Sindlinger-Burchartz, 1998. 160 pp., illus. [On a few families in Nürtingen who belonged to the Jewish community in Bad Cannstadt.] [Cf.: Besprechung (Joachim Hahn) [in]: Zeitschrift für württembergische Landesgeschichte, Jg. 58, Stuttgart, 1999. pp. 420–421.]

36393. NUREMBERG. FROMMER, HARTMUT/WESTNER, KATHRIN: *"Ein Justizcollegium weit schlimmer wie eine Diebesbande". Die Vernichtung von Leo Katzenberger durch das Sondergericht Nürnberg.* [In]: Mitteilungen des Vereins für Geschichte der Stadt Nürnberg. [On the judicial murder of Leo Katzenberg and Christiane Kohl's book 'Der Jude und das Mädchen' (see No. 35138/ YB XLIII). Also on the unsatisfactory post-war prosecution of this crime.]

36394. NUREMBERG. *Gedenkbuch für die Nürnberger Opfer der Schoa.* Hrsg. von Michael Diefenbacher und Wiltrud Fischer-Pache. Bearb. von Gerhard Jochem und Ulrike Kettner. Mit einem Essay von Leibl Rosenberg. Nürnberg: Selbstverlag des Stadtarchivs Nürnberg, 1998. LXXX, 483 pp., ports., indexes (maiden names, places of birth and of deportation, 395–440), bibl. (477–482), 2 attached maps. (Quellen zur Geschichte und Kultur der Stadt Nürnberg, Bd. 29.) [Lists 2332 names.]

36395. NUREMBERG TRIALS. ARONSON, SHLOMO: *Preparations for the Nuremberg Trial: the O.S.S., Charles Dwork, and the Holocaust.* [In]: Holocaust and Genocide Studies, Vol. 12, No. 2, Oxford, Fall 1998. Pp. 257–281, notes. [Discusses the activities of the one-man Jewish desk at the Office of Strategic Services under the direction of Dr. Charles Dwork.]

36396. NUREMBERG TRIALS. KOCHAVI, ARIEH J.: *Prelude to Nuremberg: allied war crimes policy and the question of punishment.* Chapel Hill, NC; London: The Univ. of North Carolina Press, 1998. X, 312 pp., notes (249–280), bibl. (287–296). [Deals with the discussions between the Allied Powers well before the end of the war regarding the issue of punishing war crimes and criminals, and with the joint policy leading to the Nuremberg Trials.]

36397. NUREMBERG TRIALS. MARRUS, MICHAEL R.: *The Holocaust at Nuremberg.* [In]: Yad Vashem Studies, Vol. XXVI, Jerusalem, 1998. Pp. 5–42, footnotes. [On the Nuremberg Trials.]

36398. NUSSBAUM-SOUMERAI, EVE/SCHULZ, CAROL D.: *Daily life during the Holocaust.* Westport, CT: The Greenwood Press, 1998. XXIV, 312 pp., illus., notes. [Incl. the changing lives and increasing persecution of German Jews under the Nazis; also incl. accounts of resistance and the role of rescuers.]

36399. OFER, DALIA/WEITZMAN, LENORE J., eds.: *Women in the Holocaust.* New Haven, CT: Yale Univ. Press, 1998. VII, 402 pp., notes. [Incl. chaps. (titles abbr.): Jewish women's responses to daily life in Nazi Germany, 1933–1939 (Marion Kaplan, 39–54). Ordinary women in Nazi Germany: perpetrators, victims, followers, and bystanders (Gisela Bock, 85–100). Women in Theresienstadt and the family camp in Birkenau (Ruth Bondy, 310–326). Also incl. chaps. on women in Holocaust testimonies and in Holocaust literature.]

36400. ORBACH, LARRY/ORBACH-SMITH, VIVIEN: *"Soaring Underground".* Eine Autobiographie. Aus dem Amerik. übers. von Ralf Östereich. Berlin: Kowalke, 1998. 334 pp. [Author, b. 1924 in Falkenberg nr. Stettin, lived from 1929 in Berlin, went into hiding in 1942; after denunciation in Aug. 1944, deported to Auschwitz. For orig. edn. see No. 33972/YB XLII.] [Cf.: Vom General zur Kanalratte (Susanne Klingenstein) [in]: 'FAZ', Nr. 226, Frankfurt am Main, 29. Sept. 1998, p. 48.]

36401. OSTHEIM. KINGREEN, MONICA: *Between good neighbourliness and hostility: Jewish communities amongst the rural pupulation in Germany.* [In]: Dappim le-Cheker Tekufat ha-Shoah, Vol. 13, Haifa, 1996. Pp. 231–241. [In Hebrew, title transl.] [Focuses on the town of Ostheim in the Nazi period.]

36402. PADERBORN. NAARMANN, MARGIT: *"Von ihren Leuten wohnt hier keiner mehr". Jüdische Familien in Paderborn in der Zeit des Nationalsozialismus.* Köln: SH-Verlag, [1997]. 607 pp., illus., facsims., lists, bibl. (Paderborner Historische Forschungen, Bd. 7.)

36403. PALESTINE. BALKE, RALF: *Die NSDAP in Palästina – Profil einer Auslandsorganisation.* [In]: Tel Aviver Jahrbuch für deutsche Geschichte, Bd. 27, 1998, Gerlingen, 1998. Pp. 221–250, footnotes. [Also on the antisemitism of Germans in Palestine.]

36404. PERRY, YARON: *Exchange of Germans for Eretz-Israeli citizens, 1941–1944.* [In]: Dappim le-Cheker Tekufat ha-Shoah, Vol. 13, Haifa, 1996. Pp. 149–164. [In Hebrew, title transl.]

36405. POPPLER, BERNHARD: *Das Glück steht vor der Tür. Österreich im Berliner Schwank und der Berliner Operette (Im weißen Rößl)*. [In]: Modern Austrian Literature, Vol. 31, No. 1, Riverside, CA, 1998. Pp. 20–38, notes. [Deals with the revival of Ralph Benatzky's operetta 'Im weißen Rößl' and the fate of earlier productions under the Nazis, when the mostly Jewish writers, composers, and actors were forced into exile. Also refers to a production in Westerbork in 1943.]

——— PROSECUTION OF NAZI CRIMES. BAUER, FRITZ: *Die Humanität der Rechtsordnung*. Ausgewählte Schriften. Hrsg. von Joachim Perels und Irmtrud Wojak. [See No. 36780.]

36406. PROSECUTION OF NAZI CRIMES. BOLL, BERND: *Wehrmacht vor Gericht. Kriegsverbrecherprozesse der Vier Mächte nach 1945*. [In]: Geschichte und Gesellschaft, Jg. 24, Göttingen, 1998. Pp. 595–616, footnotes.

36407. PROSECUTION OF NAZI CRIMES. EBBINGHAUS, ANGELIKA: *Der Prozeß gegen Tesch & Stabenow. Von der Schädlingsbekämpfung zum Holocaust*. [In]: 1999. Zeitschrift für Sozialgeschichte des 20. und 21. Jahrhunderts. Jg. 13, H. 2, Hamburg, Sept. 1998. Pp. 16–71, tabs., footnotes.

36408. PROSECUTION OF NAZI CRIMES. PERELS, JOACHIM: *Der Umgang mit Tätern und Widerstandskämpfern nach 1945*. [In]: Kritische Justiz, Jg. 30, Baden-Baden, 1997. Pp. 357–374, footnotes. [Deals also with the problems of restitution.]

——— PROSECUTION OF NAZI CRIMES. PERELS, JOACHIM: *Der Umgang mit Tätern und Widerstandskämpfern im Nachkriegs-Deutschland, ein lehrreiches Exempel*. [See in No. 36137.]

36409. RADOK, RAINER: *Von Königsberg nach Melbourne. Vertreibung aus Ostpreußen im Dritten Reich*. Für das Ostpreußische Landesmuseum in Lüneburg bearb. und hrsg. von Ronny Kabus. Lüneburg: Institut Nordostdeutsches Kulturwerk, 1998. 185 pp., illus. [Memoirs; author, b. 1920 in Königsberg, professor of applied mathematics, son of a Jewish father, emigr. 1939 to England, was interned and sent on the SS Dunera to Australia. Deals also with the family history of his father, the Radok and the Pincus families.]

36410. RAVENSBRÜCK. TILLION, GERMAINE: *Frauenkonzentrationslager Ravensbrück*. Aus dem Franz. von Barbara Glaßmann. Mit einem Anhang "Die Massentötungen durch Gas in Ravensbrück" von Anise Postel-Vinay. Lüneburg: zu Klampen, 1998. 410 pp., footnotes, bibl., plans, [First publ. in French 1973. Author, a member of the Résistance, was deported to Ravensbrück in 1942.]

36411. REFUGEE POLICY. CAESTECKER, FRANK: *Holocaust survivors in Belgium 1944–1949; Belgian refugee policy and the tragedy of the 'Endlösung'*. [In]: Tel Aviver Jahrbuch für deutsche Geschichte, Bd. 27, 1998. Gerlingen, 1998. Pp. 353–382. [Also on refugees from German-speaking countries.]

36412. REFUGEE POLICY. MEYER, KATHARINA: *Keiner will sie haben. Die Exilpolitik in England, Frankreich und den USA zwischen 1933 und 1945*. Frankfurt am Main; New York: Lang, 1998. 148 pp. (Europäische Hochschulschriften, Reihe 31: Politikwissenschaft, Bd. 352.) [Cf.: Besprechung (Perdita Ladwig) [in]: Zeitschrift für Geschichtswissenschaft, Jg. 47, H. 1, Berlin, 1998, pp. 85–88.]

36413. REFUGEE POLICY. STADELMANN, JÜRG: *Umgang mit Fremden in bedrängter Zeit. Schweizerische Flüchtlingspolitik 1940–1945 und ihre Beurteilung bis heute*. Zürich: Orell Füssli, 1998. VIII, 395 pp., illus., tabs., maps, notes (309–356), bibl. (357–367), chronol., indexes (381–395). (Zeitgeschichte.) Zugl.: Zürich: Univ., Diss., 1997. [Cf.: Besprechung (Georg Kreis) [in]: Schweizerische Zeitschrift für Geschichte, Vol. 49, Nr. 1, Basel, 1998, pp. 164–165.]

36414. REITER, ANDREA: *Die Erfahrung des Holocausts und ihre sprachliche Bewältigung*. [In]: literatur für leser, Jg. 21, H. 3, Frankfurt am Main, 1998. Pp. 275–286, footnotes.

36415. RESCUE OF JEWS. AHARONI, ADA: *Not in vain: an extraordinary life.* San Carlos, CA: Ladybug Press, 1998. 219 pp. [Based on notes by Thea Wolf, a German-Jewish nurse in the Jewish hospital in Alexandria during World War II, the book depicts the role the Egyptian-Jewish community played in saving Jews from Europe.]

36416. RESCUE OF JEWS. GEIER, ARNOLD: *Heroes of the Holocaust.* Illus. by T. G. Friedman. Introd. by Abraham Foxman. New York: Berkley Books, 1998. XXIII, 280 pp., illus., ports., maps, plans, chronol., bibl. [Collection of interviews with survivors and rescuers, incl. from Germany and Austria.]

36417. RESCUE OF JEWS. GUSHEE, DAVID P.: *Die Gerechten des Holocaust.* Warum nur wenige Christen den Juden halfen. Ins Deutsche übertragen von Eugen Pietras. Wuppertal: One Way Verl., 1997. 414 pp., bibl. (303–326), notes (327–412). (Beiträge zur jüdisch-christlichen Geschichte.) [For orig. edn. see No. 31837/YB XL.]

36418. RESCUE OF JEWS. HALTER, MAREK: *Stories of deliverance: speaking with men and women who rescued Jews from the Holocaust.* Transl. by Michael Bernard. Chicago, Open Court Press, 1998. XVI, 304 pp. [Author, a Polish Jew, interviewed rescuers in many countries. Several chaps. on German rescuers, mainly in Berlin. Incl. the story of Inge Deutschkron.]

36419. RESCUE OF JEWS. KELLERMAN-KLUGER, INGRID: *The saved and their saviours: a comparative study of the testemonies of sixty Jews who were hidden by non-Jews, 1941–1945.* [In]: German History, Vol. 16, No. 1, London, 1998. Pp. 56–57. [Dissertation abstract.]

36420. RHEURDT (Rhineland). *Gegen das Vergessen.* Gedenkschrift zum 60. Jahrestag der Reichspogromnacht. Recherchiert, zus.-gest. und bearb. von Theo Mäschig. Rheurdt: Gemeinde Rheurdt, 1998. 62 pp., illus.

——— RIGA. OBENAUS, HERBERT: *Die Deportation deutscher Juden nach Riga.* [See in No. 36137.]

36421. RITVO, ROGER A./PLOTKIN, DIANE M.. eds.: *Sisters in sorrow: voices of care in the Holocaust.* Foreword by Harry James Cargas. College Station TX: Texas A & M Univ. Press, 1998. XVIII, 314 pp., illus., facsims., appendixes, notes (259–286), bibl. (287–294). [Personal memoirs, also by German-, Austrian- and Czech-Jewish nurses and doctors at Theresienstadt and other camps. Incl. descriptions by non-Jewish helpers liberating the camps.]

36422. ROMANIA. KOLAR, OTHMAR: *Rumänien und seine nationalen Minderheiten 1918 bis heute.* Wien: Böhlau, 1997. 584 pp., footnotes, bibl. (516–540), map, tabs., docs., indexes (places; names, 573–584). [Incl. the chaps.: Die nationalsozialistischen Irrwege der deutschen Volksgruppe (176–187). Rumänien und der Holocaust (188–201).]

36423. ROSEN, NORMA: *The Holocaust and popular literature: history, morality and mass art.* [In]: Dimensions, Vol. 11, No. 2, New York, 1997. Pp. 17–21, illus., ports. [Deals with the proliferation of new Holocaust literature, both fiction and non-fiction.]

36424. ROSENTHAL, GABRIELE: *The Holocaust in three generations: families of victims and perpetrators of the Nazi regime.* Main transl. from German and revision of transl. text by Catherine Johnson. London; Washington: Cassell, 1998. X, 308 pp., family trees, gloss., notes, bibl. 297–308, no index. [Study conducted by a team of sociologists, psychologists and political scientists from Israel and Germany who interviewed families of victims and of perpetrators of the Holocaust in both Germany and Israel.]

36425. ROTH, KARL HEINZ: *Hehler des Holocaust: Degussa und Deutsche Bank.* [In]: 1999. Zeitschrift für Sozialgeschichte des 20. und 21. Jahrhunderts, Jg. 13, H. 2, Hamburg, Sept. 1998. Pp. 137–144, facsims., docs., footnotes.

36426. ROTHER, BERND: *Rassenwahn und Rassenstolz. Sephardische Reaktionen auf die Judenverfolgung.* [In]: Menora 1997, Bodenheim, 1997. Pp. 199–229, notes. [Deals mainly with Sephardim in France and The Netherlands.]

36427. RÜTTEN, THOMAS: *Hitler with – or without – Hippocrates? The Hippocratic Oath during the Third Reich*. [In]: Korot, Vol. 12 [1996–1997], Jerusalem, 1998. Pp. 91–106. [On Nazi physicians.]

36428. SAARBURG. MÜLLER, RUDOLF: *Vor 60 Jahren: Reichspogromnacht und "Entjudung" der deutschen Wirtschaft. Das Beispiel Saarburg 1938/39*. [In]: Landeskundliche Vierteljahrsblätter, Jg. 44, H. 4, Trier, 1998. Pp. 163–174, notes.

36429. SAKAMOTO, PAMELA ROTNER: *Japanese diplomats and Jewish refugees: a World War II dilemma*. Westport, CT: Praeger, 1998. XVI, 188 pp., ports. [Detailed investigation of how more than 24,000 European Jews reached Japan and Japanese-occupied Shanghai.]

36430. SALINGER, ELIYAHU KUTTI: *"Nächstes Jahr im Kibbuz". Die jüdisch-chaluzische Jugendbewegung in Deutschland zwischen 1933 und 1943*. Edition und Vorwort: Irmgard Klönne. Paderborn: KoWAG, Univ. Paderborn, 1998. 232 pp., illus., bibl., gloss. (Paderborner Beiträge zur politischen, wirtschaftlichen und kulturellen Weiterbildung, Neue Reihe, Bd. 14.) [Author, b. 1915 in Schnackenburg/Elbe, grew up in Berlin, joined the Haschomer Hazair in 1931, emigr. from Switzerland to Palestine in 1943. Lives in Kfar Menachem.]

36431. SAMSON, SHLOMO: *Between darkness and light: 60 years after "Kristallnacht"*. Transl. from the German by Mary Harber. Ed. by Shira Twersky-Cassell. Jerusalem: Rubin Mass 1998. 498 pp., illus., ports., facsims., scores, plans. [Author tells of experiences under the Nazis in Leipzig, then subsequent flight to the Netherlands and imprisonment in Westerbork and Bergen-Belsen. For German edn. see No. 34088/YB XLII.]

36432. SCHÄFER, KURT: *Verfolgung einer Spur (Raphael Weichbrodt)*. Frankfurt am Main: Fritz Bauer Institut, 1998. 43 pp., frontis., illus., docs. [Author's account of life and death of R.W., a Jewish doctor and univ. teacher, b. in Bromberg, who taught and practised in Frankfurt am Main and died in a concentration camp 1942.]

36433. SCHEUER, LISA: *Vom Tode, der nicht stattfand. Theresienstadt, Auschwitz, Freiberg, Mauthausen: eine Frau überlebt*. Aachen: Shaker, 1998. 154 pp. [Cf.: Jahrgang 1907 (Doris Bulau) [in]: 'Allgemeine', Jg. 53, Nr. 17, Bonn, 20. Aug. 1998, p. 15.] [L.Sch., b. 1907 in Leipa, Bohemia, lives since 1968 in Cologne.]

36434. SCHLESWIG-HOLSTEIN. *Geschichte und Biografie. Jüdisches Leben, Nationalsozialismus und Nachkriegszeit in Schleswig-Holstein*. Festschrift für Erich Koch. Hrsg. vom Arbeitskreis zur Erforschung des Nationalsozialismus in Schleswig-Holstein e.V. (Akens). Kiel: Akens, 1998. 239 pp., illus., notes. [Selected articles (titles partly abbr.): Juden in Leck (Bettina Reichert, 13–22). Herbert Hagen, der Judenreferent des SD aus Neumünster (Gerhard Paul, 63–78). Dr. Arnold Kalisch – ein verfolgter Pazifist und Jude (Bernd Philipsen, 79–96; on a jurist from Berlin seeking refuge in Danmark, later in Sweden). Mit einem Kindertransport nach Großbritannien. Drei ehemalige Kieler erinnern sich (Bettina Goldberg, 121–140). Die Situation der Juden in Schleswig-Holstein 1945–1950 im Spiegel der Zeitungen 'Undzer Schtime', 'Wochnblat' und 'Jüdisches Gemeindeblatt' (Sigrun Jochims, 153–174). Die Entschädigungsakten als Quelle für die Exilforschung (Thomas Pusch, 189–212). Briefe aus Konzentrationslagern und Ghettos (Frauke Dettmar, 213–218).]

36435. SCHLESWIG-HOLSTEIN. PAUL, GERHARD/GILLIS-CARLEBACH, MIRIAM, eds.: *Menora und Hakenkreuz. Zur Geschichte der Juden in und aus Schleswig-Holstein, Lübeck und Altona (1918–1998)*. Eine gemeinsame Publ. des Forschungsprojektes 'Zur Sozialgeschichte des Terrors' am Inst. für schlesw.-holst. Zeit- und Regionalgesch. an der Bildungswiss. Hochschule Flensburg – Univ. (Schleswig) und des Joseph-Carlebach-Inst. an der Bar Ilan-Univ. (Ramat Gan), Israel. Neumünster: Wachholtz, 1998. 943 pp., illus., notes (815–916), bibl. (917–924), indexes (persons; places, 927–940). [Cont. 59 contribs. arranged under the sections: I. *Das jüdische Milieu (vor und nach 1933)* (31–180). II. *Verfolgung und Selbstbehauptung (1933–1945)* (181–604). *Neuanfänge (1930–1998)* (605–720). IV. *Vergangenheit, die nicht vergeht (1945–1998)* (721–812).] [Cf.: Besprechung (Arno Herzig) [in]: Aschkenas, Jg. 9. H. 1, Wien, 1999, pp. 289–291.]

36436. SCHMIDT, HERBERT: *"Beabsichtige ich die Todesstrafe zu beantragen"*. Die nationalsozialistische Sondergerichtsbarkeit im Oberlandesgerichtsbezirk Düsseldorf 1933–1945. Essen: Klartext, 1998. 342 pp., footnotes, docs., bibl. (329–341). (Düsseldorfer Schriften zur neueren Landesgeschichte, Bd. 49.) Zugl.: Düsseldorf, Univ., Diss. [Incl. trials against Jews.]

—— SCHMITZ-BERNING, CORNELIA: *Vokabular des Nationalsozialismus*. [See No. 36164.]

36437. SCHOENBERNER, GERHARD, ed.: *Zeugen sagen aus. Berichte und Dokumente über die Judenverfolgung im "Dritten Reich"*. Berlin: Aufbau-Taschenbuch-Verl., 1998. 445 pp., illus.

36438. SCHOEPS, JULIUS H.: *Das Gewaltsyndrom. Verformungen und Brüche im deutsch-jüdischen Verhältnis*. Berlin: Argon, 1998. 189 pp., footnotes, index (194–197). [A collection of essays and revised and enlarged book reviews dealing with antisemitism, Holocaust, Jewish life in Germany, Jewish identity, Max Liebermann, Goldhagen debate, and Jewish resistance. Hitherto unpubl. essays are listed according to subject.]

36439. SCHUBERT, WERNER: *Die Stellung der Frau im Familienrecht und in den familienrechtlichen Reformprojekten der der NS-Zeit*. [In]: Frauen in der Geschichte des Rechts. Von der Frühen Neuzeit bis zur Gegenwart. Hrsg. von Ute Gerhard. München: Beck, 1998. Pp. 828–870, footnotes. [Incl. a section on 'mixed marriages'.]

36440. SCHWERDT, OTTO/SCHWERDT-SCHNELLER, MASCHA: *Als Gott und die Welt schliefen*. Biografie. Viechtach: Lichtung, 1998. 112 pp. [O. Schw., b. 1923 in Braunschweig, in 1936 fled with his family to Poland, deported in 1943 to Auschwitz-Birkenau. Lives in Regensburg.]

36441. SCOTT, JACK: *Nie wieder in Deutschland leben*. Von Gelsenkirchen, Gera und Fürth durch Belgien, Frankreich, Spanien und mit der britischen Armee nach Deutschland zurück. Jüdische Schicksale 1924–1947. Hrsg. von Erhard Roy Wiehn. Unter Mitarbeit von Julia Nowotny-Iskandar. Konstanz: Hartung-Gorre, 1998. 191 pp., illus., facsims. [Memoirs; author, orig. Jakob Schloß, b. 1924 in Gelsenkirchen, lives in England.]

36442. SEIDLER, E.: *Die Schicksale jüdischer Kinderärzte im Nationalsozialismus*. Ein Vorbericht. [In]: Monatsschrift Kinderheilkunde, H. 8, Heidelberg, 1998. Pp. 744–753, facsims., tabs., bibl.

36443. SEKI, KUSUKO: *Japans Germanistik unter dem Faschismus*. [In]: Doitsu Bungaku, No. 100, Tokyo, Frühling 1998. Pp. 64–76, notes. [Deals with the very critical attitude of Japanese writers to Nazi Germany, the persecution of Jewish writers, the bookburnings.]

36444. SHANGHAI. JAHN, HAJO, ed.: *Zwischen Theben und Shanghai*. Jüdische Exilanten in China – chinesische Exilanten in Europa. Almanach zum V. Else-Lasker-Schüler-Forum "Flucht in die Freiheit". Berlin: Oberbaum Verl., 1998. 255 pp., illus., facsims., notes. [Selected essays: Zeitbrücken im Jahr des Büffels (ed., 11–25). Nazi-Organisationen in Shanghai (Astrid Freyeisen, 51–66). Splitter aus einem Leben. Max Mohr in Shanghai (Stefan Weidle, 67–86). Zuflucht in Shanghai – Schutz vor Nazideutschland (Peter Finkelgrün, 87–100). Friedrich Schiff – ein österreichischer Künstler in Shanghai (Simon Wachsmut, 107–143, illus. (by Schiff). KZ Dachau – Ghetto Shanghai – heute New York. Zu Lebensweg und Werk des Künstlers David L. Bloch (Rosamunde Neugebauer, 135–155, illus. by Bloch). Exiltheater in Shanghai 1939–1947 (Michael Philipp, 157–168). Willy Haas: von Prag nach Indien (Jürgen Serke, 169–180). Zwischen Shanghai und Berlin (181–185; abbr. reprint of an article on the arrival of 295 refugees returning to Berlin in 1947). Sonderfall – die "Wiedergutmachung" bei den Shanghai-Flüchtlingen (Winfried Seibert, 187–224; incl.: Auszug aus dem Urteil des OLG Neustadt vom 3. Juni 1960).]

36445. SHANGHAI. WASSERSTEIN, BERNARD: *Secret war in Shanghai: treachery, subversion and collaboration in the Second World War*. London: Profile Books, 1998. XIV, 354 pp., illus., maps, notes (293–330), bibl. (331–342), index (345–354). [Incl. German and Austrian refugees from Nazi-occupied Europe.]

384   *Bibliography*

36446. SHARFMAN, GLENN R.: *The dilemma of German-Jewish youths in the Third Reich: the case of the Bund deutsch-jüdischer Jugend, 1933–1935.* [In]: Shofar, Vol. 16, No. 3, West Lafayette, IN, Spring 1998. Pp. 28–41, footnotes.

36447. SHEFFI, NA'AMA: *Yishuv intellectuals and the approaching of the Third Reich.* [Title condensed.] [In]: Qesher, No. 20, Tel-Aviv, Nov. 1996. Pp. 104–115. [In Hebrew, with English summary. Engl. transl. of full title: Intellectuals and the approaching catastrophe; Hebrew publicists and their attitude towards German culture in the time of the Third Reich.]

36448. SILESIA. HANKE, WOLF: *In aller Unschuld schuldig.* [In]: Jüdischer Almanach 1999 des Leo Baeck Instituts, Frankfurt am Main, 1998. Pp. 33–41, illus. [Childhood reminiscences of life in Löwenberg (today: Lwowek), Silesia during the Nazi era seen through the eyes of a non-Jew.]

36449. SOBIBOR. SCHELVIS, JULES: *Vernichtungslager Sobibór.* Aus dem Holl. von Gero Deckers. Berlin: Metropol, 1998. 334 pp., footnotes, illus., facsims., tabs., bibl., indexes. (Dokumente – Texte – Materialien, Bd. 24.) [Orig. Dutch edn.: Vernietigingskamp Sobibor. Amsterdam: De Bataafsche Leew, 1993. Incl. list of survivors, among them a few German-speaking Jews.]

36450. SPAIN. ROTHER, BERND: *Franco und die deutsche Judenverfolgung.* [In]: Vierteljahrshefte für Zeitgeschichte, Jg. 46, H. 2, München, April 1998. Pp. 189–220, footnotes. [Incl. policy towards German-speaking Jews seeking asylum in Spain.] [Cf.: Das papierene Privileg (Paul Ingendaay) [in]: 'FAZ', Nr. 203, Frankfurt am Main, 2. Sept. 1998, p. N 5.]

36451. STAFFA, CHRISTIAN/KLINGER, KATHERINE, eds.: *Die Gegenwart der Geschichte des Holocaust: intergenerationelle Tradierung und Kommunikation der Nachkommen.* Beiträge einer Konferenz in Berlin am 26. und 27. Jan. 1997. Berlin: Inst. für Vergl. Geschichtswiss., 1998. 255 pp., bibl. (Schriftenreihe des Inst. für Vergl. Geschichtswiss., Bd. 2.)

———— STEIMAN, LIONEL B.: *Paths to genocide: antisemitism in Western history.* [See No. 37093.]

36452. STEINBERG, PAUL: *Chronik aus einer dunklen Welt.* Ein Bericht. Aus dem Franz. von Moshe Kahn. München: Hanser, 1998. 166 pp. [Recollections of a German-born Auschwitz survivor deported from Paris in 1943; orig. title 'Chronique d'ailleurs', publ. 1996.] [Cf.: Mein Freund Henri. Paul Steinbergs dunkle Chronik (Gerhard Schulz) [in]: 'FAZ', Nr. 113, Frankfurt am Main, 16. Mai 1998, p. V, Beilage.]

36453. STEINER, JOHN M./CORNBERG, JOBST FRHR. VON: *Willkür in der Willkür. Befreiungen von den antisemitischen Nürnberger Gesetzen.* [In]: Vierteljahrshefte für Zeitgeschichte, Jg. 46, H. 2, München, April 1998. Pp. 143–187, footnotes. [Cf.: Launen des Diktators. Ausnahmen von den Nürnberger Gesetzen (Milos Vec) [in]: 'FAZ', Nr. 58, Frankfurt am Main, 10. März 1999, p. N 5.]

36454. *Studies in Contemporary Jewry.* An annual, Vol. 13 [with the issue title]: The fate of the European Jews, 1939–1945: continuity or contingency? Ed. by Jonathan Frankel. Jerusalem: The Avraham Harman Institute of Contemporary Jewry, the Hebrew Univ.; Oxford, New York: Oxford Univ. Press, 1997. 1 issue, notes. [Incl.: Continuities, discontinuities and contingencies of the Holocaust (Gavin I. Langmuir, 9–29). The camps: eastern, western, modern (Zygmunt Bauman, 30–40). Radical historical discontinuity: explaining the Holocaust (Steven T. Katz, 41–55). Forced emigration, war, deportation and Holocaust (Götz Aly/Susanne Heim, 56–73). Memory and method: variance in Holocaust narrations (Dan Diner, 84–99). What are the contexts for German antisemitism? Some thoughts on the origins of Nazism, 1800–1945 (Geoff Eley, 100–132). Understanding the Jewish dimension of the Holocaust (Dan Michman, 225–252). The origins of the myth of the "new Jew": the Zionist variety (Anita Shapira, 253–270).]

36455. SULZBACH, ANNY: *Eine deutsche Jugend; Speyer – Bergen-Belsen: Lebensgeschichte von Anny Sulzbach.* Übers. aus dem Franz. von Gisela Glänzel [et al.]. Speyer: Stadtverwaltung, 1998. 132 pp., illus. (Schriftenreihe der Stadt Speyer, Bd. 9.)

36456. SWITZERLAND. Moorehead, Caroline: *Dunant's dream: war, Switzerland, and the history of the Red Cross.* London: HarperCollins, 1998. XXXI, 780 pp., illus., ports., facsims., appendixes, chronol., notes (723–743). [Incl. question of how much the International Red Cross knew about the persecution of the Jews, and how it reacted. Also discusses Swiss refugee policy and the reluctance to admit Jews; Swiss handling of Jewish assets.]

36457. SWITZERLAND. Pritzker-Ehrlich, Marthi, ed.: *Jüdisches Emigrantenlos 1938/39 und die Schweiz.* Eine Fallstudie. Bern; New York: Lang, 1998. 324 pp., illus., facsims., chronol., footnotes. (Exil-Dokumente, Bd. 1.) [Incl.: Vorwort (Konrad Feilchenfeldt, 13–17). Einleitung (ed., 19–22). Incl. family letters written between Feb. 1938 and Sept. 1939; also suppl. dealing with the Ehrlich, Mittler and Schidorsky families from Eydtkuhnen (East Prussia), Berlin, Vienna and Zurich.]

36458. SWITZERLAND. Sarasin, Philipp/Wecker, Regina, eds.: *Raubgold, Réduit, Flüchtlinge. Zur Geschichte der Schweiz im Zweiten Weltkrieg.* Mit Beiträgen von Peter Hug, Harold James [et al.] sowie dem Forschungsprogramm der Unabhängigen Expertenkommission Schweiz – Zweiter Weltkrieg von Jacques Picard. Zürich: Chronos, 1998. 181 pp., docs., notes. [Incl.: Zwischen humanitärer Mission und inhumaner Tradition. Zur schweizerischen Flüchtlingspolitik der Jahre 1938–1945 (Georg Kreis, 121–140).]

36459. SWITZERLAND. Silberman, Henri: *Jüdische Asylanten in Büsserach während des Zweiten Weltkrieges.* [In]: Jahrbuch für Solothurnische Geschichte, Bd. 71, Solothurn, 1998. Pp. 171–210, illus., facsims., docs. [Cont. the author's diary (written in 1942 in French, with German transl.) about his life in a camp in Switzerland after his flight from France, where he and his family had been living since their emigration from Germany after 1933.]

36460. SWITZERLAND. Zeder, Eveline: *Ein Zuhause für jüdische Flüchtlingskinder. Lilly Volkart und ihr Kinderheim in Ascona 1934–1947.* Zürich: Chronos, 1998. 146 pp., illus., notes, bibl. [Incl. list of refugee children.]

36461. SWITZERLAND (JEWISH ASSETS). König, Mario: *Die Finanzdrehscheibe Schweiz im Ruch der Kollaboration.* [In]: 1999. Zeitschrift für Sozialgeschichte des 20. und 21. Jahrhunderts. Jg. 13, H. 1, Hamburg, März 1998. Pp. 174–182, footnotes. [Review essay.]

36462. SWITZERLAND (JEWISH ASSETS). Levin, Itamar: *Switzerland: from denial to the beginning of restitution.* [In]: Jewish Spectator, Vol. 62, No. 4, Calabasas, CA, Spring 1998. Pp. 30–31.

36463. SWITZERLAND (JEWISH ASSETS). Schröder, Dieter/Surmann, Rolf: *Raubgold. Schweizer Positionen.* [In]: Mittelweg 36, Jg. 7, H. 4, Hamburg, 1998. Pp. 53–56. [Review essay.]

36464. SWITZERLAND (JEWISH ASSETS). Zabludoff, Sidney: *Movements of Nazi gold: uncovering the trail.* London: Institute of the World Jewish Congress, 1997. 27 pp., illus., map, tabs. (Policy study 10.) [Incl. SS booty from concentration camps.]

36465. THERESIENSTADT. Karný, Miroslav/Kemper, Raimund/Kárná, Margita, eds.: *Theresienstädter Studien und Dokumente 1997* [see No. 36231.] [Incl. the following contribs. related to Theresienstadt: Der geistige Widerstand in Theresienstadt; Kultur als Lebenselixier (Livia Rothkirchen, 118–140). Die tschechisch-jüdische Widerstandsbewegung in Theresienstadt (Frantisek Fuchs, 141–156; deals also with Richard Friedmann from Vienna, a former inmate of Theresienstadt). Fritz Ullmann und seine Hilfe für die Theresienstädter Häftlinge (Miroslav Kryl, 184–215; on the exile years of Dr. Fritz Ullmann in Geneva, who worked from 1939 to 1946 for the Jewish Agency). Jakob Edelsteins letzte Briefe (Miroslav Kárný, 216–229; cont. 6 letters to and from Edelstein written in German). Das Aufbaukommando und ein Jahr in den Gruben von Kladno (Jirí Kosta, 230–247; personal memoirs of author, b. 1921, about forced labour in Theresienstadt between Nov. 1941 and Feb. 1942). Theater in Theresienstadt (Eva Sormová, 266–274). Deutsche Literatur in Theresienstadt (Ludvík E. Václavek, 275–289). Zeitzeugen sprechen (Ruth Elias, 308–314).]

36466. THERESIENSTADT. Kárný, Miroslav/Kemper, Raimund/Kárná, Margita, eds.: *Theresienstädter Studien und Dokumente 1998.* Prag: Stiftung Theresienstädter Initiative; Academia, 1998. 388 pp., illus., facsims., notes, index (381–388). [Cont. (titles partly abbr.): Die Ausschaltung der Juden aus dem öffentlichen Leben des Protektorates und die Geschichte des "Ehrenariertums" (Miroslav Kárný, 7–39). Der Okkupationsapparat und die Vorbereitung der Transporte nach Lodz (Jaroslava Milotová, 40–69; on the five transports of 5,000 Jews from Prague Oct. 16 – Nov. 3, 1941). Das Schicksal der jüdischen Bevölkerung der Stadt Iglau 1938–1942 (Jens Hampel, 70–99). Das Schicksal der alten Frauen aus Deutschland im Ghetto Theresienstadt (Anita Tarsi, 100–130; incl. the section: Tschechische und deutsche Juden. Kreuzungen der Kulturen). .Von einem Haus im Theresienstädter Ghetto (Ludmila Chládková, 131–141; deals with a diary written by a woman from Germany in house L 415). Theresienstädter Erziehung; Berichte zum ersten Jahrestag der Theresienstädter Heime in L 417 (Anita Franková, 142–180; introd. and reprint of reports written in summer 1943 on the education of the young by Otto Zucker, Albert Fischer, Egon Redlich, Franz Kahn, Ota Klein, G. Bäumle). Ein interessanter Vorgänger: Der erste Theresienstadt-Film (1942) (Karel Margry, 181–212; incl. the orig. synopsis of the script). Die Akademie des Überlebens (Jelena Makarová unter Mitarbeit von Alex Leljtschuk et al., 213–238; on a collection of more than 2,280 lectures given in Theresienstadt by 500 lecturers). Arbeitskommando Wulkow (Miroslav Franc, 239–256; personal memoirs on forced labour in a camp north of Berlin in March 1944). Episoden aus dem Leben eines Überlebenden (Hans H. Sladk, 257–276; memoirs by author, a German-speaking Jew, imprisoned in Theresienstadt from Nov. 1941 until May 1945).Überleben (Ruth Bondy, 277–287). Flucht aus Zamosc; hrsg. und kommentiert von Raimund Kemper (Jan Osers, 288–321; on the escape of the author and another inmate, Jan Bachrich, and their ensuing separate odysseys through Nazi-occupied Europe). Erinnerungen an die Widerstandsbewegung (Milos Pick, 322–342). Entwicklungskonzeptionen der Gedenkstätte Theresienstadt und die Motivationsstruktur ihrer Besucher (Jan Munk, 342–355). Zur Erfassung der Verstorbenen im Theresienstädter Ghetto (Zlatuse Kukánová/Lenka Matusíková, 356–367). Der Fall der Jeanette Jenny (Michal Frankl, 368–378).]

36467. THERESIENSTADT. Randt, Alice: *Die Schleuse. Drei Jahre im Ghetto Theresienstadt.* Hrsg., überarb. und ergänzt von Horst Bethmann. 37124 Rosdorf: H. Bethmann, 1997. 136 pp., illus., facsims., footnotes. [A.R., née Seligmann, 1895 Hanover – 1980 Munich; her memoirs about her imprisonment in Theresienstadt were written in 1945 after liberation.]

36468. THERESIENSTADT. Roubickova, Eva Mandlova: *We're alive and life goes on: a Theresienstadt diary.* Transl. by Zaia Alexander. Foreword by Virginia Euwer Wolff. New York: Holt, 1998. XV, 189 pp., illus., ports., facsims., maps. [Author, b. 1921 into a German-speaking family in Bohemia.]

36469. THERESIENSTADT. Tarsi, Anita: *Late diaries and memoirs: elderly women from the Reich in the Theresienstadt ghetto.* [In]: Dappim le-Cheker Tekufat ha-Shoah, Vol. 14, Haifa, 1997. Pp. 149–186. [In Hebrew, title transl.]

36470. THERESIENSTADT. Weissová, Helga: *Zeichne, was Du siehst. Maluj, co vidíš. Draw what you see.* Zeichnungen eines Kindes aus Theresienstadt/Terezín. Göttingen: Wallstein, 1998. 167 pp., illus. [Titles and texts in German, Czech and English. Incl.: Kinder im Konzentrationslager Theresienstadt (Rudolf M. Wlaschek, 145–149). 62 drawings by the artist Helga Hosková-Weiss, made between Dec. 1941 and 1945/1946. H.W. was imprisoned as a twelve-year old in Theresienstadt, later in Auschwitz, Freiberg and Mauthausen. Lives in Prague.]

36471. THERESIENSTADT. Toll, Nelly: *When memory speaks: the Holocaust in art.* Westport, CT: Praeger, 1998. XVIII, 125 pp., illus., bibl. [Documents the Holocaust through sketches of camp life drawn surreptitiously by victims. Incl. German, Austrian and Czech artists. Also incl. contemporary paintings and sculpture.]

36472. TOMASZEWSKI, JERZY: *The expulsion of Jewish Polish citizens from Germany on October 28–29, 1938.* [In]: Acta Polonia Historica, Vol. 76 [with the issue title]: Jewish Studies, Warszawa, 1997. Pp. 97–122, footnotes.

36473. TRIER. *Vorläufiges Gedenkbuch für die Juden von Trier 1938–1943.* Zusammengestellt von Reiner Nolden. 2. überarb. u. korr. Aufl., Trier, 1998. IX, 135 pp. [Privately printed.]

36474. *The triumphant spirit: portraits and stories of Holocaust survivors: their messages of hope and compassion.* Created and photogr. by Nick Del Calzo. Ed. by Linda J. Raper. Stories written by Renee Rockford. Introd. by Thomas Keneally. Denver, CO: Triumphant Spirit, 1997. 172 pp., illus., ports., notes, bibl. [Series of interviews by N. Del Calzo a.o. with several German, as well as Austrian and Czech survivors, all now living in the US.]

36475. *Unternehmen im Nationalsozialismus.* Hrsg. von Lothar Gall und Manfred Pohl. München: Beck, 1998. 143 pp., footnotes, indexes. (Schriftenreihe zur Zeitschrift für Unternehmensgeschichte, Bd. 1.) [Papers given at a conference in Frankfurt am Main, June 20 – 21, 1997. Cont.: Einleitung (eds., 7–13). Unternehmen unter dem Hakenkreuz (Henry A. Turner, 15–24). Die Rolle der Banken im Nationalsozialismus (Harold James, 25–36; with comments by Carl-Ludwig Holtfrerich and Christopher Kopper, 37–44). Erfahrungen mit der Geschichte der Volkswagen GmbH im Dritten Reich (Hans Mommsen, 45–54; with comments by Manfred Grieger, Marie-Luise Recker, Mark Spoerer and a reply by Hans Mommsen, 55–72). Die Deutsche Reichsbahn 1933–1945 (Klaus Hildebrand, 73–90). Hugo Stinnes und der Nationalsozialismus (Gerald D. Feldman, 91–98). Robert Bosch und der Widerstand gegen den Nationalsozialismus (Joachim Scholtyseck, 99–106). Die I.G.-Farbenindustrie (Peter Hayes, 107–116; with comments by Avraham Barkai and Anthony Nicholls (117–124). Podiumsdiskussion (125–138). All contribs. also deal with antisemitism, "aryanisation", persecution of Jews and forced labour.]

36476. VAN ALPHEN, ERNST: *Caught by history: Holocaust effects in contemporary art, literature, and theory.* Stanford, CA: Stanford Univ. Press, 1997. XII, 233 pp., illus., facsims., notes, bibl. [Incl. chap.: Autobiography as resistance to history: Charlotte Salomon 'Life or Theater' (65–85).]

36477. VIENNA. SEIFERT, OTTO: *Bücherverwertungsstelle Wien 1, Dorotheergasse 12.* [In]: Jahrbuch 1998 des Dokumentationsarchivs des österr. Widerstandes, Wien, 1998. Pp. 88–94, footnotes. [On the 'aryanisation' of the book trade and libraries in Austria after the 'Anschluß'.]

36478. VIENNA. TRAHAN, ELIZABETH WELT: *Walking with ghosts: a Jewish childhood in wartime Vienna.* New York, Bern: Lang, 1998. 252 pp., illus. (Literature and the sciences of man, 17.) [For German edn. and data see No. 33881/YB XLII.]

—— VORDTRIEDE, KÄTHE: *"Mir ist noch wie ein Traum, dass mir diese abenteuerliche Flucht gelang": Briefe nach 1933 aus Freiburg im Breisgau, Frauenfeld und New York an ihren Sohn Werner.* [See No. 37012.]

—— WALK, JOSEPH: *Changes in religious teaching in Germany in the Nazi period.* [In Hebrew; see in No. 36700.]

36479. WEISSER, ELKE: *Fürs Leben lernen.* Deutsche Reformpädagogik an jüdischen Schulen bis 1939. [In]: Neue Sammlung, Vierteljahres-Zeitschrift für Erziehung und Gesellschaft, Jg. 38, H. 3, Seelze-Velber, 1998. Pp. 281–296, footnotes.

36480. WEISS, YFAAT: *The encounter between German and Polish Jewry during the Nazi period.* Tel-Aviv: Tel-Aviv Univ., 1996. 2 vols., 399, XVI pp. [Diss.; in Hebrew, with English summary.]

36481. WEISS, YFAAT: *The transfer agreement and the boykott movement: a Jewish dilemma on the eve of the Holocaust.* [In]: Yad Vashem Studies, Vol. XXVI, Jerusalem, 1998. Pp. 129–172, footnotes. [On the Haavara Transfer agreement of 1933.]

36482. WESTPHALIA. Meynert, Joachim/Mitschke, Gudrun: *Die letzten Augenzeugen zu hören. Interviews mit antisemitisch Verfolgten aus Ostwestfalen.* Bielefeld: Verl. für Regionalgeschichte, 1998. 192 pp., footnotes, bibl. (Quellen zur Regionalgeschichte, Bd. 3.) [A CD is attached to the book. Incl. interviews with people from Bielefeld, Minden, Rheda, Gütersloh; also with those who went after 1945 to Detmold and Paderborn.]

36483. WESTPHALIA. Meynert, Joachim: *Jüdische Geschichte und regionale Identität.* Beiträge zur Geschichte der jüdischen Minderheit in Ostwestfalen. Bielefeld: Verl. für Regionalgeschichte, 1998. 116 pp. (Texte und Materialien aus dem Mindener Museum, Bd. 13.) [Incl. 8 articles, some of them previously publ., mainly dealing with the Jews in Bielefeld, Lippe and Minden-Ravensberg during the Nazi period and with aspects of collective memory and "Vergangenheitsbewältigung".]

36484. WESTPHALIA. Mitschke, Gudrun: *Erinnerte Geschichte. Interviews mit antisemitisch Verfolgten aus Ostwestfalen.* [In]: Lippische Mitteilungen, Bd. 67, Detmold 1998. Pp. 231–247, footnotes. [Analyses individual processes of memory.]

36485. Wildt, Michael: *Before the "Final Solution": the Judenpolitik of the SD, 1935–1938.* [In]: Leo Baeck Institute Year Book XLIII, London, 1998. Pp. 241–269, footnotes.

36486. Wollenberg, Jörg: *Den Blick schärfen – Gegen das Verdrängen und Entsorgen. Beiträge zur historisch-politischen Aufklärung.* Mit einem Vorwort von Arno Klönne. Bremen: Donat, 1998. 287 pp., notes. [Incl. essays, written over the last ten years, on "Aryanisation", November Pogrom, Nuremberg Trials, Kurt Waldheim; also on Walter Fabian.]

36487. Wrocklage, Ute: *Fotografie und Holocaust.* Annotierte Bibliographie. Frankfurt am Main: Fritz Bauer Institut, 1998. 96 pp., index (places, 89–91). [Bibl. of illus. books, catalogues etc. of concentration camps and of memorials.]

36488. Yahil, Leny: *Die Shoah: Überlebenskampf und Vernichtung der europäischen Juden.* Aus dem Amerik. von H. Jochen Bußmann. München: Luchterhand, 1998. 1055 pp., tabs., maps, notes (895–987), bibl (988–1020), index (1021–1055). [First edn. in Hebrew publ. in 1987; American edn. with the title 'The Holocaust' publ. in 1990. Incl.: Geleitwort (Eberhard Jäckel, 21–22). Vorwort zur deutschen Ausgabe (Leni Yahil, 23–25). Book deals with the period between 1932 and 1945.]

36489. Zimmerman, Herman: *Ein Engel an meiner Seite. Eine Geschichte vom Überleben im Holocaust.* Aus dem Amerik. von Karl Herzer. Mit einem Geleitwort von Johannes Rau. Zweite Aufl. Heidelberg: HVA, 1998. 185 pp., illus. [1st edn. publ. 1997; incl.: Geleitwort (Johannes Rau, 9–12). Nachwort des Übersetzers (178–184); personal recollections.] [H.Z., b. in Cologne into an Eastern-Jewish family, fled in 1938 via The Netherlands, Belgium and France to Switzerland, in 1945 returned to France, emigr. 1949 to the US.]

36490. Zuckermann, Moshe: *Zweierlei Holocaust. Der Holocaust in den politischen Kulturen Israels und Deutschlands.* Göttingen: Wallstein, 1998. 181 pp., notes. [A collection of essays, dealing with collective memory, instrumentalisation of the Holocaust in Israel and the attitude of German intellectuals confronted by the Holocaust; incl. an analysis of a debate between Günter Grass and Yoram Kaniuk.] [Cf.: Besprechung (Axel Schmitt) [in]: Aschkenas, Jg. 9. H. 1, Wien, 1999, pp. 284–285.]

——— Zuckermann, Moshe: *Perspektiven der Holocaust-Rezeption in Israel und Deutschland.* [See in No. 36664.]

36491. Zweig, Ronald W.: *Feeding the camps: allied blockade policy and the relief of concentration camps in Germany, 1944–1945.* [In]: Historical Journal, Vol. 41, No. 3, Cambridge, Sept. 1998. Pp. 825–851, footnotes.

B. Jewish Resistance

36492. GEISEL, EIKE: *Störenfriede der Erinnerung. Die jüdische Widerstandsgruppe Herbert Baum*. [In]: Triumph des guten Willens [see in No. 36549.]. Pp. 130–147.

36493. *Konflikte aus der Geschichte*. [Section title of] Konfliktforschung aktuell, Jg. 6, H. 3–4, Berlin, 1998. 1 issue. [Selected contribs.: Kurzbiographien von Teilnehmern am antifaschistischen Widerstand gegen das NS-Regime in Berlin 1933–1945 – Klärungsansätze und Materiallage (Klaus Keim/Klaus-Peter Pforte, 55–65). Interview mit dem Berliner Antifaschisten Walter Sack, Jg. 1915 (Editha Nagl/Wolfgang Kögel, 99–120).]

36494. LUSTIGER, ARNO: *Rotbuch: Stalin und die Juden*. Die tragische Geschichte des Jüdischen Anti-faschistischen Komitees und der sowjetischen Juden. Berlin: Aufbau, 1998. 428 pp., bibl. (399–403), notes (404–416), index (417–428). [Deals also with the Rote Kapelle and the fate of German-Jewish Communists and other Jews in the early years of the GDR.]

36495. ROHRLICH, RUBY, ed.: *Resisting the Holocaust*. Oxford; New York: Berg, 1998. 264 pp., notes. [Cont. 12 contribs. dealing with resistance in many European countries, as well as in concentration camps. Incl.: Culture and remembrance: Jewish ambivalence and antipathy to the history of resistance (Martin Cohen, 19–38). Resistance histories in post-war Germany: the missing case of intermarried Germans (Nathan Stoltzfus, 151–178, notes).]

36496. SCHOEPS, JULIUS H.: *Gab es einen jüdischen Widerstand? Abwehrstrategien gegen Hitler und den NS-Terror*. [In]: Das Gewaltsyndrom. Verformungen und Brüche im deutsch-jüdischen Verhältnis [see in No. 36438]. Pp. 133–147.

36497. SCHUR, MAXINE ROSE: *Hannah Szenes: a song of light*. Philadelphia: Jewish Publication Society, 1998. 106 pp. [First publ. in 1986, tells the story of the Hungarian resistance fighter H.S. who fled to Palestine, but volunteered with Haganah to be parachuted behind enemy lines in Hungary and was later caught and shot.]

36498. STEINBACH, PETER: *Widerstand von Juden*. Anmerkungen zum Widerstandsbegriff. [In]: Menora 1998, Bodenheim, 1998. Pp. 31–69.

36499. STROBL, INGRID: *Die Angst kam erst danach. Jüdische Frauen im Widerstand in Europa 1939–1945*. Frankfurt am Main: Fischer Taschenbuch Verlag, 1998. 479 pp., illus., notes (409–459), bibl. (460–474). [Focuses on France, Belgium, The Netherlands, Hungary and Poland. Incl. also the involvement of German-speaking refugee women in resistance and rescue activities.]

36500. TEICHMANN, SEPP: *Jüdischer Widerstand oder Widerstand von Juden? Zur Geschichte und Rezeption von Widerstand*. [In]: Gedenkdienst aktuell, Nr. 2, Wien, 1998. Pp. 12–13.

IV. POST-1945

A. General

36501. AUSTRIA. *Displaced Persons. Jüdische Flüchtlinge nach 1945 in Hohenems und Bregenz*. [Hrsg.: Esther Haber]. Innsbruck: Studien Verl., 1998. 112 pp., illus., notes. (Schriften des Instituts für Zeitgesch. der Univ. Innsbruck und des Jüdischen Museums Hohenems, Bd. 3.) [Incl. (titles partly abbr.): Vorwort (ed., 7–10). Zwischenstation im Dreiländereck. Jüdische DPs und Flüchtlinge nach 1945 in Hohenems und Bregenz (Thomas Albrich, 11–56). Auf der Suche nach den DPs (Erik Weltsch, 57–62). Über Erinnerungsinterviews mit Zeitzeugen aus Hohenems und Bregenz zu den jüdischen Displaced Persons in Vorarlberg (Esther Haber, 63–74). Ein ehemaliger DP erzählt (75–80). Also documents the exhibits relating to DPs in the Jüdisches Museum Hohenems.]

36502. AUSTRIA. Embacher, Helga: *Neubeginn ohne Illusionen. Juden in Österreich nach 1945.* Wien: Picus, 1998. 322 pp., illus., notes (263–305), bibl. (308–321). [Also on displaced persons, antisemitism, restitution, Waldheim affair.]

36503. AUSTRIA. Pelinka, Anton/Mayr, Sabine, eds.: *Die Entdeckung der Verantwortung. Die Zweite Republik und die vertriebenen Juden.* Eine kommentierte Dokumentation aus dem persönlichen Archiv von Albert Sternfeld. Hrsg. von Anton Pelinka und Helmut Reinalter. Wien: Braumüller, 1998. XIV, 306 pp., port., footnotes, bibl. (239–300), index (301–305). (Vergleichende Gesellschaftsgeschichte und politische Ideengeschichte der Neuzeit, Bd. 10.) [Incl. docs. about A. Sternfeld's assistance in establishing in 1995 a restitution fund in Austria for Nazi victims (Nationalfonds der Republik Österreich für Opfer des Nationalsozialismus); also interviews with A. St., who emigr. from Vienna to the UK in 1938 and returned to Vienna in 1966.]

36504. AUSTRIA. Pelinka, Anton: *Jüdische Identität in Österreich.* [In]: Jahrbuch 1998 [des Dokumentationsarchivs des österreichischen Widerstandes]. Wien, 1998. Pp. 103–110. [Focuses on Jews in Austria after World War II.]

36505. AUSTRIA. Zelman, Leon with Armin Thurnher: *After survival: one man's mission in the case of memory.* Transl. from the German by Meredith Schneeweiss. New York: Holmes and Meier, 1998. X, 166 pp. [Story of a Polish Jew, a DP in Austria at the end of World War II, who remained there and now writes about present-day Jews and Austrian attitudes towards them.]

36506. BERLIN. Kessler, Judith: *Jüdische Immigration seit 1990. Resümee einer Studie mit 4000 Zuwanderern aus der früheren Sowjetunion in Berlin.* [In]: Trumah 7, Berlin, 1998. Pp. 87–100, footnotes.

36507. Bodemann, Y. Micha: *Die Koffer gepackt und doch geblieben.* Verweilen zwischen Nähe und Ferne: die Situation jüdischer Zuwanderer in der Nachkriegszeit. [In]: 'FAZ', Nr. 241, Frankfurt am Main, 17. Okt. 1998. Beilage, p. II.

——— Brenner, Michael: *Deutsch-jüdische Geschichte nach 1945 – nur ein Epilog?* [See in No. 36147.]

36508. Brumlik, Micha, ed.: *Zuhause, keine Heimat? Junge Juden und ihre Zukunft in Deutschland.* Gerlingen: Bleicher, 1998. 216 pp., ports. [Incl. introd. essay by the ed. and 15 personal accounts of Jews living in Germany.]

36509. Bubis, Ignatz: *Reflexionen eines deutschen Juden.* Die jüdische Gemeinschaft in Deutschland und ihr Verhältnis zu Israel. [In]: Fünfzig Jahre Israel: Vision und Wirklichkeit [see No. 37043]. Pp. 214–221.

——— Cohn, Matthias: *"Damit das Wissen lebendig bleibt". Zum Selbstverständnis der Zweiten Generation in der Bundesrepublik lebender Juden.* [See in No. 36172.]

36510. COLOGNE. Ginzel, Günther B./Güntner, Sonja, eds.: *"Zuhause in Köln …": jüdisches Leben 1945 bis heute.* Köln: Böhlau, 1998. 211 pp., illus., bibl., indexes (subjects; persons). [Articles are arranged under the following sections: *Prolog* (9–40; contribs. by Ralph Giordano/Günther B. Ginzel, Rachel Salamander/Sonja Güntner, Werner Jung). *Das Gestern im Heute. Vom Mut zum Neuanfang und den Schatten der Vergangenheit* (41–70; contribs. by Monika Grübel, Sammy Maedge, Johannes Ralf Beines, Thomas Blisniewski). *Jüdisches Leben heute. Innenansichten* (71–90; contribs. by Miguel Freund, Annette Vesper, Michael Lawton, Judith Preugschat). *Juden in Köln. Erlebte Geschichte in Texten und Bildern* (91–146, eds.,). *Germania Judaica. Kulturelle Begegnungen* (147–174; contribs. by Willehad Paul Eckert, Jutta Bohnke-Kollwitz, Annette Haller, Jürgen Wilhelm, Benedikt von und zu Hoensbroech). *Juden und Nichtjuden. Wahrnehmungen, Erfahrungen, Bemühungen* (175–204; contribs. by Johannes Rau, Willehad Paul Eckert, Klaus Heuge). Selected articles are listed according to subject.]

36511. Dietrich, Susanne/Schulze Wessel, Julia: *Zwischen Selbstorganisation und Stigmatisierung.* Die Lebenswirklichkeit jüdischer Displaced Persons und die neue Gestalt des Antisemitismus in der deutschen Nachkriegsgesellschaft. Stuttgart: Klett-Cotta, 1998. 232 pp., illus., facsims., tabs., footnotes, bibl. (227–231). (Veröff. des Archivs der Stadt Stuttgart, Bd. 75.) [First part (Susanne Dietrich, 13–131) deals with displaced persons in the Stuttgart DP-camps; second part (Julia Schulze Wessel, 133–226) deals with antisemitism, based on an analysis of Stuttgart police files 1945–1948.)]

36512. FÜRTH. BERTHOLD-HILPERT, MONIKA: *Die frühe Nachkriegsgeschichte der jüdischen Gemeinde Fürth (1945–1954)*. [In]: Menora 1998, Bodenheim, 1998. Pp. 361–380, notes.

36513. GEIS, JAEL: *"Ja, man muß seinen Feinden verzeihen, aber nicht früher, als bis sie gehenkt werden"*. Gedanken zur Rache für die Vernichtung der Juden im unmittelbaren Nachkriegsdeutschland. [In]: Menora 1998, Bodenheim, 1998. Pp. 155–180, notes. [Analyses the debates about revenge in German-language Jewish newspapers and periodicals.]

36514. GELSENKIRCHEN. GRÜNFELD, JEHONATHAN OLIVER: *Die Migration jüdischer Jugendlicher und junger Erwachsener aus der ehemaligen Sowjetunion nach Gelsenkirchen*. Gelsenkirchen: Privately printed, 1998. 98 pp., footnotes, suppl. (XIII pp.). [Available at the Bibliothek Germania Judaica, Cologne.]

36515. GROSSMANN, ATINA: *Trauma, memory, and motherhood: Germans and Jewish Displaced Persons in post-Nazi Germany, 1945–1949.* [In]: Archiv für Sozialgeschichte, Bd. 38, Bonn, 1998. Pp. 215–239, footnotes.

——— GUTTMANN, MICHA: *Jüdische Geschichte in Nordrhein-Westfalen*. [See in No. 35912.]

36516. HERF, JEFFREY: *Zweierlei Erinnerung: die NS-Vergangenheit im geteilten Deutschland*. Aus dem Amerik. von Klaus-Dieter Schmidt. Berlin: Propyläen, 1998. 558 pp., notes (457–525), bibl. (526–544), index. [For American edn. see No. 35258/YB XLIII.]

36517. *Juden in Deutschland, Juden in der Fremde. Über die politische und kulturelle Bedeutung jüdischer Diaspora.* [Hrsg.: Sybille Fritsch-Oppermann]. Rehburg-Loccum: Ev. Akademie Loccum, 1998. 177 pp. (Loccumer Protokolle 67/95.) [Incl. contribs. (partly in English) on Jews in today's Germany (Ignatz Bubis, Rafael Seligmann, Michael Fürst); on antisemitism (Erich Zenger).]

36518. KEYNAN, IRIT: *Holocaust survivors and the emissaries from Eretz-Israel, Germany 1945–1948.* Tel-Aviv: Ha-Amuta le-Cheker Ma'arakhot ha-Ha'apalah al-shem Shaul Avigur, Tel-Aviv Univ.; Am Oved, 1996. 263 pp. [In Hebrew.]

36519. KRAUSS, MARITA: *Projektion statt Erinnerung: Der Umgang mit Remigranten und die deutsche Gesellschaft nach 1945.* [In]: Exil. Forschung, Erkenntnisse, Ergebnisse, Jg. 18, Nr. 1, Frankfurt am Main, 1998. Pp. 5–16.

36520. LEIPZIG. HOLLITZER, SIEGFRIED: *Eugen Gollomb. Mosaiksteine zu einem Lebensbild.* [In]: Forschungsstelle Judentum, Mitteilungen und Beiträge 14, Leipzig, April 1998. Pp. 4–25, footnotes. [E.G., Jan 19, 1917 Breslau – Jan. 1, 1988 Leipzig, escaped from an outcamp of Auschwitz, joined the Polish resistance, went to Leipzig in 1947, where he became chairman of the small Jewish congregation.]

——— LEZZI, EVA: *Leben und älter werden in Deutschland: Alltagserfahrung und Erinnerungsformen*. [See in No. 36172.]

36521. MERTENS, LOTHAR: *Alltäglicher Antisemitismus in der deutschen Provinz? Der Fall Gollwitz.* [In]: Jahrbuch für Antisemitismusforschung 7, Frankfurt am Main; New York, 1998. Pp. 208–225, notes. [Deals with the reaction of the local population to the settlement of 60 Russian-Jewish immigrants in a small town in Brandenburg. See also No. 36534.]

36522. MERTENS, LOTHAR: *Ein Führungswechsel findet statt. Jüdisches Leben in den neuen Bundesländern.* [In]: Sachor, Bd. 8 (1998) [see No. 36567]. Pp. 97–102.

36523. MIRON, GUY: *The Holocaust survivors in the DP camps in Germany.* [In]: Alon le-Morei ha-Historia, No. 7, Jerusalem, 1998. Pp. 40–48. [In Hebrew, title transl.]

36524. NOLDEN, THOMAS: *"Aus der Vergangenheit herausgewandert".* *Überlegungen zur Lyrik jüdischer Autoren der Gegenwart.* [In]: Colloquia Germanica, Bd. 31, H. 3, Tübingen, 1998. Pp. 259–276, notes.

36525. OFFENBERG, ULRIKE: *"Seid vorsichtig gegen die Machthaber": die jüdischen Gemeinden in der SBZ und der DDR 1945–1990.* Berlin: Aufbau, 1998. 334 pp., illus., gloss., tabs., bibl. (280–289), notes (290–325), index. Zugl.: Berlin, Freie Univ., Diss., 1997. [Cf.: Sozialistische Arisierung (Jacques Schuster) [in]: 'FAZ', Nr. 191, Frankfurt am Main, 19. Aug. 1998, p. 7.]

36526. PELZ-BERGT, JUTTA: *Die ersten Jahre nach dem Holocaust; Odyssee einer Gezeichneten.* Hrsg. von Sigrid Jacobeit. Berlin: Ed. Hentrich, 1997. 180 pp., illus. ((Reihe deutscher Vergangenheit.) [Memoirs focusing on the post-war experiences of a survivor of Auschwitz and Ravensbrück.]

36527. REGENSBURG. MOOSBURGER, UWE/WANNER, HELMUT: *Schabbat Schalom: Juden in Regensburg – Gesichter einer lebendigen Gemeinde.* Regensburg: Mittelbayerische Druck- und Verl.-Ges., 1998. 151 pp., illus.

36528. RESTITUTION. PROSS, CHRISTIAN: *Paying for the past: the struggle over reparations for surviving victims of the Nazi terror.* Transl. by Belinda Cooper. Baltimore: Johns Hopkins Univ. Press, 1998. XXII, 265 pp., illus., tabs., gloss., appendixes, notes, bibl.

36529. RESTITUTION. SCHLEIER, BETTINA: *Das Umzugsgut jüdischer Auswanderer – von der Enteignung zur Rückerstattung.* [In]: Bremisches Jahrbuch, Bd. 77, Selbstverl. des Staatsarchivs Bremen, 1998. Pp. 247–265, footnotes.

——— RESTITUTION. SEIBERT, WINFRIED: *Sonderfall – die "Wiedergutmachung" bei den Shanghai-Flüchtlingen.* [See in No. 36444.]

36530. RESTITUTION. ZWEIG, RONALD W.: *Refugee assets and refugee rehabilitation – the Jewish experience.* [In]: Tel Aviver Jahrbuch für deutsche Geschichte, Bd. 27, Gerlingen, 1998. Pp. 383–400, footnotes. [On reparations and the restitution process; the Luxembourg agreement of 1952; Jewish voluntary organisations.]

36531. RHEINZ, HANNA: *Die jüdische Frau. Auf der Suche nach einer modernen Identität.* Gütersloh: Gütersloher Verl.-Haus, 1998. 160 pp., notes (154–157), gloss. (Gütersloher Taschenbücher, 717.) [A collection of essays dealing with Jewish life in post-war Germany, focusing on Jewish women; also on assimilation, mixed marriages and conversions, relationship to Israel and the image of Jews in Germany in other countries of the Galut, the limited authority of rabbis in Germany, "shtetl-nostalgia" of non-Jews.]

36532. ROKAHR, GERD: *Mir geht es gut, ich bin gesund. Briefe aus deutschen Konzentrationslagern (1933–1945).* Begleitheft zu einer Ausstellung im Jüdischen Museum August-Gottschalk-Haus in Esens. Hrsg. vom Ökumenischen Arbeitskreis Juden und Christen in Esens. Esens: Ökum. Arbeitskreis, 1998. 47 pp.

36533. SCHEIN, ADA: *Homeless Displaced Persons as partners in the Zionist enterprise; survivors in German and Austrian DP camps and the Jewish National Fund.* Jerusalem: Research Institute for the History of the Keren Kayemeth le'Israel, Land and Settlement, 1997. 75, XXX pp. [In Hebrew and English. The XXX pp. are in English.]

36534. SPÜLBECK, SUSANNE: *Ordnung und Angst. Russische Juden aus der Sicht eines ostdeutschen Dorfes nach der Wende.* Eine ethnologische Studie. Frankfurt am Main; New York: Campus, 1998. 298 pp., notes (245–279), bibl. (283–298). (Schriftenreihe des Zentrums für Antisemitismusforschung, Bd. 5.). Zugl.: Berlin, Techn. Univ., Diss. [On the reaction of the local population to seventy Russian-Jewish immigrants, who were sent to live in a village in Brandenburg in 1990.] [Cf.: Das Erbe des Antisemitismus als Hindernis bei der Annäherung (Carsten Klingemann) [in]: Das Parlament, Jg. 48, Nr. 38, Bonn, 11. Sept. 1998, p. 15. See also No. 36521.]

36535. TAKEI, AYAKA: *Wiederaufbau und Konsolidierung der jüdischen Gemeinden im Nachkriegsdeutschland (1945–1955)*. Magisterarbeit an der Abt. europäisch- und amerik. Geschichte, Philos. Fak. der Waseda Univ., Tokio. Tokio: [Typescript], 1998. 208 pp. [In Japanese, with German title; availabe at the Zentralarchiv zur Erforschung der Geschichte der Juden in Deutschland, Heidelberg.]

36536. TOBIAS, JIM G.: *Der Kibbuz auf dem Streicher-Hof. Zur Geschichte der jüdischen Kollektivfarmen 1945–1948*. [In]: Menora 1998, Bodenheim, 1998. Pp. 381–399, notes.

36537. TOBIAS, JIM G.: *Der Kibbuz auf dem Streicher-Hof*. Die vergessene Geschichte der jüdischen Kollektivfarmen 1945–48. Begleitbuch zur Ausstellung. Nürnberg: Jim G. Tobias [Sulzbacher Str. 45], 1997. 95 pp., illus., facsims., bibl. [Deals with the Hachsharot-Kibbuzim for Jewish displaced persons in Franconia, mainly with "Kibbuz Nili", established by the US military government on an estate formerly owned by Julius Streicher. Book accompanies an exhibition and a documentary film with the same title.]

36538. VIENNA. COYNE, NANCY ANN: *Picturing memory: Holocaust field work in Vienna*. [In]: The Jewish Quarterly, Vol. 45, No. 3, London, Autumn 1998. Pp. 55–61, illus., ports. [Author interviewed and photographed 50 Jewish survivors in Vienna in the late 80s. The painter Georg Eisler, the actress Charlotte Becher, and Moritz Einziger, an administrator for the JOINT, are featured in detail.]

36539. WEISS, YFAAT: *Homeland as shelter or as a refuge? Repatriation in the Jewish context*. [In]: Tel Aviver Jahrbuch für deutsche Geschichte, Bd. 27, Gerlingen, 1998. Pp. 195–220, footnotes. [On the phenomenon of remigration; also on Polish Jews in Nazi Germany and on displaced persons.]

B. Education and Teaching. Memorials

36540. AACHEN. *Mahnmal und Gedenkstätte an der Aachener Synagoge: (Simon-Schlachet-Gemeindezentrum)*. Hrsg. von Wolfgang Krücken und Alexander Lohe im Auftrag der Ges. für Christl-Jüd. Zus.-arbeit e.V. Aachen: Shaker, 1998. 33 pp., illus.

36541. AUSCHWITZ. *Auschwitz. Einen Ort sehen*. Hrsg. von Knut Dethlefsen und Thomas B. Hebler. Berlin: Hentrich, 1997. 175 pp., illus. [Contribs. in German and Polish on Auschwitz as a memorial site, different approaches to commemoration, the Internationale Jugendbegegnungsstätte Auschwitz.]

36542. BERLIN. KATTAGO, SIOBHAN: *Representing German victimhood and guilt: Die neue Wache and unified German memory*. [In]: German Politics and Society, Vol. 16, No. 2, Berkeley, CA, Summer 1998. Pp. 86–104, notes. [Deals with the restoration of the old war memorial 'Die neue Wache' in Berlin as a central memorial for the victims of war and tyranny, and with the controversy over treating German victims and victims of German atrocities alike.]

36543. BERLIN, HOLOCAUST MEMORIAL. PETERSDORFF, ULRICH VON: *Das Berliner Holocaustdenkmal. Zur Namensnennung der NS-Opfer auf Denkmälern*. [In]: Geschichte in Wissenschaft und Unterricht, Jg. 49, H. 2, Stuttgart, 1998. Pp. 115–118, footnotes.

36544. BERLIN, HOLOCAUST MEMORIAL. TANAKA, J.: *Streit um die Erinnerung. Über das Mahnmal für die ermordeten Juden Europas in Berlin*. [In]: Doitsu Bungaku, H. 101, Tokyo, Herbst 1998. Pp. 87–97, footnotes. [With Engl. summary.]

36545. BRINK, CORNELIA: *Ikonen der Vernichtung*. Öffentlicher Gebrauch von Fotografien aus nationalsozialistischen Konzentrationslagern nach 1945. Frankfurt am Main; New York: Campus, 1998. 266 pp., illus. (Schriftenreihe des Fritz Bauer Instituts, Bd. 14.) [Cf.:

Wieviel Wirklichkeit verträgt die Wirksamkeit? Cornelia Brink erklärt, warum die fotografische Dokumentation der nationalsozialistischen Greueltaten nicht lehrreich ist (Carlos Collado Seidel) [in]: 'FAZ', Nr. 287, Frankfurt am Main, 10. Dez. 1998, p. 11.]

36546. *Dimensions: A Journal of Holocaust Studies, Vol. 12, No. 1* [with the issue title] *Holocaust education: traditions, touchstones and taboos.* New York, 1998. 1 issue, notes. [Cont. (titles abbr.): Moralizing the Holocaust (Lawrence L. Langer, 306, ports.). The lessons of the Holocaust (Omer Bartov, 13–20, illus., ports., incl. post-war Germany). The German historians and the burden of the Nazi past (Georg G. Iggers, 21–28, illus., incl. popular reaction to Goldhagen and the Wehrmacht exhibit). How can the significance of the Holocaust be taught? (Robert F. Drinan, S.J., 29–31, illus., ports.). Teaching the Holocaust (Karen Friedman, 33).]

—— FAULENBACH, BERND/SCHÜTTE, HELMUTH, eds.: *Deutschland, Israel und der Holocaust. Zur Gegenwartsbedeutung der Vergangenheit.* [See No. 37041.]

36547. *Fondation Auschwitz: Bulletin trimestriel.* No. spécial 60 [with the issue title]: *La Mémoire d'Auschwitz dans l'art contemporain/The memory of Auschwitz in contemporary art.* Actes du Colloque International/Proceedings of the International Conference, Bruxelles, 11–13 décembre 1997. Bruxelles, juillet–sept. 1998. 1 issue, 352 pp. [Cont. introd. speeches, 34 papers and discussions arranged under the following sections: To survive and paint; Art and life: combatting Auschwitz; Witnesses and legacy: transmitting through art; Representation and figures of absence. Art when art seems impossible; Art as a memorial space; The Memorial Monument (on the Berlin Holocaust memorial); Closing speeches.]

36548. FRANKFURT am Main. JÜDISCHES MUSEUM FRANKFURT AM MAIN.: *Zehn Jahre Jüdisches Museum Frankfurt am Main 1988–1998.* Frankfurt am Main: Jüd. Museum der Stadt Frankfurt am Main, 1998. 64 pp., illus. [Incl.: Zehn Jahre Jüdisches Museum Frankfurt am Main. Ein Bericht (Georg Heuberger, 8–13).]

36549. GEISEL, EIKE: *Triumph des guten Willens. Gute Nazis und selbsternannte Opfer. Die Nationalisierung der Erinnerung.* Hrsg. von Klaus Bittermann. Berlin: Ed. Tiamat. 207 pp., bibl. (Critica Diabolis, 75.) [A collection of 21 essays and reviews by author who died in 1997, on (a.o.) memorials, collective memory, 'Vergangenheitsbewältigung', Jewish resistance, Hannah Arendt, Adolf Eichmann. Incl.: Nachwort (ed., 197–202).]

36550. GELSENKIRCHEN. INSTITUT FÜR STADTGESCHICHTE, ed.: *Historische Spuren vor Ort – Gelsenkirchen im Nationalsozialismus.* Bearb. von Ludger Breitbach [et al.]. Essen: Klartext, 1998. 109 pp., illus., maps. [Incl. places relevant to the history of Jews in Gelsenkirchen, Buer and Horst (incorporated in 1930 into Gelsenkirchen).]

36551. HOFFMANN, DETLEF, ed.: *Das Gedächtnis der Dinge: KZ-Relikte und KZ-Denkmäler 1945–1995.* Frankfurt am Main; New York: Campus, 1998. 351 pp., illus., notes. (Wissenschaftliche Reihe des Fritz-Bauer-Instituts, Bd. 4.) [Cont.: Das Gedächtnis der Dinge (ed., 6–35). Dachau (ed., 36–91). Buchenwald (Volkhard Knigge, 92–173). Neuengamme (Ute Wrocklage, 174–205). Die südfranzösischen Lager (ed./Volkhard Knigge, 206–223). Bilder von den südfranzösischen Lagern (Werner Reuber, 224–237). Four contribs. on Auschwitz (Cornelia Brink, Katharina Menzel, Ines Rensinghoff, Ute Wrocklage, 238–324). Über den Umgang mit den Orten des Schreckens (Jörn Rüsen, 330–343). Nachwort (ed., 344–350).]

36552. KIEL. CLAUSEN, SIGRUN: *Führungen durch eine Ausstellung über den Holocaust – ein Erfahrungsbericht.* [In]: Kieler Blätter zur Volkskunde, Jg. 29, Kiel, 1997. Pp. 169–175, footnotes.

—— KORN, SALOMON: *Deutsch-jüdische Gedenkkultur nach dem Holocaust.* [See in No. 36162.]

36553. *Lessons and legacies II: teaching the Holocaust in a changing world.* Ed. and introd. by Donald G. Schilling. Evanston, IL: Northwestern Univ. Press, 1998. XII, 233 pp., appendix, notes (193–230). [11 essays, incl. contribs. by Christopher Browning, Michael R. Marrus,

Gerhard L. Weinberg a.o. on various aspects of teaching the Holocaust. Several essays deal with new research on the motivations of both perpetrators and rescuers.]

36554. LOWER SAXONY. OBENAUS, HERBERT: *Gedenkstätten in Niedersachsen.* [In]: Menora 1997, Bodenheim, 1997. Pp. 342–368, notes.

36555. *Mahnung und Erinnerung.* Hrsg. von Hans-Jochen Vogel und Rita Süssmuth. München: Saur, 1998. 223 pp. (Jahrbuch des Vereins "Gegen Vergessen – Für Demokratie", Bd. 2.) [Cont. 24 essays, some of them dealing with the "New Right", Holocaust denial and revisionism, the former GDR's dealings with the Nazi past and Holocaust, memorials, teaching projects and "Erinnerungskultur". Selected articles are listed according to subject.]

36556. MAUTHAUSEN. BOTZ, GERHARD [et al.]: *Mauthausen als "Erinnerungsort": Probleme der "Authentizität" und des österreichischen "kollektiven Gedächtnisses".* [In]: Jahrbuch 1998 des Dokumentationsarchivs des österr. Widerstandes, Wien, 1998. Pp. 15–29.

36557. MINDEN. *Versöhnung in Minden: Chronik der Begegnungswoche deutsch-jüdischer Altbürger Mindens; 24.-30. Mai 1994.* Aufgezeichnet von Pery Gurwitz. Hrsg. von Friedrich-Wilhelm Steffen, Kulturbüro der Stadt Minden. Minden: Kulturbüro, 1998. 123 pp.

36558. MÖNCHENGLADBACH. WIESEN, BRIGITTE [et al.]: *Das Hans Jonas Denkmal und seine Übergabe.* [In]: Rheydter Jahrbuch 24, Mönchengladbach, 1998. Pp. 163–180, notes. [Docs. the speeches held in Mönchengladbach, June 3, 1998. Also in this issue: Brief von Hans Jonas an Lisel Haas (Hans Hoster, 181–187, port., illus., notes; letter written to a cousin in Oct. 1945).]

36559. MOLLER, SABINE: *Die Entkonkretisierung der NS-Herrschaft in der Ära Kohl.* Die Neue Wache – Das Denkmal für die ermordeten Juden Europas – Das Haus der Geschichte der Bundesrepublik Deutschland. Mit einem Vorw. von Joachim Perels. Hannover: Offizin, 1998. 155 pp., illus. (Diskussionsbeiträge des Inst. für Polit. Wiss. der Univ. Hannover, Bd. 24.)

36560. MONTEATH, PETER: *Erinnerung an Holocaust und Literaturpolitik in der DDR: Der Fall Rolf Weinstock.* [In]: Jahrbuch für Antisemitismusforschung 8, Frankfurt; New York, 1998. Pp. 288–306, notes. [On the fate of a Jewish Auschwitz survivor's recollections, written in 1945, publ. in 1950 in the GDR and immediately taken off the market and suppressed; also on the GDR's policy of indifference in the post-war era to the fate of the Jews under the Nazis.]

36561. MOYSICH, JÜRGEN/HEYL, MATTHIAS, eds.: *Der Holocaust – ein Thema für Kindergarten und Grundschule?* Hamburg: Krämer, 1998. 324 pp., footnotes. [Cont. 24 contribs. arranged under the sections: Grundsatzartikel (23–160). Erfahrungsberichte aus der pädagogischen Sicht (161–324).]

36562. *Never again: the Holocaust's challenge for educators.* Ed. by Helmut Schreier and Matthias Heyl. Hamburg: Krämer, 1997. 214 pp., illus., notes. [For previous publ. in German of some of these essays see No. 33134/YB XLI. Incl. the first Engl. transl. of Theodor Adorno's 1966 essay: Education after Auschwitz.]

36563. NORTH-RHINE WESTPHALIA. *Forschen – Lernen – Gedenken.* Bildungsangebote für Jugendliche und Erwachsene in den Gedenkstätten für die Opfer des Nationalsozialismus in Nordrhein-Westfalen. Düsseldorf: [no publ. given], 1998. 124 pp., illus. [Incl.: Grußwort (Gabriele Behler, 3–4). Vorwort (Angela Genger, 5–6). Entwicklungen und Veränderungen in der pädagogischen Arbeit der Gedenkstätten in Nordrhein-Westfalen (Angela Genger/ Kerstin Griese, 7–18). Contribs. on the institutions in Gelsenkirchen, Cologne, Dortmund, Wewelsburg, Bonn, Krefeld, Siegen, Wuppertal, Düsseldorf, Essen, Münster. Also on youth exchange projects.]

——— OSNABRÜCK. FELIX-NUSSBAUM-MUSEUM: *Triumph des Todes?* Museumsbau von Daniel Libeskind gilt Felix Nussbaum. [See No. 36913.]

36564. Ossenberg, Ursula: *Sich von Auschwitz ein Bild machen? Kunst und Holocaust.* Ein Beitrag für die pädagogische Arbeit. Frankfurt am Main: Fritz Bauer Institut, 1998. 84 pp., illus. (Pädagogische Materialien, Nr. 4.)

36565. RAVENSBRÜCK. Eschebach, Insa: *Elemente einer nationalen und religiösen Formensprache im Gedenken.* Religionswissenschaftliche Überlegungen zu den Gedenkräumen im "Zellenbau" der Gedenkstätte Ravensbrück. [In]: Zeitschrift für Religions- und Geistesgeschichte, Jg. 50, H. 4, Leiden, 1998. Pp. 339–355, footnotes.

36566. RHINELAND. Schrader, Ulrike: *". . . wie ein Mann, der gräbt." Erinnerungszeichen für die vertriebenen und ermordeten Juden im Bergischen Land.* [In]: Romerike Berge, Jg. 48, H. 2, Burg an der Wupper 1998. Pp. 12–27, illus., notes. [On memorials and their inscriptions.]

36567. *Sachor.* Zeitschrift für Antisemitismusforschung, jüdische Geschichte und Gegenwart. Bd. 8 (1998) [with the issue title] *Alltags-und Lokalgeschichte: Ein geschärfter Blick?* Hrsg. von der Stud. Arbeitsgemeinschaft für Antisemitismusforschung (StAGA) e.V. Verantw. Redakteure: Heike Catrin Bala und Andrea Löw. Essen: Klartext, 1998. 1 issue. [Incl. (titles partly abbr.): Erkenntnisgewinn durch Regional-, Lokal- und Alltagsgeschichte? (Mark Stagge, 10–23). Ausgestellte Geschichte. Die Alte Synagoge und das Jüdische Museum Westfalen im Vergleich (Jens Brockschmidt/Andrea Löw, 24–40). Der Novemberpogrom in der Lokalgeschichte (Oliver Willnow, 41–65). Befreit, verschwunden und vergessen? "Displaced Persons" im Ruhrgebiet nach 1945 (Dirk Walter, 66–75). Incl. also bibl. notes and reviews on the topic and an article on the Berlin Holocaust memorial (Ralf Molkenthin, 103–109). One further essay is listed according to subject.]

36568. Shapira, Anita: *The Holocaust: private memories, public memory.* [In]: Jewish Social Studies, Vol. 4, No. 2, Bloomington, IN, Winter 1998. Pp. 40–58, notes.

36569. VIENNA. Jüdisches Museum der Stadt Wien: *Wiener Jahrbuch für jüdische Geschichte, Kultur & Museumswesen.* Bd. 3, 1997/1998 [with the issue title] *Über Erinnerung.* [Red.: Hannes Sulzenbacher]. Hrsg. vom Jüdischen Museum der Stadt Wien. Wien: Brandstätter, 1998. 159 pp., illus. [Incl. 11 contribs. dealing with exhibitions and memorials related to Jewish themes and concentration camps by Felicitas Heimann-Jelinek, Eva Grabherr, Vera Bendt, Viktoria Schmidt-Linsenhoff, James E. Young, Detlef Hoffmann, Isolde Charim, Hannes Sulzenbacher.]

V. JUDAISM

A. Jewish Learning and Scholars

36570. Abrams, Daniel: *Sexual symbolism and merkavah speculation in medieval Germany: a study of the Sod ha-egoz texts.* Tübingen: Mohr Siebeck, 1997. XIV, 146 pp., illus., facsims. of plates of Hebrew text, tabs., footnotes, bibl. (105–120). (Texts and studies in medieval and early modern Judaism, Vol. 13.) [Incl. Eleazar of Worms, and other German rabbis.]

36571. BAECK, LEO. Wallas, Armin A.: *Drei Briefe von Leo Baeck an Paul Graf Thun-Hohenstein.* [In]: Jüdischer Almanach 1999 des Leo Baeck Instituts, Frankfurt am Main, 1998. Pp. 9–23, notes. [Incl. letters written 1924 and 1950.]

36572. BARKAI, RON: *A history of Jewish gynaecological texts in the Middle Ages.* Leiden: Brill, 1998. X, 241 pp. (Brill's series in Jewish studies, Vol. 20.)

36573. Brämer, Andreas: *Qol qore – David Heymann Joels hebräischer Aufruf zu einer Rabbinerversammlung 1846. Ein Quellenbeitrag zur Frühgeschichte des Konservativen Judentums.* [In]: Frankfurter Judaistische Beiträge, 25, Frankfurt am Main, Dez. 1998. Pp. 121–146, footnotes. [Incl. the text of the 'appeal' in Hebrew and transl. into German.]

36574. BREUER, ISAAC. BREUER, SHLOMO: *Dr. Isaac Breuer, portrait of a "Talmud Jew"*. [In]: Ha-Ma'an, Vol. 37, No. 1, Jerusalem, Sept.-Oct. 1996. Pp. 55–57. [In Hebrew, title transl.] [A speech made by his grandson in Jerusalem on the 50th anniversary of his death.]

36575. BREUER, ISAAC. BREUER, MORDECHAI (BEN SHIMSHON): *The people of the Torah or the people of God*. [In]: Ha-Ma'yan, Vol. 37, No. 3, Jerusalem, April 1997. Pp. 33–44. [In Hebrew, title transl.] [On the ideas of R. Isaac Breuer.]

——— BUBER, MARTIN. CRESTI, SILVIA: *Aporien der jüdischen Identität. Literatur und Judentum in der Zeitschrift 'Der Jude' von Martin Buber*. [See in No. 35925.]

36576. BUBER, MARTIN. EDEN, YOHAI: *Truth without method: studies in the Jewish philosophy of Martin Buber*. [In]: Akdamot, No. 2, Jerusalem, Feb. 1997. Pp. 33–50. [In Hebrew, title transl.]

36577. BUBER, MARTIN. LUZ, EHUD: *Historio-collective memory in the philosophy of Martin Buber*. [In]: Eshel Beer-Sheva, Vol. 4, Beer Sheva, 1996. Pp. 366–378. [In Hebrew, title transl.]

36578. CARMILLY-WEINBERGER, MOSHE: *Wolf Jonas Eybeschütz: an "enlightened" Sabbatean in Transylvania*. [In]: Studia Judaica, Jg. 6, Cluj, 1997. Pp. 7–26.

36579. ELIAV, MORDECHAI/HILDESHEIMER, ESRIEL: *The Rabbinical Seminary in Berlin 1873–1938: the background to its establishment and its students throughout the years*. Jerusalem: Leo Baeck Institute, 1996. 125 pp. [In Hebrew, title transl.]

365780. GEIGER, ABRAHAM. HESCHEL, SUSANNAH: *Abraham Geiger and the Jewish Jesus*. Chicago: Univ. of Chicago Press, 1998. XII, 317 pp., illus., notes (243–300).

36581. HESCHEL, ABRAHAM JOSHUA. *Between God and man: an interpretation of Judaism from the writings of Abraham J. Heschel*. Selected, ed., and introd. by Fritz A. Rothschild. With a new foreword by David Hartman. New York: Free Press, 1997. 298 pp. [First publ. in 1959.]

36582. HESCHEL, ABRAHAM JOSHUA. *On the 25th anniversary of his death*. With contribs. by Susannah Heschel and others. [In]: Tikkun, Vol. 13, No. 1, Oakland, CA, Jan./Feb. 1998. Pp. 33–46, illus., ports.

36583. HESCHEL, ABRAHAM JOSHUA. KAPLAN, EDWARD K./DRESNER, SAMUEL H.: *Abraham Joshua Heschel: a prophetic witness*. New Haven, CT: Yale Univ. Press, 1998. X, 402 pp., illus., ports., notes, bibl. [First vol. of a comprehensive biography, dealing with H.'s early years until his arrival in the US in 1940.] [Cf.: The contradictions of Abraham Joshua Heschel (Jon D. Levenson) [in]: Commentary, Vol. 106, No. 1, New York, July 1998. Pp. 34–38.]

36584. HESCHEL, ABRAHAM JOSHUA. KAPLAN, EDWARD/DRESNER, SAMUEL H.: *Heschel in Vilna*. [In]: Judaism, Vol. 47, No. 3, New York, Summer 1998. Pp. 278–295, notes.

36585. HESCHEL, ABRAHAM JOSHUA. WOLF, ARNOLD JACOB: *Abraham Joshua Heschel after twenty-five years*. [In]: Judaism, Vol. 47, No. 1, New York, Winter 1998. Pp. 108–114, notes. [On the 25th anniversary of Heschel's death.]

36586. HIRSCH, SAMSON RAPHAEL. FRISCH, AMOS: *The approach of Rabbi S.R. Hirsch to the sins of the Patriarchs according to his commentary on the Book of Genesis*. [In]: Ahrend, Moshe/Feuerstein, Shmuel, eds.: Biblical studies and teachings. [In Hebrew]. Ramat-Gan: Bar-Ilan Univ., 1997. Pp. 181–197. [In Hebrew.]

36587. HIRSCH, SAMSON RAPHAEL. HABERMAN, JACOB: *Kaufmann Kohler and his teacher Samson Raphael Hirsch*. [In]: Leo Baeck Institute Year Book XLIII, London, 1998. Pp. 73–102, port., footnotes. [K.K., Fürth 1843 – New York 1926, rabbi, went to the US in 1869, president of Hebrew Union College, Cincinnati 1903–1921.]

36588. HIRSCH, SAMSON RAPHAEL. KAPLAN, LAWRENCE: *"Torah u-madda" in the thought of Rabbi Samson Raphael Hirsch*. [In]: BDD-Bekhol Derakhekha Daehu, No. 5, Ramat-Gan, Summer 1997. Pp. 5–31.

36589. HOFFMANN, DAVID ZEVI. SHAPIRA, MELEKH: *Letters and responsa by Rabbi David Zevi Hoffmann*. [In]: Ha-Ma'yan, Vol. 37, No. 4, Jerusalem, July 1997. Pp. 1–14. [In Hebrew, title transl.] [D.H., 1843 Hungary – 1921 Berlin, Judaist and Rector of the Berlin Rabbinerseminar.]

36590. HOROWITZ, SHABBETAI SHEFTEL. SACK, BRACHA: *On "the secret of cause and effect" in the writings of R. Shabbetai Sheftel Horowitz of Prague*. [In]: Mehkerei Yerushalayim be-Mahshevet Yisrael, No. 12, Jerusalem, 1996. Pp. 201–216. [In Hebrew, with English summary] [S.S. Horowitz, 1565–1619.]

36591. JUDAH BEN SAMUEL he-HASID. TA-SHMA, ISRAEL M.: *'Sodot ha-Tefilla' by R. Judah the Pious*. [In]: Tarbiz, Vol. 65, No. 1, Jerusalem, Sept.-Dec. 1995. Pp. 65–77. [In Hebrew, with English summary.] [J.b.S. of Regensburg, fl. 1200, founder of mysticism in Ashkenaz.]

36592. JUDAH BEN SAMUEL he-HASID. TA-SHMA, ISRAEL M.: *The pamphlet "Zekher assah le-nifla'otov" by Rabbi Judah he-Hasid*. [In]: Kobez al-Yad, No. 12, Jerusalem, 1994. Pp. 121–146. [In Hebrew, title transl.]

36593. KATZ, NAPHTALI BEN ISAAC. LIEBES, YEHUDA: *A profile of R. Naphtali Katz of Frankfurt and his attitude towards Shabbateanism*. [In]: Mehkerei Yerushalayim be-Mahshevet Yisrael, No. 12, Jerusalem, 1996. Pp. 293–305. [In Hebrew, with English summary.] [First publ. in Engl. 1995, see No. 33169/YB XLI.]

36594. MAIMON, SALOMON. WADE, MARA: *Enlightenment self-fashioning in the German vernacular: Salomon Maimon's autobiography*. [In]: Lessing Yearbook, Vol. XXIX, 1997. Detroit; Göttingen, 1998. Pp. 175–198, notes. [On Maimon's two-part autobiography 'Salomon Maimons Lebensgeschichte von ihm selbst erzählt'(1792–1793), which, for the first time in German, describes life in the East European shtetl.]

36595. MEIR BEN BARUCH of ROTHENBURG. GROSSMAN, AVRAHAM: *Meir ben Baruch of Rothenburg and Eretz-Israel*. [In]: Cathedra, No. 85, Jerusalem, July 1997. Pp. 63–84. [In Hebrew, with English summary.]

36596. MEIR BEN BARUCH of ROTHENBURG. LÜBKE, MIRJAM: *Die jüdisch-christlichen Rechtsbeziehungen im Spiegel der Responsen des R. Meir ben Baruch von Rothenburg*. Duisburg, [Univ. of Duisburg: Mag.-Arbeit], 1998. 89 pp., footnotes, bibl. [Available at the Bibliothek Germania Judaica, Cologne.]

36597. MENDELSSOHN, MOSES. BENJAMIN, LYA: *Moses Mendelssohn in the Jewish Press of Romania*. Brief analytical survey. [In]: Studia Judaica, Vol. 6, Cluj, 1997. Pp. 27–36.

36598   MENDELSSOHN, MOSES. BRODY, MYLES: *Irving Greenberg: Moses Mendelssohn's unacknowledged disciple*. [In]: Jewish Spectator, Vol. 62, No. 4, Calabasas, CA, Spring 1998. Pp. 21–27. [Discusses Mendelssohn's philosophy and compares him with the contemporary American-Jewish theologian Greenberg.]

36599   MENDELSSOHN, MOSES. GOETSCHEL, WILLI: *Neue Literatur zu Moses Mendelssohn*. [In]: Lessing Yearbook, Vol. XXIX, 1997. Detroit; Göttingen, 1998. Pp. 199–209, notes. [Review essay dealing with numerous recent publications on M. M.]

36600   MENDELSSOHN, MOSES: *Moses Mendelssohn: philosophical writings*. Ed. and transl. by Daniel O. Dahlstrom. Cambridge; New York: Cambridge Univ. Press, 1997. XXXIX, 321 pp. (Cambridge texts in the history of philosophy.)

36601   MENDELSSOHN, MOSES. *Moses Mendelssohn. Dokumente II. Die frühen Mendelssohn-Biographien*. Bearb. von Michael Albrecht. Mit Isaak Euchels Mendelssohn-Biographie. Übersetzt und mit einer Nachschrift von Reuven Michael. Stuttgart-Bad Cannstadt: Fromann/ Holzboog, 1998. XXVI, 444 pp., footnotes, index (437–444). (Gesammelte Schriften, Jubiläumsausgabe, Bd. 23.) [Cont.: Einleitung (Michael Albrecht, IX-XXVI). 44 biographies resp. biogr. articles publ. between 1759 and 1827.]

36602.   ROSENZWEIG, FRANZ. AMIR, YEHOYADA: *Man's part of the truth; the concept of truth in 'The Star of Redemption'*. [In]: Mehkerei Yerushalayim be-Mahshevet Yisrael, No. 13, Jerusalem, 1996. Pp. 557–586. This issue of the journal = Rivkah Shatz-Uffenheimer Memorial Volume, Vol. II. [In Hebrew, with English summary.]

36603   ROSENZWEIG, FRANZ. BIENENSTOCK, MYRIAM: *Rosenzweig, Franz (1886–1929)*. [In]: Routledge Encyclopedia of Philosophy, London; New York: Routledge, 1998. Pp. 357–363.

36604.   ROSENZWEIG, FRANZ. HORWITZ, RIVKA: *Hamann and Rosenzweig on language – the revival of myth*. [In]: Daat, No. 38, Ramat-Gan, 1997. Pp. V-XXVIII.

36605   ROSENZWEIG, FRANZ. *Franz Rosenzweig's "New thinking"*. Ed. and transl. by Alan Udoff and Barbara E. Galli. Syracuse, NY: Syracuse Univ. Press, 1998. 128 pp., notes. (Library of Jewish philosophy.) [Incl. four reviews of 'The star of redemption', and R.'s 1917 letter to Rudolf Ehrenberg.]

36606.   ROSENZWEIG, FRANZ: *God, man, and the world: lectures and essays*. Ed. and transl. by Barbara E. Galli. Introd. by Michael Oppenheim. Syracuse, NY: Syracuse Univ. Press, 1998. XXXIV, 152 pp. (Library of Jewish philosophy.)

36607.   ROSENZWEIG, FRANZ. WIEHL, REINER: *Zeit und Ewigkeit in Franz Rosenzweigs 'Stern der Erlösung'*. [In]: Trumah 7, Berlin, 1998. Pp. 135–146, footnotes.

36608.   ROTHSCHILD, FRITZ A., ed.: *Christentum aus jüdischer Sicht*. Fünf jüdische Denker des 20. Jahrhunderts über das Christentum und sein Verhältnis zum Judentum. [Transl. by Ursula Rudnick and Ruth Olmesdahl.] Berlin: Inst. Kirche und Judentum, 1998. 380 pp., illus. (Veröff. aus dem Inst. Kirche u. Judentum, Bd. 25.) [On Leo Baeck, Martin Buber, Franz Rosenzweig, Will Herberg and Abraham J. Heschel. Incl. introductory essays by J. Louis Martyn, Ekkehard Stegemann, Bernhard Casper, Bernhard W. Anderson and John C. Merkle. American orig. edn. publ. in 1990 (paperback edn. in 1996); see No. 27514/YB XXXVI.]

36609.   SAMSON HA-NAKDAN. BEN-MENAHEM, DAVID: *"The Shimshoni"* – *Rabbi Samson ha-Nakdan and his book*. [In]: Hagigei Giv'ah, No. 4, Givat Washington, 1996, Pp. 57–78. [In Hebrew, title transl.]

36610.   SCHOLEM, GERSHOM. BROCKE, MICHAEL: *Gershom Scholem: Wissenschaft des Judentums zwischen Berlin und Jerusalem*. [In]: Freiburger Rundbrief, N.F., Jg. 5, H. 3, Freiburg, 1998. Pp. 178–186, footnotes.

36611.   SCHOLEM, GERSHOM. IDEL, MOSHE: *Subversive catalysts: gnosticism and messianism in Gershom Scholem's view of Jewish mysticism*. [In]: Zmanim, No. 61, Tel-Aviv, Winter 1998. Pp. 64–76. [In Hebrew.] [First publ. 1995.]

36612.   SCHOLEM, GERSHOM. SCHMIDT, CHRISTOPH: *Der häretische Imperativ*. Gershom Scholems Kabbala als politische Theologie? [In]: Zeitschrift für Religions- und Geistesgeschichte, Jg. 50, H. 1, Leiden, 1998. Pp. 61–83, footnotes. [Also in this issue: Soziologische Überlegungen zur jüdischen Mystik im Werk von Gershom Scholem (Johannes Twardella, 84–90).]

36613.   SCHOLEM, GERSHOM. *On the possibility of Jewish mysticism in our time and other essays*. Ed. and selected, with an introd. by Avraham Shapira. Transl. by Jonathan Chipman. Philadelphia: Jewish Publication Society, 1997. XIX, 244 pp. [Collection of 23 shorter pieces, most of them in English for the first time; orig. publ. between 1926 and 1977.]

36614. SCHOLEM, GERSHOM. SHEDLETZKY, ITTA: *In search of Judaism lost.* [In]: Zmanim, No. 61, Tel-Aviv, Winter 1998. Pp. 78–87. [In Hebrew.] [On Scholem's personality.]

36615. SCHOLEM, GERSHOM. TSUR, MUKY: *With Gershom Scholem.* [In]: Zmanim, No. 61, Tel-Aviv, Winter 1998. Pp. 88–96. [In Hebrew.] [A personal view of Scholem.]

36616. SCHWEID, ELIEZER: *Demythologisation and remythologisation of Judaism (Mythos and Judaism in the philosophies of Kaufman, Buber and Baeck).* [In]: Eshel Beer-Sheva, Vol. 4, Beer Sheva, 1996. Pp. 342–365. [In Hebrew, title transl.]

36617. *Tradition renewed: a history of the Jewish Theological Seminary.* Ed. by Jack Wertheimer. New York: The Jewish Theological Seminary of America, 1997. 2 vols., XXV, 854 pp.; 872 pp. [Incl. chaps.: Wissenschaft des Judentums comes to America: a chapter in immigration history, 1890–1935 (Robert Liberles, 327–352 pp., illus., notes). The Seminary during the Holocaust years (Marsha L. Rozenblit, 271–308, notes).]

36618. WASSERMANN, HENRY: *"Der Habilitand hat sich stets durchaus unjüdisch bescheiden gehabt . . .". Zur Geschichte der Judaistik an der Leipziger Universität.* Leipzig: Simon-Dubnow-Institut für jüd. Gesch. und Kultur e.V., 1998. 44 pp., footnotes, doc. [Incl.: Vorwort (Stefi Jersch-Wenzel, 3–4). Deals with Lazar Gulkowitsch (1898 Zirin (Russia) – 1941 Tartu (Dorpat, Estonia), who taught at Leipzig University 1924 – 1933.] [Cf.: Besprechung (Judith Kashti) [in]: 'MB', Jg. 67, Nr. 44, Tel Aviv, März-April 1999, p. 11.]

36619. WEINBERG, JECHIEL JACOB. WEINGORT, AVRAHAM: *A study on the thought of Rabbi J.J. Weinberg.* [In]: Ha-Ma'yan, Vol. 37, No. 3, Jerusalem, April 1997. Pp. 24–32. [In Hebrew, title transl.] [J.J.W., 1884 Lithuania – 1966 Lausanne, rabbi, talmudist, Rector of the Berlin Rabbinerseminar.]

36620. ZUNZ, LEOPOLD. NIEHOFF, MAREN R.: *Zunz's concept of Haggadah as an expression of Jewish spirituality.* [In]: Leo Baeck Institute Year Book XLIII, London, 1998. Pp. 3–24, footnotes.

36621. ZUNZ, LEOPOLD. TRAUTMANN-WALLER, CÉLINE: *Philologie allemande et tradition juive. Le parcours intellectuel de Leopold Zunz.* Paris: le Cerf, 1998. 1 vol. [Cf.: Revue (Norbert Waszek) [in]: Les cahiers du judaisme, No. 3, automne 1998, pp. 135–137.]

B. Perception and Identity

——— CRESTI, SILVIA: *Aporien der jüdischen Identität. Literatur und Judentum in der Zeitschrift 'Der Jude' von Martin Buber.* [See in No. 35925.]

36622. DISCHEREIT, ESTHER: *Übungen, jüdisch zu sein.* Frankfurt am Main: Suhrkamp, 1998. 215 pp., frontis. (edition suhrkamp 2067.) [A collection of essays on various aspects of being Jewish in Germany after 1945. Incl.: Gespräch mit Wolfgang Benz (119–214).]

36623. FRAIMAN, SARAH: *Jüdische Identität und Identitätskrise. Bewußtes und Unbewußtes bei Lion Feuchtwanger und Jakob Wassermann.* [In]: Aschkenas, Jg. 8, 1998, H. 2, Wien, 1999. Pp. 511–524, footnotes.

36624. GEBHARDT, MIRIAM: *"Vom Ghetto zur Villa" – familiale Erinnerungsstrategien im emanzipierten Judentum.* [In]: Clemens Wischermann, ed.: Die Legitimität der Erinnerung und die Geschichtswissenschaft. Stuttgart: Steiner, 1996. Pp. 175–188. [On concepts of identity as depicted in Jewish autobiographical texts 1871–1933.]

36625. GILMAN, SANDER L./JÜTTE, ROBERT/KOHLBAUER-FRITZ, GABRIELE, eds.: *"Der schejne Jid". Das Bild des "jüdischen Körpers" in Mythos und Ritual.* Wien: Picus, 1998. 163 pp., illus., notes, index. [Publ. on the occasion of an exhibition with the same title, held at the Vienna Jewish Museum Sept. 16, 1998 – Jan. 24, 1999. Incl. 11 essays on racism, Jewish hygiene, images and perceptions of Jews and non-Jews by Susanne Belovari, Christina von Braun, John M.

Efron, Sander L. Gilman, Susannah Heschel, Robert Jütte, Gabriele Kohlbauer-Fritz, Sybilla Nikolow, Rhoda Rosen, Thomas Schlich and Joachim Schlör.]

36626. GILMAN, SANDER L.: *Die schlauen Juden. Über ein dummes Vorurteil*. Aus dem Amerikanischen von Brigitte Stein. Hildesheim: Claassen, 1998. 311 pp., notes. [For orig. edn. publ. 1996, and annot. see No. 34306/YB XLII.]

36627. GOMBRICH, ERNST H.: *Jüdische Identität und jüdisches Schicksal*. Eine Diskussionsbemerkung. Mit einer Einleitung von Emil Brix und einer Diskussionsdokumentation von Frederick Baker. Hrsg. von Emil Brix und Frederick Baker. Wien: Passagen, 1997. 78 pp., notes, bibl. Deutsche Erstausg. (Passagen forum.) [Incl. Einleitung (Emil Brix, 11–32). Two essays by Ernst H. Gombrich (transl. by Dorothea McEwan): Jüdische Identität und jüdisches Schicksal. Zum Wiener Kunstleben um 1900 (33–54). Betrachtungen zur Tragödie des Judentums (55–64). Diskussionsdokumentation (65–72). G.'s essays were first publ. in English by Österreichisches Kulturinstitut, London (Occasions, Vol. 1).]

36628. GRÖZINGER, KARL E., ed.: *Sprache und Identität im Judentum*. Wiesbaden: Harrassowitz, 1998. 265 pp., footnotes, index. (Jüdische Kultur, Bd. 4.) [Incl.: Zur Einführung (ed., 7–14). Sprache, Sprechen und Übersetzen: Überlegungen zu Bertha Pappenheim und ihrem Erzählungsband 'Kämpfe' (Inge Stephan, 29–42; deals also with Pappenheim as Josef Breuer's and Sigmund Freud's patient Anna O.). Sprache und Identität – Das Hebräische und die Juden (ed., 75–90). "... lügt auch bei wörtlichen Zitaten". Anmerkungen zur Zerstörung jüdischer Sprach-Identität (Manfred Voigts, 151–172; on the impact of Hans Blüher and other antisemites on German-Jewish intellectuals such as Max Brod, Fritz Mauthner, Moritz Goldstein, Lion Feuchtwanger a.o.). Further selected essays are listed according to subject.]

36629. HÖPFNER, CHRISTIAN: *Heinrich Heines Suche nach Identität*. Stuttgart: Metzler, 1997. 319 pp., footnotes, bibl. (278–314), index. (Heine-Studien.)

36630. KAUFFMANN, KAI: *Rudolf Borchardts und Walter Benjamins Berliner Kindheiten um 1900*. [In]: Zeitschrift für Germanistik, N.F., Bd. VIII, H. 1, Bern; New York, 1998. Pp. 374–386, footnotes.

36631. KONZETT, MATTHIAS: *The politics of recognition in contemporary Austrian Jewish literature*. [In]: Monatshefte für deutschen Unterricht, deutsche Sprache und Literatur, Vol. 90, No. 1, Madison, WI, Spring 1998. Pp. 71–88. [Deals with national or ethnic categorisations and questions of Jewish identity in a play by Elfriede Jelinek, a novel by Robert Schindel and a story by Doron Rabinovici.]

36632. KURZ, GERHARD: *Hirsch-Hyazinth. Zu einer Selbstdeutungsfigur Heines*. [In]: Aschkenas, Jg. 8, 1998, H. 2, Wien, 1999. Pp. 501–524.

36633. PICKUS, KEITH H.: *Images of God and country: Jewish national and religious identities in Wilhelmine Germany*. [In]: Aschkenas, Jg. 8, 1998, H. 2, Wien, 1999. Pp. 425–438, footnotes.

36634. REICHMANN, EVA, ed.: *Habsburger Aporien? Geisteshaltungen und Lebenskonzepte in der multinationalen Literatur der Habsburger Monarchie*. Bielefeld: Aisthesis, 1998. 195 pp., notes. [Selected essays: Aufzeichnungen aus der Welt des Extraterritorialen. Lebensflüchtlinge und Vorstadt-Ahasvers. Albert Ehrensteins (un)sentimentale Reise in die Untergründe Kakaniens (Armin A. Wallas, 77–112). "Der Segen des ewigen Juden". Zur 'jüdischen Identität' Joseph Roths (Andreas Herzog, 113–132). "Kannst Du Dir etwas Verwandteres denken als die Begriffe: Heimat und Kuchengeruch?". Heimatlosigkeit als Heimat im Werk Joseph Roths (Eva Reichmann, 133–146). Max Brods deutsch-jüdischer Nachsommer von 1932: "Die Frau, die nicht enttäuscht" (Werner Kummer, 163–174).]

——— RHEINZ, HANNA: *Die jüdische Frau. Auf der Suche nach einer modernen Identität*. [See No. 36531.]

36635. SCHMID, HANS-DIETER: *Theodor Lessing und die Israelitische Gartenbauschule Ahlem – eine Legende*. [In]: Hannoversche Geschichtsblätter, Bd. 52, Hannover, 1998. Pp. 289–295, illus., footnotes. [Deals with the false assertion made by L. in his autobiography, that he had been educated at Ahlem.]

36636. SONINO, CLAUDIA: *Der Jude Gundolf und der "Fall" Heine*. [In]: Menora 1997, Bodenheim, 1997. Pp. 231–254, notes. [On Friedrich Gundolf's ambivalent attitude towards Heinrich Heine.]

36637. STUHLDREIER-MARAIS, ANTOINETTE C.: *Posttraditionale Identitäten deutscher Juden und Jüdinnen im Hinterhaus und in der Bel Étage an der Wende vom 19. zum 20. Jahrhundert. Sozialstrukturelle Kontextualisierungsansätze im Vergleich*. [In]: "... was also ist der Mensch ....": Geschichte und Anthropologie im Gespräch. Festgabe für Anton H. Viktor zum 60. Geburtstag. Hrsg.: Gesine Winterhalter [et al.]. Berlin: Monopteros-Verl., 1998. Pp. 43–54, footnotes.

——— *Theodor Lessing und seine Zeitgenossen – eine Würdigung zum 65. Todestag*. [See No. 36887.]

——— ZEHENDREITER, FERDINAND: *Überlegungen zum Judentum Arnold Schönbergs aus der Perspektive einer Theorie des künstlerischen Handelns*. [See No. 36941.]

C. Jewish Life and Organisations. Genealogy

36638. *Avotaynu*. The International Review of Jewish Genealogy. Vol. XIV, Nos. 1–4. Teaneck, NJ, 1998. 4 issues. [Incl. contribs. on German-Jewish families and their genealogical source material. No. 1 incl.: Literary sources for genealogical research on Jews with German roots (Angelika G. Ellmann-Krüger with Edward David Luft, 31–35, bibl.). No. 3 incl.: Jewish family name adoption in Mecklenburg (Anne Feder Lee/Jacqueline London, 35–39; with list of names). No. 4 incl.: Yad Vashem database will document all Jews caught up in the Holocaust (Sallyann Amdur Sack, 4–5). Further contribs. are listed according to subject.]

36639. *Babylon*. Beiträge zur jüdischen Gegenwart. H. 18, Frankfurt am Main, Okt. 1998. 1 issue. [Incl.: Editorial (Micha Brumlik, Dan Diner, Gertrud Koch, Cilly Kugelmann, Martin Löw-Beer, 7–8). This issue incl. essays dealing with (a.o.) Jewish fundamentalism in the 19th and 20th cent. and Orthodoxy; also an interview with the Lubavitch rabbi Zalman Gurevitch, at present working in Frankfurt, and also review essays.]

36640. BERGBAUER, KNUT: *Der "Schwarze Haufen": eine deutsch-jüdische Jugendgruppe zwischen pädagogischem Anspruch und politischer Realität*. Köln: Fachhochschule, Dipl.-Arbeit, 1998. 92 pp. [Available at the Bibliothek Germania Judaica, Cologne.]

36641. BREUER, MORDECHAI: *On the uniqueness of the prayer rituals in Ashkenaz*. [In]: Dukhan, No. 14, Jerusalem, Dec. 1995. Pp. 43–53. [In Hebrew, title transl.]

36642. BRODER, HENRYK M.: *Die jiddische Mamme. Angriff auf einen Mythos*. [In]: Kursbuch 132, [with the title] *Unsere Mütter*, Berlin, Juni 1998. Pp. 128–135.

36643. CONRAD, ANNE [et al.], eds.: *Das Volk im Visier der Aufklärung. Studien zur Popularisierung der Aufklärung im späten 18. Jahrhundert*. Hamburg: Lit, 1998. 266 pp. (Veröffentlichungen des Hamburger Arbeitskreises für Regionalgeschichte HAR, Bd. 1.) [Incl.: Jüdische Armenfürsorge und obrigkeitliche Armenpolitik (Arno Herzig, 99–113). Tod und Judentum in der Zeit der Aufklärung am Beispiel des jüdischen Begräbniswesens in Altona (Gaby Zürn, 215–227).]

36644. DAXELMÜLLER, CHRISTOPH: *Der jüdische Tod. Von Legenden, Morden, Bräuchen, Scheintoten und Tänzen, aus denen in Auschwitz Wirklichkeit wurde*. [In]: Christoph Daxelmüller, ed.: Tod und Gesellschaft – Tod im Wandel. Begleitband zur Ausst. im Diözesanmuseum Obermünster Regensburg. Regensburg, 1996. (Kunstsammlungen des Bistums Regensburg, Diözesanmuseum Regensburg; Kataloge und Schriften, Bd. 18.). Pp. 81–87.

36645. DORON, YEHOYAKIM: *The Jewish youth movements in Germany 1909–1939*. Jerusalem: Rubin Mass, 1996. 340 pp. [In Hebrew]

36646. ESHKOLOT, ZEEV, ed.: *The Eskeles genealogy*. Haifa: [no publ.], 1995. 272 pp. [Pp. 9–30 and 249–264 contain an essay by Ruth Eitan, in English and in Hebrew – "Historical background to the history of the Jews of Germany". The rest of the book contains biographies, genealogical charts, photographs of graves, and addresses of family members.]

36647. FRIEDLER, ERIC: *Makkabi chai – Makkabi lebt. Die jüdische Sportbewegung in Deutschland 1898–1998*. Unter Mitarbeit von Barbara Siebert. Mit 138 Abbildungen in duotone. Wien: Brandstätter, 1998. 111 pp., illus., notes, index.

36648. GLASENAPP, GABRIELE VON/VÖLPEL, ANNEGRET: *Jüdische Kinder-und Jugendbuchverlage im 19. und 20. Jahrhundert*. Ein Überblick. [In]: Buchhandelsgeschichte, [Beilage zum] Börsenblatt für den Deutschen Buchhandel, Jg. 164, Nr. 2, Frankfurt am Main, 16. Juni 1998. Pp. B 62–B 73, notes, bibl.

36649. GUENZBURG FAMILY. GUENZBURG, SIGMAR (SIMCHA): *The history of the Guenzburg family during ca. 450 years*. [Ma'ayan Zvi: Privately printed], 1996. 66 pp. [In Hebrew, title transl.]

36650. GUGGENHEIM FAMILY. HEINZELMANN, JOSEF: *Die Herkunft der Guggenheim*. [In]: Archiv für Familiengeschichtsforschung, Jg. 1, H. 2, Limburg, 1997. Pp. 113–118, facsims., footnotes.

36651. HEINRICH, GERDA: *Akkulturation und Reform. Die Debatte um die frühe Beerdigung der Juden zwischen 1785–1800*. [In]: Zeitschrift für Religions- und Geistesgeschichte, Jg. 50, H. 2, Leiden, 1998. Pp. 137–155, footnotes. [Focuses on discussions in Prussia, esp. on Marcus Herz's 'Über die frühe Beerdigung der Juden. An die Herausgeber des hebräischen Sammlers' (1787) and Salomon Seligmann Pappenheimer's 'An die Barmherzigen zu Endor, oder über die zu früh scheinende Beerdigung der Juden' (1798).]

36652. HEINZELMANN, JOSEF: *Carl Zuckmayers Ahnen. Ein Beitrag zum 100. Geburtstag des Dichters*. [In]: Genealogisches Jahrbuch, Bd. 37/38, Neustadt an der Aisch, 1998. Pp. 201–243. [Incl. genealog. lists.]

36653. *Jüdisches Kinderleben im Spiegel jüdischer Kinderbücher*. Eine Ausstellung des Universitätsbibliothek Oldenburg mit dem Kindheitsmuseum Marburg. Hrsg. von Helge-Ulrike Hyams [et al.]. Oldenburg: BIS, 1998. 475 pp., illus., facsims., notes, indexes (persons, titles, 451–466). [Incl. (titles partly abbr.): Einleitung (Helge-Ulrike Hyams, et. al., 13–14). Jüdische Kindheit in Deutschland (Helge-Ulrike Hyams, 17–28). Jüdische Kindheit und die jüdischen Feste (Jürgen Scheunemann, 29–42). Zum jüdischen Schulwesen von der Aufklärung bis zur Zerstörung (Friedrich Wißmann/Klaus Klattenhoff, 43–58). Haskalah und Philanthropismus: Begegnung und Austausch (Hanno Schmitt, 59–66). Jüdische Kindheit in Deutschland am Ende des 19. und Anfang des 20. Jahrhunderts (Ursula Blömer/Detlef Garz, 67–80). Jüdische Jugendschriften im Umfeld der deutschen Jugendbewegung vor und nach dem ersten Weltkrieg: Zwischen Diskriminierung und Identitätssuche (Gottfried Mergner, 81–100). Das Leben jüdischer Kinder im "Dritten Reich" bis 1939 (Werner Fölling, 101–108). Das jüdische Kinder- und Landschulheim Caputh. Wirkungen und Nachwirkungen (Ilse Meseberg-Haubold, 109–114). Jüdische Kindheit im Schatten des Holocaust (Michael Fritsche/Ulrike Peper, 115–124). Israel – Land der Jugend: "Wir kehren zurück und bauen auf" (Wolfgang Grieb, 125–136). Jüdische Kindheit im Nationalsozialismus (Klaus Klattenhoff/Friedrich Wißmann, 137–160). Die Haggadah des Kindes (Helge-Ulrike Hyams, 161–166). Jüdische Grundschulbücher aus drei Jahrhunderten (Renate Hinz/Wilhelm Topsch, 167–192). Jüdische Märchen als Kinderliteratur in Deutschland bis 1938 (Reinhard Pirschel, 193–204). Deutsch-jüdische Mädchenliteratur zwischen Kulturwahrung und Emanzipation (Annegret Völpel, 205–214). Das Bild des Arabers in deutsch-zionistischen Jugendbüchern zur Zeit der dritten Alija (Andreas Wirwalski, 215–224). Moses, das göttliche Kind (Waltraud Strickhausen, 225–234). Jiddische Kinderliteratur (Karina Kranhold, 235–244). Die Bedeutung der hebräischen Sprache für das jüdische Kind (Reinhard Heitzenröder/Helge-Ulrike Hyams, 245–252). Die Prinzessin mit der Nas'. Wiedersehen mit einem verlorengeglaubten Kinderbuch (Laureen Nussbaum, 253–256). Die Pessach-Haggadah (Gesine Brakhage, 257–260). Die Sammlung Hyams (Helge-Ulrike Hyams, 261–266). Jüdische Kinder- und Jugendbuchverlage des späten 19. und frühen 20. Jahrhunderts (Gabriele von Glasenapp/Annegret Völpel, 267–282). Annotationen (286–450; partly illustr. annotations to the 416 books shown in 1998 in Oldenburg and thereafter in numerous other places.]

36654. NELKI, ERNA & WOLFGANG: *Nelki: the story of a German-Jewish family as recorded in 1997 from research material by Wolfgang Nelki*. London: Privately printed, 1997. 43 pp., illus., ports., facsims., map. [Available at the Wiener Library in London; deals with a German-Jewish family from Berlin who left Germany between 1933–34; some members settled in England.] [For orig. German publ. in 1991, see No. 28373/YB XXXVII.]

36655. SCHINDLER, THOMAS: *"Was Schandfleck war, ward unser Ehrenzeichen ..."*. Die jüdischen Studentenverbindungen und ihr Beitrag zur Entwicklung eines neuen Selbstbewußtseins deutscher Juden. [In]: "Der Burschen Herrlichkeit" – Geschichte und Gegenwart des studentischen Korporationswesens. Hrsg. von Harm-Hinrich Brandt und Matthias Stickler. Würzburg: Stadtarchiv Würzburg, 1998. (Historia Academia, Bd. 36; Veröff. des Stadtarchivs Würzburg, Bd. 8.)

36656. *Stammbaum*. The Journal of German-Jewish Genealogical Research. Issue 13 & 14. New York: Leo Baeck Institute, May & Dec. 1998. 32 & 36 pp. [Issue title of Issue 13: *Mostly Holocaust: Sources & resources*; a special feature prepared by Peter Landé (ed. by George Arnstein); cont. the chaps.: German Jews and the Holocaust – the 1939 Census. The German government's 'Gedenkbuch'. Memorial books for specific states and localities. Austrian victims – the mystery remains. Deportations from other countries. Concentration camps, killing centers & ghettoes. Explanatory notes for lists of German Jews. German Jews in Stutthof and other camps. Survivors of the Holocaust. Issue 14 cont. contribs. by George E. Arnstein, Carol Davidson Baird, Susan Fisher Boyer, Werner L. Frank, Rolf Hofmann, Peter W. Landé, Anne Feder Lee, Levy, Fred and Carol Kahn Strauss on the genealogy of German-speaking Jews, archival collections, cemeteries; also book reviews and search notices.]

36657. THIEBERGER, FRIEDRICH: *Jüdisches Fest, jüdischer Brauch*. Unter Mitwirkung von Else Rabin. Frankfurt am Main: Jüdischer Verl., 1997. 436 pp., illus. [Reprint of book, orig. publ. in 1937, first reprint in 1967.] [Cf.: Besprechung (J. Friedrich Battenberg) [in]: Archiv für hess. Geschichte und Altertumskunde, N.F., Bd. 56, Neustadt an der Aisch, 1998, pp. 483–484.]

D. Jewish Art and Music

——— *Architektur und Kunst*. [Section title (with contribs. by Salomon Korn, Annette Weber and Hannelore Künzl), see in No. 35999.]

——— *Benno Elkan. Ein jüdischer Künstler aus Dortmund*. [See No. 36813.]

36658. COHEN, RICHARD I.: *Jewish icons: art and society in modern Europe*. Berkeley: Univ. of California Press, 1998. XVIII, 358 pp., illus., ports., notes (261–318), bibl. (319–348) [Incl. Jewish art and depiction of Jews in Germany (particularly Frankfurt, Berlin) over three centuries. Also Jewish art in post-war museums and exhibitions.]

36659. KOGMAN-APPEL, KATRIN: *The Sephardic picture cycles and the rabbinic tradition: continuity and innovation in Jewish iconography*. [In]: Zeitschrift für Kunstgeschichte, München, 1997. Pp. 451–478, footnotes, illus. [Deals also with the relationship to Askenazic Jewish art.]

36660. LEWANDOWSKI, LOUIS. SCHLEIFER, ELIYAHU: *The music of Lewandowski in historical perspective*. [In]: Dukhan, No. 14, Jerusalem, Dec. 1995. Pp. 133–143. [In Hebrew, title transl.]

36661. OFFENBACH, ISAAC. Kaufmann, Jacobo: *Isaac Offenbach und sein Sohn Jacques oder "Es ist nicht aller Tage Purim".* Tübingen: Niemeyer, 1998. XII, 226 pp., frontis., illus., facsims., bibl. (Conditio Judaica, 21.) [Incl.: Zum Geleit (Hans Otto Horch, XI-XII; also on the author, b. 1939 in Buenos Aires, son of German-Jewish parents, music director, dramatist, author of opera libretti; lives in Jerusalem). Book incl.: Verzeichnis sämtlicher bekannter Werke Isaac Offenbachs (incl. synagogue music).] [I.O. (1779/81 – 1850), music teacher, cantor, composer, lived in Deutz and Cologne.]

36662. SULZER, SALOMON. Schleifer, Eliyahu: *The Cantor Salomon Sulzer and his influence from his own times until today.* [In]: Dukhan, No. 14, Jerusalem, Dec. 1995. Pp. 144–151. [In Hebrew, title transl.]

——— *Theodor Harburger. Die Inventarisierung jüdischer Kunst- und Kulturdenkmäler in Bayern.* [See No. 35964.]

——— Weber, Annette: *Jüdische Kultgegenstände aus westfälischen Gemeinden des 18. und 19. Jahrhunderts.* [See in No. 36081.]

——— Weyl, Robert/Weyl, Martine: *La fresque de la cour du bain des Juifs à Strasbourg.* [See No. 36089.]

VI. ZIONISM AND ISRAEL

36663. *Aus Politik und Zeitgeschichte.* Beilage zur Wochenzeitung Das Parlament. B 14/98, Bonn, 27. März 1998. 1 issue. [Incl.: Essays by Michael Wolffsohn, Moshe Zimmermann and Ilan Pappe on 50 years of Israel, Zionism and the Israeli-Palestinian conflict; also: Perspektiven der Holocaust-Rezeption in Israel und Deutschland (Moshe Zuckermann, 19–29).]

36664. Avineri, Shlomo: *Profile des Zionismus.* Die geistigen Ursprünge des Staates Israel. 17 Portraits. Aus dem Amerik. von Eileen Bayer [et al.]. Gütersloh: Gütersloher Verlagshaus, 1998. 264 pp. [Incl. Moses Hess, Theodor Herzl, Max Nordau.] [Cf.: Besprechung (David Krochmalnik) [in]: Freiburger Rundbrief, N.F., Jg. 6, H. 4, Freiburg, 1999, pp. 286–287.]

36665. Bodenheimer, Alfred/Hessing, Jakob: *"Wer sagt denn, das Leben sei kein dialektischer Prozeß?" Ein Gespräch mit Josef Burg.* [In]: Jüdischer Almanach 1999 des Leo Baeck Instituts, Frankfurt am Main, 1998. Pp. 169–181, illus. [J.B., born 1909 in Dresden, Israeli politican, long-term leader of the National Religious Party (Misrachi).]

36666. Bondy, Ruth: *Der Dornenweg deutscher Zionisten in die Politik. Felix Rosenblüth in Tel Aviv.* [In]: Menora 1998, Bodenheim, 1998. Pp. 297–314.

36667. Dowty, Alan: *Zionism's greatest conceit.* [In]: Israel Studies, Vol. 3, No. 1, Bloomington, IN, Spring 1998. Pp. 1–23, notes. [Incl. the early history and ideology of German Zionism and how, over time, the orig. ideology has been changed.]

36668. Friedlander, Albert H.: *The 100th anniversary Theodor Herzl conference (held at the Stadtcasino Basel 27–30 August 1997).* [In]: European Judaism, Vol. 31, No. 1, London, Spring 1998. Pp. 114–120. [Conference held in commemoration of the First Zionist Congress in 1887.]

36669. Friedman, Isaiah: *Germany, Turkey, and Zionism, 1897–1918.* With a new introd. by the author. New Brunswick, NJ: Transaction Books, 1998. XX, 461 pp., appendixes, bibl. (429–451). [For orig. edn., publ. in 1977, see No. 14475/YB XXIII.]

36670. Gilbert, Martin: *Israel: a history.* New York: William Morrow, 1998. XVI, 750 pp., illus., ports., maps, gloss., bibl. [Incl. early Zionism, Theodor Herzl, German-Jewish emigration to Palestine; deals also with German-Jewish contrib. to culture; the Eichmann trial.]

—— GRANACH, GAD: *Heimat los! Aus dem Leben eines jüdischen Emigranten.* [See No. 36994.]

36671. GRÖZINGER, ELVIRA: *Abschied vom Zionismus? Der "Held" in der modernen israelischen Literatur.* [In]: Menora 1997, Bodenheim, 1997. Pp. 280–310, notes. [Deals with the influence of German culture on Israeli literature; also with Israeli writers from Germany and Austria.]

36672. HALAMISH, AVIVA: *Exodus affair: Holocaust survivors and the struggle for Palestine, 1947.* Transl. from the Yiddish by Ora Cummings. Syracuse, NY: Syracuse Univ. Press, 1998. 356 pp., illus., map, notes.

36673. HALPERN, BEN/REINHARZ, JEHUDA: *Zionism and the creation of a new society.* New York; Oxford: Oxford Univ. Press, 1998. 293 pp., notes (273–275), bibl. (277–279). [Incl. the history of German Zionism; also the immigration of German Jews into Palestine.]

36674. HAUMANN, HEIKO, ed.: *Der Traum von Israel. Die Ursprünge des modernen Zionismus.* Mit Beiträgen von Heiko Haumann, Alex Carmel [et al.]. Weinheim: Beltz Athenäum, 1998. 329 pp., footnotes. [Cont. (some titles abbr.): Zionismus und die Krise jüdischen Selbstverständnisses. Tradition und Veränderung im Judentum (Heiko Haumann, 9–64). "Jerusalem muß unser werden". Titus Tobler und der "Christenstaat" (Alex Carmel, 65–88). Leopold Hamburger und Sigismund Simmel: Zwei frühe deutsche Zionisten in Palästina (Erik Petry, 89–107). Abraham Mapus "Zionsliebe". Die Geburt einer neuen Zionsidee in Osteuropa (Verena Dohrn, 108–139). Palästina aus ostjüdischer Sicht (Desanka Schwara, 140–169). Tsarist policy toward Zionism in Russia (Aleksandr Loksin, 170–185). Von Chatam Sofer zu Theodor Herzl. Zum Verhältnis von Orthodoxy und Frühzionismus im Königreich Ungarn während des 19. Jahrhunderts (Walter Pietsch, 186–204). Der Erste Zionistenkongress im Spiegel der jüdischen Presse Ungarns (Peter Haber, 204–231). Die ersten Zionistenkongresse aus der Sicht der damaligen Basler Publizistik (Patrick Kury, 232–249). Die "Protokolle der Weisen von Zion" und der Basler Zionistenkongreß von 1897 (Michael Hagemeister, 250–273). Kampf gegen die Assimilation und gegen die Politik der Alliance Israélite Universelle: Der elsässische Zionist Alfred Elias (1865–1940) (Astrid Starck, 274–294). Die Wahlen zum Rat der Jüdischen Gemeinde Petrograds 1917: Ein Sieg der Zionisten (Valerij Jul. Gessen, 295–300). Michael Schabad und der Revisionismus in der Schweiz (Bettina Zeugin, 301–318). Von der Ausgrenzung zum Nationalstolz. "Weibische" Juden und "Muskeljuden" (Monica Rüthers, 319–329).]

36675. HEID, LUDGER: *Nächstes Jahr in Jerusalem. Der Traum vom jüdischen Staat.* [In]: Fünfzig Jahre Israel: Vision und Wirklichkeit [see No. 37043]. Pp. 11–24, bibl. notes.

36676. HEIDECKER, FRITZ JOSEPH: *Die Brunnenbauer. Jüdische Pionierarbeit in Palästina 1934–1939.* Hrsg. von Erhard Roy Wiehn. Konstanz: Hartung-Gorre, 1998. 258 pp., illus., facsims., bibl. (255–256). [Incl. the diary written in Palestine by the author between 1939 and 1940 in German.] [F.J.H., b. Dec. 22, 1912 in Georgensmünd (Franconia), emigr. 1933 to France, 1934 to Palestine, where he became a leading activist of the Moshav-movement.]

36677. HERZL, THEODOR: *Die Judensache (The Jewish Cause): diaries.* Introd.: Shlomo Avineri. Transl.: Josef Wenkert. Vol. 1: June 1895 – October 1898. Jerusalem: Bialik Institute; The Zionist Library of the World Zionist Organization, 1997. 733 pp.

36678. HERZL, THEODOR: *The Jews' state.* A critical English translation. Transl. and with an introd. by Henk Overberg. Northvale, NJ: Jason Aronson, 1997. XII, 271 pp. [Orig. title 'Der Judenstaat', first publ. in 1896.]

36679. HERZL, THEODOR. ALMOG, SHMUEL: *Was Herzl a Jewish nationalist?* [In]: Yahadut Zemanenu, Vol. 11–12, Jerusalem, 1998. Pp. 3–21. [In Hebrew, with English summary.]

36680. HERZL, THEODOR. AVINERI, SHLOMO: *Herzl's path towards formation of a Jewish national consciousness.* [In]: Alpayim, No. 15, Tel-Aviv, 1997. Pp. 254–287. [In Hebrew, title transl.]

36681. HERZL, THEODOR. Boyarin, Daniel: *Colonial drug; Zionism, gender, and mimicry.* [In]: Theoria u-Vikoret, No. 11, Tel-Aviv, Winter 1997. Pp. 123–144. [In Hebrew, with English summary.]

36682. HERZL, THEODOR. Gluzman, Michael: *Longing for heterosexuality; Zionism and sexuality in Herzl's 'Altneuland'.* [In]: Theoria u-Vikoret, No. 11, Tel-Aviv, Winter 1997. Pp. 145–162. [In Hebrew with English summary.]

36683. HERZL, THEODOR. Graetz, Michael: *Sprache und Politik – Herzls 'Judenstaat' und die Macht der Rhetorik.* [In]: Trumah 7, Berlin, 1998. Pp. 101–112, footnotes.

36684. HERZL, THEODOR. Gutwein, Daniel: *Herzl and the struggle within the Jewish plutocracy; the Rothschilds, Baron Hirsch and Samuel Montagu.* [In]: Zion, Vol. 62, No. 1, Jerusalem, 1997. Pp. 47–74. [In Hebrew, with English summary.]

36685. HERZL, THEODOR. Hadomi, Leah: *Nationalism and universalism in Herzl's plays.* [In]: Bamah, No. 147–148, Jerusalem, 1997, Pp. 32–41. [In Hebrew.]

36686. HERZL, THEODOR. Harel, Nira: *A small large heart: the story of Herzl.* Tel-Aviv: Rakhess, 1996. 95 pp. [In Hebrew, title transl.] [A book for children on the life of H.]

36687. HERZL, THEODOR. Harel, Chaya: *Herzl and Eretz Israel; dream and action.* [In]: Kivunim, No. 11–12 [48–49], Jerusalem, Dec. 1997. Pp. 36–48. [In Hebrew, title transl.]

36688. HERZL, THEODOR. Harel, Chaya: *Herzl's "Jewish State".* [In]: Alon le-Morei ha-Historia, No. 6, Jerusalem, 1997. Pp. 26–38. [In Hebrew, title transl.]

36689. HERZL, THEODOR. Harel, Chaya: *Herzl's call to the Jews of South Africa.* [In]: Kivunim, No. 11–12 [48–49], Jerusalem, Dec. 1997. Pp. 75–81. [In Hebrew, title transl.]

36690. HERZL, THEODOR. Heymann, Michael: *Herzl and religion.* [In]: Daniel Carpi; Jubilee volume. A collection of studies on the history of the Jewish people presented to Daniel Carpi on his 70th birthday by his colleagues and students. Tel-Aviv: Tel-Aviv Univ., 1996. Pp. 97–107. [In Hebrew.]

36691. HERZL, THEODOR. Mann, Rafi: *Herzl and the press: from "sword of steel" to cable newspaper.* [In]: Qesher, No. 21, Tel-Aviv, May 1997. Pp. 20–36. [In Hebrew, with English transl.] [On H.'s career in journalism.]

36692. HERZL, THEODOR. Pawel, Ernst: *Herzl in the labyrinth of exile: a biography.* [Transl. from the English by Bruria Ben Barach.] Tel-Aviv: Mahbarot le-Sifrut, 1997. 410 pp. [In Hebrew, title transl. First publ. in 1989, see No. 26707/YB XXXV.]

36693. HERZL, THEODOR. Rabi, Ya'akov: *Herzl as foreign correspondent.* [In]: Qesher, No. 21, Tel-Aviv, May 1997. Pp. 37–43. [In Hebrew, with English summary.] [On his period as the Paris correspondent for the 'Neue Freie Presse', 1891–1895.]

36694. HERZL, THEODOR. Seewann, Harald: *Theodor Herzl und die akademische Jugend.* Eine Quellensammlung über die Bezüge Herzls zum Korporationsstudententum. Graz: Eigenverlag Harald Seewann [Postfach 358], 1998. 223 pp. (100 pp. of illus. and docs.).

36695. HERZL, THEODOR. Shahar, David: *The development of Th. Herzl's attitude towards antisemitism from 'Diary of Youth' (1882) to 'The Jewish State' (1896).* [In]: Ma'of u-Ma'asseh, No. 3, Be'er-Turiah, Jan. 1997. Pp. 79–101. [In Hebrew, title transl.]

36696. *Israel – Geschichte in Texten.* Aus dem Jüdischen Almanach des Leo Baeck Instituts in Jerusalem. Hrsg. und zusammengestellt von Jakob Hessing. Frankfurt am Main: Suhrkamp Taschenbuch Verlag, 1998. 160 pp., illus.

36697. KARK, RUTH: *Kaiser in Jerusalem.* [In]: Eit-mol, No. 139, Tel-Aviv, July 1998. Pp. 3–6. [In Hebrew, title transl.] [On the visit of Emperor William I. to Palestine in Oct. 1898.]

36698. KAUFMANN, RICHARD. STERN, SHIMON: *Richard Kaufmann as a city planner in the Jewish Yishuv of Eretz-Israel at the beginning of the Mandate period.* [In]: Zeev Zafrai/Yvonne Friedman, eds.: Hikrei Eretz; studies in the history of the Land of Israel, dedicated to Prof. Yehuda Feliks [In Hebrew]. Ramat-Gan: Bar-Ilan Univ. 1997. Pp. 365–390. [In Hebrew.]

36699. KOUTS, GIDEON: *Herzl and Nordau as critics of the press.* [In]: Qesher, No. 21, Tel-Aviv, May 1997. Pp. 44–48. [In Hebrew, with English summary.]

36700. LAMM, ZVI, ed.: *Moulding and rehabilitation. Papers in memory of Prof. Akiva Ernst Simon and Prof. Carl Frankenstein.* Jerusalem: Magnes Press, Hebrew Univ., 1996. 350 pp. [In Hebrew.] [Cont. 21 articles and a bibl. of the writings of the two professors dealing with E.S. and C.F., their theories on education and educational studies; bibls. of their publs. Incl.: Changes in religious teaching in Germany in the Nazi period (Joseph Walk, 148–153).] [See also No. 37010.]

36701. LÜHE, BARBARA VON DER: *Die Musik war unsere Rettung! Die deutschsprachigen Gründungsmitglieder des Palestine Orchestra.* Tübingen: Mohr Siebeck, 1998. XVIII, 356 pp., footnotes, bibl. (321–344), index. (Schriftenreihe wissenschaftlicher Abhandlungen des Leo-Baeck-Instituts, 58.)

36702. MEIER, AXEL: *Die kaiserliche Palästinareise 1898. Theodor Herzl, Großherzog Friedrich I. von Baden und ein deutsches Protektorat in Palästina.* Konstanz: Hartung-Gorre, 1998. 122 pp., footnotes, bibl. (Konstanzer Schriften zur Schoah und Judaica, Bd. 5.) [Cf.: Besprechung (Reuven Assor) [in]: 'MB', Jg. 66, Nr. 140, Tel Aviv, Okt.-Nov., 1998, pp. 11–12.]

———— MEYER-MARIL, EDINA: *Deutsche Einflüsse auf die Architektur Israels und der Beitrag deutsch-jüdischer Emigranten.* [See in No. 36731.]

36703. MIRON, GUY: *Autobiographies as sources in social history: German Jewry in Palestine/Israel as a test case.* [In]: Historia, No. 2, Jerusalem, Aug. 1998. Pp. 103–132. [In Hebrew, with English summary.]

36704. *Modern Judaism.* Vol. 18, No. 3 [with the issue title]: *100 years of Zionism and the 50th anniversary of the State of Israel.* Baltimore: Johns Hopkins Univ., Oct. 1998. 1 issue, notes. [Cont.: Zionism as revolution? Zionism as rebellion? (David Vital, 205–216). Zionism in the age of revolution (Anita Shapira, 217–226). Cultural Zionism's image of the educated Jew: reflections on creating a secular Jewish culture (Paul Mendes-Flohr, 227–240). Thoughts on Zionism as a utopian ideology (Yosef Gorny, 241–152). Reflections on the state of Zionist thought (Arnold M. Eisen, 253–266). Zionism in retrospective (Eliezer Don-Yehiya, 267–276). Incl. early German Zionists and the German Zionist movement.]

36705. MÖDING, NORI: *Immigration nach Palästina – Befunde der "Oral History" aus den 1980ern und 1990ern.* [In]: Tel Aviver Jahrbuch für deutsche Geschichte, Bd. 27, Gerlingen, 1998. Pp. 513–528. [On interviews with immigrants who came from Germany 1933–1939; presents and analyses one biography.]

36706. Naphtali, Fritz Peretz. RIEMER, YEHUDA: *Fritz Peretz Naphtali: a Social-Democrat in two worlds.* Jerusalem: Hassifria Haziyonit, 1996. 384 pp. [In Hebrew.]

36707. NORDAU, MAX. SCHULTE, CHRISTOPH: *Fin de siècle, Dreyfus, Zionismus – Max Nordau als Beobachter der III. Republik.* [In]: Jüdischer Republikanismus in Frankreich. Hrsg. von Christoph Miething. Tübingen: Niemeyer, 1998. Pp. 50–60, footnotes.

36708. NORDAU, MAX. ZUDRELL, PETRA: *Der pathologisierende Diskurs im Kontext literarischer und zionistischer Debatten um die Jahrhundertwende: Zur zeitgenössischen Rezeption der Werke von Max Nordau.* [In]: Aschkenas, Jg. 8, 1998, H. 2, Wien, 1999. Pp. 439–476, footnotes.

36709. RATZABI, SHALOM: *Immigrants from Central Europe in "Brit Shalom" and the question of use of force.* [In]: Zmanim, No. 58, Tel-Aviv, 1997. Pp. 78–85. [In Hebrew.] [The context is the Jewish-Arab conflict in Palestine.]

36710. RÖHL, JOHN C.G.: *Wilhelms seltsamer Kreuzzug.* [In]: Die Zeit, Nr. 42, Hamburg, 8. Okt. 1998. Pp. 30–36, illus. (Zeitläufte spezial.)

36711. ROLNIK, ERAN J.: *Mit Freud nach Palästina – Zur Rezeptionsgeschichte der Psychoanalyse.* [In]: Tel Aviver Jahrbuch für deutsche Geschichte, Bd. 27, 1998. Gerlingen, 1998. Pp. 273–300.

36712. SALZBERGER, ELI M./OZ-SALZBERGER, FANIA: *The German tradition of the Israeli Supreme Court.* [In]: Iyyunei Mishpat, Vol. 21, No. 2, Tel-Aviv, April 1998. Pp. 259–294. [In Hebrew, with English summary.] [On the influence of German-born and German-educated (Jewish) jurists on Israeli legal and political discourse in the formative years of the state.]

36713. SALZBERGER, ELI/OZ-SALZBERGER, FANIA: *The secret German sources of the Israeli Supreme Court.* [In]: Israel Studies, Vol. 3, No. 2, Bloomington, IN, Fall 1998. Pp. 159–192, notes.

36715. SCHLÖR, JOACHIM: *"Alija Chadascha und öffentliche Meinung". Das Mitteilungsblatt des Irgun Olei Merkas Europa (Tel-Aviv) als historische Quelle.* [In]: Menora, Bodenheim, 1997. Pp. 70–97. [Deals with the 'MB' from its beginnings in 1932 until 1943.]

36716. SCHLÖR, JOACHIM: *In weiter Ferne: Berlin. Bilder der Stadt in der Erinnerung deutsch-jüdischer Emigranten.* [In]: Menora 1998, Bodenheim, 1998. Pp. 267–296. [Based on the recollections of German Jews in Tel Aviv. Also on a similar topic by the same author: *Kaffee verkehrt. Notate an Kaffeehaustischen in Tel Aviv* [in]: Jüdischer Almanach 1999, Bodenheim, 1998. Pp. 151–158.]

36717. SCHLÖR, JOACHIM: *Kanton Iwrit. Schwierigkeiten mit der deutschen Sprache im jüdischen Palästina.* [In]: Sprache und Identität im Judentum [see No. 36627]. Pp. 231–252.

36718. SCHWARZ-GARDOS, ALICE: *Die Jekkes. Ein besonderes Kapitel der israelischen Geschichte.* [In]: Fünfzig Jahre Israel: Vision und Wirklichkeit [see No. 37043]. Pp. 52–63.

36719. SHAPIRA, ANITA, ed.: *Independence; the first fifty years*; collected essays. Jerusalem: Zalman Shazar Center for Jewish History. 1998. 581 pp. [In Hebrew.] [Incl. articles (in Hebrew): The Jewish State in the political philosophy of Martin Buber (1942–1965) (Shalom Ratzaby, 195–214). The way to "the other Germany". David Ben-Gurion and his attitude towards Germany, 1952–1960 (Yechiam Weitz, 245–266).]

36720. SHASHAR, MICHAEL: *"The transient dream": German Jewry's contribution to religious life in Israel.* Jerusalem: Shashar Publishing, 1997. 321 pp. [In Hebrew.]

36721. SHEFFI, NA'AMA: *German in Hebrew: translations from German into Hebrew in Jewish Palestine, 1882–1948.* Jerusalem: Yad Izhak Ben-Zvi; Leo Baeck Institute, 1998. 295 pp. [In Hebrew.]

36722. SHEFFI, NA'AMA: *Rejecting the other's culture – Hebrew and German in Israel 1933–1965.* [In]: Tel Aviver Jahrbuch für deutsche Geschichte, Bd. 27, 1998, Gerlingen, 1998. Pp. 301–320.

——— SIMON, ERNST A.: *Sechzig Jahre gegen den Strom. Briefe von 1917 – 1984.* Hrsg. vom Leo Baeck Institut Jerusalem. [See No. 37010.]

36723. WEINER, HANNAH: *Youth in ferment within a complacent community: Zionist youth movements and Hechaluz in Germany.* Vol. 1. Ramat Efal: Yad Tabenkin; Tel-Aviv: Tel-Aviv Univ., 1996. 495 pp. [In Hebrew.]

36724. WILTMANN, INGRID: *Nur Ewigkeit ist kein Exil. Lebensgeschichten aus Israel.* Mit einem Nachwort von Anat Feinberg. Mohlin/Villingen: Rauhreif, 1998. 476 pp. [Cont. 29 interviews, most of them with people from German-speaking countries.]

36725. Wistrich, Robert S.: *Zionism and its Jewish "assimilationist" critics (1897–1948)*. [In]: Jewish Social Studies, Vol. 4, No. 2, Bloomington, IN, Winter 1998. Pp. 59–111, notes.

36726. Yekutiel, Perez: *Masterman, Muehlens and malaria, Jerusalem 1912–1913*. [In]: Korot, Vol. 12 [1996–1997], Jerusalem, 1998. Pp. 107–123. [Dr. E.W.G. Masterman, chief of the English Mission Hospital of the London Jews' Society in Jerusalem; Dr. Peter Muehlens, department head in the Institut für Schiffs- und Tropenkrankheiten in Hamburg; went to Jerusalem in Aug. 1912 leading a malaria expedition.]

36727. Zertal, Idith: *From catastrophe to power: Holocaust survivors and the emergence of Israel*. Berkeley: Univ. of California Press, 1998. XIII, 344 pp., illus., ports., gloss., notes (275–324). [Incl. German Jews who emigrated to Palestine; also deals with the Exodus affair.]

36728. *Zionismus: Annäherung an die jüdische Nationalbewegung – Standpunkte zum Jubiläum des Ersten Zionistenkongresses 1897 in Basel*. Zionismus 1897 – 1997: eine Serie der Basler Zeitung. Basel: Buchverl. Basler Zeitung, 1997. 87 pp., illus.

36729. Zucker, Ruth: *"Im Auftrag für Israel". Mein Leben als Spionin*. [Cover title: Meine Jahre als Spionin]. München: Deutscher Taschenbuch Verlag, 1998. 242 pp., illus. Originalausgabe. [Author, née Ruth Amelie Koopmann, b. 1914 in Bonn, graphologist, psychologist, emigr. in 1934 to Palestine, where she joined the Haganah.]

VII. PARTICIPATION IN CULTURAL AND PUBLIC LIFE

A. General

36730. *Die Achtundvierziger. Lebensbilder aus der deutschen Revolution 1848/49*. Hrsg. von Sabine Freitag. München: Beck, 1998. 352 pp., illus., bibl. notes (303–342), index (349–352). [Incl.: Karl Blind: Ein Talent in der Wichtigmacherei (Rudolf Muhs, 81–98). Gabriel Riesser: Der Advokat der Einheit (Erik Lindner, 160–170). Ludwig Bamberger: Mit Dampf und Elektrizität für ein modernes Deutschland (Christian Jansen, 200–213).]

36731. *Architektur- und Ingenieurwesen zur Zeit der nationalsozialistischen Gewaltherrschaft 1993–1945*. [Hrsg.] Ulrich Kuder. Im Auftrag des Rektorats und des Zentrum für Technik und Gesellschaft der Brandenburgischen Technischen Universität Cottbus. Berlin: Gebr. Mann, 1997. 177 pp., illus., footnotes. [Incl.: Deutsche Einflüsse auf die Architektur Israels und der Beitrag deutsch-jüdischer Emigranten (Edina Meyer-Maril, 14–41). Georg Schlesinger. Vom Wirken eines großen Ingenieurs (Günter Spur, 69–95, bibl., bibl. G.Sch.; G. Sch., 1874 Berlin – 1949 UK, mechanical engineer, leading design engineer at Ludwig Loewe & Co., Berlin, since 1904 the only Jewish 'Ordinarius' for machine tools and production at the TH Charlottenburg, dismissed in 1933, emigr. via Zurich and Brussels in 1939 to the UK). Jüdische Architekten vor und nach 1933 (Myra Wahrhaftig, 157–177.]

———— ARNHOLD FAMILY. Lässig, Simone: *Juden und Mäzenatentum in Deutschland*. Religiöses Ethos, kompensierendes Minderheitsverhalten oder genuine Bürgerlichkeit? [See No. 35988.]

———— ARNHOLD FAMILY. Lässig, Simone: *Nationalsozialistische "Judenpolitik" und jüdische Selbstbehauptung vor dem Novemberpogrom. Das Beispiel der Dresdner Bankiersfamilie Arnhold*. [See No. 36238.]

36732. Barth, Boris: *Deutsch-jüdisch-europäische Privatbankengruppen vor und nach dem Ersten Weltkrieg*. Hrsg.: Carl-Ludwig Holtfrerich. Frankfurt am Main: GUG, 1998. 29 pp. (Arbeitspapier/ Gesellschaft für Unternehmensgeschichte e.V., Arbeitskreis für Bankgeschichte; 1997, Nr. 5.)

36733. Diethe, Carol: *Towards emancipation: German women writers of the nineteenth century*. Oxford; New York: Berghahn Books, 1998. VIII, 214 pp., illus., ports. footnotes, bibl. (200–210).

[Incl. chap.: The Berlin salons and the Jewish question: Henriette Herz, (1764–1854); also chaps. on Rahel Varnhagen and Fanny Lewald.]

36734. DÜWELL, FRANZ JOSEF/VORMBAUM, THOMAS, eds.: *Recht und Juristen in der deutschen Revolution 1848/49*. Baden-Baden: Nomos, 1998. 258 pp., footnotes. (Juristische Zeitgeschichte: Abt. 2, Forum juristische Zeitgeschichte, Bd. 3.) [Incl.: Eduard von Simson (Gerd Pfeiffer, 5–46). Gabriel Riesser. Für verfassungsrechtliche Freiheit und Gleichstellung der Juden (Wilfried Fiedler, 47–92).]

36735. EXILE. ALTER, PETER, ed.: *Out of the Third Reich: refugee historians in post-war Britain*. Foreword by Peter Wende. Introd. by Peter Alter. London; New York: I.B. Tauris; London: German Historical Institute, 1998. XXIV, 271 pp., illus., ports., notes, bibls. [Anthology of 14 brief memoirs by the historians Julius Carlebach, Francis L. Carsten (see also No. 36792), Edgar J. Feuchtwanger, J.A.S. Grenville, E.P. Hennock, Helmut Koenigsberger, Wolf Mendl, Werner E. Mosse, Helmut Pappe, Arnold Paucker, Sidney Pollard, Peter Pulzer, Nicholai Rubinstein, Walter Ullmann.]

36736. EXILE. ASH, MITCHELL G.: *Wissenschaftswandel durch Zwangsauswanderung – Kurt Lewin und Else Frenkel-Brunswik nach 1933*. [In]: Tel Aviver Jahrbuch für deutsche Geschichte, Bd. 27, 1998, Gerlingen, 1998. Pp. 251–272.

——— EXILE. DÜWELL, KURT [et al.], eds.: *Vertreibung jüdischer Künstler und Wissenschaftler aus Düsseldorf 1933–1945*. [See No. 36239.]

36737. EXILE. *Exil*. Forschung, Erkenntnisse, Ergebnisse. Jg. 18, Nr. 1 & 2. Hrsg. von Edita Koch und Frithjof Trapp. Frankfurt am Main: E. Koch (Postfach 17 0 34), 1998. 2 issues, 105; 108 pp., notes. [No. 1 deals with several aspects of remigration; selected contribs. are listed according to subject. No. 2 incl.: Preisfragen zu einem Leben in Deutschland vor und nach 1933 – das Beispiel Karl Löwith (Liliane Weissberg, 14–23; on a competition initiated by Gordon W. Allport and two other Harvard professors in 1939). Fritz Hirsch – ein deutscher Operettenkönig in den Niederlanden (Andreas Oertel, 24–33). Zum Leben und Werk von Menachem Birnbaum (Georg Schirmers, 34–53, illus.). Erinnerungen an Menachem Birnbaum (Mirjam Birnbaum, 54–56; on the artist M.B., son of Nathan B., lived in Berlin, emigr. 1933 to the Netherlands, deported to Sobibor March 1943, later to Auschwitz, where he died 1944/1945. Die Zeit, die Liebe und der Tod – 'Jarmila' von Ernst Weiß im Kontext seiner Erzählungen (Josef Quack, 77–84). "Sein tiefstes Gesetz schreibt sich jeder allein". Erich Frieds Exillyrik vor und nach dem 13. Oktober 1943 (Jörg Thunecke, 85–107). Nachruf auf den deutsch-jüdischen Schriftsteller Robert Muller (Barbara Müller-Wesemann, 77–78). Also book reviews.]

36738. EXILE. *Exilforschung*. Ein internationales Jahrbuch. Bd. 16, 1998: Exil und Avantgarden. Hrsg. im Auftrag der Gesellschaft für Exilforschung/Society for Exile Studies von Claus-Dieter Krohn [et al.]. München: Text + Kritik, 1998. 275 pp., illus., notes. (Exilforschung, Bd. 16.) [Selected contribs. dealing with German-speaking émigrés: Gedächtnis – Erinnern – Eingedenken. Walter Benjamins 'Passagenarbeit' und Dani Karavans 'Passagen' in Portbou (Peter Rautmann, 12–31). Avantgarde im Exil? Anmerkungen zum Schicksal der bildkünstlerischen Avantgarde Deutschlands nach 1933 und zum Exilwerk Richard Lindners (Rosamunde Neugebauer, 32–55). Auf der Spitze des Mastbaums. Walter Benjamin als Kritiker im Exil (Stephan Braese, 56–86). Etwas Anständiges, das auch etwas Wind macht. Zu Anna Seghers' Briefwechsel mit der Redaktion der Zeitschrift 'Das Wort' (Dieter Schiller, 87–104). Avantgarde und Exil. Else Lasker-Schülers 'Hebräerland' (Doerte Bischoff, 105–126). Das Scheitern der Wirtschaftsmacht an den politischen Umständen. Robert Neumanns Exilerzählung 'Sephardi' (Thomas Hilsheimer, 127–141). Das Eigene im Fremden. Die Wirkung der Exilanten und Exilantinnen auf die amerikanische Germanistik (Jost Hermand, 157–173). Filmavantgardisten im Exil (Helmut G. Asper, 174–193). "Ich brauche mich mit 'Geschäften' nicht mehr zu befassen, nur mit Kunst". Alexander László und die Weiterentwicklung seiner Farblichtmusik im amerikanischen Exil (Jörg Jewanski, 194–228). "Wenn ich eines richtig gemacht habe ...". Berliner Sexualwissenschaftler in Palästina/Israel (Joachim Schlör, 229–252).]

36739. EXILE. *German Life & Letters,* New Series, Vol. 51, No. 2 [with the issue title]: *Exile studies special number.* Oxford: Blackwell, April 1998. 1 issue, notes. [Selected articles (titles abbr.): The Americanisation of Günther (Guy Stern, 153–164). Rudolf Kommer from Czernowitz – 'that spherical, remorselessly shaved, enigmatic "dearest friend"' (Deborah Vietor-Engländer, 165–184). German-speaking women in exile in Britain, 1933–1945 (Charmian Brinson, 204–224). Jewish women authors and the exile experience: Claire Goll, Veza Canetti, Else Lasker-Schüler, Nelly Sachs, Cordelia Edvardson (Dagmar C.G. Lorenz, 225–239). The Rohme episode in Arnold Zweig's 'Das Beil von Wandsbek' (Jost Hermand, 240–249). The earliest reception of the Holocaust: Ernst Sommer's 'Revolte der Heiligen' (Anthony Grenville, 250–265). Kurt Hiller – a 'Stänkerer' in exile 1934–1955 (J.M. Ritchie, 266–286). Deutschsprachiges Exil in Skandinavien: Die Gastländer Dänemark, Norwegen, Schweden (Helmut Müssener, 302–323). Incl. also contribs. on Thomas, Klaus and Erika Mann.]

36740. EXILE. HAGEMANN, HARALD, ed.: *Zur deutschsprachigen wirtschaftswissenschaftlichen Emigration nach 1933.* Marburg: Metropolis, 1997. 608 pp., notes, bibl. [Cont. German and English contribs.]

——— EXILE. *Handbuch der deutschsprachigen Emigration 1933–1945.* [See No. 36159.]

36741. EXILE. *Keine Klage über England? Deutsche und österreichische Exilerfahrungen in Großbritannien 1933–1945.* Hrsg. von Charmian Brinson [et al.]. München: Iudicium, 1998. 333 pp., footnotes, index (327–333). (Zugl.: Publications of the Institute of Germanic Studies, Bd. 72.) [Cont. 23 essays, most of them dealing with Jewish exiles. Selected essays: (titles partly abbr.): H.G. Adler: a Prague writer in London (Jeremy Adler, 13–30; see also No. 36769). Kampf um Ätherwellen; die deutschsprachigen Satiren der BBC im zweiten Weltkrieg (Uwe Naumann, 31–38). Karl Otten at the BBC (Richard Dove, 39–47). Gabriele Tergits Roman 'Effingers' (Irmela von der Lühe, 48–61). Stella Rotenbergs Exildichtungen (Beate Schmeichel-Falkenberg, 62–73). Exil und literarische Produktion: das Beispiel Mela Hartwig (Sigrid Schmid-Bortenschlager, 88–99). Kindheitserlebnisse und Frauengestalten in den Romanen von Anna Gmeyner (Edward Timms, 100–111). Zur kulturellen Identität bei Hilde Spiel (Esther V. Schneider-Handschin, 112–123). Beyond Dachau: Irmgard Litten in England (Marian Malet, 124–136). Ruth Heinrichsdorff: an SAP activist in British exile (Charmian Brinson, 157–174). 'Die Kultur haben wir ihnen aufgehoben. Sie wurde nur nicht abgeholt' (Jennifer Taylor, 175–189; on Grete Fischer). Language and identity in the autobiographical writings of Judith Kerr and Charles Hannam (Gillian Lathey, 190–199). Two typographer- calligraphers: Berthold Wolpe and Elizabeth Friedlander (Pauline Paucker, 200–214, illus.). Dr Rosa Schapire – art historian and critic in exile (Shulamith Behr, 215–223). Emigré germanists and the University of London (John L. Flood, 224–240). Deutschsprachige Wirtschaftswissenschaftler im britischen Exil (Harald Hagemann, 241–262; incl. list of names). Willy Sternfeld and exile studies in Great Britain (J.M. Ritchie, 263–275). Paul Frischauer: österreichischer Schriftsteller und britischer Geheimagent (Ursula Prutsch, 276–285). The unpublished correspondence between Stefan Zweig and Sir Siegmund Warburg (Jeffrey B. Berlin, 286–301). Heinz Liepmann im englischen Exil (Wilfried Weinke, 302–316).]

36742. EXILE. SAINT SAUVEUR-HENN, ed.: *Zweimal verjagt. Die deutschsprachige Emigration und der Fluchtweg Frankreich – Lateinamerika 1933–1945.* Berlin: Metropol, 1998. 248 pp., footnotes. (Dokumente – Texte – Materialien, Bd. 25.) [Cont. (titles partly abbr.): Vorwort (ed., 9–10). Zur Erfahrung der Emigration (Alfred Grosser, 11–14). Essays are arranged under the following sections: I. *Frankreich: ein provisorisches Exil*; cont.: Deutsche und österreichische Emigranten in Frankreich 1933–1942 (Gilbert Badia, 16–33). Deutschsprachige Emigranten in den französischen Internierungslagern 1939–1942 (Christian Eggers, 34–47). II. *Fluchtwege und Fluchthilfe nach Lateinamerika: eine neue Rettung*; cont.: Fluchtweg Spanien – Portugal. Die deutsche Emigration und der Exodus aus Europa 1933–1945 (Patrik von zur Mühlen, 50–60). Aus der zweiten Heimat vertrieben. Susanne Eisenberg (Bach) und ihre Fluchthelfer (Christine Hohnschopp, 61–65). Der Vatikan und die Brasilien-Visa 1940–1941 (Klaus Voigt, 66–75). III. *Die literarische Übertragung der doppelten Emigration*; cont.: Flucht aus Frankreich. Der Weg von Anna Seghers nach Mexiko (Alexander Stephan, 78–89). Frankreich in Lateinamerika? Frankreichbezüge im mexikanischen Exil der Anna

Seghers (Fritz Pohle, 90–87). Erich Arendts Gedichte im Exil (Suzanne Shipley, 98–105). Autobiographisches Schreiben über das Exil heute: Lisa Fittko (Ursula Seeber-Weyrer, 106–118). IV. *Literatur und Politik*; cont.: Gustav Regler zwischen zwei Erdteilen (Guy Stern, 120–132). Stefan Zweigs Freitod und das "Brasilien-Buch". Gerüchte und Zusammenhänge (Gerhard Drekonja-Kornat, 133–139). Die drei Leben des Otto Katz alias Rudolf Breda alias André Simone (Marcus G. Patka, 140–154). Leopold von Andrian – ein Legitimist im Exil (Ursula Prutsch, 155–166). V. *Die Nachwirkungen der doppelten Emigration auf die künstlerische Produktion*; cont.: Paul Walter Jacob und die Freie Deutsche Bühne in Argentinien (Frithjof Trapp, 168–175). Brigitte Alexander, Bodo Uhse und Walter Reuter im Exil in Frankreich und Mexiko (Renata von Hanfstengel, 176–181). Die österreichische kulturelle Emigration in der Auseinandersetzung mit der "neuen Welt" (Edith Blaschitz, 184–191). Alfredo Bauers "Die Antwort" (1944) als Modell des österreichischen Exiltheaters in Argentinien (Jean-Marie Winkler, 192–198). Die historisch-politische und kulturelle "Exzeption" des österreichischen Exils 1938–1945 (Felix Kreissler, 199–208). VII. *Zwischen Ursprungs- und Gastland*; cont.: "Sie strandeten wie Schiffbrüchige am La Plata." Eine neue Identitätsfindung der "zweimal Verjagten"? (Anne Saint Sauveur-Henn, 210–222). VIII. *Berichte von Zeitzeugen und Zeitzeuginnen* (223–244; essays by Franz Blum, Charlotte Janka, Alfredo Bauer, Sophie Marum and Lenka Reinerová).]

36743.   EXILE. WALTON-JORDAN, ULRIKE: *Voices of exile: the contributions of German-speaking refugees to British culture and public life.* Leo Baeck Lodge Lecture delivered on Oct. 18 in London. London: The B'nai Brith Leo Baeck Lodge, Leo Baeck Hall, Oct. 18, 1998. 1 issue.

36744.   EXILE LITERATURE. "*In Spuren gehen...*". Festschrift für Helmut Koopmann. Hrsg. von Andrea Bartl [et al.]. Tübingen: Niemeyer, 1998. XI, 512 pp., footnotes. [Section VI with the title '*Exil und innere Emigration*' incl.: Judentum – Kirche – Habsburg. Joseph Roths antinationalistische Vorstellungen der dreißiger Jahre (Alfred Riemen, 375–398), Das Exil als geistige Lebensform. Über den Emigranten Hans Sahl – mit einer vergleichenden Abschweifung zu Thomas Mann (Lothar Pikulik, 399–412). Hermann Hesse, der Nationalsozialismus und die Juden (Egon Schwarz, 413–431). A further contrib. is listed according to subject.]

36745.   EXILE LITERATURE. *Mit der Ziehharmonika.* Zeitschrift für Literatur des Exils und des Widerstands. Hrsg. Siglinde Bolbecher, Konstantin Kaiser. Red.: Evelyn Adunka [et al.]. Jg. 15, Nos. 1–3. Wien, 1998. 3 issues, 67; 59; 55 pp., illus., facsims., bibl. notes. [Nr. 1/Doppelnummer with the issue title '*Exil in Mexiko*' incl. contribs. on Mexico, on the "Anschluß", poems and book reviews. Nr. 2 with the issue title '*Zerrissene Landschaft*' incl. contribs. on/by Hedwig Katscher, Wolfgang Georg Fischer, Hermann Hakel, Herbert Kuhner, Theodor Kramer, Vladimir Vertlib, obituaries (Gerda Rodel-Neuwirth, Hermann Levin Goldschmidt), poems, book reviews. Nr. 3 with the issue title '*Literatur und Literaturkritik*' incl. essays on literary critic, on/by exile authors (Fritz Beer, Peter Siemsen, Maria Leitner, Herbert Haber, Konrad Merz), personal recollections, poems, book reviews. Selected articles are listed according to subject.]

————   EXILE LITERATURE. *Sanary-sur-Mer. Deutsche Literatur im Exil.* [See No. 36266.]

36746.   EXILE LITERATURE. STERN, GUY: *Literarische Kultur im Exil/literature and culture in exile.* Gesammelte Beiträge zur Exilforschung/collected essays on the German-speaking emigration after 1933. (1989–1997). Dresden: Dresden University Press, 1998. X, 428 pp., index (409–426). (Philologica, Dresdner Beiträge zur Literatur-, Kultur- und Mediengeschichte, Reihe A, Bd. 1.) [Cont. essays partly in English, partly in German. Incl. also autobiographical essays.] [Cf.: Opfer, Helden und Warner. Die Gegenwart im Blick: Guy Sterns Beiträge zur Exilforschung (Helmut Hirsch) [in]: 'FAZ', Nr. 50, Frankfurt am Main, 28. Feb. 1998, p. 34.] [G.St., b. 1922 in Hildesheim, Germanist and lit. historian, emigr. 1937 to US, 1942–1945 served in US Military Intelligence, after WW II professor at various US univs.; member of the Exec. Board. of the LBI in New York since 1967.]

36747.   EXILE LITERATURE. WIEMANN, DIRK: *Exilliteratur in Großbritannien 1933–1945.* Opladen: Westdt. Verl., 1998. 377 pp., footnotes, bibl. (363–377). (Kulturwiss. Studien zur deutschen Literatur.) Zugl.: Oldenburg, Univ., Diss., 1997. [Incl. a.o. Arnold Bender, Anna Maria

Jokl, Arthur Koestler, Karl Mannheim, Robert Neumann, Anna Sebastian (= Friedl Benedikt).]

36748. FRANKFURT SCHOOL. Gur-Zeev, Ilan: *The Frankfurt School and the history of pessimism.* Jerusalem: Magnes Press, Hebrew University, 1996. 307, IV pp. [In Hebrew, with English summary.]

36749. *Intermezzo Berlin. Wiener in Berlin 1890–1933* Hrsg.: Bernd Evers. Berlin: Staatl. Museen zu Berlin/Preußischer Kulturbesitz, 1998. 84 pp., illus., notes, index. (Sammlungskataloge der Kunstbibliothek.) [Catalogue of an exhibition of the same name in Berlin, Nov. 11, 1998 – Jan. 10, 1999; incl. numerous Jewish publishers, actors, musicians, composers and artists.]

36750. Kempter, Klaus: *Die Jellineks 1820–1955. Eine familienbiographische Studie zum deutschjüdischen Bildungsbürgertum.* Düsseldorf: Droste, 1998. VIII, 631 pp., illus., footnotes, bibl. (555–621), index. (Schriften des Bundesarchivs, 52.) [On the Jellinek family originally from Moravia; incl. Adolf J., rabbi and scholar in Leipzig and Vienna; Hermann Jellinek, writer, journalist, revolutionary; Georg and Walter J., jurists and univ. professors, Camilla Jellinek, women's movement activist. Also on antisemitism and defence of antisemitism. See also No. 36356.]

36751. Kernmayer, Hildegard: *Judentum im Wiener Feuilleton (1848–1903): exemplarische Untersuchungen zum literarästhetischen und politischen Diskurs der Moderne.* Tübingen: Niemeyer, 1998. VIII, 326 pp. (Conditio Judaica, 24.) Zugl.: Graz, Univ., Diss., 1997.

36752. Klemmer, Klemens: *Jüdische Baumeister in Deutschland. Architektur vor der Shoah.* Stuttgart: Deutsche Verlags-Anstalt, 1998. 288 pp., illus.

36753. Koelbl, Herlinde: *Jüdische Portraits. Photographien und Interviews.* Frankfurt am Main: Fischer Taschenbuch Verlag, 1998. 411 pp., illus., index. [Paperback edn. of No. 25948/YB XXXV (first publ. 1989).]

36754. Lamping, Dieter: *Von Kafka bis Celan. Jüdischer Diskurs in der deutschen Literatur des 20. Jahrhunderts.* Göttingen: Vandenhoeck & Ruprecht, 1998. 206 pp., notes (164–191), bibl. (192–203), index.

36755. Lehming, Hanna, ed.: *Jüdische Denker im 20. Jahrhundert.* Hamburg: E.B.-Verl., 1997. 184 pp. [Incl. a.o.: Theodor W. Adorno, Hannah Arendt, Leo Baeck, Walter Benjamin, Martin Buber, Abraham J. Heschel, Franz Rosenzweig.]

36756. Lindner, Erik: *Buchhändler und Verleger in der Paulskirche 1848/49.* Eine Annäherung. [In]: Buchhandelsgeschichte, [Beilage zum] Börsenblatt für den Deutschen Buchhandel, Jg. 164, Nr. 22, Frankfurt am Main, 17. März 1998. Pp. B 2–12, illus., notes. [Incl. the Jewish publishers: Moritz Veit, Friedrich Wilhelm Levysohn.]

36757. Maas, Utz: *Verfolgung und Auswanderung deutschsprachiger Sprachforscher 1933–1945.* Bd. 1: Einleitung und Biobibliographische Daten A–F. Osnabrück: Sec Kommunikation und Gestaltung GmbH, 1996. 288 pp. [Incl. 62 short biographies.] [Cf.: Besprechung (Anne Christine Nagel) [in]: Berichte zur Wissenschaftsgeschichte, Bd. 21, Weinheim, 1998, pp. 198–199.]

——— *Medizinische Bildung und Judentum.* [See No. 35928.]

36758. MENDELSSOHN FAMILY. Kühn, Helga-Maria: *"In diesem ruhigen Kleinleben geht so schrecklich viel vor". Rebecka Lejeune Dirichlet, geb. Mendelssohn Bartholdy in Göttingen 1855–1858.* [In]: Göttinger Jahrbuch, Bd. 46, Göttingen, 1998. Pp. 115–125, illus., facsims., footnotes. [Deals with a sister of Felix and Fanny.]

36759. Nissel, Muriel: *Married to the Amadeus: life with a string quartet.* London: Giles de la Mare, 1998. XI, 184 pp., illus., facsims., tabs., appendixes. [English-born author describes her life as the wife of Siegmund Nissel, who together with two other Austrian-Jewish refugees, Norbert Brainin and Peter Schidlof, founded the Amadeus Quartet when interned on the Isle of Man.]

36760. POST WORLD WAR II. BRAESE, STEPHAN [et al.], eds.: *Deutsche Nachkriegsliteratur und der Holocaust.* Frankfurt am Main; New York: Campus, 1998. 417 pp., footnotes. (Wiss. Reihe des Fritz Bauer Instituts, Bd. 6.) [Cont. 21 contribs. dealing with Jewish and non-Jewish writers, incl. some exile writers such as Nelly Sachs, Paul Celan, Ruth Klüger, Peter Weiss, Jurek Becker, Edgar Hilsenrath, Jean Améry. Selected contribs. are listed according to subject.]

36761. POTTER, PAMELA MAXINE: *Most German of the arts: musicology and society from the Weimar Republic to the end of Hitler's Reich.* New Haven, CT: Yale Univ. Press, 1998. XX, 364 pp., notes (267–340), bibl. (341–356). [Incl. Jews in the university before 1933; Jewish contribs. to music as composers, conductors; racial and political purge of music faculties.]

——— REICHMANN, EVA, ed.: *Habsburger Aporien? Geisteshaltungen und Lebenskonzepte in der multinationalen Literatur der Habsburger Monarchie.* [See No. 36634.]

36762. ROTHSCHILD FAMILY. FERGUSON, NIALL: *The world's banker: the history of the house of Rothschild.* London: Weidenfeld & Nicolson, 1998. XXII, 1309 pp., illus., facsims., tabs., family tree, appendixes, notes, bibl.

36763. SCHÖNHOVEN, KLAUS/VOGEL, HANS-JOCHEN, eds.: *Frühe Warnungen vor dem Nationalsozialismus. Ein historisches Lesebuch.* Mit einem Geleitwort von Rita Süssmuth. Bonn: Dietz Nachf., 1998. 399 pp., footnotes, docs., tabs., index (391–398). [Incl. parliamentary debates from 1922 – 1933 on the ideology and politics of National Socialism (with introductions). Among the speakers were Siegfried Aufhäuser, Ernst Hamburger, Ernst Heilmann, Rudolf Hilferding.]

36764. SIEGMUND-SCHULTZE, REINHARD: *Mathematiker auf der Flucht vor Hitler.* Quellen und Studien zur Emigration einer Wissenschaft. Hrsg.: Deutsche Mathematiker-Vereinigung. Braunschweig: Vieweg, 1998. XIV, 368 pp., ports., docs., footnotes, bibl. (322–344), indexes (subjects; persons, 345–368). (Dokumente zur Geschichte der Mathematik, Bd. 10.) [Also on life and work of émigré mathematicians in the USA.] [Cf.: Hätten Akademiker sich selbst ausrechnen sollen. Doch die Mathematiker, die aus Hitlers Deutschland fliehen konnten, hatten das Böse nicht einkalkuliert (Ernst Horst) [in]: 'FAZ', Nr. 256, Frankfurt am Main, 4. Nov. 1998, p. 10.]

36765. WISTRICH, ROBERT S.: *Exil, Entfremdung und "gelobte Länder".* Marx, Freud und Herzl. [In]: Menora 1997, Bodenheim, 1997. Pp. 53–69, notes. [Deals with alienation as a source for inventiveness and creativity.]

B. Individual

36766. *Abschied und Wiederkehr. Abraham Jaskiel – Zeev Yaskil – Amos Yaskil.* Eine Künstlerfamilie. Leipzig: [Ephraim Carlebach Stiftung Leipzig in Zusammenarbeit mit der Dresdner Bank Leipzig und der Galerie an der Mühle, Hänigsen/Hannover], 1998. 142 pp., illus. [Texts also in English and Hebrew.] [A.Jaskil, 1894 Czenstochow (Poland) – 1987 Haifa, painter, lived in Germany from 1914, from 1920 in Leipzig. Emigr. to Palestine in 1933. His sons (b. 1929 in Leipzig and 1935 in Haifa) also became artists.]

36767. ADELSBERGER, LUCIE. BAADER, GERHARD: *Lucie Adelsberger: a forgotten Jewish pioneer allergist.* [In]: Korot, Vol. 12 (1996–1997), Jerusalem, 1998. Pp. 137–143. [L.A. worked at the Robert-Koch-Institut in Berlin.]

36768. ADLER, FELIX. RADEST, HOWARD B.: *Felix Adler. An ethical culture.* New York; Berlin: Lang, 1998. XII, 181 pp. (American liberal religious thought, Vol. 5.) [F.A., 1851 Alzey – 1933 New York, philosopher, teacher, social reformer, son of a rabbi, went to the US in 1857, founder of the Ethical Culture Societies (1876) and of the Ethical Culture Fieldstone Schools.]

36769. ADLER, H.G.. ADLER, JEREMY: *H.G. Adler – Der Wahrheit verpflichtet.* Interviews, Gedichte, Essays. Gerlingen: Bleicher, 1998. 247 pp., notes, bibl. [Incl. autobiographical texts, essays on concentration camps, Theresienstadt, resistance; also an essay by H.G. Adler's son Jeremy Adler (Der Wahrheit verpflichtet, 205–234).] [H.G. Adler, July 2, 1910 Prague – Aug. 20, 1988 London, historian. writer, poet; for further data see 25665/YB XXXV.]

36770. AGNON, SHMUEL JOSEF. SCHLÖR, JOACHIM: *Gestern und vorgestern und heute – einem Buch und einer Reise hinterher.* [In]: Tel Aviver Jahrbuch für deutsche Geschichte, Bd. 27, Gerlingen, 1998. Pp. 491–512. [On Agnon's travel report 'Gestern, vorgestern', first publ. in 1946.]

36771. ALONI, JENNY. STEINECKE, HARTMUT: *Fremde Heimat. Die "westfälischen" Erzählungen der Droste-Preisträgerin Jenny Aloni.* [In]: Literatur in Westfalen. Beiträge zur Forschung 4. Im Auftrag des Landschaftsverbandes Westfalen Lippe. Hrsg. von Walter Gödden. Paderborn: Ferd. Schöningh, 1998. Pp. 199–217, footnotes. [Emphasises the autobiographical aspects of Aloni's stories.] [J.A., née Rosenbaum, 1917 Paderborn – 1993 Israel, writer. An edn. of her works was publ. 1990–1997: Gesammelte Werke in Einzelausgaben. Hrsg. von Friedrich Kienecker und Hartmut Steinecke. Paderborn: Schöningh, 1990–1997. 10 vols.]

36772. ARENDT, HANNAH. ASCHHEIM, STEVEN E.: *Nazism, culture and the origins of totalitarianism. Hannah Arendt and the discourse of evil.* [In Hebrew, title transl.] Jerusalem: Leo Baeck Institute, 1998. 28 pp.

36773. ARENDT, HANNAH. LAQUEUR, WALTER: *Der Arendt-Kult. Hannah Arendt als politische Kommentatorin.* [In]: Europäische Rundschau, Jg. 26, Nr. 4, Wien, 1998. Pp. 111–125, notes.

36774. ARENDT, HANNAH. LEIBOVICI, MARTINE: *Judentum und Aufklärung in der Sicht Hannah Arendts.* [In]: Judentum und Moderne in Frankreich und Italien. Hrsg. von Christoph Miething. Tübingen: Niemeyer, 1998. Pp. 224–243.

36775. ARENDT, HANNAH. PRINZ, ALOIS: *Beruf Philosophin oder Die Liebe zur Welt. Die Lebensgeschichte der Hannah Arendt.* Weinheim: Beltz & Gelberg, 1998. 326 pp.

36776. ARENDT, HANNAH. VOWINCKEL, ANNETTE: *Hannah Arendt und Martin Heidegger. Geschichte und Geschichtsbegriff.* [In]: Politisches Denken, Jahrbuch 1998, Stuttgart, 1998. Pp. 175–203, footnotes. [Engl. summary on p. 203; analyses the correspondence between the two philosophers and shows Heidegger's influence on H.A.'s concept of history.]

36777. AUERBACH, ELLEN. *Ellen Auerbach. Berlin – Tel Aviv – London – New York.* Mit Beiträgen von Ute Eskilden [et al.] sowie einem Interview von Susanne Baumann. München: Prestel, 1998. 103 pp., illus. [Catalogue of exhibition at the Akademie der Künste in Berlin, May 17 – July 7, 1998.] [Cf.: "Ich bin eine unzureichende Weltbürgerin. Ein Gespräch mit der Photographin Ellen Auerbach in New York (Tekla Szymanski) [in]: Aufbau, Vol. 64, No. 13, New York, June 19, 1998, pp. 16–17.] [E.A., née Rosenberg, b. 1906 in Karlsruhe, photographer, emigr. 1933 to Palestine, 1936 to the UK, 1937 to the US. Lives in New York.]

36778. AUSLÄNDER, ROSE. RYCHLO, PETER: *"Der Jordan mündete damals in den Pruth".* Aspekte des Judentums bei Rose Ausländer. [In]: Ein Leben für Dichtung und Freiheit. Festschrift zum 70. Geburtstag von Joseph P. Strelka. Hrsg. von Karlheinz F. Auckenthaler. Tübingen: Stauffenberg-Verl., 1997. (Stauffenberg-Festschriften.) Pp. 175–194.

36779. BARON, HANS. SCHILLER, KAY: *Hans Baron's humanism.* [In]: Storia della Storiografia, No. 34, Milano, 1998. Pp. 51–99, footnotes. [Deals with life and work of H.B.] [H.B., b. June 22, 1900 in Berlin, historian of Late Middle Ages, Renaissance and Reformation, dismissed from his position as lecturer in Berlin in 1933, emigr. 1936 to UK, 1938 to US, Professor at various US universities.]

36780. BAUER, FRITZ: *Die Humanität der Rechtsordnung.* Ausgewählte Schriften. Hrsg. von Joachim Perels und Irmtrud Wojak. Frankfurt am Main; New York: Campus, 1998. 440 pp., index. (Wissenschaftliche Reihe des Fritz Bauer Instituts, Bd. 5.) [Cont. reprint of articles orig. publ. between 1955 and 1968. Incl.: Einleitung der Herausgeber: Motive im Denken und

Handeln Fritz Bauers (9–34). Articles are arranged under the following sections: Die Humanität der Rechtsordnung. Aufarbeitung der NS-Verbrechen. Widerstandsrecht. Reform des Strafrechts. Gegen autoritäres Recht. Für eine humane Rechtsordnung. Also incl. a selected bibl. Fritz Bauer.] [F.B., July 16, 1903 Stuttgart – June 30, 1968 Frankfurt am Main, lawyer. Emigr. in 1936 to Denmark, fled to Sweden in 1943, active with the SOPADE-group in Stockholm and co-founder (with Willy Brandt) of the 'Sozialistische Tribüne', returned to Germany 1949, where he was prominent in the SPD and in jurisprudence, prosecutor in Nazi war-crimes' trials, incl. the Auschwitz trial.]

36781. BECKER, JUREK. JUNG, THOMAS: *"Widerstandskämpfer oder Schriftsteller sein ...". Jurek Becker – Schreiben zwischen Sozialismus und Judentum*. Eine Interpretation der Holocaust-Texte und deren Verfilmung im Kontext. Frankfurt am Main; New York: Lang, 1998. 255 pp., illus. (Osloer Beiträge zur Germanistik, Bd. 20.) [Incl. biography and list of works of J.B.; deals mainly with 'Jakob der Lügner', 'Der Boxer', 'Bronsteins Kinder' and 'Die Mauer'.]

——— BENJAMIN, WALTER. ASAI, K.: *'Geborgensein' und 'Ausgesetztsein'. Walter Benjamins Berlin*. [See No. 35968.]

36782. BENJAMIN, WALTER. BULLOCK, MARCUS: *Walter Benjamin and Ernst Jünger: destructive affinities*. [In]: German Studies Review, Vol. 21, No. 3, Tempe, AZ, Oct. 1998. Pp. 563–581, notes.

36783. BENJAMIN, WALTER. KLEY, STEFAN: *Walter Benjamin: mysteriöser Tod im Exil*. [In]: Damals, Jg. 30, H. 7, Stuttgart, 1998. Pp. 36–42, illus.

36784. BENJAMIN, WALTER. MARCUS, LAURA/NEAD, LYNDA, eds.: *The actuality of Walter Benjamin*. London: Lawrence & Wisehart, 1998. 224 pp., illus., notes, no index. [Collection of essays on different aspects of B.'s writings and personality.]

——— BENJAMIN, WALTER. PARINI, JAY: *Benjamin's crossing*. [See No. 37134.]

36785. BERNEY, ARNOLD. MATTHIESEN, MICHAEL: *"Verlorene Identität". Der Historiker Arnold Berney und seine Freiburger Kollegen 1923–1938*. Göttingen: Vandenhoeck & Ruprecht, 1998. 131 pp., frontis., bibl. [Deals with the relation between A.B. and his colleagues Hermann Heimpel and Gerhard Ritter.] [A.B., data see No. 30971/YB XXXIX.]

36786. BLOCH, ERNST. *Bloch-Almanach*. Periodicum des Ernst-Bloch-Archivs, des Ernst-Bloch-Zentrums der Stadt Ludwigshafen am Rhein. Hrsg. von Karlheinz Weigand. [Bd. 17, Mössingen-Talheim, 1998. 1 issue, 192 pp., footnotes. [Cont. one text by E.B. and 6 contribs. on E.B.'s philosophy; also a bibl. E.B. (179–188). Selected contrib.: Ein Zuhause für den Philosophen. Ernst Bloch in Leipzig (Jürgen Teller, 157–170).]

36787. BLUM, RUDOLF. ECKERT, BRITA: *Zuflucht in Italien*. Auszug aus dem Lebensbericht von Rudolf Blum. [In]: Buchhandelsgeschichte, [Beilage zum] Börsenblatt für den Deutschen Buchhandel, Jg. 164, Nr. 3, Frankfurt am Main, 15. Sept. 1998. Pp. B 114–B 136, illus., facsims., notes. [Introduction by B.E. is followed by an excerpt of B.'s memoirs dealing with his years in Florence, 1936–1943.] [R.B., 1909 Berlin – 1998, of Jewish descent, librarian, philologist, historian. See also obit.: Rudolf Blum und der Börsenverein. Erinnerungen und Gedanken zu seinem Tode (in): Buchhandelsgeschichte Jg. 164, Nr. 1, 17. März 1998, pp. B 59–B 60.]

36788. BREDIG, GEORG. WEHEFRITZ, VALENTIN: *Pionier der Physikalischen Chemie Prof. Dr. phil. Dr. med. h.c. Dr. sc.techn. h.c. Georg Bredig (1868–1944)*. Ein deutsches Gelehrtenschicksal im 20. Jahrhundert. Mit einem Geleitwort des Rektors der Universität Karlsruhe (TH) Prof. Dr.-Ing. Sigmar Wittig. Dortmund: [Universitätsbibl. Dortmund], 1998. 96 pp., port., footnotes. (Universität im Exil; Biogr. Archiv verfolgter Universitätsprofessoren 1933–1945 an der Univ.-bibl. Dortmund, Nr. 3.) [Incl. bibl. Georg Bredig.] [G.B., Oct. 1, 1868 Glogau – April 24, 1944 New York, chemist, converted to Protestantism, prof. at Karlsruhe TH 1911–1933, emigr. 1939 via the Netherlands to the US.]

36789. BROCH, HERMANN. Bernáth, Arpád [et al.], eds.: *Hermann Broch. Persepektiven inter-disziplinärer Forschung.* Akten des internationalen Symposions Hermann Broch, József-Attila-Universität, Szeged. Tübingen: Stauffenberg Verl., 1998. XIII, 326 pp., footnotes. [Cont. 24 essays dealing with different aspects of Broch's work and its reception.]

36790. BROCH, HERMANN. Sandberg, Glenn: *Hermann Broch and Hermann Cohen: Jewish messianism and the golden age.* [In]: Modern Austrian Literature, Vol. 31, No. 2, Riverside, CA, 1998. Pp. 71–80, notes. [Discusses the influence of Hermann Cohen's messianic writings on Hermann Broch's 'Der Tod des Vergil'.]

36791. CANETTI, ELIAS. Murphy, Harriet: *Canetti and Nietzsche: theories of humor in 'Die Blendung'.* Albany: State Univ. of New York, 1997/ IX, 444 pp. (Suny series the margins of literature.) [Deals with Nietzsche's influence on Canetti's writing.]

36792. CARSTEN, FRANCIS L. *Obituaries Francis Carsten:* Obituary Francis Carsten (Henry J. Cohn) [in]: German History, Vol. 17, No. 1, London, 1999. Pp. 95–101. New light on the Reich (Richard J. Evans) [in]: The Guardian, London, July 7, 1998. [F.L. Carsten, June 25, 1911 Berlin – June 23, 1998 London, historian, 1933–1936 member of the Socialist resistance group 'Neu Beginnen', 1936–1939 Amsterdam, 1939 to UK; from 1947 university lecturer in London; from 1961 held Masaryk Professor of Central European History at the School of Slavonic and East European Studies, Univ. of London. Author of: The German workers and the Nazis. Aldershot: Scolar Press, 1995; German edn.: Widerstand gegen Hitler. Die deutschen Arbeiter und die Nazis. Aus dem Engl. vom Verfasser. Frankfurt am Main: Insel, 1996.] [See also in No. 36735.]

36793. CASSIRER, ERNST. Habermas, Jürgen: *Die befreiende Kraft der symbolischen Formgebung. Ernst Cassirers humanistisches Erbe und die Bibliothek Warburg.* [In]: Vorträge aus dem Warburg-Haus, Bd. 1, Hrsg. von Wolfgang Kemp [et al.]. Berlin: Akademie-Verl., 1997. Pp. 1–29, footnotes. [Deals with Cassirer's frequent visits to the Warburg Library in the early 1920s.]

36794. CELAN, PAUL. Felstiner, John: *Paul Celan: poet, survivor, Jew.* The Leo Baeck Memorial Lecture 41. New York: Leo Baeck Institute, 1998. 22 pp., bibl.

36795. CELAN, PAUL. Shmuel, Ilana: *Letters to the "East", on Paul Celan's letter to a childhood friend and on his meridian.* [In]: Moznaim, Vol. 72, No. 5, Tel-Aviv, Feb. 1998. Pp. 29–31. [In Hebrew, title transl.]

36796. COHEN, HERMANN. Bernstein-Nahar, Avi: *Hermann Cohen's teaching concerning modern Jewish identity (1904–1918).* [In]: Leo Baeck Institute Year Book XLIII, London 1998. Pp. 25–46, footnotes.

36797. COHEN, HERMANN. Sieg, Ulrich: *Das Testament von Hermann und Martha Cohen.* Stiftungen und Stipendien für jüdische Einrichtungen. [In]: Zeitschrift für Neuere Theologiegeschichte, Bd. 4, H. 2, Berlin, 1997. Pp. 251–264, footnotes. [Incl. Hermann Cohen's will of 1915 discovered by the author in the Marburg Staatsarchiv, providing considerable sums for Jewish institutions; the will was never executed after his widow's deportation from Berlin to Theresienstadt where she died in Sept. 1942.]

36798. DÖBLIN, ALFRED. *Alfred Döblin. Im Buch. Zu Haus. Auf der Straße.* Vorgestellt von Alfred Döblin und Oskar Loerke. Mit einer Nachbemerkung von Jochen Meyer. Marbach am Neckar: Dt. Schillergesellschaft, 1998. 212 pp., frontis., ports., illus. (Marbacher Bibliothek, 2.) [Cont. the autobiogr. text 'Erster Rückblick' (5–126). Das bisherige Werk Alfred Döblins (Oskar Loerke, 127–200; both texts were first publ. in 1928). Nach siebzig Jahren (Jochen Meyer, 201–211).]

——— DÖBLIN, ALFRED. Kojima, H.: *Die Großstadt Berlin und Alfred Döblin.* [See No. 35970.]

36799. DRUCKER, MARTIN. Lang, Hubert: *Martin Drucker – Das Ideal eines Rechtsanwalts.* Hrsg.: Ephraim Carlebach Stiftung Leipzig. Leipzig: E. Carlebach Stiftung, 1997 [?].

116 pp., illus., facsims., docs. [M.D., 1869 Leipzig – 1947 Leipzig, lawyer, Notar, president of the Deutscher Anwaltverein until 1933.]

36800. ECKSTEIN, HARRY. *Comparative Political Studies*. Vol. 31, No. 4, [with the issue title] *A tribute to Harry Eckstein*, London, 1998. 1 issue. [Incl.: A tribute to Harry Eckstein (James A. Caporaso/Alec Stone Sweet, 411–422). Harry Eckstein as political theorist (Gabriel A. Almond, 505 ff.). Also 3 further essays on aspects related to H.E.'s work and one essay by H.E.] [H.E., b. 1924 in Schotten, social scientist and political theorist, emigr. in 1936 to the US.]

36801. EDINGER, LUDWIG. KREFT, GERALD: "*. . . wie sich der ganze Mensch gebildet hat.*" *Wissenschaftlicher Erfolg und jüdische Familiengeschichte in Leben und Werk Ludwig Edingers (1855–1918)*. [In]: Medizinische Bildung und Judentum [see No. 35928]. Pp. 29–46.

36802. EDINGER, LUDWIG. KREFT, GERALD: *The work of Ludwig Edinger and his Neurology Institute*. [In]: Horst-Werner Korf/Klaus-Henning Usadel (eds.): Neuroendocrinology. Retrospect and perspectives. Heidelberg; New York: Springer, 1997. Pp. 407–424, ports., notes. [Deals also with the fate of the Neurology Institute and its Jewish scientists during the Nazi period.] [L.E., 1855 Worms – 1918 Frankfurt am Main, neurologist, founder of modern comparative neuroanatomy; lived and worked in Frankfurt am Main.]

36803. EHRLICH, PAUL. BÄUMLER, ERNST: *Paul Ehrlich. Forscher für das Leben*. 3., durchges. Aufl. Frankfurt am Main: Wötzel, 1997. 367, 24 pp., illus., geneal., notes (307–317), bib. (335–357), index. [American edn. (revised and extended, first publ. 1984): Scientist for life. New York: Holmes & Meier, 1997.]

36804. EHRLICH, PAUL. LEDERER, SUSAN E./PARASCANDOLA, JOHN: *Screening syphilis: 'Dr. Ehrlich's Magic Bullet' meets the public health service*. [In]: Journal of the History of Medicine and Allied Sciences, Vol. 53, No. 1, Oxford, Jan. 1998. Pp. 345–370, footnotes, illus. [On a Hollywood film (1940) on Paul Ehrlich, starring Edward G. Robinson, which Jack Warner used to promote a positive view of Jewish contributions to society in the light of Nazi antisemitism.]

36805. EHRLICH, PAUL. WITKOP, BERNHARD: *Der unbekannte Paul Ehrlich*. [In]: Akademische Geburtstagsfeier für Universitätsprofessor Dr. med. Dr. h.c. Hans Schadewaldt 7. Mai 1998. Düsseldorf: Triltsch, 1998. (Düsseldorfer Arbeiten zur Geschichte der Medizin, Beiheft XIII.) Pp. 39–57, illus., port.

36807. EINSTEIN, ALBERT. GRUNDMANN, SIEGFRIED: *Einsteins Akte. Einsteins Jahre in Deutschland aus der Sicht der deutschen Politik*. Berlin; New York: Springer, 1998. XVI, 535 pp., illus., docs., notes (419–476), name index (477–516), bibl. (517–533). [Covers the years 1919 until 1934 as reflected in a file held in the Geheimes Staatsarchiv Preußischer Kulturbesitz.]

36808. EINSTEIN, ALBERT. TONIETTI, TITO M.: *Albert Einstein and Arnold Schönberg correspondence*. [In]: 'NTM', Internationale Zeitschrift für Geschichte und Ethik der Naturwissenschaftem, Technik und Medizin, N.S., Vol. 5, Basel, 1997. Pp. 1–22.

36809. EINSTEIN, CARL. *Etudes Germaniques*. Vol. 53, No. 1 [with the issue title]: Carl Einstein, Paris, Janvier-Mars 1998. 272 pp., footnotes. [Incl. 13 contribs. on C.E. and a bibliography.]

36810. EINSTEIN, CARL. GORSEN, PETER: *Die Irrationalisierung der Welt*. Carl Einstein, ein Grenzgänger, Lebensphilosoph und Surrealist. [In]: 'FAZ', Frankfurt am Main, Nr. 113, Frankfurt am Main, 16. Mai 1998. P. II, Beilage. [C.E., 1885 Neuwied – 1940 France (suicide), art historian, lived from 1928 in Paris.]

36811. ELIAS, NORBERT. MENNELL, STEPHEN/GOUDSBLOM, JOHAN: *The Norbert Elias reader: a biographical selection*. Oxford; Malden, MA: Blackwell, 1998. X, 295 pp., notes, bibl. (The heritage of sociology.)

36812. ELIAS, NORBERT: *On civilization, power, and knowledge: selected writings*. Ed. by Stephen Mennell and Johan Goudsblom. Chicago: Univ. of Chicago Press, 1998. IX, 302 pp., notes.

36813. ELKAN, BENNO. *Benno Elkan. Ein jüdischer Künstler aus Dortmund.* [Text]: Fritz Hofmann, Peter Schneider. Mit Fotografien von Jürgen Spiler. Hrsg.: Rosemarie E. Pahlke, Museum am Ostwall/Stadtsparkasse Dortmund. Essen: Klartext, 1998. 128 pp., illus. [Incl. a chap. on E.'s 'Große Menorah' (Jerusalem); also a chap. 'Jüdische Kunst'.] [B.E., Dec. 2, 1877 Dortmund – Jan. 10, 1960 London, sculptor, lived from 1919 in Frankfurt am Main, emigr. to London in 1934.]

36814. ETTLINGER, KARL. Hock, Sabine: *"Ich bin ein Spötter nur, ein loser."* Karl Ettlinger (1882–1939) und seine Mitarbeit bei der Münchner Wochenschrift "Jugend" in der Zeit von 1902 bis zum Beginn des Ersten Weltkrieges. Nidderau: Verl. Michaela Naumann, 1998. 340 pp., footnotes, bibl. K.E. (320–326), bibl. (327–340). Zugl.: Frankfurt am Main: Univ., Diss., 1997. [K.E., Jan. 22, 1882 Frankfurt am Main – May 29, 1939 Berlin, writer.]

36815. FACKENHEIM, EMIL. Braiterman, Zachary: *Fideism redux: Emil Fackenheim and the State of Israel.* [In]: Jewish Social Studies, Vol. 4, No. 1, Bloomington, IN, Fall 1997. Pp. 105–120, notes.

36816. Federn, Ernst: *Versuche zur Psychologie des Terrors: Material zum Leben und Werk von Ernst Federn.* Hrsg. von Roland Kaufhold. Gießen: Psychosozial-Verl., 1998. 244 pp., bibl. [Cont. texts on and by E.F. Some (on concentration camps) were written by E.F. in 1945/1946. Selected articles: Das Leben Ernst Federns im absoluten Terror des nationalsozialistischen Lagersystems (Bernhard Kuschey, 111–127). Überleben im Terror – Ernst Federns Geschichte. Zur Entstehung des Filmes mit Ernst Federn und Hilde Federn (Wilhelm Rösing/Martha Barthel-Rösing, 128–144). Zum Briefwechsel zwischen Bruno Bettelheim und Ernst Federn (Roland Kaufhold, 145–174). Der Terror als System: Das Konzentrationslager (1945). Mit einer Einführung von W. Rösing (Ernst Federn, 175–218). Dokumentation des Briefwechsels Bruno Bettelheim – Ernst Federn (219–236).] [E.F., b. Aug. 26, 1914 in Vienna, psychotherapist, social worker, imprisoned from 1938 to 1945 in Dachau and Buchenwald, after liberation emigr. to Brussels, 1948 to the US. Remigr. 1972 to Austria, lives in Vienna.]

36817. FEIGEL, SIGI. *Schweizer auf Bewährung. Klara Obermüller im Gespräch mit Sigi Feigel.* Zürich: Chronos, 1998. 171 pp., illus., docs. [Incl. antisemitic letters written to S.F.] [S.F., b. 1921 in Zurich, son of Ukrainian immigrants, lawyer, for 16 years president (at present honorary president) of the Israelitische Cultusgemeinde Zurich.]

36818. FEUCHTWANGER, LION. Jaeger, Roland: *"He just wanted books".* Lion Feuchtwanger als *Büchersammler.* [In]: Aus dem Antiquariat, [Beilage zum] Börsenblatt für den Deutschen Buchhandel, Jg. 165, Nr. 43, Frankfurt am Main, 29. Mai 1998. Pp. A 330–A 341, illus., notes.

36819. FEUCHTWANGER, LION. Levesque, Paul: *Mapping the other: Lion Feuchtwanger's topographies of the Orient.* [In]: The German Quarterly, Vol. 71, No. 2, Cherry Hill, NJ, Spring 1998. Pp. 145–165, notes. [On Feuchtwanger's views on the Jew as an Oriental, also on 'Jud Süss'.]

36820. FLECHTHEIM, OSSIP K. *Obituaries Ossip K. Flechtheim.* In memoriam: Ossip K. Flechtheim (John H. Herz) [in]: Aufbau, Vol. 64, No. 6, New York, March 13, 1998. P. 22. Ossip K. Flechtheim (1909–1998). Wissenschaftler und Aktivist (John H. Herz) [see in No. 36239]. [Ossip K. Flechtheim, May 5, 1909 Nikolayev (Russia) – March 4, 1998 Berlin, political scientist, for further data see No. 28704/YB XXXVII.]

36821. FORST, SIEGMUND. *Siegmund Forst: a lifetime in arts & letters.* Ed. by Cynthia Elyce Rubin. New York: Yeshiva Univ. Museum, 1997. 76 pp., illus., ports. [S.F., b. 1904 in Vienna, illustrator, calligrapher, now lives in the US. Catalogue publ. as a companion to the exhibition on S.F. held at the Yeshiva Univ. Museum, Sept. 27, 1997 – July 31, 1998.]

36822. FRANKL, VIKTOR EMIL. Längle, Alfried: *Viktor Frankl.* Ein Porträt. München: Piper, 1998. 335 pp., illus., graphs., bibl. [See also No. 36992.] [Cf.: Unorthodox als Psychotherapeut und Jude. Eine neue Biographie des Psychologen Viktor Emil Frankl, des

Vaters der Logotherapie (Yizhak Ahren) [in]: Allg. Jüd. Wochenzeitung, Jg. 54, Nr. 5, Berlin, 4. März 1999, p. 7, port.] [See also No. 36992.]

36823. FREUD, SIGMUND. RHEINZ, HANNA: *Unentdeckte Obsessionen. Tierbilder und Tierlieben im Werk des Sigmund Freud.* [In]: Jüdischer Almanach 1999 des Leo Baeck Instituts, Frankfurt am Main, 1998. Pp. 103–117, illus, notes.

36824. FREUD, SIGMUND. ZAHAVI, ELIAHU, ed.: *Freud – soul and sex.* Haifa: Dimyon, 1997. 151 pp. [In Hebrew.] [A collection of brief aphorismic sentences and passages from F.'s works, transl. from English edns. by Nurit Schreiber-Kalati.]

36825. FRIED, ERICH. *Erich Fried. Eine Chronik.* Leben und Werk: das biographische Lesebuch. Hrsg. von Christiane Jessen, Volker Kaukoreit und Klaus Wagenbach. Berlin: Wagenbach, 1998. 127 pp., frontis., illus., facsims.

36826. FRIED, ERICH. LAWRIE, STEVEN: '*Das grosse Trauerfeld, auf dem sie sich versuchen': Erich Fried's work for German radio.* [In]: German Life & Letters, Vol. 51, No. 1, Oxford, Jan. 1998. Pp. 121–146, footnotes.

36827. FRIEDLANDER, ELIZABETH. PAUCKER, PAULINE: *New borders: the working life of Elizabeth Friedlander.* Oldham: Incline Press, 1998. 92 pp., illus. [E.F., 1903 Berlin – 1984 Kinsale, Ireland. Graphic designer. Worked for Ullstein Press, emigr. 1936 to Italy, 1939 to UK. During the war worked for 'Black Propaganda' outfit, faking German documents. After the war re-started career as free-lance designer (Penguin, Monotype et al.), retiring to Ireland in 1961.] [Cf.: Le beau métier d'Elizabeth (Claude Weber) [in]: Gréngespoun, No. 190, Luxembourg, June 15, 1999, p.9.]

36828. FUCHS, WOLFGANG. MILNE ANDERSON J. [et al.]: *Wolfgang Heinrich Johannes Fuchs (1915–1997).* [In]: Notices of the American Mathematical Society, Vol. 45, No. 11, Washington, DC, Dec. 1998. Pp. 1472–1478, ports., notes. [Obituary, dealing with F.'s life and work.] [W.F., May 19, 1915 Munich – Feb. 24, 1997, Ithaca, NY, mathematician, went to Cambridge, UK, in 1933, his parents following him in 1939; from 1948 at Cornell University, becoming member of the faculty in 1950.]

36829. GANS, EDUARD. WASZEK, NORBERT: *Gans'Erbrecht als rechtshistorische Anwendung der Hegelschen Geschichtsphilosophie und im Kontext des rechtswissenschaftlichen Methodenstreits seiner Zeit.* [In]: Hegels Vorlesungen über die Philosophie der Weltgeschichte. Hrsg. von Elisabeth Weisser-Lohmann und Dietmar Köhler. Bonn: Bouvier, 1998. Pp. 185–203, footnotes.

36830. GELLNER, ERNEST. *The social philosophy of Ernest Gellner.* Ed. by John A. Hall and Ian Jarvin. Amsterdam; Atlanta, GA, 1996. 730 pp., footnotes. (Poznan studies in the philosophy of the sciences and the humanities, Vol. 48.) [Cont. 32 essays on several aspects of Gellner's work, two of them dealing with his life and intellectual background; also a reply by Gellner and a complete bibl. of his work (687–718). Cf.: Obituary Ernest Gellner (S.N. Eisenstadt) [in]: Proceedings of the American Philosophical Society, Vol. 142, No. 1, Philadelphia, PA, March 1998. Pp. 134–137, port.] [Ernest André G., Dec. 9, 1925 Paris – Nov. 5, 1995 Prague, philosopher, born into a German-speaking Czech family, educated in an English school in Prague, emigr. to the UK in 1938, professor of philosophy at the London School of Economics, and at Cambridge Univ., from 1993 closely connected with the Central European Univ. in Prague.]

36831. GLASER, CURT. STROBL, ANDREAS: *Curt Glaser und die 'Deutschen Meister' des Insel-Verlags.* [In]: Aus dem Antiquariat, [Beilage zum] Börsenblatt für den Deutschen Buchhandel, Jg. 165, Nr. 3, Frankfurt am Main, 31. März 1998. Pp. A 166–A 183, illus., notes. [C.G., art historian, for data see No. 27682/YB XXXVI.]

36832. GLÜCKEL VON HAMELN. TURNIANSKY, CHAVA: *A Jewish woman's life. The memoirs of Glikl (Hamel).* [In]: Sexuality and the family in history; collected essays. Ed. by Israel

Bartal and Isaiah Gafni. Jerusalem: Zalman Shazar Center for Jewish History, 1998. Pp. 177–191.

36833. GOLDHABER, GERTRUDE SCHARFF. Bond, Peter D.: *Obituary Gertrude Scharff Goldhaber*. [In]: Physics Today, Vol. 51, Washington DC, July 1998. Pp. 82–83, port. [G. Sch.G., July 14, 1911 Mannheim – Feb. 2, 1998 Patchogue, NY, nuclear physicist, emigr. to England in 1935, to the US in 1939, professor at the Univ. of Illinois and at the Brookhaven National Laboratory, elected to the National Academy of Sciences in 1972.]

36834. GOLDSTEIN, KURT. Kreft, Gerald: *"... weil man es in Deutschland einfach verschwiegen hat ...". Kurt Goldstein (1878–1965), Begründer der Neuropsychologie in Frankfurt am Main*. [In]: Forschung Frankfurt, H. 4, Frankfurt am Main, 1998. Pp. 78–90, ports., illus., facsims., bibl. [K.G., Nov. 6, 1878 Kattowitz (Upper Silesia) – Sept. 19, 1965 New York, neurologist, 1922 – 1930 director of the Frankfurt Institute of Neurology, 1930 – 1933 director of the Department of Neurology of the Krankenhaus Moabit in Berlin, emigr. 1933 via Switzerland to The Netherlands, in 1935 to the US.]

36835. GRÜNHUT, MAX. Fontaine, Ulrike: *Max Grünhut (1893–1964). Leben und wissenschaftliches Wirken eines deutschen Strafrechtlers jüdischer Herkunft*. Frankfurt am Main; New York: Lang, 1998. 176 pp., footnotes, bibl. (169–176). (Schriften zum Strafrecht und Strafprozeßrecht, Bd. 31.) Zugl.: Göttingen, Univ., Diss., 1997. [M.G., 1893 Magdeburg – 1964 Oxford, baptised, criminologist and penal reformer, univ. professor, evicted from Bonn Univ. in 1933, emigr. to the UK in 1939. Became reader of criminology at Oxford Univ.]

36836. GRUNWALD, CLARA. Schürings, Hans: *Clara Grunwalds Weg von Rheydt nach Auschwitz*. [In]: Rheydter Jahrbuch 24, Mönchengladbach, 1998. Pp. 69–78, illus., notes. [C.G., educator, data see No. 33372/YB XLI.]

36837. GUMPERT, MARTIN. Ittner, Jutta: *Augenzeuge im Dienst der Wahrheit: Leben und literarisches Werk Martin Gumperts (1897–1955)*. Bielefeld: Aisthesis, 1998. 508 pp., illus., chronol., bibl. (462–479), bibl. M.G. (483–497). Zugl.: Hamburg, Univ., Diss., 1995. [M.G., Nov. 13, 1897 Berlin – April 18, 1955 New York, physician, writer, medical journalist, emigr. in 1936 to the US.]

36838. GUTTMANN, WALTER. Voswinckel, Peter: *Um das Lebenswerk betrogen: Walter Guttmann (1873–1941) und seine 'Medizinische Terminologie'*. Oder: von den Fallstricken und Versäumnissen deutscher Biblio- und Historiographie und den Folgen unkritischen Kompilierens im Computerzeitalter. [In]: Medizinhistorisches Journal, Bd. 32, H. 3/4, Jena, 1997. Pp. 321–354, footnotes, facsims., tabs. [On the 'aryanisation' of medical literature.] [W.G. (from 1920: Walter Marle), Jan. 26, 1873 Hirschberg – Sept. 18, 1941 Berlin, converted to Protestantism, senior medical consultant, medical writer.]

36839. HABER, FRITZ. Szöllösi-Janze, Margit: *Fritz Haber 1868–1934*. Eine Biographie. München: Beck, 1998. 928 pp., illus., notes (709–851), bibl. (incl. bibl. F.H., 855–905), indexes (persons, institutions, 870–928). [Cf.: Besprechung (Notker Hammerstein) [in]: Historische Zeitschrift, Bd. 268, H. 3, München, Juni 1999, pp. 699–701. Besprechung (Jörg Hackeschmidt) [in]: Zeitschrift für Geschichtswissenschaft, Jg. 47, H. 1, Berlin, 1999, pp. 58–60. Deutscher als der Kaiser. Das tragische Leben des Chemikers Fritz Haber (Dirk van Laak) [in]: Die Zeit, Nr. 24, Hamburg, 4. Juni 1998, p. 36. Insignien der Moderne. Margit Szöllösi-Janzes vortreffliche Biographie des Wissenschaftlers Fritz Haber (Udo Schumacher) [in]: 'FAZ', Nr. 183, Frankfurt am Main, 10. Aug. 1999.]

36840. HECHT, OTTO. Hering, Rainer: *"... daß sie im Gefühle eigener Schuld so reagieren möchten, wie ich es von Ihnen erhoffe." Ein Briefwechsel über das "Dritte Reich" zwischen den Tropenmedizinern Erich Martini und Otto Hecht 1946/47*. Prof. Dr. Peter Borowsky zum 60. Geburtstag am 3. Juni 1998. [In]: Zeitschrift des Vereins für Hamburgische Geschichte, Bd. 84, Hamburg, 1998. Pp. 185–224, ports., illus., footnotes. [Incl. letters of O.H. and his former superior E.M., anatomist, zoologist, since May 1933 active member of the NSDAP.] [O.H., 1900 Ulm – 1973

Mexico City, chemist, zoologist, dismissed from the Hamburg "Tropeninstitut" in 1933, emigr. in the same year to Palestine, in 1940 to Venezuela, in 1945 to Mexico.]

36841. HEINE, HEINRICH. ARENDT, DIETER: *Heine – ein Tribun mit der Schellenkappe oder: ein politischer Don Quichote.* [In]: Sprache und Literatur, Jg. 28, H. 2, Paderborn, 1997. Pp. 3–20, footnotes.

36842. HEINE, HEINRICH. ELONI, YEHUDA: *Heinrich Heine as a journalist.* [In]: Qesher, No. 22, Tel-Aviv, Nov. 1997. Pp. 32–41. [In Hebrew, with English summary.]

36843. HEINE, HEINRICH. *Die Jahre kommen und vergehn! 10 Jahre Heinrich-Heine-Universität Düsseldorf.* Hrsg. von Holger Ehlert [et al.] Düsseldorf: Grupello, 1998. 299 pp., frontis., illus., notes. [A collection of 46 articles, some of them dealing with various aspects of Heine's life, his work and reception, others with the controversy over the re-naming of Düsseldorf university and related political issues.]

36844. HEINE, HEINRICH. LOSSIN, YIGAL: *On behalf of the persecuted Jews of Damascus: a chapter in the journalistic history of Heinrich Heine.* [In]: Qesher, No. 22, Tel-Aviv, Nov. 1997. Pp. 48–59. [In Hebrew, with English summary.]

36845. HEINE, HEINRICH. MAYER, HANS: *Der Weg Heinrich Heines.* Versuche. Frankfurt am Main: Suhrkamp, 1998. 117 pp. [A collection of five previously publ. articles on H.H.]

36846. HEINE, HEINRICH. PETERS, GEORGE F.: *Review essay: Heinrich Heine at 200.* [In]: The German Quarterly, Vol. 71, No. 3, Cherry Hill, NJ, Summer 1998. Pp. 284–298, notes. [Lists recent publications on Heine.]

36847. HEINE, HEINRICH. SCHÄRF, CHRISTIAN: *Die Selbstinszenierung des modernen Autors. Heinrich Heines "Ideen. Das Buch Le Grand".* [In]: literatur für leser, Jg. 21, H. 4, Frankfurt am Main, 1998. Pp. 301–311, footnotes.

36848. HEINE, HEINRICH. SCHLINGENSIEPEN, FERDINAND/WINDFUHR, MANFRED, eds.: *Heinrich Heine und die Religion, ein kritischer Rückblick.* Ein Symposium der Evangelischen Kirche im Rheinland vom 27.-30. Oktober 1997. Düsseldorf: Archiv d. Evang. Kirche, 1998. 244 pp., footnotes. (Schriften des Archivs der Evang. Kirche im Rheinland Nr. 21.) [Incl. 11 essays by Manfred Windfuhr, Peter Guttenhöfer, Alfred Bodenheimer, Edith Lutz, Ferdinand Schlingensiepen, Beate Wirth-Ortmann, Hubert Wolf, Wolfgang Schopf, Joseph A. Kruse, Wilhelm Gössmann and Michael Schmidt.]

36849. HEINE, HEINRICH. SCHULZ, JÜRGEN MICHAEL: *Heine – the link between literature and journalism.* [In]: Qesher, No. 22, Tel-Aviv, Nov. 1997. Pp. 42–47. [In Hebrew, with English summary.]

36850. HEINE, HEINRICH. WOLF, HUBERT [et al.]: *Die Macht der Zensur. Heinrich Heine auf dem Index.* Düsseldorf: Patmos, 1998. 272 pp., footnotes, docs., bibl. (260–270). [Incl.: A. Zwischen Amboß und Hammer: Heinrich Heine unter staatlicher und kirchlicher Zensur (Hubert Wolf/Dominik Burkhard, 11–143). B. Dokumentation der Indexverfahren (154–190). C. Analyse der Gutachten (Gisbert Lepper, 191–219). D. Heinrich Heine: Religionskritik, Zensur und Selbstzensur (Wolfgang Schopf, 220–259).]

36851. HERMANN, GEORG. CASPARY, ARPE: *Vom hellen Grund der Vernunft. Zum 55. Todesjahr des Schriftstellers Georg Hermann.* [In]: Aufbau, Vol. 64, No. 24, New York, Nov. 20, 1998. Pp. 5–6, port.

36852. HESS, MOSES. SHULMAN, MARY: *Moses Hess and his times.* [In]: Jewish Frontier, Vol. 45, No. 2, New York, March/April 1998. Pp. 24–27.

36853. HEYM, STEFAN. TAIT, MEG: *Stefan Heym's 'Radek': the conscience of a revolutionary.* [In]: German Life & Letters, Vol. 51, No. 4, Oxford, Oct. 1998. Pp. 496–508, notes.

36854. HILFERDING, RUDOLF. Smaldone, William: _Rudolf Hilferding: the tragedy of a German Social Democrat._ DeKalb: Northern Illinois Univ. Press, 1998. 271 pp., illus., frontis., notes (213–245), bibl. (247–262). [R.H., 1877 Vienna – 1941 France (suicide), Socialist politician, finance minister in the Weimar Republic.]

36855. HINTZE, HEDWIG. Kaudelka, Steffen: _Ein Lebenslauf mit Geschichte._ Manche führten den Krieg der Geister, Hedwig Hintze hatte Geist und entdeckte die Schicksalsgemeinschaft der Völker. [In]: 'FAZ', Nr. 235, Frankfurt am Main, 10. Okt. 1998. Beilage, p. IV, port. [H.H., née Guggenheimer, 1884 Munich – July 19, 1942 Utrecht (suicide), historian, university lecturer, wife of Otto Hintze (1861–1940).]

36856. HIRSCH, RAHEL. Chevallier, Sonja: _Fräulein Professor: Lebensspuren der Ärztin Rahel Hirsch 1870–1953._ Düsseldorf: Droste, 1998. 220 pp., illus., chronol. [R.H., 1870 Frankfurt am Main – 1953 nr. London, physician, from 1903–1919 at the Charité, Berlin, emigr. 1938 to the UK.]

36857. HÖNIGSWALD, RICHARD. Grassl, Roswitha: _Der junge Richard Hönigswald._ Eine biographisch fundierte Kontextualisierung in historischer Absicht. Würzburg: Königshausen & Neumann, 1998. 304 pp., footnotes, bibl. (251–298), index. (Studien und Materialien zum Neukantianismus, Bd. 13.) Zugl.: Mannheim, Univ., Diss., 1997. [Incl.: Zur Biobibliographie Richard Hönigswalds (205–241).] [R.H., July 18, 1875 Ungarisch-Altenburg – July 11, 1947 New Haven, CT, philosopher, dismissed from Munich Univ. in 1933, emigr. to the US in 1939.]

36858. HOLLÄNDER, LUDWIG. Miron, Guy: _Between integration and isolation._ [In]: Yahadut Zemanenu, Vol. 11–12, Jerusalem, 1998. Pp. 99–124. [In Hebrew, with English summary.] [On the writings of Ludwig Holländer, C.V. director, lawyer, publisher.]

36859. HORKHEIMER, MAX. Wiggershaus, Rolf: _Max Horkheimer zur Einführung._ Hamburg: Junius, 1998. 129 pp., bibl., chronol. [On H.'s life and work.]

36860. HOROVITZ, BELA. Spivey, Nigel: _For ordinary mortals: the birth of the Phaidon Press and the rebirth of "aura"._ [In]: TLS, London, April 3, 1998. P. 14, illus. [Deals with B. H., 1898 Budapest – 1955 New York, publisher, founder of the Phaidon Press (orig. in Vienna) and the East & West Library, which publ. the Leo Baeck Institute Year Book from 1956–1971.]

36861. ISING, ERNST. Kobe, Sigismund: _Ernst Ising – physicist and teacher._ [In]: Journal of Statistical Physics, Vol. 88, Nos. 3/4, New York, 1997. Pp. 991–995, port., notes. [Obituary by the same author: Das Ising-Modell – gestern und heute (in): Physikalische Blätter, Jg. 54, Nr. 10, Weinheim, 1998. Pp. 917–920, ports., notes.] [E.I., May 10, 1900 Cologne – May 11, 1998 Peoria, IL, theoretical physicist, teacher, 1934–1938 teacher and headmaster of the Jewish Landschulheim Caputh, survived the war in Luxembourg, emigr. to the US in 1947, where he was professor of physics at Bradley University, Peoria, from 1948 until 1976.]

36862. JONAS, HANS. Seidel, Ralf & Roman: _Hans Jonas._ Mönchengladbach: Gladbacher Bank, 1997. 81 pp. (Zeugen städtischer Vergangenheit, 15.)

36863. KAFKA, FRANZ. Arbib, Marina: _"Faith as the tool of the guillotine": on Kafka and his Jewish thoughts in his diaries and in his aphorisms._ [In]: Moznaim, Vol. 72, No. 5, Tel-Aviv, Feb. 1998. Pp. 7–9. [In Hebrew, title transl.]

36864. KAFKA, FRANZ. Karl, Frederick, R.: _In the struggle between you and Kafka, back yourself._ [In]: American Imago, Vol. 55, No. 2, Baltimore, Summer 1998. Pp. 189–204, notes. [Discusses Kafka's life, incl. his Jewish background.]

36865. KAFKA, FRANZ. Philipp, Frank, ed.: _The legacy of Kafka in contemporary Austrian literature._ Riverside, CA: Ariadne Press, 1997. 231 pp. (Studies in Austrian literature, culture, and thought.)

36866. KAFKA, FRANZ. Voigts, Manfred: *Kafka und die jüdische Frau. Die Diskussionen um Erotik und Sexualität im Prager Zionismus.* [In]: Aschkenas, Jg. 8, H. 1, Wien, 1998. Pp. 125–177, footnotes.

36867. KANTOROWICZ, ERNST H.. *Geschichtskörper. Zur Aktualität von Ernst H. Kantorowicz.* Hrsg. von Wolfgang Ernst und Cornelia Vismann. München: Fink, 1998. 239 pp., footnotes, index. [Cont. 14 essays, two of them dealing with biographical aspects: Ein Posener Itinerar zu Kantorowicz (Adam S. Labuda, 73–103, illus.; deals with the Jews of Posen and particularly with the Kantorowicz family and their business). Ernst H. Kantorowicz. Eine archäobiographische Skizze (Peter Th. Walther/Wolfgang Ernst, 207–233).] [Cf.: Zu den Sternen sah er führerlos hinan. Wie Ernst Kantorowicz Orientierung suchte und gab (Michael Borgolte) [in]: 'FAZ', Nr. 33, Frankfurt am Main, 9. Feb. 1999, p. 53.]

36868. Keilson, Hans: *Wohin die Sprache nicht reicht.* Essays – Vorträge – Aufsätze 1936 – 1996. Mit einem Nachwort von Wolfdietrich Schmied-Kowarzik. Gießen: Ricker'sche Univ.-Buchhandlung, 1998. 264 pp., frontis., notes, bibl. [Incl. personal recollections, essays dealing with K.'s work as a therapist with Jewish orphans, with trauma, antisemitism of the Left.] [H.K., born 1909, psychotherapist and writer; further data see No. 28743/YB XXXVII.]

36869. Kerr, Alfred: *"Ich sage, was zu sagen ist".* Theaterkritiken 1893–1919. Hrsg. von Günther Rühle. Frankfurt am Main: S. Fischer, 1998. 959 pp., frontis., chronol. (Alfred Kerr/Werke in Einzelbänden, Bd. VII, 1.)

36870. KISCH, EGON ERWIN. Patka, Marcus G., ed.: *Der rasende Reporter Egon Erwin Kisch.* Eine Biographie in Bildern. Mit einem Vorwort von Hellmuth Karasek. Berlin: Aufbau, 1998. 303 pp., illus.

36871. KLEMPERER, VICTOR. *Leben in zwei Diktaturen: Victor Klemperers Leben in der NS-Zeit und in der DDR.* Eine Tagung der Friedrich-Ebert-Stiftung in Zusammenarbeit mit dem Verein "Gegen das Vergessen – Für Demokratie" am 19. und 20. Sept. 1997 in Dresden. [Red.: Christoph Wielepp/Hans-Peter Lühr]. Dresden: Friedrich-Ebert-Stiftung, Büro Dresden, 1997. 81 pp.

36872. KLEMPERER, VICTOR. Stammen, Theo: *Zeitzeugenschaft. Die Tagebücher von Victor Klemperer 1933–1945.* [In]: Edith Stein Jahrbuch, Bd. 4, Würzburg, 1998. Pp. 391–409, footnotes.

36873. KLEMPERER, VICTOR. Watt, Roderick H.: *Victor Klemperer's 'Sprache des Vierten Reichs': LTI=LQI?* [In]: German Life & Letters, Vol. 51, No. 3, Oxford, July 1998. Pp. 360–371, notes.

36874. KOESTLER, ARTHUR. Cesarani, David: *Arthur Koestler: the homeless mind.* London: Heinemann, 1998. X, 646 pp., illus., ports., notes (577–621), bibl. (622–627), bibl. of K.'s works. [Incl. his Jewish background and upbringing, his interest in Zionism and his experiences under Communism and Nazism.]

36875. KOLMAR, GERTRUD. Jäger, Gudrun: *Gertrud Kolmar: Publikations- und Rezeptionsgeschichte.* Frankfurt am Main; New York: Campus, 1998. 297 pp., illus., facsims., footnotes, bibl. (270–297). (Campus Judaica, 12.)

——— KOLMAR, GERTRUD. Yamaguchi, Y.: *Berlin im Roman "Eine jüdische Mutter" von Gertrud Kolmar.* [See No. 35972.]

36876. KOMPERT, LEOPOLD. Wittemann, M. Theresia: *Draußen vor dem Ghetto. Leopold Kompert und die 'Schilderung jüdischen Volkslebens' in Böhmen und Mähren.* Tübingen: Niemeyer, 1998. VI, 399 pp., footnotes, bibl. (355–384), illus., index (persons). (Conditio Judaica, 22.) Zugl.: München, Univ., Diss., 1997. [L.K., 1822 Münchengrätz, Bohemia – 1886 Vienna, writer.] [Cf.: Besprechung (Ritchie Robertson) [in]: Aschkenas, Jg. 9. H. 1, Wien, 1999, pp. 258–258.]

36877. KORTNER, FRITZ. Critchfield, Richard: *Fritz Kortner and anti-semitism*. [In]: Literatur und Geschichte. Festschrift für Wulf Koepke zum 70. Geburtstag. Hrsg. von Karl Menges. Amsterdam; Atlanta, GA: Rodopi, 1998. (Amsterdamer Publikationen zur Sprache und Literatur, 133.). Pp. 205–219, notes. [Deals with K.'s encounters with antisemitism during his childhood years in Vienna and his pre- and post-exile years in Berlin as an actor and theatre director.]

36878. KRACAUER, SIEGFRIED. Belke, Ingrid: *Neue Veröffentlichungen zu Siegfried Kracauer*. [In]: Soziologische Revue, Jg. 21, München, 1998. Pp. 307–313. [Review essay.]

36879. KRAUS, KARL. Leshem, Giora: *The painters of wolves; on Karl Kraus and his unique achievement*. [In]: Moznaim, Vol. 72, No. 5, Tel Aviv, Feb. 1998. Pp. 44–48. [In Hebrew, title transl.]

36880. KUCZYNSKI, JÜRGEN. *Selected obituaries*. Nachruf Jürgen Kuczynski 1904–1997 (Jan Peters) [in]: 1999. Zeitschrift für Sozialgeschichte des 20. und 21. Jahrhunderts, Jg. 13, H. 1, Hamburg, März 1998. Pp. 240–245. Jürgen Kuczynski tot (Hans G. Helms, 3–6) [in]: Marginalien, H. 47, Wiesbaden, 1997. Pp. 3–5. Der letzte seiner Art (Stan Schneider) [in]: 'Allgemeine', Jg. 52, Nr. 17, Bonn, 21. Aug. 1997. P. 6. Dissident auf Linie. Zum Tode von Jürgen Kuczynski, Großbürger und Sozialist (Klaus Hartung) [in]: Die Zeit, Nr. 34, Hamburg, 15. Aug. 1997. P. 18. See also No. 37002.] [J.K., 1904 Elberfeld – 1997 Berlin, Marxist historian, emigr. 1936 to the UK, from 1946 professor at the Humboldt Univ. in East Berlin, founder and long-time director of the Akademie-Institut für Wirtschaftsgeschichte.]

36881. KUTTNER, STEPHAN GEORGE. Tierney, Brian: *Stephan George Kuttner* [Obituary]. [In]: Proceedings of the American Philosophical Society, Vol. 142, No. 3, Philadelphia, PA, Sept. 1998. Pp. 486–491, port. [St.G. K., Aug. 24, 1907 Bonn – Aug. 12, 1996, historian of canon law, born into a family of Jewish descent, brought up as a Lutheran, converted to Catholicism, emigr. in 1933 to Italy, in 1940 to the US, professor at the Catholic Univ. of America in Washington, DC, at Yale and at the Univ. of California at Berkeley.]

36882. LANDAUER-LACHMANN, HEDWIG. Seemann, Birgit: *Hedwig Landauer-Lachmann. Dichterin, Antimilitaristin, deutsche Jüdin*. Frankfurt; New York: Campus, 1998. 146 pp., illus., footnotes, bibl. (138–146). (Campus Judaica, Bd. 11.) [Incl. bibl. of H. L.-L.'s works.] [H.L., data see No. 31073/YB XXXIX.]

36883. Lasker-Schüler, Else: *Werke und Briefe*. Kritische Ausgabe, B. 3, I: Prosa 1903–1920. Bearb. von Ricarda Dick. Frankfurt am Main: Jüd. Verlag, 1998. 544 pp., illus., indexes.

36884. LASKER-SCHÜLER, ELSE. *Deine Sehnsucht war die Schlange*. Else Lasker-Schüler Almanach. Hrsg. von Anne Linsel und Peter von Matt. Red.: Manfred Escherig. Wuppertal: Hammer Verlag; Else-Lasker-Schüler-Ges., 1997. 256 pp., notes. (Else-Lasker-Schüler-Almanach, Bd. 3.) [Cont. ten essays.]

36885. LASKER-SCHÜLER, ELSE. Frank, Bernhard: *Eve's song: observations on the poetry of Else Lasker-Schüler*. [In]: Judaism, Vol. 47, No. 3, New York, Summer 1998. Pp. 298–310, notes.

36886. LEICHTER, KÄTHE. Steiner, Herbert, ed.: *Käthe Leichter. Leben, Werk und Sterben einer österreichischen Sozialdemokratin*. Wien: Ibera und Molden, 1997. 520 pp. [K.L., née Pick, Aug. 20, 1895 Vienna – Feb. 1942, nr. Magdeburg, SDAP politician, publicist, arrested in May 1938, sent to Ravensbrück in May 1940, murdered in Feb. 1942.]

36887. LESSING, THEODOR. *Zeitschrift für Religions- und Geistesgeschichte*. Jg. 50, H. 3 [with the issue title]: *Themenschwerpunkt: Theodor Lessing und seine Zeitgenossen – eine Würdigung zum 65. Todestag*. Leiden, 1998. 1 issue, footnotes. [Incl. (titles abbr.): Vorwort (Redaktion: Julius H. Schoeps/Christoph Schulte/Christine Stumpfe, 193–194). Theodor Lessing im Geiste seiner Zeitgenossen (Elke-Vera Kotowski, 193–218). Überlegungen zu Identität und Projektion in Theodor Lessings Essay "Der jüdische Selbsthaß" am Beispiel der Fallstudie über Maximilian Harden (Andrea Boelke-Fabian, 219–241). Theodor Lessings Kampf gegen den Lärm (Matthias Lentz, 242–264). Theodor Lessings Philosophie der Not (Rainer Marwedel, 265–277).]

36888. LEVY, ALEXANDER. MEYER-MARIL, EDINA: *Alexander Levy. Ein deutsch-jüdischer Architekt zwischen Berlin, Tel Aviv, Paris und Auschwitz.* [In]: Menora 1998, Bodenheim, 1998. Pp. 315–337, notes. [A.L., Dec. 21, 1883 Berlin – Auschwitz, architect, lived and worked in Palestine 1926–1927, emigr. to Paris in 1933, deported to Auschwitz in Aug. 1942.]

36889. LEVY, KURT. BERANKOVA, LJUBA/RIEDEL, ERIK: *Heimat Exil Heimat: Emigration und Rückkehr des jüdischen Malers Kurt Levy (1911–1987).* [Hrsg.: Jüdisches Museum; Stadt Frankfurt am Main]. Sigmaringen: Thorbecke, 1998. 128 pp., illus. (Schriftenreihe des Jüdischen Museums Frankfurt am Main, Bd. 6.)

36890. LIEBERMANN, MAX. *Festakt zu Ehren Max Liebermanns.* [In]: Jahrbuch Preußischer Kulturbesitz, Bd. XXXIV, Berlin: Gebr. Mann, 1998. Pp. 195–210. [Incl.: Max Liebermann als Künstler und Kulturpolitiker (Peter Paret, 195–203). Max Liebermann zu Ehren (Walter Jens, 204–210).]

36891. LISSAUER, ERNST. ALBANIS, ELISABETH: *Ostracised for loyalty: Ernst Lissauer's propaganda writing and its reception.* [In]: Leo Baeck Institute Year Book XLIII, London, 1998. Pp. 195–224, port., footnotes.

36892. LUBARSCH, OTTO. PRÜLL, CAY-RÜDIGER: *Otto Lubarsch (1860–1933) und die Pathologie an der Berliner Charité von 1917 bis 1928.* Vom Trauma der Kriegsniederlage zum Alltag eines deutschnationalen Hochschullehrers in der Weimarer Republik. [In]: Sudhoffs Archiv, Bd. 81, H. 2, Stuttgart, 1997. Pp. 193–210. [O.L., pathologist, converted to Protestantism, cofounder of the Alldeutscher Verband.]

36893. LUXEMBURG, ROSA. ENDERLEIN, KLAUS: *"Dresden ist ein herrliches Städtchen" – Rosa Luxemburg: Fakten, Erinnerungen, Reflexionen.* Dresden [A.-Altus-Str. 16]: K. Enderlein, 1997. 44 pp., illus.

36894. LUXEMBURG, ROSA. HIRSCH, HELMUT: *Rosa Luxemburg.* Mit Selbstzeugnissen und Bilddokumenten dargestellt von Helmut Hirsch. Reinbek: Rowohlt Taschenbuch Verlag, 1998. 160 pp., illus., facsims., notes, chronol., bibl. (148–156), index. [20th (revised) edn.; first publ. in 1969.]

36895. LUXEMBURG, ROSA. SEIDEMANN, MARIA: *Rosa Luxemburg und Leo Jogiches: die Liebe in den Zeiten der Revolution.* Berlin: Rowohlt, 1998. 186 pp., illus., bibl. (Paare.)

36896. MAIMON, SALOMON. SCHULTE, CHRISTOPH: *Salomon Maimons Lebensgeschichte. Autobiographie und moderne jüdische Identität.* [In]: Sprache und Identität im Judentum [see No. 36627]. Pp. 135–150.

36897. MANNHEIM, ERNST. WELZIG, ELISABETH: *Die Bewältigung der Mitte. Der Soziologe und Anthropologe Ernst Mannheim.* Wien: Böhlau, 1997. 292 pp., illus. [Cf.: Besprechung (Michael Neumann) [in]: Mittelweg 36, Jg. 8, H. 3, Hamburg, Juni/Juli 1999, pp. 56–57.] [E.M., b. 1900 in Budapest, cousin of Karl Mannheim, expelled from Leipzig university in 1933, in the same year emigr. to England, in 1937 to the US, where he became professor of sociology at the Univ. of Kansas City.]

36898. MARCUSE, HERBERT: *Feindanalysen. Über die Deutschen.* Hrsg. von Peter-Erwin Jansen und mit einer Einl. von Detlev Claussen. Lüneburg: Zu Klampen, 1998. 149 pp. [A collection of unpubl. texts written between 1939 and 1947, mostly from M.'s work at the US Office of War Information.] [Cf.: Besprechung (Wolfram Stender) [in]: Mittelweg 36, Jg. 7, H. 3, Hamburg, 1998, pp. 33–35.]

36899. MARCUSE, HERBERT: *Technology, war and Fascism: collected papers.* Vol. 1. Ed. by Douglas Kellner. Transl. by Richard Wolin. London; New York: Routledge, 1998. XVII, 278 pp., illus., ports., facsims. [Incl. exchange of letters with Heidegger in 1947–48.]

36900. MARCUSE, HERBERT. HABERMAS, JÜRGEN: *Die verschiedenen Rhythmen von Philosophie und Politik; zum 100. Geburtstag Herbert Marcuses.* [In]: 'NZZ', Nr. 164, Zürich, 18./19. Juli 1998. P. 61, port.

36901. MARUM, LUDWIG. EXNER-SEEMANN, KONRAD: *Ludwig Marum: Landespolitiker und NS-Opfer in Kislau/Bad Mingolsheim.* [In]: Badische Heimat, H. 2, Konstanz, Juni 1998. Pp. 195–217, port., illus., notes. [L.M., jurist, politician, data see No. 33429/YB XLI.]

36902. MARX, KARL. COWLING, MARK, ed.: *The Communist Manifesto: new interpretations.* Transl. by Terrell Carver. Edinburgh: Edinburgh Univ. Press, 1998. XVV, 209, notes. [Incl. the full text of the manifesto in transl. by T.C.]

36903. MARX, KARL. *The Communist Manifesto: a modern edition.* Introd. by Eric Hobsbawm London, N.Y.: Verso, 1998. 87 pp. [150th anniversary edn.]

36904. MARX, KARL. OBERMANN, KARL: *Karl Marx und die "Neue Rheinische Zeitung".* [In]: Fritz Bilz/Klaus Schmidt, eds.: Das war 'ne heiße Märzenzeit. Revolution im Rheinland 1948/49. Köln: PapyRossa, 1998. Pp. 43–48.

36905. MARX, KARL. WOOD, ELLEN MEISKINS: *Principles of Communism. The Communist Manifesto 150 years later.* Transl. by Paul M. Sweezy. New York: Monthly Review Press, 1998. XI, 112 pp., notes.

36906. MASSARY, FRITZI. STERN, CAROLA: *Die Sache, die man Liebe nennt. Das Leben der Fritzi Massary.* Berlin: Rowohlt, 1998. 378 pp., illus., bibl. (343–364), chronol., index (373–378). [F.M., orig. Friederike Massarik, March 21, 1882 Vienna – Jan. 30, 1969 Beverly Hills, CA, soprano, operetta diva, wife of the actor Max Pallenberg, emigr. 1937 to the UK, 1939 to the US.]

36907. MAYER, GUSTAV. PRELLWITZ, JENS: *Jüdisches Erbe, sozialliberales Ethos, deutsche Nation: Gustav Mayer im Kaiserreich und in der Weimarer Republik.* Mannheim: Palatium, 1998. 252 pp., footnotes, bibl. (235–246), index (247–252). (Mannheimer historische Forschungen, Bd. 17.) Zugl.: Mannheim, Univ., Diss., 1998. [Also on G.M.: Fortschritt als Lebensgeschichte. Gustav Mayer, Historiker der Arbeiterbewegung und Engels-Biograph, war ein Prophet des deutschen Niedergangs (Benedikt Stuchey) [in]: 'FAZ', Nr. 44, Frankfurt am Main, 21. Feb. 1998. Beilage, p. IV.] [G.M., Oct. 4, 1871 Prenzlau – Feb. 21, 1948 London, historian.]

36908. MEITNER, LISE. LEWIN SIME, RUTH: *Lise Meitner and the discovery of nuclear fission.* [In]: Scientific American, New York, Jan. 1998. Pp. 58–63, illus.

36909. MENDELSOHN, ERICH. STEPHAN, REGINA, ed.: *Erich Mendelsohn – Architekt 1887 – 1953 – gebaute Welten: Arbeiten für Europa, Palästina, Amerika.* Mit Beiträgen von Charlotte Benton [et al.]. [Übers.: Katja Steiner et al.] Ostfildern/Ruit: Verl. Gerd Hatje, 1998. 344 pp., illus.

36910. MOSSE, GEORGE L.. MOSSE, GEORGE L./STRAUSS, MONICA: *German-Jewish culture: "What could have been and what may be".* A talk in New York with the historian George L. Mosse. [In]: Aufbau, Vol. 64, No. 25, New York, Dec. 4, 1998. P. 11, port., illus. [An interview.] [G.L.M., Sept. 18, 1918 Berlin – Jan. 22, 1999 Madison, WI, historian, emigr. 1933 to the UK, 1939 to the US, professor emer. at the Univ. of Wisconsin and the Hebrew Univ. in Jerusalem.]

36911. MÜHSAM, PAUL. LEVI-MÜHSAM, ELSE: *Paul Mühsam, von seiner Tochter gesehen.* [In]: Exil. Forschung, Erkenntnisse, Ergebnisse, Jg. 18, Nr. 1, Frankfurt am Main, 1998. Pp. 85–98.

36912. NEUMANN, HUGO. KIRCHNER, GERRIT: *Hugo Neumann and his "Kinderhaus"; a pioneer of social pediatrics in Berlin.* [In]: Korot, Vol. 12 [1996–1997], Jerusalem, 1998. Pp. 151–159.

36913. NUSSBAUM, FELIX. Jasse, Astrid: *Triumph des Todes? Museumsbau von Daniel Libeskind gilt Felix Nussbaum.* [In]: Aufbau, Vol. 64, No. 22, New York, Oct. 23, 1998. Pp. 8. [On F.N. and the Felix-Nussbaum-Museum in Osnabrück, opened in July 1998.]

36914. NUSSBAUM, FELIX. Kaster, Karl Georg, ed.: *Felix Nussbaum: art defamed, art in exile, art in resistance: a biography.* 4th enl. and fully rev. edn. of the catalogue for the exhibition of the same title, May 6 to Aug. 26, 1990, Kulturgesch. Museum Osnabrück. Transl. by Eileen Martin. With contribs. by Eva Berger [et al.]. New York: The Overlook Press, 1997. 496 pp., chiefly illus., bibl. [German edn.: Bramsche: Rasch, 1997. (Osnabrücker Kulturdenkmäler, Vol. 3.)] [F.N., 1904 Osnabrück, – 1944 Auschwitz, painter, 1932 – 1935 in Italy, later in Belgium; went into hiding in 1941, after denunciation deported to Auschwitz in Aug. 1944.]

36915. NUSSBAUM, FELIX. Zerull, Ludwig: *Felix Nussbaum.* Hrsg. durch die Niedersächsische Lottostiftung. Hannover: Th. Schieder, 1998. 85 pp., ports., illus. (Kunst der Gegenwart aus Niedersachsen, Bd. 50.)

36916. OFFENBACH, JACQUES. Fischer, Ralph: *Der späte Offenbach (1870–1880).* H. 1. Bad Ems: Verein für Geschichte/Denkmal- und Landschaftspflege e.V., Bad Ems, 1998. 45 pp. (Bad Emser Hefte, Nr. 171.)

36917. OPPENHEIMER, FRANZ. Yassour, Avraham: *'Individualism' and 'collectivism' in Franz Oppenheimer's theory.* [In]: Shorashim, Vol. 10, Tel-Aviv, 1997. Pp. 18–27. [In Hebrew, with English summary.]

36918. PAZI, MARGARITA. Bauschinger, Sigrid: *Obituary.* [In]: The German Quarterly, Vol. 71, No. 1, Cherry Hill, NJ, Winter 1998. Pp. 61–62. [M. P., 1920 Altstadt (Czechoslovakia) – Feb. 2 1997 Tel Aviv, literary historian, emigr. in 1938. After 5 years of internment in Mauritius, finally reached Palestine in 1945.] [Cf.: Obit. (Mark H. Gelber) [in]: Modern Austrian Literature, Vol. 31, No. 1, Riverside, CA, 1998, pp. 170–174, port.]

36919. PHILIPPSON, ALFRED. Mehmel, Astrid: *Alfred Philippsohn (1.1.1864 – 28.3.1953) – ein deutscher Geograph.* [In]: Aschkenas, Jg. 8, 1998, H. 2, Wien, 1999. Pp. 353–390, footnotes.

36920. POPPER, KARL. Hacohen, Malachi H.: *Karl Popper, the Vienna Circle, and Red Vienna.* [In]: Journal of the History of Ideas, Vol. 58, No. 1, Baltimore, MD, 1997. Pp. 711–734.

36921. POPPER, KARL. *The significance of Popper's thought.* Proceedings of the conference Karl Popper: 1902–1994, March 10–12, 1995. Graduate School for Social Research Warsaw. Ed. by Stefan Amsterdamski. Amsterdam; Atlanta, GA: Rodopi, 1996. 1 vol. (Poznan Studies in the Philosophy of the Sciences and the Humanities, 49.) [A collection of 6 contribs; incl. a personal portrait: Karl Popper – the thinker and the man (Ernest Gellner, 75–85).]

36922. POPPER-LYNKEUS, JOSEF. Wolf, Efraim: *Josef Popper-Lynkeus, a great humanist and a multiface thinker.* Jerusalem; Kibbutz Dalia: Ma'arekhet, 1996. 153 pp. [In Hebrew.] [Transl. from the Russian, first publ. in 1988.] [J.P.-L., pseud. Lynkeus, 1838 Kolin, Bohemia – 1921 Vienna, physicist, social reformer, philosopher.]

36923. RATHENAU, WALTHER. Mikuteit, Johannes: *Der Parlamentarismus im Urteil von Walther Rathenau.* [In]: Der Staat, Bd. 36, Berlin, 1997. Pp. 95–117, footnotes.

36924. REICHMANN, EVA G. Paucker, Arnold: *The Germany that didn't succumb.* [In]: The Guardian, London, Sept. 30, 1998. [Obituary.] [E. R., Jan. 16, 1897 Lublinitz, Upper Silesia – Sept. 16, 1998 London, historian, long-serving member of the Executive of the London LBI.]

36925. REUSS, LEO. Haider-Pregler, Hilde: *Überlebenstheater: der Schauspieler Reuss.* Mitarb.: Isabella Suppanz. Wien: Holzhausen, 1998. X, 319 pp., illus. [Incl.: Rollenverzeichnis (250–293).] [Cf.: Schein oder nicht Schein. Der Jude, der die Nazis foppte: Der Fall Reuss, dramatisiert (Ulrich Weinzierl) [in]: 'FAZ', Nr. 23, Frankfurt am Main, 28. Jan. 1998, p. 35.] [L.R., orig. Leon Mauriz Reiss (in the USA: Lionel Royce), 1891 Galicia – 1946 USA, actor, emigr. before the 'Anschluß' from Vienna to the US.]

36926.   ROSENSTOCK-HUESSY, EUGEN. Stahmer, Harold/Gormann-Thelen, Michael: *Rosenstock-Huessy, Eugen (1888–1973)*. [In]: Theologische Realenzyklopädie. In Gemeinschaft mit Horst Balz [et al.] hrsg. von Gerhard Müller. Bd. XXIX, Religionspsychologie – Samaritaner. Berlin; New York, de Gruyter, 1998. Pp. 413–418, bibl. [Eugen Rosenstock (since 1925: Rosenstock-Huessy), converted to Protestantism in 1906, philosopher, sociologist, social reformer, professor of legal history at Breslau Univ., emigr. 1934 to the US.]

36927.   ROSENZWEIG, FRANZ. Zak, Adam: *Rosenzweig, Franz (1886–1929)*. [In]: Theologische Realenzyklopädie. In Gemeinschaft mit Horst Balz [et al.] hrsg. von Gerhard Müller. Bd. XXIX, Religionspsychologie – Samaritaner. Berlin; New York: de Gruyter, 1998. Pp. 418–424, bibl.

36928.   ROTHSCHILD, MEYER AMSCHEL. Elon, Amos: *Der erste Rothschild. Biographie eines Frankfurter Juden*. Deutsch von Matthias Fienbork. Reinbek: Rowohlt, 1998. 255 pp., illus., notes (229–240), bibl., index. [Cf.: "Halt mir dein Geschwister beisammen" (Sibylle Fritsch) [in]: Illustr. Neue Welt, Nr. 3, Wien, März 1999, p. 19. Das Ethos der Rothschilds (Willi Jasper) [in]: Die Zeit, Nr. 47, Hamburg, 12. Nov. 1998, p. 69.] [For orig. edn. see No. 34488/YB XLII.]

36929.   SACHS, NELLY. Lermen, Birgit/Braun, Michael: *Nelly Sachs: "an letzter Atemspitze des Lebens"*. Bonn: Bouvier, 1998. 308 pp., frontis., illus., facsims., notes (257–288), chronol. (Lebensspuren – deutsche Dichter des 20. Jahrhunderts, Bd. 2.) [On life and work of N.S.; incl.: Briefwechsel zwischen Hilde Domin und Nelly Sachs (217–256; 35 letters, with the exception of three, hitherto unpubl.).]

36930.   SALOMON, ALICE. Berger, Manfred: *Alice Salomon: Pionierin der sozialen Arbeit und der Frauenbewegung*. Frankfurt am Main: Brandes und Apsel, 1998. 95 pp., illus. (Wissen & Praxis, 76.)

36931.   SALOMON, CHARLOTTE. Belinfante, Judith [et al.], eds.: *Charlotte Salomon: life? Or theatre?* Zwolle: Waanders; London: Royal Academy of Arts, 1998. 796 pp., chiefly col. illus., ports., facsims., bibl. [Publ. for the Royal Academy as a companion volume to the exhibition 'Life? or theatre?: work of Charlotte Salomon at the Royal Academy of Arts, London, 22 Oct. 1998 – 17 Jan. 1999.] [Cf.: The 'wildly unusual' work of Charlotte Salomon (Astrid Schmetterling) [in]: The Jewish Quarterly, Vol. 45, No. 3, London, Autumn 1998, pp. 48–54, illus. 'Take care of it – it is my whole life' (E. Jane Dickson) [in]: The Daily Telegraph, London, Oct. 3, 1998.] [See also No. 36476.]

36932.   SCHAAL, ERIC. *Eric Schaal – Photograph*. Bonn: Weidle, 1998. 125 pp. [mostly ports.]. [Publ. on the occasion of an exhibition of Deutsche Bibliothek Frankfurt, Deutsches Exilarchiv 1933–1945 in 1998; incl.: Eric Schaal: Brief an Max Mohr (120–121). Eric Schaal – ein Photograph der Künstler (Klaus Honnef, 122–123). Interview mit Miriam Schaal (Barbara Weidle, 124–126).] [E.Sch., 1905 Munich – 1994, Männedorf nr. Zurich, photographer, emigr. in 1936 to the US.]

———   SCHLESINGER, GEORG. Spur, Günter: *Georg Schlesinger. Vom Wirken eines großen Ingenieurs*. [See in No. 36731.]

36933.   SCHLESINGER, MORITZ. Blamont, J.: *Moritz, dit Maurice Schlesinger, éditeur de musique (Berlin, 3 octobre 1797 – Baden-Baden, 25 février 1871)*. [In]: Archives Juives, No. 31/1, 1er semestre, Paris, 1998. Pp. 125–127.

36934. SCHNITZLER, ARTHUR. PLENER, PETER: *Arthur Schnitzlers Tagebücher oder Die Textur der Erinnerung*. [In]: Jahrbuch der ungarischen Germanistik 1997, Budapest, 1997. Pp. 33–50, notes.

36935. SCHNITZLER, ARTHUR. STRELKA, JOSEPH P., ed.: *Die Seele ... ist ein weites Land*. Kritische Beiträge zum Werk Arthur Schnitzlers. Bern; New York: Lang, 1997. 201 pp., illus., footnotes. (New Yorker Beiträge zur österreichischen Literaturgeschichte, Bd. 8.) [Cont. English and German articles.]

36936. SCHNITZLER, ARTHUR. *Text+Kritik*. H. 138/139 [with the issue title] *Arthur Schnitzler*. München, April 1998. 1 issue, 174 pp., notes, port. [on issue cover]. [Cont. 11 essays. Selected essays (some titles abbr.): Fin de siècle in Wien. Zum bewußtseinsgeschichtlichen Horizont von Schnitzlers Zeitgenossenschaft (Gotthart Wunberg, 3–23). Zur Lektüre von Arthur Schnitzlers Tagebüchern (Markus Fischer, 24–35). Der falsch gewonnene Prozeß. Das Verfahren gegen Arthur Schnitzlers Reigen (Heinz-Ludwig Arnold, 114–122). Vita Arthur Schnitzler (Michael Scheffel, 138–150). Internationale Arthur-Schnitzler-Bibliographie (Nicolai Riedel, 151–172).]

36937. SCHNITZLER, ARTHUR. TWERASER, FELIX W.: *Political dimensions: Arthur Schnitzler's late fiction*. Columbia, SC: Camden House, 1998. 163 pp. (Distrib. in UK by Boydill & Brewer, Woodbridge.)

36938. SCHÖNBERG, ARNOLD. GRADENWITZ, PETER: *Arnold Schönberg und seine Meisterschüler*. Berlin 1925–1933. Mit einem Beitrag von Nuria Schoenberg-Nono. Wien: Zsolnay, 1998. 359 pp., frontis., ports., facsims. (music), bibl., index (349–359).

36939. SCHÖNBERG, ARNOLD. GREISSLE-SCHÖNBERG, ARNOLD: *Arnold Schönberg und sein Wiener Kreis*. Erinnerungen seines Enkels. Wien: Böhlau, 1998. 260 pp., illus., facsims.

36940. SCHÖNBERG, ARNOLD. SINKOVICZ, WILHELM: *Mehr als zwölf Töne. Arnold Schönberg*. Wien: Zsolnay, 1998. 329 pp., frontis., illus., facsims., indexes. [On Sch.'s life and work.]

36941. SCHÖNBERG, ARNOLD. ZEHENTREITER, FERDINAND: *Überlegungen zum Judentum Arnold Schönbergs aus der Perspektive einer Theorie des künstlerischen Handelns*. [In]: Hubert Knoblauch [et al.], eds.: Religiöse Konversion. systematische und fallorientierte Studien in soziologischer Perspektive. Konstanz: UVK, Univ.-Verl. Konstanz, 1998. (Passagen & Transzendenzen.) Pp. 147–167, footnotes, bibl. [Deals with Sch.'s conversion to Protestantism in 1898 and his return to Judaism in 1933.]

36942. SCHÖNDORFF, ALBERT & HERMANN. SCHWARZ, EGBERT F.: *Zur Geschichte der Gebrüder Schöndorff AG (1890–1933)*. [In]: Geschichte im Westen, Jg. 13, Köln, 1998. Pp. 189–207, illus., footnotes. [On the Düsseldorf coachbuilding firm, its founders and its "aryanisation".]

36943. SCHOLEM, GERSHOM. MYERS, DAVID N./RUDERMAN, DAVID B., eds.: *The Jewish past revisited: reflections on modern Jewish historians*. New Haven, CT: Yale Univ. Press, 1998. XI, 244 pp. (Studies in Jewish culture and society.) [Incl. Gershom Scholem.]

36944. SCHREKER, FRANZ. ZIBASO, MAGALI: *Franz Schreker – ein vergessener Komponist*. [In]: Jüdischer Almanach 1999 des Leo Baeck Instituts, Frankfurt am Main, 1998. Pp. 91–102, illus., notes. [F.S., composer, son of a Jewish father and a Catholic mother, March 23, 1878 Monaco – March 21, 1934 Berlin.]

36945. SCHWEITZER BRESSLAU, HELENE. MÜHLSTEIN, VERENA: *Helene Schweitzer Bresslau. Ein Leben für Lambarene*. München: Beck, 1998. 298 pp., illus. [H.B., wife of Albert Schweitzer, for further data see No. 29914/YB XXXVIII.]

36946. SCHWERIN, LUDWIG. *Von Deutschland ins "Land der Väter" (Israel)* Menschen, Tiere, Landschaften. gesehen von Ludwig Schwerin (Buchen 1897–1983 Ramat Gan). Ausstellung im Bezirksmuseum Buchen 7. Mai bis 28. Sept. 1997. Hrsg.: Stadt Buchen/Odenwald;

Verein Bezirksmuseum e.V. Buchen-Walldürn: Druckerei Odenwalder, 1997. 124 pp., illus. [L.Sch., July 10, 1897 – July 2, 1983, Ramat Gan, painter, book illustrator, emigr. in 1938 via Switzerland to Palestine.]

36947. SEELER, MORIZ. ELBIN, GÜNTHER: *Am Sonntag in die Matinee. Moriz Seeler und die Junge Bühne.* Eine Spurensuche. Mannheim: persona, 1998. 125 pp. [M.S., 1896 Greifenberg (Pomerania) – 1942 (deportation to Riga), theatre director, film producer, writer, in 1921 founded "Junge Bühne" in Berlin.]

36948. SEGHERS, ANNA. RINSER, LUISE: *Hoffnung und Glaube der Anna Seghers.* [In]: ndl, neue deutsche literatur, Jg. 46, H. 518, Berlin, März/April 1998. Pp. 131–143.

36949. SINSHEIMER, HERMANN. LAMPERT, LISA: *"Oh my daughter!": "Die schöne Jüdin" and "Der neue Jude" in Hermann Sinsheimer's 'Maria Nunnez'.* [In]: The German Quarterly, Vol. 71, No. 3, Cherry Hill, NJ, Summer 1998. Pp. 254–270, notes.

36950. SINSHEIMER, HERMANN. SKOLNIK, JONATHAN: *Dissimilation and the historical novel: Hermann Sinsheimer's 'Maria Nunnez'.* [In]: Leo Baeck Institute Year Book XLIII, London, 1998. Pp. 225–237, footnotes. [On 'Maria Nunnez; eine jüdische Überlieferung, first publ. in 1934 in Berlin, dealing with a young "conversa" in sixteenth-cent. Portugal.] [H.S., Freinsheim 1883 – London (?) 1950, theatre critic, essayist, novelist, emigr. to the UK in 1939.]

36951. SIODMAK, CURT. HÄRTEL, CHRISTIAN: *"Eine Geschichte zu verkaufen war eine Riesensache!"* Dem Autor Curt Siodmak auf der Spur. [In]: Juni, Magazin für Literatur & Politik, Nr. 28, Mönchengladbach, 1998. Pp. 81–98, notes.

36952. SIODMAK, ROBERT & CURT. JACOBSEN, WOLFGANG/PRINZLER, HANS HELMUT, eds.: *Siodmak Bros. Robert und Curt Siodmak.* Berlin – Paris – London – Hollywood. Mit Beiträgen von Rolf Aurich [et al.]. Berlin: Argon, 1998. 438 pp., illus., docs., bibl., index. (Stiftung Deutsche Kinemathek und Int. Filmfestspiele Berlin, Retrospektive 1998.) [Incl. biographical essays and other texts; also letters, short stories and filmographies.] [R.S., Aug. 8, 1890 Dresden – March, 10, 1973 Locarno, film producer, emigr. in 1933 to Paris, in 1939 to the US, returned to Europe in 1951. – C.S., for data see No. 35741/YB XLIII.]

36953. SPIEGEL, HENRY WILLIAM. *Remembrance and appreciation roundtable. Dr. Henry William Spiegel (1911–1995): émigré economist, historian of economics, creative scholar, and companion.* [In]: The American Journal of Economics and Sociology, Vol. 57, No. 3, New York, July 1998. Pp. 345–361, footnotes. [Incl. contribs. on Spiegel's life and work by Samuel H. Bostaph, Craufurd Goodwin, Harald Hagemann, Ingrid H. Rima, Warren J. Samuels and Cecile Spiegel. Ed. by Laurence S. Moss.] [H.W.Sp., 1911 Berlin – 1995 New York (?), emigr. in 1936 to the US.]

36954. SPIELMAN, FRED (Fritz Spielmann). *Spring came back to Vienna: Fritz Spielmann Festival.* Ed. by the Orpheus Trust, Vienna. Vienna: Dokumentationsstelle für neuere österreichische Literatur, 1998. 79 pp., illus., ports., facsims., scores, discography (74–77), film score (78). (Zirkular, Sondernummer 52.) [F.S., 1906 Vienna – 1997 New York, composer, pianist, singer, emigr. 1938 via Paris to the US. Brochure was publ. in conjunction with the festival held in Vienna from March 22 – May 14, 1998.]

36955. STECKEL, LEONHARD. RUEB, FRANZ, ed.: *Leonard Steckel, Schauspieler und Regisseur.* Zürich: Innaron-Verl., 1998. 232 pp., illus. [Cf.: Erinnerung an ein Bühnenmonster (M.D.) [in]: 'NZZ', Nr. 236, Zürich, 12. Okt. 1998, p. 34.] [L.St., Jan. 8, 1901 Knihinin, Hungary – Feb. 9, 1971 Bavaria (train accident), actor, stage director, emigr. 1933 to Switzerland, long-time member of the Zurich Schauspielhaus.]

36956. STEIN, EDITH. MÜLLER, ANDREAS UWE/NEYER, MARIA AMATA: *Edith Stein. Das Leben einer ungewöhnlichen Frau.* Biographie. Zürich: Benziger, 1998. 287 pp., illus., notes, chronol.

36957. STEIN, EDITH. PETERMEIER, MARIA: *Die religiöse Entwicklung der Edith Stein.* Eine Untersuchung zur Korrelation von Lebens- und Glaubensgeschichte. Frankfurt am Main; New York: Lang, 1998. 244 pp., illus. (Elementa Theologiae – Arbeiten zur Theologie und Religionspädagogik, Bd. 10.)

36958. STEINSCHNEIDER, HERMANN alias HANUSSEN. KUGEL, WILFRIED: *Die wahre Geschichte des Hermann Steinschneider.* Düsseldorf: Grupello, 1998. 304 pp., illus., facsims. [Cf.: Der furchtsame Hellseher. Eine knochentrockene Hanussen-Biographie erledigt Legenden (Corona Hepp) [in]: 'FAZ', Nr. 257, Frankfurt am Main, 5. Nov. 1998, p. 12.] [H.St., 1889 – March 24, 1933 Berlin (shot by members of SA), pseud.: Hanussen, hypnotist, mesmerist, clairvoyant.]

36959. STERN, SELMA. *Apropos Selma Stern.* Mit einem Essay von Marina Sassenberg. Frankfurt am Main: Verl. Neue Kritik, 1998. 138 pp., illus. (Apropos, 14.) [Incl. texts by and about S. St.] [Selma Stern-Täubler, July 24, 1890 Kippenheim – Aug. 17, 1981 Basle, historian, emigr. 1941 to the US, lived from 1960 in Switzerland.]

36960. STERNBERG, THEODOR. BARTELS-ISHIKAWA, A.: *Theodor Sternberg – ein Wegbereiter des Freirechts in Deutschland und Japan.* [In]: Zeitschrift der Savigny-Stiftung für Rechtsgeschichte, Bd. 114, Germanistische Abt., Wien, 1997. Pp. 398–414, footnotes. [Th. St., 1878 Berlin – 1947 Tokyo (?), jurist, since 1913 professor of jurisprudence in Tokyo (=Todai).]

36961. STRAUß, LUDWIG: *Gesammelte Werke. Prosa und Übertragungen.* Gesammelte Werke, Band 1. Hrsg. von Hans Otto Horch. [Textred.: Kerstin Rückwald]. Göttingen: Wallstein, 1998. 607 pp., notes (543–565). (Gesammelte Werke in vier Bänden/Ludwig Strauß; Veröff. der deutschen Akademie für Sprache und Dichtung Darmstadt, Bd. 73.) [Incl.: Nachwort des Herausgebers (566–607).] [Cf.: Es dürstete den Trank nach dem Trinkenden. Revolutionäres Denken mit gegenrevolutionären Skrupeln: Ludwig Strauß ist zu entdecken (Gert Mattenklott) [in]: 'FAZ', Nr. 255, Frankfurt am Main, 3. Nov. 1998, p. L 12, port.]

36962. STRAUß, LUDWIG: *Schriften zur Dichtung.* Gesammelte Werke, Band 2. Hrsg. von Tuvia Rübner. [Textred.: Till Schicketanz]. Göttingen: Wallstein, 1998. 493 pp., footnotes, notes (388–458), index. (Gesammelte Werke in vier Bänden/Ludwig Strauß; Veröffentlichungen der Deutschen Akademie für Sprache und Dichtung Darmstadt, Bd. 73.) [Incl.: Nachwort (ed., 459–480).]

36963. TORBERG, FRIEDRICH: *Wien oder Der Unterschied.* Ein Lesebuch. Hrsg. von David Axmann und Marietta Torberg. München: Langen Müller, 1998. 286 pp. [A collection of essays, some of them autobiographical.]

36964. TUCHOLSKY, KURT. HEPP, MICHAEL: *Kurt Tucholsky.* Dargestellt von Michael Hepp. Reinbek bei Hamburg: Rowohlt, 1998. 187 pp., illus., bibl. Orig.-Ausg. (Rowohlts Monographien, 50512.)

36965. VARNHAGEN, RAHEL. TEWARSON, HEIDI THOMANN: *Rahel Levin Varnhagen: the life and work of a German Jewish intellectual.* Lincoln: Univ. of Nebraska Press, 1998. XI, 262 pp., illus., ports., notes (227–253). (Text and context.)

36966. VARNHAGEN, RAHEL. WÄGENBAUR, BIRGIT: *"Ich denke mir es sehr möglich, dass wir einander verständen".* Der Briefwechsel zwischen Rahel Levin Varnhagen und Karoline von Fouqué. [In]: Zeitschrift für deutsche Philologie, Bd. 117, Berlin, 1998. Pp. 189–209, footnotes.

36967. VARON, BENNO WEISER: *A different kind of homecoming.* [In]: Midstream, Vol. 44, No. 3, New York, April 1998. Pp. 25–26. [The author, a diplomat and journalist, describes his impressions during a recent, government-sponsored visit to Vienna which he had left in 1938 as a refugee.]

36968. VIERTEL, BERTHOLD. *Traum von der Realität: Berthold Viertel.* Hrsg. im Auftrag der Theodor Kramer Gesellschaft von Siglinde Bolbecher [et al.]. Wien: Th. Kramer Ges.;

Döcker, 1998. 297 pp., frontis., index (291–297). (Zwischenwelt, 5.) [Cont. 19 contribs. on B.V., his life and work in Berlin, during exile in the UK, and, after the war, in Vienna by Helmut G. Asper, Matthias Braun, Fritz Beer, Marianne Brün-Kortner, Evelyn Deutsch-Schreiner, Ernst Glaser, Wolfgang Glück, Kevin Gough-Yates, Marianne Gruber, Hans Heinz Hahnl, Hilde Haider-Pregler, Johann Holzner, Irene Jansen, Konstantin Kaiser, Felix Kreissler, Peter Roessler, Gerhard Scheit, Hans Viertel and Klaus Völker.]

36969. WALLICH, PAUL. Neite, Werner: *Paul Wallich. Von der Leidenschaft des Büchersammelns.* [In]: Aus dem Antiquariat, [Beilage zum] Börsenblatt für den Deutschen Buchhandel, Jg. 165, Nr. 8, Frankfurt am Main, 28. Aug. 1998. Pp. A 572–A 574, illus., notes. [P.W., Aug. 10, 1882 Potsdam – Nov. 11, 1938 Cologne (suicide), banker, economic historian.]

36970. WARBURG, ABY M.. McEwan, Dorothea: *"Mein lieber Saxl!" – "Sehr geehrter Herr Professor!". Die Aby Warburg – Fritz Saxl Korrespondenz zur Schaffung einer Forschungsbibliothek 1910 bis 1919.* [In]: Archiv für Kulturgeschichte, Bd. 80, H. 2, Köln, 1998. Pp. 417–434, footnotes. [Fritz Saxl, Jan. 8, 1890 Vienna – March 22, 1948 London, art historian, director of Warburg Library (later Institute).]

36971. WARBURG, ABY M.. Schoell-Glass, Charlotte: *Aby Warburg und der Antisemitismus. Kulturwissenschaft als Geistespolitik.* Frankfurt am Main: Fischer Taschenbuch Verlag, 1998. 317 pp., illus., footnotes, docs., bibl. (281–315), index. (Veröff. des Franz Rosenzweig Zentrums für deutsch-jüdische Literatur und Kulturgesch., Hebr. Univ. Jerusalem.) Orig.-ausg. [Analyses the deep impact the prevalent antisemitism in Imperial and Weimar Germany had on Warburg's work.] [Cf.: Sonette an Orpheus. Wie Aby Warburg den Dämon des Antisemitismus zu bannen suchte (Volker Gebhardt) [in]: 'FAZ', Nr. 44, Frankfurt am Main, 22. Feb. 1999, p. 56. Bollwerke gegen den Antisemitismus. Charlotte Schoell-Glass rückt Aby Warburgs kulturwissenschaftliches Projekt in ein neues Licht (Barbara Hahn) [in]: Die Zeit, Nr. 14, Hamburg, 31. März 1999, p. 49.]

———— WARBURG, ABY M.. Wuttke, Dieter: *Aby M. Warburg-Bibliographie 1866 bis 1995.* Werk und Wirkung. Mit Annotationen. [See No. 36167.]

36972. WASSERMANN, JAKOB. Eidelberg, Shlomo: *Jakob Wassermann, the Jewish-German writer who opposed Herzl and the Jewish state.* [In]: Ha-Umma, No. 130, Tel-Aviv, Winter 1997–98. pp. 190–199. [In Hebrew, title transl.]

36973. WASSERMANN, JAKOB. Koester, Rudolf: *Jakob Wassermann's anti-Semitism and German politics.* [In]: Orbis litterarum, Vol. 53. Copenhagen, 1998. Pp. 179–190.

36974. WEIL, ERIC. Kirscher, Gilbert: *Eric Weil (1904–1977). Der Philosoph in seiner Zeit.* [In]: Politisches Denken. Jahrbuch 1998. Stuttgart, 1998. Pp. 91–107, footnotes. [Incl. Engl. summary.] [E.W., June 8, 1904 Parchim (Mecklenburg) – Feb. 1, 1977 Nice, philosopher, emigr. to France in 1933; professor of philosophy in Lille and Nice.]

36975. WEIL, GRETE. Exner, Lisbeth: *Land meiner Mörder, Land meiner Sprache.* Die Schriftstellerin Grete Weil. [Hrsg.: Landeshauptstadt München, Kulturreferat; Monacensia, Literatur-Archiv u. Bibliothek]. München: A-1-Verl., 1998. 127 pp., illus., bibl. (monAkzente, 6.) [Cf.: Distanz und Leidenschaft (Irene Armbruster) [in]: Aufbau, Vol. 64, No. 15, New York, July 17, 1998, pp. 9–10, port. See also No. 37014.]

36976. WEISS, PETER. Cohen, Robert: *The political aesthetics of Holocaust literature: Peter Weiss's 'The Investigation' and its critics.* [In]: History & Memory, Vol. 10, No. 2, Bloomington, IN, Fall 1998. Pp. 43–67, notes.

36977. WERFEL, FRANZ. Cohen, Raya: *Franz Werfel and 'the Armenian fate', 1933–1943.* [In]: Zion, Vol. 62, No. 4, Jerusalem, 1997. Pp. 369–385. [In Hebrew, with English summary.]

36978. WILDER, BILLY. Hutter, Andreas: *Billy Wilder: eine europäische Karriere.* Wien: Böhlau, 1998. 253 pp., illus., notes, bibl., index. [Focusses on B.W.'s pre-emigration career as a reporter and script writer in Vienna and Berlin. Incl.: Filmographie (230–239).] [B.W., orig. Samuel Wilder, b. June 22, 1906 in Sucha (Galicia), film director, emigr. 1934 to the US.]

————— WISTRICH, ROBERT S.. BERKOWITZ, MICHAEL: *Robert S. Wistrich and European Jewish history: straddling the public and scholarly spheres.* [See No. 35902.]

36979. ZUCKMAYER, CARL. ALBRECHT, RICHARD, ed.: *Facetten der internationalen Carl-Zuckmayer-Forschung.* Beiträge zu Leben – Werk – Praxis. Mainz: Verlag für Zukunfts-Forschung, 1997. 1 issue. (Theater- und Kulturwissenschaftliche Studien, Bd. II.) [Incl. contribs. on life, work and reception of Z. by Mario Adorf, Richard Albrecht, Horst Claus, Christine Funk, Siegfried Mews, Franz Schüppen, Christian Strasser and Hans Wagener.]

————— ZUCKMAYER, CARL. HEINZELMANN, JOSEF: *Carl Zuckmayers Ahnen. Ein Beitrag zum 100. Geburtstag des Dichters.* [See No. 36652.]

36980. ZUCKMAYER, CARL. SUPERSAXO, OTTO: *Carl Zuckmayer, ein Leben auf steinigen Wegen.* Visp: Rotten-Verl., 1998. 78 pp., illus.

36981. ZWEIG, STEFAN. MATUSCHEK, OLIVER: *"Ich kenne den Zauber der Schrift." Stefan Zweig als Autographensammler.* [In]: Aus dem Antiquariat, [Beilage zum] Börsenblatt für den Deutschen Buchhandel, Jg. 165, Nr. 9, Frankfurt am Main, 30. Jan. 1998. Pp. A 15–A 20, illus., notes.

VIII. AUTOBIOGRAPHY, MEMOIRS, LETTERS

36982. ARENDT, HANNAH/HEIDEGGER, MARTIN: *Briefe 1925–1975 und andere Zeugnisse.* Aus den Nachlässen hrsg. von Ursula Ludz. Frankfurt am Main: Klostermann, 1998. 435 pp., illus., notes (263–362), bibl. (405–422), index (429–435). [Incl.: Nachwort (ed., 385–401).] [Cf.: Ein Paar, gespalten (Dieter Thomä) [in]: Die Zeit, Nr. 42, Hamburg, 8. Okt. 1998, p. 45.]

36983. ASKIN, LEON: *Der Mann mit den 99 Gesichtern.* Autobiographie. In der deutschsprachigen Bearbeitung von Hertha Hanus. Wien: Böhlau, 1998. 381 pp., illus. [Orig. American edn. was publ. 1989: Leon Askin/C. Melvin Davidson: Quietude and quest. Protagonists and antagonists in the theatre, on and off stage. Riverside, CA: Ariadne Press, 1989.] [L.A., orig. Leon Aschkenasy, b. 1907 in Vienna, actor, emigr. 1938 to France, 1940 to the US. Returned to Vienna in 1994.]

36984. AUERBACHER, INGE: *Beyond the yellow star to America.* New York: Royal Fireworks Press, 1995. 200 pp., illus. [Memoirs starting from the time after the author's liberation in Theresienstadt to the present. Cf.: "Kein Mensch wird zum Hassen geboren". Die Schriftstellerin Inge Auerbacher über ihre Arbeit mit Kindern (Tanja Matuszis) [in]: Aufbau, Vol. 64, No. 17, New York, Aug. 14, 1998, pp. 4–5, illus.] [I.A., b. 1934 in Kippenheim (Baden), went to the US in 1946; lives in New York.]

36985. BENJAMIN, WALTER: *Gesammelte Briefe.* Hrsg. vom Theodor W. Adorno-Archiv. Bd. IV, 1931–1934. Hrsg. von Christoph Gödde und Henri Lonitz. Frankfurt am Main: Suhrkamp, 1998. 593 pp., indexes. [Cf.: Mit halbem Herzen. Walter Benjamins Bekenntnis zum Kommunismus (Christoph Menke) [in]: Die Zeit, Nr. 5, Hamburg, 28. Jan. 1999, p. 44.]

36986. BERMANN, RICHARD A. ALIAS HÖLLRIEGEL, ARNOLD: *Die Fahrt auf dem Katarakt.* Eine Autobiographie ohne einen Helden. Mit einem Beitrag von Brita Eckert, hrsg. von Hans-Harald Müller. Wien: Picus, 1998. 352 pp., notes, index. (Spuren in der Zeit.) [Cont.: Vorwort (ed., 9–12). Richard A. Bermann im Ständestaat und im Exil (Richard A. Bermann, 325–347).] [Memoirs, written between July 1938 in France and the author's death (Sept. 5, 1939) in the US. Covering the time up to 1917, the memoirs are complemented by 8 further autobiogr. texts. Also by R.A.B.: Arnold Höllriegel: *In 80 Zeilen durch die Welt. Vom Neopathetischen Cabaret bis nach Hollywood.* Hrsg. von Christian Jäger und Gregor Streim. Mit Photos von Hans G. Casparius. Berlin: Transit, 1998. 128 pp.; a collection of articles publ. orig. in the 'Berliner

Tageblatt'.] [Cf.: Der Fernwehkorrespondent. Die letzten Tage Kakaniens in den Erinnerungen Richard Bermanns (Ulrich Weinzierl) [in]: 'FAZ', Nr. 231, Frankfurt am Main, 6. Okt. 1998, p. L 6.]

36987. BLUMENFELD, ERWIN: *Einbildungsroman.* Frankfurt am Main: Eichborn, 1998. 436 pp., illus. [Autobiography. Incl.: Ein Nachwort. Erwin Blumenfelds Panoptikum des Lebens (Rudolf Trefzer, 421–428). Illust. with B.'s photographs. First edn. (in a French transl. with the title 'Jadis et Daguerre') publ. 1975, first German: 1976, a new edn.: 1988, both edns. with the title 'Durch tausendjährige Zeit'.] [E.B., Jan. 26, 1897 Berlin – July 4, 1969 Rome, photographer, for further data see No. 35497/YB XLIII.]

36988. BURG, MENO: *Geschichte meines Dienstlebens.* Erinnerungen eines jüdischen Majors der preußischen Armee. Mit einem Geleitwort von Ludwig Geiger. Vorwort von Hermann Simon. Teetz: Hentrich & Hentrich, 1998. XXVIII, 193 pp., illus., notes., gloss., index. (Jüdische Memoiren, Bd. 1.) [Reprint of an enlarged edn., publ. in 1916; the first edn. was publ. in 1854.] [M.B., 1790 Berlin – 1853 Berlin.]

36989. CARSTEN, FRANCIS L.: *From Berlin to London.* [In]: Leo Baeck Institute Year Book XLIII, London, 1998. Pp. 339–349. [Memoirs.] [F.L.C., 1911 Berlin – 1998 London, historian. For obits. see No. 36792.]

36990 EINSTEIN, ALBERT: *The collected papers of Albert Einstein.* Vol. 8, Parts A and B. The Berlin years: correspondence, 1914–1918. Ed. by Robert Schulmann [et al.]. Princeton, NJ.: Princeton Univ. Press, 1998. XXXIII, XXVIII, 1118 pp., illus., facsims., tabs., chronol., appendix, notes, bibl. (1035–1066). [These two vols. comprise 677 letters, most previously unpubl., all in their orig. language. A compendium volume with English transl. was also publ. in 1998. For earlier vols. see Nos. 30992, 30993/YB XXXIX; No. 33335/YB XLI.]

36991. EPSTEIN, HELEN: *Dreifach heimatlos: die Suche einer Tochter nach der verlorenen Welt ihrer Mutter.* Aus dem Amerik. von Gaby Wurster und Heike Schlatterer. München: Diana, 1998. 366 pp., illus. [For orig. edn. and details see No. 35709/YB XLIII.]

36992. FRANKL, VIKTOR E.: *Was nicht in meinen Büchern steht.* Lebenserinnerungen. München: Quintessenz; MMV Medizin Verl., 1995. 113 pp., frontisp., illus., facsims [V.F.'s autobiography (not fully listed previously); for Engl. edn. see No. 35710/YB XLIII. See also No. 36822.] [V.E.F., 1905 Vienna – 1997 Vienna, psychotherapist, survivor of Theresienstadt, Auschwitz, Kaufering III and Türkheim, Prof. of Neurology and Psychiatry at the Univ. of Vienna, also at numerous US universities.]

36993. FRIEDLÄNDER, SAUL: *Wenn die Erinnerung kommt.* Aus dem Franz. von Helgard Oestreich. München: Beck, 1998. 192 pp. (Beck'sche Reihe.) [New edn. with new publisher; for details and data see No. 28813/YB XXXVII.]

36994. GRANACH, GAD: *Heimat los! Aus dem Leben eines jüdischen Emigranten.* Aufgezeichnet von Hilde Recher. Augsburg: Ölbaum, 1997. 183 pp., illus. [Based on conversations with Hilde Recher, Henryk M. Broder, and Michel Bergmann; deals with the author's upbringing in Berlin, Hachshara in Hamburg between 1933 and 1936, Kibbuz life in Palestine and later years in Jerusalem.] [G.G., orig. Gerhard G., b. March 29, 1915 in Rheinsberg., son of the actor Alexander G., emigr. 1936 to Palestine. Lives in Jerusalem.]

36995. GRUBEL, FRED: *Schreib das auf eine Tafel die mit ihnen bleibt. Jüdisches Leben im 20. Jahrhundert.* Wien: Böhlau, 1998. 322 pp., illus., facsims. [Memoirs; incl. 2 chaps. on the Leo Baeck Institute.] [F.G., orig. Fritz Grübel, Oct. 22, 1908 Leipzig – Oct. 11, 1998 New York, jurist, emigr. to England in 1939, to the US in 1940. 1966 – 1996 director of the New York Leo Baeck Institute.] [Cf.: Mit Stumpf und Stil. Fred Grubels Wirken gegen die Gefräßigkeit der Zeit (Ulrich Weinzierl) [in]: 'FAZ', Nr. 202, Frankfurt am Main, 1. Sept. 1998, p. 47. Erlebte Erinnerung an eine große Vergangenheit (Guy Stern) [in]: Aufbau, Vol. 64, No. 13, New York, June 19, 1998, pp. 5. In memoriam Fred Grubel: Ein Leben für das Vermächtnis des deutschsprachigen Judentums (Guy Stern) [in]: Aufbau, Vol. 64, No. 22, New York, Oct. 23, 1998, p. 21, port.]

36996. HARTMANN, HEINZ: *In search of self, in the service of others: reflections of a retired physician on medicine, the Bible and the Jews.* Amherst, NY: Prometheus Books, 1998. 198 pp., illus., bibl. (195–198). [H.H., b. in Ostrow (Posen) in 1913, physician, went in 1939 to Syracuse, NY; for his earlier memoirs see No. 23719/YB XXXII.]

36997. HERRMANN, DORIS: *Geboren im Zeichen des Känguruhs.* Basel: Friedr. Reinhardt Verl., 1998. 342 pp., illus. [Autobiography of a Swiss Jewess.]

36998. HIRSCHBERG, MAX: *Jude und Demokrat. Erinnerungen eines Münchener Rechtsanwaltes 1883 bis 1939.* Bearb. von Reinhard Weber. München: Oldenbourg, 1998. 334 pp., footnotes, illus., bibl., index. (Biographische Quellen zur Zeitgeschichte, Bd. 20.) [Incl.: Geleitwort (Hans-Jochen Vogel, 7–8). Einleitung (Reinhard Weber, 9–50).] [Cf.: Jude und Demokrat (Ellen Presser) [in]: Allg. Jüd. Wochenzeitung, Jg. 53, Nr. 17, Bonn, 20. Aug. 1998, p. 13.] [M.H., Nov. 13, 1883 Munich – June 21, 1964 New York, lawyer, played active role in defending Communists and Socialists in numerous political trials, a.o. in the (Felix) Fechenbach case 1922. Emigr. 1934 via Switzerland to Italy, 1939 to the US.]

36999. HOFMANNSTHAL, HUGO VON/HARDEN, MAXIMILIAN. SCHEDE, HANS-GEORG, ed.: *Hugo von Hofmannsthal – Maximilian Harden: Briefwechsel.* [In]: Hofmannsthal. Jahrbuch zur europäischen Moderne, Jg. 6, Freiburg, 1998. Pp. 7–115, illus., footnotes. [Cont.: Einleitung (ed., 7–21); letters written between 1896 and 1908.]

37000. KISCH, EGON ERWIN: *Briefe an Jarmila.* Hrsg. und mit einem Vorwort versehen von Klaus Haupt. Berlin: Das Neue Berlin, 1998. 303 pp., ports., illus., facsims., chronol. (257–295), index. [Cont. letters written to K.'s friend Jarmila Abrozová, a Czech translator and journalist, between 1923 and 1946; also letters by his wife and secretary.]

37001. KLEMPERER, VICTOR: *I shall bear witness: the diaries of Victor Klemperer, 1933–1941.* Abr., transl. and introd. by Martin Chalmers. London: Weidenfeld & Nicolson, 1998. XXIIII, 500 pp., illus., ports., chronol., maps, notes. [American edn. under the title: I will bear witness: a diary of the Nazi years, 1933–1941. Vol. 1. New York: Random House, 1998. XXII, 519 pp.] [For various German edns. see Nos. 33500, 33501/YB XLI, No. 35723/YBXLIII.] [Cf.: The Jew who fought to stay German (Amos Elon) [in]: The New York Times Magazine, New York, March 24, 1996, pp. 52–55. Speech and blood (Laurence Birken) [in]: Shofar, Vol. 17, No. 1, West Lafayette, IN, Fall 1998, pp. 122–136, footnotes. Destiny in any case (Gordon Craig) [in]: New York Review of Books, Vol. 45, No. 19, New York, Dec. 3, 1998, pp. 3–6, illus. A starred witness takes the stand (Peter Heinegg) [in]: Cross Currents, Vol. 47, No. 1, Ann Arbor, MI, Spring 1997, pp. 86–91. Victor Klemperer (1881–1960): reflections on his 'Third Reich' diaries (Hans Reiss) [in]: German Life and Letters, Vol. 51, No. 1, Oxford, Jan. 1998, pp. 65–92. notes.]

37002. KUCZYNSKI, JÜRGEN. *Jürgen Kuczynski – Freunde und gute Bekannte: Gespräche mit Thomas Grimm.* Berlin: Schwarzkopf und Schwarzkopf, 1997. 345 pp., illus. Orig.-Ausg. (Jürgen Kuczynski.) [For obits. J.K. see No. 36880.]

37003. LAMBERG, ROBERT F.: *Schwierigkeiten mit der NZZ. Jugenderinnerungen eines späteren Korrespondenten.* [In]: 'NZZ', Nr. 173, Zürich, 29. Juli 1998. P. 13. [Author, b. 1929 in Reichenberg (Czechoslovakia) to a German-speaking Jewish family, long-time foreign correspondent of the 'NZZ', survived in hiding in Pressburg/Bratislava.]

37004. MAYER, BERNHARD: *Interessante Zeitgenossen. Interesting Contemporaries. Lebenserinnerungen eines jüdischen Kaufmanns und Weltbürgers. Memoirs of a Jewish merchant and cosmopolitan 1866–1946.* Hrsg. von/ed. by Erhard Roy Wiehn. [Engl. transl. by Gabriele Merzbacher-Mayer et. al.] Konstanz: Hartung-Gorre, 1998. 382 pp., illus., facsims., docs. [Also on B.M.: Eine kleine Kollektion grosser Meisterwerke. Die rekonstruierte Sammlung Bernhard Mayer im Kunsthaus Zürich (Thomas Ribi) [in]: 'NZZ', Nr. 167, Zürich, 22. Juli 1998, p. 167.]

[B.M., 1866 Laufersweiler (Hunsrück) – 1946 Zurich, furrier, art collector, since 1915 Swiss national, lived in Belgium and Switzerland, emigr. to the US in 1941.]

37005. MAYER, HANS: *Zeitgenossen.* Erinnerung und Deutung. Frankfurt am Main: Suhrkamp, 1998. 374 pp. [A collection of essays (incl. personal reminiscences), some of them previously publ.]

37006. MEITNER, LISE. LEMMERICH, JOST: *Lise Meitner – Max von Laue. Briefwechsel 1938–1948.* Berlin: ERS-Verlag, 1998. 560 pp., frontis. [Lise Meitner], notes (539–541), index (persons, 542–553), bibl. (554–560). (Berliner Beiträge zur Geschichte der Naturwissenschaften und der Technik, 22.) [Incl. biographical introductions to Meitner and von Laue.]

37007. RIEGNER, GERHART: *Ne jamais désespérer. Soixante années au service du peuple juif et des droits de l'homme.* Paris: Les Editions du Cerf, 1998. 1 vol. [Cf.: Erster Warner vor Hitlers "Endlösung". Die Erinnerungen von Gerhart Riegner (Walter Laqueur) [in]: 'NZZ', Nr. 249, Zürich, 27. Okt. 1998, p. 65.] [G.R., b. Sept. 12, 1911 Berlin, Jewish functionary, emigr. 1933 to France, 1934 to Switzerland; in 1942 transmitted first information on the mass exterminations of Jews in Nazi-occupied countries. Lives in Geneva.]

37008. RUDIN, WALTER: *So hab ich's erlebt. Von Wien nach Wisconsin – Erinnerungen eines Mathematikers.* Aus dem Amerikanischen von Ina Paschen mit der freundlichen Unterstützung von Walter Rudin. München: Oldenbourg, 1998. 181 pp., illus. [First publ. in 1997 by the American Mathematical Society with the title "The way I remember it". Part I (1–126) cont. personal memoirs, Part II (129–181) cont. 11 mathematical essays.] [W.R., b. May 2, 1921 in Vienna, mathematician, emigr. in 1938 via Switzerland to France, to England in 1940, joined the Forces Françaises Libre, later the Pioneer Corps and, in 1944, the Royal Navy. Emigr. in 1945 to the US. Lives in Madison.]

37009. SCHMUCKLER, MALKA: *Gast im eigenen Land. Emigration und Rückkehr einer deutschen Jüdin.* Autobiografie. Ratingen: Melina-Verl., 1997. 155 pp. [Author, b. 1927 in Nuremberg, emigr. 1937 to Palestine, returned to Germany (Cologne) in the 1960s.]

37010. SIMON, ERNST A.: *Sechzig Jahre gegen den Strom.* Briefe von 1917– 1984. Hrsg. vom Leo Baeck Institut Jerusalem. [Hrsg.: Sarah Fraiman (with Dafna Mach)]. Tübingen: Mohr Siebeck, 1998. VI, 296 pp., frontis., footnotes, gloss. (287–289), index (290–296). (Schriftenreihe wissenschaftlicher Abhandlungen des Leo-Baeck-Instituts, 59.) [Incl.: Geleitwort (Yehoshua Amir, V–VI).] [E.A.S., March 15, 1899 Berlin – Aug. 18, 1988 Jerusalem, Zionist, historian, educationalist, emigr. 1928 to Palestine.]

37011. VARNHAGEN, RAHEL. *Rahels erste Liebe. Rahel Levin und Karl Graf von Finckenstein in ihren Briefen.* Nach den Orig. hrsg. und erl. von Günter de Bruyn. 2. Aufl. Berlin: Arani, 1998. 364 pp., illus., bibl. (Märkischer Dichtergarten.)

37012. VORDTRIEDE, KÄTHE: *"Mir ist noch wie ein Traum, dass mir diese abenteuerliche Flucht gelang . . .": Briefe nach 1933 aus Freiburg im Breisgau, Frauenfeld und New York an ihren Sohn Werner.* Hrsg. von Manfred Bosch. Lengwil: Libelle, 1998. 396 pp. [K.V., née Blumenthal, 1891 Hannover – 1964 New York, journalist, lived in Freiburg until her flight to Switzerland in 1939; in 1941 emigr. to the US.] [Cf.: "Gewöhne Dir bitte an, mein Schicksal als äusserst normales zu sehen". Die Freiburger Journalistin und Emigrantin Käthe Vordtriede (Manfred Bosch) [in]: 'NZZ', Nr. 200, Zürich, 31. Aug. 1998, p. 27.]

37013. WEILL, KURT. *Sprich leise wenn du Liebe sagst. Der Briefwechsel Kurt Weill/Lotte Lenya.* Hrsg. und übersetzt von Lys Symonette und Kim H. Kowalke. Köln: Kiepenheuer & Witsch, 1998. 558 pp., illus., footnotes, bibl. (531–534), index (535–548). [Incl.: Zur Einführung & Prolog (eds. 11–48). Teil I. Die deutsch geschriebenen Briefe (49–274). Teil II. Die englisch geschrieben Briefe (transl. into German, 275–492). Epilog: Nach seinem Tod (493–503). Nachwort (503–509). Incl. also a list of K.W.s works. For American edn. see No. 34561/YB XVII.]

37014. WEIL, GRETE: *Leb ich denn, wenn andere leben.* Zürich: Nagel & Kimche, 1998. 255 pp., illus., ports. [Autobiography.] [Also on G.W.: The bible and Greek dramas as intertexts: Grete Weil's adaptation of her sources (Guy Stern) [in]: Literatur und Geschichte. Festschrift für Wulf Koepke zum 70. Geburtstag. Hrsg. von Karl Menges. Amsterdam; Atlanta, GA: Rodopi, 1998. (Amsterdamer Publikationen zur Sprache und Literatur, 133.). Pp. 221–231, notes. [See also No. 36975.]

37015. WUNSCH-MAINZER, ILSE: *Zurück nach vorn. Mein Leben mit Prometheus.* Frankfurt am Main: Stroemfeld (Roter Stern), 1998. 368 pp., illus., facsims. [Autobiography; author, née Wunsch, born 1911 in Berlin, pianist, emigr. with her first husband, the pianist Max Janowski, to Japan, later to the US, where she met her second husband, the writer Otto Mainzer, on whom the book focuses. Incl. also letters written by her mother from Berlin before deportation.] [Cf.: Zurück zum Leben gefunden. Im Gespräch mit 'Aufbau': Ilse Wunsch Mainzer (Evelyn Sander) [in]: Aufbau, Vol. 64, No. 24, New York, Nov. 20, 1998, pp. 15 & 17.]

37016. ZADEK, PETER: *My way: eine Autobiographie, 1926–1969.* Köln: Kiepenheuer & Witsch, 1998. 606 pp., illus., ports., facsims., index (587–606). [Incl.: Werkverzeichnis Peter Zadek (557–583).] [P.Z., b. May 19, 1926 in Berlin, theatre director, emigr. to England as a child, in the late 1950s returned to Germany, where he is still working.]

37017. ZUCKMAYER, CARL. ZUCKMAYER, CARL/HINDEMITH, PAUL: *Briefwechsel.* Ediert, eingeleitet und kommentiert von Gunther Nickel und Giselher Schubert. St. Ingbert: Röhrig, 1998. 122 pp., frontis., ports., illus., facsims., footnotes. (Zuckmayer-Schriften, Bd. 1.) [Incl. letters written betweeen 1940 and 1964.]

37018. ZWEIG, STEFAN. *Alfons Petzold – Stefan Zweig.* Briefwechsel. Eingeleitet und kommentiert von David Turner. Frankfurt am Main; New York: Lang, 1998. 190 pp., notes (129–178), index. (Austrian Culture, Vol. 27.) [Incl. unpubl. letters written betweeen 1911 and 1923.]

IX. GERMAN-JEWISH RELATIONS

A. General

37019. BADRUS, NADIA: *Das Bild der Siebenbürger Sachsen über die Juden.* Einige Anhaltspunkte. [In]: Das Bild des Anderen in Siebenbürgen. Stereotype in einer multiethnischen Region. Hrsg. von Konrad Gündisch [et al.]. Köln: Böhlau, 1998. (Siebenbürgisches Archiv, Bd. 33.) Pp. 85–107, footnotes. [Incl. Engl. and French summaries. Deals with the attitudes of the 'Saxons' in Transylvania towards the Jews, reflecting latent hostility and, in the 20th cent., antisemitism.]

37020. BODEK, JANUSZ: *Ein "Geflecht aus Schuld und Rache"? Die Kontroversen um Fassbinders' Der Müll, die Stadt und der Tod'.* [In]: Deutsche Nachkriegsliteratur und der Holocaust [see No. 36760]. Pp. 351–384.

37021. BRAESE, STEPHAN, ed.: *In der Sprache der Täter.* Neue Lektüren deutschsprachiger Nachkriegs- und Gegenwartsliteratur. Opladen: Westdeutscher Verl., 1998. 255 pp., footnotes. [Book consists partly of the revised papers presented at a conference at the Hebrew Univ. in Jerusalem in Dec. 1996. Cont. (titles partly condensed): Einführung (ed., 7–12). Der Holocaust im Geschichtsnarrativ. Über Variationen historischen Gedächtnisses (Dan Diner, 13–30). Zum Begriff der Lyrik by Adorno (Moshe Zuckermann, 31–42). Irmgard Keun im Nachkriegsdeutschland (Stephan Braese, 43–78). Zur Prosa Johannes Bobrowskis (Holger Gehle, 79–102). Wolfgang Koeppen und Ruth Klüger (Jakob Hessing, 103–116). George Taboris 'Die Kannibalen' (Rachel Perets, 117–136). Shoah-Literatur: Weder Fiktion noch Dokument (Jürgen Nieraad, 137–148). Zur Jugendautobiographie Georges-Arthur Goldschmidts (Alfred Bodenheimer, 149–166). W.G. Sebalds 'Die Ausgewanderten' (Sigrid Korff, 167–198). Zu Esther Dischereits Romanen, Hörspielen und Gedichten (Itta Shedletzky, 199–226). Incl. also a contrib. on Christoph Ransmayr by Amir Eshel.]

37022. ECKERT, PAUL WILLEHAD: *Shylocks Rückkehr. Juden und jüdische Themen auf deutschen Bühnen nach 1945*. [In]: "Zuhause in Köln ...": jüdisches Leben 1945 bis heute [see No. 36510]. Pp. 148–160.

37023. FOSCHEPOTH, JOSEF: *Für junge Juden kaum noch attraktiv*. Die Geschichte der Gesellschaften für Christlich-Jüdische Zusammenarbeit. [In]: 'FAZ', Nr. 292, Frankfurt am Main, 16. Dez. 1998. P. 9.

37024. HORWITZ, RIVKA: *On historiosophy, mythos and Christian-Jewish dialogue in Germany at the beginning of the 19th century*. [In]: Eshel Beer-Sheva, Vol. 4, Beer-Sheva, 1996. Pp. 317–341. [In Hebrew, title transl.]

37025. JUNG, THOMAS: *Nicht-Darstellung und Selbst-Darstellung: Der Umgang mit der "Judenfrage" in der SBZ und der frühen DDR und dessen Niederschlag in Literatur und Film*. [In]: Monatshefte für deutschen Unterricht, deutsche Sprache und Literatur. Vol. 90, No. 1, Madison, WI, Spring 1998. Pp. 49–70. [Incl. Engl. abstract on p. 89.]

37026. KUMME, ANDREA: *Die "Wiener Apokalypse" in Inge Merkels Roman "Das andere Gesicht"*. [In]: Modern Austrian Literature, Vol. 31, No. 1, Riverside, CA, 1998. Pp. 50–83, notes. [Novel incl. Jewish themes and has a rabbi as protagonist.]

37027. LOTTER, FRIEDRICH: *Zur christlich-jüdischen Kontroverse im Mittelalter*. Quellen und Literatur der Jahre 1993–1996. [In]: Aschkenas, Jg. 8, H. 2, Wien, 1998. Pp. 525–544, footnotes. [Review essay.]

37028. MÜLLERS, ANNEGRET: *Tradition and change: the difficulty of living in the present*. [In]: European Judaism, Vol. 31, No. 1, London, Spring 1998. Pp. 71–78, notes. [Paper given at the 25th Standing Conference of Jews, Christians, and Muslims in Europe, held in Bendorf near Koblenz and co-sponsored by the Leo Baeck College. Author discusses Germans' problems in coming to terms with their past and draws on examples from her own life.]

37029. PASTO, JAMES: *Islam's "strange secret sharer": Orientalism, Judaism, and the Jewish Question*. [In]: Comparative Studies in Society and History, Vol. 40, No. 3, Cambridge, July 1998. Pp. 437–474, footnotes. [Deals mainly with liberal Protestant German theologians, their critical study of the Bible and Judaism and their part in the political discussion of the "Jewish Question".]

37030. ROBERTS, ULLA: *Spuren der NS-Zeit im Leben der Kinder und Enkel; drei Generationen im Gespräch*. München: Kösel, 1998. 236 pp. [Incl. chap.: Deutsch-jüdische Gruppentreffen von Angehörigen der dritten Generation (115–139).]

37031. ROBERTSON, RITCHIE: *Freedom and pragmatism: aspects of religious toleration in 18th-century Germany*. [In]: Patterns of Prejudice, Vol. 32, No. 3, London, July 1998. Pp. 69–80, notes. [Incl. emancipation of the Jews, discusses religious tolerance and attitudes towards Jews as expressed by G.E. Lessing.]

37032. SÖLÇÜN, SARGUT: *Moralität der Doppelmoral oder Chancen des jüdischen Lebens im deutschen Exil – Autobiographische Erkundungen*. [In]: literatur für leser, Jg. 21, H. 3, Frankfurt am Main, 1998. Pp. 287–198, footnotes. [Deals with Laura Waco's 'Von zu Hause wird nichts erzählt. Eine jüdische Geschichte aus Deutschland', see No. 35749/YB XLIII.]

37033. WEILER, CHRISTEL: *"Verzeihung, sind Sie Jude?". Über einen möglichen Umgang des Theaters mit Geschichte*. [In]: Theater seit den 60er Jahren: Grenzgänge der Neo-Avantgarde. Hrsg.: Erika Fischer-Lichte. Tübingen: Francke, 1998. (UTB für Wiss.) Pp. 375–387.

B. German-Israeli Relations

37034. AUSTRIA. EMBACHER, HELGA/REITER, MARGIT: *Gratwanderungen. Die Beziehungen zwischen Österreich und Israel im Schatten der Vergangenheit.* Wien: Picus, 1998. 387 pp., illus., notes (289–364), bibl., chronol., index.

37035. BARZEL, NEIMA: *Relations between Israel and Germany – from the boycott policy to complex relations.* [In Hebrew]. [In]: The first decade 1948–1958. [In Hebrew, title transl.] Ed. by Zvi Zameret and Hannah Yablonka. Jerusalem: Yad Izhak Ben-Zvi, 1997. Pp. 197–214.

37036. BENZ, WOLFGANG: *Antisemitismus und das Verhältnis der Deutschen zu Israel.* [In]: Kulturchronik, Jg. 16, Nr. 4, Bonn, 1998. Pp. 24–26.

37037. BERGMANN, WERNER: *Realpolitik versus Geschichtspolitik. Der Schmidt-Begin-Konflikt von 1981.* [In]: Jahrbuch für Antisemitismusforschung 7, Frankfurt; New York, 1998. Pp. 266–281, notes.

37038. *Brücken in die Zukunft. NRW – Israel 1998: Wege zur Verständigung – Brücken bauen. Ein Jugend-projekt des Minist. für Frauen* [et al.] *und des Minist. für Schule* [et al.] *des Landes Nordr-hein-Westfalen.* [Projektltg.: Helle Becker. Red. Bearb.: Marita Klink]. Hrsg.: Minist. für Frauen [et al.]; Minist. für Schule [et. al.]. Essen: Klartext, 1998. 176 pp., illus. [Incl.: Geleitwort (Johannes Rau, 5–7). Vorwort (Gabriele Behler & Birgit Fischer, 8–10). Einführung (Helle Becker, 11–17). 17 contribs. by young non-Jewish and Jewish participants of the 'Jugendprojekt'.]

37039. EISLER, JAKOB: *Hessische Kolonisationspläne für Palästina 1848–1850.* [In]: Jahrbuch '99 [des Landkreises Kassel], Kassel, 1998. Pp. 36–40, notes. [On the Verein zu Frankfurt am Main für eine deutsche Kolonie im Gelobten Land.]

37040. EYLON, LILI: *The Wagner controversy.* [In]: Ariel, No. 103, Jerusalem, 1996. Pp. 13–16. [On the question whether to play Wagner's music in Israel.]

37041. FAULENBACH, BERND/SCHÜTTE, HELMUTH, eds.: *Deutschland, Israel und der Holocaust. Zur Gegenwartsbedeutung der Vergangenheit.* Essen: Klartext, 1998. 138 pp., illus., footnotes. [Papers given at a conference in Hattingen 1996. Cont. (some titles abbr.): Deutschland und Israel – eine besondere Beziehung auf Dauer? (Frank von Auer, 11–18). Der Weg zum Völkermord an den europäischen Juden (Hans Mommsen, 19–30). Der Holocaust in der Erinnerung (Detlef Hoffmann, 31–44). Die Bedeutung des Holocaust für das kollektive Bewußtsein und die Politik Israels (Moshe Zimmermann, 45–54). Über Variationen historischen Gedächtnisses (Dan Diner, 55–70). Berliner Beispiele öffentlicher Erinnerung an die nationalsozialistische Gewaltherrschaft (Peter Reichel, 71–88). Die DDR und der Holocaust (Annette Leo, 89–104). Podium: Die Last der Vergangenheit – die Zukunft des deutsch-israelischen Verhältnisses (Annette Leo, Anke Martiny, Gas Shimron, Siegfried Vergin, Bernd Faulenbach, 105–140).]

37042. JASPER, WILLI/PRIMOR, AVI: *"Ein abschließendes Urteil über die Geschichte kann man nicht willkürlich fällen".* Ein Gespräch über Deutschland und Israel. [In]: Menora 1998, Bodenheim, 1998. Pp. 338–347.

37043. LICHTENSTEIN, HEINER/ROMBERG, OTTO R., eds.: *Fünfzig Jahre Israel: Vision und Wirklichkeit.* Bonn: Bundeszentrale für pol. Bildung, 1998. 359 pp., illus. (Schriftenreihe, Bd. 353.) [A collection of articles first publ. in 'Tribüne'. Incl. 3 contribs. on German-Israeli relations by Markus A. Weingardt, Dieter Schulte, Dieter H. Vogel; further selected articles are listed according to subject.]

37044. MARIENFELD, WOLFGANG: *Das Georg-Eckert-Institut für Internationale Schulbuchforschung in Braunschweig. Die deutsch-israelischen Schulbuchempfehlungen.* [In]: Menora 1997, Bodenheim, 1997. Pp. 369–402, notes.

37045. *Mein Israel. 21 erbetene Interventionen.* Hrsg. von Micha Brumlik. Frankfurt am Main: Fischer Taschenbuch Verlag, 1998. 176 pp., bibl. notes. (Originalausgabe.) [A collection of essays by non-Jewish and Jewish authors from Germany (Wolf Biermann, Maxim Biller, Detlev Claussen, Ralph Giordano, Susannah Heschel, Stefan Heym, Peter Stephan Jungk, Nadja Klinger, Cilly Kugelmann, Friedrich-Wilhelm Marquardt, Peggy Parnass, Julius H. Schoeps, Valentin Senger, Dorothee Sölle, Michael Walzer, Markus Wolf; also by Israeli authors (Dan Diner, Jakob Hessing, Gabriel Motzkin, Moshe Zimmermann, Moshe Zuckermann).]

37046. WATZAL, LUDWIG: *Von Normalität kann noch keine Rede sein. Die deutsch-israelischen Beziehungen.* [In]: Das Parlament, Jg. 48, Nr. 14, Bonn, 27. März 1998. Pp. 8. [Issue title: *Fünfzig Jahre Israel 1948–1998.* This issue incl. also: Die Gründung des Staates Israel war die zwingende und beste Antwort auf den Holocaust (Dina Porat, p. 9. Ein Land, ein Grundkonsens und viele Stimmen; Variationen des Zionismus in Israel (Dan Diner, p. 1).]

———— ZUCKERMANN, MOSHE: *Zweierlei Holocaust. Der Holocaust in den politischen Kulturen Israels und Deutschlands.* [See No. 36490.]

C. Church and Synagogue

37047. *Auf dem Weg zum christlich-jüdischen Gespräch.* 125 Jahre Evangelisch-lutherischer Zentralverein für Zeugnis und Dienst unter Juden und Christen. Hrsg. von Arnulf H. Baumann. Münster: Inst. Judaicum Delitzschianum, 1998. 1 vol. (Münsteraner Judaistische Studien, Bd. 1.) [Cont. 8 essays dealing with the Zentralverein, Franz Delitzsch, Gustav Dalman, Otto von Harling, Hans Kosmala, Karl Heinrich Rengstorf in particular and the Christian-Jewish encounter in general by Arnulf H. Baumann, Hermann Brandt, Karin Haufler-Musiol, Benno Kosmala, Hermann Lichtenberger, Werner Monselewski and Jürgen Roloff. For a further essay on the present role of the Zentralverein by Arnulf H. Baumann, see in No. 37111 (pp. 218–220).]

37048. BURMEISTER, HEIKE A.: *Der "Judenknabe": Studien und Texte zu einem mittelalterlichen Marienmirakel in deutscher Überlieferung.* Göppingen: Kümmerle, 1998. 378 pp., illus. (Göppinger Arbeiten zur Germanistik, 654.) Zugl.: Marburg, Univ., Diss., 1997.

37049. GILLIS-CARLEBACH, MIRIAM/VOGEL, BARBARA, eds.: *"Wie ein Einheimischer soll der Fremdling bei euch sein – und bringe ihm Liebe entgegen wie dir selbst". Toleranz im Verhältnis von Religion und Gesellschaft.* Die dritte Joseph-Carlebach-Konferenz. Hamburg: Dölling und Galitz, 1997. 230 pp. (Publications of the Joseph-Carlebach-Institute.) [Papers presented at a conference in Ramat Gan 1996.]

37050. KEDAR, BENJAMIN Z.: *The forcible baptisms of 1096: history and historiography.* [In]: Forschungen zur Reichs-, Papst- und Landesgeschichte. Peter Herde zum 65. Geburtstag von Freunden, Schülern und Kollegen dargebracht. Hrsg. von Karl Borchardt und Enno Bünz. Teil 1, Stuttgart: Hiersemann, 1998. Pp. 187–200, footnotes. [On the First Crusade.]

37051. KRAUSS, SAMUEL: *The Jewish-Christian controversy from the earliest times to 1789.* Vol. I: *History.* Ed. and revised by William Horbury. Tübingen: Mohr Siebeck, 1996. XIV, 310 pp. (Studien zum Antiken Judentum, 56.) [Hitherto unpubl. book by author, emigr. from Vienna to Cambridge in 1938, written in German and transl. into English shortly before author's death in 1948, aged 92.] [Cf.: Review (Hanne Trautner-Kromann) [in]: Frankfurter Judaistische Beiträge, 25, Frankfurt am Main, Dez. 1998, pp. 174–175.]

37052. KRIENER, KATJA/SCHMIDT, JOHANN MICHAEL, eds.: *Gottes Treue. Hoffnung von Christen und Juden.* Die Auseinandersetzung um die Ergänzung des Grundartikels der Kirchenordnung der Evangelischen Kirche im Rheinland. Neukirchen-Vluyn: Neukirchener Verl., 1998. 320 pp., footnotes.

37053. LOTTER, FRIEDRICH: *Ritualmord.* [In]: Theologische Realenzyklopädie, Bd. XXIX, Religionspsychologie – Samaritaner. In Gemeinschaft mit Horst Balz [et al.] hrsg. von Gerhard Müller. Berlin; New York, 1998. Pp. 253–259, bibl.

37054. RENDTORFF, ROLF: *Christen und Juden heute: neue Einsichten und neue Aufgaben.* Neukirchen-Vluyn: Neukirchener Verl., 1998. 154 pp. [A collection of 7 articles publ. between 1990 and 1998.]

—— ZUPANCIC, ANDREA: *Das Judenbild in der christlichen Ikonographie des Mittelalters.* [See in No. 36081.]

D. **Antisemitism**

37055. ARIELI-HOROWITZ, DANA: *The Jew as 'destroyer of culture' in National Socialist ideology.* [In]: Patterns of Prejudice, Vol. 32, No. 1, London, Jan. 1998. Pp. 51–67, footnotes.

37056. BÄRSCH, CLAUS EKKEHARD: *Die politische Religion des Nationalsozialismus.* Die religiöse Dimension der NS-Ideologie in den Schriften von Dietrich Eckart, Joseph Goebbels, Alfred Rosenberg und Adolf Hitler. München: Fink, 1998. 406 pp., footnotes. [Also on the antisemitic elements in the 'political religion' of the Nazi protagonists.]

37057. BEN-ITTO, HADASSA: *"Die Protokolle der Weisen von Zion" – Anatomie einer Fälschung.* Aus dem Engl. von Helmut Ettinger und Juliane Lochner. Berlin: Aufbau, 1998. 418 pp., illus., bibl., index. [Orig. title: 'The lie that wouldn't die'.] [Cf.: Besprechung (Uri R. Kaufmann) [in]: Aschkenas, Jg. 8, H. 2, Wien, 1998, pp. 590–591.]

37058. BENZ, WOLFGANG: *Diffamierung aus dem Dunkel. Die Legende von der Verschwörung des Judentums in den "Protokollen der Weisen von Zion".* [In]: Grosse Verschwörungen. Staatsstreich und Tyrannensturz von der Antike bis zur Gegenwart. Hrsg. von Uwe Schultz. München: Beck, 1998. Pp. 205–217, notes.

37059. BERESWILL, MECHTHILD/WAGNER, LEONIE: *"Eine rein persönliche Angelegenheit". Antisemitismus und politische Öffentlichkeit als Konfliktfeld im "Bund Deutscher Frauenvereine".* [In]: Die Philosophin. Forum für feministische Theorie und Philosophie, Nr. 15, Tübingen, April 1997. Pp. 9–23, footnotes.

37060. BERESWILL, MECHTHILD/WAGNER, LEONIE, eds.: *Bürgerliche Frauenbewegung und Antisemitismus.* Tübingen: Edition diskord, 1998. 125 pp., footnotes. [Cont.: Einleitung (eds., 7–12). Aufbruch in eine neue Gesellschaft? Erwartungen jüdischer Frauen an die deutsche Frauenbewegung und die Grenzen der Zusammenarbeit (Helga Krohn, 13–44). 'Eine rein persönliche Angelegenheit'. Antisemitismus und politische Öffentlichkeit als Konfliktfeld im "Bund Deutscher Frauenvereine" (eds., 45–63; previously publ. in 1997, see No. 37059). "Woran erkennen wir die Prostituierte?". Sittlichkeit, Großstadtdiskurs und Antisemitismus im Kontext der Frauenbewegung (Susanne Omran, 65–87). Antijudaismus – Antisemitismus: Zum Zusammenhang von christlichen Traditionen und antijüdischen Stereotypen (Dagmar Henze, 89–99). Die Eine und der Andere. Moderner Antisemitismus als Geschlechtergeschichte (Johanna Gehmacher, 101–120).]

—— BERGMANN, WERNER/WETZEL, JULIANE: *"Der Miterlebende weiß nichts". Alltagsantisemitismus als zeitgenössische Erfahrung und spätere Erinnerung (1919–1933).* [See in No. 35925.]

37061. BERGMANN, WERNER: *Antisemitismus und deutsch-jüdische Geschichte.* [In]: Jahrbuch Extremismus & Demokratie, Bd. 10, Baden-Baden, 1998. Pp. 255–275. [Review essay.]

37062. CORNISH, KIMBERLEY: *The Jew of Linz: Hitler, Wittgenstein and their secret battle for the mind.* London: Century, 1998. 298 pp., illus., ports., appendix, notes (235–284). [German edn. publ. under the title: *Der Jude aus Linz: Hitler und Wittgenstein.* Aus dem Engl. von Angelus Johansen. Berlin: Ullstein, 1998. 432 pp.] [Based on the fact that Hitler and Wittgenstein for a short time attended the same school in Linz, author argues the tenuous theory that they influenced each other and world events by holding a grudge which made one an antisemite, and the other a Soviet spy at Cambridge. Incl. chap.: Wagner and Judaism in music.] [Cf: Changing the course of history (Frank McLynn) [in]: The Sunday Times, London, March 15, 1998, p. 6.]

37063. CYMOREK, HANS: *Georg von Below und die deutsche Geschichtswissenschaft um 1900.* Stuttgart: Steiner, 1998. 374 pp., footnotes, bibl. (316–363), index. (Vierteljahrschrift für Sozial- und Wirtschaftsgeschichte, Beihefte, Nr. 142.) Zugl.: Berlin, Humboldt-Univ., Diss., 1995 u.d.T. Georg von Below. [Deals also with Below's antisemitism, esp. in the chap. 'Antimodernismus und Antisemitismus' (296–302).]

37064. DIETRICH, STEFAN J.: *Gewalt und Vorurteil. Antijüdische Ausschreitungen 1948 in Nordbaden.* [In]: Badische Heimat, H. 1, Konstanz, März 1998. Pp. 71–81, facsims., notes.

37065. ERB, RAINER: *Antisemitismus und Antizionismus.* [In]: Fünfzig Jahre Israel: Vision und Wirklichkeit [see No. 37043]. Pp. 222–232.

37066. FISCHER, KLAUS P.: *History of an obsession: German Judeophobia and the Holocaust.* London: Constable; New York: Continuum, 1998. IX, 532 pp., notes (439–487), bibl. (489–511). [Deals with antisemitism from 18th to 20th century.]

37067. FUGMANN, MARKUS: *Moderner Antisemitismus.* Frankfurt am Main: Diesterweg, 1998. 114 pp., illus., bibl. (Brennpunkt Geschichte.)

37068. GRÖZINGER, ELVIRA: *"Judenmauschel". Der antisemitische Sprachgebrauch und die jüdische Identität.* [In]: Sprache und Identität im Judentum [see No. 36627]. Pp. 173–198.

37069. GUBSER, MARTIN: *Literarischer Antisemitismus. Untersuchungen zu Gustav Freytag und anderen bürgerlichen Schriftstellern des 19. Jahrhunderts.* Göttingen: Wallstein, 1998. 325 pp., notes, bibl. (315–326). Zugl.: Fribourg, Univ., Diss., 1995.

37070. HOLZTRÄGER, HANS: *Antisemitismus unter Siebenbürger Sachsen in Nord-Transylvanien.* [In]: Halbjahresschrift für südosteuropäische Geschichte, Literatur und Politik, Jg. 9, Ippesheim, 1997. Pp. 88–97.

37071. HORTZITZ, NICOLINE: *[D]ie Art kan nicht nachlassen [...] (Rechtanus 1606) – rassistisches Denken in frühneuzeitlichen Texten?* [In]: Aschkenas, Jg. 8, H. 1, Wien, 1998. Pp. 71–104, footnotes.

37072. IGGERS, GEORG: *Academic anti-semitism in Germany 1870–1933.* A comparative perspective. [In]: Tel Aviver Jahrbuch für deutsche Geschichte, Bd. 27, Gerlingen, 1998. Pp. 473–489, footnotes. [Also on different assessments of academic antisemitism.]

37073. JOHNSON, WILLIS: *The myth of Jewish male menses.* [In]: Journal of Medieval History, Vol. 24, No. 3, Amsterdam, 1998. Pp. 273–295, footnotes. [Examines previous interpretations of Christian medieval texts.]

37074. KEITH, GRAHAM: *Hated without a cause? A survey of antisemitism.* Carlisle, Cumbria: Paternoster Press, 1997. XII, 301 pp., notes, bibl. (284–292). [Incl. sections on German antisemitism (incl. Nazi period), Luther and the Jews.]

37075. KERCHNER, BRIGITTE: *"Unbescholtene Bürger" und "gefährliche Mädchen" um die Jahrhundertwende.* Was der Fall Sternberg für die aktuelle Debatte zum sexuellen Mißbrauch an Kindern bedeutet. [In]: Historische Anthropologie, Jg. 6, H. 1, Weimar, 1998. Pp. 1–32, footnotes. [Deals also with antisemitic aspects of a "sex scandal" in 1900.]

37076. KÖLLING, BERND: *Tod eines Handlungsreisenden. Die Affäre Helling und der Antisemitismus in der Weimarer Republik.* [In]: Jahrbuch für Antisemitismusforschung 7, Frankfurt am Main; New York, 1998. Pp. 151–174, notes. [Deals with an incident in Magdeburg 1926.]

37077. LEMHÖFER, LUTZ: *Schwarz-braune Verschwörungstheorien. Anmerkungen zum Programm eines "frommen" Szene-Verlages*. [In]: Jahrbuch für Antisemitismusforschung 7, Frankfurt am Main; New York, 1998. Pp. 322–331. [On the catholic publisher Anton Schmid in Durlach, who in his publs. also reveals antisemitic ideas.]

37078. LEVIN, DAVID J.: *Richard Wagner, Fritz Lang and the Nibelungen: the dramaturgy of disavowal.* Princeton, NJ: Princeton Univ. Press, 1998. XI, 207 pp., illus., notes (151–187), bibl. (189–198). [Deals with Lang's film on the Nibelungen and compares it to Wagner's operas by exploring the relationship between aesthetics and antisemitism.]

37079. LEWIS, BERNARD: *Semites and Anti-Semites: an inquiry into conflict and prejudice.* London: Phoenix, 1997. 285 pp., notes (273–286), index. [First publ. 1986; see No. 23820/YB XXXII. Incl. preface and afterword to the new edn.]

37080. LIST, MARTIN: *Antisemitismus in Deutschland – einige neuere Studien im Lichte der Goldhagen-Debatte.* [In]: Politische Vierteljahresschrift, Jg. 39, Opladen 1998. Pp. 113–125, notes. [Review essay.]

37081. MAEDGE, SAMMY: *Vom alltäglichen Antisemitismus und Rechtsextremismus. Erfahrungen in Köln.* [In]: "Zuhause in Köln . . .": jüdisches Leben 1945 bis heute [see No. 36510]. Pp. 56–57.

37082. MARISSEN, MICHAEL: *Lutheranism, anti-Judaism, and Bach's 'St. John Passion'.* With an annot. literal transl. of the libretto. New York; Oxford: Oxford Univ. Press, 1998. XII, 109 pp., appendixes, footnotes, indexes. [Incl. chaps.: Lutheran concepts of Jews and Judaism; Jew-hatred and the St. John Passion; Appendix 1: notes on anti-Judaism and Bach's other works.]

37083. MATTIOLI, ARAM, ed.: *Antisemitismus in der Schweiz 1848–1960.* Mit einem Vorwort von Alfred A. Häsler. Zürich: Orell Füssli, 1998. X, 594 pp. [Covers the period between 1848 and 1960.]

37084. *Methodenprobleme der Antisemitismusforschung.* [In]: Jahrbuch für Antisemitismusforschung 7, Frankfurt am Main; New York, 1998. Pp. 103–150, notes. [Section with above title cont.: Sozialwissenschaftliche Methoden in der Antisemitismusforschung. Ein Überblick (Werner Bergmann/Rainer Erb, 103–120). Antisemitismus, jüdische Geschichte und Jüdische Studien (Johannes Heil, 121–139). Das "Bild des Juden in der Literatur". Berührungen und Grenzen von Literaturwissenschaft und Antisemitismusforschung (Mona Körte, 140–150).]

37085. MÜLLER, ANGELIKA: *Der "jüdische Kapitalist" als Drahtzieher und Hintermann. Zur antisemitischen Bildpolemik in den nationalsozialistischen Wahlplakaten der Weimarer Republik 1924–1933.* [In]: Jahrbuch für Antisemitismusforschung 7, Frankfurt am Main; New York, 1998. Pp. 175–207, notes, illus.

37086. MURPHY, DAVID T.: *Familiar aliens: German antisemitism and European geopolitics in the inter-war era.* [In]: Leo Baeck Institute Year Book XLIII, London, 1998. Pp. 175–191, footnotes.

37087. *Der Prozeß um den Brand der Synagoge in Neustettin.* Antisemitismus in Deutschland ausgangs des 19. Jahrhunderts, Bearb. von Gerd Hoffmann. Mit einer Einführungsbibliographie und bibliographischen Anmerkungen zu Ernst Henrici, Hermann Makower, Erich Sello. Schifferstadt: Hoffmann, 1998. 329 pp., illus., footnotes, bibl. (306–314), (bibl. notes (315–329). [On antisemitism in Imperial Germany as reflected in the arson of the synagogue in Neustettin (Pomerania) in Feb. 1881 followed by trials in Köslin, Leipzig and Konitz between Oct. 1882 and March 1884. Incl. chaps. on the two defence lawyers Hermann Makower and Erich Sello and the antisemitic agitator Ernst Henrici; also the reprint of 'Schlußbetrachtung' (Erich Sello, 209–246) orig. publ. in 1884 in 'Die Nation'.]

37088. QUAST, BRUNO: *Anthropologie des Opfers. Beobachtungen zur Konstitution frühneuzeitlicher 'Verfolgungstexte' am Beispiel des "Endinger Judenspiels".* [In]: Zeitschrift für Germanistik, N.F., Bd. VIII, H. 1, Bern; New York, 1998. Pp. 349–360, footnotes. [On a blood libel case in the 15th cent. and a passion play from the 16th cent.]

37089. REGNERI, GÜNTER: *Salomon Neumann's statistical challenge to Treitschke: the forgotten episode that marked the end of the Berliner Antisemitismusstreit.* [In]: Leo Baeck Institute Year Book XLIII, London, 1998. Pp. 129–153, footnotes.

37090. RENSMANN, LARS: *Kritische Theorie über den Antisemitismus.* Studien zu Struktur, Erklärungspotential und Aktualität. Berlin: Argument-Verl., 1998. 386 pp., footnotes, bibl. (367–386). (Edition Philosophie und Sozialwissenschaften, 42.) [Incl. a chap. on the Goldhagen debate.]

37091. SAMMONS, JEFFREY L., ed.: *Die Protokolle der Weisen von Zion.* Die Grundlage des modernen Antisemitismus – eine Fälschung. Text und Kommentar. Göttingen: Wallstein, 1998. 128 pp., footnotes. [Author also traces the origin of the "Protocols" (Einführung, 7–26).]

——— *"Der schejne Jid".* Das Bild des "jüdischen Körpers" in Mythos und Ritual. [Hrsg. von Sander L. Gilman, Robert Jütte, Gabriele Kohlbauer-Fritz.] [See No. 36624.]

37092. SCHNELL, RALF: *Dichtung in finsteren Zeiten.* Deutsche Literatur und Faschismus. Reinbek: Rowohlt Taschenbuch Verlag, 1998. 207 pp., notes (186–189), bibl. (190–201), index. (Rowohlts Enzyklopädie.) Originalausgabe. [Incl. the chap.: Auschwitz, ein deutsches Trauma – ohne Ende, ohne Anfang (7–26; deals also with antisemitic traditions).]

37093. STEIMAN, LIONEL B.: *Paths to genocide: antisemitism in Western history.* Basingstoke; London: Macmillan; New York: St. Martin's Press, 1998. XV, 284 pp., notes (245–260), bibl. (267–276). [A survey of nearly two thousand years of Christian antisemitism in all its forms; incl. chaps.: The age of Reformation: Luther and the Jews; Imperial Germany and Habsburg Austria: ideology, politics, culture; Nazi Germany: the Final Solution.]

37094. TANNER, JAKOB: *"Bankenmacht": politischer Popanz, antisemitischer Stereotyp oder analytische Kategorie?* [In]: Zeitschrift für Unternehmensgeschichte, Jg. 43, Nr. 1, Stuttgart, 1998. Pp. 19–34, footnotes. [Incl. Engl. abstract.]

——— VOIGTS, MANFRED: *". . . lügt auch bei wörtlichen Zitaten".* Anmerkungen zur Zerstörung jüdischer Sprach-Identität. [See in No. 36627.]

37095. WAGNER, GOTTFRIED: *Wer nicht mit dem Wolf heult. Autobiographische Aufzeichnungen eines Wagner-Urenkels.* Mit einem Vorwort von Ralph Giordano. Köln: Kiepenheuer & Witsch, 1997. 409 pp., notes, index. [Engl. edn.: *He who does not howl with the wolf. The Wagner legacy: an autobiography.* Preface by Rabbi Julia Neuberger. Transl. by Della Couling. London: Sanctuary, 1998. 355 pp., ports., illus., facsims., index.] [R.W's. great grandson's autobiography also deals extensively with the antisemitism and Nazi associations of the Wagner family.]

E. Noted Germans and Jews

37096. BACH, JOHANN SEBASTIAN. HOFFMANN-AXTHELM, DAGMAR: *Die Judenchöre in Bachs Johannes-Passion.* Der Thomaskantor als Gestalter lutherischer Judenpolitik. [In]: Freiburger Rundbrief, N.F., Jg.5, Freiburg, 1998. Pp. 103–111, footnotes. [Abbr. version of article publ. 1989.]

37097. BRECHT, BERTOLT. VOIGTS, MANFRED: *Brecht and the Jews.* [In]: Schnittpunkte/Intersections. Das Brecht-Jahrbuch 21/The Brecht Yearbook 21. Madison, WI, 1996. Pp. 100–123, notes, illus. [Incl. German, French and Spanish abstracts.]

37098. BURCKHARDT, JACOB. DEBRUNNER, ALBERT M.: *Eine verdrängte Seite. Die antisemitischen Äusserungen von Jacob Burckhardt.* [In]: Israelitisches Wochenblatt, Jg. 98, Nr. 8, Zürich, 20. Feb. 1998. Pp. 6–7, port.

37099. FONTANE, THEODOR. FLEISCHER, MICHAEL: *"Kommen Sie, Cohn." Fontane und die "Judenfrage".* Berlin: Michael Fleischer [privately printed], 1998. 402 pp., illus., chronol., notes

(339–372), bibl. (373–380), index (381–391). [Cf.: Besprechung (Hans Otto Horch) [in]: Fontane Blätter, Jg. 67, Potsdam, 1999, pp. 135–141.

37100. GRILLPARZER, FRANZ. REEVE, WILLIAM C.: *"In the beginning...": the opening scene of Grillparzer's 'Die Jüdin von Toledo'*. [In]: Modern Austrian Literature, Vol. 31, No. 1, Riverside, CA, 1998. Pp. 1–19, notes.

37101. HAUFF, WILHELM. CHASE, JEFFERSON S.: *The wandering court Jew, and the hand of God: Wilhelm Hauff's 'Jud Süss' as historical fiction*. [In]: Modern Language Review, Vol. 93, No. 3, Leeds, 1998. Pp. 724–740, footnotes.

37102. HAUPTMANN, GERHART. SPRENGEL, PETER: *Phantom des Reichstags: fremde Blicke Hauptmanns auf Rathenau*. [In]: Zeitschrift für Germanistik, N.F., Bd. VIII, H. 1, Bern; New York, 1998. Pp. 97–107, footnotes.

37103. HEIDEGGER, MARTIN. BEVILACQUA, GIUSEPPE: *Heidegger a Celan*. Una lettera senza risposta. [In]: Belfagor, Vol. 8, No. 3, Firenze, May 31, 1998. Pp. 355–358. [Incl. letter written in Jan. 30, 1968.] [Also on Heidegger and Celan: "Mit einer Hoffnung auf ein kommendes Wort". Die Begegnung von Paul Celan und Martin Heidegger (Stephan Krass) [in]: 'NZZ', Nr. 176, Zürich, 2./3. Aug. 1997, p. 57.]

37104. HEIDEGGER, MARTIN. JONES, MICHAEL T.: *Heidegger the fox: Hannah Arendt's hidden dialogue*. [In]: New German Critique, No. 73, Ithaca, NY, Winter 1998. Pp. 164–192, footnotes. [Discusses their relationship and correspondence, incl. H.'s pronouncements on the 'Jewish Question'.]

37105. HEIDEGGER, MARTIN. LANG, BEREL: *Heidegger's silence*. Ithaca, NY: Cornell Univ. Press, 1996. XI, 129 pp., notes, bibl. [Cf.: "A specter that will not go away": review essay (Anson Rabinbach) [in]: Jewish Social Studies, Vol. 4, No. 3, Bloomington, IN, Spring/Summer 1998. Pp. 168–172.]

37106. HEIDEGGER, MARTIN. SAFRANSKI, RÜDIGER: *Martin Heidegger: between good and evil*. Transl. from the German by Ewald Osers. Cambridge, MA: Harvard Univ. Press, 1998. XVII, 474 pp., chronol., notes (435–452), works cited (453–459), bibl. (461–464). [Incl. Heidegger's relationship with H. Arendt; also chap.: Is Heidegger antisemitic?] [Cf.: Not very good at being in the world (Roger Scruton) [in]: The Times, London, April 30, 1998, p. 44.]

——— HESSE, HERMANN. SCHWARZ, EGON: *Hermann Hesse, der Nationalsozialismus und die Juden*. [See in No. 36744.]

37107. HUMBOLDT, ALEXANDER VON. SLONIMSKI, CHAIM SELIG: *Zur Freiheit bestimmt*. Alexander von Humboldt – eine hebräische Lebensbeschreibung. Hrsg. von Kurt-Jürgen Maaß. Aus dem Hebr. übers. von Orna Carmel. Bonn: Bouvier, 1997. 1 vol. [First German edn. of a Hebrew biography of A.v.H., publ. in Berlin in 1858 by the mathematician and astronomer Ch.S.S. (1810 Bialystok – 1904 Warsaw) with the financial aid of the Berlin Jewish community and presented to A.v.H. on his 88th birthday. Incl. an essay entitled: Alexander von Humboldt und die Juden (Peter Honigmann; first publ. in 1987, see No. 24854/YB XXXIII).]

37108. KLEPPER, JOCHEN. WECHT, MARTIN JOHANNES: *Jochen Klepper. Ein christlicher Schriftsteller im jüdischen Schicksal*. Düsseldorf: Archiv der Evang. Kirche im Rheinland, 1998. XIV, 658 pp., illus. (Studien zur Schlesischen und Oberlausitzer Kirchengeschichte, 3.) [For data on J.K. see No. 30045/YB XXXVIII.]

37109. LESSING, GOTTHOLD EPHRAIM. ROBERTSON, RITCHIE: *'Dies hohe Lied der Duldung'? The ambiguities of toleration in Lessing's 'Die Juden' und 'Nathan der Weise'*. [In]: The Modern Language Review, Vol. 93, No. 1, Leeds, 1998. Pp. 105–120.

37110. LICHTENBERG, GEORG CHRISTOPH. Schäfer, Frank: *Lichtenberg und das Judentum.* Göttingen: Wallstein, 1998. 175 pp., footnotes, bibl. (163–175). (Lichtenberg-Studien, Bd. 10.) [Analyses L.'s writings and letters dealing with Jews and Judaism, some of which contain outspoken antisemitic invectives.] [CF.: Philologie des Verdachts. Peinliche Befragung: Frank Schäfer über Lichtenberg und die Juden (Thomas Wirtz) [in]: 'FAZ', Nr. 33, Frankfurt am Main, 9. Feb. 1999, p. 48.]

37111. LUTHER, MARTIN. Sherman, Franklin: *Luther and the Jews. An American perspective.* [In]: Siegert, Folker/Kalms, Jürgen U., eds.: Internationales Josephus-Kolloquium Münster 1997. Vorträge aus dem Institutum Judaicum Delitzschianum. Münster: Inst. Judaicum Delitzschianum, 1998. Pp. 210–217.

37112. MAHLER-WERFEL, ALMA. *Diaries, 1898–1902.* Selected and transl. by Antony Beaumont. From the German edn. transcribed and ed. by A. Beaumont and Susanne Rode-Breymann. London: Faber, 1998; Ithaca: Cornell Univ. Press, 1999. 494 pp., illus., facsims., index of A.M.-W.'s compositions. [Incl. Alma's early relationship with Gustav Mahler and her friendship with numerous Jewish personalities of her day.]

37113. MANN, HEINRICH & THOMAS. Thiede, Rolf: *Stereotypen vom Juden. Die frühen Schriften von Heinrich und Thomas Mann.* Zum antisemitischen Diskurs der Moderne und dem Versuch seiner Überwindung. Berlin: Metropol, 1998. 236 pp., footnotes, bibl. (227–236). (Reihe Dokumente, Texte, Materialien, Bd. 23.) [Orig. publ. in 1995 as a diss. (Johns Hopkins Univ., 1993).]

37114. MANN, THOMAS. Levenson, Alan: *Christian author, Jewish book? Methods and sources in Thomas Mann's 'Joseph'.* [In]: The German Quarterly, Vol. 71, No. 2, Cherry Hill, NJ, Spring 1998. Pp. 166–178, notes. [Discusses Mann's use of Midrash and the general influence of Judaism on the novel.]

37115. MÜLLER, WILHELM. Hartung, Günter: *Müllers Verhältnis zum Judentum.* [In]: Kunst kann die Zeit nicht formen. 1. internationale Wilhelm-Müller-Konferenz Berlin 1994. Hrsg. von Ute Bredemeyer und Christiane Lange. Berlin: Int. Wilh.-Müller-Ges. e.V., 1996. Pp. 195–222, notes.

37116. NIETZSCHE, FRIEDRICH. Niemeyer, Christian: *Nietzsches rhetorischer Antisemitismus.* [In]: Nietzsche-Studien, Bd. 26/1997. Berlin; New York, 1998. Pp. 162, footnotes.

37117. PARACELSUS, PHILIPPUS AUREOLUS THEOPHRASTUS. Benzenhöfer, Udo/ Finsterbusch, Karin: *Antijudaismus in den medizinisch-naturwissenschaftlichen und philosophischen Schriften des Paracelsus.* [In]: Sudhoffs Archiv, Bd. 81, H. 2, Stuttgart, 1997. Pp. 129–138. [Incl. summary.]

37118. Riem, Andreas: *Apologie für die unterdrückte Judenschaft in Deutschland.* Mit einer Einleitung zu Leben und Werk des Autors von Walter Grab. Tübingen: Niemeyer, 1998. VIII, 90 pp., footnotes. (Conditio Judaica, 25.) [Incl. introduction: Deutsche Aufklärung und Judenemanzipation. Andreas Riems Weg vom bibelkritischen Neologen zum revolutionären Demokraten. Judentum und Naturrecht (ed., 1–40); three texts by Andreas Riem, first publ. 1797 and 1798.] [Cf.: Besprechung (Arno Herzig) [in]: Aschkenas, Jg. 9, H. 1, Wien, 1999, pp. 256–257.]

37119. Rinser, Luise: *Begegnungen mit dem Judentum.* Impressionen und Reflexionen. [In]: Edith Stein Jahrbuch, Bd. 4, Würzburg, 1998. Pp. 391–410.] [Personal recollections of the author, b. 1911.]

37120. SCHILLER, FRIEDRICH. Misch, Manfred: *Spiegelberg und sein Judenstaatprojekt.* [In]: "In Spuren gehen. Festschrift für Helmut Koopmann [see No. 36744]. Pp. 127–138, footnotes. [On Schiller's 'Die Räuber'.]

37121. TREITSCHKE, HEINRICH VON. Langer, Ulrich: *Heinrich von Treitschke. Politische Biographie eines deutschen Nationalisten.* Düsseldorf: Droste, 1998. 445 pp., footnotes, chronol., bibl.

(402–440), index. [Deals also with T.'s antisemitism and the 'Berliner Antisemitismus-streit'.]

37122. WAGNER, RICHARD. COHEN, MITCHELL: *Wagner as a problem.* [In]: German Politics and Society, Vol. 16, No. 2, Berkeley, CA, Summer 1998. Pp. 94–130, notes. [Discusses whether Wagner's operas reflect his antisemitic views.]

37123. WAGNER, RICHARD. LEESON, DANIEL N.: *Antisemitism in Richard Wagner's music dramas.* [In]: Midstream, Vol. 44, No. 7, New York, Nov./Dec. 1998. Pp. 9–12.

371254. YOVEL, YIRMIYAHU: *Dark riddle: Hegel, Nietzsche, and the Jews.* Oxford: Polity Press; University Park: Pennsylvania State Univ. Press, 1998. XX, 235 pp., notes (197–217), bibl. (218–224). [Hebrew edn. publ. in 1996 (Jerusalem: Schocken). Deals with the two philosophers' relationship to Judaism, as well as to their Jewish contemporaries.]

X. FICTION AND POETRY

37125. APPELFELD, AHARON: *The conversion.* Transl. from the Hebrew by Jeffrey M. Green. New York: Schocken Books, 1998. 240 pp. [Story of a converted Jew, set against the background of small-town Austria between the wars.]

37126. APPELFELD, AHARON: *The iron tracks.* Transl. from the Hebrew by Jeffrey M. Green. New York: Schocken, 1998. 195 pp. [Story of an Austrian Holocaust survivor who is a perpetual traveller on the railway.]

37127. BERNAYS, ISAAK (d.i. HERMANN SCHIFF): *Schief-Levinche mit seiner Kalle oder Polnische Wirtschaft.* Ein Ghetto-Roman. Nachwort, hrsg. und kommentiert von Renate Heuer. Frankfurt am Main; New York: Campus, 1996. 212 pp. (Campus Judaica, 8.) [Incl. Nachwort (ed., 199–210; on ghetto-novels and the writer Schiff, who publ. his novel in 1848 under the pseud. 'Isaak Bernays'.] [Cf.: Besprechung (Wilfried Weinke) [in]: Zeitschrift des Vereins für Hamburgische Geschichte, Bd. 83/2, Hamburg, 1997, pp. 334–336.] [Hermann Schiff, orig. David Bär Sch., 1801 Hamburg – 1867 Hamburg, writer, cousin of Heinrich Heine.]

37128. *Beyond lament: Poets of the world bearing witness to the Holocaust.* Ed. by Marguerite M. Striar. Evanston, IL: Northwestern Univ. Press, 1998. 565 pp. [Anthology, incl. German-, Austrian-, Czech-Jewish poets; Separate chap. with their biographies.]

37129. GRONEMANN, SAMMY: *Schalet.* Beiträge zur Philosophie des "Wenn schon". Mit einem Nachwort von Joachim Schlör. Leipzig: Reclam, 1998. 249 pp. (Reclam-Bibliothek, Bd. 1619.) [Author (1875–1952), Berlin lawyer, writer and Zionist, in a humorous way depicts Jewish life in Berlin during the 1920s; orig. edn. publ. in 1927.] [S.G., 1875 Strasburg, W. Prussia – 1952 Tel Aviv, jurist, humorist, writer.]

37130. HEYMANN, WALTHER: *Gedichte, Prosa, Essays, Briefe.* Hrsg. von Leonhard M. Fiedler und Renate Heuer. Frankfurt am Main; New York: Campus, 1998. 229 pp., illus., ports. (Campus Judaica, Bd. 13.) [Incl.: Rekonstruktion der Biographie (Renate Heuer, 10–35). Heymanns Lyrik (Rainer Brändle, 37–45). Heymanns Prosa (Thomas Pachunke, 114–117).] [W.H., May 19. 1882 Königsberg – Jan. 9, 1915 Soisson (fallen in battle), lyricist, writer, whose collection is kept in the Deutsches Literaturarchiv – Schiller Nationalmuseum Marbach and in the Archiv Bibliographia Judaica Frankfurt am Main.]

37131. HOFFMANN, YOEL: *Bernhard.* Transl. from the Hebrew by Alan Treister. New York: New Directions, 1998. 192 pp. [A collage of brief vignettes about the experiences of Bernhard Stein, a middle-aged German Jew who, in the 1930s, emigr. from Berlin to Palestine.]

37132. LANDSBERGER, ARTUR: *Berlin ohne Juden.* Hrsg. und mit einem Nachwort von Werner Fuld. Bonn: Weidle, 1998. 218 pp. [First publ. 1925.] [Cf.: Auf der dünnen Decke der Begeisterung. Zur Neuauflage eines alten Romans (Joachim Schlör) [in]: Der Tagesspiegel, Nr. 16 539, Berlin, 6. dez. 1998, p. W 8.]

———— MORGENSTERN, SOMA: *Flucht in Frankreich.* Ein Romanbericht. Hrsg. und mit einem Nachwort von Ingolf Schulte. [See No. 36380.]

37133. PARINI, JAY: *Benjamin's crossing.* London: Anchor; New York: Holt, 1997. 305 pp. [Fictionalised account of the life and death of Walter Benjamin.]

37134. PLAIN, BELVA: *Legacy of silence.* New York: Delacorte Press, 1998. 344 pp. [Novel; begins in 1939 in Germany and ends in the present in the US. Story of two women who lose their parents in the Holocaust and flee to Switzerland.]

37135. RÜHLE-GERSTEL, ALICE: *Verlassenes Ende.* Gedichte. Hrsg. und mit einer biographischen Skizze von Marta Marková. Innsbruck: Ed. Löwenzahn, 1998. 63 pp., illus. (Skarabäus.) [Alice Gerstel, 1894 Prague – 1943 Mexico (suicide), writer, emigr. with her husband Otto Rühle in 1936 to Mexico.]

37136. SCHOPFLOCHER, ROBERT: *Wie Reb Froike die Welt rettete.* Erzählungen. Göttingen: Wallstein, 1998. 179 pp. [Incl. short autobiographical text.] [R.Sch., agriculturalist, businessman, writer, b. 1923 in Fürth, emigr. with his parents to Argentina in 1937; author of several books in Spanish. This book, depicting life among Jewish emigrants in South America, is the first one written in his mother tongue.]

37137. SELIGMANN, RAFAEL: *Schalom meine Liebe.* Roman. München: Deutscher Taschenbuch Verlag, 1998. 271 pp. Orig.-ausg. [Based on the author's script of a television film with the same title (ARD); deals with a young Frankfurt Jew vacillating between life (and women) in Israel and Germany.]

Index to Bibliography

List of Contributors

BORUT, Jacob, Ph.D., b. 1956 in Jerusalem. Historian at Yad Vashem Archives, Jerusalem. Formerly editor of the German section of *Pinkasei Ha-Kehillot*. Author of i.a. *"A New Spirit among our Brethren in Ashkenaz": The Change in Direction of German Jewry at the End of the 19th Century* (1999); co-editor of *German Anti-Semitism Reconsidered* (1999); and numerous articles on German and German-Jewish history. (Contributor to Year Books XXXVI and XLI.)

BREUER, Edward, Ph.D., b. 1960 in Montreal. Associate Professor of Jewish Studies at Loyola University, Chicago. Author of *The Limits of Enlightenment* (1996); articles in *Zion*, *Jewish History* and *Hebrew Union College Annual*.

CARMILLY-WEINBERGER, Moshe, Ph.D., b. 1908 in Budapest. Professor Emeritus of Jewish Studies at Yeshiva University, New York; Doctor Honoris Causa of Babes-Bólyai University, Cluj-Napoca. Formerly Chief rabbi of Cluj-Kolozsvár; educator and civil servant in Israel; Author of *Censorship and Freedom of Expression in Jewish History* (1977); *The Rabbinical Seminary of Budapest, 1877–1977: A Centennial Volume* (1986); *Memorial Volume for the Jews of Cluj-Kolzsvár* (1988 2nd edn.); *The Road to Life* (1994); *The History of the Jews in Transylvania, 1623–1944* [Hungarian] (1995); co-editor of *Studia Judaica*. Awarded the Wilhem Bacher Memorial Medal, 1996.

ELLENSON, David, Ph.D., b. 1947 in Brookline, MA. I.H. and Anna Grancell Professor of Jewish Religious Thought at Hebrew Union College – Jewish Institute of Religion, Los Angeles. Author of *Tradition in Transition* (1989); *Rabbi Esriel Hildesheimer and the Creation of a Modern Jewish Orthodoxy* (1990); *Between Tradition and Culture* (1994). (Contributor to Year Book XL.)

FEIL, Katharina S., DHL, b. 1960 in Stuttgart. Senior Administrator of Books and Manuscripts Auctions and Curator of Private Collections at Sotheby's, New York. Assistant researcher for *Great Books from Great Collectors*, exhibition at the Library of the Jewish Theological Seminary of America; researcher for *From Court Jews to the Rothschilds, 1600–1800*, exhibition at the Jewish Museum, New York.

GELDERMANN, Barbara, M.A., b. 1966 in Aachen. Currently working on her Ph.D. thesis about the Sephardic Jewish community in Shanghai. Author of 'Die bagdadisch-jüdische Gemeinde von Shanghai (1844–1945). Akkulturation oder Paria. Jüdische Identität in einer kolonialen Ära', in *Le Travaux du Centre*

Marc Bloch (2000); 'Shanghai: City of Immigrants', in *Exil Shanghai. Schriftenreihe des Vereins Aktives Museum Faschismus und Widerstand in Berlin* (2000).

GOLOMB, Jacob, Ph.D., b. 1947 in Wroclaw. Professor of Philosophy at the Hebrew University of Jerusalem and philosophical editor of the Hebrew University Magnes Press. Author of *Nietzsche's Enticing Psychology of Power* (1989); *Introduction to Existentialism* (1990); *In Search of Authenticity from Kierkegaard to Camus* (1995). Editor of *Nietzsche and Jewish Culture* (1997); co-editor of *Nietzsche and Depth Psychology* (1999).

KOLINSKY, Eva, D.Phil., b. 1940 in Schmalkalden, Germany. Professor of Modern German Studies and Director of the Centre for the Study of German Culture and Society at Keele University. Author of numerous books on post-war German society i.a. *A Companion to Modern German Culture* (1998) and *Jewish Culture in German Society Today* (1999). Author of several articles on the treatment of the Holocaust in German history textbooks.

NAGEL, Michael, D.Phil., b. 1950 in Bonn. Lecturer and member of the Deutsche Presseforschung institute at Bremen University. Author of *"Emanzipation des Judem im Roman" oder "Tendenz zur Isolierung"? Das deutsch-jüdische Jugendbuch in der Diskussion zwischen Aufklärung, Reform und Orthodoxie, 1780–1860* (1999) and other publications on the history of children's literature; the history of the periodical press in the eighteenth and nineteenth centuries; storytelling; German-Jewish literature and children's literature.

PELLI, Moshe, Ph.D., b. 1936 in Haifa. Professor of Judaic Studies and Director of the Judaic Studies Program at the University of Central Florida. Formerly Associate Professor of Modern Hebrew Literature and Language at Yeshiva University, New York; editor of *NIV*; founding editor of *Lampishpahah*. Author of i.a. *Moses Mendelssohn: Bonds of Tradition* (1972); *The Age of Haskalah* (1979); *Struggle for Change: Studies in Hebrew Enlightenment Literature* (1988); *Sugot Vesugyot Besifrut Hahaskalah Haivrit* (1999); and numerous papers on the Hebrew Enlightenment and modern Hebrew literature. (Contributor to Year Books XX, XXII, XXIV and XXVII.)

THIEM, Sabine, M.A., b. 1965 in Herne. Currently working on the anthropology of nineteenth century public and civic art in the Habsburg Empire. Author of 'Kontroverse in Königsberg: Jüdische Nationalitäten in Ostpreussen in der Weimarer Republik' in *Nordost-Archiv* (1998).

WEISS, Yfaat, Ph.D., b. 1962 in Haifa. Assistant Professor for Jewish History at the Ludwig Maximilians University, Munich. Author of *Schicksalsgemeinschaft im Wandel. Jüdische Erziehung im nationalsozialistischen Deutschland 1933–1938*, vol. XXV of Hamburger Beiträge zur Sozial- und Zeitgeschichte (1991).

WELCH, Steven R., Ph.D., b. 1953 in Denver, Colorado. Lecturer in Modern German History at the University of Melbourne. Author of ' "Our India": Nazi

Plans for the East', in *Genocide: History and Fictions* (1997); 'The Court-Martialling of German and American Deserters in World War II' in *Modern Europe: Histories and Identities* (1998); ' "Harsh but Just"? German Military Justice in World War II: A Comparative Study of the Court-Martialling of German and U.S. Deserters' in *German History*, vol. XXVII (1999).

General Index to Year Book XLIV
of the Leo Baeck Institute

Religiöses Leben von Juden in den nationalsozialistischen Konzentrationslagern

Thomas Rahe

»Höre Israel«

Jüdische Religiosität
in nationalsozialistischen
Konzentrationslagern

Sammlung Vandenhoeck

Thomas Rahe

„Höre Israel"

Jüdische Religiosität in nationalsozialistischen Konzentrationslagern

Sammlung Vandenhoeck.
1999. 263 Seiten, Paperback
DM 38,– / öS 277,– / SFr 36,60
ISBN 3-525-01378-7

Im Angesicht der Verbrechen in
den nationalsozialistischen Konzentrationslagern stellten sich Fragen nach Gott und nach der Recht-
fertigung Gottes in bis dahin un-
vorstellbarer Schärfe. Das religiöse
Denken und Handeln jüdischer
Häftlinge ist eine wichtige Dimension der Lagerwirklichkeit, eine
Dimension, die bisher in der historischen und theologischen Literatur
nicht oder nur sehr verkürzt zur
Kenntnis genommen wurde.
Der Kosmos von Tod, Angst, Ver-
zweiflung, Hunger und Krankheit
in den Konzentrationslagern bildete
nicht nur den Hintergrund für das
religiöse Handeln von Juden, sondern prägte und veränderte es.
Thomas Rahe stellt die Bandbreite
religiöser Verhaltensweisen jüdischer Häftlinge dar und fragt nach
der Bedeutung der Religion für die
Juden in den Konzentrationslagern.
Unter welchen Voraussetzungen
spielte sich das jüdisch-religiöse
Leben in den Konzentrationslagern
ab? Wie veränderte sich das religiöse Denken und Handeln unter den
Bedingungen der Lagerexistenz? In-
wieweit konnte die Religion helfen,
eine Identität zu bewahren? Welche
Folgen hatten religiöse Aktivitäten
für die Überlebenschancen? Wie
wurde der Holocaust religiös-theo-
logisch gedeutet? Im Mittelpunkt
dieser Darstellung stehen Selbstzeugnisse von jüdischen Häftlingen
wie Tagebücher, Gebete, Gedichte,
die in den Lagern entstanden sind,
Erinnerungsberichte und Interviews.
Thomas Rahe vermeidet vorschnelle
Urteile und Verallgemeinerungen;
er betrachtet vielmehr die unmittel-
bare Wirklichkeit in den Lagern und
hört hin, was die Opfer zu sagen
haben.

Weitere Informationen:
Vandenhoeck & Ruprecht, Geschichte,
D-37070 Göttingen. Fax: 0049-551-54782-14

V&R
Vandenhoeck
& Ruprecht

YEAR BOOK I

The absorbing story of Jewish Life and Spiritual Resistance in Hitler Germany, 1933 - 1939

1956

PUBLISHED FOR THE INSTITUTE BY THE

EAST AND WEST LIBRARY

LONDON

The CD-ROM of the first forty volumes opens up a wealth of information on German speaking Jewish life history and culture made easily accessible for the first time with the assistance of an advanced search mechanism.

LEO BAECK INSTITUTE

YEAR BOOK

1995

RESISTANCE AND LIBERATION
ASSIMILATION AND SELF-PERCEPTION
JUDAICA

German and Austrian Jews in the Fight against National Socialism
Jewish Conversion from the Seventeenth to the Nineteenth Century
German Jews in the Age of Emancipation
Responses to Persecution in the 1930s
Judaica
Historiographical Review

Bibliography for 1994

XL

PUBLISHED FOR THE INSTITUTE
SECKER & WARBURG
LONDON

The CD-ROM is published by Berghahn Books, ISBN 1571811834. Orders should be placed with:

Plymbridge Distributors	Books International
Estover Road	P.O. Box 605
Plymouth	Herndon
PL6 7PY	VA 20177
UK	USA
Tel. +44 1752 202 300	Tel. (800) 540 8663 (toll free)
Fax +44 1752 202 333	Fax +1 703 689 0660
e-mail orders@plymbridge.com	e-mail intpubmkt@aol.com
Price: £260	Price: US $399

JEWISH STUDIES
FROM BERGHAHN BOOKS

June 1999: JEWISH LAW: *Essays and Responsa*

Edited by Walter Jacob and Moshe Zemer

The Bible presents only a small portion of the laws necessary for a state to function. Nevertheless, whole tractates of the Talmud discuss a wide variety of legal issues both civil and criminal. Although the jurisdiction of the beth din was limited in every land where Jews have lived, the scholars felt that it was important to develop a system which dealt with every aspect of life. Quite a few of the issues were discussed at a purely theoretical level. But faced with specific problems in their respective communities, the rabbinic scholars were forced to be practical and go beyond the traditional halakhah in order to protect the community. This mixture of idealism and reality shape the later rabbinic discussions, some elements of which have been incorporated into modern Israeli law, but also shape modern Jewish thinking in the Diaspora. This area of the halakhah has been rather neglected, but this volume will no doubt stimulate further research.

ISBN: 1 57181 197 4   Paperback   £12.50

EUROPEAN JUDAISM:
A Journal for a New Europe

Editors: Jonathan Magonet, Principal,
Leo Baeck College. London and Albert H.
Friedlander, Rabbi,Westminster Synagogue, London.
Published in association with the Leo Baeck College
and the Michael Goulston Education Foundation

For over 25 years, European Judaism has provided a voice for the postwar Jewish World in Europe. It has reflected the different realities of each country and helped rebuild Jewish consciousness after the Holocaust.

"European Judaism *makes an important contribution to the quest for a global ethic. It explores the inner workings of the Jewish world, with particular insight into the psychological and spiritual challenges of life after the Shoah. But at the same time it is a medium for dialogue, examining in particular the relationship between Judaism, Christianity, and Islam. It is indeed a jornal for the 'new' Europe".* **Professor Dr. Hans Kueng, Tuebingen**

"*By setting current problems and issues against the background of tradition with such scholarly precision and insight, European Judaism is making an invaluable contribution to the effort to restore to European Jewry the continuity which was so tragically ruptured during the Holocaust".* **Karen Armstrong**

Recent themes include: New Agendas for Europe; Jewish Geography; Two Teachers: Lévinas and Levi; The Inner Landscape

Subscription Rates, Volume 32/1999 (Two issues per year/ISSN: 0014-3006):
Institutional Rate: £60.00/$90.00   Individual Rate: £18.00/$27.00
Student Rate: £15.00/$22.00   Individual Issues: £10.00/$15.00

BERGHAHN BOOKS ARE PLEASED TO ANNOUNCE THAT AS OF OCTOBER 2000 THEY WILL TAKE OVER THE PUBLICATION OF THE LEO BAECK INSTITUTE YEAR BOOK WHICH IS PUBLISHED IN HARDBACK EACH YEAR.

For further information contact:
Berghahn Books, 3 New Tec Place, Magdalen Road, Oxford,
OX4 1RE, UK. Tel: +1865 250011 Fax: +1865 250056
Email: BerghahnUK@aol.com

Berghahn Books, 55 John Street, 3rd Floor, New York
NY 10038, USA. Tel: 212 233 1075 Fax: 212233 2501
Email: BerghahnUS@aol.com

Desanka Schwara
»Ojfn weg (Lebenswelten osteuropäischer
schtejt a bojm« Juden, Band 5)
Jüdische Kindheit und 1999. 490 Seiten. 7 s/w-
Jugend in Galizien, Abbildungen. Broschur.
Kongreßpolen, Litauen DM 88,–/sFr 80,–/öS 642,–
und Rußland 1881–1939 ISBN 3-412-07898-0

Bislang unveröffentlichte Tagebücher von jüdischen Jungen und Mädchen erlauben einen Blick aus ihrer Sicht auf das alltägliche Leben im »Schtetl«. Die Eindrücke, Gedanken und Gefühle der Jugendlichen spiegeln die epochalen Umwälzungen wider, denen sich das Ostjudentum um die Jahrhundertwende gegenübersah.

Susanne Marten-Finnis (Lebenswelten osteuropäischer
Heather Valencia Juden, Band 4)
Sprachinseln 1999. 144 Seiten. 5 s/w-Abbil-
Jiddische Publizistik in dungen. Broschur.
London, Wilna und Berlin DM 39,80/sFr 37,–/öS 291,–
1880–1930 ISBN 3-412-02998-X

Das Jiddische hatte sich stets in einer besonderen Sprachsituation befunden. Jiddisch war weder Landes- noch Mehrheitssprache und hat daher immer als Sprachinsel funktioniert. Hier soll der Leser mit jiddischen Zeitungen, Zeitschriften und Flugblättern bekannt gemacht werden. Im Mittelpunkt stehen dabei zentrale Publikationen, die 1884 in London, 1905 in Wilna und 1922 in Berlin entstanden sind.

THEODOR-HEUSS-STR. 76, D-51149 KÖLN, TELEFON (0 22 03) 30 70 21

Hamburger Beiträge zur Sozial- und Zeitgeschichte (HBSZ)

Herausgegeben von der
Forschungsstelle für Zeitgeschichte in Hamburg (FZH)
vormals: Forschungsstelle für die Geschichte des Nationalsozialismus in Hamburg

In den »Hamburger Beiträgen zur Sozial- und Zeitgeschichte«
werden vornehmlich Darstellungen und Quellen zur deutschen Geschichte des
20. Jahrhunderts veröffentlicht. Besondere Berücksichtigung finden
Untersuchungen und Dokumentationen zu den Voraussetzungen und Strukturen,
Entwicklungen und Folgen der nationalsozialistischen Diktatur.

Bisher erschienen: Bände 1-36

Christians Verlag
Kleine Theaterstraße 10 · 20354 Hamburg · Germany
Tel.: ++49(0)40/35 60 06-0 · Fax: ++49(0)40/35 60 06-26

Avraham Barkai

Hoffnung und Untergang
Studien zur deutsch-jüdischen
Geschichte des
19. und 20. Jahrhunderts

Mit einer Einführung
von Ursula Büttner
Darstellungen, Band 36

1998, geb., 296 Seiten
ISBN 3-7672-1316-8
DM 42,- / Euro 21,50

Die hier zumeist erstmals in deut-
scher Sprache veröffentlichten
Aufsätze des international bekann-
ten israelischen Historikers
Avraham Barkai geben einen
Überblick über wirtschaftliche und
gesellschaftliche Aspekte jüdischen
Lebens in Deutschland.
»Die Auswahl ist ebenso wohlüber-
legt getroffen wie angeordnet
worden.«
H-SOZ-U-KULT

Hamburger Beiträge zur Sozial- und Zeitgeschichte (HBSZ)

Quellen

Band 1

Christa Fladhammer, Michael Wildt (Hrsg.)

Max Brauer im Exil

Briefe und Reden aus den Jahren 1933-1946

»[...] an interesting contribution to a little-investigated chapter of German exile history«.

Oxford Journals

1994, geb., 360 S. ISBN 3-7672-1219-6
DM 42,- / Euro 21,50

Band 2

Ursula Büttner, Angelika Voß (Hrsg.)

Alfred Kantorowicz: Nachtbücher

Aufzeichnungen im französischen Exil 1935 bis 1939

»Die Herausgeberinnen [...] zeigen uns Kantorowicz ohne falsche Rücksicht. In ihrem mustergültigen Apparat steckt ein Handbuch der deutschen Emigration in Frankreich [...]«

Die Welt

1995, geb., 336 S. ISBN 3-7672-1247-1
DM 48,- / Euro 24,60

Band 3

Peter Witte (u. a.)

Der Dienstkalender Heinrich Himmlers 1941/42

»...it will influence scholarship for years to come.«

The Guardian

1999, geb., 800 S. ISBN 3-7672-1329-x
DM 128,- / Euro 65,50

Darstellungen

Bisher erschienen: Band 1 – 36
Lieferbare Titel (Auswahl):

Band 25

Yfaat Weiss

Schicksalsgemeinschaft im Wandel

Jüdische Erziehung im nationalsozialistischen Deutschland 1933-1938

»Vor 1933 [...] war ein eigentlich jüdisches Schulwesen nur wenig ausgeprägt [...] Wie und warum sich dies in der neuen Situation nach 1933 durchgreifend änderte, ist das mit beeindruckender Umsicht und ausgeprägter Sachkenntnis dargestellte Thema von Weiss.«

Aschkenas

1991, geb., 228 S. ISBN 3-7672-1127-0
DM 29,80 / Euro 15,30

Band 33

Michael Zimmermann

Rassenutopie und Genozid

Die nationalsozialistische »Lösung der Zigeunerfrage«

»Mit Zimmermanns Buch liegt ein umfassender Überblick über die NS-Zigeunerverfolgung in Europa vor, das jetzt schon als wichtiges Standardwerk Geltung hat.«

Zeitschrift für Geschichtswissenschaft

1996, geb., 576 S. ISBN 3-7672-1270-6
DM 68,- / Euro 34,80

Band 34

Patrick Wagner

Volksgemeinschaft ohne Verbrecher

Konzeptionen und Praxis der Kriminalpolizei in der Zeit der Weimarer Republik und des Nationalsozialismus

»Ein ungewöhnliches und ein ungewöhnlich gutes Buch, das ein wichtiges Thema auf einfallsreiche Weise bearbeitet und zudem auch noch vorzüglich geschrieben ist.«

Berliner Zeitung

1996, geb., 548 S. ISBN 3-7672-1271-4
DM 68,- / Euro 34,80

Band 35

Frank Bajohr

»Arisierung« in Hamburg

Die Verdrängung der jüdischen Unternehmer 1933-1945

»Mit seiner exemplarischen Fallstudie [...] hat Frank Bajohr [...] Licht in das Dunkel dieses in der neueren deutschen Geschichte einzigartigen Besitzwechsels gebracht. Ihm ist es erstmals umfassend gelungen, die verschiedenen Gruppen zu beleuchten, die [...] materiellen Vorteil aus Vertreibung und Holocaust zogen.«

Die Zeit

1997, 2. Aufl. 1998, geb., 420 S. ISBN 3-7672-1302-8
DM 54,- / Euro 27,60

The History of the 'Palestine Orchestra' and the Collected Letters of Ernst A. Simon

Sechzig Jahre gegen den Strom
Ernst A. Simon-Briefe
Herausgegeben vom
Leo Baeck Institute

The collected letters of Ernst Simon are a contemporary document about a German Jew who had strong ties not only to the German culture but also to his Jewish heritage. Ernst Simon was a student, colleague and friend of Martin Buber. He came from a largely assimilated Jewish home in Berlin, and in 1928 he emigrated to Palestine, where he became a member of the 'Brith Shalom', an organization which was trying to improve relations with the Arabs living in the country. Ernst Simon demonstrated his complete commitment to the reconciliation between Germany and Israel after the Shoah. These letters show Ernst Simon's lifelong unceasing attempt to understand dissenters, to build bridges between people and to fight for human values and dignity.

1998. VII, 295 pages (Schriftenreihe wissenschaftlicher Abhandlungen des Leo Baeck Insituts 59). ISBN 3-16-147000-1 cloth DM 98.00

Barbara von der Lühe
Die Musik war unsere Rettung
Die deutschsprachigen Gründungs-mitglieder des Palestine Orchestra
Mit einem Geleitwort
von Ignatz Bubis

Using interviews of contemporary witnesses and previously unpublish-ed written sources, Barbara von der Lühe studies the professional and private lives of 50 German-speaking Jewish musicians and musicologists who were persecuted in Germany, Austria and Czechoslovakia from 1933 on and who emigrated to Palestine up to the year 1939 where they founded the 'Palestine Orchestra'. She analyzes the emi-grants' acculturation and integration into their new home as well as their influence on the cultural and musi-cal history of Palestine, showing in particular the large influence that the emigration of German-speaking musicians had on the development of the modern music industry and thus on the culture of Palestine/ Israel in general.

1998. XX, 356 pages (Schriftenreihe wissenschaftlicher Abhandlungen des Leo Baeck Instituts 58). ISBN 3-16-146975-5 cloth DM 128.00

Mohr Siebeck
http://www.mohr.de

bóhlau Wien neu

Albert Lichtblau (Hg.)
Als hätten wir dazugehört
Österreichisch-jüdische Lebensgeschichten aus der
Habsburgermonarchie
1999. Ca. 608 S. Ca. 100 SW-Abb. Geb.
ISBN 3-205-98722-5

Die gesammelten Lebenserinnerungen gewähren viel-
fältige Einblicke in das Leben der österreichischen Juden
zwischen 1848 und 1918. Die Memoiren behandeln das
Leben der Juden in den Kronländern Böhmen und
Mähren, Galizien und Bukowina, den Alpenländern und
vor allem der k.k. Haupt- und Residenzstadt Wien.
Unter den Autoren befinden sich etwa der wegen seines
Kontaktes mit Theodor Herzl berühmt gewordene konservative Rabbiner Moritz Güdemann und der Maler
Josef Floch. – Die meisten Autorinnen und Autoren
zählen jedoch nicht zu den berühmt gewordenen, sondern schrieben ihre Geschichte für die eigene Familie
oder Bekannte. Es geht darin um das Alltagsleben oder
das Wohnen, die Liebe zur Kultur in jüdischen Familien
oder die Übernahme von Werten der bürgerlichen
Gesellschaft, die Vielfältigkeit des jüdischen Lebens, das
konkrete Zusammenleben mit Nichtjuden im Bereich der
Arbeit oder in der Schule oder die Erfahrung von jüdischen Kindern und Jugendlichen. Gemeinsam ist fast
allen Lebenserinnerungen die Würdigung Kaiser Franz
Josephs als Garant der jüdischen Emanzipation.

Zu beziehen über:
Minerva, Wissenschaftliche
Buchhandlung, A-1201 Wien, Sachsenplatz 4-6, Pf 88,
Fax: +43/1/330 24 39

bóhlau Wien

Jewish Studies

Jacobo Kaufmann

Isaac Offenbach und sein Sohn Jacques oder »Es ist nicht alle Tage Purim«

1998. XII, 226 Seiten mit 33 Abb. Kart. DM 136.–/ €69.54. ISBN 3-484-65121-0 (Conditio Judaica. Band 21)

Jacques Offenbach (1819–1880) hat sich durch drei Kulturen inspirieren lassen, in denen er gleichermaßen zu Hause war: durch die deutsche, die französische und – was bisher in der Forschung viel zu wenig Beachtung fand – durch die jüdische Kultur. Diese wurde ihm insbesondere durch seinen Vater Isaac (Ben) Juda Eberst (später Offenbach) vermittelt. Dessen Bild und das seiner Familie, insbesondere auch seines weltberühmten Sohnes, gewinnt eine bisher nicht erreichte Tiefenschärfe: Zum einen durch eine profunde historisch-werkbiographische Einleitung, zum andern durch eine Auswahl seiner weltlichen und geistlichen Dichtungen aus dem Nachlaß.

M. Theresia Wittemann

Draußen vor dem Ghetto

Leopold Kompert und die ›Schilderung jüdischen Volkslebens‹ in Böhmen und Mähren

1998. VIII, 399 Seiten. Kart. DM 172.– / €87.94. ISBN 3-484-65122-9 (Conditio Judaica. Band 22)

Die böhmischen bzw. mährischen Ghettonovellen Leopold Komperts (1822–1886), Eduard Kulkes (1831–1897) u. a. haben die jüdische Lebenswirklichkeit im 19. Jahrhundert oft detailgetreu für die Nachwelt bewahrt. Erstmals werden sie im Rahmen einer kulturanthropologischen Studie als literarische Quellen zur Rekonstruktion jüdischer Alltagswelt ausgewertet. Darüber hinaus steht die Problematik jüdischer Assimilation bzw. Akkulturation im Zeitalter der Emanzipation, die auch in Heinrich Heines berühmtem »Rabbi von Bacherach« (1840) thematisiert wird, im Zentrum der vorliegenden Untersuchung.

Mark H. Gelber

Melancholy Pride

Nation, Race, and Gender in the German Literature of Cultural Zionism

Ca. 350 Seiten. Kart. ca. DM 112.– / €57.26. ISBN 3-484-65123-7 (Conditio Judaica. Band 23)

The study attempts to analyze the multi-faceted and complicated relationship between the Central European, Germanic-Austrian cultural milieu and the Jewish national literature and culture which evolved within it at the turn of the last century. Issues regarding the construction and differentiation of a modern Jewish national identity and culture as an aspect of Cultural Zionism are central to this project, as are the problematical literary and cultural partnerships forged in an age of rising racialist thought, growing feminist consciousness, and increasing secularism.

Paris un Wiene

Ein jiddischer Stanzenroman des 16. Jahrhunderts von (oder aus dem Umkreis von) Elia Levita
Eingeleitet, in Transkription herausgegeben und kommentiert von ERIKA TIMM
unter Mitarbeit von GUSTAV ADOLF BECKMANN

1996. CLI, 251 Seiten. Geb. DM 68.– / €34.77. ISBN 3-484-60174-4

In der europäischen Erzählliteratur des 16. Jahrhunderts ist ein neuer Stern erster Größe sichtbar geworden. »Paris un Wiene«, die von dem Humanisten Elia Levita oder einem seiner Schüler geschaffene jiddische Stanzenfassung des aus Frankreich nach Italien gekommenen gleichnamigen Prosa-Liebesromans, hebt diesen auf eine ganz unerwartete Höhe – erzähltechnisch durch eine vor allem an Ariost geschulte Verskunst und Tiefenperspektivik, inhaltlich durch eine geniale, *avant la lettre* ›realistische‹; Beobachtungsgabe, die auf Schritt und Tritt das Erhabene und das hinreißend Komische zur Deckung zu bringen vermag. Trotz dieser unverkennbaren Herkunft aus Renaissance-Italien ist das Werk auf eine verhaltenere, erst bei eindringlicher Lektüre hervortretende Weise, in die jüdische Glaubens- und Denkwelt eingebettet. Seit Jahrzehnten ein Geheimtip der Handvoll Fachleute des Altjiddischen, blieb es lange unediert, weil das erste Drittel des Werkes verloren schien. 1986 wurde ein vollständiges Exemplar bekannt, 1988 erschien ein Faksimile-Nachdruck, im Erscheinen begriffen ist die von dem Jerusalemer Jiddisten Chone Shmeruk erstellte große Ausgabe in hebräischen Lettern. Im vorliegenden Band wird das Werk erstmalig in lateinschriftlicher Transkription auch dem abendländischen Leser zugänglich gemacht. Der minutiöse fortlaufende Kommentar hilft ihm über eventuelle sprachliche Schwierigkeiten hinweg, und die ausführliche Einleitung soll ihm ermöglichen, die reich orchestrierte Symphonie, die das Werk darstellt, zu rezipieren in möglichster Vielfalt der strukturellen wie der genetischen Aspekte, der europäischen wie der spezifisch jüdischen Bezüge.

Max Niemeyer Verlag GmbH
Postfach 21 40 · D–72011 Tübingen